Business Communication
Strategies and Skills   Second Edition

Business Communication
Strategies and Skills   Second Edition

Richard C. Huseman *University of Georgia*
James M. Lahiff *University of Georgia*
John M. Penrose, Jr. *University of Texas*
John D. Hatfield *University of Georgia*

The Dryden Press
Chicago   New York   Philadelphia   San Francisco   Montreal   Toronto
London   Sydney   Tokyo   Mexico City   Rio de Janeiro   Madrid

Acquisitions Editor: Anne E. Smith
Project Editor: Nancy Shanahan
Managing Editor: Jane Perkins
Design Director: Alan Wendt
Production Manager: Mary Jarvis
Permissions Editor: Doris Milligan

Text and Cover Designer: Jeanne Calabrese
Copy Editor: Kathy Richmond
Indexer: Lois Oster
Compositor: The Clarinda Company
Text Type: 10/12 Univers 45

Library of Congress Cataloging in Publication Data
Main entry under title:

Business communication.

Includes bibliographical references and index.
1. Communication in management.
I. Huseman, Richard C.
HF5718.B794   1984   658.4′5
84-6022
ISBN 0-03-062512-7

Address orders:
383 Madison Avenue
New York, NY 10017

Address editorial correspondence:
One Salt Creek Lane
Hinsdale, IL 60521

CBS College Publishing
The Dryden Press
Holt, Rinehart and Winston
Saunders College Publishing

Cover photography by Gary Gladstone.
Copyright Gary Gladstone, The
Gladstone Studio, Ltd., New York.

Contents

The Dryden Press Series in Management

Preface

Whether you live in a metropolis like New York City or in Shady Grove, Oklahoma, with a population of two, you are surrounded by change. Some changes, such as those in mass transit systems, have been necessitated by the growth of population centers. Other changes, such as the development of emission control standards for automobiles, have been triggered by a growing concern over some aspect of the quality of life. Still other changes, such as the growth of the fast-food industry, have resulted from changing personal preferences.

While some organizations have been able to anticipate changes and have made smooth transitions, others have been forced to react to changes with little time for planning. Some did so successfully; others did not.

Since organizations and individuals are both affected by change, it follows that their communication practices are similarly influenced. A special challenge in developing this second edition was to present timely and relevant information that would directly assist the reader in improving as a communicator.

The second edition differs from its predecessor in many ways. Every chapter has been updated. However, the most significant features of the second edition are:

- A separate chapter on the visual aspects of business writing and on the means of altering the impact of appearance (Chapter 4);
- More thorough coverage of long reports whereby the planning and writing of reports are now the subjects of separate chapters (Chapters 8 and 9);
- A separate chapter on listening (Chapter 12), a skill in which deficiencies are seemingly universal;
- An expanded chapter on public presentation (Chapter 14), with greater emphasis on team presentations;

□ A chapter on using the electronic office (Chapter 18)—an environment in which many of the readers will be employed;

□ An appendix on the legal aspects of business communication—a topic of growing significance in this litigious society (Appendix B); and

□ Additional new cases and revised learning objectives.

Our objective has been to develop the most comprehensive text and supplementary package for the business communication course. We have developed a book of readings and applications with its own *Instructor's Manual* to accompany the text, providing the instructor with a wide range of options in terms of course emphasis. Finally, an *Instructor's Manual* to accompany the text includes test questions, course outlines for both quarter and semester systems, and transparency masters.

The improvements in the second edition are attributable to a variety of sources. We have implemented many of the suggestions made by colleagues and students. The following reviewers merit special thanks for playing a major role in improving the second edition:

E. Paul Alworth—The University of Tulsa
Martha Bickley—Illinois State University
Betty Cochran—Northeast Missouri State University
Nancy Darsey—Lamar University
Marie E. Flatley—San Diego State University
Retha H. Kilpatrick—Western Carolina University
David O. Lewis—The University of North Carolina at Wilmington
Mary Ellen Raleigh—The University of Michigan–Flint
Diana C. Reep—The University of Akron

We especially appreciate the contributions of Janette Reints, R. David Ramsey, and Wesley King. Professor Reints, of Grossmont College, was solely responsible for the preparation and writing of Chapter 18, "Using the Electronic Office." Appendix A, "Recognizable Patterns of Language," which appeared in the first edition, was revised by its author, Professor R. David Ramsey, of Southeastern Louisiana University. Wesley King, a recent graduate of the University of Georgia Law School, wrote Appendix B, "The Legal Environment of Business and Business Communication."

We are deeply indebted to Anne E. Smith, associate publisher, and to Debbie Karaszewski, editorial assistant, of The Dryden Press. Their combined efforts and suggestions facilitated the meeting of deadlines with a minimum of confusion and a maximum of goodwill. Doris Milligan, permissions editor, also contributed significantly to the final product. Finally, we owe special thanks to Jackie Ogletree, Nancy Parks, Karen Turner, and Melanie Barber for their help in typing various portions of the manuscript.

Richard C. Huseman
James M. Lahiff
John M. Penrose, Jr.
John D. Hatfield   December 1984

Acknowledgments

A Costly Misunderstanding
Larry R. Smeltzer
Louisiana State University

The Big Bite: A Costly
Transaction
Vivienne Hertz
Southern Illinois University

The Wonderful Opportunity
Dan Viamonte
Radio/TV/Film Department
Professor, North Texas State
University

Nick's Crisis
Jim Stull
San Jose State University

Schmitz Clothing Company
Dr. Beryl D. Hart
West Liberty State College

Communicate or Perish
John A. Muller
Air Force Institute of Technology

The Dilemma: Length versus
Format
Richard Pompian
St. John's University

A Letter Worth Examining
Peter M. Stephan
Writing and Editing Consultant

Assessing the Assessors
Randy E. Cone
Department of Business
Communication and Office
Systems
University of New Orleans

Easy to Judge, Hard to Correct
Lynne K. Anderson
Tidewater Community College

An Embarrassment of Riches
R. Eugene Hughes
West Virginia University

Car Trouble
Robert Underwood
Ball State University

The Nirvana Alarm Clock
Robert Underwood
Ball State University

Planning the Report
Kath Ralston
Chisholm Institute of Technology
Victoria, Australia

The Long Report: Sunny Orange
Juice
Robert J. Olney
Southwest Texas State University

Breaking the Lockstep
James M. Lahiff
University of Georgia

Why Students Choose a
University
Anthony S. Lis
Professor of Business
Administration
The University of Oklahoma
Norman, Oklahoma

Clear and Concise
Communication
Jeremiah J. Sullivan
University of Washington

Enthusiast or Maverick?
Basil Livingston Cleare, Ph.D.
Borough of Manhattan
Community College
City University of New York

Policies in a Crisis
Smiley W. Weatherford, Jr.
President
The Valmont Group, Inc.
Athens, Georgia

The Drop
Smiley W. Weatherford, Jr.
President
The Valmont Group, Inc.
Athens, Georgia

Communication Mismatch
Martha Shoemaker
Coca-Cola Company U.S.A.

The Disappointing Interview
Mary Jane Nelson Riley
Central State University

Body Language
Mildred W. Landrum
Kennesaw College

The Campus Planning Meeting
Julie C. Burkhard
Charlottesville, Virginia

The City Council Meeting
Julie C. Burkhard
Charlottesville, Virginia

The Realty Tangle
Doris D. Phillips
The University of Mississippi

The Hemphill Company
Elizabeth Plunkett
West Georgia College

Communication and Conflict
Sherry Rhodes
Human Relations Consultant
Sherry Rhodes and Associates
Dallas, Texas

Boss Man
Karen L. Reiter
Walsh College

A Hair-Raising Situation
Amanda Copeland
Southwestern Oklahoma State
University
Kathy B. White
University of North Carolina at
Greensboro

The Interview Dilemma
Ann Maloy Kane
Rose State College
Midwest City, Oklahoma

The Expanding System
Mike Rausenberger
MBS Software
San Diego, California

Who's Interviewing Whom?
Jim Stull
San Jose State University

Lost Opportunity
Michael T. O'Neill
Personnel Finders of Arlington,
Inc.

Accomplishments Lead to
Interviews
Ann Perry
Assistant Director for Placement
Services
University of Louisville, Belknap
Campus

The Resume: Path to an
Interview—and a Job
Richard J. Barnhart
San Francisco State University

Chapter 18   Using the
Electronic Office
Janette Reints
Grossmont College
El Cajon, California

Appendix A
Recognizable Patterns of
Language
Richard David Ramsey
Southeastern Louisiana
University
Hammond, Louisiana

Appendix B
The Legal Environment of
Business
and Business Communications
Wesley C. King, Jr.
University of Georgia; Member
Georgia Bar

About the Authors

Richard C. Huseman, Ph.D. (University of Illinois), has been teaching at the University of Georgia for the past 19 years and currently is serving as Chairman of the Department of Management and as Director of the Georgia Executive Program. His major area of interest is communication and human performance. In addition to this text, he has co-authored the following: *Readings in Interpersonal and Organizational Communication; Interpersonal Communication in Organizations;* and *Readings in Organizational Behavior.* In addition to his academically related duties, he has been active as a trainer and consultant for numerous private corporations. During his 19 years at the University of Georgia, he has participated in more than 150 training programs at the supervisory, middle management, and executive levels. He currently is a regular speaker at the I.B.M. Management Development Center.

James M. Lahiff, Ph.D. (Pennsylvania State University), is Associate Professor of Management in the College of Business Administration at the University of Georgia. His research interests include organizational behavior, personnel interviewing, compensation administration, and time management. He has written many articles which have appeared in academic and practitioner-oriented publications. In addition to this text, he is coauthor of *International Communication in Organizations.* He has done training and consulting for such organizations as U.S. Chamber of Commerce, Wrigley Company, and Union Carbide.

John M. Penrose, Jr., Ph.D. (University of Texas, Austin), is a senior lecturer in business and organizational communication and has been the coordinator of the 10-member business communication division in the College of Business Administration and the Graduate School of Business at the University of Texas at Austin. Since 1966, he has taught business communication, marketing, and management at Ohio University, Southern Illinois University, and the University of Texas. Each academic year he teaches six different topics in business communication including nonverbal communication, public relations, organizational communication, and data communication systems. In addition to 53 articles and book reviews, he has authored several chapters in books and textbooks. American Business Communication Association activities include serving as regional program coordinator for a Midwest meeting, the program chair for the 1981 Southwest meeting, and program chair at the 1982 international convention in New Orleans. He has served on the Teaching Methodology Committee and chairs the Graduate Studies

Committee. He is serving a 4-year term on the Board of Directors, where he functions as Vice President, Southwest.

John D. Hatfield, Ph.D. (Purdue University), is Associate Professor of Management and Graduate Coordinator in the Department of Management, College of Business Administration, University of Georgia. In addition to this text, he has written numerous articles and is coauthor of *Interpersonal Communication in Organizations.* He also has extensive training and consulting experience with such organizations as the U.S. Chamber of Commerce, Georgia Power Company, Westinghouse, and Duke Power Company.

Business Communication
Strategies and Skills   Second Edition

1 *Introduction*

Communication in Business: An Overview

Learning Objectives
1. To recognize the extent to which organizations depend upon communication.
2. To identify some of the monetary and nonmonetary costs of communication to the organization.
3. To recognize the reasons for the increasing importance of business communication.
4. To understand the value of training for improvement in sending and receiving messages.
5. To understand the environment in which the business organization functions.
6. To recognize the effect of this environment upon business communication.

*S*ven Nordberg emigrated to the United States at age sixteen in 1906 with an English vocabulary of ten words and a burning desire to get ahead. His first job was with a clothing company in what was later called a sweatshop. He started as a common laborer, and he learned the business while he learned the language.

Sven stayed with the company until he retired in 1956 as a first-line supervisor. He earned a good living, raised a family, and enjoyed a comfortable life. One of the few regrets of his life, however, was that he was never promoted beyond first-line supervisor. He had learned English almost as quickly as he had mastered the different types of equipment used at the company.

By the time he reached 35 and was promoted to supervisor, he was recognized throughout the company as one of its best mechanics. When other promotions were not forthcoming, his boss would explain it by saying he was "too valuable a machine man" and that "Your best skills are mechanical ones." Thinking back, he realized this was a subtle way of telling him that he didn't work well with people.

In 1972 Kristin Nordberg, Sven's granddaughter, graduated from college, the first family member to do so. She earned a degree in business with a concentration in computers. She had many job offers and went to work for a leading international corporation. After three years, during which the promotions didn't come as quickly as she expected, she quit her job. Since her skills were in demand and the economy was strong she had no problem finding another good job. Several times since then she has changed jobs upon becoming unhappy with her career progression.

Kristin now recognizes that technical competence in itself does not insure managerial ability. As she explains, "Possessing the necessary knowledge is a step in the right direction, but it isn't enough. You've got to be able to present information, to write and speak in a way that others will understand. You've also got to be able to listen, read, and create a climate in which people are encouraged to share information. In short, you've got to be able to communicate."

Although separated by more than half a century, Sven and Kristin learned the same lesson: a knowledge of the language, even when coupled with superior technical ability, does not necessarily mean that a person is a good communicator. ∎

Communication: Its Pervasive Nature

When a former president of Shell Oil Company said, "This business of communicating has become as important as finding more oil,"[1] he succinctly stated a belief held by many. Regardless of the type of organization in which you work now or will work in the future, this business of communicating is all-important. Communication is significant to organizations and to individuals alike.

Even the monster in the classic *Frankenstein* became aware of the significance of communication.[2] While hiding in the woods, the monster observed the family of a shepherd for several days.

I found that these people possessed a method of communicating their experiences and feelings to one another by articulate sounds. I perceived that the words they spoke sometimes produced pleasure or pain, smiles or sadness, in the minds and countenances of the hearer. This was indeed a godlike science and I ardently desired to become acquainted with it. ■

Regardless of where communication occurs or who is involved, the basics of the transaction are identical. Just as the corporation requires certain kinds of information to survive, an individual depends on communication with others to maintain a balanced perspective and to feel a sense of belonging.

Frank Rhodes didn't work for any vast business organization. He owned and operated a small wholesale janitorial supplies company. The work force consisted of five warehouse workers, one secretary, and three outside salespersons. He encountered problems regularly caused by such things as salespersons not completing their order forms, warehouse workers losing bills of lading, and a secretary who sometimes misfiled important papers. Frank found that the more closely he observed his workers and the more he talked with them, the less frequently such problems occurred. No matter how hard he worked at it, however, problems involving information seemed to arise. Sometimes a message didn't go where it was supposed to. Other times information was distorted by the time it got to the intended recipient. ■

Much of the information exchanged by individuals on the job has little to do with the job itself, but it is nevertheless vital to the individual. Human beings are sometimes referred to as social animals, for they need to communicate even when there is nothing urgent for them to express. In fact, much of the conversation in which we engage may appear purposeless on the surface but is actually purposeful in satisfying our need to interact with others. To recognize the importance people attach to such communication, one need only consider what is generally regarded as the ultimate punishment for troublesome prison inmates, solitary confinement. The person placed in solitary confinement is thereby absolutely deprived of the opportunity and right to communicate with others.

Although human communication often appears purposeless, it is not.

Because communication is recognized as being crucial, many organizations seek to train employees to become better communicators. Training programs may be structured around any one of many different aspects of communication. For example, a recent catalog of the American Management Association included the following communication courses among the courses offered by that organization.[3]

□ Interpersonal Skills Lab
□ Effective Executive Speaking
□ Projecting a Positive Executive Image
□ Memory and Listening Skills for Executives
□ Negotiating Skills
□ How to Sharpen Your Business Writing Skills
□ Strategies for Developing Effective Presentation Skills
□ The Manager's Guide to Effective Business Interviewing
□ Improving Business Writing Skills for Secretaries and Administrative Assistants
□ Self-Improvement and Interpersonal Skills Development for Secretaries
□ Recruiting, Interviewing, and Selecting New Employees
□ Strengthening Interviewing Skills: Role-Playing Demonstrations
□ Interpersonal and Technical Skills for Personnel Assistants
□ Performance Appraisal of Professionals: Appraising, Coaching, and Counseling Skills
□ Sales Presentations that Win
□ Telephone Selling Skills
□ Successful Sales Calls—How to Improve Your Face-to-Face Effectiveness with the Customer

The list suggests just how varied the nature of communication courses is as well as the many organizational activities in which communication is vital.

Organizations devote much effort to improving communication.

Monetary Costs

The government regulates and monitors the activities of business organizations in various ways and at various levels. Local governments impose zoning restrictions and thereby limit business expansion. Though state and federal governments may be further removed from the business site, their observations are close and their monitoring is constant.

The business organization is obligated to provide the information that the government requires. Providing this information often taxes the best of communication systems. The federal government demands very many types of information from business organizations, and the expense involved in satisfying such demands is high. A Senate subcommittee investigating the expense of regulation found that small busi-

The government requires much information from business organizations.

nesses spend $18 billion a year in the completion of forms for agencies of federal, state, and local governments.

The federal government and its various agencies have a voracious appetite for information. When business seeks to satisfy this appetite, its involvement is time consuming and expensive. Extensive communication is required to satisfy governmental requests for information; such requirements also help to explain the increased emphasis on business communication.

It requires much time and effort to satisfy the government's information demands.

In the mid-1970s the Commission on Federal Paperwork was established to eliminate needless paperwork without depriving the government of information necessary for it to operate effectively. The commission estimated that at that time the total costs of federal government paperwork exceeded $100 billion a year.[4] According to the commission's calculations, federal paperwork then cost each person in this country approximately $500 per year. There is no reason to believe that this cost has diminished.

The expense of federal government paperwork has been documented.

Figure 1.1 shows the estimated costs of federal paperwork to some of the major segments of society. For example, private industry spends from $25 billion to $32 billion per year on paperwork required by the federal government.

Remember that the commission's findings pertain only to federal government paperwork. Communication between management and employees is not included nor is communication between management and consumers, stockholders, other companies, and so on. In fact, most of the communication that typifies a business organization was not even included in the commission's findings. If it could be calculated, the total cost of business communication would indeed be staggering.

Research has shown that much of an average work day is devoted to communication. According to one study, the time spent on one or another phase of communication in a typical manufacturing plant comprises between 40 and 60 percent of an average work day. Although it is a cliche, "time is money" is nonetheless true. The tremendous cost of business communication partially accounts for the intense interest in it.

Consider the cost of a single letter to a business organization. The cost of the average business letter in 1982, from dictation to mailing, was $7.11. This represents an increase of 7.2 percent over the 1981 cost of $6.63. When the first Dartnell survey on this subject was conducted in 1930, incidentally, the cost of a business letter was $.30.[5]

Nonmonetary Costs

Monetary costs are important to an organization, but many other less tangible costs of communication are also important. For instance, it is difficult to compute the cost of communication failures. It is obvious, however, that such failures often cause long-felt repercussions.

Figure 1.1   Estimated Annual Costs of Federal Government Paperwork

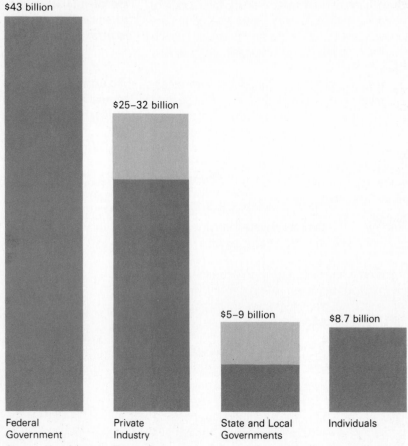

Source: *Final Summary Report,* Commission on Federal Paperwork, October 3, 1977, p. 5.

*W*hen Fred Adkins, a lathe operator, misunderstood the tolerances required for the fittings he was working on, his mistake was not noticed until he had completed half of the order. The completed fittings had to be scrapped, and he had to start over. Other orders he was to work on were delayed, and the work schedules for some of the other operators were disrupted. The customer waiting for the fittings was also inconvenienced and may reconsider before placing another order with Fred's employer.

   Fred believed that his supervisor had been at fault and had given incorrect instructions. The supervisor denied this, and for the next week Fred was really disgusted with his boss and with his job. His friends at work sympathized with him and the shop productivity temporarily dropped. After several weeks things returned to normal, but Fred still talks occasionally about finding another job. ■

The repercussive nature of communication failures may make it difficult to determine the exact financial costs involved. There is no question, however, that ineffective communication does result in errors, misunderstanding, poor performance, and negative feelings.

There are many intangible costs involved in communication.

Internal and External Communication

Internal communication refers to messages sent and received within the organization. Such communication may be either formal or informal. It is formal when the messages are sent through channels of communication developed by management. Expense statements, trip reports, and safety bulletins are examples of formal internal communication. Much of the communication that goes on in any organization, however, is informal; it does not go through regular channels. Instead, information is exchanged between individuals who, although not formally connected, do interact by telephone conversation, social or chance meetings, and even on the golf course.

Much of the communication conducted by an organization is with individuals or groups outside the organization. This is external communication, and it may involve any of the many different segments of the public with which the organization interacts.

Advertising is a highly structured form of external communication. Through advertising most organizations have the greatest number of public contacts. Whether the approach involves television commercials, printed ads, or brochures sent by the company to persons on a select mailing list, advertising characterizes external communication.

Advertising is the most structured type of external communication.

Most external communication is less formal than a company's advertising, however. When the management of a plant keeps the neighboring community aware of how the company contributes to the local economy, that is external communication. News releases and public speeches by executives are examples of external communication.

All external communication is not planned and purposeful, however. There is another type. For example, you play many different roles in the course of a day, and the roles are sometimes difficult to separate. For that reason all employees are unofficial spokespersons for their employers. Even though you may seldom talk to outsiders about your work or about your employer, you are still representing your employer.

Not all external communication is planned.

Satisfied employees are often the best advertisement for the company. Often community members form their impressions of the company through the comments of its employees.

*T*im Crowley manages a daycare center. He says that he can always tell what kind of a day Marlene Bauer has had when she comes to pick up her child. Marlene works as a welder at Arena, Inc.

According to Tim, "Some days she comes in all friendly and talkative. Other days she is a completely different person."

One day Marlene arrived very grim-faced, and Tim asked her how her job was going. "You wouldn't believe the bosses out there," she said. "They don't know the first thing about welding and they won't listen to anyone who does."

Marlene stood there for ten minutes and talked about how bad things were at Arena. "From that time on," Tim says, "whenever anyone would mention Arena, I would think of what a terrible place to work Arena must be." Sometimes Tim would repeat Marlene's comments to others and, unintentionally, influence their perceptions of Arena. ■

Growth of Business Organizations

Most business organizations are much larger today than they were even a generation ago. Much organizational growth has occurred through mergers and acquisitions. In organizations that even a decade ago were small enough to allow managers to know personally a sizable share of the employees such expansion has now made close contact more difficult. As an organization grows, so do its communication problems. Organizational development through planned expansion or consolidation may result in one or more levels being added to the organization. Figure 1.2 shows the organizational chart for a medium-size food-products company. The increased distances among the different levels of management are a result of growth and greatly complicate transmission of information.

Specialization of Tasks

In recent years many companies have become more diversified in the products or services they provide. Such diversification is intended to make a company more profitable by making it less susceptible to the ups and downs of one segment of the economy. As organizations grow, whether through diversification or other ways, management seeks ways of creating greater and greater efficiency. One means of increasing efficiency is to make the individual worker's duties more specific. As duties are narrowed down, there are several consequences: (1) individual workers become competent and more productive faster since less training is required for them to master their highly specialized jobs; and (2) the use of sublanguage or jargon increases.

Organizational growth often leads to communication problems.

Business communication is affected significantly by the use of jargon, a verbal shortcut that allows specialists to communicate together more easily. An accountant, for example, will use certain terms which are likely to be understood by other accountants when communicating with them. The use of jargon is based on the assumption that specialists in

The use of jargon will facilitate communication between specialists.

Figure 1.2   Organizational Chart of a Food-Products Company

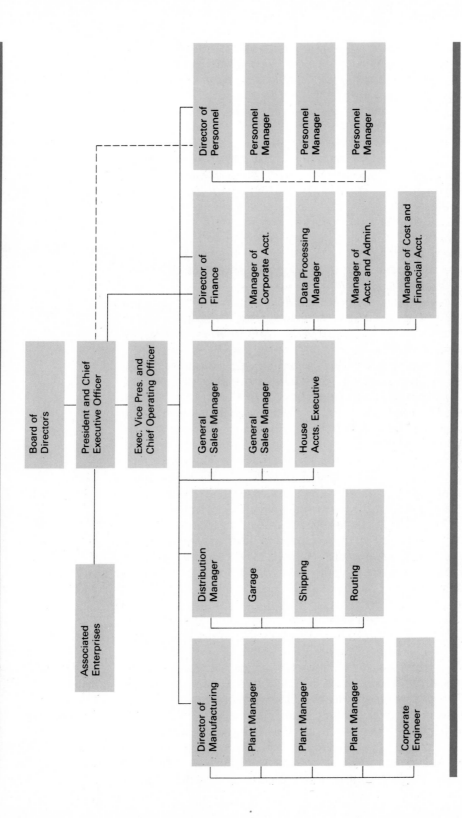

the same discipline share a similar level of knowledge; people may be briefer and more specific through the use of appropriate jargon. Consequently, jargon saves time and achieves understanding readily—as long as both individuals are specialists of the same sort.

However, problems occur when a specialist uses jargon to communicate with someone who is not the same sort of specialist in the same area. When one counselor tells another counselor of a client who ventilated, both counselors understand that the client spoke in anger. A person unfamiliar with the terminology might think that the client opened a window. Economists sometimes use the term *negative saver* to describe people who spend more than they earn. This term may convey the intended meaning to other economists but not to the general public. The longer specialists work within their chosen fields, the more inclined they become to try to deal with everyone else through jargon. When that happens, misunderstandings and frustrations inevitably follow.

Jargon is functional only when the interactants possess similar occupations.

At one time management researchers viewed specialization as a solution to many of the problems confronting business organizations. Through specialization many companies become more productive and more efficient.

Years ago, for example, a single carpenter would build most of a house alone. This was both time consuming and expensive, however, so work teams were developed. Individual workers became highly specialized, and each had a specific job to perform. Rather than work on a single house from start to completion, an individual would do one job and move on to another building project. Through specialization it was possible to construct large housing developments in little more time than was formerly devoted to building a single house.

Managers now realize, however, that specialization is not the panacea they once thought. When management narrows jobs and turns people into specialists, these people become more dependent upon the efforts of other specialists. For specialization to be effective, whether in construction or in any other endeavor, there must be good communication among the specialists.

Without good communication specialization would be ineffective.

Lack of Skill in Sending

Many people consider oral communication to be as natural as breathing, eating, and sleeping. They maintain that with maturity one naturally develops into a proficient communicator. One need not be overly perceptive, however, to recognize that this is not true. Each day we observe many walking examples who are testimonials to the falsity of that position.

Without training, one cannot reach full potential as a communicator.

The ability to communicate ranks high among those attributes that employers seek in a potential employee. Business leaders frequently bemoan the lack of this ability among many college graduates. Workers often cite an inability to communicate as a prime shortcoming of their superior.

Lack of Skill in Receiving

Until recently people did not recognize that the receiver played an important role in the communication process. The communicator was invariably held responsible for any communication problems. Popular opinion held that if information were transmitted properly, there would be effective communication. If not, the communicator was at fault. Now, people realize that, whether the message is spoken or written, getting the desired response from the receiver depends partly on whether it is received as intended.

Many communication problems are the fault of the receiver.

We spend almost 50 percent of our average work day listening to others. One's listening ability can be improved, and several tape-recorded courses are available for this purpose. Listening is also the subject of many training courses conducted in business and governmental organizations.

Through training, listening ability can be improved.

Since Brenda enjoyed working with numbers, she was especially pleased when hired as a payroll clerk. That job was an eye-opening experience for her, however. She had always thought that a payroll clerk spent most of the day working with numbers.

After six months on the job, Brenda said, "I like my work, but it's different from what I expected. At least half of my time is spent getting and giving information. Mathematical ability is important to do this job, but the ability to communicate with others is just as important." ∎

Educators regularly express alarm at an apparent national decline in reading abilities. Some companies provide remedial reading instruction for employees unable to read and to comprehend at an acceptable level. Certain employers consider reading to be so important that they provide this instruction completely at company expense. The worker attends these classes at full pay.

Companies and individuals daily pay the price for problems caused by a lack of skill in receiving information. The drill-press operator who did not listen carefully to the supervisor explain how to work with the new alloy destroyed $300 worth of drill bits and wasted $1,000 worth of raw materials. When provisions of the group-health insurance plan were changed, a memo detailed the changes. It became apparent several weeks later that the maintenance workers had misunderstood the memo. An inability to receive information accurately contributes greatly to communication problems and partially explains the great importance now attached to communication.

Improper reception of information can be costly to an organization.

Relationship between Communication and Organizational Effectiveness

The widespread recognition of the importance of communication has spawned much research in business communication. The researchers have discovered that effective communication enhances much of what is considered important in business organizations.

Management considers worker morale to be an important indicator of a healthy organization. Better communication is usually accompanied by better morale. Managers who are concerned about low morale should create additional communication opportunities for workers.

Improved communication usually leads to better morale.

Job satisfaction is another important consideration, and many managers strive to make jobs more satisfying for the workers. A close link exists between job satisfaction and morale. Research in business organizations has revealed that interpersonal relationships among workers greatly influence job satisfaction. Workers are also more likely to be satisfied with their jobs if they are satisfied with the amount of information that they receive on the job. When workers believe they are actually a part of their work group, they will be more satisfied than if they feel left out.

There is a relationship between communication and such factors as job satisfaction and relationships with coworkers.

The following statements are among the factors that explain the importance of communication to the business organization:

- Growth of business organizations
- Increased specialization of tasks
- Lack of skill among senders and receivers
- Increased monitoring of business by government
- Relationship between communication and other vital signs of an organization.

The Organizational Environment

This society has become communication-oriented. The U.S. Postal Service, for example, handled 106.3 billion pieces of domestic mail in 1980, an increase of more than 22 billion pieces since 1970. In 1960 the volume was 63 billion pieces.

In approximately 98 percent of households in the United States there is now a telephone. Approximately 98 percent of households have a television set, and in the average household, television was watched 6.5 hours each day in 1981. The advent and growth of cable television further exemplifies the emphasis on communication. During the past decade the number of subscribers to cable TV increased from 4.5 million to 15.5 million.

We live in a communication-oriented society.

The abundant communication opportunities should ensure an informed society. Such an abundance, however, is also the source of

An emphasis on communication does not ensure an informed society.

problems. The multitude of messages that compete for the individual's attention presents a severe challenge for the responsible communicator.

Some dramatic changes in the work force have had an impact on communication in organizations. The sheer growth in the size of the work force has been as impressive as its growing diversity. In 1970 the labor force in the United States totaled 85.9 million workers; in 1981 it was 108.8 million.

Shifts have occurred in the composition of the labor force. In the period from 1970 to 1981 the percentage of women in the labor force grew from 36.7 percent to 42 percent, and they are staying on the job longer. Women who began work in 1977 can expect to work 27.7 years as compared to 25.7 in 1970.

An increasingly diverse work force provides new challenges for the communicator.

The trend toward more white-collar workers and shrinking numbers of blue-collar workers has been apparent for some time and is continuing. While white-collar workers comprised only 43 percent of the total labor force in 1960, that group had expanded to 52.9 percent by 1981.

Such changes plus many others contribute to the turbulence in today's business organization. Much organizational turbulence, however, can be controlled and managed through effective communication.

The Interpersonal Environment

Turbulence within organizations causes repercussions which extend beyond organizational boundaries. Pressures emanating from the organizational environment affect the interpersonal environment and thereby influence our relationships and interactions with others.

Some of the changes in the work force described above have resulted in a greater diversity of workers who possess fewer shared goals and interests. This heterogeneous work force represents differing frames of reference which exert pressures toward divisiveness and misunderstanding. With reduced commonalities communication problems are more prevalent.

Communication problems are intensified in a heterogeneous work force.

Changing lifestyles affect us both interpersonally and organizationally. A growing interest in leisure-time activities may result in a declining interest in one's job. On the other hand, the word *workaholic* has become a common part of our language because there are people who become obsessed with their work to the point that other aspects of their lives suffer.

Personal problems, even though removed from the work place, have an effect on job performance. For example, a person going through a divorce may seek to alleviate pressures through altered on-the-job behaviors. Since the presence of family problems in general affect one's work, repercussions from such problems will affect the work environment.

Personal problems affect job performance.

Coping with stress is one of the challenges of modern living. Some of the sources of stress are occupational while others are not. Regardless of source, however, the effects are far-reaching. *Burnout* is used to describe exhaustion caused by making excessive demands on one's energy or strength.

Social phenomena such as divorce, leisure-time pursuits, or burnout, to name a few, profoundly affect every dimension of one's life. Such phenomena intensify communication problems both of an interpersonal and organizational nature.

The Computerization of the Business Organization

Many authorities predicted that the advent of modern technology would eliminate jobs and reduce the volume of paperwork in business organizations. Advanced high-speed printing machines and modern photocopiers have instead contributed to the already high volume of communication. These devices so simplify the preparation process that paperwork is now disseminated more widely than ever. Some authorities are calling it an *information explosion*.

Modern technology has contributed greatly to organizational effectiveness, but problems remain.

Computers with the capacity of processing and storing tremendous amounts of information have truly detonated the information explosion. Equipped with a high-speed printer, a computer can turn out reams of paper daily and, in the process, inundate management with information.

Computerization has neither eliminated jobs nor reduced paperwork. Peter F. Drucker, a foremost management authority, says:

At present the computer is the greatest possible obstacle to management information because everybody has been using it to produce tons of paper. Now, psychology tells us that the one sure way to shut off all perception is to flood the senses with stimuli. That's why the manager with reams of computer output on his desk is hopelessly uninformed.[6]

Due to computerization, there is a greater need for skilled communicators than ever before.

Modern technology has contributed greatly to management's access to information. It has also enhanced management's ability to transmit information quickly and economically. Modern technology has not, however, replaced the human communicator. If anything, computerization has increased the importance of the human communicator's role, for it is the manager who must ultimately determine the information to be retrieved and those to whom it should be sent.

More information is available now than ever before, and growing numbers of organizations now employ a director of communication, a job title virtually unheard of until recently. The director of communication is responsible for managing the flow of information within the organization and for solving communication problems. No matter how sophisticated technology becomes, individuals who are skilled in communication and aware of the vital components in the communication process will always be needed. Chapter 2 describes the communication process.

Summary

This chapter has provided an introduction to the field of business communication. Although communication has been studied much more frequently in recent years, it has always been an important activity in business organizations regardless of the size of the organization. It is vital to the goals of the organization and to the individuals within the organization. Management constantly seeks ways to improve internal and external communication, many times by providing communication training for employees.

The exact cost of communication to an organization is difficult to calculate. It is even more difficult to arrive at the intangible costs of communication. Communication failures in organizations, however, have many repercussions and affect individuals far removed from the site of the problem.

Communication has assumed such significance in business for a number of reasons. The tremendous growth of organizations makes managing more difficult and necessitates improved communication. As workers become more specialized, they become more dependent upon others and must exchange more information with them. Most individuals are not naturally skillful in sending and receiving messages, but these abilities can be learned. Business organizations must provide the government with a great deal of information, and this responsibility is met only through communication. Research in business organizations has shown that effective communication enhances workers' attitudes and encourages behavior that business considers desirable.

Footnotes

[1] Robin D. Willits, "Company Performance and Interpersonal Relations," *Industrial Management Review* 7 (1967): 91–107.

[2] Mary W. Shelley, *Frankenstein* (London: Oxford University Press, 1969), p. 112.

[3] *American Management Association Course Catalog* (New York: American Management Association, March–October 1982).

[4] *Final Summary Report,* Commission on Federal Paperwork, October 3, 1977, p. 5.

[5] *Dartnell Target Survey* (Chicago: The Dartnell Corporation, 1982).

[6] Peter F. Drucker, *Technology, Management and Society* (New York: Harper & Row, 1970), pp. 174–175.

Review Questions

1. What is meant by the pervasive nature of communication?
2. Why are humans sometimes referred to as social animals?
3. Which type of costs, monetary or nonmonetary, can be more accurately computed? Why?

4. Define internal communication.
5. Define external communication.
6. Compare formal channels to informal channels.
7. Explain how task specialization affects communication between individuals within an organization.
8. Define jargon.
9. Give one example of the effect government monitoring of business has upon business communication.
10. In what ways does computerization facilitate business communication? How does computerization complicate business communication?

Case

A Costly Misunderstanding
Larry R. Smeltzer
Louisiana State University

Mr. Kenneth Newson is a middle-level manager in a large chemical company. With over fifteen years of managerial experience, Mr. Newson has experienced many difficult communication situations. His effective communication skill is one reason for his steady record of increased responsibilities and promotions.

Mr. Newson recently decided to invest a rather large sum of money he had been saving. He thoroughly reviewed several alternatives such as stocks, bonds, treasury certificates, and real estate. He was especially interested in a new small apartment building located near his home.

Mr. Jacobs, the real estate agent, was very persuasive while explaining the tax advantages and potential income of a newly-built apartment building. Mr. Newson had confidence in the real estate agent and agreed to buy the building at the asking price contingent upon three things: first, landscaping had to be completed; second, a fence had to built around the back patios and; third, mail boxes were to be installed along the street. Due to his managerial experience, Mr. Newson insisted that each of these items be written into the contract.

Approximately 45 days after taking possession of the building from the builder, the mail boxes had been installed but neither the fence nor landscaping had been completed. Mr. Newson called Mr. Jacobs to ask about the delay. Mr. Jacobs replied that the contractor told him the job had been completed. Mr. Newson then called the builder directly and again he was told the conditions of the contract had been met.

Mr. Newson was furious. He didn't believe that the two pine trees in the front yard were "landscaping"; furthermore, short fences between the patios but no back enclosure did not meet the terms of the agreement. He believed that nearly $1000 worth of services and goods had not been supplied. The contractors replied that they provided everything that was agreed upon and additional work could not be expected because of the low price at which the building was purchased. No agreement could be reached so Mr. Newson filed a suit against the contractor for breach of contract.

■ ■ ■

Case Questions

1. Mr. Newson, Mr. Jacobs, and the building contractor are all experienced, well-meaning business people. What caused the misunderstanding in this situation?
2. How could the parties involved prevent the extra expense of a law suit?
3. How would you define fence? Landscape? Why are these difficult terms to define?

Case

The Big Bite: A Costly Transaction

Vivienne Hertz
Southern Illinois University

Rachel Ruddy, a 50-year-old professional mid-level manager at the City Bank of New Rochelle, had been considering for quite some time having some extensive dental work. Although she made a point of having yearly checkups and cavities filled, she felt her appearance was affected by a badly discolored incisor, misaligned teeth, and noticeable fillings. In a growing awareness of the importance of self-image and its relationship to job mobility, she decided to invest in having her teeth crowned.

She enlisted the professional services of her regular dentist, Dr. Luke, who also happened to be a casual social acquaintance with whom she shared some friends and interests in common. Her first step was to ask Dr. Luke about possible improvements. He explained that he would initially take an impression and then discuss a total diagnostic package. The cost of the first phase would be $75, a charge to be subtracted later if she chose to have the work done.

After completing the impression, Dr. Luke explained the total procedure to Rachel at a professional appointment. She was so shocked at the initial figure ($4,900 for work that she assumed would cost half that amount) that she asked few questions at that session, hesitant to pay so much just to improve her appearance.

Later, upon reflecting upon the importance of her appearance in her job and her desire never to have to wear dentures, she returned for another appointment to clarify her understanding of the process and charges. Most of her questions dealt with the process itself.

From this appointment, she understood that the charge included five years of maintenance. In fact, Dr. Luke mentioned that at one time he offered ten years, but found that figure unrealistic. He stressed that the decision to have this work done was the patient's. But he did mention that saving one's teeth and avoiding later problems with the temporomandibular joint were investments. And, of course, if one compared the cost to that of a new car, it did not seem exorbitant.

Rachel had the work done, but she found that the diagnostic fee was not subtracted from the bill. The doctor's billing secretary maintained that Rachel misunderstood the initial figure, and the doctor had already subtracted the fee. Rachel did not believe that was so, but decided that it was not worth making an issue of $75.

A year later, however, Rachel was billed for $20 after a regular appointment with the doctor's dental hygienist. When she protested this charge, she was told that she had misunderstood. The package was for one year of maintenance, but certainly a reasonable person would not expect to have "free" dental care for five years. The five-year period was for replacement of crowns that may not have adapted to the mouth.

Rachel has no intention of going to court or changing dentists. She is fairly satisfied with the work, but not with the coloring of one tooth. Dr. Luke has told her not to worry as within a year the shading will conform through natural staining. He has been right with other predictions about the teeth, but she is uncomfortable that if she waits too long she might be charged for any changes or new crowns.

■ ■ ■

Case Questions

1. Who is at fault—the dentist for not putting his diagnosis in writing or the patient for not fully understanding the services?
2. How could some of these misunderstandings have been avoided?
3. What services should be communicated orally and what ones in writing?

2

The Nature of Communication

Learning Objectives
1. To understand the nature and purpose of communication.
2. To learn how reinforcing and aversive stimuli can affect the behavior of others in the communication exchange.
3. To comprehend the myths and realities of communication.
4. To improve your ability to exchange information through an awareness of the different variables in the communication process.
5. To master the encoding and decoding skills of effective communication and thereby avoid communication breakdowns.
6. To identify your major strengths as a communicator.

Item: **A student concerned about her grade in a psychology class has a conference with her professor. While the professor has given no tests, the students have turned in a number of short papers on various aspects of psychology. At the conference the professor assures the student she is doing good work. When the final grades come out the student receives a C. Later, when she meets with the professor again and says that she thought she was doing good work and expected an A, the instructor replied that a C was good in his class.**

Item: **The owner of a restaurant telephones her supplier and tells him that she wants her order of Thanksgiving turkeys cut in half. When the order arrives, she is shocked to receive the same number of turkeys that she ordered last year—with each bird cut neatly in half.**

Item: **An employee in an organization is told that his work is outstanding and he is going to receive the highest raise in an office of five people. Later the employee finds out that while his raise was the largest, it was just a few dollars more per month. Even more significant is the fact that one person (who got the lowest raise) tells the other four people in the office that the supervisor told her that he will have a private office built for her. The other four members of the office will continue to work in one large open office. What are the rewards for outstanding work?**

The above items point out that there are many ways of communicating. Many times what we hear is not what the other person said, and consequently, what we say frequently can be interpreted in an entirely different manner by the listener.

As pointed out earlier, the major purpose of this book is to help you understand the nature of communication and how to communicate effectively. While most of this book focuses on developing effective communication skills, this chapter provides a theoretical framework that we hope will enable students to become more effective communicators. In this chapter we set forth the nature and purpose of communication, examine myths and realities about communication, present variables in the communication process, discuss encoding and decoding skills, and help you identify your major strengths as a communicator.

The Nature and Purpose of Communication

A basic goal of any organization is survival. If campus organizations fail to meet the needs of their members, they cease to exist. Many student government organizations on campuses in the United States have gone out of business because members found the organization no longer met any particular goals. In private business a major goal is making a profit. When businesses fail to make a profit, they eventually cease to function.

What factors enable organizations to meet their goals and continue to exist? The major element that enables organizations to meet goals is the behavior of people in a particular organization. Whether or not a business organization is successful depends largely upon the behavior of the people in that organization. The judgments, decisions, and efforts put forth by organization members determine to a large extent the profitability of a business. Admittedly, there are some factors, such as government intervention and regulation, competing businesses, and natural disasters that also influence profits, but the behavior of people in organizations has great influence. The fundamental question is one of motivation. How does one motivate others to behave in the desired manner?

As a starting point, we must realize that just as the behavior of others affects us, our behavior affects others. For example, have you ever found an item at a garage sale that really caught your interest? "That's a good deal for the price," you said to yourself, "but it's more than I have to spend. This scenerio may have occurred:

"That item over there that you have marked $10—does it work?"

"Sure it works; it's almost brand new."

"If it works I'd be interested in it for $5, but I don't think it's worth much more than that."

"You kidding? Those sell for $20 new and that's if you can find one. I got a new one for Christmas. That's why I'm selling this one. I'd have to have at least $8 for it."

"Yeah. It's probably worth that, but I only have $7.25 with me. If you'll take that, I'll buy it."

"Okay."

"Wow!" you thought. "I'd have paid the whole $10 if I'd had to. What an opportunity!"

"I'd have let that old thing go for $5. Hope that person comes back," the seller thought.

A basic goal of organizations is survival.

The behavior of people is what enables organizations to meet goals.

Just as your behavior influenced the seller, so did the seller's behavior influence you. Interpersonal behavior elicits responses—it is not one-way communication.

Influencing the Behavior of Others

We now realize that the behavior of organization members determines whether an organization reaches its goals and that our behavior affects others' behavior. To understand how we influence the behavior of others we need a brief examination of *reinforcing* and *aversive* stimuli.[1]

Reinforcing stimuli have a positive impact on our behavior. We find these stimuli pleasant, and in many cases we seek them out. Reinforcing stimuli are experienced through our senses in such forms as the taste of good food or drink, the sight of an attractive man or woman, or the smell of perfume or cologne. In brief, a reinforcing stimulus is one we seek out and want to experience. This type of stimulus is positive and can have a motivating effect upon behavior. It is sometimes called *positive reinforcement.*

Aversive stimuli have quite the opposite effect upon our behavior. Aversive stimuli are also sensory experiences and can include the taste of rotten food, a nasty smell, or the sight of something or someone we find ugly. These stimuli influence our behavior in a negative way in that we seek to avoid aversive stimuli. They are sometimes called *negative reinforcement.*

Perhaps some of the most forceful stimuli, both reinforcing and aversive, come to us as *auditory* verbal stimuli, those that arrive through the sense of hearing. For example, the statement, ''you are doing good work,'' can be a reinforcing stimulus that will encourage one to work long and hard. Likewise, the phrase, ''you really muffed that one,'' can have an aversive effect that will cause a person to reduce effort and perhaps skip a day of work. Frequently aversive stimuli may cause an employee to quit the job altogether!

By this point it has probably occurred to you that what is reinforcing to one person may be aversive to another. For example, drinking blood is aversive to most people in this country, but in some parts of the world it is reinforcing. Or perhaps more realistically, some find drinking alcoholic beverages aversive, while others find this activity reinforcing. Any stimulus can be reinforcing or aversive depending upon the person and the situation. The basic question is how does a stimulus become reinforcing or aversive?

Any stimulus paired or linked with a (positive) reinforcer becomes a reinforcing stimulus. Any stimulus paired or linked with an aversive (negative) stimulus becomes an aversive stimulus. An example of a reinforcing stimulus is found in advertisements in statements such as ''Eating yogurt leads to a long life.'' An example of an aversive stimulus pairing is part of the learning process of a young child who puts a finger on the

Our behavior is influenced by reinforcing and aversive stimuli.

Reinforcing stimuli have a positive impact on behavior.

Aversive stimuli have a negative impact on behavior.

Auditory stimuli are some of the most forceful.

A paired stimulus produces either a reinforcing or an aversive reaction.

hot stove; the pain in the finger (stimulus) is associated with the stove, which is now avoided (aversion).

Many important pairings take place in conversations. The statement, "Karen thinks you are doing a bad job," will cause you to react less favorably to Karen the next time you see her. Likewise, the statement, "John says you are one of our best sales reps," will be reinforcing to how you behave with John.

Many important pairings take place in conversations.

This discussion of stimuli contains three important points. First, it is the behavior of people that enables most organizations to meet their goals. Second, behavior is greatly influenced by reinforcing and aversive stimuli. Third, some of the most powerful reinforcing and aversive stimuli come to us through the auditory sense, the sense of hearing. From this discussion the role and importance of communication in the business setting becomes clear. Communication is the major way we influence the behavior of our business colleagues. *Indeed, the verbal and nonverbal communication of managers influence profits more than any other factor.*

Communication is the major way we influence the behavior of others.

Since communication is a major influence in organizations, it is appropriate that we examine in greater detail the nature of this activity. Many people give little thought to communication because they have been talking for as long as they can remember. What is communication really? For many of us communication is speaking. For some of us it is primarily writing. For a few of us communication is primarily listening.

Seven Myths and Realities about the Nature of Communication

In order to understand more about the nature of communication, we must confront some of the common misunderstandings or myths about the nature of communication.

The Myth: **We communicate only when we consciously and deliberately choose to communicate.**

We may think we control our communication. For example, we make a decision to send a letter to a prospective employee several days after an employment interview to make a job offer. Or, we make a decision to call a staff meeting to discuss an important problem. Some of the time we consciously and deliberately control the way we communicate. However, there are many aspects of communication we are unaware of, and we are often surprised when our communication brings a different result than we had anticipated.

In the example above the writer of the letter is shocked to learn that the prospective employee has already accepted a job at a lower salary with a lesser firm. Why? In a follow-up telephone call, the candidate said that since several days had passed after the employment inter-

[1]
The myth is that we communicate only when we intend to. The reality is that we frequently communicate messages we are not aware of.

view, he assumed he was not going to get the offer or, at least, he was not the company's first choice. The prospective employee received a message of disinterest just as if the message had been communicated face-to-face.

The Reality: **We communicate many times when we are not consciously aware that we are communicating.**

Continuing the example, the reason that several days passed before the applicant received the job offer was that one secretary was ill and the other was busy typing a lengthy report. The reality of the situation is that the employer offering the job communicated a message he was unaware of. Indeed, all of us frequently communicate messages that we do not intend to communicate.

The Myth: **Words mean the same thing to our listener as they do to us.**

[2]
The myth is that we communicate as if words themselves had specific meanings. The reality is that words do not have meaning; rather meanings are in terms of people's experiences.

The basis for this myth is that we assume words have the same meanings for everyone. In a large organization, for example, one of the sales representatives phones in a special order and asks that it be shipped right away. A few days later, the rep is back in the office and is upset when the customer calls to say the order has not been received. Upon checking with the shipping department, the rep learns that while she telephoned on Monday to have the order immediately shipped, the order was not shipped until Friday. "I thought I told you to ship the order right away," she yells. "We did ship it right away," retorts the shipping department supervisor. To the salesperson anxious to receive a commission, the words *right away* mean in the next 15 minutes. To the person in shipping who receives dozens of calls daily demanding, "get it out right away," "ship it now," "rush it," or "ship it yesterday," the phrase *ship it right away* takes on a totally different meaning: *right away* means *get it shipped some time this week.*

To illustrate further, when the word *apple* is spoken, some will hear or see a red apple, some a yellow apple, and still others perhaps will think of an apple pie. Why does the same word mean different things to different people?

The Reality: **Words do not really have meanings; meanings are in terms of people's experiences and perceptions.**

In the example, the words *ship it right away* mean different amounts of time to the sales representative and the shipping supervisor because of the different perceptions they each hold. Because of the myth that words have specific meanings, we assume that others will get exactly the same message from a set of words that we do. The reality is that words, in fact, mean different things to different people.

Meanings of words can be divided into denotative and connotative parts. *Denotative* meanings are those that have commonly agreed upon or standard meanings. These are the sorts of meanings we find in a dictionary. Thus, *chair* yields the denotative meanings of a support one sits on, usually alone, probably with a back and four legs. However, when you internalize—that is, add your own meaning to the words—you are using the connotative aspect. *Chair,* for example, might bring to mind a dentist's chair or a barber chair if your day's activities include them.

We tend to agree on denotative meanings, but we seldom share the same connotative meanings. It's our use and perception of words with connotative meanings that create problems.

The Myth: We communicate primarily with words.

Many of us believe that a communicated message is one that is either spoken or written. For example, you go to your professor's office to discuss a topic for your term paper. You hand the professor an outline of your proposal. The professor responds, after quickly glancing over the outline. "The outline looks good. Go ahead with the paper." But you feel somewhat uneasy about going ahead with the paper. Why? After leaving the professor's office, you realize that your uneasiness stems from the fact that she looked over the paper very quickly and several times glanced at her watch, as if she were late for a meeting. You now realize that something far more important than the outline for your term paper was on her mind. Indeed, the professor did communicate with words, but she also communicated without words—nonverbally.

The Reality: The majority of the messages we communicate are not based on words but rather on nonverbal symbols.

In recent years we have become much more aware of nonverbal communication. Books, such as *Body Language* and *How to Read a Person Like a Book,* have stated that many times our tone of voice, eye contact, body movement, or even the clothes we wear communicate much more than the words we use. Albert Mehrabian, an expert on nonverbal communication, has calculated that as much as 93 percent of our attitudes are formed by nonverbal messages, while only 7 percent are the result of verbal stimuli.[2]

Frequently our nonverbal communication undermines our verbal communication. For example, at a lecture the speaker begins by saying, "I am pleased to be here and talk about my favorite topic—human motivation." However, his nonverbal communication denies it: he wears a wrinkled suit, he looks at his notes instead of the audience, and he speaks in a monotone. The real message that has been communicated to you is that it is going to be a long and boring afternoon.

When there is a contradiction between what is communicated ver-

[3]
The myth is that we think we communicate primarily with words. The reality is that the majority of the message is based on nonverbal communication.

bally and what is communicated nonverbally, why do we usually choose to believe the nonverbal message? Primarily because it is easier for people to manipulate words than to manipulate nonverbal behavior. Most of us believe that nonverbal messages are the most accurate reflection of what a person really is thinking. There really is some truth in the old adage, "actions speak louder than words."

The Myth: Nonverbal communication is the silent language.

The term *body language* is often misused in place of nonverbal communication. Many think nonverbal communication is never heard—that it is only seen.

The Reality: Nonverbal communication is received through all the five senses.

Gestures, body positions, and the way we walk are silent nonverbal messages—so are the tone of our voice, the clapping of our hands, and the touch of a handshake. Nonverbal messages can be felt, heard, smelled, and tasted, as well as seen.

The Myth: Communication is a one-way activity.

The basis for this myth is the assumption that our message moves uninterrupted to the receiver and ends there. All of us at one time or another have had people communicate in this fashion, talking *at* us rather than *with* us. For example, the supervisor communicates with such a tone of voice that you are reluctant to ask any questions or provide any responses other than a passive, affirmative nod. Or, when a subordinate fails to carry out an assignment correctly, we hear his boss say, "I *told* him exactly how to do it." All of us have been guilty of *telling* people rather than *communicating with* people.

The Reality: Communication is a two-way activity.

Most of us have played a parlor game similar to "Pass the Message" where people sit in a circle and one member of the group whispers a message to the person on the right. The message is passed in turn from one person to the next. Each person repeats the message only once, and no one can ask any questions about the message. When the message finally gets to the last person, that person says the message aloud. Usually there is little, if any, resemblance to the original message. This game is a classic example of one-way communication. The message is passed quickly but inaccurately.

Using the same group of people, one can play the game so that each member, after hearing the message, is allowed to ask questions about the message. There are two dramatic differences from the first version

[4]
The myth is that nonverbal communication is silent. The reality is that actually it can be heard, tasted, smelled, and felt.

[5]
The myth is that communication is a one-way activity of *telling* people. The reality is that communicating is a two-way activity in which feedback from the other party is crucial.

of the game. First, it takes longer to play the game. Two-way communication always takes longer than one-way communication. The second and more important difference is that the message is passed along much more accurately. The major reason for the increased accuracy is due to *feedback*.

Feedback is simply the reaction that the listener has to the sender's verbal and nonverbal message. A major function of feedback is that it allows the senders to see how well they are accomplishing the objectives of the original communication. In brief, what distinguishes effective from ineffective communication is the ability to accurately interpret the feedback provided by the other party.

The Myth: **The message we send is identical to the message received by the listener.**

We all have a tendency to assume that the message we send is received by our listener *exactly* as we sent it. For example, suppose you send a letter to a friend in another state inviting that person to be your guest during homecoming next month. When you receive no response to your letter, you become irritated. Why did your friend not respond? Perhaps the problem is not that your friend did not reply, but that the post office lost your letter. Perhaps the problem is that you inadvertently left out a page of the letter when you sealed the envelope and your friend never received the message. The message that we send may be perfectly clear to us but not to our listener because of some influence that neither we nor our listener can control.

The Reality: **The message as it is finally received by the listener is never exactly the same as the message we originally sent.**

Part of the reason the message is never the same was mentioned earlier: words do not convey specific meanings. Meanings are in people, and those meanings are there in terms of experiences. Since no two of us have had exactly the same set of experiences, the message received by one person can never be exactly the same as the message sent by another individual.

The Myth: **You can never give someone too much information.**

Sometimes in organizations we hear someone say, "Nobody ever tells me, I just work here." Indeed, there are times when people do not receive the information that they need to perform their jobs properly. In an effort to keep employees informed, some organizations have adopted communication policies that send an abundance of information on all types of topics to all employees. The prevailing idea is that if some communication is good, more is better. The vast array of office equipment makes it possible to generate multiple copies of all kinds of infor-

[6]
The myth is that the message we send is identical with the message received. The reality is that the message received by the listener is *never* identical to the message intended by the sender.

[7]
The myth is that you can never give someone too much information. The reality is that people can be given too much information. This overload can be just as much of a problem as not having enough information.

mation to keep the employees informed. We frequently assume that the more information we provide employees, the more productive they will be. Unfortunately, there are times when people get so much information they become less productive.

The Reality: **There are times when people can be given too much information and thus suffer from an information overload.**

Information overload is a more common problem than most of us realize. In the last 50 years the development of copying machines and other types of mechanical reproduction have vastly increased our ability to generate and transmit information. But our capacity as humans to handle and process information has remained virtually unchanged during the past 50 years. We speak at about the same rate as we did 50 years ago. We listen and understand at about the same level as we did 50 years ago. It is not surprising, therefore, that information overload (having too much information to make intelligent use of it) is a major problem for people in many organizations. We need to understand that we do not solve problems simply by providing more and more communication. We need to be concerned not so much with the *quantity* of communication but rather with the *quality* of communication.

Having looked briefly at these seven myths and realities about the nature of communication, it is apparent that communication can be a confusing activity. We have been at it so long and so frequently that communication has become almost a subconscious activity. To understand communication breakdowns, let's examine the variables in the communication process.

Variables in the Communication Process

Communication can be defined broadly as the transmission of a message between two or more people. While many writers discuss intrapersonal communication—that which occurs within the individual—our concern here is to examine interpersonal communication which occurs *among* people.

Communication between people involves many factors. The major variables in the communication process include:

1. Sender/Encoder   **4.** Receiver(s)/Decoder(s)
2. Message   **5.** Perception
3. Channel   **6.** Feedback

The way in which these six variables interact is illustrated in Figure 2.1, a model of the communication process. Too many of us take the art of communication for granted because we are ignorant of the mechanics involved. This model is intended to increase your awareness of the variables responsible for successful communication.

Communication is the transmission of a message between two or more people.

The communication process includes six variables.

Figure 2.1   A Communication Model

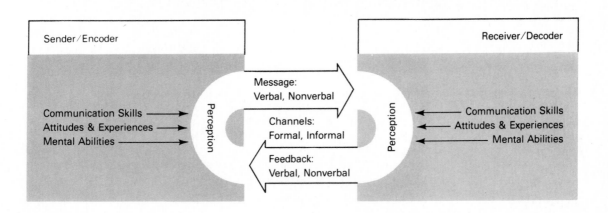

The Sender/Encoder

The sender in the communication process has the responsibility for formulating the message in a way that accurately conveys an idea to the receiver. Since communication is essentially a process of creating understanding, there is a need for concerted effort on the part of the sender and receiver to arrive at a similar meaning. The sender, however, bears the major burden. The sender must mentally see the communication from the receiver's viewpoint. The sender's task is to search for and use communication symbols and communication skills that will bring about understanding in the mind of the receiver.

Specifically, the sender should use verbal and nonverbal symbols that are on the receiver's level and should secure feedback from the receiver. These two concepts will be discussed later in the section on encoding and decoding.

The sender's basic task is to search for and use communication skills that will bring understanding to the receiver.

The Message

The message part of the communication process consists of the verbal and nonverbal symbols that represent the information we want to transmit. Each message we send is an attempt to convey an idea to our receiver. Some of the messages we attempt to communicate are relatively simple. An example of a simple message is a stop sign. While we may not always obey the sign, the message is clear and straightforward. Other messages are more complex and thus are more difficult to impart to the receiver. For example, we may wish to convey to a group of employees that we want simultaneously to increase production and improve quality control. Achieving understanding of that message by the

Many of the important messages we convey are complex.

entire group of employees could be difficult because the two components of the message, *improve quality control* and *increase production,* seem incompatible on the surface.

The Channel

What is the appropriate channel for any given message? Should it be communicated face-to-face or on paper? The question of whether an oral or written channel should be used can be partially answered by reviewing the following questions:

1. Is immediate feedback needed? Is it important to get the receiver's reaction to your message? If so, then oral communication provides the quickest feedback. Although feedback can be gained from written communication, it generally comes slowly. For many messages there is a need for immediate feedback, and oral communication provides that opportunity.

2. Is there a question of acceptance? Frequently there may be resistance to the message we are attempting to communicate. If acceptance is likely to be a problem, oral communication is better than written communication. When people receive a written communication, they feel they have had no chance for input. In face-to-face communication, adapt your message to the receiver to seek the receiver's feedback.

3. Is there a need for a documented record of the communication? Many times in organizations the messages we send may need to be verified or monitored at a later date. Frequently the receiver of a message is expected to be accountable for information contained in the message. In cases where accountability is important, written communication is superior to oral communication.

4. Is there a need for detailed accuracy? If the message being communicated contains detailed or exacting information, or if it explains a complicated procedure, again, the written method is a superior means of communication.

Finally, we should note that no one communication method is universally superior to another method. In many cases the message can best be communicated by a combination of *both* written and oral channels. Frequently individuals will follow a conversation with a written summary. In other cases people will hand carry a written communication so that they can provide a few words of explanation and ensure acceptance of the written statement.

Whatever your choice of communication channel, be sure to weigh both its benefits and its costs. For example, most managers are always short on time, a precious resource. The high cost of time can determine which channel of communication is most appropriate. A company directive announcing an increase in employee health benefits should ob-

Frequently there is a need for both written and oral communication.

viously not be communicated face-to-face to all 2,000 employees; it would take too much time. Rather, a written memo is the more appropriate channel of communication in light of the number of people and the nature of the message. On the other hand, relaying a new business strategy against competitors to the director of marketing would definitely call for a face-to-face conference to ensure complete understanding of the company's revised approach. Determination of the communication channel depends on its cost (time, people, equipment) and the derived benefits (more effective message and more efficient means of message dissemination).

One other characteristic of channels is that they are either *formal* or *informal.* The formal channels include downward, upward, and horizontal communication.

Downward Channels. There are several types of downward communication. Katz and Kahn, in *The Social Psychology of Organizations,* identify the major types of downward communication as job instruction, job rationale, policy and procedure, feedback, and indoctrination.[3]

Downward channels of communication include several types of information.

1. **Job instructions** explain how a task is to be done. The instructions come from written specifications, training manuals, training sessions, or on-the-job training.
2. **Job rationale** tells workers how their task relates to other jobs in the organization. Specialization in many organizations has made it difficult for workers to see how their particular task fits into the rest of the organization. For this reason, job rationale communications are an important downward channel.
3. **Policy and procedure** communications explain to workers the regulations and personal benefits that are provided by their employer. An example of policy is "You receive a three-week paid vacation after three years with the company." Policy and procedure communication may be thought of as "the way we do things around here."
4. **Feedback** includes messages that inform employees about whether their work is being performed satisfactorily. Feedback should be provided daily as well as in the form of systematic performance-appraisal reviews.
5. **Indoctrination** communications seek employee support of a particular organizational objective. For example, "Acme Company would like all employees to participate in the blood drive."

One additional note about downward channels of communication: as messages travel downward in organizations, they tend to become distorted. In many cases much of the message never gets through to the intended receiver. One study of downward communications in 100 firms attempted to determine how much of what top management said actually penetrated the organizational structure.[4] The results of that study are:

1. Employees at the vice-presidential level understood 65 percent of what they heard from top management.
2. Employees at the general-supervisor level got 56 percent.
3. Employees at the plant-manager level got 40 percent.
4. Employees at the foreman level got 30 percent.
5. Finally, employees on the production line got only 20 percent of the message!

Much of the message is lost as it is passed down the organizational structure.

Upward Channels. Upward channels are important because they are the major means of getting information to higher organizational levels where important decisions are made. Essentially, upward communication means following the chain of command. The individual employee communicates a request or a problem to the immediate supervisor; if the immediate supervisor is not able to respond or make the decision, the message is passed to the person at the next higher level.

Katz and Kahn point out that communication moving upward in the organization consists of the following types of information:

1. What the employee has done.
2. What those under the employee have done.
3. What the employee's peers have done.
4. What the employee's problems are.
5. What the problems of the employee's department are.
6. What the employee thinks needs to be done.
7. What the employee's perceptions of his or her job performance are.
8. What organizational policies and practices need adjusting.

Upward channels of communication contain several types of information.

Horizontal Channels. The last type of formal communication channel is horizontal channels. Goldhaber identifies four major purposes for using horizontal channels.[5]

1. Task coordination
2. Problem solving
3. Sharing information
4. Conflict resolution

Horizontal channels of communication have four important uses.

Because horizontal communication occurs among employees of about the same level in the hierarchy, it has a different tone from communication between superiors and subordinates. The tone is likely to be consultative, persuasive, or suggestive rather than directive.

Informal Channels. Although we have emphasized formal channels of communication, we should not underestimate the importance of informal channels. We know less about them than we do about formal channels, yet informal channels are nevertheless critical to the communication process.

Informal channels of communication are frequently referred to as the *grapevine*.

Messages that do not conform to upward, downward, or horizontal channels are classified as informal. Informal communication in organizations is referred to frequently as the *grapevine*. While many writers assume that grapevine communication is inaccurate, at least one researcher maintains that between 75 percent and 95 percent of grapevine information is correct.[6] In addition, informal channels usually provide information faster than formal ones and play an important role in coordination of organizational tasks.

Informal messages are also called by other names: *nonjob-oriented, task, social,* or *maintenance communication.* At times communication can follow the chain of command but still be informal; this is especially true when the topic is not related to the organization or the job. An example is when various levels of employees discuss nontask topics on the golf course or at the company picnic.

The Receiver/Decoder

The receiver can be viewed in many ways. How much does the receiver know about the topic? Is the receiver likely to be receptive to the message and the sender? What experience has the receiver had with the sender? These questions and many others determine the impact of the message upon the receiver.

The basic skills employed by the receiver are listening and providing feedback to the sender.

Specifically, the receiver is primarily concerned with two types of behavior: listening and providing feedback to the sender. Both of these skills will be discussed in the section on encoding and decoding.

Perception

Perception is one of the most important variables in communication. As shown in Figure 2.1, perception is an integral part of both the sender's and the receiver's involvement in the communication process. As a perceiver, each of us is a product of all of our *experiences.* Our *attitudes* toward the surrounding environment also modify our perception of what's being communicated. Of course, our *mental abilities,* or intelligence, greatly determine our capacity to discern the communication experience accurately. Finally, *communication skills,* whether in the area of speaking or listening, will influence the way we send a message and the way we receive feedback about that message. In all likelihood each sender and receiver will bring different attitudes, experiences, mental abilities, and communication skills to bear on the communication process. This does not mean that an understanding cannot be reached. Rather, an awareness and sensitivity to these differences in perception can facilitate an open and productive communication experience.

Perception greatly affects how we send and receive messages.

The position a person occupies in an organization strongly influences perception. Katz and Kahn cite the different perceptions of supervisors and subordinates as an example. They report that 76 percent of the foremen "always or almost always" sought ideas from subordinates in seeking solutions to job problems. However, only 16 percent of the workers thought their foremen actually sought their opinions.[7] There can be little question that perception greatly influences the way we send and receive messages.

Feedback

Feedback is the reaction that the receiver has to your message. The receiver may agree or disagree. The feedback may be verbal or nonverbal; it can be written or oral. Feedback is important because it provides guidance for the next message that we send to the receiver. In brief, we can evaluate the effectiveness of our communication by the feedback we receive.

The ability to interpret feedback accurately is an important skill to master. As we will see later, feedback is an essential part of the encoding and decoding process.

Now that we have briefly examined the major variables in communication, we can examine encoding and decoding skills.

Feedback is the reaction the receiver has to your message.

Encoding-Decoding Skills

Encoding is the process of translating an idea into a message. Imagine that you want to write a letter to a company about possible summer job openings. You have certain ideas you want to communicate in that letter. For example, you should offer reasons why you chose that particular company. Also, you should provide some general information about your qualifications in the letter accompanying your resume. As these ideas form in your mind and you put them on paper, the encoding process is occurring. Encoding includes your decisions whether to use verbal or nonverbal channels; which communication channels, such as writing or speaking, are within your selection; which words to use and with how much emphasis; and when and how to deliver the message.

Decoding is the process of translating a message into an idea. Imagine the personnel manager of the company you have written as she opens your letter of inquiry.

She notes that you are asking about a summer job. At the same time she makes decisions about you and your qualifications. She decodes information about your work by how neat and attractive the layout of your letter and resume are. She decodes information about your work experience, courses you are taking, and interests you seem to have.

All the decisions the personnel manager makes about your message are the end result of what we call the *decoding process.*

Perhaps our descriptions of encoding and decoding make them appear to be simple processes. They are not. As you learned from the discussion of the myths and the realities of communication, people rarely assign the same meanings to our intended messages. Somewhere in the encoding-decoding processes, breakdowns in communication can occur. Communication breakdowns can be avoided if we know what problems contribute to them. Therefore, in the next section we review major barriers to communication, and we outline skills both the sender and receiver should have in order to overcome such breakdowns. The most important responsibility of the sender is to create understanding in the receiver's mind. In turn, receivers must make every effort to help senders create understanding and must make them aware of what has been understood.

Encoding-decoding skills help avoid communication breakdowns.

Communication Barriers

There are several barriers to communication which affect the six major variables in the communication process that we discussed earlier in this chapter. One of the earliest and most complete lists of these barriers is presented by Thayer, who includes seven major categories.[8]

1. **Meaning barriers:** problems with meaning, significance, and the sending and reception of the meaning of the message.
2. **Organizational barriers:** problems with physical distance between members; specialization of task functions; power, authority, and status relationships; and with information ownership.
3. **Interpersonal barriers:** problems with the climate of the relationship, values held, and negative attitudes held by the participants.
4. **Individual barriers:** problems with individual competencies to think and act, which would include physical ailments or handicaps, and problems with individual skills in receiving and transmitting information, which would include poor listening and reading skills and psychological considerations.
5. **Economic, geographic, and temporal barriers:** problems with time and dollar costs, different locations, and the effects of time upon reception of the message.
6. **Channel and media barriers:** problems that confront the issue of how to best communicate a message; for example, it is sometimes best to transmit a message face-to-face rather than in writing.
7. **Technological barriers:** problems with too much information for the capacity of the recipient.

There are three main encoding/decoding skills that can help overcome common breakdowns: analyzing the other person, getting and giving feedback, and understanding perception.

Analyzing the Other Person

1. The First Skill We Must Have Is the Ability to Analyze the Other Person. As a sender, we should know that different receivers react to the same message in different ways. Imagine a football coach criticizing a player's performance: "Wilson, you couldn't stop that halfback with a cannon." How will Wilson react? Some people will try harder. Their pride is hurt, or they want to avoid future criticism. Other people might stop trying altogether and quit the team. Many of us at one time or another have "quit the team," whether it involved football, playing the piano, attending a class, or any other activity where someone important criticized our work. Still others have succeeded in an activity, in part because someone prodded us to improve. We react differently to the same message.

Receivers of our messages are all unique individuals. They are of different races and sexes. They have different family backgrounds and come from different parts of the country or the world. Their personalities are different. And to the extent that they are unique, that is the extent to which they will react in their unique ways to what we encode.

As a receiver we should analyze the sender's frame of reference, too. On the telephone:

Martha   **"Jim, I've *got* to have that report on my desk by 9 a.m. tomorrow."**

Jim   **"Impossible. I'll be up all night working on it."**

Martha   **"I'm sorry, but I've got to have it by nine."**

As Jim puts his phone back on the receiver, he thinks, "This is terrible. . . . I can't believe how unfair she is. . . . She'll get her report all right. . . . but it's the last time." At the same time Martha is thinking, "If he doesn't get that report to me by nine, I'll never be ready for the board meeting. . . . It's unfair. . . . Why can't they give us more time?"

It's easy for Jim to be angry. Martha hasn't told him why the 9 a.m. deadline is so important. Yet, would he feel different had Martha justified the deadline? Perhaps not. He would need to work all night anyway. However, Jim needs to understand why Martha acts in such an adverse manner. She is pressuring him, but she also has pressures on her.

When receiving messages, we must analyze our senders. They are just as unique as we are. And to the extent that they are unique, that is the extent to which they'll encode messages in different ways.

Sidebar notes:

Encoding-decoding skill number 1: Analyzing the other person.

The sender realizes that receivers are unique—and treats them that way.

The receiver analyzes the sender's frame of reference—and responds accordingly.

Feedback

2. A Second Encoding-Decoding Skill Is Getting and Giving Feedback. As a sender, we need to create a climate where the receiver will feel comfortable and be willing to provide feedback to us. Immediate feedback, of course, seldom occurs when we use written communication: that is one of the disadvantages of writing letters or memos instead of speaking face-to-face with our receiver. However, in verbal situations we must try to get as much immediate feedback as possible to determine whether we have created the understanding we want.

It's important to realize, of course, that the *recipient* of a message has certain obligations, too. As receivers, we should try to apply the guidelines to better listening that are presented in Chapter 12. We should avoid false feedback and should seek agreement on message meaning. As we said earlier, communication is a two-way activity.

Listed below are several questions many managers ask to get feedback from their employees about instructions or directions.

- □ "Do you understand?"
- □ "Repeat that to me, will you?"
- □ "Got any questions?"
- □ "What'd I forget to tell you?"

As you evaluate each question, think about three things. Will the question get useful feedback? How will the receiver react to each question? Is the receiver likely to return false or expected feedback?

For example, "Do you understand?" is a very common question following a set of instructions: "Here, type this double-spaced except for tables. I need one-inch margins all around, two inches at the bottom. Don't forget the enclosures. Do you understand?" We say it almost unconsciously. At the same level of consciousness our secretary responds, "Yes." In some oganizations "Repeat that" is used as a matter of policy, especially in areas where misunderstood instructions might endanger the safety of employees. Yet what would you think if your own supervisors asked you that question every time they gave you instructions?

Your analysis of these questions should lead you to conclude there is no one sure way of getting accurate and willing feedback. In many situations, though, if we ask questions or perhaps pause momentarily, our receiver will give us the feedback we need.

Since a sender will have difficulty getting useful feedback in all situations, you can see that giving feedback is an important responsibility of the receiver. Feedback is the way we tell senders about the understanding or misunderstanding they have created. There are several characteristics of effective feedback listed in the following section.

Encoding-decoding skill number 2: Receiving and giving feedback.

Getting useful feedback involves more than phrasing questions. Feedback is a receiver's responsibility.

Characteristics of Good Interpersonal Feedback

□ *It is specific rather than general.*
To be told, "You are dominating," is not as constructive as to be told, "You did not listen to what others said and thereby curtailed their suggestions."

□ *It is descriptive rather than evaluative.*
By avoiding evaluative language, such as, "You handled that badly," you reduce the need for the individual to react defensively.

□ *It takes into account the needs of both the receiver and the giver of feedback.*
Feedback can be destructive when it serves only your needs and fails to meet the receiver's needs.

□ *It is directed toward behavior the receiver can do something about.*
Frustration is increased when people are reminded of some shortcoming over which they have no control.

□ *It is well-timed.*
In general, feedback is most useful at the earliest opportunity after a given behavior—depending, of course, on the other person's readiness to hear it. There are occasions when a cooling-off period should occur.

□ *It is two-way.*
You get feedback about the feedback.

□ *It is tailored to the individual.*
A successful communicator recognizes the different needs and abilities of each person and interacts with each accordingly. You must guard against the desire to remake others in your own image. Changes in behavior must be within the framework of each individual's personality and skills.

Understanding Perception

3. Understanding Perception Is a Third Skill the Encoder and Decoder Must Share in Order to Ensure Effective Communication. Perception is the process of assigning meaning to a message. Consider the following sentence:

Uncle Ned is a moderate smoker.

Now, estimate how many cigarettes Uncle Ned smokes on an average day. Ten? Twenty? Fifty? When you selected a number, you were perceiving the word *moderate*. You assigned meaning to the message.

Perception is a major cause of communication breakdowns. One underlying reason is that we are simply not careful when we perceive other people and their messages. In fact, there are several ways in which we misuse our perceptual skills.

Encoding-decoding skill number 3: Understanding perception.

Figure 2.2 A Test of Visual Perception

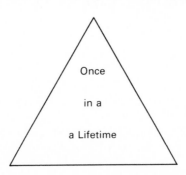

First, our experiences influence our perceptions of messages. Consider this old riddle: a father and his son are driving to work one morning. A terrible accident occurs. The father is killed instantly, and the son is badly injured. An ambulance arrives at the accident scene. The attendants place the son in an ambulance and rush him to the hospital. When they carry him into the emergency room, the nurse says, "He's in terrible shape. We've got to get him to surgery." They rush him down the hall to surgery. The surgeon walks in, takes one look at him, and says, "I'm sorry. I can't operate on him. He's my son." How can this be?

Perhaps he is the father's stepson. Perhaps the "father" is a Catholic priest. Perhaps the boy was adopted. Other explanations abound. Yet actually the surgeon was the boy's mother. Why couldn't we think of this correct answer? Simply because our experiences have convinced us that surgeons are male.

We interpret messages according to our past experiences.

Read aloud the sentences in the two triangles pictured in Figure 2.2. Did you notice two *the's* in the first triangle and two *a's* in the second? If not, then your experiences ("I've read this before") are controlling your ability to perceive and, in this case, to read.

Second, we often fill in missing information about messages we receive. Consequently, we sometimes perceive them wrongly. See if you can follow instructions. What appears in Figure 2.3 is the Roman numeral nine. Your instructions are to add one line to this Roman numeral

We fill in missing information.

Figure 2.3 A Test of Mental Perception

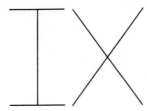

and make 6 out of it. Possibly, you placed an *S* in front of the *IX* and created *SIX.* If you tried to create a Roman numeral six, then you filled in missing information. Reread the instructions. They do not specify that you must use Roman numerals.

Many times, when we are faced with an unclear message, we fill in information and hope for the best. In our earlier example of the sales representative who asks for the order to be shipped right away, the shipper assumed the rep meant by the end of the week. Without feedback and further information, the shipper simply assigned his own meaning to the salesperson's message.

Third, we often perceive messages so that they are consistent with our own attitudes and beliefs. Tom and Bill are playing tennis:

Tom **"You play much tennis?"**

Bill **"Every day."**

Tom **"Wow. Don't you miss a lot of class?"**

Bill **"Yeah. I only went to Math 104 twice last quarter."**

Tom **"How'd you do?"**

Bill **"Flunked."**

Tom **"You failed?"**

Bill **"Yeah. Prof gave really tricky tests. Besides that, I don't think she liked me."**

We are often inclined to interpret messages so that they satisfy our impression of the world. We see the world, in essence, through rose-colored glasses, shaded the hue of personal attitudes about ourselves, others, and life in general. In brief, an understanding of encoding and decoding is crucial to effective communication.

Now that we have considered the encoding and decoding skills involved in the communication process, we are ready to identify your particular strengths as a communicator.

> **We interpret messages according to our own attitudes and beliefs.**

Identifying Your Communication Strengths

Effective communication often depends on assuming the appropriate communication style for the occasion. The trick, of course, is to correctly analyze the occasion and to have the ability to modify your communication to meet that situation. Knowing more about the various styles of communication will prepare you for these situations. In the balance of this chapter, we examine four major communication styles and evaluate ourselves to see which style we favor.

Communication Styles

There is no agreed upon number of categories of communication styles; some authorities state there are as few as one while others list as many as eight. Most of the styles do seem to cluster around four dimensions, however. Those four are the blaming, directing, persuasive, and problem-solving styles.[9]

A person who uses the *blaming style* is trying to find fault or discover who is to blame for a problem. At the extreme, the tone is accusatory and negative. "This is what you did wrong" is a typical blaming expression. This tone, as you might expect, evokes a negative feeling in the receiver. The results, therefore, are not likely to be positive. Usually this style is to be avoided; it might be selected when all other styles have failed or when the facts of the situation are absolutely clear.

The second style is the *directing style.* A directing person tells others, particularly subordinates, how to do their jobs or how to solve problems. Discussion is minimized; communication is predominantly one-way. "This is the way you'll do it" exemplifies a directing tone. Don't confuse the directing style with the more positive instructional tone which involves more feedback. Keep in mind the unidirectional aspect of the directing style.

The directing style can be effective in certain situations. The school teacher who finally becomes exasperated with note passing in the fourth-grade class states, "(You will) Be quiet!" and thus re-establishes authority. The acceptance of the command may not be heartfelt, but the command is followed.

The *persuasive* tone employs information sharing and acceptance techniques. Instead of directing the audience to do something, the message is presented for their evaluation and active acceptance. The goal of the message is often to have the receiver(s) want to do what you present, but because *they* chose the decision. Because the recipient makes the decision, much greater acceptance of the action is likely than with the blaming or directing approaches. Frequently the truly persuasive person is able to establish a need in the receiver and present a plan of action that meets that need. The action, of course, is the original goal.

The final style is the *problem-solving style.* This approach seeks mutual acceptance from both sender and receiver of the final action; compromise is usually frequent. Two-way communication is required. Ideas are jointly explored and evaluated. Personalities may emerge but are not used in deciding the final action, as they are in the other three styles. Discussions between both parties may lead to fruitful plans of action and mutual respect. On the other hand, they may also lead to disagreements, confusion, and frustration when consensus is evasive. The style is especially valuable when group behavior change is sought.

During this discussion, you may have noted how the blaming and problem-solving approaches, from the sender's viewpoint, are almost opposites and how the directing and persuasive approaches are bipolar. Further, the blaming and the directing techniques have little feedback while the persuasive and problem-solving methods build on this interaction. Figure 2.4 illustrates these relationships. Another diagrammatical technique which outlines other relationships between the four styles places them on a continuum from blaming to problem solving. See Figure 2.5.

If you know which style is your dominant style, you can better prepare for the occasion with the correct style—whether it is your first choice or another one. Complete the self-assessment instrument in Figures 2.6 and 2.7 and follow the instructions for scoring it.

How to Interpret Your Scores.   Refer to Figure 2.4. Blaming is opposed to problem solving; this is also the case in Figure 2.5. Thus, if we can evaluate our blaming and problem-solving styles, we should also be able to determine our abilities on the two styles between the extremes. This self-evaluation instrument measures your tendency to use blaming and problem-solving styles.

If your score for the left column was between 21 and 28, you are probably a moderate blamer; a score of 29 or higher suggests you rely somewhat heavily on the blaming style. Examination of your communication style is necessary.

Figure 2.4   Four Communication Styles Compared by Degree of Interaction

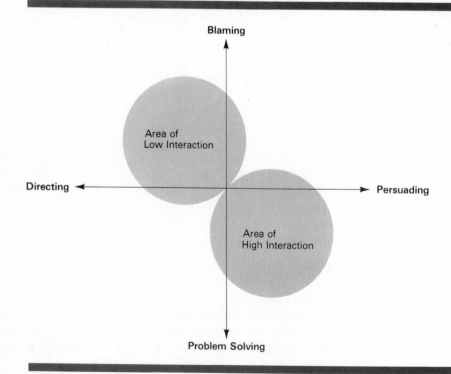

Figure 2.5   Four Communication Styles Compared by Extent of Participant Involvement

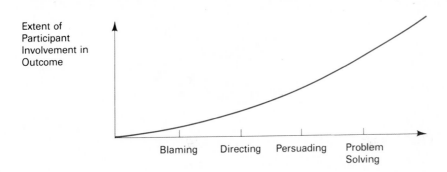

Figure 2.6   Self-Assessment of Communication Style

Indicate the degree to which you do the following:

	Very Little	Little	Some	Great	Very Great
1. Make judgments early in the conversation.	————	————	————	————	————
2. Share my feelings with others.	————	————	————	————	————
3. Talk about the issues.	————	————	————	————	————
4. Have analyzed others' motives.	————	————	————	————	————
5. Talk about the person.	————	————	————	————	————
6. Use clear and precise language.	————	————	————	————	————
7. Decide on the action before the conversation.	————	————	————	————	————
8. Encourage the other person to discuss feelings.	————	————	————	————	————
9. Am open for new information.	————	————	————	————	————
10. Ask questions which seek agreement with me.	————	————	————	————	————
11. Talk the majority of the time.	————	————	————	————	————
12. Ask questions which get others to describe events.	————	————	————	————	————
13. Talk half the time or less.	————	————	————	————	————
14. Others defend their position to me.	————	————	————	————	————

Source: Sandra E. O'Connell, *The Manager as Communicator,* (San Francisco: Harper & Row, Publishers, Inc., 1979), p. 25. Reprinted by permission of Harper & Row, Publishers, Inc.

Figure 2.7   Score Sheet for Self-Assessment

Scoring Sheet

Item No.		Score
1	_____	
2		_____
3		_____
4	_____	
5	_____	
6		_____
7	_____	
8		_____
9		_____
10	_____	
11	_____	
12		_____
13		_____
14	_____	
Totals	_____	_____

Total column 1 _____
Total column 2 _____
Interpretation of scores:
very little = 1 point, little = 2 points, some = 3 points, great = 4 points,
and very great = 5 points

Source: Sandra E. O'Connell, *The Manager as Communicator,* (San Francisco: Harper & Row, Publishers, Inc., 1979), pp. 25–26. Reprinted by permission of Harper & Row, Publishers, Inc.

Similarly, if your score on the right column is from 21 to 28, you fall in the moderate problem-solving style category. A score of 29 or higher indicates a strong leaning toward problem solving as your dominant technique.

Don't assume that blaming is always bad and problem solving is always good. There are occasions when you need to be directive and perhaps even blame. Problem solving can be both tedious and time consuming; it is not a panacea for all ills. Become familiar with the four styles and with your own strengths and weaknesses, then try to select the appropriate style for the occasion.

Summary

In this chapter we discussed the nature of communication. We began by noting that the behavior of people is what enables organizations to achieve their goals. We use verbal and nonverbal communication to influence the behavior of others.

We identified several myths and realities about the nature of communication.

Myth 1: We only communicate when we intend to.
Reality: We frequently communicate messages we are not aware of communicating.

Myth 2: We communicate as if words had specific meanings.
Reality: Words do not have meanings; rather, meanings are within people based on their experiences.

Myth 3: We communicate primarily with words.
Reality: The majority of the messages we communicate are based on the nonverbal aspects of communication.

Myth 4: Nonverbal communication is the silent language.
Reality: Some nonverbal communication is silent, but much of it is not silent.

Myth 5: We communicate as if communication were a one-way activity.
Reality: Communication is a two-way activity in which feedback from the other party is crucial.

Myth 6: The message we communicate is identical to the message received.
Reality: The message finally received by the listener is never identical to the message sent.

Myth 7: You can never give someone too much information.
Reality: People can be given too much information. An information overload can be just as much of a problem as not having enough information.

We examined a model of communication and discussed the encoding and decoding skills necessary for effective communication and helpful in overcoming communication breakdowns. Special attention was directed at the importance of perception in the communication process. Indeed, the ability to perceive the other person's frame of reference accurately is something we will mention time and again as we discuss oral and written communication in this book. Finally, you were provided an opportunity to assess your communication style in an attempt to improve your interpersonal skills.

Footnotes

[1]For a more detailed discussion of reinforcing and aversive stimuli, see David Thompson, *Managing People—Influencing Behavior* (St. Louis: The C.V. Mosby Company, 1978).

[2]Albert Mehrabian, "Communication without Words," *Psychology Today* (September 1968) 2:53–55.

[3]Daniel Katz and Robert Kahn, *The Social Psychology of Organizations* (New York: John Wiley & Sons, 1978), p. 440.

[4]Ray Killian, *Managing by Design . . . for Executive Effectiveness* (New York: American Management Association, 1968), p. 254.

[5]Gerald M. Goldhaber, *Organizational Communication,* 3rd ed. (Dubuque, Iowa: William C. Brown Co., 1983), pp. 162–163.

[6]Keith Davis, "Care and Cultivation of the Corporation Grapevine," *Dun's Review* (July 1973), p. 46.

[7]E. Jacobson, "Foremen-Steward Participation Practices and Work Attitudes in a Unionized Factory," unpublished doctoral thesis (Ann Arbor: University of Michigan, 1951).

[8]Lee Thayer, *Communication and Communication Systems* (Homewood, Ill.: Richard D. Irwin, 1968), pp. 195–203.

[9]Much of this discussion is taken from Sandra O'Connell, *The Manager as Communicator* (San Francisco, Calif.: Harper & Row, 1979).

Review Questions

1. In what ways can reinforcing or aversive stimuli have an impact on behavior?

2. Discuss the seven myths and realities about the nature of communication. Support your discussion with an example of each myth/reality.

3. What is the sender's major responsibility in the communication process?

4. The more information we provide employees, the more productive they will be. Comment on this statement.

5. What important criteria determine whether an oral or a written channel of communication is most appropriate in sending a message?

6. What are downward, upward, and horizontal channels of communication? Suggest several situations in which these channels should be used.

7. How does informal communication differ from formal communication?

8. Name the encoding and decoding skills that both sender and re-

ceiver should master to prevent communication breakdowns. Within the context of a business setting, give an example of each.

9. What are the characteristics of good feedback? Who bears the primary responsibility for good feedback? How can good feedback facilitate an accurate and willing information exchange?

Case

The Wonderful Opportunity

Dan Viamonte
Professor, North Texas State University
Radio/TV/Film Department

Bob Anderson had been a trade specialist with the state Agricultural Development Division for almost two years. He was attracted by the philosophy of the new administration to attract international trade. Although Bob's background was in music, he had acquired some business experience with a small food-processing company in the western part of the state.

During the past year, Bob attended several statewide training sessions designed to inform and develop interest in international trade. Many food producers, packaging firms, and brokers were not accustomed to dealing with foreign markets.

Bob traveled throughout the state in the months that followed trying to establish a network of participants eager to supply quality food products. The task was difficult. Trade opportunities went to other states. Somehow the typical obstacles and problems the growers and trade brokers faced were not easily dealt with and the Agricultural Development Division was not helping to solve them.

At one of the regional trade meetings sponsored by the state, Bob met Dr. Beldon, a former college professor who was now an international trade consultant representing business associates from the Middle East. They both agreed that the state had tremendous resources at its command but lacked the critical sophistication, contacts, cultural understanding, and experience to negotiate with the Middle Eastern markets. Bob was very excited about this new foreign market opportunity and returned to his office vowing to get something started.

Three days later, Bob called Dr. Beldon and shared a rumor that the governor was planning an unofficial business trip to the Middle East within two months. Would some of Dr. Beldon's associates be willing to prepare letters of introduction? Dr. Beldon responded that coincidently, several major agricultural businessmen from the Middle East had decided to tour parts of the United States on their way to an international trade show in Japan. Although this was short notice, Bob suggested that perhaps the Agricultural Development Division could invite the Middle Eastern businessmen next week to tour the state's facilities and meet with interested agribusinessmen. It would also be an excellent opportunity for the governor to meet with delegates from three Middle Eastern countries.

Dr. Beldon had some reservations as he listened to Bob's enthusiastic idea. He had been involved in several unpleasant experiences before with previous state officials. He knew that the foreign businessmen could be persuaded to come, but they would require assurances that they could meet with people who were authorized to negotiate. Once they heard that the governor was interested they would be disappointed if he did not appear.

Almost by instinct, Bob sensed that Dr. Beldon was worried. He assured him that all would work out well. He promised to send an official letter of invitation to the foreign businessmen the very next day but realized that he had to get approval from his superiors.

Bob was surprised to discover that several of his peers were skeptical about the value of a meeting with businessmen from the Middle East. The director of the Agricultural Development Division seemed interested but warned that these things had to be handled carefully. It was suggested that the Agricultural Development Division send an official letter to the department requesting a state agricultural tour.

Not knowing quite how to resolve this impasse, Bob ignored several telephone messages from Dr. Beldon. With only a few days remaining before the Middle Eastern businessmen had to leave the U.S. for Japan, Bob received an urgent message from the governor's office. Who was Dr. Beldon? What trade delegation was he talking about? Was the governor planning to attend some agricultural exposition in Japan?

Dr. Beldon, in a final attempt to insure that his telex to the Middle Eastern associates in New York was correct, had placed a direct telephone call to the governor. He spoke with several members of the governor's staff and tried to explain the urgency of the situation. Nobody seemed to know anything about the proposed meeting. He was told that someone from the staff would talk to the governor that evening. The governor was attending a regional conference of governors outside of the state but would be checking in with his office later that evening. Two hours later, the governor's chief assistant had returned Dr. Beldon's call and explained that some mix-up had occurred. The governor was not aware of any trade delegation visiting the state. The staff person had just talked with the director of the Agricultural Development Division at his home and had been told that no such contact had been authorized. Perhaps Dr. Beldon had misunderstood Bob Anderson's enthusiasm.

Everyone in the governor's office agreed it was a wonderful idea and suggested that perhaps at some later date a meeting could be arranged with the businessmen to discuss the state's interest in agriculture. Apologies were given for any inconvenience or embarrassment that may have been caused.

■ ■ ■

Case Questions

1. What assumptions did Bob Anderson make?
2. What channels of communication did Bob Anderson establish to insure the success of the venture? What might he had done to improve communication lines?
3. Why did the director of Agricultural Trade Division tell the governor's staff that no such contact had been authorized?
4. What reservations did Dr. Beldon have concerning this proposed meeting?
5. How would you have written a letter of introduction for the governor?
6. Why was there confusion about the governor's trip?
7. How might this whole situation been handled to insure that the growers, packagers, and brokers could meet with the businessmen from the Middle East directly?

Case

Nick's Crisis
Jim Stull
San Jose State University

Nick Young has worked as manager of the information services division of World Business Machines (WBM) for 12 years. His department's ratings have always been superior, and he is well liked by everyone with whom he works.

Because of energy shortages in the paper industry and because of new developments in the high-technology industry, WBM plans to make some significant modifications in the information services division. Any personnel changes resulting from these modifications will be subject to strict adherence to affirmative action guidelines.

Both Nick and his boss agree that the changes will be for the benefit of the organization, will improve the working conditions for current employees, and will result in additional employment opportunities for members of the community. Nick's boss has asked Nick to avoid discussing any of these planned changes until all of the details have been finalized.

Many of Nick's subordinates have noticed that whenever they make suggestions about improving work procedures, Nick acts a little nervous and says, "Let's talk about this later." Additionally, Nick's administrative assistant unknowingly leaked to one of Nick's subordinates that "some big changes are going to take place, and they have something to do with affirmative action."

Nick's subordinates begin to talk. Rumors are spread about layoffs. Morale begins to drop noticeably. Tardiness and absenteeism rise sharply. Work begins to pile up, and work quality starts to drop. Nick starts to spend most of his time disciplining his employees and writing reports for their personnel files.

Nick becomes very dissatisfied with his job; his boss picks up on Nick's signals and calls Nick into his office for some counseling.

■ ■ ■

Case Questions

1. What are some of the variables that have led to Nick's crisis? Be sure to discuss internal and external variables, upward and downward communication, formal and informal channels, verbal and nonverbal messages, and similar factors.

2. At what point in the case might Nick have taken action to possibly avoid getting into the crisis?

3. What advice should Nick's boss give Nick about (a) Nick's boss's responsibility for the crisis, (b) Nick's responsibility, and (c) what to do next to try to restore peace in the department?

2 *Written Strategies*

Characteristics of Effective Written Communication

Learning Objectives
1. To understand ten characteristics that make writing effective.
2. To recognize writing that does not contain the ten characteristics.
3. To understand how the ten characteristics work in combination to make writing effective.
4. To learn different techniques for building the ten characteristics into your own writing.

In order to provide a mechanism by which students may air their problems concerning academic courses, the university has established the following grievance procedure for all undergraduate students. First, the student should attempt to resolve his grievance with the course instructor. If not satisfied, then he may petition the head of the department in question, who will respond to the grievance in writing. If the student is not entirely satisfied, then his grievance may be submitted to the Undergraduate Petitions Committee, a three-man panel composed of two faculty members and one student who will render a final decision concerning the grievance. ■

Imagine that you have just received your final term grades. One of them is a very unpleasant surprise—a grade two letters lower than what you expected. First, you call the course instructor, who says that he doesn't have time to see you. Angered by this response, you call the dean of student affairs. She tells you to consult your student handbook. There you will find a specific procedure to follow in handling your problem. You open the handbook, and what appears is the material printed above.

Reread the material. As you do, make a mental list of the things you find wrong with it. Remember that whatever you *think* is wrong probably is. After all, it was written for students—you're the audience.

This chapter introduces ten characteristics that make written communication effective:

1. Readable
2. Tactful
3. Personal
4. Positive
5. Active

6. Unified
7. Coherent
8. Clear
9. Concise
10. Mechanically sound

Our goals are to help you learn to analyze the communication of others and, in doing so, to become a better communicator yourself. As we discuss each characteristic, we'll rewrite the material from the student handbook so that you can see how written communication, if approached systematically, can be improved.

Characteristic 1: Readable

Saying that something is readable means that it is understandable because of its clear style of writing. Many of us write to impress our readers. We purposefully choose long words and write lengthy, complicated sentences in order to show off our command of the language and perhaps even our intelligence. Any idea, no matter how simple, can be written in such a way as to make it difficult or even impossible for our readers to understand. This often happens when we sacrifice understanding for the impression we hope to make.

This chapter's primary purpose is to facilitate and otherwise enhance an individual's proficiency in translating cognitions into appropriately presented written material which effectively satisfies a minimum of ten salient criteria.

When readers become aware of our writing style, they no longer concentrate on the meaning of our message. The best writing style is one that does not draw attention to itself.

What is your impression of the material from the student handbook? It is more complicated than it needs to be, yet the style of writing is fairly typical of much communication in business, including student handbooks.

Readability has been a popular written communication topic since the late 1940s when mathematical formulas were developed to judge the degree of complexity of written material. We will show you how to use one of these formulas, Gunning's Fog Index.[1] The index works best with text of at least 200 words. Only prose can be evaluated; the Fog Index doesn't work on nonsentence material, such as letterheads, inside addresses, or balance sheet information.

Steps in Computing Readability

Robert Gunning's Fog Index is intended to gauge the grade level of written material; that is, what level of education will the audience need to have in order to understand something that is written. Analyze the material from the student handbook following these steps.

1. **Count the number of words in the passage.** There are 100 words in the handbook material; of course, you can apply the Fog Index to longer or shorter passages.
2. **Count the number of complete thoughts in the passage.** Note that a simple or complex sentence has one complete thought; a compound sentence has two thoughts. We counted four complete thoughts.
3. **Compute the average sentence length.** To do this, divide the number of words in the passage (100) by the number of complete thoughts (4); the answer is 25.
4. **Compute the percentage of "hard words."** These are words having three or more syllables. However, do *not* include:
   a. proper names (e.g., Kennedy, Carolina)
   b. combinations of short, easy words (e.g., bookkeeper, homemaker, however)
   c. verb forms made three syllables by adding -ed or -es (e.g., created, trespasses).

   To compute the percentage, divide the number of hard words (we counted 15) by the total number of words in the passage (100). The answer is 15 percent.

5. **Add the average sentence length** (25) **and the percent-age of hard words** (15—notice we've removed the decimal point). The answer is 40.

6. **Multiply the answer in Step 5 by the constant, 0.4.** (The answer is 16.0) The number 16, then, is the Fog Index.

Interpreting the Fog Index

We can interpret the Fog Index by comparing it to a grade level. For example, if the index is 6, then the material is written at the sixth-grade level. Our index of 16 for the material from the student handbook means that it is written at the level of a senior in college.

Is this level appropriate? Hardly. Gunning states that anyone who writes at a level greater than 12 is inviting misunderstanding.[2] Many publishers urge authors of college textbooks to write at the ninth-grade level.[3] Popular magazines, such as *Time* and *Reader's Digest,* are usually written at tenth- or eleventh-grade levels.

The readability index corresponds to a grade level.

Using Readability Formulas

As you determine the readability of the material from the student hand-book, you might realize that two things will raise a readability index— long sentences and long words. Therefore, use the Fog Index with care. Applying the formula too strictly in your own writing might result in short, choppy sentences that could become monotonous and per-haps offensive to your readers. Also, longer words often add precision to what we are saying. Yet the readability formula can serve as a guide in your writing—a warning that you may be trying to impress rather than communicate for understanding.

Try to write at a level at or below your audience's educational level. Always avoid writing above their level. Try to write at a level below their educational level, but never allow your message to sound like you are writing down to your audience. Your goal is quick understanding and easy comprehension by your audience. Insulting your audience by writing too far below them, however, is quite detrimental.

Just because a Fog Index level is low doesn't mean it must sound childish or immature. One mark of an effective writer is the ability to write clearly at a low index level while maintaining an intelligent tone. Journalists, for example, sharpen these skills. *Time* or *Newsweek* don't sound immature to most of us, yet they regularly average a level of advanced high school, tenth to twelfth grade.

Using the fog index goes beyond applying the formula alone; there are three steps in all: (1) quantitative evaluation through the Fog Index formula, (2) interpretation and analysis of the index score, and (3) revi-sion as necessary. Once you have determined your typical index level or

Readability formulas are only guides to better writing.

the level for a specific piece of writing, compare that to the educational level of your intended audience. If your level is higher than their educational level, then make adjustments in your writing.

Gunning shares 10 suggestions for clearer writing, many of which have direct influence on the Fog Index level.

1. Keep sentences short. Aim for an average of 20 words or fewer.
2. Use the simple over the complex; this applies to sentences as well as words and thoughts.
3. The familiar word is best.
4. Avoid unnecessary words.
5. Use action verbs; avoid the passive tense.
6. Write like you talk. Your writing should have a conversational tone rather than a stilted or affected tone.
7. Use terms your reader can picture. Avoid abstract words.
8. Try to relate to your reader's experience.
9. Vary your words, sentence length, and sentence construction to sustain interest.
10. Write to express ideas, not to impress the reader.

For its many values, the Fog Index has several shortcomings. First, it is oblivious to the connotations of words; only the number of words and the number of difficult words are noted. Second, the index works only with text and nonsentence writing cannot be evaluated. Third, the index is English language-oriented. Finally, reader interest in the material is not determined. Clearly, an interested reader will put up with difficult writing more than a disinterested reader.

We've redone the student handbook material to show you that readability can be improved. At the same time we've removed some of the hard words that have more than two syllables.

So that students can air their problems about courses, the university has adopted the grievance procedure described below for all undergraduate students. First, the student should try to resolve his grievance with his instructor. If this doesn't work, then his grievance may be filed with the head of the department in question. The department head will respond to the student in writing. If the student is still not satisfied, then his grievance may be submitted to the Undergraduate Petitions Committee. This committee is a three-man panel made up of two faculty members and one student. Its decision will be final. ∎

Here is the readability index of the revised material:

1. 100 words
2. 7 complete thoughts
3. Average sentence length = 14.3
4. Percentage of hard words = 6
5. 14.3 + 6 = 20.3
6. 20.3 × .4 = 8.1.

Although the readability of the student handbook material is now satisfactory, the material contains other problems. The second characteristic of effective written communication will help us identify some of them.

Characteristic 2: Tactful

Material that is written tactfully does not offend the reader. Unfortunately, too many of us assume that what is inoffensive to us is inoffensive to everyone else. Not every person enjoys off-color jokes. Nor does everyone appreciate ethnic jokes or religious anecdotes. As we pointed out in Chapter 2, one skill the effective encoder of messages has is the ability to analyze the receiver. An outcome of such an analysis should be more tactful writing, which should contain the following elements:

1. Tactful writing does not insult the reader's intelligence. We mean this both ways—write *to* your reader, neither above nor below. For example, with high levels of readability in our writing, tact does not become a problem until the readers *realize* we are trying to impress. A low Fog Index is also inoffensive so long as the readers don't think we are writing down to them.

> You can insult your reader by writing at too high or too low a level.

Avoid other forms of demeaning communication as well. "You're looking much better than usual," is not likely to be well-received, even if it slipped out without malicious intent. And such blatant an insult as, "I really thought you could handle the job. I guess I was wrong!" is sure to bring out a negative reaction. Demeaning language, of course, is to be avoided in written communication just as judiciously as in spoken communication.

2. Tactful writing does not categorize the reader. Consider the following:

People such as you like a good bargain. That's why we're offering you these fantastic discounts on . . .

As the sender of this message, you might safely assume that all customers like good bargains. However, many of your customers will think of themselves as being different from other customers. *People such as you* puts the customer in the same category with everyone else. To the extent that you offend only one, two, or several customers with such categorizations, that's the extent to which your potential sales could decline. Imagine being a personnel manager who receives several hundred resumes from potential employees each year. Many of these resumes are accompanied by a cover letter whose salutation reads *Dear Personnel Manager*. To some managers there is quite a difference between such a salutation and one containing the manager's name.

> You can insult your reader by categorizing him or her.

3. Tactful writing is not sexist. We can insult at least half our readers by using sexist language. Reexamine the student handbook material. Taken literally, it was written only for males. Notice that the Undergraduate Petitions Committee is "three-man." Whether you are offended by such language is irrelevant. Someone in your audience could be.

> You can insult your reader by using sexist language.

One problem in removing sexist language is that we often change *he* to *he or she* (or perhaps *s/he*) and *him* to *him or her*. Such phrasing can become cumbersome unless it is used sparingly. With this problem in mind, here are some ways of removing sexist language from your writing:

a. Use the word *person*. For example:

Sexist: **Turn your finished product in to your supervisor. He will check its quality.**

Nonsexist: **Turn your finished product in to your supervisor. This person will check its quality.**

b. Use plurals. For example:

Sexist: **An employee will be promoted based upon his ability and seniority.**

Nonsexist: **Employees will be promoted based upon their ability and seniority.**

Sexist: **A good manager develops his subordinates.**

Nonsexist: **Good managers develop their subordinates.**

c. Use the words *you* or *your*. For example:

Sexist: **An employee should punch his time card promptly each morning.**

Nonsexist: **Punch your time card promptly each morning.**

Many commonly used words in business communication are potentially sexist. Here are some examples of those words and their more contemporary replacements:[4]

Don't Say	Say
Businessman	Businessperson, business executive, manager
Chairman	Chairperson, moderator, chair
Manmade	Manufactured, handmade
Salesman	Salesperson, sales agent, sales representative
Spokesman	Spokesperson, representative

Don't Say	**Say**
Workmen	Workers
Foreman	Supervisor
Stockboy	Stock clerk

Finally, be sure that you don't fall victim to sexual stereotypes when writing about people who have assumed roles once reserved for a single sex. Such phrases as *male nurse, female attorney,* and *woman manager* merely call attention to the sex of the role occupant rather than the role itself.

4. Tactful writing is not offensive.   Obviously, a reader can find our use of sexist language to be offensive. However, other just as offensive uses of language include the following:

> **Sexist writing is not the only offensive use of language.**

a.   **Humor in bad taste.** Witness the collection message that began:

> *Maybe you've heard this one: Why are little birds so sad in the morning? Answer: Because their little bills are all "over-dew." It may remind you that we have a little bill that is over-due. If you feed it a check . . . .*[5]

b.   **An accusatory tone:** When your writing contains an accusation, whether implied or expressed, you risk offending your reader. Compare these two sentences:

Accusatory: **Perhaps you didn't follow the instruction manual that accompanied your Expresso Coffeemaker.**

Nonaccusatory: **Please recheck the instruction manual that accompanied our Expresso Coffeemaker.**

As you work toward increasing tact in your writing, remember that your own perception of tact is not what counts. All that really counts is the meaning your receiver assigns to the message.

To make the student handbook material tactful, we need to remove the sexist language. To do so, we've removed the words his, his, his, and man.

So that students can air their problems about courses, the university has adopted the grievance procedure described below for all undergraduate students. First, the student should try to resolve the grievance with the instructor. If this doesn't work, then the grievance may be filed with the head of the department in question. The department head will respond to the student in writing. If the student is still not satisfied, then the grievance may be submitted to the Undergraduate Petitions Committee. This committee is a three-person panel made up of two faculty members and one student. Its decision will be final. ■

Characteristic 3: Personal

By personal we mean that what you write should convey a "you" attitude. Such an attitude means that you focus on the receiver's needs and interests—not on yourself, the writer. In terms of writing technique, using the you attitude means you deemphasize the use of *we* and *I* and emphasize *you* and *your*. Here are some examples:

We and I	**You**
We've mailed a check.	You'll receive your check in the mail.
Our savings accounts pay 6 percent interest.	You'll earn 6 percent interest from your savings account.
I want to express my appreciation . . .	Thank you for your help with . . .

The "you" attitude puts the reader first.

Notice that using *you* and *your* makes the reader the center of attention in the message. This *you* attitude has two levels. The first is fairly mechanical and easy. Go through your draft and spot each *I* reference. Then work on the elimination of these words. You won't be able to remove all the references but the tone improves with each removal. Now go through that same draft and insert some *you* references. Up to the point where the *you's* become bothersome and noticeable, they are valuable interest developers. Once or twice in a letter the person's name can be spliced into the message for special emphasis.

The second level of applying the *you* attitude is more elusive and difficult. At this level you are going beyond the mere substitution of *you's* for *I's* and are seeking a between the lines tone that the message is to the reader instead of from the author. This is the level and tone you should strive toward.

Compare these two short messages:

The company wishes to encourage employees to take part in the suggestion system that it has provided; the system has produced many money-saving ideas in the past.

Employees are the heart of XYZ Company, and each employee's ideas are enthusiastically sought and carefully evaluated. Many employee-volunteered ideas have produced time- and effort-saving changes.

Note that neither passage has an *I* nor a *you,* but the second one has a tone that is directed to the employee rather than from the company.

Clearly, tactful and personal writing are related. As you've probably already discovered, using the *you* attitude is a convenient way to avoid sexist language. However, tactful writing sometimes requires that you avoid the *you* attitude in order not to offend the reader. Consider the following:

We and I	**You**
We didn't receive a check.	You didn't send your check.
Employees who are late three days with no excused reason will be dismissed.	If you are late three days with no excused reason, then you will be dismissed.

In the first example, "You didn't send your check" contains an accusatory tone. The *we* and *I* approach implies that the check did not arrive for reasons other than the reader's not having sent it. The second example is less explicit in its absence of tact. The *you* version communicates an expectation that every reader is considering taking three free holidays. The more appropriate *we* and *I* version succesfully communicates the company's policy but avoids the implication that all employees are irresponsible.

Generally, you'll want to put the reader first. Write from his or her point of view. However, if making the reader the center of attention might bring offense, then shift to the *we* and *I* approach.

Here, then, is a new (but not perfect) version of the student handbook material.

So that you can air your problems about your courses, the university has adopted for you the grievance procedure below. First, you should try to resolve your grievance with your instructor. If this fails, then your grievance may be filed with the head of the department in question. The department head will respond to you in writing. If you are still not satisfied, then your grievance may be submitted to the Undergraduate Petitions Committee. This committee is made up of three persons (two faculty members and one student). Its decision will be final. ∎

If your approach might offend the reader, use we and I instead.

Characteristic 4: Positive

Effective written communication is written in a positive tone. How people react to your writing depends in part upon the climate of communication you establish with them. Such a climate can clearly be positive or negative. In Figure 3.1 compare these messages posted on the walls of two different doctors' offices. Both messages have the same meaning. Yet they convey different ideas about the relationship the sender wants to establish.

When writing in business, we want to create as positive a climate and as much good will as possible. Thus, we avoid using negative words such as *delay, can't, impossible, inconvenience,* and *trouble.*

A positive tone develops a positive relationship.

Figure 3.1 Two Doctors' Offices Messages

NO
SMOKING

PLEASE REFRAIN
FROM
SMOKING

Here are some examples:

Negative   You *failed* to enclose a check with your order; therefore, it is *impossible* to send you the merchandise.

Positive   As soon as your check arrives, we'll send your order via
parcel post.

Negative   There can be *no* exceptions to this policy.

Positive   This policy must apply equally and fairly to everyone.

Negative   The oven *doesn't* come with a 40-inch cooktop.

Positive   The oven is available with either a 30-inch or a 36-inch
cooktop.

Negative   The paint is guaranteed not to *dull, chip,* or *scratch* for
two years.

Positive   The paint is guaranteed to stay bright and smooth for
two years.

Negative   We *regret* having *forgotten* to include your refund
check.

Positive   You will receive your refund check by the end of the
week.

Negative   We *cannot* meet until Monday morning.

Positive   We can meet on Monday morning.

The tone we employ sets the climate for our communication. A positive climate means we use a positive tone.

Other than careful word selection, there are two other ways to enhance a positive message; both relate to emphasis. The first approach employs the concept of *reversal words*. These words change the direction or tone of a message from positive to negative or from negative to positive. When they occur at a transition point they identify the upcoming change. This identification can be valuable when you are moving from bad news to good news for the reader knows that the negative is finished.

The change from a positive message to a negative message is unpleasant. For this reason, try not to add extra emphasis to the negative information by saying, in effect, "Brace yourself, here it comes."

Reversal words change the direction or tone of a message.

In summary, we might wish to use reversal words between negative and positive thoughts, but we should always avoid reversal words prior to negative thoughts. *However, on the other hand, but,* and *unfortunately* are examples of reversal words and phrases. *Unfortunately* should especially be avoided since it is a negative word that is used only before a negative thought.

The second approach to gain maximum benefit from your message is emphasis through location. When we use *place emphasis* we place our information at either the beginning or the end of the message since those are the locations of maximum emphasis. The opposite of this works, too; putting negative information in the middle of a message— away from the beginning or ending emphasis locations—draws as little attention to it as possible.

Mass emphasis uses repetition for emphasis. A positive message might be repeated in both similar and different ways throughout the piece of writing.

Let's take a look at the student handbook material. Obviously, we are dealing with inherently negative material in a grievance procedure. We must use the word *grievance;* after all, that is the subject of the procedure. Yet, there are ways of giving the procedure a more positive tone.

So that you can air your problems about your courses, the university has adopted the grievance procedure below for you. Please help us by following each step. Try to resolve your grievance with your instructor. After talking to your instructor, if still unsatisfied, your grievance may be filed with the head of the department in question. The department head will respond to you in writing. If you want further consideration, your grievance may be submitted to the Undergraduate Petitions Committee. This committee is made up of two faculty members and one student. Its decision will be final.

Characteristic 5: Active

Which sentence seems more emphatic to you?

1. Effective business writers use the active voice.
2. The active voice is used by effective business writers.

Sentence 1 was written in the active voice, where the subject performs the action expressed by the verb. Sentence 2 is in the passive voice; the subject receives an action expressed by the verb. The active voice helps make your sentences come alive. Since people usually talk in the active voice, they are more accustomed to dealing with it when you put your words on paper. Active is strong because the subject is acting. Passive is weak because the subject is being acted upon. Consider the following:

Use the active voice to emphasize ideas.

Passive	**A refund will be sent to you.**
Active	**You will receive a refund.**

Passive	**The report was written by Jim.**
Active	**Jim wrote the report.**

Passive	**The product's safety has been shown by laboratory tests.**
Active	**Laboratory tests have shown the product's safety.**

Sometimes you'll want to use the passive voice, especially if you want to de-emphasize a point. Again, we are concerned about tact in writing:

Use the passive voice to de-emphasize ideas.

Passive	**Your payment has not been received.**
Active	**You didn't send in your payment.**

Passive	**Your credit was checked.**
Active	**We checked your credit.**

The passive voice need not always be used to de-emphasize an idea. We can rewrite "Your credit was checked" in the active voice and still be tactful: "To assure that the use of credit is in the best interest of the applicant, we do check all credit references."

Using the active voice guideline, we should make two changes in the student handbook material. In Step 2 the phrase *Your grievance may be filed* should be changed to "You may file your grievance." And the Step 3 "Your grievance may be submitted" should read "You may submit your grievance."

Characteristic 6: Unified

Each sentence and paragraph in business communication should contain only one idea. When writing a sentence, your goal is to make sure that two unrelated ideas don't appear. Meeting this goal is easy if you write nothing but simple sentences. Limiting yourself to simple sentences, however, will result in a choppy writing style characteristic of a first-grade reader: "See Dick. See Jane. See Spot run."

Experienced writers combine simple, compound, and complex sentences to vary their writing style. Yet using compound and complex sentences brings the danger of lack of unity:

Poor	**Better**
Thank you for placing your order, and your new Beachcraft Towels should reach you by July 15. (Compound sentence.)	Thank you for placing your order. Your new Beachcraft Towels should reach you by July 15. (Two simple sentences.)

Poor	**Better**
When you start the engine, adjust the motor speed immediately, and check your owner's manual if you have any further problems. (Compound-complex sentence.)	When you start the engine, adjust the motor speed immediately. If you have any further problems, please check your owner's manual. (Two complex sentences.)

Remember that sentence variety is important. Also don't sacrifice unity for the sake of variety.

Unity applies in much the same way to writing paragraphs. In this case our goal is to be sure that no paragraph contains more than one central idea. However, many times our thoughts get mixed together:

We need to talk about expansion plans tomorrow. The report is due next month, and I'm afraid we're running short on time. I can't figure out last month's profit statement. Need to go over it with you. We're over budget. Enclosed is a bill from the printer. Impossible! Did you authorize this?

You can see that this writer is dealing with three separate ideas—expansion plans, the profit statement, and the printer's bill. The paragraph can be improved by making three paragraphs out of it:

We need to talk about expansion plans tomorrow. The report is due next month, and I'm afraid we're running short on time.

I can't figure out last month's profit statement. Need to go over it with you. We're over budget.

Enclosed is a bill from the printer. Impossible! Did you authorize this?

Paragraph unity: one central idea per paragraph.

Besides reading more smoothly, the material is presented so as to tell the reader that these are three important ideas, as opposed to only one.

Perhaps the best way to make sure that your paragraphs are unified is to begin all of them with a topic sentence. Then do not write any other sentence not related to the topic sentence. Save unrelated ideas for future paragraphs.

Since our student handbook material is so brief, paragraph unity is not a problem. In practice, however, you'll find that most paragraphs are quite lengthy and require careful attention to unity.

Characteristic 7: Coherent

Coherence is also a quality important to both sentences and paragraphs. If sentences or paragraphs are coherent, the ideas in them are clearly tied together and easy to understand.

Sentences often lack coherence because we use pronouns such as *this, that,* and *it* ambiguously.

Unclear	**Your Grasscutter electric mower will operate quietly and quickly, and this will save you money.**
Clear	**Your Grasscutter electric mower will operate quietly and quickly. Its speed will save you money.**
Unclear	**They rented furniture for their apartment that cost $100 per month.**
Clear	**For their apartment, they rented furniture that cost $100 per month.**

Dangling constructions also make sentences incoherent:

Unclear	**Being a preferred customer, I am sure you'll be interested in this.**
Clear	**Since you are a preferred customer, I'm sure you'll be interested in this.**
Unclear	**Having been run through the adding machine, the clerk rechecked his figures.**
Clear	**After running figures through the adding machine, the clerk rechecked them.**

Coherent sentences and paragraphs are understandable because they stick together.

Paragraphs can be coherent if we make a conscious attempt to use certain devices to help the reader along. Unfortunately, we too often assume the reader can read our mind along with our writing, and we produce paragraphs like the following:

Four devices for improving paragraph coherence: parallel structure, linking words, enumerating, and signposting.

You'll want to own a Washamatic clothes dryer for several reasons. It costs only 9¢ for the average load and has a one-year guarantee on all parts. It comes in three brilliant colors—harvest gold, fresh green, and sunflower yellow.

One device for improving the coherence of this paragraph is the use of *parallel structure:*

You'll want to own a Washamatic clothes dryer for several reasons. It costs only 9¢ for the average load. It has a one-year guarantee on all parts. And it comes in three brilliant colors—harvest gold, fresh green, and sunflower yellow.

Parallel structure simply emphasizes all three of the reasons equally.

Another way to improve coherence is to use linking words:

You'll want to own a Washamatic clothes dryer for several reasons. It costs only 9¢ for the average load. Also, it has a one-year guarantee on all parts. In addition, the Washamatic comes in three brilliant colors—harvest gold, fresh green, and sunflower yellow.

Linking words perform the same function as transitions between paragraphs. Other examples of them include *however, and, consequently,* and *therefore.*

A third device for enhancing paragraph coherence is called *enumerating.* Here we give a specific numeric or chronological label to each of our ideas:

You'll want to own a Washamatic clothes dryer for several reasons. First, it costs only 9¢ for the average load. Second, it has a one-year guarantee on all parts. And third, the Washamatic comes in three brilliant colors—harvest gold, fresh green, and sunflower yellow.

Finally, we can *signpost,* that is, assign brief headings to our major ideas:

You'll want to own a Washamatic clothes dryer for several reasons:
Cost—only 9¢ for the average load.
Guarantee—one year on all parts.
Colors—three brilliant colors: harvest gold, fresh green, and
sunflower yellow.

If you examine the student handbook material, you'll find that coherence was added to the procedure when we made other wording changes. Coherence can also be achieved through careful outlining, and outlining will share its benefits with improved clarity as well. Coherence and clarity tend to go hand-in-hand.

Coherent Writing through Careful Outlining

The better you organize your written material, the easier it will be to understand. And the better you outline your ideas, the more organized they will become as you put them on paper. Outlining is one key to reader understanding.

We'll discuss outlining in detail in Chapter 9. However, you can use an outline for any lengthy written communication—memos, letters, policies, and procedures.

An outline is a convenient way to organize paragraphs and groups of paragraphs into a logical arrangement. Imagine, for a moment, that you need to write a memo to employees about timeliness. They are late reporting to work in the morning, they take extended breaks, and their 30-minute lunch hours often last from 45 minutes to one hour. Somehow, you need to communicate to them and influence them to abide by company policies. The first step in writing this memo is to outline your ideas on paper. You might, for example, follow the AIDA (Attention, Interest, Desire, Action) sequence, a formula for persuasive writing we'll discuss in more detail in Chapter 7 on persuasive letters, and construct an outline similar to this:

I. Attention
    A. Some statistics about output per hour
    B. Some statistics about lost output because of lost time
II. Interest
    A. Employees' role in company success
    B. Reference to time policies
        1. Tardiness
        2. Break time
        3. Lunch time
III. Desire
    A. Consequences of conforming to time policies
    B. Consequences of not conforming to time policies
IV. Action
    A. Simple call for conformity
    B. Expression of appreciation for conformity

Since we have outlined four basic ideas (Attention, Interest, Desire, and Action), at least four paragraphs are needed in our memorandum. Also, we might easily have two paragraphs under Interest and perhaps two under Desire. In any case, we are planning our memo logically. If the material is well-organized, our chances of having it understood are increased.

Characteristic 8: Clear

Clarity in writing applies to word choice, to sentence and paragraph structure, and to the overall organization of whatever you write, be it a letter, a memo, or a report. Clarity is a general concept meaning that what we write is understandable to the reader. Naturally, readability (being understandable due to *style* of writing) is important to clarity. Unity and coherence are also important. Clarity also involves several additional techniques we have discussed: choosing your words carefully, using topic sentences in your paragraphs, and outlining your ideas before you begin writing.

Clear writing includes readability, unity, and coherence.

Clear Writing through Word Choice

You may remember that one step in computing Gunning's Fog Index is to determine the percentage of hard words. According to Gunning, hard words have three or more syllables. Yet some long words are easy to understand (for example, hippopotamus, buffalo, and supervisor). More important, though, is that readers may not understand some short words, particularly technical jargon.

Figure 3.2   Avoid Technical Jargon

*Writing clearly means avoiding jargon.
Why didn't he just say: "All the fish
died!"*

Source: Copyright International Paper Company

Avoid Technical Jargon.   Every field of business has its own special language. A blow to the head is a subdural hematoma to a doctor. What the military calls a protective reaction strike is nevertheless dropping bombs. And if you do poorly in school, you'll probably be called an underachiever.

When writing in business, you should avoid using jargon unless you are sure the reader will understand it. Read the accompanying piece from *Consumer Reports,* (Figure 3.3). It contains only four hard words, but notice the impact of the technical jargon.

Avoid Unfamiliar Words.   Jargon basically consists of words that are unfamiliar to us. But many often-used words aren't really jargon, although they create just as much misunderstanding. Try this paragraph:

Fully cognizant of the *inoperative nature* of his *vehicle,* George's *initial* response was to *institute* repairs. *Prior* to *modifying* the timing, he found a *defective* wire in the *anterior portion* of the engine.

We have italicized the unfamiliar words. See if these changes make the paragraph more understandable:

Knowing well that his car was *not working,* George's *first* response was to *begin* repairs. *Before changing* the timing, he found a *faulty* wire in the *front part* of the engine.

Even the simplest ideas can be made almost unintelligible if we use unfamiliar words. Get out your dictionary and see if you can translate these old sayings into their familiar form:

**Technical jargon will
impress your reader
only with the
impression you're trying
to make.
Using familiar words
can improve reader
understanding.**

Figure 3.3   Hey There, Plainspeak Fans . . .

A number of our readers have been bemused by the following gem, enclosed with one of their monthly credit-card statements:

Any holder of this consumer credit contract is subject to all claims and defenses which the debtor could assert against the seller of goods or services obtained pursuant hereto or with the proceeds hereof. Recovery hereunder by the debtor shall not exceed amounts paid by the debtor hereunder.

Well, that's easy enough to understand—if you're a lawyer. If you're not, a translation (as it applies to credit sales) might go something like this:

When you buy a product on credit, you incur a debt. Your creditor may sell that debt to a third party. That third party can't duck responsibility for making good to you on an unsatisfactory product by claiming that he or she is not the one who sold it to you. But you can't get more back than you've paid for the product.

The insert, as is shown above, was sent out by the Mobil Oil Credit Corp. But the legalese wasn't Mobil's fault. As the insert also noted: "The Federal Trade Commission rule on preservation of consumer claims and defenses requires that creditors give you this notice."

Source: Copyright 1978 by Consumers Union of United States, Inc., Mount Vernon, N.Y. 10550. Reprinted by permission from CONSUMERS REPORTS, March 1978.

- He who expresses merriment subsequent to everyone else expresses merriment of most superior quality.
- Precipitation entails negation of economy.
- Pulchritude is not evinced below the dermal surface.

To help make your writing clear, use words that are familiar to your reader. Here are some examples:

Don't Say	Say
Prior to	Before
Subsequent to	After
Accomplish	Do
Reimburse	Pay
Determine	Find out
Transmit	Send
Advantageous	Helpful

Don't Say	Say
Locality	Place
Facilitate	Help
Encounter difficulty in	Find it hard to
Pursuant to your request	As you asked

Clear Writing through Topic Sentences

A unified paragraph, you may remember, has only one central idea. Usually, you'll express this idea in the topic sentence. This sentence clearly states the central idea of the paragraph.

The topic sentence should be placed at either the beginning or the end of the paragraph. In business communication the topic sentence usually appears at the beginning. However, you might place your topic sentence at the end of the paragraph if (1) the main topic of your paragraph will be unclear unless the reader is first exposed to some details, or (2) you are attempting to persuade the reader, and his or her reaction might be unfavorable. In the second case, presenting details first will help you support the position you take in the topic sentence.

The topic sentence presents the main idea of your paragraph.

These two examples should help you understand how the topic sentence (in italics) can make writing clearer:

Burns Brick Company has several employee relations problems. The turnover rate is 39 percent, up 10 percent from last year. Absenteeism has increased almost 25 percent this year. And the number of grievances has more than doubled during the past six months.

The turnover rate at Burns Brick Company is 39 percent, up 10 percent from last year. Absenteeism has increased almost 25 percent this year. And the number of grievances has more than doubled during the past six months. *Obviously, the company is faced with several important employee relations problems.*

By using topic sentences and by ensuring that every sentence in the paragraph is related to the topic sentence (unity), the reader better understands our written message.

Characteristic 9: Concise

Conciseness deals with the specific words you choose to use. It means saying what you want to say in the fewest possible words. The opposite of conciseness is wordiness. You can become a concise writer if you'll avoid (1) wordy expressions, (2) trite phrases, (3) useless repetition, and (4) abstract words.

Avoid Wordy Expressions

Wordy expressions are simply deadweight in a sentence. Many sentences beginning with *there are, it is,* or *there is* are wordy sentences. Notice how you can say the same thing without phrases that make your sentences begin slowly:

Don't say	Say
There are three fine restaurants on Broad Street.	Three fine restaurants are on Broad Street.
It is important that all employees read the company handbook.	All employees should read the company handbook.
There is little time left for us to make a decison.	We have little time left to make the decision.

Slow-starting sentences create wordiness.

In just these three examples we have saved six words at no expense to understanding.

"More matter, with less art" were Queen Gertrude's words to the rambling, wordy Polonius in Shakespeare's *Hamlet.* As she encouraged him to speak more concisely, we encourage you to write more concisely by avoiding such phrases as:

Wordy	Concise
A long period of time	A long time (or two weeks)
At the present time	Now (or the present date)
Consensus of opinion	Consensus
Due to the fact that	Because
During the month of November	During November
For the purpose of	For
For the reason that	Because
In many cases	Often
In some cases	Sometimes
In the near future	Soon
In the event that	If
In the state of Illinois	In Illinois

Wordy phrases are dead weight no matter where they appear in your sentences.

Wordy	Concise
In view of the fact that	Because, since
With regard to	About
With reference to	About
The jar which is blue	The blue jar

Avoid Trite Phrases

Trite phrases are worn-out, commonplace expressions. Because they are overused, trite phrases have lost their meaning, are deadweight in your sentences, and can reduce your credibility as a writer.

Although some trite phrases can simply be deleted from a sentence, others have fresher replacements. Here are some examples:

Don't Say	Say
Advise	Tell
Enclosed please find	Enclosed is
Numerous and sundry	Many
Permit me to say	-Nothing-
It has come to my attention	I have learned
Under separate cover	separately
Please be advised	-Nothing-
Up to this writing	Until now
In accordance with your request	As you requested
Kindly	Please

Trite phrases can make you appear shallow.

Avoid Useless Repetition

Sometimes we repeat ideas for effect—to impress them in the reader's mind. Television advertisements repeat the product's name many times so that we won't forget it. When you write, you might also repeat ideas. Yet one careless mistake we sometimes make is useless repetition of the same idea:

- The two cars were exactly identical. (exactly)
- His pay raise was small in size. (in size)
- We join together in wishing you well in your new job. (together)
- If you can't use the new typewriter, return it back to me. (back)

Repeat ideas for effect, not because you forgot to proofread.

□ What we need are some new changes. (new)
□ Please see me at 3:30 p.m. in the afternoon. (in the afternoon)

The words in parentheses can be omitted from each sentence with no loss of understanding.

Avoid Abstract Words

Abstract words contribute to unclear writing because they are so vague that our reader is not sure what we are trying to say. Concrete words, the opposite of abstract words, have clear, specific meanings. They help readers create the image that we want created in their minds.

Vehicle is an abstract word. When we say, "A vehicle was parked at the curb," the reader is not sure just what kind of vehicle we mean— truck, bus, car, or other vehicle. To create a more vivid image for the reader, we should move from the abstract to the concrete:

Abstract words create unclear images in the reader's mind.

From Abstract . . . . . .
Vehicle→Car→Pontiac→1985   Pontiac→Grand Prix→Brown   and gold 1985 Pontiac Grand Prix

. . . . . . to Concrete

Thus, we should say, "A brown and gold 1985 Pontiac Grand Prix was parked at the curb." Notice how much clearer this image is than when we simply say vehicle.

Here are some examples of the use of abstract versus concrete language:

Abstract	**Concrete**
Your savings account will earn the *highest* possible interest.	Your savings account will earn the *maximum* 6.5 percent interest each year.
The *majority* of our stockholders voted for the new plan.	*Sixty-four percent* of our stockholders voted for the new plan.
Your new, *lightweight* Electro Typewriter can be carried easily from *room* to *room*.	Your new Electro Typewriter is *feather light. Weighing only twelve pounds,* it can easily be carried from *office* to *office*.
You will receive your refund check *soon*.	You will receive your full $132.19 by *July 15.*

In summary, you can write concisely if you avoid using wordy expressions, trite phrases, useless repetitions, and abstract words. Writing more concisely usually means reducing the number of words used, thus saving the reader time and energy. Yet, as in the case of abstract words, conciseness may mean increasing the actual number of words to create a more vivid image.

Return to the student handbook material at the beginning of this chapter. Much of the wordiness was removed when we improved the material's readability. For example, we replaced *in order to* with *so that.* Otherwise, the material needed few changes to make it more concise.

Characteristic 10: Mechanically Sound

Mechanically sound writing is free of two kinds of defects—errors in grammar and format problems. You've probably wondered many times how an English teacher you once had could have been so cruel as to reduce your grade on a theme by three points for every comma splice. Phrases such as *dangling construction, faulty reference,* and *subject-verb agreement* may nauseate you, yet one reason correct grammar is so important is that, at the very least, it helps ensure reader understanding. Consider these examples:

Correct grammar enhances understanding.

▫ A newspaper headline: City Council Bans Gambling Behind Closed Doors
▫ From a letter to an invited speaker: Your speech will be followed by dinner, to begin promptly at 7:30 P.M.
▫ From a newspaper article: An audience of nearly 200 heard her lecture on "The Future of Endangered Species." A number of them have already perished.

Of course we're aware that written communication can often be understood in spite of grammatical errors. However, a second reason for correct grammar is it improves your credibility as a writer. No matter how good your ideas are, if they are presented on paper with poor grammar, many readers will discount the ideas because the grammar detracts from them. Advertisers know that the package sells the product. You'll find that many business people are just as concerned about correct grammar as your English teacher was. Grammar is the package that helps sell your ideas. (Appendix B contains material to help you refresh your grammar skills.)

Correct grammar enhances credibility.

As you read the following chapters about letters, memos, policies and procedures, and reports, you will find there are certain formats for each. Business letters, for example, typically have a heading, inside address, salutation, body, and complimentary closing. As a writer of business letters, you are expected to adhere to this format.

One format requirement for procedures such as the one in the student handbook material is that they be written in step-by-step fashion. Our example is not. In fact, the grammar and format of the handbook material can be improved in at least two ways. First, the word *this* in

Format refers to the physical arrangement of written material.

the phrase *if this fails* has no antecedent. Of course, we understand what the antecedent is, but for the sake of credibility, we should alter the phrase to read *if this attempt fails.* We should also alter the format of the presentation so that it has an orderly appearance. Our new product, then, is this:

So that you can air your problems about your courses, the university has adopted the grievance procedure below for you. Please help us by following each step:

1. *Try to resolve your grievance with your instructor.*
2. *After talking to your instructor, you may, if still unsatisfied, file your grievance with the head of the department in question. The department head will respond to you in writing.*
3. *If you want further consideration, you may submit your grievance to the Undergraduate Petitions Committee. This committee is made up of two faculty members and one student. Its decision will be final.*

Figure 3.4   Evaluation of Student Handbook Final Draft

___√___ Readable	The material now has an index of 7.2.
___√___ Tactful	We've removed the sexist language. The material does not insult your intelligence.
___√___ Personal	Very you oriented.
___√___ Positive	As positive as possible for a grievance procedure, where you must use some negative words.
___√___ Active	Only one sentence in passive voice.
___√___ Unified	Sentences appear to have only one major idea.
___√___ Coherent	All sentences and paragraphs are clearly tied together. Enumerating is used to enhance coherence.
___√___ Clear	Much more understandable than the material at the beginning of the chapter.
___√___ Concise	Deadweight has been removed.
___√___ Mechanically sound	Meets all the format specifications for a procedure. Grammar correct.

In Figure 3.4, we evaluate this procedure against our ten characteristics of effective written communication.

Summary

Finally, let's compare our final product with the handbook material at the beginning of the chapter. We haven't done a perfect job, but we've come a long way from writing for ourselves toward analyzing and writing for our readers.

As you work your way through the remaining chapters in this section, look for ways to incorporate these ten characteristics into your writing. We hope you've learned to apply these ideas to other people's writing. Now you should apply them to your own written communication.

Footnotes

[1]Robert Gunning. *The Technique of Clear Writing* (New York: McGraw-Hill, 1952). Gunning's Fog Index is only one of many formulas for measuring readability. You might be interested in another: Rudolph Flesch, *The Art of Readable Writing,* (New York: Harper & Rox, 1949).

[2]Ibid, p. 38.

[3]*Chronicle of Higher Education,* October 15, 1974, p. 11.

[4]Carolyn Crawford Dolecheck, "Are You Teaching Affirmative Action Writing?" *ABCA Bulletin* 41, no. 4, (December 1978): 21.

[5]Herta A. Murphy and Charles E. Peck, *Effective Business Communication* (New York: McGraw-Hill, 1976), p. 457.

Review Questions

1. How do we interpret Gunning's Fog Index?
2. What do we mean by tactful written communication?
3. What are some ways of avoiding sexist language when we write?
4. Why should we adopt the you attitude when we write?
5. Why is correct grammar important to mechanically sound written communication?
6. When should you use the passive voice? Active voice?
7. How can we ensure paragraph unity?
8. What are some ways of improving paragraph coherence?
9. How can we enhance the clarity of our writing?
10. Suggest some ways of writing concisely.
11. What is meant by positive tone?

Exercises

1. Get a copy of the student handbook for your college or university. As we have done in this chapter, evaluate part of it against the ten characteristics of effective written communication. Then rewrite the part you have evaluated and try to improve it.

2. Get copies of *Time* and *Reader's Digest.* Compute the readability index on three randomly selected paragraphs from each magazine. Compare the average index for each magazine. Are there readability differences between these two publications? If so, why?

3. Write a paragraph containing problems involving at least five of the ten characteristics of effective written communication. Either rewrite the paragraph yourself or trade papers with a classmate and rewrite one another's paragraph.

4. Write a 200-word paper entitled "Almost Everything in this Chapter is the Opposite of What My High School English Teacher Told Me to Do," or "Why I Feel Uneasy about the Ten Characteristics." Discuss in class or with a classmate the differences between writing English themes and writing in business.

5. Write a set of instructions about how to start a car. Use sexist language in your instructions. Have five females who are not in your class read the instructions. Ask them if anything offends them about the instructions. Keep track of those who point to the sexist language and those who don't. Ask those who are not offended by the language why they weren't. Report the results of your survey to the class.

6. Examine the material below. It was written for Teaneck employees only. Customers will not see it.
    a. Compute and interpret the material's readability.
    b. Find at least five other effective writing problems in the material.
    c. Rewrite the material so that all writing problems are removed.

    Customer Refunds
    Teaneck Department Store will refund a customer's money in the event that the customer is dissatisfied with his merchandise. If the merchandise is being returned by the customer, it should be accompanied by a sales slip. The merchandise should be examined by the salesman for potential abuse. Subsequent to merchandise inspection, the salesman should fill out a retail credit check form and acquire the appropriate approval (in the form of a signature) from his supervisor. The customor should be asked to sign the credit check and then refund the money. The credit check should be placed beneath the cash drawer.

7. Rewrite the following sentences so that they conform to the ten characteristics of effective written communication. Each sentence contains at least one error.

    a. Our regional director, a girl with substantial years of experience, will audit your accounts.

    b. If you don't pay promptly, a substantial discount won't be received by you.

    c. In view of the fact that you've had the merchandise for only six months, it goes without saying that your warranty covers the repair.

    d. If the employee has a grievance, the employee should take his grievance to the grievance committee.

    e. Smelling of liquor, the policeman arrested the driver.

    f. It is believed by the Board of Trustees that the new plan will work.

    g. Despite your delay in paying the bill, we will not cancel the account.

    h. I can say at this time that a lawyer could provide a solution to this problem, but that he would necessarily need to be a tax specialist.

    i. There can be no exceptions to this policy.

    j. A full report will be sent to you by the department chairman.

    k. Decentralization of the word processing center was suggested by the report to improve work flow and reduce noise.

    l. You are not allowed to miss work if you don't have a good reason.

    m. At the present time the consensus of opinion is that employee turnover will increase during the month of May.

    n. Your performance was totally unsatisfactory.

    o. The purposes of the meeting was: (1) to communicate personnel policies; (2) encouragement of participation in in-service training programs; and (3) introducing several new employees.

    p. The report was intended for Fred and I, not for John and Susan.

    q. Each of the following pages have been proofread by the editorial staff.

    r. In accordance with your request, attached herewith is the surplus inventory report.

    s. Smoking is not permitted anywhere except in the lobby.

    t. We beg to inform you that unless you act soon, the contract will expire.

Case

Schmitz Clothing Company
Dr. Beryl D. Hart
West Liberty State College

Schmitz Clothing Company is a West Virginia firm which specializes in making tailor-made dress shirts for men and women. The firm has been in business for 15 years. Business has tripled in volume since it started. Your tailor-made shirts are sold in some specialty men's stores across the United States, and a majority is made to order and sold directly to customers who appreciate high-quality tailoring.

This morning you received a letter from an influential customer, Mrs. Ralph Cocoa of Huntington, West Virginia. Her November 15 order for ten tailor-made dress shirts which she ordered as a Christmas present for her husband totaled $550. Her letter reported that when the shirts were delivered by carrier, the box was damaged and all of the shirts were stained with blue. Naturally she is furious. She has requested immediate replacements so she will have them in time for Christmas. In the 15 years you've been in business, this is the first time the carrier has lost or damaged an order. After inspecting the shipping cartons, the carrier reported they were in bad condition, and they agreed to pay you $250.

Your dilemma is that you cannot duplicate the entire shipment in the five weeks before Christmas. You will try to complete five shirts.

■ ■ ■

Case Questions

1. Considering the above information and the feelings of Mrs. Cocoa, determine how you will write the letter. Use the effective letter-writing principles which you have learned.
2. What is the purpose of the letter? What will be your opening paragraph? What will be your explanation? What will be your closing paragraph?

Case

Communicate or Perish
John A. Muller
Air Force Institute of Technology

Pilot Smith wishes to fly from Airfield Alfa to Airfield Beta. The route between Alfa and Beta is over country seldom higher than 50 feet above sea level, but Airfield Beta itself is circled by low hills which are almost 400 feet above sea level. Weather stations along the route Smith intends to fly report the ceiling, the height of the cloud layer, in written reports every four hours. Smith checks the available data just prior to his departure for Beta and discovers that the last report, the 8:00 p.m. observation, only one hour old, states that the ceiling is unlimited all the way to the hills around Beta, at which point it is 1,000 feet.

Smith takes off from Alfa at 9:10 p.m. in unsettled weather and heads directly for Beta. As he nears Beta, he discovers that the ceiling is much lower than he had read in the report. He is forced to fly under 500 feet to stay in visual contact with the ground. His aircraft is not equipped to operate blind, and Smith has no experience flying on instruments only, so he has to maintain visual contact with the ground. Smith manages to get into Beta by slipping between hilltops and the clouds at great risk to his life. Occasionally he must fly through the clouds, risking collision with the higher hills.

When he gets on the ground, very frightened by his experience, he almost immediately meets the weather observer whose report of the 1,000-foot ceiling led Smith to fly to Beta that evening. Smith's fear rapidly turns to anger, and he berates the observer severely, telling him that he is stupid and incompetent, that the inaccurate report endangered the lives of everyone flying into Beta that night, and that he, Smith, intends to report the observer to the local authorities.

Suppose you are the local authority. Smith reports the incident to you, and your subsequent investigation reveals that the facts are as he says. In order to eliminate this dangerous situation, you call in an expert. After consultation you write and issue a directive designed to prevent a repetition of the incident.

■ ■ ■

Case Questions

1. Write a narrative description of the incident starting with the 8:00 p.m. measurement of the ceiling by the observer at Beta and ending with the instructions to pilots and observers which will prevent a recurrence of the problem. Explain exactly what the problem was and include definitions of term *ceiling* at all significant points in your narration.
2. What knowledge or experience must a person have to understand the word and idea *ceiling?*
3. The observer's measurement of the cloud cover was quite scientific, as are all weather measurements. In view of the problems Smith had, why bother with weather reports at all? Especially written reports?

Letters: The Visual Dimension

Learning Objectives
1. To acknowledge the importance of the appearance of letters.
2. To enhance the appearance of a letter by adjusting margins in accordance with the length of the letter.
3. To identify the eight major parts of a letter.
4. To identify those additional letter parts which are used occasionally.
5. To type letters using the four major styles of placement.
6. To recognize the advantages and disadvantages of the four styles of placement.

*W*hile a student, Bill Lipton looked forward to three things: graduation, getting a job, and having his own secretary. He had expected the three events to occur more or less simultaneously, but that wasn't the way it worked out. At the time he graduated Bill did not have a job; in fact, it took him six months to find one. Two years ago he was hired as an assistant office manager, the position he presently holds. He does not yet have his own secretary, and he isn't likely to get one in the near future. When he needs a secretary, he uses one from the secretarial pool—that is, if one is available. "It's not exactly as I expected it would be," Bill says. "For example, it's not enough to know how to compose a good letter; you'd better be able to put the thing together."

After several unpleasant experiences, Bill learned that the availability of a secretary does not insure accuracy. When his boss found errors in two of Bill's reports, Bill blamed them on secretarial mistakes. That was when Bill learned he was responsible for the content and appearance of his correspondence and reports, regardless of who typed them. As his boss expressed it, "When you sign it, you're testifying to its accuracy." Bill learned the hard way that he must be knowledgeable about every aspect of business communication. ■

As it will be described in Chapter 13, much of the meaning of any message is nonverbal; it goes beyond words. If, when talking with someone, you closed your eyes you would miss a large part of the message. The same principle pertains to business writing. The reader has access to many cues in addition to the verbal message. These cues, which together constitute appearance, create the first impression that the reader forms of the message and of its writer.

Too often business people overlook the importance of appearance in written communication. The effect of hours of effort spent developing a logical and coherent message may be neutralized by a displeasing appearance. Such factors as quality and color of paper, spacing, margins, and size of type will influence a reader's receptivity to a message.

The appearance of a message influences reader receptivity to it.

While the content of a message is certainly more important than its appearance, an appropriate appearance increases the likelihood of its being read. A written message must meet certain expectations if it is to be read and seriously considered. In this chapter we focus on those expectations and what you should do to meet them. Since message content is of primary importance, a cardinal rule to remember in business writing is that appearance should not call attention to itself. Instead, by meeting the reader's expectations, the appearance of a message should subtly facilitate communication.

The appearance of a message should not call attention to itself but it should meet reader expectations.

Stationery

One of the first things a reader notices upon opening a letter is the stationery on which it is typed. A unique characteristic of stationery, of course, is that it is both seen and felt.

Since stationery should not detract from the message thereon, it should be the same quality as stationery used in most business organizations. A good quality paper will meet public expectations and enhance the image of your organization.

The most common paper size is 8½ by 11 inch sheets, but some executives use Monarch-size sheets of 7¼ by 10½ inches. Half sheets, 8½ by 5½ inches, are often used for brief internal messages such as memos or notes.

The range of stationery weights is 16 to 20 pounds. If lighter than 16 pounds, it is too fragile, and if heavier than 20 pounds, it is too bulky and hard-to-fold, as well as expensive.

White continues to be the standard color for business stationery, although greater use is being made of pastels. Colored paper is used more often in sales letters than in other types of correspondence.

Many companies personalize their stationery with a watermark which is impressed on the paper during production. A watermark is a faint design which can be seen when the paper is held up to the light. The company logo, or some other identifying symbol, is often used as a watermark. Envelopes and second pages should be of the same quality as the company stationery.

> **Stationery should not detract from the message thereon.**

> **The weight of business stationery should be between 16 and 20 pounds.**

> **Business stationery is often personalized with a watermark.**

Letterhead

The printed heading on stationery is called a *letterhead*. A letterhead lends legitimacy to any business organization. Virtually all business organizations, whether one-person operations or much larger, use letterhead stationery.

At one time a letterhead took up a large part of a piece of stationery. It was not unusual to include such things as names of company officers and pictures of the company's plant along with the routine identifying information. A modern letterhead does not include such extraneous details and usually occupies the top two inches of the paper.

The letterhead includes the company name, address, and ZIP code. The letterheads of many firms also include their telephone number, including the area code. Companies engaging in international business often include a code address for cablegrams in the letterhead.

Planning is necessary if one is to avoid having to send letters with an unattractive or disorganized appearance, an appearance likely to detract from the message itself. The placement of the letter on the page is an important determinant of appearance.

A letter which is balanced on the page is more attractive than one that is not. By surrounding your message with ample margins you can achieve a framing effect. Side margins are commonly 1½ inches, and top and bottom margins are approximately 2 inches. By varying the top and side margins on the basis of the message length, you can produce a letter with eye appeal.

> **Modern letterheads are subtle and not distracting.**

> **The placement of a letter on a page greatly influences its appearance.**

> **By varying margin sizes on the basis of message length you are able to enhance its appearance.**

Standard Parts of a Business Letter

Compare pieces of correspondence from a variety of companies and immediately you will notice obvious differences. There may be considerable variation in such factors as size of type, margins, and general appearance.

Although letters may differ in appearance, they are similar in the basic parts they include.

While there will be diversity in stylistic features, you will find agreement in the parts of a letter. No matter how unusual a company's correspondence format is, its letters will contain the same basic parts. Regardless of the purpose of the letter, the reader has certain information needs that the following parts satisfy:

1. Return address of the sender
2. Date the letter was written.
3. Inside address of the receiver
4. Salutation
5. Attention line
6. Body of the letter
7. Close
8. Signature block

There are eight standard parts of a business letter.

Return Address

The letters of most business organizations are written on stationery that has the company letterhead, including address, at the top. When writing a letter on plain paper, allow a margin of at least 1½ inches from the top of the sheet. There are two ways to arrange the return address of the sender: 1) begin each line at the center of the page, or 2) arrange the return address so that the longest line ends at the right margin. The date should be typed at least a double space beneath the lowest part of the letterhead. If there is no letterhead, the date is below the final line of the return address, as shown in Figure 4.5. Since the return address is the first information on the page, it establishes the top and right margins. When using plain paper, the sender does not include his or her name in the sender's address. In either case the sender's address must include street number and name, or post office box number, and city, state and ZIP code.

In the absence of a letterhead, there are two ways to arrange the return address of the sender.

Date

All letters and reports should be dated, since the date tells the reader something about the context in which the letter was written. The date also simplifies the filing of a letter: correspondence within a given file folder is usually arranged chronologically, according to the dates of the materials. The standard form for dates is month, day, and year—for example, November 19, 1986. Companies that do international busi-

The date is an important part of any business letter.

ness often use a day, month, year sequence such as 19 November 1986.

The date should be typed three space lines below the sender's address, whether or not there is a letterhead. If there is no letterhead there will be more line spaces between the date and the top of the page. There will be an equal number of line spaces after the close.

In the full-block or simplified style, the date begins at the left margin. In the modified-block style, the date may be horizontally centered or begun at the center.

Inside Address of Receiver

The first line of the inside address determines the left margin for the letter. The inside address includes the name, title, and address of the person to whom the letter is being sent. Be very careful that all of this information is correct. Letter writers create unnecessary obstacles to their intended goal when they misspell receivers' names or state incorrect job titles.

Information in the receiver's address is arranged in descending degrees of specificity. The most specific information, the receiver's name, if known, is presented first and followed by the receiver's professional title, the name of the organization, mailing address, city, state, and ZIP code. It is customary, although not mandatory, to abbreviate the names of states, districts, and territories. The U.S. Postal Service recommends the abbreviations presented in Figure 4.1. The two-

> **Letter recipients are often irritated by misspelling or inaccuracies in their name or title.**
>
> **Information in the receiver's address is arranged from specific to general.**

Figure 4.1 Recommended Abbreviations for State, District, and Territory Names

Alabama	**AL**	Iowa	**IA**	North Dakota	**ND**
Alaska	**AK**	Kansas	**KS**	Ohio	**OH**
Arizona	**AZ**	Kentucky	**KY**	Oklahoma	**OK**
Arkansas	**AR**	Louisiana	**LA**	Oregon	**OR**
California	**CA**	Maine	**ME**	Pennsylvania	**PA**
Panama		Maryland	**MD**	Puerto Rico	**PR**
Canal Zone	**CZ**	Massachusetts	**MA**	Rhode Island	**RI**
Colorado	**CO**	Michigan	**MI**	South Carolina	**SC**
Connecticut	**CT**	Minnesota	**MN**	South Dakota	**SD**
Delaware	**DE**	Mississippi	**MS**	Tennessee	**TN**
District		Missouri	**MO**	Texas	**TX**
of Columbia	**DC**	Montana	**MT**	Utah	**UT**
Florida	**FL**	Nebraska	**NE**	Vermont	**VT**
Georgia	**GA**	Nevada	**NV**	Virgin Islands	**VI**
Guam	**GU**	New Hampshire	**NH**	Virginia	**VA**
Hawaii	**HI**	New Jersey	**NJ**	Washington	**WA**
Idaho	**ID**	New Mexico	**NM**	West Virginia	**WV**
Illinois	**IL**	New York	**NY**	Wisconsin	**WI**
Indiana	**IN**	North Carolina	**NC**	Wyoming	**WY**

letter state abbreviation should be separated from the ZIP code by a single space.

Inside addresses are typically arranged in this manner:

Dr. John Robinson
Affirmative Action Officer
Central States College
Administration Building
Macon, MO 63552

Modern Office Supply
2226 Main Street
Buckeye, NM 88212

Salutation

By asking yourself how well you know your correspondent, you should be able to select an appropriate salutation. Some frequently used salutations in business letters are *Dear Mr., Ms., Mrs.;* although the use of *Dear* is declining. The better you know the correspondent, the more informal you may be. By the time you have written several times and perhaps talked on the telephone with that person, you will probably be on a first-name basis with your correspondent.

Your knowledge of your correspondent will affect the style of the salutation and of the close.

In the past, salutations of *Gentlemen, Sirs,* and *Madam* were not only acceptable but widely used. These terms are used less today, even when a letter is addressed to a company. Instead a writer, unaware of an individual's name, may address a job title or use a subject line:

Many writers, unaware of a receiver's name, will address a job title.

Purchasing Agent
Kennan Paper Company
Hoffman, NC 28347

Twin Cities Software, Inc.
14162 Perimeter Road
Groton, VT 05046

Dear Agent

SUBJECT: Cash Discounts

The following are examples of typical salutations:

- Dear Mr. Dooley and Mr. Paterno
                or
- Dear Messrs. Dooley and Paterno
- Dear Mrs. Ross and Mrs. Warwick
                or
- Dear Mmes. Ross and Warwick
- Dear Ms. Landers and Ms. Manners
                or
- Dear Mses. Landers and Manners

A business letter writer has the choice of two styles of punctuating the salutation and the close of a letter. With open punctuation there is no punctuation following the salutation or the close. When using mixed punctuation, the salutation is followed by a colon and the close by a comma.

A letter writer may choose between open and mixed punctuation.

Open—Dear Sir   Sincerely

Mixed—Dear Ms. Ladd: Cordially,

When the recipient has a title, it should be used in the salutation (e.g., Dear Captain Watson:). It is sometimes difficult to decide how to address high-level officials in government or dignitaries in the church. Figure 4.2 illustrates appropriate forms of address and salutation for corresponding with certain individuals.

There are appropriate forms of address and salutation for corresponding with high-level governmental or church officials.

Figure 4.2   Forms of Address

Addressee	Address (envelope and letter)	Salutation
U.S. Officials		
The President	The President The White House Washington, DC 20500	Dear Mr. or Madam President:
The Vice-President	The Vice-President United States Senate Washington, DC 20510	Dear Mr. or Madam Vice- President:
Senator	The Honorable (full name) United States Senate Washington, DC 20510	Dear Senator (surname):
Representative	The Honorable (full name) House of Representatives Washington, DC 20515	Dear Mr. or Madam (surname):
Canadian Officials		

Member of House of
    Commons
	(Mr., Ms., Miss or Mrs.) (full
	    name), M.P.
	House of Commons
		Formal: Dear Sir: or Madam:
		Informal: Dear (Mr., Ms.,
		    Miss or Mrs.) (surname):

Canadian minister	(Mr., Ms., Miss or Mrs.) (full
	    name)
	Canadian Minister to (country)
	(city), (country)
		Formal: Sir: Madam:
		Informal: Dear (Mr., Ms.
		    Miss or Mrs.) (surname):

Members of provincial
    governments
	(Mr., Ms., Miss or Mrs.) (full
	    name) M.L.A.
	Member of the Legislative
	    Assembly
	(name) Building
	(city), (province)
		Formal: Dear Sir: or Madam:
		Informal: Dear (Mr., Ms.,
		    Miss or Mrs.) (surname):

Mayor	His or Her Worship (full name) City Hall (city), (province)	Dear Sir: or Madam:
Religious Leaders		

Minister, pastor, or
    rector
	The Reverend (full name)
	(title), (name of church)
	(local address)
		Dear (Mr., Ms., Miss or
		    Mrs.) (surname):

(continued)

Figure 4.2 (continued)

Religious Leaders

Rabbi	Rabbi (full name) (local address)	Dear Rabbi (surname):
Catholic bishop	The Most Reverend (full name) Bishop of (province) (local address)	Formal: Your Excellency: Informal: Dear Bishop (surname):
Catholic priest	The Reverend (full name) (initials of order, if any) (local address)	Formal: Reverend Sir: Informal: Dear Father (surname):
Protestant Episcopal bishop	The Right Reverend (full name) Bishop of (name) (local address)	Formal: Right Reverend Sir or Madam: Informal: Dear Bishop (surname):
Protestant Episcopal dean	The Very Reverend (full name) Dean of (church) (local address)	Formal: Very Reverend Sir or Madam: Informal: Dear Dean (surname):
Anglican archbishop	The Most Reverend Archbishop of (province) (local address)	Formal: Most Reverend (full name) Informal: Dear Archbishop:
Anglican Bishop	The Right Reverend (full name) Bishop of (name) (local address)	Formal: Right Reverend Sir: Informal: Dear Bishop:
Anglican canon	The Reverend Canon (full name) (local address)	Formal: Reverend Sir: Informal: Dear Canon:
Methodist bishop	The Reverend (full name) (local address)	Formal: Reverend Sir: Informal: Dear Bishop (surname):

Miscellaneous

President of a university or college	Dr., Mr., Ms., Mrs., or Miss) (full name) President, (name of institution) (local address)	Dear Dr. or President (surname):
Dean of a college or school	Dean (full name) School of (name) (name of institution) (local address)	Dear Dean (surname):
Professor	Professor (full name) Department of (name) (name of institution) (local address)	Dear Professor (surname):

Some writers use what we call a *salutopening* instead of a traditional salutation. A salutopening presents the first few words of the opening paragraph and the reader's name in place of the salutation.

Yes, Ms. Jefferson:
You are right to expect extended service . . .

Salutopenings are sometimes used in place of a traditional salutation.

After the name in the salutopening, the sentence continues into the letter body which is a double space lower.

Salutopenings eliminate the artificiality of greeting strangers as *Dear*. Conventional salutations, however, continue to be used much more frequently than salutopenings.

Attention Line

The attention line indicates the specific person who should read the letter. It should be placed between the inside address of the receiver and the salutation. The letter is not addressed to that person, however, nor is that person named in the salutation. In fact, the attention line and the salutation are rarely used simultaneously. Either may be used with or without a subject line. (A subject line is used in Figure 4.6.)

An attention line may be used with or without a subject line.

Allied Lenses, Inc.
1418 Industrial Drive
Carbondale, IL 62901

Attention: Mr. Robert Jenkins

Subject: Insurance Plans for Lenses

Some writers use an attention line when they know the receiver's name but do not know the receiver's sex. For example:

Quality Printing Co.
124 East Frontage
Lobo, TX 79855

Attention: W.C. Brown

The Body

The main message of a letter is contained in the body. The body begins a double space below the salutation or attention line. Use a single space within paragraphs and double space between paragraphs.

The body of the letter should convey the necessary information without leaving significant questions unanswered. Many writers believe they are obligated to fill an entire sheet even when a shorter message would

The body of a letter should be long enough to cover the topic but no longer than necessary.

accomplish the same purpose. The body should be no longer than necessary.

Use short paragraphs. Short paragraphs make it easy for a reader to scan a letter and identify important points. Longer paragraphs make the letter more difficult to read. Some authorities consider an average of four to six lines per paragraph to be reasonable.

The Close

There should be a double space between the last lines of the body and the close of the letter. The close should match the salutation in formality or informality. Form letters, especially sales messages, frequently do not match salutations and closes. For example, one may contain a salutation of "Dear Resident" and close with "Sincerely yours" or some variation thereof.

Truly, sincerely, respectfully, and *cordially* are the words most commonly used in closing letters. Each may be used with *yours* and sometimes with *very.* Some common and appropriate closes are:

□	Yours truly	□	Sincerely yours
□	Sincerely	□	Respectfully
□	Cordially	□	Respectfully yours

When one uses the simplified style (shown in Figure 4.7), both the salutation and close are excluded.

The close and the salutation should be of equal formality.

Signature Block

Leave four lines of space below the close and type your name. If the letter is a business letter, type your job title directly beneath your name. The title can be typed on the same line as the name if both are short. In some organizations, the name of the company appears in capital letters two spaces below the close and before the four spaces that precede the typed name. This format was originally used to clarify the company's legal responsibility for the letter. It is no longer considered necessary, and the practice is diminishing.

Through the signature block, correspondents may indicate how they prefer to be addressed.

The writer's name and job title comprise the signature block in a business letter.

Sincerely   *Yours truly*

PHOENIX INDUSTRIES

                                                    Wanda L. Sinclair, Editor

Kenneth E. Booth
Director of Public Relations

Additional Parts of a Business Letter

The standard parts described in the preceding pages are routinely found in business letters. There are some additional parts you should be familiar with since you will use them on occasion.

Reference Initials, Enclosures, and Copies

Reference initials appear at the left margin a double space below the last line of the signature block. When the sender's initials are used, they should be unspaced capitals. The sender's initials should precede the typist's initials, which are lowercase without spaces. A colon, dash, or diagonal separates the two sets of initials. It is not necessary to include the sender's initials, however, if the sender's name is typed below the signature.

If something in addition to the letter is included in the envelope, an enclosure notation should be made one or two spaces below the reference initials. Enclosure may be spelled out or abbreviated *Encl.* or *Enc.* If more than one enclosure is sent, the number should be indicated. Enclosures may be listed although this is not required.

If someone other than the intended receiver will be sent a copy of a letter, that person should be identified at the very end of the letter. List the names of those who are to receive copies after the single letter *c.* This may be used to refer to copies made by any means such as carbon or photocopies. This information is typed at the very end of the letter and appears one or two spaces below the reference initials, enclosure notation, or signature block.

If the sender signs the letter, it is not necessary to include the sender's initials.

At the very end of the letter you should identify persons, other than the intended receiver, who will be sent a copy.

JTD:nvp	*np*
Enclosures 3	*Enclosures: 1. Brochure*
	2. Registration Form
c: Mr. Jenkins	
Ms. Phillips	*c: B. Kelly*

A company may send copies of letters to someone without the receiver or addressee being made aware that this is being done. Such copies are called *blind copies* and noted with *bc.* This notation is typed on the letter copies but not on the original and appears directly below the usual copy notation.

Blind copies are copies of which the addressee is unaware.

Postscripts

A postscript conveys thoughts added to a letter after it has been completed. If a message is planned and well-organized, a postscript would not be necessary. Postscripts are not often used today; when used, they are usually for emphasis. A postscript is often preceded by *P.S.,* but this is not necessary. A postscript should appear at the bottom of the letter, one or two spaces below the last line typed on the page.

Second-Page Headings

When a letter continues beyond one page, each subsequent page should be headed by the receiver's name, page number, and date. While the first page may be typed on letterhead stationery, subsequent pages should be on plain paper.

Subsequent pages of a letter should be headed by receiver's name, page number, and date.

The heading should be typed one or two inches from the top of the page, and the body of the letter should resume four spaces below the heading. Two or more lines of the body must be included to warrant a second page; never begin a second page solely for the signature block. These second-page headings are commonly used:

Wilcox Tool Company   -2-   May 14, 19___

Mr. Frank Settles, July 31, 19___, page 2

*Ms. Tanya Berancourt
March 15, 19___
Page 2*

The date that appears in the heading of the second and subsequent pages should be the same as the date on the first page. This is true even though subsequent pages may be typed on a different date from the first page.

Letter Placement

As stated earlier, companies differ somewhat in the format of letters written by their employees. In general, however, the writer single spaces within the parts of a letter and double spaces between the parts. Some organizations provide employees with a manual or style sheet prescribing a certain style.

The writer has four main styles of letter placement from which to choose: full-block, modified-block, traditional (a modification of full-block), and simplified styles.

The four main styles of letter placement are full-block, modified-block, traditional, and simplified style.

In the full-block style, every line begins at the left margin including the date, close, and signature block. Because of the focus on the left margin, a typist need not make many adjustments on the typewriter; thus it is fast. Critics of this style contend that it results in an unbalanced, left-leaning appearance. The full-block style is shown in Figure 4.3.

In the modified-block style, the date begins at the center of the page or is centered horizontally. The close and the signature block are normally aligned with the date. This style is shown in Figure 4.4

The full-block style contributes to fast typing.

Figure 4.3   Full-Block Style

International Publishing Company ———————————————————   **Letterhead**
Mercantile Building, Suite 20
Miami, Florida 33101

January 5, 19__ ——————————————————————————————————————   **Date**

Professor Laurence Gray ———————————————————————————————   **Receiver's Address**
Mobile Technological College
Post Office Box 1412
Mobile, Alabama 36601

Dear Professor Gray: ————————————————————————————————   **Salutation**

As a prominent educator in the field of business communication, you have
corrected the writing faults of numerous students of business administration. Since you are well aware of current trends in business communication,
would you please share some of your thoughts with us at International?

Over the years different surveys have shown a wide variety of writing
problems experienced by students. What do you think are the most common
problems that your students display in the writing they do for you? As a   ——————   **Body**
professor, how do you help your students overcome these problems? Lastly,
what do you especially look for when selecting a text on business communication?

By devoting a few minutes to writing a one-page response to these questions,
you will accomplish two purposes: 1) you will help us produce textbooks
which directly meet your needs, and 2) you will receive from us a
complimentary prepublication copy of the revised edition of International
Directory of Business Communicators.

By responding today you will be benefiting from the Directory within ten
days.

Sincerely, ———————————————————————————————————————   **Close**

(Ms.) Beverly A. Dolan ————————————————————————————   **Signature Block**
Customer Service Agent

jo

Figure 4.4   Modified Block Style

Mobile Technological College
Post Office Box 1412
Mobile, Alabama 36601

January 8, 19__

International Publishing Company
Mercantile Building, Suite 20
Miami, Florida 33101

Attention: Beverly A. Dolan

During my career as a business communication educator I have become aware
of certain recurring problems which students experience in their business
writing. I am pleased to be asked to share my thoughts on this subject.

Students are never taught to recognize good writing, and this constitutes
a major problem. While they may learn some basic principles of effective
communication, they complete their education still unaware of the
characteristics of good writing.

It seems to me that another problem lies in the unrealistic expectations
possessed by so many students. Too many see themselves in positions of
authority in which someone else will be responsible for correcting their
writing faults. Such unrealistic expectations result in some students
not taking their business communication course as seriously as they
should.

I try to correct these and other such problems by bringing into the classroom many samples of good writing without limiting it to business writing.
In the process, I point out the universal characteristics of superior
writing.

The best way to combat those harmful unrealistic expectations seems to be
to use many realistic case studies and, when possible, to bring in former
students to discuss their experiences involving business communication.
It has been my experience that former students are almost always much
more appreciative of their communication training than is the current
crop of students.

When I select a business communication textbook, I look for one that
presents a balance of theory and practical information in a readable
fashion. Interesting anecdotes, believable problems, and margin notes
also contribute much to student learning. Regardless of the textbook used,
I always recommend <u>The Elements of Style</u> by William Strunk, Jr. and E. B.
White as a supplement.

Figure 4.4   (continued)

```
International Publishing Company
January 8, 19__
Page 2




I hope that you find my comments helpful, and I look forward to receiving
the Directory.


                         Cordially,


                         Laurence Gray
                         Professor of Business

bn
```

Figure 4.5 Traditional Style

```
                                         1628 Ludington Street
                                         Mobile, Alabama 36603
                                         January 14, 19__


        Ms. Beverly A. Dolan
        International Publishing Company
        Mercantile Building, Suite 20
        Miami, Florida  33101

        Dear Ms. Dolan:

             Several days ago in class Professor Gray told us of your interest in
        business communication problems.  He described the way in which he had
        responded to your letter, and, since I don't agree with what he told you,
        I am presenting my own point of view.

             It seems to me that most of what we learn in business communication
        class is useless.  When I graduate from college, I don't plan on spending
        my time organizing and writing letters and reports.  That's what secretaries
        are for.  The way I see it, I'll dictate the main ideas and my secretary
        will do the rest.

             Professor Gray considers spelling to be a major problem, but I don't
        see it that way.  I have lost plenty of points in my business communication
        assignments because of misspelled words.  He shouldn't take off points for
        spelling because, after graduation, I'll make sure that I have a secretary
        who is a good speller.

             Things like communication principles, neatness, and correct spelling
        are truly irrelevant for me.  I intend to deal with important activities
        such as business strategy and long-range planning.  In case you're curious,
        I have already accepted a job offer and will begin work in early June for
        Multinational Industries.

             I wrote this letter so that you would get a student's point of view.
        Please consider it as you plan your next textbooks.  I am sending copies
        of this letter to the officers of Multinational.


                                         Sincerely yours,



                                         Stanley H. Sedgwick

        cc:  Buckminster Sedgwick
             Peter Sedgwick
             Suzanne Sedgwick
             Hunter Sedgwick
```

In the traditional style, each paragraph is indented five spaces. Except for that, the traditional style is identical to the modified-block style. The modified-block style and the traditional style are the most popular styles. The traditional style is shown in Figure 4.5.

In the simplified style developed by the Administrative Management Society, neither a salutation nor a close is used.[1] A subject line replaces the salutation. As in the full-block style, all lines begin at the left margin. With the influx of word processing into modern offices, the simplified

The traditional style is characterized by indented paragraphs.

The simplified style is becoming increasingly popular.

Figure 4.6   Simplified Style

```
                        Pro-Am Sportswear
                        Ivy, Virginia    22945




        January 16, 19__



        Ms. Beverly A. Dolan
        Customer Service Agent
        International Publishing Company
        Mercantile Building, Suite 20
        Miami, Florida   33101

        PROBLEMS IN BUSINESS COMMUNICATION

        The impact of communication upon any business organization is indisputable,
        so it was with great interest that I received your recent letter.  I am
        glad to have the opportunity to express some of my thoughts on the subject.

        The skills and qualities emphasized in business communication courses are
        the skills and qualities in shortest supply in the current work force.  It
        is common for people who hold degrees, whether they be associate, bachelor,
        or master degrees to have severe difficulties in communicating.

        Organizing ideas seems to present problems for many.  This is evident in
        many reports which I read which completely lack continuity.  Letters which
        require follow-up letters for complete explanation should not be necessary
        but often are.

        Students who are unable to make presentations or conduct meetings are
        receiving degrees in business.  It is important that business communication
        courses develop these abilities since they are so crucial to a person's
        success in business.

        The communication course I took as an undergraduate contributed more to my
        own success than did any other single course.  To this day, I continue to
        refer to the textbook used in that course.  Over the years I have partici-
        pated in various training programs on communication in order to reinforce
        those principles learned so long ago.

        Being so aware of the importance of communication, I am especially pleased
        to have the opportunity to express my thoughts on the subject.  I have
        enclosed two brochures with which we communicate our fringe benefits to
        our employees.  What do you think of the brochures?



        Harrison Burke
        President

        kt
        Enclosures 2
```

style is becoming increasingly popular because it contributes to greater typing efficiency. The simplified style is shown in Figure 4.6.

Be aware of the differences in the four main styles of letter placement as described above. Table 4.1 indicates some specific characteristics of the four preceding sample letters.

Most of the business letters you will send or receive will represent one of the four placement styles discussed in this chapter. These are not the only styles of placement, however. Writers will sometimes devise

Special letter formats are sometimes devised to attract the reader's attention.

special formats to get the reader's attention by using devices such as unusual margins, color, and boxes that enclose important information. Sales letters frequently have unusual formats, but even those types of letters are comprised of the standard parts presented in this chapter.

Figure 4.7 identifies the parts of a letter and appropriate spacing. Remember to center the letter vertically by leaving the same number of line spaces between the date and the top of the page as between the

Flexibility in spacing between letterhead, date, and receiver's address allows for balancing the letter on the sheet.

Figure 4.7 Spacing Layout

	Letterhead
xxxxxxxxxxxxxxxxxxx	
xxxxxxxxxxxxxx	
xxxxxxxx	
xxxxxxxxxxxxx	Date
xxxxxxxxxxxxxxxxx	Receiver's Address
xxxxxxxxxxxxxxxxxxxxxxxx	
xxxxxxxxxxxxxxxxxxxx	
xxxxxxxxxxxxxxx	
xxxxxxxxxxxx	
xxxxxxxxxxxxxxxxxxxx:	Salutation
xxxxxxxxxxxx...	
	Body
xxxxxxxxxxxxxxxx,	Close
xxxxxxxxxxxxxxxxxxxxxx	Signature Block
xxxxxxxxxxxxxxxxxxxxxx	
xx	Reference Initial
xxx	Enclosure
xx	Copy

Table 4.1   Characteristics of Letter Placement Styles in Sample Letters

Style	Figure	Punctuation	Return Address	Greeting	Reference Initials	Enclosures	Copies
Full-Block	4.3	Mixed	Letterhead	Salutation	Yes	No	No
Modified Block	4.4	Mixed	Letterhead	Attention line	Yes	No	No
Traditional	4.5	Mixed	Typed	Salutation	No	No	Yes
Simplified	4.6	Open	Letterhead	Subject line	Yes	Yes	No

signature block and the bottom of the page. The spacing between the other letter parts is constant regardless of the style of letter placement used.

Summary

The visual dimension of a letter is its appearance, and it can enhance or detract from the image of the organization or individual that sends it. Such factors as stationery and letterhead are a significant part of the visual dimension.

The eight standard parts of a business letter are the return address, date, inside address of receiver, salutation, attention line, body, close, and signature block. Each part has a definite and important function.

Proper spacing adds much to the appearance of a letter. By adjusting the vertical space above and below the date, a typist can center the letter on the page and thereby make it more attractive. Ordinarily the body is single-spaced within paragraphs and double-spaced between paragraphs.

The four main styles of letter placement are full-block, modified-block, traditional, and simplified. Each style possesses distinct characteristics and conveys a definite image. Occasionally writers devise special styles, especially in sales letters, to attract attention.

Footnote

[1]*The Simplified Letter,* a brochure published by the Administrative Management Society, Willow Grove, Penn.

Review Questions

1. What are the most visible characteristics of business stationery?
2. What information is usually contained in a letterhead?
3. How must letter writers compensate for the absence of letterhead stationery?
4. How does one achieve a framing effect in one's letters?
5. What are the eight basic parts in a business letter?
6. Between which of the basic parts is the writer allowed some flexibility in spacing to adjust the length of the letter?
7. For what reasons might a writer use a subject line?
8. What four words are most commonly used in closing letters?
9. What are the differences between the four main placement styles of a business letter?
10. What is a blind copy? What is its purpose?

Exercises

1. Collect three or more samples of plain business stationery (without letterheads). Write a one-page analysis of the similarities and differences of the three samples.
2. Imagine that you are about to start your own business. Describe the kind of business it will be and create a letterhead for your business stationery. Write a brief analysis of the image you try to convey through your letterhead.
3. Collect three or more samples of letterhead stationery and write a brief analysis of each letterhead.
4. Write the mailing addresses for the following individuals:
   a. Director of the local Chamber of Commerce.
   b. Tax assessor of your area.
   c. Local army recruiter.
   d. President, or chief administrator of the college, university, or school you attend.
   e. Local superintendent of schools.
5. Interview one or more of the following about the style of letter placement that he/she/they prefer(s). Find out why that style is preferred and write a brief analysis of what you learned from your interview(s).
   a. An office manager.
   b. The supervisor of a typing pool.
   c. A typing teacher.

Case

The Dilemma: Length versus Format
Richard Pompian
St. John's University

Mark Rothmark is a recent college graduate who was hired as a personnel consultant by a management consulting firm. The personnel

Figure 4A.1   Letter from Mark R. Rothmark, Consultant

```
                    The Gandlope Company, Consultants
                              P.O. Box 1144
                         Hinsdale, Illinois  60521


                                            June 25, 1984

        Mr. C.M. Robins, director of personnel
        Smith & Smith Mfg. Co.
        2000 Smith Bros. Rd.
        Mildred, MI 47047

        Dear Mr. Robins:

            This is in response to your April 30 request for a study to determine
        employee information needs.  We find that your employees' high morale and
        efficiency have partially been lost as a result of the many personnel
        transfers occuring recently.  We therefore recommend that a company
        newspaper be established as soon as possible.  As you know,many of your
        employees have been transferred to other plants or departments because the
        company has grown so much and so quickly over the past year. This growth
        was due in part to the high morale of the employees, who had formed tightly
        knit and efficient work units. The many transfers have caused those
        efficient work units to break up, in turn causing a number of problems for
        the company. Morale has declined somewhat as a result of the dissolution
        of the "family structure" that was created. Employees have been accusing
        the management of becoming "cold and impersonal" as a result of the
        breakups.  Declining morale has led to declining production.  The decline in
        production has been aggravated because employees frequently call or visit
        ex-members of the group on company time.  The entire situation sets a poor
        example for newly hired workers, who see the work place as a "goof-off"
        opportunity (which will further hurt production). Means must be found to
        re-establish employee morale, eliminate or reduce time away from the work
        place, improve current production, and set an appropriate example for new
        employees.  Although nothing short of a full-scale employee relations
        program can be expected to meet your needs fully, I am proposing a company
        newspaper as part of that program, one which can be implemented very quickly.
            I believe that the newspaper will help combat many of the problems
        indicated above.  In order to help solve your current problems and meet the
        needs outlined above, the company newspaper should help re-establish the
        "family atmosphere" that led to your early success; re-establish respect
        for management by showing that management still cares about the employee;
        provide sufficient news about transferred employees so that remaining
        employees do not spend so much time inquiring about or making contact with
        those transferred; and through all of the above, convince new employees
        that they are to take their work seriously.  If you can accomplish those
        four objectives, you should be on your way to increased productivity.  The
        newspaper could be a 17" x 11" sheet folded to 8-1/2" x 11", printed on
        both sides in one or two colors.  Editorially, I recommend that the
        newspaper focus on news and events directly related to the employees'
        interests.  Management notices and general news about the company should
        be included, but the paper must not be allowed to become a "puff sheet"
        for management.  Instead, it must be "of, by, and for the employees" in
        order for it to accomplish its objectives.
            The paper must be published frequently in order for it to become part
        of the work environment. I recommend that it be published once a week if
        possible, and no less than twice monthly.  If it can not be published at
```

Figure 4A.1   (continued)

The Gandlope Company
June 25, 1984
Page 2

least twice monthly, I withdraw my recommendation, for the paper will
contain "stale news" and not have the intended effect. A survey of
employees indicates that they would like to see the following items:
employee transfers, employee promotions, personnel and family news,community
announcements,company news, and "getting ahead" articles. I will furnish
additional information if you are interested in following up.

Sincerely,

Mark R. Rothmark   P.S.: *I will call you*
Mark R. Rothmark, consultant   *next Thursday*
                                            about this matter.

director at Smith and Smith Manufacturing believed company employees seemed to be spending more time finding out the latest gossip about each other than working. Therefore, the personnel director asked the consulting firm for a study of the employees' information needs, and Mark was assigned to the project.

Mark knew that his supervisor, the son of the owner of the consulting firm, liked one-page letters and memoranda. Mark is generally a pretty good writer. Although he had a lot of information to convey about the project, he tried to put everything in a one-page letter, even though in this instance, he was not instructed to do so.

Fortunately, Mark showed the letter to his boss before sending it. The boss called it "terrible, very poorly written" and told Mark to redo it. Mark is trying to figure out what to do because he thinks the writing is pretty well-organized and clear. He realizes, however, that the problem may be with the format.

■ ■ ■

Case Question

1. What specifically could be done to make the letter more attractive and inviting to read? Give *at least* a half-dozen suggestions. Where and how should your suggestions be implemented?

Case

A Letter Worth Examining
Peter M. Stephan
Writing and Editing Consultant

Acme Widget Company, Inc.
1234 Main Street
Bigtown, State 98799

February 15, 1984

ABC Company
P. O. Box 3333
Anytown, State 43299

Attention: William R. Smith, Vice President, Purchasing

Gentlemen:

Our meeting this past week was short, but much was accomplished. I
always feel satisfied when I come away from such a meeting.

I understand our agreement as follows. We are developing a new widget,
model 23-A-1.2b, which should work better than our previous model that has
given you so much trouble. When you buy one of our new 23-A-1.2b widgets,
we will train fifteen of your people to run it. If you want more than
fifteen people trained, however, you will have to buy another widget; we
provide free training for only fifteen people per widget purchase.

You ought to be more satisfied with this widget than with our previous
models. If not, we should have another model on the market in a year or
so. Maybe it will be more satisfactory.

We will be delivering your widget as soon as we get the bugs out of our
production line. Then we can set up the time for the training session.
As soon as you identify your training session participants, call your
training director (I forget his name) to work out the logistics. We will
be back in touch with you soon.

Call if you have problems, solutions, or questions.

Respectfully,

John Adamson
Vice-President, Sales

Case Questions

1. What behavior does Adamson want to get from Smith? What behavior is he likely to get if Smith reads this letter?

2. Write a revised letter that will achieve the desired goals.

Good-News and Neutral Letters

Learning Objectives
1. To identify the characteristics of the good-news letter and the neutral letter and the kinds of situations for which these letters are appropriate.
2. To recognize the strategic decisions that must be made in planning good-news and neutral messages.
3. To make effective requests through letters.
4. To develop appropriate written responses to the requests of others.
5. To identify the advantages and disadvantages of form letters and the kinds of situations for which form letters are appropriate.

When Bill Ellis was hired as a secretary for a professional baseball team, he expected his job to have variety and excitement. He thought that he would get to know the players and that he would experience the highs and lows that are a part of any athletic team.

His job proved to be interesting, but there was not a great deal of variety or excitement. While he did meet a few of the lesser-known players, he did not see much of any of them. It surprised him to learn that most of his duties were identical to those he performed on his previous secretarial jobs at a bank and at a steel company.

Bill spent much of his time in all three jobs handling routine correspondence. Although the specific purposes for writing letters differed in each organization, he recognized certain similarities.

Many of the letters to which Bill now responded had been written by children. Thus, misspelled words, poor grammar, and a lack of clarity were commonplace.

One young fan wrote, "I think you're teem is the best one. Pleas send a picture that will fit the frame Grandma gave me. Thanks a lot, Tony Brown." As was true of many such letters, Tony did not provide his address. Another fan wrote, "Send me a picture of your best player so I can see how good he is."

While one does not expect children to be polished letter writers, many of the inappropriate letters that Bill sees were written by adults. Based on his experience Bill says, "If everyone would simply learn the basics of letter writing and become familiar with the vital parts of a letter, communication would improve immeasurably." ∎

A knowledge of the basics of letter writing will improve your communication.

Despite the growing use of the telephone and other electronic media for business communication, the letter continues to play a crucial role in the conduct of business. While organizations have developed multitudes of forms that make it easier to convey certain kinds of information, the letter is still most important in many situations. For instance, letters provide the most personal contact that much of the public has with business organizations or governmental agencies; frequently letters are the organization's sole contact with many individuals. Thus, the receiver forms an impression of an organization through such letters.

The wider use of the telephone has not made letters less important.

When a letter is readable and thorough, it contributes to building and maintaining the goodwill of the customer. A letter that is vague or poorly organized has the opposite effect. When a customer receives a letter that is not thorough, and thus necessitates additional correspondence, there is an erosion of that goodwill upon which any business depends. The impact of a letter extends far beyond the factual transmission of information.

In this chapter we present an approach for writing letters that transmit either good news or neutral information effectively. We also discuss the use of form letters.

The Importance of Appropriate Letters

No matter what other skills may be necessary to perform a job well, the ability to communicate is certainly one such skill. Employers frequently hire and promote on the basis of communication skills; an example of one such skill is the ability to write effective letters.

Figure 5.2 is a two-page advertisement that appeared as part of a series in *Newsweek* magazine.[1] The fact that a major corporation chose to sponsor this ad suggests the importance business gives written communication. There is no question that a company's written communication greatly influences the way a reader perceives the company.

For example, when Robert Hill was no longer able to find air filters for his 20-year-old lawn mower, he wrote to the manufacturer about the problem. The company replied with the letter in Figure 5.1.

Robert didn't like the letter he received for several reasons. All he had asked for was help in finding some air filters, and the firm's suggestion was pretty well buried in the letter. Besides that, having owned a Kleenkutter for 20 years, he hardly had to be sold on the product. After reading the letter, Robert said, "They must think I'm an idiot, telling me to read the owner's manual. In 20 years of operating this mower I've practically memorized the manual." Overall, Robert did not like the tone of the letter. The writer seemed to presume that his reader knew nothing about the mower, ignoring the fact that Robert was a long-time satisfied user.

We seldom receive a letter that has absolutely no effect on us: some letters are pleasing, others are displeasing. Robert was definitely displeased with the response he received. Sometimes we get a letter and are impressed with its cleverness; we marvel at the writer's ability to select just the right word. Sometimes we are so aware of the letter writer's flair that, minutes after reading a letter, we may remember a certain phrase but may forget the purpose of the letter. At other times a letter may be so dull that we remember nothing about it or throw it away after reading the first line.

It is not easy to write letters that work, but it can be simplified through a systematic approach. The primary purpose of this chapter is to provide a systematic approach that will simplify and clarify the task of the writer. The approach for each type of letter is described in terms of the strategy upon which each is based.

The situations for which good-news and neutral letters are written may vary, but the characteristics of effective written communication remain important. Review these characteristics as presented in Chapter 3. Any letter, regardless of type, should possess those same characteristics. In addition to adhering to the systematic approach described in this chapter, therefore, you must also incorporate the characteristics presented in Chapter 3. In other words, good business writing is also good writing.

Employers expect those they hire to possess communication skills.

A company's written communication influences public perception of the company.

Each letter you receive greatly influences the way you feel about the writer.

A letter will work for its writer only to the extent that its purpose is clear to the reader.

Figure 5.1   An Inappropriate Letter

March 1, 1984

Mr. Robert Hill
1215 Oakdale Drive
Trenton, New Jersey 08600

Dear Mr. Hill:

We are pleased to learn of your satisfaction with the Q-11 Kleenkutter. Although our products may cost a little more than the products of some of our competitors, they are designed to last longer and perform better.

Since the Q-11 was finely tuned at the factory, it should require very little in the way of maintenance. When servicing is required, however, one must be sure to follow all of the instructions provided on pages 12-19 of the owner's manual. For the best in servicing and repair, it is advisable that you deal with a registered company technician.

Since the Q-11 went out of production fifteen years ago, it has become difficult to find some of the parts for it, but air filters designed for the Q-13 or Q-14 are readily available and may be adapted to the Q-11. Any one of our registered technicians is able to do this, and the cost would be moderate.

The next time you visit a Kleenkutter dealer, why not inspect the Q-14, our newest and most efficient mower? You'll find that it has the same basic design as the Q-11 with some advanced features intended to simplify its operation.

Yours truly,

William W. Dunbar
Customer Service

Writing Good-News and Neutral Letters

In many letters you will transmit either good news or routine, neutral information to the reader. Good-news and neutral letters are easy to write because of the nature of the message. Some typical situations in which such a letter is written are:

Readers are usually receptive to good-news and neutral letters.

- You write to place an order.
- You receive an order which will be filled promptly.

Figure 5.2   A Public Statement on Letter Writing

How to write a business letter

Some thoughts from Malcolm Forbes
President and Editor-in-Chief of Forbes Magazine

International Paper asked Malcolm Forbes to share some things he's learned about writing a good business letter. One rule: "Be crystal clear."

A good business letter can get you a job interview.

Get you off the hook.

Or get you money.

It's totally asinine to blow your chances of getting *whatever* you want—with a business letter that turns people off instead of turning them on.

The best place to learn to write is in school. If you're still there, pick your teachers' brains.

If not, big deal. I learned to ride a motorcycle at 50 and fly balloons at 52. It's never too late to learn.

Over 10,000 business letters come across my desk every year. They seem to fall into three categories: stultifying if not stupid, mundane (most of them), and first rate (rare). Here's the approach I've found that separates the winners from the losers (most of it's just good common sense)—it starts *before* you write your letter:

Know what you want

If you don't, write it down—in one sentence. "I want to get an interview within the next two weeks." That simple.

List the major points you want to get across—it'll keep you on course.

If you're *answering* a letter, check the points that need answering and keep the letter in front of you while you write. This way you won't forget anything—*that* would cause another round of letters.

And for goodness' sake, answer promptly if you're going to answer at all. Don't sit on a letter—*that* invites the person on the other end to sit on whatever you want from *him*.

Plunge right in

Call him by name—not "Dear Sir, Madam, or Ms." "Dear Mr. Chrisanthopoulos"—and be sure to spell it right. That'll get him (thus, you) off to a good start.

(Usually, you can get his name just by phoning his company—or from a business directory in your nearest library.)

Tell what your letter is about in the first paragraph. One or two sentences. Don't keep your reader guessing or he might file your letter away—even before he finishes it.

In the round file.

If you're answering a letter, refer to the date it was written. So the reader won't waste time hunting for it.

People who read business letters are as human as thee and me. Reading a letter shouldn't be a chore—*reward* the reader for the time he gives you.

Write so he'll enjoy it

Write the entire letter from his point of view—what's in it for *him?* Beat him to the draw—surprise him by answering the questions and objections he might have.

Be positive—he'll be more receptive to what you have to say.

Be nice. Contrary to the cliché, genuinely nice guys most often finish first or very near it. I admit it's not easy when you've got a gripe. To be agreeable while disagreeing—that's an art.

Be natural—write the way you talk. Imagine him sitting in front of you—what would you *say* to him?

Business jargon too often is cold, stiff, unnatural.

Suppose I came up to you and said, "I acknowledge receipt of your letter and I beg to thank you." You'd think, "Huh? You're putting me on."

The acid test—read your letter *out loud* when you're done. You

"Be natural. Imagine him sitting in front of you—what would you say to him?"

might get a shock—but you'll know for sure if it sounds natural.

Don't be cute or flippant. The reader won't take you seriously. This doesn't mean you've got to be dull. You prefer your letter to knock 'em dead rather than bore 'em to death.

Three points to remember:

Have a sense of humor. That's refreshing anywhere—a nice surprise

- You are able to make an adjustment as requested by the customer.
- You receive an application for credit, and you are able to grant it.
- You receive a request for information, and you oblige the writer.

When writing a good-news or neutral letter, arrange your ideas directly. In a direct or deductive arrangement, you present your main idea first

Figure 5.2   (continued)

in a business letter.

Be specific. If I tell you there's a new fuel that could save gasoline, you might not believe me. But suppose I tell you this:

"Gasohol"–10% alcohol, 90% gasoline–works as well as straight gasoline. Since you can make alcohol from grain or corn stalks, wood or wood waste, coal–even garbage, it's worth some real follow-through.

Now you've got something to sink your teeth into.

Lean heavier on nouns and verbs, lighter on adjectives. Use the active voice instead of the passive. Your writing will have more guts.

Which of these is stronger? Active voice: "I kicked out my money manager." Or, passive voice: "My money manager was kicked out by me." (By the way, neither is true. My son, Malcolm Jr., manages most Forbes money–he's a brilliant moneyman.)

"I learned to ride a motorcycle at 50 and fly balloons at 52. It's never too late to learn anything."

Give it the best you've got

When you don't want something enough to make *the* effort, making an effort is a waste.

Make your letter look appetizing –or you'll strike out before you even get to bat. Type it–on good-quality 8½″ x 11″ stationery. Keep it neat. And use paragraphing that makes it easier to read.

Keep your letter short–to one page, if possible. Keep your paragraphs short. After all, who's going to benefit if your letter is quick and easy to read?

You.

For emphasis, underline impor-

tant words. And sometimes indent sentences as well as paragraphs.

Like this. See how well it works? (But save it for something special.)

Make it perfect. No typos, no misspellings, no factual errors. If you're sloppy and let mistakes slip by, the person reading your letter will think you don't know better or don't care. Do you?

Be crystal clear. You won't get what you're after if your reader doesn't get the message.

Use good English. If you're still in school, take all the English and writing courses you can. The way you write and speak can really help –or *hurt*.

If you're not in school (even if you are), get the little 71-page gem by Strunk & White, *Elements of Style*. It's in paperback. It's fun to read and loaded with tips on good English and good writing.

Don't put on airs. Pretense invariably impresses only the pretender.

Don't exaggerate. Even once. Your reader will suspect everything else you write.

Distinguish opinions from facts. Your opinions may be the best in the world. But they're not gospel. You owe it to your reader to let him know which is which. He'll appreciate it and he'll admire you. The dumbest people I know are those who Know It All.

Be honest. It'll get you further in the long run. If you're not, you won't rest easy until you're

found out. (The latter, not speaking from experience.)

Edit ruthlessly. Somebody ~~has~~ said that words are ~~a lot~~ like inflated money–the more ~~of them that~~ you use, the less each one ~~of them~~ is worth. ~~Right on.~~ Go through your entire letter ~~just~~ as many times as it takes. ~~Search out and~~ Annihilate all unnecessary words, ~~and~~ sentences–even ~~entire~~ *paragraphs*.

"Don't exaggerate. Even once. Your reader will suspect everything else you write."

Sum it up and get out

The last paragraph should tell the reader exactly what you want *him* to do–or what *you're* going to do. Short and sweet. "May I have an appointment? Next Monday, the 16th, I'll call your secretary to see when it'll be most convenient for you."

Close with something simple like, "Sincerely." And for heaven's sake sign legibly. The biggest ego trip I know is a completely illegible signature.

Good luck.

I hope you get what you're after.

Sincerely,

Malcolm S. Forbes

then provide the secondary details. You will notice this arrangement throughout our coverage of good-news and neutral letters:

1. Start with the main ideas.
2. Present the secondary details.
3. Close on a positive note.

Neutral and good-news letters should be arranged deductively—the main idea should precede the secondary details.

1. Main Idea. Because you are conveying positive or neutral information, resistance or disagreement is unlikely. For that reason, present your main idea immediately. By getting to the point immediately a shorter message will result. Such an approach elicits the goodwill of the reader while saving time—both yours and the reader's.

Present your main idea immediately.

2. Secondary Details. In a good-news or neutral letter, secondary details are usually explanatory. If you are acknowledging an order, the secondary details may pertain to such factors as method and time of shipment. In a letter of adjustment, the secondary details may explain why the problem occurred in the first place. When you present the secondary details, you should respond to whatever questions the reader may have asked. At the same time anticipate and respond to other likely questions.

In presenting secondary details, respond to likely questions.

3. Positive Note. The letter should end in as straightforward a fashion as it began. If you are acknowledging an order, a suggestion of future business would be appropriate. Be brief and direct in your positive note.

The main function of the positive note is to close or complete the message. Its omission will have no significant effect on the message. Do not end with a cliche such as:

Do not hesitate to contact me if I can be of further help.

You would be wiser to omit the close or, better yet, end with a brief and direct statement such as:

Write me again when I can help.

Avoid the use of cliches in closing letters.

The main difference between a good-news letter and a neutral letter is found in the first paragraph. In a good-news letter you begin with the good news, the main point of the letter. Rhonda Davis arranged her ideas in this sequence to respond to a dissatisfied customer's request for a full refund on the purchase price of a five-pound package of grass seed:

It is in the first paragraph that a good-news letter differs from a neutral letter.

Main Idea   Here is a check for the refund you requested.

Secondary   Slight soil irregularities occasionally minimize the effectiveness of any grass seed. Your satisfaction is important to us.

The neutral letter, as the name suggests, presents a message which is neither good nor bad. You begin with the main idea which, as the name suggests, is neutral rather than good news.

Frank Lofton wanted to write Amco, Inc. to request information for a term paper. In planning the letter he arranged his ideas in this sequence:

Main Idea   Please send information on the products manufactured by Amco, Inc.

Seconday Idea(s)   1. I want the material for a term paper. 2. I am especially interested in products developed in the last ten years.

Close   Thanks for your help.

In responding for Amco, Beth Johnson also used a direct approach. She presented this sequence of ideas in her letter:

Main Idea   I am enclosing a brochure describing each of our products.

Secondary Idea(s)   1. The products described on pages 3–8 and 11 were developed during the past ten years. 2. We are pleased that you selected Amco as a subject for your paper.

Close   Good luck with your paper.

> These letters are easy to write since you are transmitting a nonthreatening and often pleasant message.

Characteristics of Good-News or Neutral Letters

In this type of letter, you are complying with the wishes of the other party, sending neutral information, or requesting routine information. The reader will not be displeased with the message. Therefore, get right to the main point. Avoid keeping the reader in suspense.

Such letters should be direct, specific, and complete. After reading the first paragraph (or preferably the first sentence), the reader should know the main idea of the letter. You should cover the topic as specifically as is necessary and thoroughly enough that the reader has no unanswered questions.

> A good-news letter should be direct.

Placing Orders

When you order something from a supplier of any sort, the process is simplified if you have an order blank from the company. When you do not, you must follow the good-news and neutral letter format.

In your letter, indicate exactly what you are ordering, the instructions for shipping, and the manner in which you intend to pay.

Please send me one X-365 workbench. I have enclosed a check for the total amount.

Since I intend to give the workbench as a birthday gift, it is important that it arrive before May 30. If, for any reason, the workbench is unavailable, please notify me immediately.

Robert Palmer works as an assistant purchasing manager for a large company. For many of the purchases he makes, he simply completes an order blank. Frequently, however, he must write letters of order.

When Robert writes a letter of order, he provides enough information

> In the absence of an order blank, the good-news and neutral letter plan should be followed in placing orders.

> Letters of order must be complete.

so that the seller does not have to request additional details. The following excerpt from one of his letters shows his approach.

Please ship the following goods to reach our Silvertown plant by December 1, 19___:

Quantity	Catalog Code	Unit Price	
12	A–812–0610	167.99	2015.88
12	A–842–1914	79.99	959.88
		Total	2975.76

Charge these goods to our account on the regular $^1/_{10}$, net 30 terms.
It is important that the goods arrive by December 1. We appreciate the promptness with which you always fill our orders.

Whether using an order form or writing an order letter, you must include all of the necessary details. Delays often occur because the order letter did not include all of the necessary information.

Incomplete order letters are responsible for many delayed orders.

Order Letter Guide

Start with your main point. *Please send* or *Please ship* are appropriate openings and are likely to result in a fast response.

Provide all the details necessary for the seller to fill the order now. If details such as catalog number, size, color, and price are omitted, further correspondence will be necessary and a delay will result.

Indicate the payment plan you will follow.

Include shipping instructions if you have a preference.

Close with your expectations of an appropriate delivery date.

This guide and the others in the letter writing chapters are intended to assist you in composing the various types of letters. The guides are not meant to be used as outlines. The situations for which an order letter is written vary so much that most letters must be written individually. By viewing each situation as unique you are more likely to write a letter that elicits the desired outcome.

By viewing each letter-writing situation as unique, you are more likely to write an appropriate letter.

Acknowledging Orders

Many business organizations live or die according to the volume of orders received. The link between orders received and business success is a clear one; the link between acknowledgments and success is less

Acknowledging orders is good business.

clear. For that reason, businesspeople have a tendency to play down the importance of letters of acknowledgment.

Many people look upon acknowledging orders as nothing but a time-consuming chore. Some organizations send only preprinted postcards in acknowledgment. Other sellers, reasoning that the promptly shipped order will soon be delivered to the buyer, send no acknowledgment. While the postcard is preferable to no acknowledgment at all, a letter is desirable and personable.

Some acknowledgment of an order is desirable; a letter is preferable.

Correspondents should recognize that while orders are routine for the seller, they may not be so routine for the buyer. Future business with the buyer often depends on the way the seller handles the present order.

The manner in which present orders are handled often determines future orders.

One practice that suggests the seller is uninterested in the customer is the tendency to overuse a message of order acknowledgment. Whether the message is in the form of a letter or a postcard, it should be changed at regular intervals. When a seller persists in sending the same message for a long time, customers may begin to feel they are being taken for granted. Customers most likely to feel this way are those who are most important—your best customers.

*F*rancis Genet has worked as a purchasing agent for three companies for a total of 18 years. During that time he has observed a wide variety of business practices on the part of suppliers. One of the most irritating practices, he believes, is the repeated use of the same letter acknowledging an order. "In some cases," Francis says, "a company will send out the same letter of acknowledgment for years. After a while you start thinking that your business means nothing to the supplier." ∎

At regular intervals a company should change the order acknowledgment letters it uses.

Order Acknowledgment Guide

Tell the buyer that the order was received and is being filled according to directions.

Identify the order clearly enough to prevent the reader from confusing it with another order.

Give the buyer the details of shipment—how it is being shipped and when the buyer should receive it.

State the financial arrangement if it was not made clear prior to shipment.

Express appreciation for the order.

Encourage more orders in the future.

No matter how small the order being acknowledged, its potential may be considerable. If handled properly, today's new customer may be tomorrow's major purchaser. Customers—whether old and valued or brand new—are receptive to a statement of appreciation and an assurance that the order will be sent promptly. Consider the impression likely to be made by each of the following approaches:

- A letter of acknowledgment
- A preprinted fill-in postcard
- A completely preprinted postcard.

The way in which an order is acknowledged will influence the receiver's perceptions of the sender.

Letter of Acknowledgment.

Your order for one X–365 workbench is being processed and will be shipped within 48 hours.

Since you included a check for the full purchase price, we are pleased to pay all of the shipping expenses. We know you will be pleased with the workbench, just as thousands of other customers have been. We believe, Mr. Morris, that you will find the table surface truly resists all types of scratches, dents, and burns. This feature, plus the stability ensured by the four sturdy legs, means you will enjoy it for many years to come.

When you decide to order tools, remember that Harris, Inc., carries a full line of manual and power tools. These tools, like the workbench, are designed to provide good service and take hard use. The drawers and shelves of the workbench were designed especially for Harris tools.

Use the enclosed order blanks and postage-paid envelope for placing your next order. We look forward to serving you again.

This letter got down to business immediately by referring to the item ordered and its shipment. It sought future orders and remains personal throughout.

Individualized letters of acknowledgment provide a personal touch and are appreciated.

Preprinted Acknowledgment.

A preprinted fill-in postcard, shown in Figure 5.3, informs the buyer that the order has been received and action is being taken. If the buyer happens to have placed several orders with Harris recently, however, this postcard may not clarify which order is being filled. Although such a postcard is completely impersonal, it does answer the buyer's most likely question about whether the order is being filled.

Certain merchandise occasionally may be out of stock, especially when the seller does a sizable volume of business. In acknowledging the order the seller must inform the buyer that the merchandise will be available soon.

Many organizations that receive a tremendous volume of orders do not acknowledge orders unless shipment will be delayed. For major re-

Even the most impersonal order acknowledgment is preferable to none, since it tells the buyer that the order is being filled.

Many organizations acknowledge only orders that will be delayed.

Figure 5.3   A Preprinted Postcard

```
Dear _____:

     Your order for _____ has been
received and will be shipped within 48 hours by United
Parcel Service.  You should receive it no later than
_____.

     Thank you for your business.

                    Robert Bates
                    Harris, Inc.
```

tailers, such as Sears, most orders are filled almost immediately—the goods arrive as quickly as any acknowledgment would.

When a delay does occur, it is acknowledged by the form in Figure 5.4. The customer's address, along with the information necessary for the customer to identify the order, is written on the front of the postcard. Without this information customers who have placed several orders do not know which order was delayed. On the other side of the card, Figure 5.4 (continued), is a sales message.

Any of the three kinds of acknowledgments is better than no acknowledgment. Even when an order is filled promptly, unless an acknowledgment is made, the customer is left wondering until the shipment actually arrives.

Figure 5.4   Postcard Informing the Consumer of a Delay in Shipment

SEARS, ROEBUCK AND CO.
Customer Relations Dept.
925 S. Homan Ave.
Chicago, Illinois 60607

Sears

THANK YOU . . . . .
. . . for your order.
The merchandise you ordered
is temporarily out of stock.
We expect to make shipment
by the date shown.
Should you write about this
order, please return this card
with your letter.

Source: Courtesy of Sears, Roebuck and Co.

Figure 5.4   (continued)

Sears

Shop and Save

the convenient Catalog way . . . Place
orders by phone or in person at your
nearest Sears Retail Catalog Order
Department, Sears Catalog Sales Office,
or Sears Catalog Merchant.

Source: Courtesy of Sears, Roebuck and Co.

The benefits of a personal letter of acknowledgment must be weighed against its cost. Such letters are expensive, but they can be justified if an opportunity for significant further business exists.

In many cases a form letter will suffice, but it is unwise to rely solely on forms to acknowledge orders. An organization will be most effective in acknowledging orders through a rational use of a combination of completely preprinted forms, fill-in forms, and personal letters.

Personal letters of acknowledgment are expensive, but the expense can often be justified.

Requesting Credit

When you request credit by letter, the sequence of ideas is identical to those in the standard order letter. As with an order letter, you should get to the point immediately and provide the necessary details immediately thereafter.

Get to the point immediately when requesting credit.

Please open a charge account for me. My name and address follow:

Marcia O. Bonner
1400 Tiffany Avenue, Apt. 980
Orlando, FL 32802

Prior to moving to Orlando I lived for three years at

1011 Live Oak Lane
Building C
New Orleans, LA 70113

While living in New Orleans I had charge accounts with Axel's Emporium, Carson's Department Store, and Michelle's Boutique.

I have worked for B&J Electronics for the past five years as a sales representative. I earn more than $25,000 per year.

My Orlando bank is Sun City Bank & Trust, where I have a checking and a savings account. In New Orleans I banked at Tri-State Bank.

Most requests for consumer credit are made by completing an application form furnished by the organization from which credit is sought. Even the person who writes a letter requesting credit will probably be asked to complete such a form. The information requested, however, will be very similar to that provided in the letter.

Most requests for credit are made on application forms.

A person opening a new business will most likely request credit by letter. The sequence of ideas will be identical to those presented by an individual consumer.

Please open a credit line of $1,500 for my company, Schief Clothiers, Inc., formerly known as Threads Unlimited.

On July 1, 1984, I purchased Threads Unlimited from the estate of Waldo Gillis. I plan to feature your Falcon line of sportswear as our highest quality offering.

I have 12 years of experience in men's clothing, the last four of which were spent owning and operating Suit City in Boise, Idaho. The Greater Boise Credit Bureau has my complete credit history on file.

The grand opening of Schief Clothiers will be held September 3–5, Labor Day weekend. By that time, I hope to have a complete inventory of Falcon sportswear.

Please send me a confirmation of a $1,500 line of credit and the payment plan you offer. Also indicate the date by which I must place an order so that I will receive it by late August.

Extending Credit

Few business organizations insist on cash payment from customers. The extension of credit has become the rule rather than the exception. Consumers are applying for credit in increasing numbers, and the degree to which it is extended grows proportionately.

A letter in which credit is granted is another example of a good-news letter.

When a person seeks credit and a business organization sees fit to extend it, the situation calls for a good-news letter. As with all such letters, directness is appropriate. What applicants want to know is whether or not they are going to be given credit. The main purpose of such a letter is to extend credit to the reader; however, this is not the sole purpose. In writing such a letter the writer should try to:

1. Tell the person seeking credit that it will be granted.
2. Compliment the person for meriting the faith implicit in any credit approval.
3. Explain the terms of the credit plan.

4. Point toward future business with the customer and express appreciation for the credit request.

We are pleased to send you a Rusk Brothers credit card. Thank you for thinking of us when you decided to open a charge account. It is through your intelligent use of credit in the past that you have earned this account.

Bills are mailed on the 20th of each month and are payable by the 15th of the next month. There is a finance charge of 1½ percent on the unpaid balance each month.

The enclosed brochure describes many of the special services we offer our charge customers. As a charge customer you may easily shop by telephone, and you will receive advance notification of sales.

We appreciate the opportunity to serve you, and we hope to merit your patronage for a long time.

A letter offering to extend credit to an applicant should contain positive phrasing. It should welcome the applicant to a preferred group of customers, and it should express acceptance and trust of the new charge customer.

A company that extends credit takes a risk. Through a careful selection of applicants the risk is reduced but still present. However, once the decision to extend credit is made, the company has determined that the customer has the capacity to use credit wisely. At this point the letter writer should not mar a pleasant occasion with overtones of distrust and apprehension. Contrast the positive tone of the previous example with the negative tone of this one:

In extending credit the writer should express acceptance and trust.

Dear Ms. Saunders:

We are pleased to grant you credit as you requested January 3. Bills are sent monthly on the 20th and must be paid by the 15th. It is our policy to charge 1½ percent interest on the unpaid balance on the 15th. Therefore, if you are wise and wish to protect your credit rating, you will be sure to pay your bill by the 15th. We appreciate the opportunity to serve you.

Sincerely,

The first letter was optimistic and hopeful; the second was neither. In each case the applicant's request was honored, but the impression created was quite different. In extending credit a company has an opportunity to develop a positive relationship with a customer. An effective letter will capitalize on this opportunity.

This is how a furniture factory informed a retailer that credit was being granted and the goods were being shipped:

The manner in which credit is extended will color the relationship between customer and creditor.

The Deltina cane-back chairs you ordered on May 1 are being shipped to your store via Statewide Motor Company. They should arrive in Augusta by May 5. The amount of this merchandise has been debited to your new account.

Your excellent record with other creditors allows us to extend to you our regular terms of 2/10, n/30. As a new customer you may carry as much as $1,000 of our products on account.

Included with your order are some suggested window and floor displays which other dealers have found helpful in attracting customers. Once customers pause to look at the chairs, they recognize their stylishness and proven durability.

Use the enclosed order forms for placing your next orders. You can always count on prompt deliveries and our full cooperation.

Unlike the earlier credit-extending letter, this one was to a dealer. A dealer is generally interested in the sales potential of a product and ways to display a product; a consumer will be more interested in price and durability.

In writing to extend credit you should certainly adapt your message to the interests of the customer. Whether writing to a dealer or to a consumer, however, the same principles apply. In either case the structure of the message is the same.

A credit extension message should be adapted to the interests of the reader, whether dealer or consumer.

Credit Extension Guide

Indicate at the start that credit is being extended.

If goods are being shipped, give the details immediately.

Specify the goods and the method of shipment.

Mention how the reader earned the credit.

Resell the reader on the wise choice.

Point to future orders in the close.

Avoid sarcasm, name-calling, and threats.

Making Routine Claims

Consumers understandably evaluate stores according to how the stores treat their customers. The way in which a store responds to a request for an adjustment is greatly influenced by the manner in which the customer seeks the adjustment.

In seeking adjustments you should indicate immediately what you seek.

When I saw your humidifier advertised on television, I thought it was just what I needed. You said that it would solve the problem of dry air and static electricity, and both of these are real problems in my house.

This information is unnecessary since it does not advance the reader's understanding of the problem.

One thing I didn't anticipate was the way its color would clash with most of the furnishings in my house. I thought that gray would blend in with the surroundings, but it doesn't.	Overly wordy and beside the point.
After using it for one week, I've decided that I can't get used to it. None of the colors in which it comes would be any better for my house.	Writer now states the problem, but reader still has no idea of the specifics of the humidifier (model, size, etc.).
I would like to return my humidifier to you. If I do so, would you please send me a full refund? I would certainly appreciate it.	Writer finally requests a specific action.

This example was wordy and rambling. It was arranged in an indirect sequence, from general (seen on television) to the specific (a full refund).

When writing to seek a routine claim, you should use the direct sequence from specific points to general ones. As you expect the claim to be readily satisfied, tell the reader the action you seek and the reasons for the request. If persuasion seems necessary to get a claim satisfied, the persuasive sequence presented in Chapter 7 is appropriate. The approach followed in seeking a routine claim is straightforward and appropriate.

The indirect sequence is inappropriate for good-news and neutral letters.

Will you please send another Flora and Fauna Dictionary to replace the one I am returning in the attached package?

This book arrived with many of the illustrations blurred, especially those between pages 200 and 300. I have enclosed the invoice which accompanied the book.

If an unsoiled copy is unavailable, I shall appreciate a full refund.

Routine Claim Guide

When making a claim, write promptly.

Request a specific action in the first sentence.

Explain why such action would be desirable.

Express confidence in the reader's judgment and appreciation for the action you are seeking.

Avoid sarcasm, name-calling, and threats.

Approving Adjustments on Claims

When a merchant is able to approve an adjustment being sought by a customer, it calls for a prompt and direct response. This approval is positive, and it includes an attempt at resale.

Granting an adjustment calls for a prompt and direct response.

You will receive a brand-new Deluxe Glide steam iron later this week. We are happy to be of service to you.

Thank you for returning the other iron to us. Our technicians are analyzing its performance in order to learn how to improve our inspection procedures. By calling the problem to our attention you are helping us to serve you better.

You should receive our summer-sale catalog next week. It is full of high-quality products which we are pleased to stand behind.

When a customer seeks an adjustment on the basis of an error made by a business, most firms grant the adjustment immediately. Many cases are not that clearcut, however. Sometimes neither party appears to be at fault. A third party may be responsible or it may be impossible to determine responsibility.

Many firms, not wanting to lose a customer, will automatically assume responsibility even though responsibility may be unclear. For example, a woman ordered a dozen plants through the mail. Upon opening the package, she found that only two of the plants appeared healthy and the remaining ones had died. She had never done business with the company before, and she requested replacements for the plants. The company responded in this way:

Many firms will assume responsibility for an error even when responsibility is unclear.

Dear _____:

A dozen healthy plants are being mailed to you today at no expense to you.

Under normal circumstances plants from Richard Brothers are extremely resistant to those conditions likely to harm lower quality plants. In the five years we have been shipping plants in our patented stay-moist containers, more than 99 percent of the plants shipped have arrived in greenhouse condition.

To insure that plants will arrive in good condition, it is important that they be removed from the carton and transplanted within 24 hours after you receive them. Doing this will result in healthy plants which will add much to your pleasures of gardening.

From now on you will receive our Green Thumb newsletter each month. It features unadvertised specials which are likely to enhance your garden at a fraction of the usual price.

Yours truly,

Adjustment Approval Guide

Indicate immediately that the adjustment is being granted.

Grant the adjustment wholeheartedly.

Play down the negative aspects by avoiding negative words.

Briefly explain the reason for the problem or imply it when describing the measures.

If the reader must take some action, indicate it specifically.

Look forward to future business in the close.

Requesting Routine Information

When you read an advertisement in a magazine about a product in which you are interested, you may have some unanswered questions. Like many other consumers, you may write directly to the company for answers.

In requesting routine information, state the request in the first sentence. In that way there is no doubt in the reader's mind about what information is desired. Next, provide whatever other details might be necessary. Last, point to the future by stating what you want the reader to do.

Note the differences between the two letters that follow.

Requests for routine information should provide whatever details are necessary but no more.

On the six o'clock news last night they showed a brief portion of the speech you gave yesterday.

The purpose is unclear. Since this letter was written to a political candidate, it is not known which speech the writer is referring to.

It sounded interesting, and I would like to learn what else you said in your speech.

This presents no new information.

Please send me a copy of the speech you gave.

Here is the request, but it doesn't clarify much. The reader still doesn't know which speech or whether the speaker's notecards or handouts would suffice in case a copy of the speech is not available.

Information Request Guide

Make a specific request immediately.

Ask whatever specific questions are necessary to get the desired information.

Avoid wordiness by asking direct questions. "Will the machine . . ." is preferable to "I am interested in . . ."

Make a positive and an appreciative reference to the action desired of the reader.

Business organizations send and receive numerous requests for routine information. The more specific a request is, the more likely it is to elicit the desired response.

Can the gas water heater (model HN422) be installed in a horizontal rather than vertical position? I would like to install it in the space under my workbench. It would be in a clean environment, and there would be no tools or equipment in direct contact with it. The room in which I hope to install it is heated. Since I am in the midst of remodeling my house, I would appreciate a prompt reply.

When making a request, be specific.

Granting Routine Requests

Directness is a desirable characteristic in any good-news or neutral letter. When you can answer yes to a request made by another, you should do so enthusiastically. Since it is the answer that the reader is hoping for, say it immediately.

Grant routine requests directly.

Yes, I will be happy to give your sixth-grade class a tour of our plant on the afternoon of May 5.

Your students will especially be interested in the assembly line, but I will also show them one of our research labs, if they care to see one.

The enclosed brochures will acquaint your students with our full line of products. If you will have them read and discuss the brochures prior to your visit, it may make the tour more interesting.

I look forward to meeting you and your class in the lobby of Building B at one o'clock next Wednesday afternoon.

When the manager of a textile plant was asked to donate the plant's scrap materials to a charity drive, he responded with enthusiasm and sincerity.

Yes, we will gladly contribute the scrap materials from our mill for the next four weeks to the Tri-County Charity Drive.

Many of the poor and elderly of the community will benefit from the Tri-County blanket-making project. It is certainly worthwhile, and we are pleased to be a part of it.

We will deliver the scraps to your temporary warehouse on each of the next four Fridays at 2:00 in the afternoon.

When granting routine requests, you should always view the reader as a potential customer. This does not mean your good-news letter must always be sales-oriented; it does mean your letters should display characteristics which are likely to instill a positive image of your firm.

You can enhance the image of your firm by the manner in which you grant routine requests.

There are certain pitfalls which must be avoided if you are to convey a positive image. The writer of the following letter, unfortunately, did not avoid them in responding to an inquiry about when a specific course would next be offered:

Thank you for your letter of February 29 in which you requested information concerning Auto Repairs for the Layperson.

This statement is obvious and unnecessary since the letter is in response to a request.

This is one of our most popular courses, and you are one of many who have expressed an interest in it. The practical nature of the course and the present shortage of auto mechanics seem to explain the popularity of this course.

This information is irrelevant. Besides doing nothing to meet the needs of the reader, the paragraph is oriented more to the writer than to the reader.

You will be happy to learn that we will offer Auto Repairs for the Layperson in the fall quarter. Classes begin on September 8 and will meet Monday and Wednesday evenings from 7:00 to 10:00.

This is the information sought by the reader. It should have been presented at the beginning of the letter.

I have enclosed the necessary registration form. Please complete the form and return it to me as soon as possible along with the tuition payment indicated on the registration form.

This information is necessary and helpful, but it is too vague. The writer should state a specific date rather than as soon as possible.

We feel sure that you will benefit greatly from this course. Please continue to think of us when you decide to enroll for additional courses.

This paragraph is unnecessary and inappropriate. Since the reader has not yet taken any course, it is not the time to sell future courses.

The writer of the above letter could have made a better impression and conveyed the information more efficiently by using the direct arrangement described in this chapter. Here is a better version of the letter:

Our course, Auto Repairs for the Layperson, will begin on September 8. The class will meet on Monday and Wednesday evenings from 7:00 to 10:00 during the fall quarter.

You may register by completing the attached form and returning it to me by September 6. By enclosing tuition payment of $75.00, you will avoid delays often encountered when paying tuition on the first night of the quarter. Many have already expressed interest in Auto Repairs for the Layperson.

Congratulations on taking a significant step in your personal development. Please call me if I can be of assistance.

Use the direct arrangement when granting a routine request.

Request Response Guide

Say yes in the first sentence.

Do so wholeheartedly.

Express interest in the request.

Point toward the future.

Prewritten Messages

There are many situations that do not necessitate a reply that is tailored to a specific individual. The expense of an individualized letter simply cannot be justified in some instances. When situations are so routine that it is impractical to compose individual letters, form letters are often a suitable alternative.

Two approaches are usually taken in the use of form letters. One approach entails the advance preparation of individual paragraphs for use in situations that frequently occur. The other approach has complete letters prepared in advance for use in certain routine situations. These prewritten messages allow an organization to respond more quickly to much of the correspondence it receives.

Form messages allow for immediate responses to predictable requests.

Form Paragraphs.   Coach Hank Sloane found that interest was growing in his summer basketball camps as he became better known through his successful basketball teams. The great number of inquiries about the camps made it difficult for Sloane and his secretary to keep up with their work. After keeping a careful record of the kinds of inquiries he received, Sloane prepared a series of paragraphs that answered the most commonly asked questions. He numbered the paragaphs and, after reading a letter, he would tell the secretary which paragraphs should be sent in response.

For example, when asked by a potential participant about the size of the camp and the possibility of tuition grants, he told his secretary to send Paragraphs 2 and 5. This is the letter that resulted.

Dear _____:

Yes, there are openings available in the July basketball camp. Enrollment is limited to 25 participants per session. As a participant, you will receive intensive coaching that will help you sharpen your skills.

Yes, partial grants are available for a limited number of participants. Please complete the enclosed application and return it to me in order to be considered for a grant. The enclosed brochure describes our camp in greater detail.

Sincerely,

After determining the kinds of information usually sought in incoming routine correspondence, writers can save time by preparing appropriate paragraphs in advance. Some organizations have a manual of such form paragraphs, and each paragraph has a reference number. The correspondent need only indicate to the typist the numbers of the paragraphs to be used and the sequence in which they are to appear.

Prewritten paragraphs may be suitable for responding to many routine types of correspondence.

Form Letters. Inquiries are sometimes so predictable that it is more efficient to go beyond form paragraphs and prepare complete form letters. The only types of information that need be added to a form letter are name, address, and date.

Most form letters in business cover routine matters, but there are some exceptions to this. According to one newspaper columnist, for example, a television network responded to viewers' complaints about a sports commentator with the form letter that follows.[2]

Most form letters cover routine matters.

Dear _____:

I appreciate your taking the time to write to express your feelings about _____. While your comments and pointed criticisms do not pass by unnoticed, I would like to state the feelings of _____ Sports regarding this matter.

Mr. _____ is an expert commentator with a vast knowledge and total recall of many sports and sports personalities. We feel his intelligence and keen mind far outweigh his sometimes controversial statements. The precision and articulation of Mr. _____ 's sports presentations rank him among the best of all sports broadcasters.

Nevertheless, we do not like to alienate our viewers. In the interest of improving all of our telecasts to the greatest possible extent, we take into consideration your comments and the comments of all viewers in connection with future programming. We look forward to winning your full support.

Sincerely,

Form letters are even more efficient than form paragraphs since they are completely prepared in advance. They are more economical than form paragraphs, and they can be dispatched more quickly. An organization's best writers should be assigned to the development of the necessary form letters for these letters are circulated widely.

Some disadvantages accompany this prepackaged approach to written communication. Form paragraphs and form letters are intended for use in highly specific situations, but they are sometimes used in situations for which they were not designed. Care must be exercised to prevent this tendency, since an inappropriate form letter may be more irritating to the receiver than no response at all. Another disadvantage of the prepackaged approach is that form paragraphs and form letters tend to become outdated quickly. Since organizational policies and practices are constantly changing, management should ensure that its prepackaged messages reflect those changes.

Appropriateness of Prewritten Messages. Careful thought should be given as to when form letters are appropriate. In general, form letters are used in situations that occur so frequently that the cost of individual letters would be prohibitive.

Department stores, for example, often use form letters to extend credit privileges to those who have sought them. Colleges may use form letters to acknowledge applications for admission. These are among the many situations in which form letters may be used effectively. An organization should be careful in sending out form letters, because there are always possible exceptions to their use. For example, a company may routinely use form letters to acknowledge orders. This is good procedure, but a form letter certainly would be inappropriate to acknowledge the initial order from a new customer whose business has been long sought.

Consider the two college students who received identical form letters denying them permission to substitute one course for another.

Bill Thompson, an excellent student, asked permission to take another accounting course in place of a required cost accounting course. He had two years of cost accounting experience. Also, the required course was scheduled for a time when Bill had to be at work. He was the sole support of his wife and two small children.

Brad Hennessey, an average student, requested permission to make a similar substitution. The required course was offered at a time that

Before using a prewritten message, management should be aware of its advantages and disadvantages.

Form messages tend to become outdated quickly.

Form letters should be used with discretion.

would conflict with his duties as volunteer photographer for the school yearbook. Although photography was only a hobby, he hoped to make it his profession eventually. ■

When the two compared their letters, they felt that they had been treated with cold indifference. Personal matters certainly deserve more personal treatment and consideration. Form letters constitute an aid to communication as long as they are used with discretion.

Personal matters deserve personal, rather than form, letters.

A major criticism of form letters is that they are too impersonal. Through the use of word-processing equipment, however, it is now possible to individualize form letters somewhat. Automatic typewriters that are controlled by magnetically recorded instructions make it possible to insert special wording for a personal touch. Although the best form letters are not as effective as individual letters, they are expedient. Most readers prefer a prompt and clear reply and thus will overlook any impersonality.

As the volume of business communication increases, there will be still greater reliance on form messages. As long as management exercises good judgment, form letters are an effective communication tool.

The growing volume of business communication suggests greater use of form messages.

Summary

Letters provide a personal link between individuals and organizations with which they do business. For that reason what people think about an organization is determined partly by the letters they receive from it.

When writing a letter that transmits either good news or neutral information, the writer should get directly to the main point. The main point should be followed by secondary details, and the letter should end on a positive note. Besides adhering to this sequence, the writer must also attend to the characteristics of effective writing presented in Chapter 3. The writer should be very specific throughout.

Some of the purposes of good-news and neutral letters are for placing and acknowledging orders, requesting and extending credit, and granting adjustments. Many such letters are also written to request or to provide routine information.

Prewritten messages are often used in order to expedite routine correspondence. In some situations, an organization may profit from the use of prewritten paragraphs. For other instances, completely prewritten form letters may be appropriate. Prewritten messages are often used in those situations that occur so frequently that the cost of individual letters would be prohibitive. This prepackaged approach to business communication is less personal than individually written messages, but it is expedient. Through the use of good judgment, businesspeople can use prewritten messages as an effective communication tool.

Footnotes

[1]International Paper Company advertisement, *Newsweek,* October 8, 1979, pp. 88–89.
[2]Jeff Denberg, "Three's a Crowd," *Atlanta Journal,* December 17, 1979, 13–B.

Review Questions

1. What is meant by the term *good-news letter?*
2. State the arguments for and against an organization acknowledging every single order received.
3. In what ways is a completely preprinted postcard as effective as an individual letter for acknowledging orders?
4. Describe the outline for a letter in which credit is extended to a new customer.
5. In extending credit to a new customer, should the writer state the penalties for late payment? Why?
6. If the seller is clearly at fault and is giving the adjustment sought by the buyer, why is it desirable to explain the problem that necessitated the adjustment?
7. Why is the direct or deductive approach most appropriate for good-news and neutral letters?
8. What criteria determine the appropriateness of a form letter for a particular situation?
9. Why has the wider use of the telephone not made letters less important?
10. What are the three categories of business letters identified by Malcolm Forbes?

Exercises

1. In response to a newspaper advertisement you ordered a bone-colored Cosmopolitan shoulder bag. The price had been reduced from $25 to $10. What especially attracted you to the purse, however, was the personalized single initial on a solid brass signet plate which adorned it. When it arrived, you were disappointed to see the faded appearance of the purse, but you were even more upset when the personalized brass signet plate fell off after one week of use. Write a letter to the company requesting that you be sent a new purse. Address the letter to Cosmopolitan Specialties, Inc., P.O. Box 146–B, Jericho, NY 11753.
2. As vice-president of Cosmopolitan Specialties much of your time is devoted to responding to customers' complaints. Sales of the Cosmopolitan shoulder bag have been better than expected, and the supply is exhausted. Since the purses were purchased at a liquidation sale by the corporate president while vacationing in Sri

Lanka, it is not possible to get any more of them. Write a letter that responds to the customer complaint in the first exercise. Since there are some spare brass signet plates available, you will send an initialed plate with the necessary glue for attaching it to the purse. Imagine that an instruction sheet will be included with the letter so you need not present the instructions. Your letter should be sent to Lois Holland, 1412 E. Boulevard, Apartment 201, Tempe, AZ 85282.

3. You own and operate a medium-size printing plant. After several years of seeking business from Foster's Department Store, you finally receive an order for five reams of letterhead stationery. Compose a letter to the office manager (Walter Davis, Foster's Department Store, P.O. Box 1010, Amston, CT 06231).

4. Presume that you have had no credit experience and that you would like a Gulf credit card. You are 20 years old and working part-time at the campus bookstore where you attend college. Write a credit application letter to Gulf Oil Company, P.O. Box 1519, Houston, TX 77001.

5. You have subscribed to *Contemporary Living* magazine for five years and have enjoyed it very much. During the past two months you have received four notices that your subscription is about to expire. These notices urge you to renew your subscription immediately. According to your records (and you have the canceled check to prove it), your present subscription still has two years to run. You renewed your subscription for three years one year ago. Write to the circulation manager of *Contemporary Living* to request that this problem be corrected. (Address: Box 9112, New York, NY 10007).

6. As circulation manager of *Contemporary Living* you have received several complaints about improper billing in the past month. The cause of the problem is a new computer system; it had been malfunctioning, but the situation has now been corrected. Write a response to the letter described in Exercise 5. The letter should be sent to Robert Strong, 1210 4th Avenue, Vilas, CO 81087.

7. You have been assigned to write a research paper on water pollution in the northeastern states. You are especially interested in the industrial causes of the problem as well as legislative changes that are currently being considered. Write a letter to Senator Justin Davis, Chairman of the Fish and Wildlife Committee and an acknowledged expert on the subject of pollution. His address is Room 410, Senate Office Building, Washington, DC 20000.

8. After buying a package of 100 paper plates to use at a church social, you discover that the package contained only 91 plates. Ninety-seven people attend the social, and you are embarrassed by the shortage. Although the plates are inexpensive, you feel that there is an important principle involved. Write a letter to Quality Paper Products, Saoli, MN 56756.

9. You are industrial relations director of Quality Paper Products. You

receive the letter described in Exercise 8 and must respond to it. You have been unable to learn how such a miscount could have occurred. Write this letter to Betty Rogers, 404 Spruce Street, Flint, MI 48500.

10. For many years, it was the policy of Classic Mail Order House to send a personal note to any customer whose order would be delayed more than a week. This chore has become too time consuming. You have been asked to draft a form letter that could be sent to customers in the case of delayed orders.

11. You are planning a week's vacation two months from now, and you are considering taking a Windjammer Cruise. You have learned the schedule and rate information from advertisements, but you have several questions: How many tourists will there be on the ship? How many of them are likely to be singles like yourself? You are aware that each tourist must perform some work on the ship each day, and you do not object to that. You wonder, however, how many hours per day and what kinds of duties you would have to perform. Write a letter seeking the above information to Windjammer Cruises, P.O. Box 1111, Miami, FL 33101.

12. Assume that you are public relations director of Windjammer Cruises. Respond to the request for information in Exercise 11. Use your imagination in responding, but remind the writer that the fare for singles is $56 higher than for double occupancy. The single-occupancy fare is $251. Write this letter to Bill Hawkin, 1220 Lake Shore Drive, Apartment 1119, Chicago, IL 60607.

13. As an automobile dealer you offer periodic service specials to persons who purchased cars from you by mailing out coupons which feature a special price list for various maintenance and repair services. Gary Brightson (1910 W. Boulevard, Indianapolis, IN 46206) brought his car in for a tune-up and presented an outdated coupon. According to the year-old coupon the cost of the tune-up was $32. The present tune-up special costs $39.50. As service manager write a letter to Gary Brightson and explain the reason why he still owes you $7.50. There is no expiration date on the coupon, only the date on which the coupon was sent out.

14. Inspired by the success of the San Diego Chicken, you purchased an appropriate costume and have become the Rochester Rooster. For $25 you will make an appearance at any sort of gathering. For $50 you will present a 20-minute act including singing and dancing. You are not especially talented, but people don't seem to expect much talent from a rooster and, besides, Rochester isn't exactly the Big Apple. Recently you were hired by Big Bill Bluss, President of Bluss Imports (4848 Lake Freeway, Rochester, MN 55901) to appear at the store and present a birthday gift to one of his long-time employees. When you arrived, a birthday party was in progress and the partygoers insisted that you entertain. Since you could not exit gracefully, you presented your complete show.

Write a letter to Big Bill requesting $50 rather than the agreed upon $25.

15. As the Rooster (from Exercise 14) you come in contact with a wide variety of audiences. At a recent appearance at a St. Patrick's Day party, sponsored by the Kelly Construction Company, the participants were overly enthusiastic. Several partygoers poured green food coloring on you in an attempt to dye your costume, and several others plucked three of your longest tail feathers. Write a letter to Sean Kelly, President, Kelly Construction Company, P.O. Box 1702, Boston, MA 02109) and request payment of $47, $25 for dry cleaning and $22 for costume repair.

16. As credit manager for Walsh Specialties (P.O. Box 143, Conyers, GA 30207), you approve Harold Smith's request for credit. He has just opened a lamp store called Let There Be Light (P.O. Box 840, Atlanta, GA 30304) in an Atlanta shopping center. You are sending him the following items on terms of 3/10, n/30:

3 solid brass shell floor lamps @ $65	$195.00
6 solid brass 6-way lamps @ $75	450.00
1 Cathay table lamp @ $40	40.00
1 clear glass hexagon table lamp @ $35	35.00
	$720.00

These lamps are fashionable as well as functional and have been popular in all parts of the country. Smith recently came to Georgia from Durham, North Carolina, where he had operated and sold a similar business. A credit report described Smith as "generally prompt in meeting financial obligations." As with all new accounts, you limit his credit to $1,000 until he proves himself to be a responsible individual. Write to Smith confirming the order and extending credit up to $1,000. Point out the three percent discount available for payment within ten days. Mention the desirability of maintaining a good credit record. Also, tell him to watch for the new Walsh catalog which he will be receiving in approximately 30 days.

17. You have always wanted to learn French and you are considering taking a one-week French Immersion vacation at the Club Miami (P.O. Box 1900, Miami Beach, FL 33139). You have read the brochures but you still have several concerns. The literature states that a variety of teaching techniques are used. You wish to learn what the teaching techniques are. Are the teachers from France or from the United States? Is the focus solely on language or is the French culture also emphasized? Since you are a daily jogger you are interested in whether there will be time and facilities available. Write to the special events director of the Club Miami to get the necessary information.

18. As special events director of the Club Miami, respond to the letter described in Exercise 17. Teaching is accomplished through lectures, group seminars, daily audio-visual language labs, and daily

French film classics. The French culture receives considerable emphasis throughout the program. The instructors are U.S. citizens, but each has lived in France for at least one year. Two hours are scheduled each afternoon for recreation and there is a park with jogging paths nearby. Remind the reader that beginning on September 1, the fee for the French Immersion vacation will increase from $375 to $450.

19. You have just opened a sporting goods store (The Right Stuff), and you want to send a note of appreciation to each customer who makes a purchase of $40 or more. Besides thanking the customer, you want to mention that you intend to offer frequent unadvertised specials. Also, entry forms will be available at your store for all of the road races and various softball, soccer, and tennis tournaments held in the community. Prepare an appropriate letter.

20. Mrs. Ruth Guffy (1638 Pine Street, Winder, GA 30680) purchased a Redi-Quik microwave oven from your store (Ace Appliances, Atlanta) six weeks ago. At that time she requested that it not be delivered until she returned from her month-long vacation. Due to a mixup in your shipping department, it was delivered the day after Mrs. Guffy left on vacation. A neighbor accepted it and stored it in her garage until Mrs. Guffy returned from vacation. She was distressed to learn that her new microwave had been delivered prematurely. There was slight water damage to the box, but the oven itself was not damaged and it worked fine. Write a letter to Mrs. Guffy in which you acknowledge the mistake and apologize. Also, point out that you are going to have a sale next month on all small kitchen appliances and many of them are color coordinated with her new microwave.

Case

Assessing the Assessors
Randy E. Cone
Department of Business Communication and Office Systems
University of New Orleans

You are the elected Supervisor of Assessments for a county in northern Illinois and are responsible for such duties as sending tax bills, "past due" notices, notices of reassessments, public sales, and the like to all owners of real property in the county. You are assisted by one assessor, one assistant assessor, and fourteen clerical employees with various job titles and responsibilities.

Last week you received a scathing letter from Donald Bowman of New Orleans, Louisiana, a former resident of your county and a long-term property owner. Mr. Bowman complained that one of his duplexes (previously zoned "commercial" and thus taxed at the lowest possible rate) was labeled "residential" and would be taxed at $583 more than last year. Bowman sent you a copy of the letter indicating that his property had been "reassessed," but it gave no reason why the building was now considered "residential" rather than "commercial." The letter (poorly written, you think) had been signed and sent by the assistant assessor; but you'd not seen it until now.

You have investigated and found that not one but a series of errors had been made by the assistant assessor in his four months on the job. In just a matter of minutes, you've learned that a letter similar to Bowman's had been sent to at least 30 county resident property owners that very morning!

In fact, Bowman's duplex *had* been reassessed but, because of a recent change in state law, it would be taxed at 25 percent of market value rather than 33.33 percent as had been done in the past. No zoning changes had been made in the area of Bowman's building, and it will remain "commercial" for tax purposes. Thus, Bowman's tax bill on this particular piece of property will be $74 *less* than in the previous year.

■ ■ ■

Case Questions

1. Write a letter to Mr. Bowman telling him the good news about his tax bill, and try to regain his confidence in you and your office.
2. What is the best method of rectifying the problems that surely will arise when the 30 local property owners receive their tax bills and letters with similar erroneous information?
3. The assessor is the person who hired the assistant assessor, and you feel that "blame" should be shared equally by those two individuals. How can you tactfully suggest more communication between those two people? What can you do to prevent recurrences?

■ ■ ■

Case

Easy to Judge, Hard to Correct
Lynne K. Anderson
Tidewater Community College

Professor Karen Cook teaches a course in business letter writing at Coastal Community College. Instead of a final examination, the students collect letters from businesses and organizations throughout the area served by their college. These letters are then organized into a report consisting of a title page, letter of transmittal, table of contents, the letters, and critiques of each of the letters based on the criteria developed throughout the course in business letter writing. Finally, each letter is assigned a grade by the student.

Every quarter many of the students' reports have letters that were sent by employees of the college. Inevitably these letters receive grades of C, D, or even lower.

Professor Cook concurs with these grades. The letters very often are typed with many unnecessary indentations, thereby adding to the cost of the letter. They are full of *I* and *We* with little emphasis on the reader. Some of the letters are so disorganized they leave the reader wondering why they were ever written. Tired phrases abound; an insincere *thank you* is tacked on at the end of many letters even when there really is nothing for which to thank the reader. Fill-ins on form letters are not aligned and often are done in different size type.

It would be a simple matter to recommend an in-house seminar on improving letter-writing skills for the staff. However, the college already employs an administrative assistant to the president who screens and approves all of the form letters that go out from the college. This assistant does not screen communications that are not mass produced. This assistant's background and experience are unrelated to business communications.

■ ■ ■

Case Questions

1. Would you recommend that the professor change the content of her course to be more in line with the letters sent out by various staff people in the college?
2. Should the professor ask the students not to include college letters in their term projects?
3. Should the professor agree with the students' critiques of college letters and do nothing to suggest improvements?
4. What other alternatives does the professor have?

Bad-News Letters

Learning Objectives
1. To recognize the strategic decisions that must be made in planning messages of refusal.
2. To learn the sequence of thoughts to be conveyed in a letter of refusal.
3. To learn the reasons for the thought sequence presented in a letter of refusal.
4. To identify the characteristics of effective letters of refusal.
5. To learn to write refusals which readers will understand as well as letters which will accomplish the intended purpose.

*H*er greatest accomplishment during her senior year, Ruth Lancaster felt, was getting a job. Because the job market for general management majors was so tight, she knew that finding a job would be a challenge. She never dreamed, however, that it would be so much of a challenge.

She originally planned to rely on the campus placement office but, after several unsatisfying interviews, she expanded her job-seeking campaign. By the time she got her job she had relied on a private employment firm as well as tips from friends. In addition, she responded to several newspaper advertisements and she sent numerous unsolicited applications for employment.

Getting a job proved to be a genuine learning experience for Ruth. Besides the experience, she also acquired a sizable file of rejection letters. She recognized three different approaches organizations took in rejecting applicants.

One small group of firms provided reasons for rejecting her. Such statements as "We need someone with sales experience," or "More of an accounting background is necessary to do this job," provided her with some worthwhile information. She appreciated this approach.

A larger group of firms sent form letters which radiated little warmth and even less tact. Such phrases as "You do not meet our needs," and "Your application will be kept on file for six months," were not at all helpful.

Another sizable group, "the real turkeys," she called them, did not respond at all. Ruth considered this practice to be the height of offensiveness. "Even the coldest form letter is better than no response," she said.

As a result of her experience Ruth now says, "No one likes to receive bad news but the manner in which it's transmitted makes all the difference in the world." ∎

Business organizations are routinely besieged with requests ranging from the acceptable to the extremely unreasonable. Regardless of the merit of a request, however, you must respond to it with restraint and with an interest in keeping the goodwill of the person making the request.

Ruth's experience taught her some of the many different ways of saying no. In addition, she discovered that the way she was turned down affected the way she felt about the company.

As presented in Chapter 5, when you are able to honor a customer's request, the approach is direct, from specific to general. A good-news letter is easy to write. Since there are always some requests that are unacceptable, however, it is necessary to write letters that bring bad news.

In this chapter we develop the strategy underlying all letters of refusal. We discuss the sequence in which ideas are most effectively organized to convey the bad news that characterizes such letters. We devote special attention to adjustment and credit refusals as well as refusals of a more general nature.

The letter of refusal is difficult to write because you are denying the reader's request. The reader is unlikely to respond favorably to such a message, so the directness of the good-news letter is inappropriate. Most authorities suggest that bad news be presented in an indirect or inductive manner.

Many experts maintain that all letters, whether good or bad news, should be direct in approach. They advise, "Get to the point!" In writing a letter of refusal, however, a writer shouldn't hit the reader right in the face. If a direct turndown appears early in a letter, the reader often reads no further and thus remains unaware of the reasons for the refusal. By refusing directly the writer lessens the probability that a reader will graciously accept the refusal. Most likely the reader will become frustrated and alienated.

While good news is transmitted most effectively in a direct manner, bad news should be presented indirectly. If the bad news is presented at the start of the letter, the reader may not bother to learn the reasons for refusal.

Strategy for the Bad-News Letter

The general strategy for a letter of refusal is to induce the reader to read the entire letter and thereby understand the reasons for the refusal. In this way it may be possible to retain the reader's approval and business. A continuing relationship might not have to be sacrificed if you can get the reader to suspend judgment until the entire message is understood.

Since a letter of refusal is not likely to make the reader a friend, the writer should prepare so that the letter has as little negative effect as possible. Before beginning to write such a letter, place yourself in the reader's position. You must decide how to lead the reader to accept your decision.

Imagine that you are the plant manager of an electrical parts manufacturing company. You receive a letter from a sixth-grade class requesting a plant tour for a 40-member group. According to company policy, tours are available only to persons 16 years of age and older and group size is limited to ten.

The company benefits from this policy because it greatly restricts the number of individuals likely to take a plant tour. There is, therefore, less disruption of plant operations. Those excluded from such tours may benefit by not being exposed to the potential dangers of the plant's machines, noise, and fumes.

An effective letter writer will strive to point out how the reader will benefit even though the request is denied. In some cases the writer may be able to make a helpful suggestion or offer an alternate plan. The plant manager, for example, might recommend a film that would introduce the students to manufacturing processes and could substitute for a tour.

Occasionally it may be impossible to point out any benefit. However,

If possible, the letter writer should point out how the reader may benefit from the refusal. If the writer cannot point out a benefit, there may be an alternative to suggest.

a writer who looks at the situation from the reader's point of view will generally find a way either to show a benefit or at least to suggest some alternative.

The key to writing letters of refusal that accomplish the intended purpose is to know the facts of the situation. While situations which require such letters are sometimes similar, they are rarely identical. By knowing the relevant facts, a writer can develop a line of reasoning that the reader is likely to understand and accept.

Steps in Transmitting Bad News

Situations necessitating letters of refusal vary greatly. However, there are certain steps that the writer should follow to produce letters that are appropriate and effective:

1. Start with a neutral comment that indicates some form of agreement.
2. Present an explanation in a positive manner.
3. Convey the refusal.
4. End on a positive note.

Following these steps will help ensure an effective letter.

1. Neutral Comment

Your opening comment should let the reader know the subject of the letter, but it should not imply either a yes or a no. After reading the first paragraph, the reader should be aware that the letter is a response to a request. Ideally the writer will indicate some form of agreement with the reader. For example, a customer wrote to complain about the auto repair service provided by a dealer. The dealer began the response by stating, "You are certainly right to expect service work that is done properly the first time." This opening accomplishes two things: it indicates the subject of the letter, and it points out an area of agreement.

Several pitfalls should be avoided in writing a neutral opening:

A neutral opening should indicate an area of agreement between writer and reader.

a.   Don't imply that the request will be granted. If the reader is led to expect acceptance, the letdown will damage the relationship. "We at Baily Motors take pride in the service we provide our customers" would be inappropriate since the reader could understandably expect acceptance.

a. Don't imply acceptance.

b.   Don't express too much pleasure in responding to the request. "We at Baily Motors are always pleased to hear from our customers" suggests that the writer is enjoying the difficulties the customer is experiencing.

b. Don't express pleasure.

c.   Don't begin the letter too far afield from the subject. The opening should clearly identify the subject of the letter. "For the

c. Don't be too far removed from subject of the letter.

past 50 years Baily Motors has been a leader in sales and in service'' will leave the reader uncertain as to the subject of the letter.

d. Don't ignore the need for a smooth transition from a neutral statement to the explanation. For that reason do not begin a sentence with such words as *however, although,* or *but.* The use of these words is a signal to the reader that a rejection is coming.

d. Don't signal a rejection.

e. Don't use negative words in the opening statement. *Won't, can't,* and *unable* are the kind of words that suggest some form of disagreement.

e. Don't use negative words.

2. Explanation

The reader will be interested enough to continue reading your letter if you have succeeded in your neutral statement. Next you should give the reasons for your decision. The reasons precede the actual denial of the request. By getting the recipients to read the reasons, you increase the likelihood that they will understand those reasons. It may be true that understanding does not guarantee acceptance of the reasons, but acceptance seldom occurs without understanding.

An explanation of the reasons for the refusal should precede the actual refusal.

In writing the explanation, watch out for these pitfalls:

a. Don't be overly apologetic when giving the reasons for your decision. "We at Baily Motors regret to tell you" reeks of insincerity. Assuming that the refusal is based on good reasons, an apology is unnecessary.

a. Don't be overly apologetic.

b. Don't fall back on company policy as a reason for refusing a request. "For 50 years Baily Motors has had a policy that prohibits" is not an adequate explanation. Organizational policies are difficult to understand. If the writer does not blame policy but explains the specific reasons plausibly, acceptance is more likely.

b. Don't use policy as a reason.

c. Don't talk down to the reader. When a writer says, "Our experience in 50 years of serving the public has taught us," it sounds like a parent addressing a child. Readers will not respond favorably.

c. Don't talk down to the reader.

d. Don't be so brief or so general that the relationship between the explanation and the problem is unclear.

d. Provide enough information so the reader will understand.

Whenever possible, emphasize reasons that might possibly benefit the reader. In order to inform a customer that a service contract would not pay for certain auto repairs, one correspondent wrote:

Your service contract pays for all necessary engine repairs as long as the car is brought in for inspection every six months. In the absence of a six-month inspection, the contract ceased to provide coverage. Regular inspections are intended to identify minor automotive problems before they become major and costly ones. Regular inspections help us to balance our work load so that each work day is quite predictable.

The writer not only explained how customers benefited from service contracts but also how the auto dealer benefited. By describing how the dealer will benefit, the writer comes across as candid and honest, and it makes the whole message more believable. Although the explanation is based on organizational policy, the writer never refers to policy. Policies are cold and impersonal, and it is difficult for people to relate to them. On the other hand, when the writer presents reasons that are clearly stated and plausible, the reasons are better received.

In some instances, of course, the only reasons for refusing a request are, plainly and simply, company reasons. In these instances the writer should not go to great lengths to try to dream up imaginary benefits for the reader. Instead, just state the company's reason or reasons and let it go at that.

3. Refusal

In the third part of the bad-news letter the writer gets to the heart of the matter, the actual refusal. If the reasons were explained clearly, the reader can probably infer a refusal even before actually reading it. Ideally the refusal flows logically from the reasons.

Sometimes it is not necessary to state the refusal directly if it can be easily implied by the reader. When a personnel director writes to tell job applicants that they are unsuitable for the position, a statement such as "We need a person who has had actual supervisory experience" will transmit the bad news. It is unnecessary to say, "You do not meet our requirements," or any highly directed equivalent.

Many refusals need not be stated directly since they can be easily implied.

These pitfalls should be avoided in stating the actual refusal:

a. Don't give any more emphasis to the refusal than is absolutely necessary. Devote enough space to the refusal to convey it, but do not belabor it.

b. Don't structure the letter so that the refusal stands out. The refusal should not call attention to itself; it should be embedded in the letter.

c. Don't make a direct negative statement of refusal. Telling the reader, "Since you forgot to oil the motor, we are unable to give you a refund," conveys the message; however, its accusatory tone may alienate the reader. "We would refund the purchase price if the maintenance instructions had been followed" is preferable.

d. Don't use the active voice in stating the rejection. "The admissions committee voted against your application for membership" is overly blunt and calls undue attention to the refusal. "Your application for membership was denied by the admissions committee" is more muted but still conveys the refusal.

If there is any chance that the message may be misunderstood, the refusal should be stated directly. The clearer the relationship between the reasons and a refusal, the less necessary it is to state the refusal explicitly.

4. Positive Ending

A letter of refusal should end on an upbeat and should leave the reader favorably disposed toward the writer (and the business). After conveying the refusal, the writer should try to regain some of the goodwill that was lost. This can be done in a number of ways. Even though you may have to turn down a person's request, you may be able to suggest an alternative. A department store, for example, may suggest its layaway service when it rejects a person's credit application. When you are unable to offer an alternative, a constructive suggestion of some sort may still be found.

Letters of refusal should end on a positive note.

To end on a positive note, avoid these pitfalls:

a. Don't bring the refusal up again.

b. Don't apologize for the refusal. You should leave the reader aware of your concern and of your good wishes rather than of the refusal. An apology will merely remind the reader of the refusal.

c. Don't resort to tired phrases in the closing. "If I can be of help in the future, please contact me" is so shopworn it is meaningless.

The purpose of the ending is to show the reader that you remain interested. Even if there is no suitable alternative, an opportunity to resell the reader on your organization may exist.

At the close of the letter the reader should be left aware of the writer's concern rather than of the refusal.

Adjustment Refusals

Customers who request adjustments generally consider themselves and their requests reasonable. Most companies take pride in their equitable adjustment policies. No matter how liberal a company's attitude toward claims is, however, certain requests are bound to be refused. Writing an adjustment refusal letter is a delicate process, for the writer implies that the request, viewed by the customer as reasonable, actually is not.

In writing an adjustment refusal you should follow the four steps described for refusals. Before starting to write, however, review the facts involved. Assuming that the facts justify a refusal, you must decide how best to transmit the refusal. As with all letters of refusal two main purposes exist: (1) to state the refusal and (2) to maintain a positive relationship with the reader. The second purpose is especially important since customers seek adjustments, and customers are more likely to

Adjustment refusals are difficult to write since you are denying a request considered reasonable by the customer.
Even though you are refusing customers' requests, you may still keep them favorably disposed toward you.

return for further business if they have been treated well. By maintaining a positive relationship with customers, the writer will usually be able to retain their business.

Imagine that you are the sales manager of a company that manufactures sporting goods. A retailer writes to ask if she might return a sizable number of skateboards that she purchased from your company. Although interest in skateboarding had been high across the nation, it never grew very popular in Green Bay where the retailer's store is located. Since interest in skateboarding is declining nationally, the skateboards would take up valuable warehouse space for some time. You decide that it is unwise to grant her request, and you write her accordingly. Here is how one correspondent did it:

Neutral Comment   It certainly was reasonable for you to expect the Rollfree skateboards to be a popular item among your customers. After all, they have been shown to be superior both in durability and in safety. Besides that, sales figures have shown it to be one of the most popular skateboards in the country.

Reasons Implied Refusal   One of the many challenges in the leisure-goods field is the speed with which the customers' interests change. Who will ever forget the hula-hoop craze and how abruptly it ended? Being in this business we realize that we have to live with the public's changing tastes, don't we? We're always willing to make adjustments if there are quality problems in our merchandise. In the absence of such problems our "all sales final" plan must be maintained.

Hopeful Note   Some analysts already predict a resurging interest in skateboarding. This resurgence, plus Rollfree's upcoming national advertising campaign, should help boost your sales. Also, I am sending you separately some new mats for newspaper advertisements which have stimulated sales in cities like Green Bay.

As mentioned earlier, the indirect approach is appropriate for most bad-news letters. The manager of a convention hotel used this approach in responding to a request for an adjustment. The president of a national student government association wrote to complain about the quantity of food the hotel provided for the Keynote Night banquet.

In refusing adjustment requests the writer should take the indirect approach.

Pleasing our customers is the foremost goal of the Elliot Plaza. Since our success depends upon your satisfaction, we appreciate your comments regarding the banquet service provided for your group.

Having catered banquets for more than 200 groups during the past year, we have established a reputation for offering quality meals at rea-

sonable prices. Our standards ensure that food will be served in generous portions. Our records show that the dinner prepared for your group was identical to portions served similar-sized groups, most of which have praised our food service. We would certainly make an adjustment if our standard servings had not been available for your group.

Many organizations are already reserving rooms for holiday banquets, and most of them are repeat customers. We would appreciate the opportunity to count you and your group among them.

When a rock-concert promoter was forced to make a substitution for a warm-up group she had advertised, she received a complaint following the concert. She sought to reject the request for a refund without sacrificing the future business of the reader in this way:

We can certainly understand why you had expected Buzzy and the Roustabouts to be the warm-up act at the concert last Friday. We only begin to advertise a concert when all of the acts on the program have agreed to perform.

Occasionally something happens which we cannot control. Since two members of the Roustabouts were hospitalized the night before the concert, there was little time to advertise the change. Most of the spectators seemed to think that the Pinnacles did an excellent job as the warm-up group. Our surveys show that most spectators attend concerts to see the headliners. Since the headline acts appeared as advertised, everyone seemed pleased with the concert.

We take our responsibilities to the public very seriously. If ever an advertised headliner is unable to appear, you can be sure that you will receive a full refund.

Loyal fans like you may soon be able to see Buzzy and the Roustabouts headlining a concert here. Our schedule for the next three months is enclosed. You're sure to find some of these concerts to your liking.

Although a small number of requests for adjustments may border on the fraudulent, most do not. Sometimes correspondents who regularly handle adjustments grow cynical, and cynicism is reflected in their letters. Such letters often include such phrases as:

> **Avoid cynicism in letters of refusal.**

You claim that the hair dryer did not work as advertised. We cannot understand how this quality-checked appliance could possibly malfunction. According to you the dryer never worked as it was supposed to.

The letters written by such correspondents are tinged with distrust and suspicion. While such letters may clearly convey the message that the requested adjustment is refused, they may lose a customer. An effective bad-news letter conveys the message yet retains the trust and business of the customer.

> **A poorly written bad-news letter can irritate and frustrate the reader.**

Occasionally a writer faces a situation in which the indirect approach is either inappropriate or unworkable. If a customer has already received a written refusal and explanation yet persists in requesting an adjust-

> **On some occasions a more direct approach is appropriate.**

Adjustment Refusal Guide

Make your opening comment neutral and relate it to the subject of the letter.

Imply neither yes nor no in the opening.

Keep the opening brief.

Convey a positive tone rather than an apologetic one in presenting the reasons for your decision.

If possible, show how the reader may actually benefit from the decision because of the reasons.

Present the reasons so that the reader anticipates a refusal.

Make your refusal clear, but don't overemphasize it.

Avoid mentioning the refusal in the ending. End the letter on a positive note.

ment, the direct approach may be suitable for a second letter. If the reader ignores the first letter refusing adjustment and simply repeats the request, the writer is justified in becoming more blunt.

To ensure that the message is unmistakably clear the writer might present the denial in the first sentence. (For example, "Until you complete the travel expense form properly, you will not be reimbursed for your business trip.") This approach may make the reader realize that the problem is serious. It is a risky approach, however, and may alienate the reader. For this reason use the direct approach only after careful consideration of how the reader is likely to respond.

The direct approach should be used only after careful consideration.

After buying a lightweight suit on sale, Bob Norris had second thoughts and wrote this request to the store:

Two weeks ago I purchased a lightweight suit at your half-price sale. Now I realize that the color isn't right for me and I'd like to return it. I have never worn the suit.

As you can see from your records, I am a long-time customer of Grenier's. In fact, almost once a month I make the 60-mile drive to shop at your store. Since I plan to go shopping within the next two weeks, please inform me promptly of your decision.

The store conveyed the bad news of an adjustment refusal in this way:

As a smart shopper you know that taking advantage of sales makes sense. You saved 50 percent by buying your suit at our recent end-of-the-season sale. Your willingness to drive 60 miles to shop at Grenier's shows that you appreciate quality, too.

Customers like you benefit from our end-of-the-season sales in several ways: not only do you enjoy tremendous savings, you also have the opportunity to select from the newest styles. Our end-of-the-season sales allow us to change our stock often and to be up-to-date.

You can be sure that any clothing you buy at Grenier's will be brand new and that you are the original purchaser. We feel that we owe that to our customers. The purchase price would, of course, be refunded on any defective merchandise.

We appreciate your loyalty and we hope to continue to earn it.

After reading the letter, Bob:

- Knew that he couldn't return the suit;
- Understood why the store was unable to take it back;
- Believed that the store was aware of the facts;
- Believed that he had been treated fairly;
- Intended to continue shopping at Grenier's.

These are the kinds of responses sought by the writer of a letter refusing a requested adjustment.

Credit Refusals

Some authorities maintain that every single business letter is a sales letter. No matter what the stated purpose of a letter, the writer must also try to sell the reader on the organization.

When you write a refusal of credit, you face a real challenge. Although you are denying a request, you should take a positive approach and try to retain the goodwill of the reader. Many people today regard credit as a right that cannot be denied them. This attitude complicates the task facing the writer.

Many writers seem to ignore the challenge of a letter of refusal. This attitude is evident in their letters. Writers who believe that you cannot deny credit and at the same time keep a friend write uninspired letters, such as:

Thank you for applying for a charge account at Wilson's Department Store. We regret to state that we are unable to extend credit to you at this time.

We appreciate your patronage.

A credit refusal like this suggests that the company has little hope of retaining the applicant's business. The letter is cold and impersonal. The writer presents the obvious message but pays no heed to the applicant's feelings or continued patronage. The person who receives such a letter is likely to become frustrated and angry.

Rather than use this type of letter as a credit denial, the writer might write it to persuade the applicant to become a cash customer. By chang-

Denying a person credit while keeping that person's business is a challenge to the writer of credit refusals.

When denying credit, the writer might strive to sell the reader on becoming a cash customer.

ing the thrust of the letter, the writer can turn a negative situation into a more positive one.

A department store de-emphasized its refusal of credit by stressing the advantages of shopping there. The writer emphasized the positive aspects of the situation.

We appreciate your recent application for a charge account at Astor Brothers.

Much information is considered before opening a new charge account, and your application was carefully considered. Once you are employed on a full-time basis, it may be possible for you to receive an Astor Brothers credit card.

Until that time please allow us to serve you on a cash basis. As our fall fashions are about to arrive, you may also enjoy our convenient layaway plan.

Of the many possible reasons for refusing a request for credit, a poor credit record is number one. Other common reasons may be that the applicant has too small or unsteady an income or, perhaps, no credit experience upon which to base a decision.

Whether the credit applicant is an individual consumer or a business organization, the letter of refusal is organized in the same way. In either case the writer will probably refer to the advantages of paying cash or making COD purchases. The writer should follow our four steps for transmitting unpleasant news. The letter to the organizational applicant may be somewhat more forthright. A letter that refuses credit to a business follows the usual pattern of neutral comment, explanation, refusal, and positive ending. Here the writer incorporates a bid for cash business in the ending.

Whether the letter rejecting credit is directed at an individual consumer or at an organization, the same steps should be followed by the writer.

Neutral Comment **Thank you for your order for 4 dozen Evenflow seed and fertilizer spreaders. Your large order suggests that you are expecting a profitable spring. We are glad to hear that.**

Explanation **Your credit references unanimously agree that you are a person of integrity and sound business principles. At this time the information about your hardware operation, however, is somewhat less positive. It is obvious that the competition for the hardware customer is indeed intense, and this always has an adverse impact on one's financial position. Current economic conditions lend additional uncertainty to the general business environment.**

Refusal **The upturn in the economy that is expected this spring will most likely improve your position considerably. For the present, however, we'll be pleased to continue serving you on a cash basis, and you in turn will continue to receive a 2 percent discount**

for cash purchases. **Another advantage of cash payment is that orders may be of any size. There is no minimum order required.**

Positive Ending **By reducing your present order by as much as one half you will still have adequate stock to meet the early spring demand.**

Please send us your instructions on the enclosed order form. Your shipment will be sent as soon as we hear from you.

Those who seek credit cannot be expected to be pleased when their applications are rejected. Too many people think a rejection of credit is a rejection of one's personal worth. Refusing credit is a delicate matter meriting thoughtful consideration. Writers often err by emphasizing the refusal rather than developing a cash customer. By de-emphasizing the refusal and stressing the advantages of cash payment, a writer can often retain customers who might otherwise be lost.

Beyond this, a person who is refused credit has the right to know the reason for the refusal. If it is based on information provided by a credit-reporting agency, the writer should say so.

Although the writer is not required to give the specific reasons in the refusal letter, according to the Fair Credit Reporting Act, customers are entitled to an explanation if they request one within 60 days of receiving the credit refusal. In order to avoid having to write an additional letter of explanation to rejected credit applicants, many organizations now include the reasons in the initial credit refusal letter. Some organizations now use forms such as the one in Figure 6.1 for refusing credit applications.

When the volume of credit applications is so great that they cannot be handled individually, such an approach serves a useful purpose in that the reader receives the necessary information. However, the approach is so impersonal that the reader's goodwill may be sacrificed.

The refusal should be de-emphasized.

Credit Refusal Guide

Begin with a neutral idea with which the reader will agree.

Explain the reasons for the decision.

State the refusal briefly and without using negative language.

If possible, offer an alternative such as paying cash or using COD purchasing.

Close with a look toward the future and without an apologetic tone.

Figure 6.1 Example of Credit Refusal Form

Date _____ 19_____

☐ Statement handed to Applicant

☐ Mailed

by: _____
Authorized Signature

Telephone: 546-1866

We would like to thank you for your recent loan application. We have given it careful consideration. However, we regret to inform you that your application has been declined.

We have provided the reason(s) for our decision in the section below. This notice is given in accordance with the various consumer credit laws and regulations applicable to our bank.

Description of account, transaction, or requested credit: _____

Description of adverse action taken: _____

Reason(s)
☐ Credit application incomplete
☐ Insufficient credit references
☐ Unable to verify credit references

☐ Insufficient income
☐ Excessive obligations
☐ Unable to verify income

☐ No credit file
☐ Insufficient credit file
☐ Delinquent credit obligations

☐ Length of employment
☐ Temporary or irregular employment
☐ Unable to verify employment

☐ Too short a period of residence
☐ Temporary residence
☐ Unable to verify residence

☐ Garnishment, attachment, foreclosure, repossession, or suit
☐ Bankruptcy
☐ Inadequate collateral

☐ We do not grant credit to anyone on the terms and conditions you request.

☐ Other-(specify) _____

DISCLOSURE OF USE OF INFORMATION OBTAINED FROM AN OUTSIDE SOURCE.

☐ Disclosure Inapplicable   ☐ Information obtained in a consumer report from: Credit Bureau of Athens, 400 College Avenue, Athens, Georgia 30601.

☐ Information obtained from an outside source other than a consumer reporting agency. Under the Fair Credit Reporting Act, you have the right to make a written request within 60 days of receipt of this notice, for a disclosure of the nature of the adverse information.

The Federal Equal Credit Opportunity Act prohibits creditors from discrimination against credit applicants on the basis of race, color, religion, national origin, sex, marital status, age, (provided that the applicant has the capacity to enter into a binding contract); because all or part of the applicant's income derives from any public assistance program; or because the applicant has in good faith exercised any right under the Consumer Credit Protection Act. The Federal Agency that administers compliance with this law concerning this creditor is:
COMPTROLLER OF THE CURRENCY, CONSUMER AFFAIRS DIVISION, WASHINGTON, D.C. 20219

Problem Orders

The success of any business organization depends to a considerable extent on the speed with which the organization can satisfy its customers. The term *turnaround time* is often used to describe how long it takes for business firms to provide customers with its goods and services.

Even the most efficient organization sometimes experiences delays in handling orders. Regardless of who is responsible for the delay it often calls for a letter in which you must convey information likely to displease a customer.

Items Not in Stock

When an item is temporarily out of stock but will be available soon you should so inform the customer. Since the customer will experience a delay, you will be transmitting bad news. At the same time you want to retain a customer's business. Here is, an example of a letter of refusal which suffers from a misplaced focus:

Thank you for your order of April 7. Unfortunately, we are presently unable to fill your order for one Classic circulating fan.

We pride ourselves on our speed in filling orders, and we usually order in ample quantities. Skyrocketing energy costs combined with customer recognition of a genuine bargain may help explain why customer demand has outdistanced our supply.

We're working hard to remedy the situation, however, and by May 15 you should be enjoying the economy and comfort that accompany a Classic circulating fan. If, due to the delay, you wish to cancel this order, please notify us promptly. We hope you won't do that, however, since we know you'll agree that a Classic circulating fan is worth waiting for.

The above letter is ineffective for several reasons. The first paragraph shows no attempt to indicate an area of agreement between writer and reader. The writer presented the bad news immediately, so it is unlikely that the disappointed reader will finish the letter. When notifying a customer of a delay in an order, you should focus on the order rather than on the delay. In the example the focus is on the delay.

Knowing that the company takes pride in filling orders quickly provides little consolation for the customer who is not benefiting from this speed. If anything, the customer will be skeptical of an organization that boasts at such an inopportune time. The second paragraph, therefore, serves no useful purpose.

The third paragraph states that the situation will be remedied soon and reminds the reader of the product's superiority. This is completely appropriate. Suggesting that the order could be canceled is not in the company's best interests. The customer may choose to cancel the order, but the writer need not suggest it. The request that the customer not cancel is weak and unnecessary. By ending the letter with a reminder of the delay, the writer incorrectly makes it the parting thought.

When informing a reader that an order will be delayed, you have two main purposes: (1) to convince the reader to wait for the order and (2)

Items that are not in stock necessitate letters of refusal.

Do not end a letter of refusal with a reminder of the bad news.

to retain the reader's business in the future. These purposes might have been accomplished better in this way.

Your order for a Classic circulating fan identifies you as a person who recognizes both quality and value.

A growing volume of orders for the Classic indicate that the public has also become aware of the superiority of the Classic. Production is increasing but the quality you associate with the Classic is being maintained.

You will be enjoying the comfort and economy of a Classic circulation fan by May 15, well before the onset of hot weather. The Classic will make the heat and humidity of summer disappear in a breeze.

Discontinued Items

In the best of all possible business worlds, as soon as a company stopped handling a certain item, all orders for that item would cease immediately. What actually happens is that orders continue to trickle in for the item long after its discontinuation.

In response to an order for a discontinued item, you must inform the customer of the discontinuation while offering an appropriate substitute. Do not, however, offer any substitute that is not clearly appropriate. It is better to lose one sale and to retain the goodwill of a customer than to provide a substitute with which the customer will be displeased.

Offer an appropriate substitute, if possible, for a discontinued item.

When a retailer ordered some T-450 videotapes from a wholesaler who had stopped carrying the T-450, the wholesaler offered an appropriate substitute.

Thank you for your order of March 17. Your customers apparently associate high quality with the Superchron name as do most people who take pride in their video investment.

As a result of its ongoing research program, Superchron has now developed a videotape that is significantly superior to anything formerly available. This new product offers 30 percent higher picture quality and 50 percent longer life than does the T-450. By refining high-energy tape particles, Superchron has created the T-900, a tape which is mirror smooth and which provides perfect pictures for replay after replay. Although you may be able to order some T-450 tapes directly from the Superchron Company, your customers will prefer the T-900 once they learn of it.

Your customers will agree that the T-900 is worth an additional $1.50 for a 60-minute cassette. Call me at (601) 592–1313 any weekday between 9 and 5. I'll fill your order that same day at a price of $15.25 per tape on orders of one dozen or more.

The savings your customers will enjoy through the longer life of the T-900 will make them glad you acquainted them with the T-900.

Too Small an Order

There are many different types of misunderstandings which may occur in the process of placing and filling orders. One instance happens when a customer places an order for a quantity too small to merit the discount expected by the customer.

In order to stimulate sales the Green-Gro Company offered a five percent discount on purchases of 100 or more 50-pound bags of lawn fertilizer. When a retailer requested the five percent discount on an order of 50 bags, the wholesaler responded in this way:

This year marks the twelfth year you have purchased your supply of Green-Gro products from us. The growth of your orders over these years suggests that your customers enjoy dealing with you as much as we do. Your adherence to sound business practices in placing orders, making prompt payment, and customer follow up have been appreciated.

For the first time ever, the Green-Gro Company has offered a special five percent discount on its lawn fertilizer, and we are passing this discount on to our customers. The one stipulation made by the Green-Gro Company is that orders must be for at least 100 fifty-pound bags in order to get the special discount.

By increasing your order to 100 bags, you will be ready for the upcoming seasonal rush and you will qualify for the special discount. Regardless of the size of your order, you will still receive our regular terms of 2/10, n/30.

You will be receiving our new catalog within three weeks. It features several new garden products that your customers will soon be seeking.

There are numerous variations of problems which arise when orders are placed. Many problems can be resolved face-to-face or over the telephone. When a letter is necessary, however, remember to use the indirect arrangement.

> **Use the indirect arrangement when refusing or modifying problem orders.**

Problem Order Guide

Begin with a noncommittal statement to which the reader is likely to respond positively.

Present the reasons for the decision.

If possible, show how the reader would benefit from the decision.

Present the refusal without belaboring it.

Avoid additional references to the refusal and point to future business in the closing.

Favor Refusals

Business organizations routinely receive requests for favors of various types. Some of the favors may be business-related, such as a special discount or preferential treatment for a particular order. Other favors may be sought by complete strangers. Charities may seek contributions. Students may write for information for research papers. A list of the types of favors sought from business organizations would be endless.

It is easy to write a letter granting a favor—that's good news! Denying a favor is somewhat more difficult, but it is best accomplished

Requests for favors must sometimes be responded to with letters of refusal.

Figure 6.2 Letter Offering A Counterproposal to Request

DELTA AIR LINES, INC.
GENERAL OFFICES/HARTSFIELD ATLANTA INTERNATIONAL AIRPORT/ATLANTA, GEORGIA 30320 U.

September 5, 1979

Mr. James M. Lahiff
Associate Professor
Department of Management
College of Business Administration
University of Georgia
Athens, Georgia 30602

Dear Mr. Lahiff:

This is just the helpful sort of reply to your good letter (of August 30th) that you imagined you'd receive. College students are likely correct in their complaints that classrooms are "far-removed" from the real world. And too many of us "out here" in the private sector must share the blame.

Unfortunately, Delta's correspondence must be considered as confidential between the company and those to whom we address letters. So, we can't "lift" from our files, forwarding copies of actual letters. However, we might be able to draft several "sample-type" examples, if you'd give us some subject ideas, and if you agree that such samples would suffice.

I have a special place in my heart for the University and its excellent College of Business Administration. My late son, Lane, graduated from your college, magna cum laude, in 1975. He thought so much of Georgia and his faculty that his younger brother, Toulmin, now a 10th grader, hopes to join you in the autumn of 1981.

You see, Professor, because of your nice comments about Delta and my special affiliation with you all, I can't let you down! Let's hear from you soon and we'll supply your sample business letters.

Thank you so much for your interest in Delta, and with best wishes, I am

Sincerely,

James L. Ewing, III
Director-Public Relations

JLE/bs

Source: Courtesy Delta Air Lines

through a carefully considered letter of refusal. If it is possible to offer a counterproposal, the writer will soften the refusal.

One of the authors of this book asked several business organizations to provide some actual letters to serve as examples in this book. Although Delta would not grant the request, it made a generous and attractive counterproposal. Note how the letter in Figure 6.2 follows the four steps: neutral comment, explanation, refusal (with a counterproposal), and a positive ending.

Sometimes you receive a request which you are unable or do not choose to honor, and no counterproposal is possible. Nevertheless, you should follow the four steps presented in this chapter. Try to convey the refusal clearly while retaining the reader's goodwill. This is how one corporation responded when solicited for a financial contribution:

> *You and the other members of the Committee to Preserve the Strand should be commended for your efforts to have the theater designated a historic site. The lives of future generations will be enriched through the success of such projects.*
>
> *We at the regional headquarters of Turflo are impressed with the large number of worthwhile projects such as yours. Several times each week we receive requests for financial support, and invariably the causes are worthy ones. Determining the worthiest recipients is a task precluded by our own time constraints.*
>
> *One way in which we try to meet our social responsibility is through our financial support of three major health-oriented organizations and the United Way. By targeting our contributions in this way we balance our support between social action goals and quality of life improvement.*
>
> *Your efforts to preserve a genuine landmark deserve widespread support. Best wishes on this project.*

When the writer is able to offer a counterproposal, the impact of the refusal will be softened.

Summary

Many of the requests made of any business organization must be refused. Since the letter of refusal conveys bad news, you should organize it in an indirect fashion proceeding from the general to the specific. This increases the chance that the reader will suspend judgment until the entire message is understood.

In writing a letter of refusal, begin with a neutral statement that makes the reader aware of the subject but implies neither an acceptance nor a refusal. Next, provide the reasons for your decision. By the time you state the refusal, the reader probably has already inferred it; the refusal should flow logically from the reasons. The ending should be positive and should not refer to the refusal.

Refusing an adjustment request is a delicate process because the writer implies that the reader's request was unreasonable. A poorly written adjustment refusal can irritate and frustrate the reader.

Since many now consider credit to be a basic human right, writing a credit refusal is difficult. In writing such a refusal, try to convey the message while retaining the friendship of the reader. A refusal of credit to a business organization is usually somewhat more forthright than one sent to an individual.

Problems in handling orders often necessitate letters in which bad news must be conveyed. When ordered items are temporarily out of stock or discontinued, the writer is challenged to satisfy the customer in some other way.

Sometimes favors are requested that cannot be granted. When you must deny a request for a favor, try to provide a counterproposal. This, of course, is not always possible. Regardless, follow the four steps presented in this chapter.

Review Questions

1. What is a letter of refusal?
2. Why should you withhold the actual refusal until well into the letter?
3. What are the functions of the neutral comment at the beginning of a letter of refusal?
4. Why should you present the reasons for your decision before the actual decision?
5. If the main purpose of a letter is to refuse a request, why should the refusal not stand out?
6. Explain the purpose of a positive ending.
7. When are direct adjustment refusals appropriate?
8. What is meant by the expression, "Every business letter is a sales letter"?
9. What are the advantages of providing the reasons for refusing credit in the initial credit-refusal letter? Are there any disadvantages?

Exercises

1. You are reservations manager for the Extravagancia, a 900-room, ocean-front hotel in Florida. The Extravagancia has an annual occupancy rate of 88 percent and it is strongly oriented toward families. In fact 90 percent of its guests bring at least one child with them.

   In recent years there has been a growing influx of college students who spend their spring break at the Extravagancia. Unfortunately, there have been several instances in which boisterous college students have upset some of the more sedate guests.

   You have decided to discourage the college trade, but you realize that today's undesirable college students will be tomorrow's desirable customers. For that reason you do not want to alienate the students when you decline to allow them to stay at the Extravagancia.

Today you received the season's first request for a reservation from a college student. Send your response to Billy Joe Harrison, 120 Finnegan Hall, Central State University, Eclipse, VA 23349.

2. Two months ago you accepted an invitation to speak to your hometown Rotary. "Social Life at State U" was to be your topic. Now, two weeks before your speech you realize that you don't have the time to make the two-hour drive to give the speech. Class assignments and your part-time job make it impossible. Write a letter to Fred Rosser, President, Murdock Rotary, P. O. Box 121, Murdock, IL 61941. Since you hope to open your own business in Murdock upon graduation, you are interested in maintaining the goodwill of this group.

3. You have just received a request from the seniors at Martin High School to allow them to conduct a sales campaign among the employees and on the premises of Rampart Insurance Company. The proceeds will be donated to a nearby children's hospital. Company policy prohibits such soliciting, and the firm's liability insurance policy would not cover solicitors. Write a letter of refusal to Robert Hocking, president of the senior class, Martin High School, Beaufort, SC 29902.

4. You are employed by Quikheat, an electrical appliance company. Approximately 10,000 toasters produced by one of your competitors, Solarist, have been declared unsafe by a governmental agency. Solarist has been ordered to repair them at no expense to the owners. This widely publicized order has been misunderstood by many Quikheat owners, who have been writing to learn what they must do to get their toasters repaired. Prepare a form letter explaining the situation for Quikheat owners who write to you.

5. Each year for the past 20 years your electrical parts company has offered free calendars to customers and to people in the local community. These calendars have become very popular because of the interesting artwork featured each year. They have also become increasingly expensive, and for this reason you decide to discontinue the practice. Instead you send greeting cards, and soon you are swamped with letters and postcards from persons asking why they did not receive a calendar. Write a form letter in response to such inquiries.

6. When you received a check from Gilson Hardware Company on November 10, you discovered that Gilson deducted the two percent discount that is available only for payment within ten days of delivery. Gilson received an order of 12 lawn mowers from your company on October 12 and was billed $1,788.00. The check dated November 8 is for $1,752.24. Gilson Hardware has been a

good customer for 10 years. Write a letter to Gilson Hardware Company (1400 Clayton Street, Farley, MO 64028) requesting a check for $35.76, the amount incorrectly deducted from the original check.

7. As faculty adviser for the Phoenix Society, it is your responsibility to notify applicants regarding the status of their applications. This is a highly select organization—for each person selected for membership, eight are rejected. Selection is based on the applicant's grade point (a minimum 3.5 is required) and on proven leadership abilities. Recommendations of faculty members are weighed heavily. Prepare a form letter that can be sent to applicants who are not selected for membership.

8. As college recruiter for the Stability Insurance Company you interview several dozen job applicants in a week. When you interview Todd Robinson, you are impressed with his academic background as well as with his maturity. You believe that he may be well-suited for an underwriting position. Several days later, however, you interview another candidate who has had more courses in insurance and who is clearly the best candidate for the job. Although you had never told Todd that he would get the job, you had been very optimistic with him. You did say, "It looks good," to him at the end of the interview. Now you must write Todd Robinson to inform him that the company will not be offering him a job. Todd's address is 258 Belmont Hall, Badger State College, Tigerton, WI 54486.

9. You are the credit manager for Midwest Wholesale Foods, a company that supplies canned foods to numerous stores in Minnesota. You receive a $2,200 order from Earnest Enterprises, and credit terms of 30 days are requested.

   Since you have never dealt with that company before, you contact the Central Merchants Credit Bureau (1200 Main Street, Riverton, MT 56476). The credit bureau informs you that Earnest Enterprises is a newly formed business owned and operated by Allen Earnest, who recently retired as a supervisor after 30 years' employment with Supreme Tire Company. The credit bureau also reports no credit record for Earnest.

   It has been Earnest's lifelong dream to own a grocery store. You believe that the area where his store is located already has more than enough stores for there are three major supermarkets within a two-mile radius. Write to Earnest (1800 North Spruce Street, Riverton, MT 56476) and tell him that he must pay cash. Do so in such a way that you will still get his business.

10. You are the promotion manager for the Multi, a large arena in a metropolitan area. Following a concert by the most popular group in the nation, the Gazelles, you receive this letter:

    My friends and I camped in front of your box office the night before tickets for the Gazelles' show went on sale. This was our first visit to the Multi. There were about 20 people ahead of us, but we were sure that we'd have seats down front.

Imagine our surprise when we went to the concert and found ourselves in the sixteenth row. Not only that, but most of the people in front of us bought their tickets on the day of the concert.

We were so mad that we went home after the concert and broke all our Gazelles' records. Besides that, we'll never attend another concert at the Multi. We may reconsider, however, if you will refund the price of our tickets. After all, fair is fair, and we should have been in the front row. I am enclosing our ticket stubs.

There had been a malfunction in the computerized ticket operation that hadn't been discovered until the day of the concert. That is how the last purchasers got the best seats.

Write a letter to Donny Zigler, 1219 Southview, Delano, TN 37325. Deny his request for a refund, but sell him on the idea of returning to the Multi for future concerts. Even though he was not in the first row, his seat was in the $12 section as he had requested.

11. You are the owner of Trash Master, Inc., a refuse collection firm that picks up trash from both residential and commercial customers. Trash Master is 15 years old, the oldest such firm in town. Until three years ago you had no competitors. Since then Trash Wiz, a national firm, arrived in the community and has taken 15 percent of your customers.

You have resisted raising your rates for the past three years but you must now do so. Your own rapidly increasing expenses dictate that rates must be raised by 15 percent. For residential customers the new monthly rate will be $9 for the usual twice-a-week pickups. The rates for commercial customers vary according to the number and size of the pickups. For example, fast-food restaurants will pay $50 per month for daily pickups. There are several differences between Trash Master and Trash Wiz: (1) Trash Master is locally owned and operated; (2) Trash Master offers residential customers two pickups per week while Trash Wiz, which uses containers one and one half times larger than those used by Trash Master, offer a single weekly pickup; (3) Trash Wiz has curbside pickup only, while Trash Master customers need not carry their trash containers down to the street; and (4) as a result of the rate increase, Trash Master residential rates will be 20 percent higher than those of Trash Wiz while the commercial rates of the two will be the same.

Write two letters: (1) a letter to all of your residential customers announcing the rate increase while trying to retain their business, and (2) a letter to your fast-food clients.

12. Your company is Luggage Unlimited, a wholesaler in Stoneham, MA 02180. You receive an order from Dallas Smith, owner of Luxury Imports, Durham, NC 27701 for one dozen #16A392 black

three-hanger Goff garment bags at $32.50 each. Luxury Imports is an occasional customer and has a good credit record.

Six months ago you stopped carrying model #16A392 since there was little demand for it. While it would be possible for you to get a dozen bags of that model, it would take six to eight weeks. You have replaced #16A392 with #28C400 five-hanger Goff garment bags at $49 each.

There are several differences between the two models. The #16A392 holds three suits, has four zippered pockets on the outside, and is constructed of double-seamed vinyl. The #28C400 holds five suits, has six zippered pockets on the outside, and is constructed of double-seamed canvas. It comes in red, blue, and tan. You also carry complete sets of matching luggage in these three colors.

Write to Dallas Smith expressing your willingness to order the requested bags as long as the delay is tolerable. Try to show that the #28C400 model is a more-than-acceptable substitute and is superior in several ways.

13. In this morning's mail you received an almost new one-half horsepower electric motor and a request for a complete cash refund. In the accompanying letter the customer noted that the motor would no longer work after only 12 hours of use. An enclosed receipt showed that the motor had been purchased one month ago. The motor is protected by a 12-month warranty. A technician tested the motor and discovered water inside it, making it appear that the motor broke because it had either been hosed down or immersed in water. The operating instructions expressly stipulate that the motor must not come in contact with water and that such an occurrence is not covered by warranty. As a customer service representative for Dynamotors, Inc., write to the customer (George Adam, 1044 Norman Lane, Lebanon, IN 46052). Deny the requested cash refund and give your reasons. Indicate that the company will repair the motor for $12 if the customer so desires. In any case the motor will be returned to Mr. Adam COD.

14. As a service representative for Worldwide Publishing, you correspond frequently with professors who are considering adopting your textbooks for classroom use. Many professors and instructors request examination copies so that they might determine whether a book is appropriate for a particular course. An examination copy is free and it is standard practice in many publishing organizations. As part of your job, you must screen out the inappropriate requests and honor the legitimate ones. The only information to base the decision on is the name of the course for which the book is being considered, the size of the class, and when the class is offered.

You receive a request for *Business Communicaton Practices* from a professor of geography who claims to be considering the book for a course in physical geography.

Write a letter to Professor Hiram Zale, Geography Deparment, Mid-State College, Sarasota, FL 33578. In the letter deny his request for an examination copy but encourage the professor to read the list of your company's geography textbooks which you have enclosed. Also, inform the professor that Worldwide Publishing offers a 20 percent discount on any book he orders regardless of its subject. You do not want to lose the goodwill of the professor for he may be interested in some of your geography books. Company policy prohibits you from sending examination copies of textbooks to any professor who does not currently teach courses in that subject area.

15. You are employed as assistant registrar at the Wilshire School, an exclusive college preparatory school for underachievers. Competition for admission to the school is keen, especially for the summer session where students can catch up on studies they have fallen behind in. Due to the demand for the summer session the school has adopted a policy of retaining each applicant's $200 registration fee unless a refund is requested prior to May 1.

    On May 25 you receive a letter from Mrs. Horace Langston requesting a complete refund of the $200 registration fee she paid for her son Larry. She wants the refund because Larry's aunt has offered to take him on a four-week tour of Europe. She believes that the trip will be as enriching for Larry as the summer session would.

    Respond to Mrs. Langston's request and deny it in such a way that she will understand your reasons and agree with you.

16. You are a building supply wholesaler. You receive an order from King Hardware for one dozen Vent Lights, a plastic domed ventilating skylight which wholesales for $185 each. Since the balance due on the King account is already $1,400, the addition of $2,200 for the Vent Lights will raise the balance over the $3,000 credit limit which you can allow Ken King, owner of the store. Write to him (225 Main Street, Joplin, MO 64810) and refuse the order as requested. You might request that the order be reduced in order to stay below the credit limit, or you might ask that part of the bill be paid in cash. Whatever you do, remember that you want to retain his business.

17. Until recently you have been successful at booking groups on tours to Greece, the Greek Isles, Turkey, Cyprus, Egypt, and Israel. The price for such a tour is $999. On the last two tours, international tensions made it impossible to visit Egypt and Israel. Instead the two tour groups visited several cities in Italy and there was no change in the length of the tour. Several customers have requested refunds of $200 to $300 since they were unable to visit Egypt and Israel as the tour had advertised.

    Write a letter to Edward Thompson (1214 N. 19th Street, Milwaukee, WI 53202) who has requested a refund of $300. Deny the request in such a way that he will continue to be a customer.

18. Write a letter to Tom Healey, President, Fort Smith Tire Co., Fort Smith, AR 72901. He recently ordered a large number of tires from you, including two dozen G78–14 Ponzi belted whitewall blems at the low price of $20 each. Upon receiving his order he observed that the Ponzi tires had some obvious defects which ranged from faded whitewalls to irregular trend patterns. Healey wishes to return the Ponzi tires to you at your expense. Being new in the tire business, Healey did not realize that *blem* means blemish and that such tires ordinarily possess visible imperfections which in no way affect safety or wear. Healey claims that he thought that blem was part of the name of the tire. It is ordinarily against your policy to take back blems since you sell them so cheaply. In your letter decline to take the tires back but point out the desirability of blems to many buyers. Try to build a positive relationship with this new dealer.

19. As the owner of a local car rental agency, you are usually able to offer prices lower than those offered by major rental agents. Not only are your prices lower, but your profit margin is smaller. For that reason you must be extremely attentive to any collection problems that arise. One of your customers (James Hansen, U.S. Petroleum, Inc., P.O. 1961, Dallas, TX 75221) rented a full-size car at the local airport for three days but did not return it to the correct drop-off point. Instead he parked it in the large airport parking lot and ten days elapsed before you could reach Hansen and learn where he had left the car. You bill him for the three-day usage as well as for the ten days during which it was misplaced. You feel justified in billing him for the ten days since you could have rented the car during that time.

Healey responds to your bill by complaining about the charge for the ten-day period saying that it was an innocent mistake. Write a letter in which you decline to cancel the bill but offer to reduce charges to $7.50 per day for the ten days. Your normal charge of $15 per day is approximately 50 percent less than the rates of your major competitors. You do not want to lose the business of U.S. Petroleum yet you feel, as a small businessperson, that you cannot completely write off the bill.

20. You have owned and operated Quality Discount, a successful mail-order business for the past 20 years and have developed a clientele of many loyal customers. In seeking ways to cut expenses you have adopted a policy of mailing (or giving) catalogs only to customers who did at least $200 business with you the previous year. This policy has upset some of your older customers who no longer buy much from you but still enjoy paging through your lavish full-color catalog.

Write a letter to Mrs. Florence Watkins (410 Shady Lane, High Point, NC 27260) in which you deny her request for a free catalog. Explain the policy and offer to send her a catalog for $5, which is what it costs you. Should she spend more than $200 this year at your business, the $5 would be credited to her account.

Case

An Embarrassment of Riches
R. Eugene Hughes
West Virginia University

Background

Hi-Tk is located in an older Midwestern city generally associated with smoke-stack industries. The company's decision to locate here was influenced by the city's proximity to the company's potential customers and the efforts of the city's Economic Development Authority (EDA). As part of the EDA's location package, one of the city's technical schools (Middle-City Technical Center) offers an intense one-year basic program in electro-mechanical servo systems.

Recently, Hi-Tk has met its hiring needs by employing graduates from two-year technical programs and 8 to 10 graduates (approximately 60% of each class) of MCTC's yearly graduating class. Immediately upon employment, all new-hires enter one- or two-year training programs specific to the separate design/production areas of the company. The ability of this hiring program to meet Hi-Tk's needs in the future is doubtful based on new production goals that will require increased levels of hiring in each of the next five years. Negotiations between Hi-Tk and MCTC have produced an agreement that will increase the number of students who can be enrolled in their program. The time necessary to implement MCTC's new program and the reluctance of Hi-Tk to hire all graduates in a class point to a probable shortfall of new-hires in the first 36 months of Hi-Tk's growth plan.

Beth's Problem

Beth Carol, the Personnel Manager for Hi-Tk, seems to be faced with an embarrassment of riches. Since word has filtered out into the community that Hi-Tk is considering a major increase in production, the Personnel Department has been swamped with applicants. A review and evaluation of the applications has identified a number of applicants who have the necessary qualifications for immediate entry into one of Hi-Tk's training programs. A somewhat larger number of applicants might easily be qualified by successfully completing the one-year basic program offered by MCTC. The largest number of applicants, however, do not seem to possess the education or work experience required for entry into MCTC's program. This latter group is of special concern to Beth because of MCTC's success rate with students admitted to the program as "special students". While special students to not meet the normal requirements for admission to the program, those who have been admitted have generally completed the program and successfully entered the labor market.

Beth is satisfied that the combination of "qualified" and "easily qualified" walk-in applicants has the potential to meet the expected near-term (24–36 months) hiring shortfall. In fact, Beth is convinced that the applicant pool will be sufficiently large that some hiring selectivity can be exercised. Beth's satisfaction with these circumstances is tempered, however, by her realization that the enlargement and maintenance of the pool of labor depends on her ability to successfully communicate with each applicant.

Beginning to outline her communications strategy, Beth immediately realizes that the three groups must be defined more precisely. She begins her outline by noting:

Qualified Group
Hiring needs for this group actually represent a 24-month time period.

Easily Qualified Group
Even with successful completion of MCTC's program, Hi-Tk cannot promise the individual a job.

Doubtful Group
Hi-Tk does not make decisions regarding entry into MCTC's program.

Successful completion of MCTC's program does not assure employment of the individual by Hi-Tk.

Reflecting on what she has written, Beth concludes that at least four general subject letters will be needed. She lists the four as:

a.   Accept.
b.   Accept—but not now.
c.   Reject—but express interest if/when qualified.
d.   Reject—but with referral.

Not sure that the four are complete or adequate, Beth begins to match the letters with the three groups of applicants.

■ ■ ■

Case Questions

1.   Has Beth adequately identified and described the groups/individuals with whom she must communicate?
2.   Are the four general letters sufficient to successfully communi-

cate with the separate groups/individuals identified in the above question?

3. Has Beth given adequate consideration to the communication medium and the personalization of the communications?

4. Prepare a communications plan that will accomplish the goals (enlarge and maintain Hi-Tk's pool of applicants) identified by Beth. Such a plan will include a draft of all appropriate and necessary communications necessary to accomplish this goal.

Case

Car Trouble
Robert Underwood
Ball State University

While visiting relatives in another state, you encounter muffler problems with your three-year-old car. You realize that there are numerous discount muffler shops available in the area where you could have your muffler repaired. However, you decide to take it to a local automobile dealer who sells and services your brand of car because you want the job done right.

You can imagine your dismay when you notice on the bill a $50 labor charge for what amounted to approximately 15 minutes' worth of work. You are upset and ask to speak with the general manager, who informs you that all labor charges in their shop are computed from a standard rate book. A set fee is charged for labor no matter how much time is actually spent on the job.

Although you pay the bill in full, you are not satisifed with this explanation. You decide to write a letter to the home office of the company which manufactured your car and request that they justify a $50 labor charge for a few minutes' worth of work. You also ask them to send you a refund because you think you have been overcharged.

Today, you receive the following impersonal, mass-produced postcard:

Dear Sir:

We have received your letter, and are sorry about the problems you have encountered. We have a district office that serves your area, and have sent them a wire about your problem. The reference number assigned to your file is 129788-43-3333-78. Please use this number in all correspondence with our company.

We have been unable to contact you by phone, and we request that you call us at the telephone number listed below at your earliest convenience.

We appreciate hearing from you and having the opportunity to be of service to you.

Owner Relations Department
Customer Service Division
(313) 337-9768

■ ■ ■

Case Questions

1. Has the appropriate psychological approach been utilized?
2. Identify the strengths and weaknesses of the communication method used by the company.
3. Suggest an improved communication method that could be used.
4. Utilizing good communication principles, write an acceptable letter to the customer.

Persuasive Letters

Learning Objectives

1. To understand the goals of the persuasion process.
2. To learn how to get and hold a receiver's attention on persuasive messages.
3. To understand what motivates people to respond favorably to persuasive messages.
4. To identify the unique characteristics of the persuasive letter and the situations for which such a letter may be appropriate.
5. To learn ways of organizing persuasive messages so that they will have the greatest impact on the receiver.
6. To write sales letters according to the four-step approach.
7. To understand the assumptions under which the various collection letters are developed.
8. To develop a collection campaign in which the twin goals of payment and goodwill are achievable.
9. To write effective letters of request.

"*T*ake one look at Lake Whaboggy and you'll never forget it," the letter promised. Gwen had received similar letters and had promptly discarded them. This letter was different, however, and she decided to take advantage of the offer. After all, for merely attending a brief orientation session of Whaboggy Enterprises she was not only guaranteed a prize, she would be reimbursed for the gasoline she used in making the 80-mile trip. As the letter stated, "You have definitely won one of the following prizes: a) a new limited-edition sportscar; b) a 25-inch color television set; c) two acres of lakefront property; or d) a name-brand digital watch."

Gwen was unprepared for what she encountered upon arriving at Lake Whaboggy. The orientation was hard-sell throughout and lasted 90 minutes, hardly what Gwen would call brief. Following the session Gwen set out to investigate the property alone. No matter where she went, however, there was always a counselor nearby. Counselor was not an accurate designation, however, since selling, rather than counseling, appeared to be the main function. The counselors all had the same message: buy today because the price is going up soon.

By midafternoon Gwen decided that she had had enough, but it took her another hour to be reimbursed for the expense of her gasoline and to collect her prize. On her return trip home she was ticketed for speeding, and shortly thereafter she had a flat tire. Two days later the digital watch she had been given stopped running. That was about the same time she discovered that she had contracted poison ivy.

Just as the letter had promised, however, Gwen did not forget Lake Whaboggy. In fact, two months after her first visit, she accidentally found the original letter. After being reminded of the joys of lakefront living, she decided to return for a second look. Now she is the proud owner of a one-acre lot at Lake Whaboggy. "The letter did it," Gwen says; "It made owning lakefront property seem like such a good idea that I couldn't resist." ∎

We face an ongoing barrage of persuasive messages from our environment. Television commercials encourage us to buy products or services, prevent forest fires or tooth decay, and watch still other television programs. Ministers, priests, and rabbis urge us to live a better life. Police officers remind us to watch our speed. And our friends seek favors from us.

Our responses to these messages vary. We barely pay attention to some so advertisers continue their search for better ways to get and hold our attention—bright colors, attractive people, catchy music, pleasing situations. Other messages do get our attention but have very little effect. Some products we simply don't want or can't afford to buy, but the commercials for them are nevertheless entertaining.

Persuasive messages have different effects.

Still other messages do effect some change in our behavior. We purchase the product or service. We slow down as we drive, especially when we near the place where we earned our last speeding ticket. We help our friends in need, often at great inconvenience to ourselves.

To write persuasive letters you must understand the process of persuasion. For that reason this chapter first describes (1) the goals of persuasion, and (2) using the sender, receiver, message, and channel to accomplish our goals.

Goals of Persuasion

Although for some of us the word *persuasion* is so mysterious that it is threatening, persuasion is nothing new. Aristotle, Plato, and Cicero wrote about persuasion almost 2,000 years ago. Popular treatments of persuasion abound today in such books as Vance Packard's *The Hidden Persuaders,* Dale Carnegie's *How to Win Friends and Influence People,* and Michael Gilbert's *How to Win an Argument.* While each of these writers took a different approach to persuasion, there is little doubt that they were all concerned about one central idea—shaping the behavior of others.

In Chapter 2 we told you that the behavior of people enables an organization to meet its goals. The essence of persuasion is to shape the behavior of others so that our goals can be reached more easily. Simply defined, persuasion is the art of getting someone to do something that they wouldn't ordinarily do if you didn't ask. By asking in a persuasive manner, we shape behavior.

> **The primary goal of persuasion is to shape someone's behavior.**

Persuading and threatening are two distinct approaches to shaping behavior. Effective persuasion results in willing compliance. Threats may elicit grudging compliance. People usually become defensive when threatened and, whatever the outcome, the relationship between the parties will be adversely affected.

When shaping others' behavior, you'll often want to influence not only what they do, but also *when* and *how* they do it. The next time you receive an invitation to enter a sweepstakes from some mail-order advertiser, notice there are extra rewards if you are a winner who entered the contest by an early deadline. Television commercials offering such consumer goods as tapes or records, books, and kitchen gadgets provide a toll-free number for you to call in your order. They also remind you to call immediately: "The supply is limited, so act now!" And many salespeople in department stores are instructed never to let a customer get out the door without having signed on the dotted line. In each case the persuader is aware that delay in shaping behavior could mean no shaping at all.

> **Sometimes we want to control *when* the behavior takes place.**

Some persuaders also want to influence *how* (or where) you perform the behavior. While the League of Women Voters simply encourages you to vote, politicians are obviously interested in controlling the way you cast your ballot: "Don't forget to vote in the October third primary. And when you do, vote for George Jenkins." Some owners of fast-food restaurants would prefer that you never prepare meals in your kitchen. Many such restaurants now offer every meal of the day. When they tell

> **We also want to control *how* the behavior is performed.**

you, "You deserve a break today," they clearly want to influence where it is you take that break.

In shaping the behavior of others, then, you'll choose at least one of the more specific goals of:

- What the behavior should be.
- When the behavior should occur.
- How (or where) the behavior should be performed.

The Persuasion Process

After selecting your specific goals, you are prepared to develop your persuasive message. Yet, as in any form of communication, certain factors will influence the success of your persuasive attempt. There are four important factors:

1. The *sender* of the persuasive message.
2. The *receiver* of the persuasive message.
3. The persuasive *message* itself.
4. The *channel* through which the persuasive message is sent.

Sender

"Consider the source," we often say if we doubt the truthfulness of some persuasive message. Indeed, the source of a persuasive message has an enormous impact on how well the message shapes behavior. This impact is one reason why baseball players sell aftershave lotion on television and why the picture of an Olympic champion is on the front of thousands of breakfast cereal boxes. In simple terms, you are more apt to respond favorably to persuasive messages when their sender is someone you respect or admire. Your response is based upon the key sender concept, *source credibility*.

The more credible the source, the more persuasive the message.

To get a better feeling of how credibility works, try this exercise: think of the best supervisor you've ever worked for. If you've never had a job, then think about the very best teacher you've ever had. Now respond to the following statements about that person by answering yes or no:

1. This person really knew the work. (Expertise)
2. This person always told the truth and kept his/her word. (Trust)
3. This person was active and energetic. (Dynamism)
4. This person would always level with me. (Objectivity)
5. This person was always interested in my personal welfare. (Goodwill)

Some components of credibility.

How many yes responses did you give? The more you gave, the more credible is the person you were thinking of.

Credibility refers to the overall image of the message sender. The exercise you just completed pointed to five important components of credibility. A receiver's image of you involves how competent, trustworthy, dynamic, objective, and well-intentioned the receiver perceives you to be. The more favorable this perception is, the more likely are you to shape the receiver's behavior.

Credibility: image of the source.

The relative importance of these components can also vary from one situation to another. Here are some persuasive situations that might apply to you now. Which components of credibility do you think are most important?

- You're turning in a term paper to your instructor one day late. The lateness is not your fault, and you want to avoid losing points because of tardiness. (Trust?)
- You're trying to convince a friend not to drop out of school. (Expertise? Objectivity?)
- You're asking someone for a date. (Trust? Goodwill?)
- You're running for an office in student government. (All of them?)

As a sender of persuasive messages you might first want to evaluate your own credibility. What is the receiver's perception of you? Notice that the word source can refer to more than simply a person. When you communicate in business, the credibility of your organization may be just as important as your own personal credibility. In summary, the first step in shaping the behavior of others is to consider your own credibility. Both within and outside of business your receivers will usually consider the source before they act.

As a business communicator, credibility of the organization and of yourself should be considered.

Receiver

As we pointed out in Chapter 2, an important encoding skill is the ability to analyze your receiver. In persuasive situations this ability is critical. Two sets of factors to consider in analyzing the receiver of your persuasive message involve attention and motivation. In short, first you get the receiver's attention and then you motivate the receiver.

The ability to analyze your receiver is vital if you are to persuade.

Attention. In any persuasive situation—be it a letter, speech, or advertisement—your first function is to get and hold your receiver's attention. Knowing several things about receivers will help you do this.

First, people will pay attention to the unexpected. Several years ago a man toured the country giving driving safety speeches to high school assemblies. He began every speech this way:

We get the receiver's attention by using the unexpected.

Look around you. Look at the person on each side of you. Ten years from now one of the three of you will be dead.

The accuracy of his statistics (one in three) was irrelevant. What caught his receivers' attention was the original, startling, and personal way he used those statistics. Other examples of using the unexpected abound. For example, The New York Racing Association, seeking buyers for its horse manure, used:

Our horses leave a lot to be desired.

The owner of a service station/restaurant along a busy highway posted a sign outside his establishment reading:

EAT HERE AND GET GAS

An orphanage for boys began its solicitation letter with:

How much is a homeless boy worth?

People heed the unexpected, and once they do, they're easier to persuade.

Second, people will pay attention to what is pleasing. Many persuaders use reinforcing stimuli simply to get the receiver's attention. Leaf through one of your favorite magazines. You will immediately notice that many products are advertised in elegant surroundings—physically attractive men and women, cheerful settings, pleasing colors. Such attention-getters are used in television commercials as well. Besides the surroundings, reinforcing words and phrases are often used to get attention:

Make Anyone Do Anything You Mentally Command—
with Your Mind Alone
One Pill Blocks 600 Calories
How to Find Someone to Love
Instant Memory—The New Way to Remember

We get attention by using reinforcing stimuli.

Once attention is obtained, then the real persuasive message begins.

Third, people pay attention to messages related to their own goals and objectives. Put simply, receivers will heed your persuasive message if that message is about something important to them. People who have dentures are more prone to watch denture-cleaner commercials on television than are people who have their original teeth. The latter pay more attention to toothpaste commercials. Pet owners pay attention to petfood commercials more carefully than those who have no pets.

We get attention by emphasizing the relevant.

In summary, three attention factors are the *unexpected,* the *reinforcing,* and the *relevant.* Which factor or combination of factors you use in developing a persuasive message depends upon your analysis of the receiver. Will he or she respond more favorably to an attention-getter that is not expected, one that is reinforcing, or one that emphasizes his or her important goals?

You might also consider your own credibility when choosing an attention factor. Low credibility can weaken any attempts at getting attention to persuade.

Low credibility can weaken any attempt to persuade.

Motivation.   Motivational factors are also involved in analyzing your receiver. Once you have gained the receiver's attention, what will make that person respond favorably to your persuasive attempt?

Many theories have been developed to explain what motivates people both at work and in their personal lives. One of these theories, developed by Abraham Maslow almost 30 years ago, says that people do things to satisfy certain needs:[1]

1. **Physiological Needs**—lower-order survival needs such as food, sleep, and air.
2. **Safety and Security Needs**—lower-order needs for personal security (for example, a safe home) and financial security (for example, a steady income or a savings account).
3. **Belonging Needs**—higher-order needs to be included in other people's activities and affection.
4. **Esteem and Status Needs**—higher-order needs to feel self-respect and respect from others.
5. **Self-Actualization Needs**—higher-order needs for self-realization or fulfillment in a vocation or avocation.

Notice the first two needs are called *lower order* and the last three needs are *higher order*. Maslow maintained that you actually progress from the first need to the fifth; that is, you first try to satisfy your physiological needs. Once they are satisfied, you are motivated to satisfy the safety and security needs, and so on until you reach the self-actualization needs. This progression from the lower to higher-order needs is why Maslow's theory is sometimes called Maslow's hierarchy of needs, illustrated in Figure 7.1.

To analyze the receiver using Maslow's hierarchy of needs, you must (1) predict which of the five levels your receiver is at at the time of your persuasive attempt, (2) create a message relevant to those needs, and (3) tell the receiver that the shaped behavior you desire will satisfy the

Maslow's five needs

Maslow identified two needs as lower order and three as higher order.

Figure 7.1 Maslow's Hierarchy of Needs

5. Self-Actualization Needs

4. Esteem and Status Needs

3. Belonging Needs

2. Safety and Security Needs

1. Physiological Needs

needs. The following three persuasive messages involve the same product, yet notice how they are adapted to different needs.

Your new Phantom will be the safest car on the highway. Heavy-duty bumpers, specially molded fenders, and our exclusive invisible roll-bar frame will protect you better than any other car on the market.

The Number 1 car in America—that's the Phantom. More than 30 million people drive Phantoms. Maybe you should think about owning one, too.

For the discriminating driver, Phantom's Marquis de Luxe is a step above luxury. It's a sign you've arrived.

Maslow's hierarchy is only one way to analyze what motivates your receiver. Another way is based upon the simple assumption that people do things for reasons, and the reasons you give in a persuasive message are built around two sets of rewards—direct and indirect.

Direct rewards come from actually buying the product or using the service; that is, these rewards come directly from your involvement with the behavior the persuasive message prompts. Think for a few moments about the rewards a consumer gets from purchasing a washing machine. There's the *convenience* of not having to visit a laundromat once or twice a week. It's more *economical* because it costs less to use a home washer than a coin-operated machine. Perhaps the clothes are *washed better* because the consumer can control the cycle, temperature, and water level of each wash. Clothes might even *wear longer,* since the home washer treats them more delicately than the commercial laundromat washer. These rewards all come directly from the consumer's having bought a washer. In that sense they are direct.

Our consumer might also receive some indirect rewards from having purchased the washer. Indirect rewards come from other people as a function of having performed the behavior. Assume that the clothes washer is the top of the line of a name brand and that our consumer is the first person in the neighborhood actually to own this superior machine. Among the indirect rewards our consumer might receive are *status, prestige, respect,* and *approval* from others in the neighborhood. Notice that you don't give these rewards to yourself. Doctors and lawyers have status only because others in the community assign that status to them. You may have heard of the phrase *conspicuous consumption* as an explanation for why many people purchase expensive consumer goods—large automobiles, color television and stereo combinations, and so on. *Conspicuous* means easy to see or obvious. Thus, conspicuous consumption means that these people buy expensive items so that others take notice of their accomplishments and assign them various kinds of indirect rewards.

You can choose from a multitude of both direct and indirect rewards when analyzing your receiver. Here are some examples:

Safety and security needs

Belonging needs

Esteem and status needs

Direct and indirect rewards

Direct rewards come from the actual, shaped behavior.

Indirect rewards come from other people as a result of our shaped behavior.

There are many direct and indirect rewards from which a persuader may choose.

Direct Rewards	Indirect Rewards
Comfort	Affection
Convenience	Appreciation
Enjoyment	Approval
Entertainment	Belonging
Health	Friendship
Less work	Pay increase
Money saved	Popularity
Personal improvement	Prestige
Problem solved	Promotion
Safety	Recognition
Satisfaction	Reputation
Sense of achievement	Respect
Variety	Status

See which of the rewards you can find in the following persuasive message. We counted at least eight.

Lonely? Never Again!
Are you a wallflower at parties? Are you afraid to approach strangers? Do you have trouble with conversation openers? Starting today, you can meet and date dozens of interesting, attractive people.

WINNING PEOPLE will show you more than 50 proven techniques for being successful with the opposite sex. For example, you will find out: How to tell immediately if someone is attracted to you. . . How to be the life of the party without making a fool out of yourself. . . How to tell someone you're attracted to them without appearing weak or foolish . . . and much, much more. WINNING PEOPLE will teach you how to win others and, in doing so, become a winner yourself.

Use of direct and indirect rewards.

For persuasive messages like this one, the writer carefully analyzes the characteristics of the intended receivers. These messages are put together to bring certain rewards to the receiver's mind as the message is read. The words are not selected haphazardly. Rather, they are carefully chosen to meet the needs of the receiver.

We will show you in the next section how these rewards are built into different kinds of persuasive messages. For now, you should understand that before you build your persuasive message, you should analyze your intended receivers in terms of factors that will get their attention and factors that will motivate them to shape their behavior in the way you plan.

Analyze potential receivers to determine factors likely to get their attention and motivate them.

So far we have described two of the four important factors in the persuasion process: (1) the sender, with special emphasis on the credibility of the source; and (2) the receiver, with emphasis on attention factors (the unexpected, reinforcing, and relevant) and motivational factors (Maslow's hierarchy plus direct and indirect rewards).

Message

A third variable in the persuasion process is the message itself. The type of persuasive message you create depends, in part, upon the channel (for example, sales letter, speech, advertisement) you intend to use. In constructing a persuasive message you should pay careful attention to both the organization of that message and the kinds of persuasive appeals you use within it.

No matter what channel you use, your message should contain at least three essential ingredients: (1) an *attention* step (as discussed earlier); (2) a *need* step (where you emphasize those needs or those direct and indirect rewards); and (3) an *action* step (where you specify the behavior the receiver should perform).

Organizing the persuasive message

While the organizational pattern provides the skeleton for your persuasive message, the persuasive appeals you use flesh out the skeleton and give the message substance. These appeals are like tools in a toolbox. You pick the one (or ones) most appropriate for your specific persuasive task. Two kinds of appeals deserve your attention—the *emotional* and the *logical*.

The appeals used give substance to a message.

Emotional Appeal. Most widely used in shaping consumer behavior, emotional appeals apply to the feelings (rather than the intellect) of the receiver. Such appeals, of course, promise the direct and indirect rewards we described earlier. To give you a better idea of how emotional appeals work, here are some examples:

Shaped Behavior	Rewards	Message
Purchase of a pair of sunglasses	Personal improvement, prestige	How good-looking can you get? Watch for those second looks as you stroll the beach in your new Sundowners. They're a sure sign you live the good life.
Joining a computer dating service	Belonging, friendships, problem-solving	Why spend time waiting for that perfect someone? You'll find them at Date-A-Match. Love is just around the corner at 100 Houston Drive.
Signing up for a cruise	Entertainment, friendships, enjoyment	There's dining, dancing, swimming . . . or, if you'd like, lounging on our spacious sundeck with the most interesting people you'll ever meet.

Emotional appeals apply to the receiver's emotions or feelings.

Some emotional appeals are technique-oriented. For example, the bandwagon technique appeals to a need to belong. This emotional appeal says, in essence, "everybody is doing it." For years a certain automobile was advertised as the number one car in America (meaning, of

The bandwagon technique is an example of an emotional appeal.

course, that everyone was buying this car). A well-known car rental agency advertises: "We're number one."

Logical Appeals.   Logical appeals are directed toward the receiver's rational thinking abilities. These appeals are used most often when persuading other businesspeople. One reason is that people in business (for example, purchasing agents) must be able to clearly justify the behavior that the persuasive message suggests. This need to justify behavior calls for appeals such as the following:

Logical appeals are used more in persuading business representatives.

Shaped Behavior	Rewards	Message
Using a collection agency for overdue accounts	Convenience, saving money	Let us show you how we can help you reduce your uncollectible bills by 25 percent. Our service also means you won't have to spend your own time dealing with delinquent accounts.
Purchasing a new typewriter	Convenience, efficiency	The porta-type memory typewriter is so light (only 15 pounds) that you can easily move it from office to office. Its computerized memory system will avoid all those retyping chores from the briefest letter to the longest report.
Purchasing a prefabricated building	Money saved, durability	The aluminum siding on Brock buildings means you'll get years of economical and long-lasting service.

Logical appeals apply to the receiver's rational thinking abilities.

Most persuasive messages are of a positive nature. That is, the message describes a reward to be attained through some positive action. Occasionally, however, a persuader will use a negative appeal to arouse emotions of fear or of self-interest. Avoiding social disapproval is sometimes the reward when a negative appeal is used.

Negative appeals are occasionally used.

Insurance companies try to sell policies by pointing out that, in the event of your death, your family will be left destitute unless you have insurance. This is a negative appeal. The persuader is predicting an unfortunate occurrence unless some action is taken. A mouthwash company may play upon our fear of rejection in advertising its product. Health care organizations publicize the fact that smokers do not live as long as nonsmokers. In other words, unless you quit smoking you will die at an earlier age. Collection letters, described later in this chapter, may sometimes include negative appeals.

The appeals used in persuasion can be either positive or negative. Positive appeals are used more frequently, but there are also situations in which negative appeals are appropriate.

Many persuasive messages contain a mixture of emotional and logical appeals. However, if you carefully analyze the television commercials you see and the magazine advertisements you read, you will notice that

Negative appeals may suggest an unfortunate occurrence unless some action is taken. Emotional appeals are used more to persuade consumers.

emotional appeals are made more frequently, especially to consumers. You will also begin to recognize the various organizational formats used in constructing persuasive messages.

In summary, the third major factor in the persuasion process is the message. In constructing the persuasive message, use the kinds of logical and emotional appeals you think will best shape the behavior of the receiver.

Channel

As a business communicator you'll probably use the persuasion process in many different situations, such as:

- Written in a collection message
- Written in a job application letter
- Written in a sales letter
- Written in a magazine or newspaper advertisement
- Written in a claim letter
- Written in a request for a favor
- Face-to-face in a public speech
- Face-to-face in an interview
- Face-to-face in a small group conference
- Face-to-face in everyday conversation
- Orally on the telephone

In all of these examples, you'll notice two basic channels of communication are emphasized—oral and written. Refer to the coverage of communication channels in Chapter 2. Sometimes you have a choice and must decide whether to use oral or written channels. For example, if you want to persuade a credit customer to mail an overdue payment, should you telephone or write a brief collection message? If you want immediate feedback and better acceptance, perhaps the oral channel is preferable. But if you need documentation, or if your message is fairly detailed, a written message might be better.

Two primary channels: oral and written

Several of the other factors we have discussed in this chapter should also enter into your decision. First, you might show more goodwill through an informal telephone conversation. Or perhaps you might be more objective in a letter. Also, your decision should be based partly upon your analysis of the customer. An unexpected telephone call might certainly get attention. However, it might be better to communicate in a letter where you can more easily control both the organization and the types of appeals you use in your message. As a persuasive source, you should weigh the channel benefits carefully when beginning your effort to shape behavior.

The appropriateness of a certain channel depends on many factors.

Persuasive Communication

Whether blatant or subtle, persuasion plays an important role in each of our lives. Your happiness and success are affected by your persuasiveness as well as by your persuadability. As a business correspondent you will be expected to be able to persuade others through your letters. The persuasive letter is one in which you seek to modify the thought and action of others in a certain direction.

Large organizations often send sales letters by the thousands. Since it is impractical to compose an individual letter for each reader, a form letter may be developed. Figure 7.2 is an example of a form sales letter developed for college students. A credit account application ordinarily accompanies such a letter.

Whether you are writing an individualized persuasive letter or a letter that will be widely distributed, the same basic principles apply. Whenever you seek to persuade someone, there are four steps you should follow. They are:

Many letters are form letters.

1. Get the reader's attention.
2. Stimulate the reader's interest.
3. Awaken a desire in the reader.
4. Encourage the reader to take a specific action.

These steps will be discussed and developed in this chapter. Thus far we have considered persuasion in general. Now we focus on those types of persuasive letters most frequently encountered in the business setting: sales letters, collection letters, and letters of special requests.

Sales Letters

Millions of unsolicited sales letters are mailed each year to consumers, many of whom routinely discard them and disparagingly refer to such letters as junk mail. That which is junk mail to many consumers is called direct mail advertising by advertisers, and it is big business. Approximately $9.9 billion is spent annually on direct mail advertising, almost as much as is spent on television advertising.[2]

Direct mail advertising is considered to be more precise than either television or newspapers, each of which is ordinarily directed at the general population. Direct mail advertising can be tailored for and sent to a narrow segment of the population. Another attractive feature of direct mail advertising is it can be scientifically tested. Sales results can be easily related to a specific letter and various versions of a letter can be compared for effectiveness.

Figure 7.2   Form Sales Letter for College Students

Richard V. Skagen
National Credit Marketing Manager
Sears, Roebuck and Co.

Dear Mrs. Lewis,

    You are invited to apply for a Sears Credit Card
-- one of the most useful and valuable credit cards a
student can have.

    It's easier to get a Sears Credit Card than you
might think. And there are so many advantages to
having a Sears Credit Card especially right now, while
you're at school. Among them:

   . Your Sears Credit Card is good at over 3400
    Sears Stores coast to coast. Wherever you
    live, travel or move, you have credit avail-
    able at a nearby Sears.

   . Your Sears Credit Card opens the door to a vast
    range of over 100,000 products and services --
    and everything Sears sells is backed by our
    famous guarantee, "Satisfaction Guaranteed or
    Your Money Back."

   . You can choose from Cheryl Tiegs™ Signature
    Sportswear, famous Kenmore Appliances, DieHard®
    Batteries, Junior Bazaar Sportswear, Free Spirit
    Bicycles and ROEBUCKS® authentic western wear.

   . You can take advantage of Sears special sales
    -- even though you may be short of cash. With
    a Sears Charge Account you can stretch your
    payments over many months if you wish.

   . You can save time and unnecessary travel by
    shopping from Sears catalogs. Just mail or
    phone in your order and say, "Charge it."

                 (over please)

Source: Sears, Roebuck, and Company.

Figure 7.2 (continued)

There are never any hidden charges. All Sears
finance charges are always fully disclosed.
And there's no annual fee, unlike some other
credit cards.

To apply for your Sears Credit Card, just fill in
and mail the enclosed form -- the postage is already
paid. Or, if it's more convenient, bring in your
application to the Credit Department of the Sears
Store in your area. Sears believes responsible young
adults deserve credit.

Why not fill it in right now, and begin enjoying
the many benefits of your Sears Credit Card as soon as
possible.

Sincerely,

Richard V. Skagen
National Credit
Marketing Manager

P.S. I strongly urge you not to pass up this
opportunity. In addition to its immediate
usefulness, your Sears Charge Account will help
establish the credit background you'll need
after you leave school.

Writing good sales letters is an art. For some people it is a full-time
occupation—and a well-paying one at that. Some of the best-known
practitioners of direct mail advertising are paid up to $25,000 to develop
a single packaged sales letter that will produce the desired results. Since
such letters are mailed in tremendous quantities, a response rate of one
to two percent is considered good.[3]

**Records are kept of the
results of specific sales
letters.**

While you may never become a part of the direct mail advertising business, much of the writing you will do is aimed at trying to persuade your reader. The obstacles you face will be similar to those encountered by the direct mail writer. In the split second that a reader may actually look at your sales letter before discarding it, you must grab the reader's attention.

When you try to persuade someone, you are trying to sell that person on an idea or a course of action. By becoming familiar with the strategy of the sales letter you will become a more effective persuader.

The reception a sales letter gets is considerably different from the reception for other types of letters. The good-news and neutral letter is easy to write because it tells readers what they want to hear. The letter of refusal, on the other hand, delivers an unfavorable response. No one wants that type of news, but a well-written letter of refusal will be read because it contains information which interests the reader. Sales letters generally fall into two categories, unsolicited and solicited.

The unsolicited sales letter does not have the advantages of other types of letters. It doesn't present information that the reader is likely to consider good news. In fact, the reader may not even be interested at first. To succeed the writer must create a message that, although unsolicited, will stimulate a relatively uninterested reader.

The solicited letter is easier since the reader has expressed interest, sought information, or made specific inquiry. The writer is responding to some needs of which the reader is already aware.

> Regardless of your occupation, much of your writing will be aimed at trying to persuade the reader.

> The principles governing sales letters pertain to all persuasive writing. When you write a sales letter, you often must stimulate an uninterested reader.

Preparation

Before beginning to write persuasively you should learn as much as possible about the idea, service, or product to be offered. You should thoroughly understand all aspects of a product before trying to sell it. You should certainly have the following information about the product:

- Exactly what it can do
- Materials from which it is made
- The expertise which developed it
- Outstanding features of the product
- Ways it differs from its competitors
- Price
- Extent of the maintenance required, and the expertise required to perform it
- Warranty, if any, that accompanies the product

> Become completely familiar with a product before trying to write a sales letter.

Without this basic information you are unlikely to sell the product successfully. This information by itself, however, is not usually enough since physical characteristics are only one dimension of a product.

Buyers will be as interested in the benefits they will derive from a product as in its physical characteristics. For that reason you should learn

> Before writing a sales letter, the writer should also become familiar with the intended customers.

as much as you can about those to whom the letter will be sent. The more you know about the readers, the more likely you are to appeal to their interests and the more successful the resulting letter will be. You will understand the readers better if you have this type of information about them:

- Income level
- Whether homes are owned or rented
- Urban or rural location
- Occupations represented
- Educational level attained
- Marital status
- Family size
- Age of family members

At times you may have to write a sales letter with little specific advance knowledge about the readers. In those instances, the product or service itself may indicate the kind of person who will read the letter. For example, if you are trying to attract customers for a lawn-care service, the letter will be geared to homeowners who live in the suburbs.

After you are fully aware of the product or idea and the potential customers, you can plan the sales message. You must determine how best to link the intended customer with what is being offered. In other words, exactly how will the reader benefit from the physical characteristics and capabilities of the product? The physical characteristics of a certain brand of running shoes are a combination of lightweight rubber, canvas, and color. The benefits to the owner of such shoes, however, would be these kinds of factors:

- Saves money because they last longer than other running shoes
- Makes the runner faster because the shoes are very lightweight
- Improves the runner's appearance because the shoes are stylish and available in many different colors
- Provides more comfort because of the specially designed arch
- Provide more safety through the unique double-deep tread

Readers are interested in the psychological benefits to be derived from a product.

Potential buyers are interested in the physical features of a product, but they are more interested in how they would benefit from them. It is the likely benefits, or psychological features, that convince the reader to buy.

Steps for Effective Sales Letters

Whenever the purpose of a letter is to elicit the cooperation of others, a certain sequence of steps should be followed. Although the terminology has varied somewhat, persuasive writers have used these same steps for years. Whether you are trying to sell something or trying to convince the reader to pursue a certain course of action, these steps have proven to be effective:

The steps for effective sales letters pertain to all types of persuasive attempts and are not limited to actual sales.

1. Attract the reader's **attention.**
2. Stimulate the reader's **interest.**
3. Develop a **desire** within the reader.
4. Encourage the reader to take a specific **action.**

1. Attention.   The first sentence of an unsolicited sales letter must grab the readers while leading them on to the remainder of the letter. In order to accomplish this you should identify one of the most significant features of the product you are trying to sell. If possible, suggest how the reader stands to benefit from using the product. (Throughout the remaining discussion of sales letters we will refer only to product even though the principles presented pertain to any persuasive writing.)

Many writers attempt to include in the first sentence that aspect of the product which will interest most readers. The manufacturer of an energy-efficient water heater, for example, considered economy to be the most important characteristic of the product. For that reason economy was emphasized in this opening:

Want to cut your water heating expense by 30 percent?

An auto dealer who believed that the product's new styling was its most interesting aspect stressed this newness:

Test drive the all-new C-7 now. Be the first in the neighborhood to own one.

No one right method of getting the reader's attention exists. Only after becoming familiar with both the product and the intended reader are you really ready to select an appropriate method. Some of the more common methods used are:

- Make a thought-provoking statement. "The best thing about our new line of purses is something you can't see."
- Present a startling fact. "Ninety-five out of 100 families would be bankrupt if they missed just three paychecks."
- Offer a bargain. "Imagine, two pairs of shoes for the price of one!"
- Describe something that currently is happening. "Today more than 500 families enjoyed the *Press Journal* with breakfast."
- Present a direct challenge. "Try to tear the enclosed piece of rubberized plastic and you'll understand why our seat covers won't wear out."
- Tell an interesting anecdote. "Until I was 25 years old I thought you had to be rich to afford a new car. The day I visited Bill Smith's Auto Market was the day I learned otherwise. That was also the day I bought my first new car."

An opening is more likely to attract attention if it is written in an original manner. When the writer uses cliches and timeworn phrases the reader is likely to discard the letter. The reader is also more likely to continue reading if the

Unless the first sentence of a sales letter attracts the reader's attention, the reader will probably discard the letter.

There are proven methods for attracting the attention of the reader.

Originality is an important characteristic in a sales letter.

Attention-Getting Guide

Present what the reader will view as the major benefit of the product that you seek to sell.

Relate the product to the reader rather than to the writer (you-centered).

Write an original opening statement.

Make the first paragraph interesting enough to appeal to the reader and so short that the reader will have to read subsequent paragraphs to get the important details.

opening paragraph is short. Brevity and conciseness are vital to an effective opening in an unsolicited letter. If the reader has already expressed interest in the product, no attention-getter is necessary.

Common Errors in Seeking Attention.   There is the possibility of a sale when you get the reader's attention. When you are unable to attract attention, a sale is unlikely. Because attention-getting is so crucial, you must try to make your approach unique. In striving to be unique, however, you risk making an error that may cause the reader to lose interest. These are some of the most common errors made in seeking attention:

Several errors are frequently made in attracting attention.

1.   Asking a foolish question. The writer will lose the reader's attention with a question that has an obvious answer, such as "How would you like to double your income and shorten your work week?"
2.   Emphasizing the writer instead of the reader. Readers want to know how they will benefit. "It looks like WKUR will be number one in the ratings soon," virtually ignores the reader.
3.   Presenting an irrelevant statement. A sales letter which begins, "There's at least one thing in life that you needn't be a millionaire to enjoy," sounds intriguing until the reader discovers that the product is a new deodorant soap. A direct link between the opening statement and the product being sold should always be made.
4.   Phrasing an idea in an unoriginal way. Avoid the use of such cliches as "a stitch in time saves nine." Refrain from using anecdotes that are already widely known. Timeworn expressions lose reader interest.

2. Interest.   Having attracted the reader's attention, you must now strive for receptive reaction. In this section you usually introduce the product and provide the reader with good reasons for buying it. Some authorities recommend that at this point the reward that is to be derived from the product should be emphasized rather than the actual product. For example, instead of selling the reader on a lawn mower, stress the

The main purpose of the interest section is to make the reader want the product.

pride associated with having an attractive lawn. In this way the reader goes beyond the product to the pleasure that results from its use. In the interest step, therefore, you are both describing the product and suggesting its value to the reader.

Now that you have the reader's attention, you must link the attention-getting step to the next step. Unless the interest step flows naturally from the attention step, the reader will probably stop reading the letter. In this letter the writer failed to link the steps:

Some things are unforgettable, and the new DMS electronic typewriter is one of them. More than 50 years of technology have produced a machine that allows revision without retyping. It features more automatic functions than any other typewriter. Because of its incredible memory it can retype virtually anything that you have typed before, and it does it automatically.

The key idea of the attention-getting step is that the typewriter has a memory *(unforgettable).* The writer does not return to that point, however, until three sentences later. There is no continuity between the attention and the interest steps.

In attempting to stimulate the reader's interest, the writer should emphasize some central selling point of the product. A central selling point is the prime reason why a person would want what a seller was offering. Any product or service has many possible central selling points. What kind of person is the customer? What are the customer's needs and interests? Answering these questions will help you identify a likely central selling point.

3. Desire. In the desire section the writer moves the reader from the "like to have that" category to the "really need that" position. Since the reader may still be balking at the letter's basic idea, the writer must justify the desire for the product.

As described earlier, there are two types of persuasive appeals: emotional and logical. Emotional appeals apply to the feelings of the receiver; logical appeals apply to the receiver's thinking abilities. By relying on an appropriate appeal, the writer helps readers justify the desire for the product.

One automobile dealer, for example, may try to sell a car on the basis of its complete warranty. This appeal is logical. Another dealer may try to sell the product through an emotional appeal: the reader will be the first one on the block to own this distinctive new model.

The product being sold will usually suggest whether to use logical or emotional appeals. Sometimes a combination of the two types of appeals is preferable.

4. Action. Now the moment of truth has arrived. The writer has pointed out the most significant features of the product as well as how the reader will benefit from its use. All that remains is for the reader to take the desired action. The writer must now tell the reader what action

There should be a natural link between the attention step and the interest step.

The writer failed to link the attention and interest steps in this example.

The writer should emphasize a central selling point throughout the letter.

The desire section should make the reader feel a need for the product.

The action close should indicate the specific action the reader should take.

to take. If you want the reader to complete the enclosed form and mail it, say so as specifically as possible. Some otherwise good sales letters are rendered ineffective by the lack of a clear action closing.

Here is an example of a sales letter in which the four steps are used:

Did you know that you don't need a college degree to get a good job?

Attention

The statement is not clever, but it is oriented toward the reader (You) and it does suggest a benefit (a good job).

You've probably read newspaper articles about how job opportunities are declining today. At the same time, however, there are occupations in which opportunities are expanding. The electronics field has a shortage of technicians. Not only is there a shortage now, but the U.S. Bureau of Labor Statistics reports that in the next ten years the demand for electronic technicians will increase by 21 percent. That means that for every ten electronics technicians now working, two more will be needed. You're probably wondering who will fill all of these new jobs. The answer is people just like you who recognize an opportunity when they see one.

The writer used the availability of jobs as a central selling point. Depending on the audience the writer might have selected a different central selling point. Selling knowledge for the sake of knowledge could be an appropriate approach with certain readers. Selling the prestige or the challenge of electronics work are other possible approaches. If you have successfully stimulated the reader's interest, that interest may now be changing to a desire for the product.

As an electronics technician you can expect to have your choice of many attractive jobs. The pay is good and so are the working conditions. One of the best aspects of an electronics education is that you don't even have to leave home to get one. People just like you have earned an electronics certificate in their leisure time at home.

Desire

The Trotter Institute of Electronics offers a one-year correspondence course which leads to a Certificate of Electronics. You could soon be on your way to a career in electronics.

You probably think that any courses offered by the Trotter Institute would have to be expensive. You're in for a surprise! You get textbooks, assignments, and consultation with our excellent instructors for only $360, and this includes employment counseling after you graduate. There may not be many bargains available these days, but this is definitely one. You can see now that getting a better job is easier than you thought.

In the desire section the writer pointed out other desirable features of the correspondence course and referred to the central selling point. The writer introduced the price but de-emphasized it by including it in a sentence that described the product's virtues.

Price should not be emphasized in a sales letter unless the price is extremely attractive.

To prepare for a better job with a great future, complete the enclosed registration form. Within ten days you'll be progressing toward an interesting and rewarding new career.

Action

The last paragraph should be brief yet purposeful. It tells the reader specifically what to do and includes a reminder of how the reader will benefit.

How Would You Like To . . .   **Attention**
1. *Make your house more attractive and valuable?*
2. *Reduce your heating and cooling expense by 35 percent?*
3. *Never again have to paint your house?*

Home ownership is an expensive proposition. It takes plenty of time   **Interest**
and money to maintain a house properly. As a homeowner you're certainly aware of your many responsibilities. If you are like most of us, you're always looking for ways to make home ownership easier. If you can do this and save money at the same time, so much the better.

Just imagine your house looking better than ever and you having more   **Desire**
time to enjoy it. How would you like to spend weekends doing what you want to do rather than painting and fixing the house? Astro Lifelong Siding will help you take a lot of the work out of home maintenance.

You can always recognize people who own homes sided with Astro Lifelong because they smile a lot. Who wouldn't smile when the heating and cooling bills are cut by 35 percent? Besides that, you can retire your paintbrush for your house will never need painting again.

You will save energy and money at the same time for only $499. You will save even more on maintenance expenses, and your house will look better than ever.

Fill out the enclosed postage-paid card and mail it today. I'll send you a   **Action**
brochure that will open your eyes. When you realize how Astro Lifelong will increase the value of your house, you'll say, "Why didn't I do this sooner?"

Sales Letter Guide

Begin with a brief statement or question that is likely to attract attention.

Be sure the opening statement clearly relates to the product offered.

Gain the reader's interest by emphasizing a central selling point that appeals to him or her.

In the desire section try to develop a need within the reader by providing additional evidence of the product's value. Also remind the reader of the central selling point.

Minimize price resistance by de-emphasizing it. Mention some of the strong points of the product while referring to price.

Indicate briefly and specifically what the reader should do, and restate the reasons the reader should take the desired action.

Although we emphasized a step-by-step approach to writing sales letters, the steps are not always separate and distinct. In some sales letters the interest and desire steps may be indistinguishable. You may not recognize the point at which one step ceases and another begins, but the sequence of ideas is obvious. It is more important that you follow this idea sequence rather than keep the steps separate.

Most effective sales letters follow the four-step sequence.

Brevity is desirable in business letters, but sales letters must usually be longer than other types of business letters. Greater length is usually required to develop a successful persuasive appeal. However, sales letters sent to dealers are usually shorter than those sent to consumers because appeals to dealers are more direct, generally emphasizing the profit to be made.

Sales letters are usually longer than other types of business letters.

Collection Letters

In most retail organizations much time and effort is invested in training employees who regularly deal with the public such as the sales personnel. Unless they are effective in face-to-face interaction with the customers, the likelihood of business success is remote.

In most organizations relationships between salespeople and customers are carefully cultivated. Yet, these same relationships are often threatened by the company's efforts to collect unpaid bills. Collecting the unpaid balance should not be the only goal of the collection process. Another important goal is to retain the goodwill and the business of the delinquent customer. Many collection letter writers completely alienate the same customers in whose loyalty the company has heavily invested. Thus, much of what is being accomplished through advertising, public relations, and skilled sales personnel can be undone through inept collection procedures.

An effective collection letter will collect the bill and maintain the customer's goodwill.

Virtually every type of business relies at least occasionally on collection letters to prod past-due accounts. These letters comprise the collection campaign, and they are written and mailed in a predetermined sequence. The early letters, sent when an account is slightly late, are mild in tone. As the account becomes more delinquent, the letters become more directive. Collection letters should never, however, become too directive:

As an account becomes more past due, collection letters become more direct in tone.

Your bill is overdue. Pay us immediately or I'll see that you never get credit in this town again.

Reasons for Collection Problems

A blacksmith shop in northern Wisconsin displayed this sign prominently: "Interested in credit? See our credit manager. Please take elevator." The building was single story. With a credit policy like this a company would have no collection problems.

The underlying reason for collection problems is obviously that we extend credit. If a business were to revoke the credit privileges of all its customers, collection problems would disappear, but this almost surely would be accompanied by a decline in profits and sales. People expect credit. It has become a part of life both for the creditor, which is the organization extending credit, and for the debtor, which is the person purchasing on credit.

In the quest for greater profits business organizations often extend credit to customers who, in an earlier time, would probably have been refused credit. As the number of these questionable accounts increases, so do collection problems increase. Estimates indicate collection problems were responsible for at least ten percent of the bankruptcies in 1980.[4] In the same year collections of past-due accounts by collection agencies were expected to exceed $1.3 billion; that means accounts of that value were declared uncollectible by the original creditor.[5] There is every reason to believe that the value of such collection accounts has increased annually since then.

There are many reasons why persons become delinquent in paying their bills, and many of these reasons are completely valid. Some credit managers refer to nonpayers as deadbeats, and they impute the motives and character of these debtors. While there may be some customers who use credit in bad faith, their number is small.

Many collection problems may be explained by such factors as illness, loss of job, or some other unexpected occurrence. In some cases collection difficulties can be traced to a debtor's misunderstanding the terms of the credit agreement. By taking greater care in explaining the operation of a charge account, companies can prevent some future collection problems. No matter how much care is taken in extending credit, however, there will be some collection problems.

> **By putting strict limits on credit, collection problems would be reduced—but so would profits.**

> **Some collection problems are due to a misunderstanding of the terms of the credit agreement.**

The Collection Campaign

Company efforts to collect past-due accounts can best be described as campaigns. As in any campaign there is a series of stages. The stages in the collection process are:

1. Reminder
2. Strong reminder
3. Inquiry
4. Urgency

You must approach each stage somewhat differently. The assumptions you make about a debtor change as the account becomes more overdue, and you write differently on the basis of the new assumptions.

Although we divide the campaign into four stages, this division does not mean that only four letters will be sent to a delinquent debtor. For any single stage, more than a single letter is usually sent.

> **The first collection letter is a reminder. The writer assumes that the customer has overlooked the bill.**

Reminder.   When a customer is first recognized as delinquent, collection efforts are restrained and mild. The assumption guiding the collection correspondent at this point is that the customer has merely overlooked the bill and needs only a reminder. At this stage, when the account is about two weeks late, many companies merely send a duplicate of the original bill with some reminder that it is overdue.

The approach in the early stages of collection is low key. This approach continues into the first actual collection letter. Since more people will pay with slight prodding, the initial letter should only prod:

Have you overlooked your unpaid balance with us? Please accept this friendly reminder and send us your check for $97.50.

The number of reminders that are sent to a delinquent customer varies from one company to another. A creditor will likely send several reminders to a customer who has a good credit history. To a customer who is viewed as a poor risk, the creditor might send only one reminder and then move to the strong-reminder stage. The process moves to the next stage quickly when it appears that the customer is not likely to respond.

Strong Reminder.   The second stage consists of a strong reminder, yet the assumption remains that the customer has simply forgotten to pay the bill. Some companies use this occasion to remind the customer of the values currently available and to point out that the customer is held in high regard despite the customer's oversight. This letter from a department store exemplifies such an approach:

> **In most organizations more reminders will be sent to a good credit risk than to a poor one.**

You will like the wide array of merchandise we now have in stock. You are sure to find something that suits your taste and your needs throughout each department.

At the time you come in, you may pay your bill of $180, which is 60 days past due. Then, let us help you look and feel great this summer.

> **In a strong reminder the writer may call the customer's attention to the value of the company's services.**

Besides reminding the customer of the past-due account, the writer has reassured the customer that credit will not be a problem at this store. The customer is reminded that this store is a reasonable place to do business.

Inquiry.   If the reminders do not have the desired effect, you must take a stronger position. Rather than continuing to assume that it is a customer's oversight, you now assume that some other reason has kept the customer from paying. This stage is called inquiry because you ask why the past-due account is not being paid. If it is not possible to elicit payment through this letter, you seek at least an explanation. If the customer responds with an explanation, there is a good chance that a payment plan will eventually result. In short, you seek customer action, preferably to pay the bill, but at least to give an explanation.

> **In the inquiry stage the writer asks the customer why the bill is past due.**

When you write a letter in the inquiry stage, you should also appeal to the reader's interest. Several appeals are often used in letters of inquiry.

By appealing to the reader's *pride* you encourage self-esteem. You may point out the pride one feels in satisfying financial obligations. Some writers emphasize pride in terms of avoiding the embarrassment of a bad credit record.

You can also appeal to the reader's *sense of equity*. The thrust of an equity appeal is that the creditor provided what the customer had requested. In all fairness, the customer should acknowledge the creditor's trust by paying the bill.

Some readers may not be swayed by appeals to their pride or their sense of equity. They may, however, respond to an appeal to their *self-interest*. Many people take credit for granted. If you can remind the reader of how valuable credit is, you may get a positive response. When readers realize how credit contributes to their self-interest, they may be more inclined to pay their bills and protect their credit rating.

This is how one writer approached the inquiry stage:

Since payments have not been received on your clothing account for either July or August, the account is delinquent.

In the past you have met your obligations promptly. We believe that something unusual has temporarily disrupted your payments. May we assist you in solving the problem?

Please send the balance due of $180 or let us know of your plan for satisfying the account.

While several letters of reminder may be sent to a delinquent customer, usually only one letter is sent in the inquiry stage. By this time the account will be approximately 90 days late. As in the example, the writer seeks to reestablish contact with the customer by making a reply easy. By suggesting that an unusual situation has caused the delinquency, the writer makes it easy for the customer to save face. At no point, however, did the writer suggest that there was any problem with the merchandise.

Urgency.   The collection process moves into the urgency stage if the inquiry did not lead to positive action by the customer. At this point the account has been delinquent for at least 120 days. A very small percentage of accounts remain delinquent for this long; however, the collection writer must be prepared to deal with the problem.

At this stage you must impress upon the customer the seriousness of the situation. To signify the gravity of the situation a higher-level executive will often sign the letter instead of a collection correspondent. You should convey the idea that this is the end of the line, although hope for a reasonable solution still exists. Avoid threats, however, for they may have an adverse effect on goodwill and usually elicit defensiveness rather than compliance.

At this point you might refer to the possibility of legal action, although not in specific terms. If several letters comprise the urgency stage, you

In the inquiry stage the writer must also appeal to the interests of the reader.

Appeals to the reader's pride, sense of equity, or self-interest are often made in the inquiry stage.

In the inquiry stage the writer is seeking to reestablish contact with the customer.

In the urgency stage the writer indicates that payments must be made now.

may not mention a specific date for action until the final letter. One writer wrote the final letter in the urgency stage in this way:

Based on your credit record we were sure that you would have contacted us regarding your delinquent account. The time has come for us to take stronger action in order to collect the $180 balance of your account.

We will expect full payment of your account within the next five days. We hope to avoid having to present your account to the Interstate Collection Association. Neither of us wishes to get involved in court actions, but it is a definite possibility.

Please send your check for $180 by October 31. By doing so you will avoid legal entanglements which will be expensive and damaging to your credit record.

In the urgency stage the tone of the letter is more demanding than persuasive. You should emphasize the need to pay rather than the reasons the customer has not paid. In that way you avoid the stridency that destroys goodwill, but leave no question in the reader's mind about the need for immediate action.

Collection strategies differ somewhat from one organization to another. In general, however, the collection correspondent's approach follows the progression we have outlined from reminder to stronger reminder to inquiry to urgent appeal. Collection campaigns require thorough planning so that past-due bills are collected without sacrificing the goodwill of the customer.

A series of collection letters used by a department store follows. Note that each letter represents one of the four stages of a collection campaign.

1. Reminder—A Gentle Prod

This is a gentle reminder that a portion of the unpaid balance on your account is overdue. This is more than likely an oversight which you will correct by making a payment within the next few days. Perhaps you have mailed your remittance already. If so, we would like to thank you for your patronage.

In sending a reminder the writers think no actual persuasion is necessary. It is assumed that payment was not made simply because the customer forgot about it.

2. Strong Reminder—A Direct Prod

Most of our customers appreciate a reminder when their account is overdue.

Therefore, we would like to remind you of your overdue account. Listed below is your present balance as well as the minimum amount due if you prefer monthly payments.

You may have already mailed a payment within the last few days. If not, won't you please do so?

As its title suggests, this letter is stronger in tone than the first one. The writer still gives the reader the benefit of the doubt, however, by assuming that the reader has merely overlooked the bill.

3. Inquiry—To Reestablish Communication

We recently wrote to you regarding the past-due balance on your charge account. With your revolving charge account you have the option of a 30-day account or monthly payments of as little as five percent of the balance. At any time, of course, you may pay more or all of your balance.

Please contact us immediately if you are unable to pay the $225 now due. Together we will be able to resolve your problem.

Use the enclosed envelope for your prompt reply.

At this point the writer wants either payment or an explanation of the delay. Reestablishing a link with the customer, preferably by receipt of payment, is the letter's goal. By reminding the reader of the charge account's convenience, the writer hopes to get a response.

4. Urgency—A Genuine Crisis

Twelve years ago this October you opened a charge account with us. Since that time we have worked hard to meet your needs. Apparently we have succeeded since you have been a regular customer.

Collection Letter Guide

Be aware of the assumption under which each letter should be written.

Get what is owed without sacrificing the goodwill of the customer.

As a collection campaign progresses, letters should become more demanding and stress collection rather than any additional sales.

Keep the reminder letter low-key and matter-of-fact.

In the strong reminder letter you may make the customer aware of the benefits of having credit.

Appeal to some interest of the reader in the inquiry stage when seeking a payment or an explanation.

In the urgency stage you should convey the seriousness of the situation and the fact that time is running out.

Because you have been such a loyal customer, it's all the more surprising that we have not heard a word from you. It's a mystery to us why you have allowed your account to become overdue after such a good credit history.

We are waiting for your check for $260 and we must have it. If your credit record is to be protected, you must act now.

Please send us a check today, or at least contact us so that a payment plan can be arranged. By acting immediately your valuable credit record may be saved.

In this letter the writer offers the debtor one last chance. The tone of the letter is serious because it is urgent that this problem be corrected.

Special Requests

Large organizations may send sales letters by the hundreds of thousands. If research shows that a particular sales letter is effective, it may be used for a long time. The same is true of collection letters. There is another kind of persuasive letter, however, which is not normally used in mass mailings; this is a letter in which you ask a favor of someone. You will write many such letters during your career.

Since there is often little reward for complying with such a request, writers usually dispense with the proven sales approach and get to the heart of the matter immediately. In this example the writer seems to think that the reader is either going to comply or not and that persuasion will have no effect:

The Public Library Guild is in the midst of its annual drive for volunteers.

Your name has been submitted as a possible volunteer. Please join us for an orientation session at the Woodword Library on Wednesday, September 8 at 7 p.m.

Through the involvement of volunteers professional librarians are freed from clerical duties and can concentrate on performing the duties for which they were actually hired. Volunteers help make the Woodword Library run more efficiently.

Please let us know that you are interested in enhancing the quality of the services provided by the Woodword Library. Your help will make a difference.

When a writer takes a fatalistic approach and assumes persuasion will have no effect, the resulting letter will be bland and a positive response is unlikely. Consider the shortcomings in the letter above:

The first paragraph is more likely to elicit a response of "who cares?" rather than the reader's attention.

In the second paragraph an invitation is extended; however, the writer made no attempt to motivate the reader to accept it. The writer points out in the next paragraph that volunteers allow professional librar-

Special requests are a common type of persuasive communication.

ians to perform their intended duties but does not explain why this is important.

The closing paragraph implies that the reader's unwillingness to volunteer would be evidence of disinterest in the library's services. Such a close is unlikely to make the reader receptive to future contact with the writer.

By adhering to the persuasive sequence, this writer was much more effective:

You have demonstrated, through your civic-mindedness in the past, the effect one dedicated person can have on a project. Now you have the opportunity again to significantly improve the services provided by one of our most important institutions.

Thomas Carlyle described the founding of a library as "one of the greater things we can do." Our entire community has enjoyed the benefits of the Woodword Library yet one obstacle prevents its continued development. A reduced budget has resulted in staff reductions and our professional librarians must now spend most of their time on clerical tasks.

Misusing professional librarians is a waste of tax money. Equally important, librarians are less accessible to those who come to learn and grow. You can help the library serve the public by performing some of the clerical duties which are so necessary for efficient operation. There will be an orientation for new volunteers on Wednesday, September 8 at 7 p.m. in the conference room of the Woodword Library. As a Woodword volunteer you will enjoy being part of a team so clearly devoted to the public good.

In this letter the writer recognized past contributions of the reader prior to describing a problem which the reader could do something about. By following the AIDA steps, the writer presented the reader with good reasons for helping prior to actually requesting assistance.

Too many writers try to avoid wasting the reader's time by leading off with the request. That is what this writer did:

Please send me a packet of the materials which you used to try to enlist public support for the recent bond referendum.

Even though the letter included additional information the reader did not read beyond the initial request. Instead, the reader immediately thought of reasons for not complying with the request and responded accordingly.

Contrast the above opening with this one:

Effective public relations practitioners are able to influence the attitudes of the public on virtually any issue. You demonstrated this ability by persuading more than 40 percent of the voters to support the recent bond referendum.

The writer presented a statement with which most public relations practitioners would agree and followed that with an acknowledgment of the reader's abilities. Since no request has yet been made, there is nothing for the reader to refuse. Since the writer has established a common ground with the reader, the reader will continue reading.

Most students preparing for a career in public relations are unaware of all that such a career entails. Their knowledge of the field is limited to the advice of professors, many of whom are long-removed from the public arena. It is only through greater contact with successful practitioners that students will become more attuned to the realities of public relations.

Here the writer laid out the problem which is of concern to practitioners such as the reader. As a practitioner the reader is uniquely qualified to alleviate the problem.

By speaking to the Mid-City Public Relations Society on Wednesday, March 15, you will contribute greatly to the development of public relations students. The meeting will begin at 7:00 and will be held at the Downtowner. All of our 75 members hope you will share your expertise with us.

In this paragraph the writer provided the reader with an opportunity to make a valuable contribution. This is a request that the reader will find hard to refuse.

Note how subtle the letter in Figure 7.3 is. At no point is an actual request made, yet it is certainly a request for support. It was sent on the letterhead stationery of a prestigious law firm and signed by the chairman of the board of trustees of the St. Jude's House.

In Figure 7.3 the writer emphasized the attention and interest steps with some specific examples. The examples will stimulate the desire of the reader to provide continued support.

The same organization took a different approach in another letter of request. The letter in Figure 7.4 follows the four steps and its appeal is more explicit than in Figure 7.3.

Many of the requests you write will be briefer and more direct than Figures 7.3 and 7.4. However, the sequence of ideas will be the same.

There are countless purposes for writing letters of special request. These are some of the more common ones:

- Recruiting a guest speaker
- Seeking financial contributions
- Recruiting a chairperson or a member for a committee
- Requesting a letter of recommendation
- Seeking cooperation for a survey

We write many letters of request, and competition is keen for the attention and cooperation of the reader. The letters that follow the persuasive strategy are more likely to elicit the desired response.

Persuasive writing is certainly not limited to letters, however. Persuasion is frequently employed in memos and reports also. Many reports, for example, include recommendations which are presented persuasively.

Figure 7.3 Letter Making a Special Request

Dear St. Jude's Benefactor:

In an effort to give you a report in the most human terms of the return on your monetary investment in St. Jude's House, it seemed appropriate to share the following vignettes with you.

First the story of Mr. D., a long-time resident of St. Jude's House, who simply could not function and live without a structured environment such as St. Jude's House, is now employed by a hospital, pays his own way, and was recently able to spend his vacation in his hometown --- Sober!

St. Jude's Director has supper once a month with a former resident who has eight years sobriety --- and he is a working, taxpaying citizen now. College educated, he came to us at St. Jude's after living in cardboard cartons under a bridge, and delivering hand-bills to finance the next drink.

Mr. C., a former resident of St. Jude's House, has remained sober for over four years. He now is an active member in Alcoholic's Anonymous. He has secured a high-paying job as a computer programmer. His last four Christmases were sober ones, the first in over twenty years!

Ms. B. has a long history of nonalcoholic drug abuse, admitted to St. Jude's House because we needed bed occupancy. Although she is on legal probation, last month she obtained a job as a clerk typist, the first job she has had in a very long time.

Mr. A., a person we have worked with over the last five years, had a kidney transplant. He was the donor --- he saved his brother's life! He now has something to be proud of and sober for the first time in twenty years! Both are recovering well.

Mr. E. is in his late twenty's and has been an alcoholic since he was fourteen. After two aborted residences, he is now settling in and making use of the community which St. Jude's has available to him. His progress is good, his outlook positive for the first time since he was fourteen.

Source: Reprinted with permission of St. Jude's House, Inc.

Figure 7.3 (continued)

Mr. F. was once a very prominent Atlantan. He now
suffers brain damage from his alcoholism, but has
been able to "hang in" at St. Jude's community. He
now works as a parking lot attendant. While his
family feels this is very beneath him, he is
beginning to come to grips with the fact that he will
never be able to return to his earlier profession.
But, he can pay his own way and become a valued
member of his community. He now has self-respect.

Although I have but scratched the surface of the human drama that
unfolds constantly day in and day out at St. Jude's House, I hope this
insight will indicate the tremendous return on your financial help at
St. Jude's House. Your money is wisely garnered and spent. The human
suffering alleviated, and the hope you provide is the most touching
thing in the world!

Sincerely,

E. Reginald Hancock
Chairman of the Board
of Trustees
St. Jude's House

ERH/sts

cc: Reverend Canon Herbert J. Beadle
     St. Jude's House Board Members

Figure 7.4   Letter of Request

October 18, 1984

In past years, you have generously supported St. Jude's, and I hope you will do so this year.

As responsible, affluent citizens we are all asked to respond to a lot of mighty good causes. These range from our church, crippled children, old folks, cancer, MS, Jerry Lewis Telethons, Atlanta Symphony, High Museum, et al. Depending on our loyalties and disposition, we make our charitable gifts. Whose heartstrings have not been touched by a crippled child --- typically a little blond, blue-eyed girl about 5 years old with shriveled up legs in a cast on crutches? It's easy to give to her.

Now, contrast that with a sloppy, falling down, filthy, bugridden, sour-smelling drunk, who has not shaved in weeks. Some think that if he was not so damned sorry, he could stay off booze and earn a good living. Of course, this overlooks the fact that he or she is a victim of a disease, too, called alcoholism.

All those other diseased folks are going to get their share of the funds. But who is going to help that dirty drunk who will cheat, lie, and steal for another shot of red-eye? St. Jude's does by providing a home, and hope, and health for the alcoholic whose family and friends have given up. The result in many cases is little short of miraculous.

It doesn't take much to give to those other needful people. I think it takes real guts, real character, to work for and give to St. Jude's House.

St. Jude's is not perfect. Anyone who knows the frustrations of fighting alcoholism will appreciate that, but we do save lives and we do give men and women an opportunity to regain their respect and return to our community. Moreover, while at St. Jude's, these men and women pay for a substantial portion of the cost of the house and, with the help of job location assistance, find jobs where they become taxpayers, no longer a drain on the tax-paying citizens of the city and country.

St. Jude's makes no pretense to being a large institution. It is modest in its size and scope, but it is the best good thing that ever happened to

Source: Reprinted with permission of St. Jude's House, Inc.

Figure 7.4 (continued)

October 18, 1984
Page 2

many people whose lives have been victimized by alcoholism. We receive no
government aid and are not a United Way agency. Rather, we have served
for 18 years because of the faithful support that you and our other friends
have given us. In this fall of 1982, we ask again for your support and
pledge our continued work to the alcoholics who turn to us for help.

Please help in whatever way you can and know that we are grateful.

Sincerely yours,

E. Reginald Hancock
Chairperson
Board of Trustees

Regardless of the format of a persuasive message, the goal is to change one's behavior or thinking. Such desired changes are more likely to result if the writer adheres to the principles of persuasion described in this chapter.

Persuasive messages are found in many formats.

Summary

Four factors are important to building an effective persuasive message: sender, receiver, message, and channel. Being aware of these factors and understanding the process of persuasion will enable you to write and speak more persuasively.

Sales letters, collection letters, and letters of request were emphasized in this chapter because of the important role such letters play in business communication.

Although some sales letters are solicited by the reader, most are not. The writer of a sales letter usually faces the challenge of securing a positive response from a reader who has expressed no interest in the product or in the ideas of the writer.

A definite strategy underlies most effective sales letters. Before writing such a letter you should learn as much as possible about the product to be sold and about the intended reader. Determine what the reader is likely to consider the most attractive feature of the product and make this the central selling point. Refer to this point throughout your letter.

In writing a sales letter you should develop your ideas in this sequence: (1) attract the reader's *attention,* (2) stimulate the reader's *interest,* (3) develop a *desire* within the reader, and (4) encourage the reader to take a specific *action.*

Although collection policies may differ among organizations, the collection process almost always progresses through four stages: (1) reminder, (2) strong reminder, (3) inquiry, and (4) urgency. Regardless of the stage of an overdue account, you must strive to maintain goodwill while collecting the unpaid balance.

In both the reminder and strong-reminder stages you should assume that the customer has simply overlooked the unpaid balance. The letters written in these stages are based on the assumption that, when reminded, the customer will pay. In the inquiry stage you should seek an explanation of the circumstances that prevent payment. This letter is more direct than the previous ones. You become insistent in the urgency stage. The theme may be that the customer can avoid greater problems only by paying now.

We often must write to request a favor which has no clear reward. Such letters of request are usually more personal than sales or collection letters, but they too follow the AIDA sequence.

Footnotes

[1] Abraham Maslow, *Motivation and Personality* (New York: Harper & Row, 1954).

[2] Jim Powell, "The Lucrative Trade of Crafting Junk Mail," *The New York Times,* June 20, 1982, p. F–7.

[3] Ibid.

[4] "Fast Answers for Slow Payments," *BusinessWeek,* March 9, 1981, pp. 88–90.

[5] "Owning-Up Time," *Time,* August 25, 1980, p. 45.

Review Questions

1. What is the primary goal of persuasion? What more specific goals does this goal encompass?
2. What is meant by source credibility? How can we use it in constructing persuasive messages?
3. What factors can you use to gain and hold the attention of a receiver?
4. Compare and contrast Maslow's theory of motivation with the direct and indirect reward approach to motivating receivers.
5. What are the four steps to follow in writing a sales letter?
6. Explain the difference between the interest step and the desire step.
7. Four common errors in seeking attention were presented in this chapter. Describe another error and provide an example of it.
8. Describe the four stages of a collection campaign.
9. In which ways is the reminder stage in the collection campaign similar to the strong-reminder stage? How are they different?
10. What is meant by central selling point?

Exercises

1. Much of the junk mail we receive consists of sales letters of various sorts. Analyze one of these sales letters. Does it follow the four-step sequence? How does the writer try to attract the reader's attention? What specific action is the writer seeking from the reader? What is the central selling point of the letter? What changes would you suggest for the letter?
2. Assume that you are a correspondent for the Ultimate Watch Company. Your company is about to introduce its first chronograph, a wristwatch designed especially for runners. These are its main features: displays hours, minutes, and seconds on a digital face; functions as a stopwatch, and displays time in minutes, seconds, and hundredths of seconds; has fewer moving parts than

any other chronograph; is shock- and water-resistant; carries a two-year warranty. Write a sales letter that will be sent to all of the subscribers to several running magazines.

3. Assume that you are sales manager of Columbia Cable Television Corporation. You must persuade the public to subscribe to Living Room Theatre, a channel featuring movies 24 hours per day. Many of the movies are recent films; none are more than one year old. The cost of Living Room Theatre is $5.50 per month or $55 per year if paid in a single payment at the time of subscribing. There are no commercials on this channel, and free maintenance is provided to any subscriber. Since Living Room Theatre has just become available in Huntington, West Virginia, you are to write a sales letter in a form that could be sent to all the residents of that area. (If you wish to name some of the movies scheduled to be shown in the near future, use your imagination.)

4. As assistant director of Shenandoah Homes one of your duties is to respond to all letters of inquiry. Shenandoah Homes is a non-profit retirement and health care facility for the elderly. A life-care contract sells for $30,000 and guarantees purchasers nutritious meals, medical care, excellent facilities for recreational and cultural activities, and a lifetime lease on a modern apartment. According to the contract, the fees cannot be increased after a contract is signed. You receive a postcard from Wesley Thornton (Box 240, Roanoke, VA 24001). He expresses interest in Shenandoah Homes and requests additional information. Write a sales letter to him.

5. Select a product and assume that you are employed by its manufacturer. Prepare a collection campaign including one letter representing each stage of the collection process. Prepare the four collection letters as form letters that could be sent to any customer.

6. Make the same assumptions as you were asked to in Exercise 5. This time, however, prepare four letters to be sent to dealers rather than consumers.

7. William Rogers has been a good customer of Meteor Finance Company for eight years. In the past ten months, however, his account has been overdue twice. At present the account is 60 days delinquent. He has missed his last two monthly payments of $120 each.

   a. Write a paragraph in which you appeal to his sense of pride.

   b. Write a paragraph in which you appeal to his sense of equity.

   c. Write a paragraph in which you appeal to his self-interest.

   d. Write a paragraph in which you appeal to something other than pride, equity, and self-interest.

   These paragraphs are not intended to appear in a single letter. Therefore, it is not necessary to relate one paragraph to another.

8. Identify the strengths and shortcomings of the following letter and rewrite it to your satisfaction:

The Program Planning Committee of the Young Business Leadership Association met yesterday to select a keynote speaker for its annual convention. The names of some very prominent business leaders were proposed for this honor but each name, for one reason or another, was dropped from consideration.

Since the YBLA includes a diversity of interests you could speak on almost any subject as long as it is somewhat related to business. Twenty to thirty minutes would be appropriate.

The YBLA was founded right here in Bismark in 1970 for the purpose of keeping businesspeople abreast of current thinking in business. We have 143 members, but they won't all attend the banquet. Last year 80 members and spouses attended the banquet and 28 outsiders attended. Just as last year, the banquet will be open to the public.

The banquet will be held at the fashionable Bismarkian Hotel at 7 p.m. on either May 28, 29, or 30 depending on your availability. We are extending this invitation four months in advance in the hope of getting a commitment from you. Select whichever date you prefer and notify us immediately so that we can proceed with our plans.

The YBLA will pay your travel and lodging expenses. If you accept our invitation, we will reserve a room for you the night of the banquet at the Econo-Rooms Inn, which is down the street from the Bismarkian.

Thank you for considering our invitation, and we hope that you will accept. We await your prompt reply.

9. You recently purchased a spacious brick ranch house and hired a painter to paint the wood trim. Your intent was to cover the beige with a light green. You returned home from a business trip to discover that the trim had been painted chartreuse. The painter acknowledges that the trim is a little bright but he assures you that the color will fade to a light green in a year or so. You do not intend to wait for it to fade. Write a letter to the painter's employer requesting that the trim be repainted at no expense to you.

10. Recently you left your car at a local car wash for a deluxe wash and wax. Shortly after retrieving the car you discover that a small camera is missing from the glove compartment. The car wash employees claim not to have seen the camera and the manager disclaims any responsibility. A large sign posted prominently at the car wash denies responsibility for missing items. Write a letter to the corporate headquarters of the car wash requesting payment for the camera which you believe was taken by one of the car wash employees.

11. You have invented a new electronic game and have established a small shop for its manufacture. The game is called Hack-Man and its most distinguishable feature is the human-like hacking sound the machine makes as points are scored. As the point total mounts

the volume of the hacking increases. Your research in your community shows that teenagers prefer Hack-Man to any other electronic game. Teenage players seem to enjoy the attention they attract when they score well. The machine is five feet tall, two feet wide, and 30 inches deep. Write a letter to be sent to the operators of game parlors. Use the letter to persuade them to send an enclosed postcard requesting that a sales representative visit. (Use your imagination and create whatever other features you care to.)

12. You have been assigned to write a research paper on universal life insurance policies. Universal life insurance is regarded by many as the most promising new approach to life insurance in years. Use the *Business Periodical Index* to locate several articles on universal life insurance. After learning what it is, write a letter to Commissioner of Insurance, State of Wisconsin, Madison, WI 53703 requesting information for your research paper. Be specific in the type of information you seek.

13. You purchased a wireless burglar alarm from a mail-order discount company and are dissatisfied with it. It was easily installed just as advertised; the problem is that the alarm goes off each time your neighbor uses her CB radio. The company has a policy of paying customer refunds only on merchandise returned within ten days of purchase. It took you more than ten days to determine that the problem could not be solved. Write a letter requesting a complete refund. Assume that you will not mail the alarm until the company has approved your request. Write the letter to Alarms Unlimited, P.O. Box 146, Warden, ME 71289.

14. You own a sporting goods store and have completed a mailing list of the members of the various bicycle clubs in your area. Prepare a sales letter to be sent to the club members in late October when a typical Minnesota winter is about to begin. Try to sell the readers on continuing to enjoy the benefits of cycling exercise by purchasing a new Exer-Bike. The Exer-Bike is manufactured in the United States, weighs only 22 pounds, and sells for $110. It is a stationary bike, 40 inches long and 30 inches high, and the handlebar is 22 inches long. The handlebar is easily adjusted, without tools, for persons of any height.

15. You volunteered to take pictures at your cousin's wedding and thereby save the newlyweds the expense of hiring a photographer. You took approximately 150 pictures and gave them to a local camera store for processing. More than half of the resulting photographs were badly blurred. Since you are an accomplished photographer, you know that you are not at fault. The owner of the camera store disclaims responsibility since he merely sent the films to another city for processing. The store owner has offered to give you free film equivalent to the amount of film that was blurred. Write a letter to the photo laboratory which processed the

film. Since you have suffered considerable embarrassment, you believe that the photo laboratory should pay you at least $100 in damages. You intend to give whatever payment you get to your cousin. Write your letter to Slic Pics Inc., P.O. Box 1212, Hilda, MO 65670.

16. In an effort to conserve energy, two years ago you replaced the caulking compound in all of the windows in your eight-room house. Now the caulking compound is badly mildewed and looks unsightly. You complain to the owner of the store where you bought the compound, but he is not sympathetic. "It's not advertised as mildew-resistant," he says. Write a letter to the manufacturer in which you request that a representative be sent to inspect your house and remedy the situation. Write your letter to Home Products, Inc., P.O. Box 290, Pottsburg, FL 32216.

17. Assume that you have developed a new electronic bug killer and call it "Black Light." It electrocutes bugs instantaneously and, unlike all other such devices, it makes no noise. It is lantern-shaped and is available in black, brown, or beige. It can be easily attached to a tree limb or it can stand upright on the ground or patio. It comes with a fluorescent bulb and sells for $22.50 wholesale. It is 16 inches tall, 4 inches wide, and 4 inches deep. It weighs 3 pounds. Write a sales letter to be sent to hardware stores and lawn supply stores throughout your state.

18. You have been assigned to write a research paper on health maintenance organizations (HMO). Read at least one article on this approach to health care before you write a letter to the manager of the largest HMO in the area. In your letter seek information on the advantages of the HMO over the traditional fee-for-service approach. Write your letter to Reginald Beatty, Manager, Reliable HMO, P.O. Box 12, Valdosta, GA 31601.

Case

The Nirvana Alarm Clock
Robert Underwood
Ball State University

You recently have begun your new job with a local advertising agency, and you have been given the assignment of writing a persuasive letter to be used in marketing the Nirvana Alarm Clock. You have been given the following description of the clock. The Nirvana Alarm Clock:

1. Automatically resets the alarm for the next day
2. Has a sturdy, non-tip base
3. Has a five-decibel buzzer
4. Has a snooze alarm

5. Is available in the following seven colors: red, pink, blue, black, purple, green, and orange
6. Is constructed of durable polystyrene
7. Has a luminous face, and projects the correct day and time on the ceiling
8. Measures six inches by six inches by two inches
9. Costs $21.95, plus $3.00 for shipping and handling
10. Comes with an unconditional two-year guarantee

Thousands of these clocks have been sold nationally, but your target market will be college-age students. Write a sales letter to be sent to these students. Remember that your letter should be built around a central theme, and that you might not want to include all the items listed above.

■ ■ ■

Case Questions:

1. What would be your central theme for this letter?
2. Which characteristics of the clock would be of most interest to a college-age student? Which characteristics would be of least interest to a college-age student?
3. List two "attention-getters" that you could use to begin your letter.

Planning the Long Report

Learning Objectives
1. To learn how to organize and outline a business report.
2. To know the difference between informational, interpretive, and problem-solving reports.
3. To learn the steps in planning the long report.
4. To be able to differentiate between primary and secondary research methods.
5. To learn the different techniques of sampling.
6. To learn how to prepare an effective questionnaire.

Stephanie wondered whether to get another cup of coffee. She'd had three cups already and felt tense. She sat at her desk waiting to see Scott, her boss at Atlantic Electronics.

She had turned in her report on employee relations problems several weeks ago, and she was confident that she had researched her topic well. The solutions to the problems were, she believed, logical and desirable; she said as much in her report. But now Scott, his superior Louise (the personnel manager), and Warren, the vice president, were, meeting. The topic of the meeting was Stephanie's first semiannual review. She had known the meeting was to take place today, and she had known who would be participating. What caught her off guard was that she saw Warren, the ranking executive in the meeting, carrying her report to the meeting. Her report was going to be used in her evaluation.

Stephanie was worried that some parts of the report—other than her research and recommendation sections—might not be correct. Although she believed she had the right information, perhaps it could have been better organized.

In the six months she had been with Atlantic, she had written about a dozen reports of various lengths for Scott. He had been gracious in guiding her to prepare the type of reports he wanted. Although her business-degree background included some report-writing instruction, she quickly found she still had a lot to learn.

So now she was wondering about her report organization, about the clarity of her conclusions, and whether she should have included more visual support, such as charts, to illustrate her findings.

Well, she thought to herself, I'll know soon. Here comes Scott. ∎

You may have had the same uneasy feeling about one of your term papers that Stephanie had about her business report. Of course, term papers differ from business reports, but both are used in performance evaluation; therefore, we may have afterthoughts about our submission of them.

The main purpose of Chapters 8 and 9 is to prepare you to write effective and appropriate business reports—reports that you want to be used in evaluating your performance. The preparation of long business reports includes two phases: planning and writing. In this chapter, we offer suggestions about how to plan the report. In Chapter 9, we discuss actual report writing. As we move through these chapters, we'll describe what Stephanie might have done to be more self-assured in her report preparation. In fact, a complete report on Stephanie's topic appears at the end of Chapter 9.

As you read the chapters, you'll find that much of the material can be applied to term paper assignments. However, several major differences between writing reports and term papers exist: (1) many term paper assignments identify your specific purpose for you, such as an assignment to describe the influence of technology on office workers. When writing business reports, you'll often need to identify your own purpose. In other words, many business reports are self-initiated. (2) Most term papers are written for a single audience, usually your instructor, while business reports typically are written for many readers. (Some reports which are written for a single reader are viewed by many more than the one intended reader.) (3) Business reports typically have standard parts that are seldom used when writing term papers.

Before we discuss how to plan and write business reports, we first need to discuss why business reports are valuable. Reports are prepared for one or more of the following reasons: (1) for documentation purposes—to provide a written record; (2) for geographical reasons—to give similar material to individuals at about the same time but in different geographical locations; (3) for financial considerations—to produce relatively inexpensive copies after the initial copy, which may be expensive; (4) for convenience, such as taking information in a briefcase for review after work; (5) for stronger organization—to edit and revise the contents of reports toward a specific goal; (6) for accuracy—to make information easier to read and verify; for example, to examine a long list of numbers for accuracy; (7) to save time—for example, writing a report may be quicker and easier than organizing a meeting for an oral presentation; and (8) for technological reasons—word processors and electronic mail are increasing the speed of report preparation and distribution while reducing the cost per report.

Why are business reports valuable?

In addition to the various values of reports, there are also a number of ways of categorizing or differentiating reports. Knowing the classification of a report frequently is a first step in deciding the report's purpose. Included in the various report classifications are: (1) formality of the report. Some reports, such as for government or high-level management, have an extremely formal tone and appearance. Other reports might be so informal that they are handwritten and quite short; (2) the length. Reports range from less than one full page to hundreds of pages; (3) The time interval of the report. Many reports are periodic, such as daily production reports, weekly progress reports, or annual financial reports. Other reports may have a time interval of one; they may occur only once.

There are many report classifications.

Other classifications are by: (4) the report's destination. Does the report go downward to subordinates or upward to superiors? Is the report directed internally, such as a report that will be used within the organization? Is the report directed externally to an audience removed from the organization, such as a local government? (5) the research category employed. The presentation of information differs depending on whether primary or secondary research is used. (6) the report's intent. Is the goal of the report to justify some action, to establish progress toward an objective, or to recommend a change? (7) the number of authors. Team-written reports frequently have a different tone than individually prepared reports. Further, team reports may incorporate individually written sections into one package or the team may work together, in both writing and editing, on each sentence in the document. (8) the extent of contribution to the decision-making process. Reports range from straightforward statements of fact to highly structured analyses that include recommendations and discussion of implications.

The Problem-Solving Report

Business reports, as mentioned in Item 8 above, can be categorized by the extent of their contribution to the decision-making process. An example of an informational report is a weekly absenteeism report that indicates only who was absent, when, the employee's department, and number of absences to date. Purely informational reports, although valuable and ever-present, add relatively little to the decision-making process compared to the other report forms.

A step above the informational report is the interpretive report. Rather than merely presenting data, this report adds meaning to the data. The facts presented in the informational report are examined and implications are drawn. To move the absenteeism report example into the interpretive report realm, the author would explain the meaning of the report: which employees are absentee problems, whether some departments experience higher rates than others, and what cost, in time, dollars, or materials, is attributable to absenteeism.

The third division of decision-making reports—and the one that makes the most contribution to the decision-making process—is the problem-solving report. Because the problem-solving report not only informs with data and interprets the data, but also analyzes the problem situation, reviews alternatives, examines implications, draws conclusions, and makes recommendations, it is frequently referred to as an *analytical report*. If our absenteeism report moved through these steps and included, for example, a recommendation that two employees be interviewed by their supervisors to determine the cause of their extreme absenteeism, the report would become an analytical report.

The reports discussed in Chapters 8 and 9, as well as the instructions on how to plan and write business reports, are the problem solving or analytical type. The problem-solving report is spotlighted because it is the most involved and difficult of the three types; it encompasses the other two forms. Thus, generally speaking, if you can write an effective analytical business report, you can probably prepare the other two categories as well.

The Planning Process

This chapter focuses on the planning of the long report. Planning involves five steps:

Steps in planning a long report

1. Determine the purpose(s)
2. Consider the receiver(s)

3. Conduct the research
4. Evaluate the results
5. Prepare the outline

Step 1: Determine the Purpose(s)

When your report is finished, what need will it satisfy? Will it supply information to be used by others in a decision-making role? Will you interpret the information? Are you to analyze the situation and supply as much information, interpretation, and specific recommendations as possible? Clearly, writing an informational report when an analytical report is desired is as inappropriate as supplying a thorough and lengthy problem-solving report when a focused and brief informational report is expected. Thus, your first step in planning the business report is deciding on the contribution to the decision-making process that this report is to serve.

In the beginning of this chapter, Stephanie had prepared a report that recommended solutions to employee relations problems. Because of the recommendations, we can assume the report is a problem-solving one.

Report contributions to decision making

Step 2: Consider the Receiver(s)

Report writing requires careful analysis of the intended audience in terms of numbers of readers and their characteristics. One reason Stephanie was concerned about seeing her report being carried into the evaluation meeting was she had not anticipated that Louise and Warren might see her report.

In considering your audience, you will want to examine several receiver characteristics:

Receiver characteristics

1. Expertise. How much do the various receivers know about the topic? Can they understand the technological jargon you might use?
2. Interests. How much detail will your receivers want? Do they prefer tables, charts, and graphs to clarify information?
3. Opinions. Will the receivers be for or against your recommendations (if you make any)? Do they have vested interests related to your recommendations? Do they think your report is important? What do the receivers think of you?
4. Hierarchical position. Are you sending a report down the organizational chart to a direct subordinate who may have little choice in whether to accept your conclusion? Is your report being shared with peers? Will the report move upward to either direct or indirect superiors?

When you write term papers, you probably spend a lot of time trying to figure out what your instructor wants. When writing long reports, your perception of your receiver(s) will dramatically influence the way you put the report together.

Step 3: Conduct the Research

Doing the research for your report means answering two questions:

1. What do I need?
2. Where can I get it?

In planning her problem-solving report, Stephanie used a procedure most good report writers employ in answering the first question. She divided her topic into three basic categories and prepared the chart in Table 8.1.

Table 8.1   What I Need: A Sample Needs Chart

Need 1 **What Is the Problem?**	Turnover information
	Absenteeism information
	Grievance information
	Morale information
	Unionization information
Need 2 **What's Causing the Problem?**	Why high turnover?
	Why high absenteeism?
	Why so many grievances?
	Why such low morale?
	Why talk of unionization?
Need 3 **What Are Some Solutions?**	More money
	More fringe benefits
	Better working conditions
	What else?

Not only did Stephanie break down her problem into three areas of need, but she also created a checklist for herself. Charts such as Table 8.1 which Stephanie prepared can help clearly define the information needs you have. Also, the chart serves as a feedback device—you can check items as you acquire the information.

With a chart such as in Table 8.1, you are ready to answer the second question: where do I get the information? Answering this question involves choosing between two kinds of information sources—primary and secondary. Primary sources are generally unpublished. You get them firsthand. Secondary sources are publications. Here are some examples:

Primary Sources	**Secondary Sources**
Questionnaires	Newspapers
Experiments	Government documents
Interviews	Books
Personal observations	Magazines
Organization files (in some cases)	Pamphlets

Primary versus secondary sources

Your choice of sources depends greatly upon how much time you have to complete your report, your budget, and your ability in using the sources.

Sometimes it is assumed that secondary research is easier and quicker than primary research. Although this may often be the case, it is not always true. Don't select a secondary research technique just because it appears to be the quickest method. A better rule of thumb— one that comes from scientific inquiry—is to do secondary research first. If someone else has already researched your topic, rely on their findings. However, you must be careful not to assume that because something is in print, it is correct or complete.

In examining secondary research, it is wise to ask: (1) is the information complete? (2) does it appear reasonable and logical? (3) is it biased? and (4) is it recent? A weakness in any one of these areas may suggest the need to conduct your own (primary) research. These same four questions should be raised before secondary research is included in the report.

By now you've had extensive experience using secondary sources and thus feel comfortable relying on them. However, you'll find that primary sources are uniquely rich, especially in terms of solving problems in organizations. To help conduct your research, we'll offer some specific suggestions about how to use both types of sources. Just as the researcher should first try to do secondary research and then, if necessary, use primary research, we will first examine secondary research sources.

Secondary Research Sources

Although secondary research is sometimes called *library research,* that does not mean that all secondary research is done in a library. Some items, such as newspapers, magazines, or pamphlets, you may have at home or at your office. However, a thorough secondary research project will likely mean a trip to the library.

You are probably familiar with using the library to locate information sources. Therefore, instead of presenting elementary instructions on how to use a library, we'll list a few reminders and hints on effective library usage.

□ Don't focus your search exclusively on books and neglect periodicals or vice versa.

□ Use the *Guide to Periodic Literature,* which may be in magazine, hardbound, or microfilm form, to find citations by title, author, or subject. The *Business Periodical Index* serves the same function but lists only articles related to business. Also consider using the *Wall Street Journal Index* and the *New York Times Index.*

□ When you find a book on your topic, use both the table of contents and the index to locate information. Skim both completely since you may not know the exact term the author uses to refer to your topic.

□ Pay special attention to the footnotes in the books and articles you find to guide you to other related sources.

□ Look for sources that survey your topic. Books of this type are sometimes entitled, *The Handbook of . . . , The (topic) Manual,* or *An Analysis of . . . .* Often these sources break the topic into outline form, may give its history, and frequently have many valuable footnotes.

□ Watch for sources with bibliographies. Sometimes entire books are bibliographies and these can be most helpful.

□ If you become frustrated or confused, seek help from a librarian; they're experts in locating information.

□ As you locate information that you think may be of some value to you, put the information on notecards.

Guidelines for library research

Let us expand on this last hint because time can be saved if several steps are taken at that point. On the top of the card write the complete citation of the source. Put it in bibliographic form (the differences between footnotes and bibliographic citations, with examples of each, are found in Chapter 9). By using cards instead of notebook paper, the cards can be sorted by topic, which can be helpful in developing your working outline. Further, an additional source card can easily be placed between two existing cards.

With the bibliographic citation at the top, the bibliography at the end of your report is easy to prepare. You just alphabetize your cards by the authors' last names. Put only one piece of information on a card, even if this means using several cards to represent one source, because it

Use notecards to organize information.

allows for easy sorting and cross-referencing. If someone else will type your report, you can give them the source cards instead of rewriting the citations. Make sure your handwriting is readable or this time-saving step fails.

Besides the bibliographic citation, jot down the information that is of value. This may be a direct quote, your own summary, or how the information relates to other sources. You may wish to put the card catalog listing on the other side of the card so you can quickly locate the source again. A sample card may look like the one in Figure 8.1.

Be sure to relate your secondary research activity to the purpose of your report. If you seek a specific person's opinion on a topic, finding a single source that gives that opinion may conclude your research. On the other hand, if you bring together a variety of opinions about a topic, clearly a number of sources will need to be examined. There's no definite way of knowing how many sources you must review to finish, but among the ways of determining an endpoint are: (1) exhausting your search (and perhaps yourself). This means locating everything you can find on the subject; (2) working until what you find starts to cluster. Once you reach the point where you find nothing new, you may be at the end of your search; (3) once you have thoroughly answered the specific question you set out to answer, you may be done. This, of

Figure 8.1   Information from a Secondary Source

Need #3

Impact of Fringe Benefits

Smith, Carlos A. "The Usefulness of Employee Benefits in Reducing Turnover," *Journal of Applied Personnel Research*, December, 1980, pp. 365 – 372.

p. 371 – "The results of most studies indicate clearly that there is no relationship between liberal doses of employee benefits and turnover rates."

p. 370 – Company	% Increase in Benefits	Change in Turnover
A.	12%	+4%
B.	25%	+1%
C.	18%	-2%

course, assumes you have a specific question, such as, 'How many cars for four or more passengers were imported from Japan in 1984?''

Primary Research Sources

There are many primary research techniques. Probably the ones we listed earlier are the most frequently used: questionnaires, experiments, interviews, personal observation, and organization files.

Questionnaires

Properly developed questionnaires can provide an enormous amount of useful data for your long report. Improperly developed questionnaires can give you misleading and often uninterpretable information. Proper use of questionnaires includes: (1) selecting an appropriate sample of respondents, (2) writing the questionnaire, (3) administering the questionnaire, and (4) tabulating the results.

Sample Selection. When you hear the results of political opinion polls, you might wonder how information obtained from as few as 1,000 persons can accurately reflect the opinions of sometimes millions of individuals. Because many opinion pollsters carefully select their samples, their predictions of election results are frequently accurate within several percentage points. Such accuracy occurs because these pollsters have clearly defined their population and, using scientific sampling guidelines, have chosen their sample from that population.

A population (also called the *universe*) is some definable group—every item, person, or thing is either in or out of the population. For national opinion pollsters in the United States, the population consists of more than 200 million citizens. On your college campus, it might be all the students or perhaps just the female undergraduate students. In an organization such as Stephanie's, the population might be all full-time employees or perhaps all hourly employees. Your first step, then, is to define your population. What group of people should the data you gather represent?

Selecting a sample involves choosing a group to represent the whole population. Ideally we would administer questionnaires to the entire population. This, however, might be time consuming and expensive. A well-conducted sample should give us similar results by contacting only a subgroup. The important assumption is that the sample represents the population.

Several types of sampling techniques exist. We'll discuss the major ones. First, in Stephanie's report writing problem, she might use a convenience sample. She might administer questionnaires to any available

Convenience sample

employees from the 500 employees in the company. Since she works in the operations department, she might distribute 50 questionnaires to the first 50 employees she encounters during the lunch hour. Such a sample is, indeed, convenient, but Stephanie's findings would probably not represent all the Atlantic Electronics employees. She might miss employees who go out for lunch or executives who do not keep regular lunch hours. Thus, convenience sampling generally is not an appropriate way of selecting a sample.

Random sampling is a second and more defensible approach to sampling. Using random sampling, Stephanie would place the names of all 500 employees in a box and draw out 50 names. Employees whose names are drawn would be asked to complete questionnaires. Despite the inconvenience of having to prepare 500 names on slips of paper for the drawing, random sampling is appropriate because each member of the population (each employee) has an equal chance of being included in the sample. This chance of being part of the sample is what makes random sampling scientifically useful and defensible. With a convenience sample, Stephanie cannot say for sure that her findings represent the opinions of all Atlantic Electronics employees. Using a random sample, Stephanie can make that important assertion.

Random sample

A third sampling technique is systematic random sampling. This technique is similar to random sampling, except that the sample draws from a list of employees and takes every *n*th one. Assume that Stephanie has in front of her a list of all 500 Atlantic employees. If she randomly picks a number between 1 and 10, such as 4, and picks every fourth person from the list, she would be conducting a systematic random sample. As with random sampling, each population member has an equal chance of being part of the sample.

Systematic random sample

Stratified random sampling is the fourth and most sophisticated technique. Again, random sampling is used, but sample members are also selected based on some important demographic characteristics (e.g., sex, race or age). The sample is stratified according to some important characteristics and usually reflects the same proportions found in the population. For example, if 47 percent of the population are female, then 47 percent of the sample would be female also. Of course, not all characteristics are important. For example, in a campus political election, sample members' hometowns may not be important. Stephanie might decide to use the following stratifications: hourly or salary, management or nonmanagement, male or female, and more than five years with Atlantic or less than five years.

Stratified random sample

Stratified random sampling is a powerful sampling technique because it ensures that sample members are selected according to one or more characteristics that might influence the findings of the questionnaire. In fact, most opinion pollsters use this technique to stratify their samples by age, income, socioeconomic status, political party affiliation, and a host of other important characteristics. Such stratification adds precision to their polls and explains why their predictions are often so accurate.

Generally speaking, a stratified sample uses fewer people in its sample but requires much more sophisticated development.

The word *questionnaire* is used in this book instead of survey because of the need for clarity: a questionnaire is always a paper-and-pencil activity completed by the respondent. On the other hand, you can either distribute a survey to respondents, or you can survey a group with a questionnaire or through interviews.

Writing the Questionnaire. A well-developed questionnaire has three basic parts: introduction, instructions, and questions. The objective of the introduction is to motivate the respondent to complete the questionnaire.

A questionnaire has an introduction, instructions, and questions.

The Introduction Includes Six Thoughts. First, it identifies the purpose of the questionnaire. Unless you are concerned that stating the actual purpose for the questionnaire will bias the respondents' answers, state specifically why you are administering the questionnaire.

Second, the introduction discusses anonymity. Because you will rarely be interested in identifying individual respondents, a statement guaranteeing their anonymity will help prevent biased responses. If their names are needed, explain why. If you need to be able to identify them but that identification will not be used in the report or shared with others, emphasize this; the emphasis may be almost as beneficial as complete anonymity in gaining their response.

Third, the introduction tells respondents what to do with the questionnaire once they have completed it. In the case of mailed questionnaires, for example, this section might contain instructions for returning the questionnaire through the mail.

Fourth, the introduction may explain why a response is important. If you are using a sample of 100 from a population of 1,000, you may explain that each respondent's opinions reflect the feelings of 10 people.

Fifth, particularly with questionnaires that appear time consuming but actually are not, indicate in the introduction the amount of time required. "Only about two and one-half minutes of your time are required," is the type of statement that may be helpful in gaining cooperation.

Finally, identify yourself in your introduction. Respondents prefer to know to whom they are responding. Your name and title humanize the message and enhance the response rate. An example introduction, as well as the balance of a questionnaire, are found in an appendix to Stephanie's report which is reproduced in Chapter 9.

The Second Portion of a Questionnaire Is the Instructions. If thorough, clear instructions are omitted, the respondents may misunderstand what they are to do. The clarity of instructions cannot be overemphasized. Assume that your reader is going to misinterpret your questionnaire—where will the error occur? Help yourself and the quality of your responses by giving clear instructions.

You may find that one set of instructions, at the beginning of the questionnaire, will guide the reader through the entire questionnaire; this is particularly true when you ask only one major category of question, such as several rank order questions. In more complex situations, however, you may need a set of instructions at the beginning and additional instructions before each new category of questions. For example, you may need new instructions as you move from a series of rank order questions to multiple choice questions.

The Final Portion Contains the Questions.   The questions are so much the heart of the questionnaire that some novices present them without introductory comments or instructions. Such approaches are doomed to failure. Many categories of questions exist. Deciding when, where, and how to use these categories is both an art and a science. Becoming familiar with the major question categories will help in the success of your questionnaire.

There are six major categories of questions; each has its own purpose, strengths, and weaknesses. Demographic questions, which frequently appear first, seek information on characteristics of the respondents. Age, sex, income, race, department, college major, and hometown are examples of demographic questions. Demographic questions have two major values: first, they can be used to break down answers to other questions. For example, you may seek a difference by sex (demographics) in the way respondents feel toward the president's foreign policy. A second value is to test the appropriateness of a random sample. If you know that your population is 35 percent college educated but your sample includes only 10 percent college educated respondents, your demographic question of education indicates that your sample appears not to be random.

Demographic questions

A second category of question is the dichotomous question—a question that elicits one of only two possible answers. Yes/no, male/female, and true/false are examples of responses to dichotomous questions. You may have noticed that dichotomous questions may also be demographic questions; "What is your sex?" fits both categories. Other categories of questions may overlap somewhat, too. Dichotomous questions allow your respondents to branch or skip irrelevant questions. An example of a branching question and instructions is "Have you earned a bachelor's degree as of today? __ Yes __ No (If yes, answer Questions 2 through 9; if no, skip directly to Question 10."

Dichotomous questions

A list question presents a list of items, thoughts, or things and asks the respondent to select one. The selection may be the greatest or the least, the largest or the smallest, the most or least important, or best or worst. Here is an example of a list question:

List and rank order questions

Which of the following do you feel is most important in determining your job satisfaction?

_____ *Money*

_____ *Praise from superiors*

_____ *Doing job well*

_____ *Respect from peers*

_____ *Fringe benefits*

Similar to the list question is the rank order question. It, too, presents a list; however, it differs because a response is given for each item in the list instead of just one item. Furthermore, the items are ranked according to some request, such as best to worst or largest to smallest. Here is an example of a rank order question:

Rank the following five items, from 1 for most important, to 5 for least important, in terms of their importance to your job satisfaction:

_____ *Money*

_____ *Praise from superiors*

_____ *Doing job well*

_____ *Respect from peers*

_____ *Fringe benefits*

Although rank order questions can gather substantial information, be careful in analyzing the rankings. Remember the rankings determine a hierarchy among the items, but that the distances between the items is not known. That is, Selections 1 and 2 may be close to each other but there might be a large gap between 2 and 3. The rankings are ordinal numbers rather than interval numbers.

A major category of question used in questionnaires is the attitude question. There are two subdivisions: direct and indirect attitude questions. The direct attitude question seeks a clear or obvious attitude. Since attitudes usually are not dichotomous (just yes or no) but are found on a scale, a Likert type of direct attitude question is often prepared. For a Likert question, the respondent gives a single reaction to each stimulus on a scale that most likely has five possible positions. Here is a Likert question:

Attitude questions

Stimulus: I enjoy my marketing classes.

Scale: Strongly agree   Agree   Neutral   Disagree   Strongly disagree

Response: _____   _____   _____   _____   _____

The semantic differential question, as opposed to the direct attitude question, seeks a deeper or more indirect attitude. Figure 8.2 shows a sample question. For each stimulus there will be a number of responses, usually about ten. A scale of five or seven positions is used between bipolar adjectives or scales.

Semantic differential questions

This category of question elicits responses that respondents might not have considered on their own. Semantic differential response can be compared group against group by which side of the neutral center

Figure 8.2   A Sample Semantic Differential Question

```
(Stimulus:)              My Marketing Classes


(Scales and
 Responses:) rewarding   ___:___:___:___:___:___:___unrewarding
             difficult   ___:___:___:___:___:___:___easy
             relevant    ___:___:___:___:___:___:___irrelevant
             messy       ___:___:___:___:___:___:___tidy
             active      ___:___:___:___:___:___:___passive
             weak        ___:___:___:___:___:___:___strong
             good        ___:___:___:___:___:___:___bad
             unnecessary ___:___:___:___:___:___:___necessary
             required    ___:___:___:___:___:___:___elective
             illogical   ___:___:___:___:___:___:___logical
             fun         ___:___:___:___:___:___:___work
```

they fall or by time period, such as current responses versus answers from a year ago.

The sixth and final question category is the open-ended question. When you are unsure about how your respondents might answer a question, when you don't want to limit them to your wording, or when you seek answers with richness and depth, consider an open-ended question. An opened-ended question is, "How do you feel about your company?" The strength of such a question lies in the richness of the answers; the weakness is it is difficult to analyze the answers statistically. You will have unique responses and therefore cannot tabulate percentages because responses may defy definite categorization.

In contrast, a closed question is one that limits the respondents' depth of answer. Thus, rank order, dichotomous, and other categories of questions can be considered closed questions.

Chapter 17 presents a thorough analysis of questions used in interviews.

Open-ended questions

Experiments

A second major primary research technique is experimentation. When you use an experiment to gather primary data, there are some implicit assumptions. First, you manipulate something and pay attention to the result. Second, you start with a specific research question or hypothesis that you test. Third, it is assumed that you are going to be objective and unbiased in your technique. Finally, most likely you will test your findings with well-defined statistical procedures. These major assumptions, plus many other guidelines and conditions, mean that experiments can be rigorous. However, if the experiment is to have meaning, the assumptions and guidelines must be met.

Since describing important methodology in any depth is beyond the scope of this text, we instead list a few guidelines and encourage you to seek additional direction elsewhere if you need it. The list of sources at the end of this chapter offers suggestions.

□ Often you will need to sample some population for your experiment. Follow the rules for sampling.

□ Always try to be unobtrusive; your presence alone can affect the data you are collecting.

□ Be careful not to overgeneralize your findings—the results you observed for a sample of 50 reflects only those 50 and not necessarily the balance of the population. Conditions may have changed, for example, in the time between the start of your experiment and when you draw conclusions.

□ Examine the secondary literature first to see if similar research has been conducted already. The mistakes of others may help you.

□ Keep your experiment simple. Try to control as many variables as possible. For example, if you wish to know the effect of raising the price of hamburgers by $.10 in the company cafeteria, don't raise the price of other items at the same time.

Guidelines for research experiments

Interviews

When using interviews to gather data for a business report, you are likely to use one of the following interview types: persuasive interviewing, information giving, or information gathering. Persuasive interviewing might be conducted to encourage subjects to take part in an experiment; information giving might be used to instruct selected subjects in how to function during an experiment. However, in terms of data gathering, you are most likely to use the information-gathering type of interview.

Two chapters in this book examine the interviewing process. Chapter 17 looks at interviewing as a management tool. Chapter 19 examines the applicant's role in the job interview. Since these chapters discuss types of questions, the interview structure, and styles of interviewing, we summarize some major concerns about data-gathering interviewing.

□ Sometimes only one or a few individuals need to be interviewed. This is particularly true when the individuals are experts. Seeking the opinion of one dietitian may be far more valuable than the opinion of many employees about the nutrition of the cafeteria food.

□ If many people need to be interviewed, do you need a random sample? Must you meet the criteria of random sampling?

□ If you are sampling and interviewing many people, are you conducting a scientific experiment, and are you therefore required to meet all the relevant scientific criteria? Not all studies need be scientific.

□ Since interviews are such obtrusive data-gathering techniques, should you consider an alternative collection method?

Guidelines for data-gathering interviews

▫ Is interviewing, which is individualized and flexible, able to justify the sometimes extensive personnel time and effort it requires?

▫ Would telephone interviewing, which has its own strengths and weaknesses, serve better than face-to-face interviewing? Telephone interviewing can gather more honest answers than face-to-face interviews since the interviewee does not have to look you in the eye. But be careful—for the same reasons telephone interviewing yields honesty, it can bring in more dishonesty. Telephone interviewing usually takes longer to conduct than you plan for it. Wrong numbers, busy signals, no answers, and number changes are part of the time to account for in telephone interviewing.

Personal Observations

A data-gathering source that is frequently overlooked is personal observation. You may be observing as you conduct an interview or run an experiment, but here we're speaking of a formal approach to answering your research question.

With the usual concerns for sampling and experimentation, observation has the additional rigors of being unobtrusive. Is your presence modifying what you're observing? Can you overcome this problem by becoming a participant within the group? Can you objectively observe the effect of raising hamburger prices in the company by joining the regular group of employees who use the cafeteria? This might have a different effect than a stranger walking about the cafeteria during lunch with a clipboard and pencil.

Organization Files

Organization files can be either primary or secondary forms of research. The placement in one camp or the other is not so important as how to use organization files.

Sometimes you find the answer to your research question by merely seeking the answer in readily available organization files. Since you are not affecting the existing data, this technique is the least obtrusive of the primary source techniques. If you raise the price of hamburgers in the cafeteria on a certain date, are you selling more or fewer hamburgers? Records may indicate the pounds of hamburger purchased before and after the change. Did the ten percent salary increase affect output? Look to the production reports, absentee reports, tardiness reports, or number of grievances sent to the company newsletter for possible changes.

Frequently some ingenuity is necessary in locating the record that meets your needs. Since the information is gathered and your presence does not affect it, using organization records can provide better quality data and take less time and effort than other research methods.

Step 4: Evaluate the Results

After having determined your purpose, considered your receiver, and conducted your research, the next step is to evaluate your results. To help in this evaluation—whether primary or secondary sources were used—test your data against this checklist. You seek a yes response to each question.

□ Are my findings reasonable and logical? If not, why?
□ Was my sample size adequate?
□ Did I apply appropriate statistical tests to my data to make it more meaningful?
□ Did I achieve appropriate depth in my research?
□ Did I answer the initial research question?

Checklist for data evaluation

Step 5: Outline the Report

Once you have gathered all your information, you are prepared to outline the report. The organization of the report is important and will affect how the report is received. Thus, as outlining is discussed, be aware that we are really discussing report organization.

There are four main organizational approaches: (1) direct versus indirect organization, (2) chronological order, (3) topic order, and the (4) problem-solving approach.

As we mentioned earlier, a long report can have many parts. For purposes of outlining, you need be concerned about only three of them: introduction, body, and conclusion. Together, these three parts make up the bulk of the report.

Direct versus indirect approach

As you outline your report, you'll have two decisions to make:

Decisions in outlining a report

Decision A　In what order do I present the introduction, body, and conclusion?
Decision B　How will I organize the body itself?

In making Decision A you have three choices:

Choice 1	Choice 2	Choice 3
Introduction	Introduction	Conclusion
Body	Conclusion	Introduction
Conclusion	Body	Body

Decision A choices

These choices may surprise you, since it seems only logical to use Choice 1. However, you'll find that Choices 2 and 3 have their own advantages. Which choice you make depends upon your analysis of the receiver(s).

In Choice 1, called the *indirect-order arrangement,* you save the conclusion (which might contain a summary and/or recommendations) until last. Why choose the indirect-order arrangement? Here are some reasons:

a. The receiver might tend to resist your conclusions because they either contain bad news or are contrary to the receiver's opinion.

b. The receiver won't understand your conclusions until he or she reads the rest of the report. Lack of understanding could be caused by the scientific or technical nature of your report or by the receiver's simple lack of familiarity with the subject of your report.

Reasons for using the indirect-order arrangement

Using the indirect-order arrangement will force your receivers to spend considerable time reading detailed information before they get to the most important part. Because of this delay, many executives will find the conclusion, no matter where it is in the report, and read it first.

Choices 2 or 3 are *direct-order arrangements.* Using this type of arrangement, you present conclusions either second (Choice 2) or first (Choice 3). Whether you choose number 2 or 3 isn't tremendously important. However, it is important to know the reasons for the direct-order arrangement.

a. The report contains good news for the receiver. Good news is best found at the top.

b. Your receiver has enough background to understand the conclusions without reading the rest of the report first.

c. The report may be easier to read, since your conclusions provide a framework around which to interpret the detailed information in the body.

d. The reader needs the conclusion first.

Reasons for using the direct-order arrangement

Choice 1, then, involves moving from specific information to general information; Choices 2 and 3, general to specific.

Decision B, you'll recall, answers the question: how will I organize the body itself? The body of the report is, of course, the longest section. Therefore, you should concisely organize it so that it flows smoothly and has the kind of impact you want.

A good outline will help you write more clearly, thereby enhancing reader understanding. When you write your outline, you must use a common set of symbols that many other writers use:

I. First-degree heading
   A. Second-degree heading
      1. Third-degree heading
      2. Another third-degree heading

Symbols and format for outline

        a. Fourth-degree heading
        b. Another fourth-degree heading
          (1) Fifth-degree heading
          (2) Another fifth-degree heading
            (a) Sixth-degree heading
            (b) Another sixth-degree heading
   B. Another second-degree heading
II. Another first-degree heading
   A. Second-degree heading
   B. Another second-degree heading

A major rule of outlining is that at least two headings must occur within the same level. Thus, I requires II and A under I must be matched with B under the I.

Two types of headings are appropriate for your outline: topic and sentence. Topic headings contain single words or short phrases; sentence headings are complete sentences. Here are some examples:

Topic headings	**Sentence headings**
I. Employee problems	**I.** Atlantic Electronics has several employee problems.
A. Turnover	**A.** Turnover is high.
1. Electronics industry rates	**1.** Turnover rates in the electronics industry are decreasing.
2. Atlantic's rates	**2.** Atlantic's turnover rate is increasing.
a. 1973–1977	**a.** From 1973 to 1977 Atlantic controlled turnover
b. 1977–present	**b.** Since 1977 turnover has increased dramatically.
B. Absenteeism	**B.** Absenteeism is at a new high.
1. etc. . . .	**1.** etc. . . .

The topic outline can be prepared more quickly than the sentence outline. However, the sentence outline will make the actual writing go faster. In fact, some of the sentences in the outline example might be good paragraph topic sentences.

Incidentally, notice that each heading in the outlines has at least two subheadings beneath it. If you break an idea down, then it must have no fewer than two parts.

Notice also the importance of parallelism: equivalent parts are the same part of speech, have the same suffix, and the same structure. For example, in the sentence heading outline above, parts I-A-1 (Turnover rates in the electronics industry are decreasing) and I-A-2 (Atlantic's turnover rate is increasing) are similar in structure.

A second approach to report organization is the chronological approach; that is, you arrange the body according to time. We're using the chronological order in describing a step-by-step procedure for planning a long report. The chronological order is especially useful for writing an informational report with a topic that can be time-sequenced. Be cautious, however. The chronological approach is often used when a time-order is not justified. So much of our lives is time-sequenced that it is easy to force our reports into this outline as well.

Chronological order

A third way to organize the report body is by topic order. Using this outlining method, you organize the body around important topics. For example, if you were writing a report to help your employer choose a location for a new plant, you could organize the report around the potential sites. Some first-degree headings for such an outline are:

Topic order

I.   Columbus, Ohio
II.   Dover, Delaware
III.   Montgomery, Alabama

Or you might organize your report using criteria your employer uses in selecting a new plant:

I.   Labor market
  A.   Columbus, Ohio
  B.   Dover, Delaware
  C.   Montgomery, Alabama
II.   Community support
  A.   Columbus, Ohio
  B.   Dover, Delaware
  C.   Montgomery, Alabama
III.   Marketing and distribution benefits
  A.   Columbus, Ohio
  B.   Dover, Delaware
  C.   Montgomery, Alabama

An advantage of the topic order is its flexibility; it can be modified to meet the organization's structure. For example, if a company has three branches, the report can be built around those branches.

A second advantage of the topic order is that the author can organize the topics in descending or ascending order of importance, such as this first-degree outline:

I. Introduction
II. Most important topic
III. Second most important topic
IV. Least important topic
V. Conclusions

Or, you can reverse the order:

I. Introduction
II. Least important topic
III. Second most important topic
IV. Most important topic
V. Conclusions

A fourth outlining method is the problem-solving order. Typically, this arrangement consists of several subparts: background, nature of the problem, solutions to the problem, and plan of action for implementing the solution. The problem-solving order is perfectly suited to Stephanie's needs since her purpose is to solve the employee relations problem. Her outline might look like this:

Problem-solving approach

I. Background: The importance of employee relations
   A. Employee relations in the industry
      1. Effects of good relations
      2. Consequences of poor relations
   B. Employee relations at Atlantic Electronics
II. Nature of Atlantic Electronics' employee relations program
   A. Grievances
      1. Recent grievances
      2. Long-standing grievances
   B. Turnover
   C. Absenteeism
      1. By department
      2. By rank
   D. Morale
      1. Methodology
      2. Return rate
   E. Unionization

Summary

This chapter presented many steps in the report planning process. In Chapter 9 we take this planning process to the next step: writing the report. First, however, test your planning against this checklist.

Checklist for Planning the Long Report

_____ **1.** Have I determined my purpose? (Have I selected the appropriate level of report as a contribution to the decision-making process?)

     _____ **a.** To inform?

     _____ **b.** To interpret?

     _____ **c.** To solve a problem?

_____ **2.** Have I analyzed the receivers?

     _____ **a.** Expertise?

     _____ **b.** Interests?

     _____ **c.** Opinions?

     _____ **d.** Hierarchical position?

_____ **3.** Have I gathered all the necessary information?

     _____ **a.** Is the needs chart finished?

     _____ **b.** Are only secondary sources used?

     _____ **c.** Are only primary sources used?

     _____ **d.** Is information on notecards?

_____ **4.** Have I analyzed my information?

     _____ **a.** Logical conclusions?

     _____ **b.** Solid information?

_____ **5.** Have I outlined my report so it will flow clearly?

     _____ **a.** Overall order for introduction, body, and conclusion chosen?

     _____ **b.** Order for body of report chosen?

References

Research

Christensen, Larry B. *Experimental Methodology.* Boston: Allyn and Bacon, 1977.

Cozby, Paul C. *Methods in Behavioral Research.* Palo Alto, Calif.: Mayfield Publishing Co., 1977.

Dominowski, Roger L. *Research Methods.* Englewood Cliffs, N.J.: Prentice-Hall, 1980.

Emory, C. William. *Business Research Methods.* rev. ed. Homewood, Ill.: Richard D. Irwin, 1980.

Mowday, Richard T., and Steers, Richard M. eds. *Research in Organizations: Issues and Controversies.* Santa Monica, Calif.: Goodyear Publishing Co., 1979.

Williams, Carol T., and Wolfe, Gary K. *Elements of Research: A Guide for Writers.* Palo Alto, Calif.: Mayfield Publishing Co., 1979.

Report Writing

Baker, Sheridan *The Complete Stylist and Handbook.* 2nd ed. New York: Harper & Row, 1980.

Brusaw, Charles T., Alred, Gerald J., and Oliu, Walter E. *The Business Writer's Handbook*. 2nd ed. New York: St. Martin's Press, 1982.

Corder, Jim W. *Handbook of Current English*. 5th ed. Glenview, Ill.: Scott, Foresman and Company, 1978.

Moyer, R., Stevens, E., and Switzer, R. *The Research and Report Handbook*. New York: John Wiley and Sons, 1981.

Review Questions

1. Why are reports prepared? Which reasons are most important? Why?
2. How are reports categorized?
3. What are the differences between informational, interpretive, and problem-solving reports?
4. What are the steps in planning the long report?
5. Identify some primary research methods. What are the strengths and weaknesses of each?
6. Differentiate between random, stratified, convenience, and systematic random samples.
7. What are the different levels of degree headings used in outlining?
8. Discuss the development of a questionnaire.
9. What are the differences between outlining and organizing a report?
10. What are the differences between the four major outlining methods?

Case

Planning the Report

Kath Ralston
Chisholm Institute of Technology
Victoria, Australia

Sally Dixon is in her final year at business college. During the past two years she has worked part-time at the local gymnasium and community center making appointments and scheduling classes conducted at the center. She enjoys working there, but she believes the management group is not very dynamic and does not take enough opportunities to promote the center's programs.

Recently Sally heard that the activities coordinator would be leaving at the end of the year. Sally would like to land the position and believes that with the combination of her practical work experience plus her business knowledge, she would make an excellent activities coordinator. She realizes that although the management group is pleased with her work, it would need more proof of her business ability if they were to consider her for the position of activities coordinator.

One evening when she arrived home she found a letter from her dentist reminding her of a dental check-up. This started her thinking about a promotional campaign for the community center where each participant could be contacted in a short time after completing their class and advised of future activities at the center. This campaign would mean setting up a new record-keeping system, but she believed that the extra business the center would obtain would far outweigh any cost.

Sally decided this was her chance to show the management group that she could apply her study of business systems and marketing in a very practical way. She thought the best approach would be to present the proposal to the management group in a report.

■　■　■

Case Questions

1. What will be the purpose of the report?
2. What aspects of the receivers will Sally have to consider?
3. What information must Sally collect for her report? Where will she get it?
4. In outlining the report, which order do you think Sally should choose? Give the reasons for your choice.

Writing the Long Report

Learning Objectives
1. To learn the effective and correct use of headings.
2. To understand the preparation of tables, graphs, and other visual matter.
3. To learn how to attribute information to its origin.
4. To understand the elements that make up the prefatory parts.
5. To understand the elements that make up the supplementary parts.
6. To know the correct order of the elements that make up a formal business report.

*A*s Stephanie looked at the business report on her desk that had just been delivered by its author, Bill Wells, she thought back to a report she had written almost ten years ago—a report that had influenced her career.

Equally new to Atlantic Electronics then as Bill is now, Stephanie had written a problem-solving report on employee relations. Unexpectedly that report had been viewed by her superiors in evaluation of her work as a personnel assistant. Although she was unsure of herself at the time, things worked out fine. The vice president had been so impressed with her ability and potential that he recommended a promotion to personnel specialist a full year before most personnel assistants are promoted. He had even made a point to stop by her desk to tell her how impressed he was with her report.

Much has happened since then, Stephanie thought to herself. Louise has taken over the vice president's job on his retirement, her immediate boss Scott Millan took a job with Burns, and she was selected to replace him. How proud I was, she thought, to be selected as the youngest personnel director to hold that job.

Well, enough reminiscing, she thought. Let's see if this report from Bill will determine his future. ■

Two of the ways business reports are classified, as we mentioned in Chapter 8, are by length and formality. Report formality is determined largely by language tone, such as using third-person singular versus first-person singular (using *the author* instead of *I*), and by the number of formal items included in the report. If the business report includes such formal elements as an authorization document or an abstract, the report becomes more formal. The more items you include, the greater the length. Therefore, formality and length are often related.

In Chapter 8 we discussed outlining the body of the report. In this chapter we'll talk about the three parts of a business report: the prefatory or preliminary parts, the text, and the concluding or supplementary parts. You'll learn about when to use, where to place, and how to construct charts and graphs. The chapter concludes with an example of a formal report.

Because the text of the report is written first and contains the major message, we'll start our discussion of business report writing with the text.

The Text

If the outline you have developed is thorough, writing the text parts should not be too difficult, although it may be time consuming. No matter in which order you've chosen to present your introduction, body, and conclusion, you should begin writing the introduction or body first.

As you write, you'll often discover that your conclusions change because the act of writing is the first time you think about your report material in real detail. Certainly you'll have some general ideas about the conclusions as they are part of your outline. But be prepared to allow your specific thinking to alter these conclusions.

The characteristics of effective written communication (discussed in Chapter 3) apply to long reports as they do to other forms of written communication.

1. Readability. Consider the education level of your receiver. You might compute a readability index on your drafts to ensure that you've written them at the appropriate level.
2. Tact. Avoid offensive language, don't insult your readers, and don't categorize them. Be especially careful to avoid sexist language.
3. Personal. Generally, do not use the *you* tone when writing the text parts of a formal business report; these reports usually demand a more impersonal writing style. However, in some circumstances a report that contains formal report items, such as an abstract or appendices, can be made more readable by using the first- or second-person tone.
4. Positive. Use a positive tone whenever possible. (But remember that some ideas aren't adaptable to a positive approach.)
5. Active. Use the active voice as much as possible. Use passive voice only to de-emphasize an idea.
6. Unity. Be sure that each sentence and paragraph contains only one central idea.
7. Coherence. Use signposts, linking words, and enumerators to give smooth and logical transitions to the text. Proper headings help coherence.
8. Clarity. Avoid unfamiliar words and use jargon only if you're sure the reader will understand you.
9. Conciseness. Avoid trite expressions, wordy phrases, unnecessary repetition, and abstract words.
10. Mechanically sound. Check and recheck for grammar errors.

Characteristics of effective written communication

Two of these characteristics, coherence and clarity, can be dramatically improved if you use two devices in your text: headings and tables and figures.

Using Headings

Headings can be taken directly from your outline. They serve as signposts and improve the reader's speed and ease in comprehending your ideas. There are many authorities who discuss the relationship between the various levels of headings. Not all authorities agree, but a few principles emerge: (1) if a heading is centered, it is more important than a heading that is against the left margin; (2) if a heading is against the left margin, it is more important than a heading that is indented; (3) if a heading is capitalized, it is more important than a heading that has only initial capital letters; (4) if a heading is underlined, it is more important than a heading that is not underlined; and (5) if a heading is placed on a line by itself, it is more important than a heading that is followed by text.

By using these principles, and intermixing them, we can develop the following hierarchy of headings and subheadings, ranging from highest to lowest:

THIS IS A FIRST-LEVEL HEADING

This Is a Second-Level Heading

This Is a Third-Level Heading

THIS IS A FOURTH-LEVEL HEADING

This Is a Fifth-Level Heading

This Is a Sixth-Level Heading

> This Is a Seventh-Level Heading
> (All caps are rarely used here; underlining is rarely used.)
> This Is an Eighth-Level Heading. This is text that follows it on

the same line. Note the period at the end of the eighth-level heading.

You will probably never need to use all eight levels of headings. However, most reports will use at least three levels. The levels you select do not need to be just the top three. You can use the principles discussed to make obvious and helpful headings. Here is an example of picking and choosing four different levels of headings for a report:

THIS MIGHT BE THE TITLE

OF THE REPORT

This Might Be a Second-Level Heading

This Might Be a Third-Level Heading

> This Might Be a Fourth-Level Heading

The important point to remember in using headings is that they must be immediately logical to your reader; which subheading is subservient to others should be obvious.

There are other formats for inserting headings in your report. For example, a numerical approach uses numbers—either with or without a phrase after the number—such as 1, 3.4, and 7.5.1 for headings. The numerical approach is used more often in formal and governmental reports. The numbers are likely to occur in technical and scientific reports and in other situations as well. No matter which format you choose, use it consistently throughout the report.

Using Tables and Figures

The report text can be divided into its prose and nonprose parts; tables and figures are subdivisions of the nonprose parts. Both tables and figures are useful for summarizing a large amount of detailed information in a small space. They also break up the text material and create a more interesting flow.

Here are some guidelines for the use of tables and figures in the text of a business report:

□ A table or figure that is one-half page or larger is placed on a page by itself. A table or figure that is less than one-half page can have text above or below it.

□ A table or figure should stand alone. That is, any viewer should be able to look at the table or figure and quickly understand the information. The viewer should not have to read the text to understand the table or figure.

□ Sometimes it is unclear whether the table or figure should be located in the text or at the end of the report in an appendix. The material should be in the text if it is necessary for the reader to view it to understand the report. If the information might be helpful but is not required, it is usually placed in an appendix. If the material is lengthy—several pages or more—it is usually placed in an appendix.

□ When a table or figure that was presented by someone else in published form is presented in your report, indicate that source much as you would use a footnote. The source indication, however, is part of the table or figure.

□ A table or figure should be referred to in the text. The table or figure then appears after that paragraph if it is to be placed on that page, or it appears on the next page if it is to receive a page unto itself. If the figure appears on a separate page, continue the text; fill the page as you normally would, then insert the table or figure on the next page.

□ If the table must be presented parallel to the long sides of the paper, place the headings so that it is read from the outside page margin of the report rather than from across the inside margin or spine.

□ In both tables and figures, the time period (years, months, and so on) is usually presented on the horizontal axis.

□ In graphs, the vertical axis should start at zero and increase upward or show a negative amount as it moves below the horizontal axis.

Tables are much more specific than figures because they show only numbers in a column and row format. For example, see Table 9.1.

Guidelines for tables and figures

Use tables to summarize quantitative information.

Table 9.1 1980–1985 Turnover Rates for Atlantic Electronics and Selected Competitors

Company	1985	1984	Turnover Rate[a] 1983	1982	1981	1980
Atlantic Electronics	13%	17%	18%	21%	21%	23%
Burns	18%	21%	16%	12%	11%	7%
Dominion	15%	14%	17%	13%	12%	15%
Southern	17%	24%	18%	16%	15%	16%

[a]These percentages are the percentage per 1,000 employees for each company.

Figures, which are also called *illustrations,* include a variety of graphs, charts, and visual matter such as maps, drawings, and photographs. The table is arranged with its title first. A footnote has been added to explain part of the information in the table.

Using Figures

Among the most popular types of figures you might use in a long report are graphs, charts, and maps. Consider using them not only to summarize information, but also to add vividness to your presentation.

Graphs. Like tables, graphs are used to present quantitative data. You'll often discover that information you intended to put into table form can be shown more effectively in a graph. Graphs show trends, comparisons, or sometimes both trends and comparisons. Four basic kinds of graphs are: pie graphs, line graphs, bar graphs, and pictographs.

Graphs can sometimes show table information more effectively.

Pie Graphs (Also Called **Circle Graphs***) Show Comparisons Only.* They contain a comparison of parts to a whole. As part of her research Stephanie might have gathered information about why former Atlantic employees had quit their jobs. The pie graph in Figure 9.1 summarizes those reasons.

These simple rules should help you construct a good pie graph:

1. Always begin your pie graph at the 12 o'clock position.
2. Enter the largest percentage first and work clockwise around the graph entering the remaining percentages in descending order according to size.
3. To compute the exact space needed for each percentage, multiply 360 (the number of degrees in a circle) by the percentage. Your product is the number of degrees the percentage should represent. (For example, $360 \times 29\% = 104$ degrees).
4. Use a protractor and ruler to draw the graph.

Figure 9.1   Reasons for Employee Separations

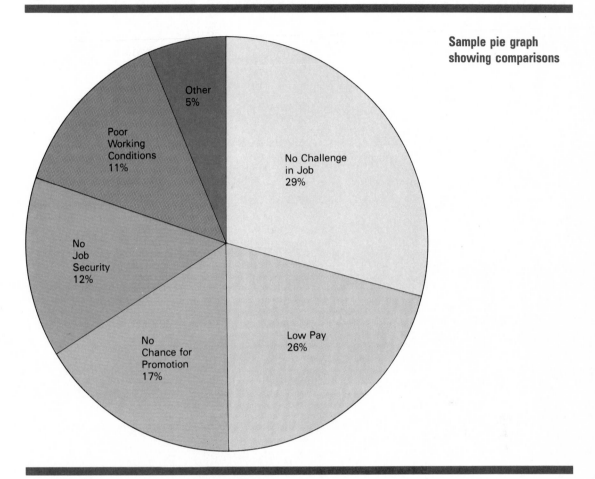

Sample pie graph showing comparisons

Other 5%

Poor Working Conditions 11%

No Challenge in Job 29%

No Job Security 12%

No Chance for Promotion 17%

Low Pay 26%

Line Graphs Are Used to Show Both Trends and Comparisons.
Single line graphs show trends. If the graph has more than one line,
then it shows both trends and comparisons.

From the variety of graphs Stephanie might have used the single line
graph in Figure 9.2 to show the trend in turnover rates at Atlantic Electronics.

Although drawing lines for all companies in Table 9.1 could be confusing, Stephanie might have compared Atlantic to its most important competitor by using a double line graph, as in Figure 9.3.

Notice that in the double line graph one line is solid, the other is
dotted. Line graphs usually contain no more than three or four lines—
too many lines will confuse your reader.

The third kind of graph, the *bar graph,* best shows comparisons. For
example, had Stephanie wanted simply to compare the Atlantic and

Figure 9.2   Atlantic Electronics Turnover Rates, 1980–1985

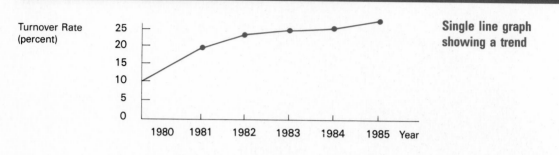

Single line graph showing a trend

Figure 9.3   Atlantic Electronics and Burns Turnover Rates, 1980–1985

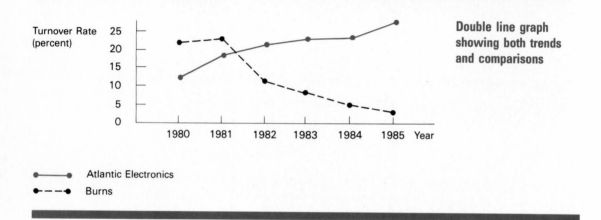

Double line graph showing both trends and comparisons

Burns turnover rates, she might have used the vertical bar graph in Figure 9.4.

If we draw the graph so that the bars extend from left to right, we call the graph a *horizontal bar graph*. There's a third type of bar graph, the *subdivided bar graph*, which can be used if you have more specific information about the contents of each bar. For example, in Figure 9.5, we see that the information about turnover rates has been subdivided by sex.

A final type of bar graph can show both positive and negative qualities. This graph is called a *bilateral bar graph*. If the information in Figure 9.5 for 1985 (23 percent turnover rate) is broken down by plant location, we develop the bilateral graph shown in Figure 9.6.

On a bilateral bar graph, the zero point is drawn through the middle of the graph. Positive quantities are entered first beginning with the largest positive quantity. Negative quantities are on the right side of the graph with the smallest negative quantity shown first.

Figure 9.4   Atlantic Electronics and Burns Turnover Rates, 1980–1985

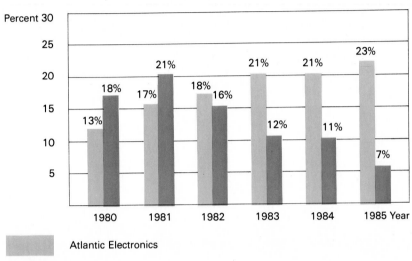

Example of a vertical bar graph showing comparisons

Atlantic Electronics

Burns

These percentages are the percentage per 1,000 employees for each company.

Figure 9.5   Comparison of Male versus Female Turnover Rates at Atlantic Electronics, 1980–1985

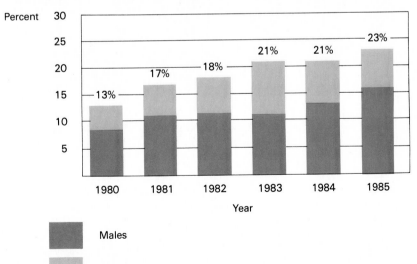

Example of a subdivided bar graph showing comparisons

Males

Females

These percentages are the percentage per 1,000 employees at Atlantic Electronics.

Figure 9.6   Breakdown of 1983 Atlantic Electronics Turnover Rate by Plant Location

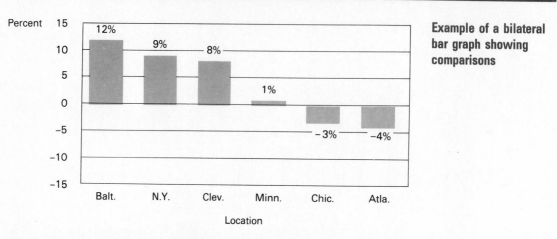

Example of a bilateral bar graph showing comparisons

Figure 9.7   Comparison of Numbers of Male and Female Employees at Atlantic Electronics, 1980–1985

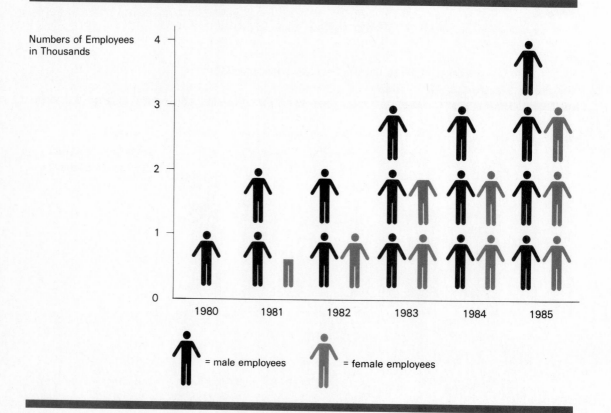

Figure 9.8 Example of an Organizational Chart for a Small Business

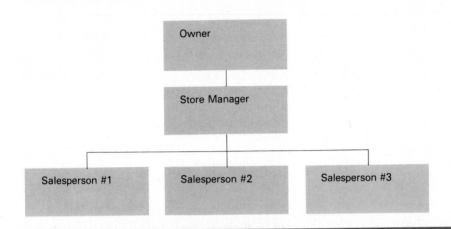

Another type of graph is the *pictograph.* This graph is similar to the bar graph except symbols rather than bars represent the quantities shown. The symbols can vary widely, from coins representing money to tractors representing farmers. Figure 9.7, on page 252, illustrates a pictograph.

In summary, the basic types of graphs are the line graph, pie graph, bar graph, and pictograph. Pie, bar, and pictographs are best for showing comparisons among quantities. Line graphs best show trends.

Unlike graphs which contain quantitative data, charts and diagrams show nonquantitative information. The differences between charts and diagrams are not always clear cut. However, most diagrams show some kind of process, while charts contain static information. The model of communication we presented in Chapter 2 is an example of a diagram. It shows the process of communication:

encoding→decoding→feedback.

Charts. An example of a chart is the organizational chart many businesses have. This chart is a picture of the organization that shows: (1) the various positions in the hierarchy, and (2) the lines of authority between and among these positions. For example, an organizational chart for a small shoe store that had one owner, a full-time manager, and three salespeople would be very simple. According to Figure 9.8, the salespeople report to the store manager, who in turn reports to the owner.

The list of charts and diagrams you might use in writing a long report is unlimited. You might use a needs chart like the one we presented earlier in this chapter to help you plan the report. Stephanie could have chosen among a variety of charts and diagrams for her actual writing:

◻ An organizational chart of Atlantic Electronics
◻ A chart showing the causes of Atlantic Electronics' employee problems
◻ A step-by-step diagram showing how to implement her solutions to the problems
◻ A diagram showing how low morale affects absenteeism and turnover
◻ A diagram showing the steps in Atlantic Electronics' current grievance procedure
◻ A chart showing the most common reasons why employees quit their jobs at Atlantic Electronics.

These brief guidelines should help you prepare charts and diagrams that will enhance your written presentation by summarizing potentially unclear information:

◻ Keep the chart or diagram as simple as possible. Don't slow your readers down by forcing them to spend unnecessary time trying to understand your drawing.
◻ Label each important part of a chart or diagram in capital letters.
◻ If you are diagramming a process, show arrows between steps or stages in the process. Arrows will help readers follow the process itself.
◻ Give the chart or diagram a number and a title. Place this information directly beneath the drawing (for example, Figure 1: Steps in Computing Compound Interest).
◻ Place the chart or diagram on the page as you would a table. Introduce it, present it, and interpret it.
◻ Don't rule out the use of color. If you only have one copy of the report to prepare, it is easy to add color, which itself adds clarity, understanding, and interest.

Guidelines for preparing a chart or diagram

Maps.   In writing long reports, maps are used less frequently than graphs, charts, and diagrams. However, maps are an interesting way to present the geographical distribution of a variety of information. For example, you might use a map of the United States to show the dollar sales for a particular company in each state. You might also break the map into territories or regions and show increases or decreases in sales for each region. Generally, you can use any map of a city, state, region, country, or larger area if it fits your report material.

Drawings and Photographs.   Occasionally, a report can be improved by adding a drawing or photograph. Drawings could include floor plans, artistic illustrations, or medical and anatomical drawings. Photographs are used for much the same purpose as drawings but photos add realism and precision because they are pictures of the actual item. Both drawings and photographs, of course, can be presented in color.

Computer-Generated Graphics. As business increasingly relies on computers for text editing and data analysis, it will also integrate special graphics tools. Besides saving time and money, computer-generated graphics are also available in colors.

The report writer now processes, examines, and manipulates the data; prepares and edits the text, and designs the maps, graphs, and drawings, all at the same computer terminal. An example of a computer-generated graph is shown in Figure 9.9.

Figure 9.9   A Sample Computer Graphic

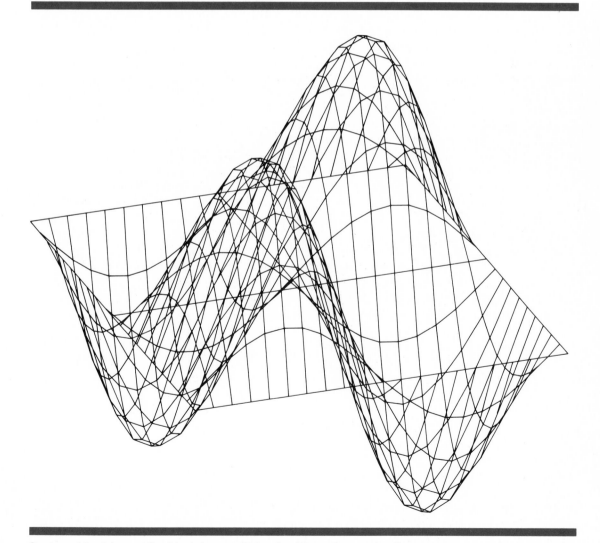

Courtesy of the Advanced Graphics Laboratory, University of Texas Computation Center.

Attribution

In Chapter 8 we talked about secondary research and how it involves the use of information that is developed by others and reported in published form. As we use that information in our business report, we must attribute it to someone else instead of claiming we developed it ourselves or leaving the reader to guess the origin of the information. In formal business reports, attribution usually appears as footnotes either at the bottom of the page or at the end of the text. In more informal reports, the attribution may be found solely in the text, such as, "David Fenton, our St. Louis marketing manager, said sales should increase by 37 percent this year." Internal attribution is more likely to be used when there are only a few sources mentioned. Once you reach four or five citations—or when you are writing a formal business report—you will need to use footnotes and a bibliography.

Footnotes may be part of the text—found at the bottom of the page where they are cited—or at the beginning of the supplementary parts. When the notes occur on a separate page at the end of the body, they are called endnotes. The bibliography is always found in the supplementary parts. Since we discuss the supplementary parts later in this chapter, we'll look now at the footnotes that appear within the text.

Three major forms of formal attribution appear to be most frequently used with text: the usual footnoting approach, the numbered bibliography technique, and the more academic author citation. Other accepted though less often used forms exist as well. The footnoting approach is traditional and is the most widely used. With this approach, a number is placed at the end of the information you are citing in the text. The number is raised one-half line and therefore is called a *superscript*. The first citation is number one, the next number two, and so on sequentially through the report. Any information cited that is taken from someone else—including both direct quotes and your paraphrasing of ideas—receives a footnote number. A block of information which is all taken from the same source in the same publication receives one number. Thus one paragraph might be attributed to one author.

Footnoting is the most common form of attribution.

On the other hand, one paragraph might include the ideas of a variety of sources. It's even possible that a single sentence can have more than one footnote; an example of this occurrence is presented below:

Many experts in finance agree with the point we have been discussing. Included in this group are Lewis,[1] Jones,[2] Harris,[3] and McWilliams.[4]

Each time you cite information you need to use a footnote. This is true even if you have cited the author earlier in the report. We often use *Ibid.* in a footnote to indicate we are referring to information from the same author and source as the one in the last footnote cited. *Op. cit.* in a footnote means the same author and publication as mentioned earlier but not the one immediately preceding. Op. cit. and, to a lesser extent, ibid. are being phased out in favor of just repeating the author's last name and the new page reference.

Either telephone or face-to-face interview attribution is handled as if the interview was a publication and the interviewee was the author. The observation in the text still receives a superscript number at the end of the quote, paraphrase, or by the author's (interviewee's) name.

As we use the superscript numbers in the text of the report, we must leave room at the bottom of the page for the footnote citation. If there are four superscript numbers in the text on page seven of your report, there must be four footnotes at the bottom of the page.

Footnoting is a precise and sometimes tedious process. Using an accepted style is necessary. The citation style varies by such considerations as number of authors and the type of publication (book, article in a periodical, a brochure, or a newspaper, for example). Because footnoting styles vary, because entire manuals are required to cover all possible formats, and because you may be directed by your organization which style to apply, we present only seven sample footnotes that show the most used variables. Pay particular attention to the Mover, Stevens and Switzer, Turabian, Knapper and Newcomb, and Brusaw, Alred, and Oliu entries since these citations focus on footnoting styles. The sample footnotes follow the University of Chicago Press *A Manual of Style,* 12th edition. The first six footnotes are for books and show various numbers of authors; the last three footnotes illustrate citations of a magazine, a brochure, and a newspaper, respectively.

[1]Charles T. Brusaw, Gerald J. Alred, and Walter E. Oliu, *The Business Writer's Handbook,* 2d ed. (New York: St. Martin's Press, 1982), pp. 215–220.

[2]Arno F. Knapper and Loda I. Newcomb, *Style Manual for Written Communication,* 2d ed. (Columbus: Grid Publishing, 1983), pp. 32–38.

[3]Ruth Moyer, Eleanour Stevens, and Ralph Switzer, *The Research and Report Handbook* (New York: John Wiley & Sons, 1981), pp. 123–168.

[4]Kate L. Turabian, *Student's Guide for Writing College Papers,* 3d ed. (Chicago: University of Chicago Press, 1976), p. 50.

[5]*A Manual of Style for Authors, Editors, and Copywriters,* 12th ed. (Chicago: University of Chicago Press, 1969), pp. 101–9.

[6]*The MLA Handbook for Writers of Research Papers, Theses, and Dissertations* (New York: Modern Language Association, 1977), p. 30.

[7]David Gabel, "Word Processing for Personal Computers," *Personal Computing,* (August 1982), pp. 82–106.

[8]*The Revolution in Software* (Berkeley, Calif.: Perfect Software, 1982), p. 3.

[9]James A. White, "Design, Sales Strategy Help Make IBM's Personal Computer a Big Hit," *The Wall Street Journal,* southwestern edition, 15 December 1982, p. 33

This footnoting style has both strengths and weaknesses. Besides being traditional and widely accepted, it is the most efficient style for the reader. Attribution is made in the text and instead of having to find the citation on some page in the supplementary parts, the reader can look directly to the bottom of the page for the information. On the other hand, the style is tedious and time consuming for the typist. If you have ever typed a page of text and tried to leave adequate room for footnotes at the bottom only to run out of room, you know the frustration it can cause!

To avoid this frustration, a modification of the standard technique is becoming widely used. Instead of presenting the footnotes at the bottom of each page as they occur, the footnotes are lifted from each page and placed in numerical order in the first of the supplementary pages. The part containing these lifted footnotes is appropriately titled Endnotes. Other than their location, the footnote citations are the same as those placed at the foot of the page. A sample endnotes page appears later in this chapter.

With the second attribution technique, there are no footnotes or endnotes. A number is placed at each location in the text where attribution is required much like the footnoting approach. Instead of using the superscript and sequential numbering, however, brackets appear around the number. The numbers refer the reader to the bibliography, which has numbers before the alphabetically presented sources. Since sources are not presented in alphabetical order, do not present the numbers sequentially. Here are two sample sentences that use this attribution style:

Jones is one of the best known authorities espousing this philosophy [6]. There are, however, other authorities who disagree with Jones [17:50], [3:63–8], [9:121].

The reader can now turn to the bibliography, find the [6] before the Jones citation, and determine the balance of the information about this source. When a specific page or pages are cited, it is customary to include this information within the brackets and after a colon. In [17:50], the 50 means page 50 in reference 17.

The third style of formal attribution differs from the ones we've described but shares some similarities, too. The third style tends to be used in academic writing, has many variations, and is rapidly gaining application. This style eliminates the footnoting process entirely, yet delivers the information required for appropriate attribution.

With this third approach, instead of using a superscript number, you present the author's last name, the year of the publication, and, if appropriate, the specific pages that were used. Citations are presented in the same fashion regardless of whether the source is an article, a book, or an interview. An exception is when the author is not known— then you present the publication name, the year, and perhaps the page numbers. Here is some sample text that utilizes the author's name attribution style. Notice the information appears in parentheses after the citation, but the author's name may be part of the sentence.

As we continue to examine the effect of increased production on job satisfaction, it is necessary to consider classical management theory. Smith (1967, p. 307), for example, feels that production is all-important.

Several other authorities agree with Smith (see, for example, McWilliams, 1956; Lewis, 1961; McAllister, 1967; Harris and Woffort, 1985; or Graber et al., 1984). Probably the most sweeping comment to the opposing view is, "Smith and her cronies are absolutely wrong! Job satisfaction is so much more important than production that it can't even be mentioned in the same breath!" (Horvath, 1985, p. 227).

When the reader confronts this attribution style, the complete citation is located in the bibliography. A bibliography presents much the same information as a footnote, but instead of being presented numerically, items are alphabetized by authors' last names. Thus, to find the Smith 1956, p. 207 citation, scan the bibliography until you alphabetically locate Smith.

If the bibliography is prepared using this attribution technique, it is the same as a standard bibliography; however, it is called references instead of bibliography.

Introduction, Body, and Conclusions

Within the body of the report, there are usually at least these three basic parts: the introduction, the body, and the conclusion.

A typical introduction tells the importance of the report topic, may give a historical perspective, and can discuss the organization of the report. The introduction includes a transition to the core of the report, which is also known as the body. You may think of this core as the body of the report. Confusion occurs since we also refer to everything between the prefatory parts and the supplementary parts as the body.

If you think of the introduction as a section that tells the reader what will soon be read, then the body is the section where the reader does this reading. In location as well as in importance, the body is central to the report; the report cannot exist without it.

The introduction tells the reader what he or she will soon read.

The conclusions section explains and summarizes what the reader has just read. The value of a conclusion section lies in its focus and emphasis—the reader is told what were the most memorable points in the report. The section may bring together for the first time divergent thoughts from the report. As you will see shortly, the conclusions section is much different than an abstract, although some people confuse the two.

The conclusion emphasizes the important points of the report.

The Supplementary Parts

Now that we have discussed the writing and appearance of the text of the formal business report, we can discuss the supplementary parts. Although the preliminary parts could be discussed and written next,

The supplementary parts include the endnotes, appendixes, bibliography, and the index.

there is one reason for giving attention to the supplementary parts first: we need to know the page numbers of the items in the concluding elements so that we can list their location by page number in the table of contents. The supplementary parts of a formal business report may contain many items but the most common ones are the endnotes page, appendixes, bibliography, and the index.

Endnotes

Endnotes are synonymous with footnotes; the only difference is they are on a separate page immediately following the text. Although you must give credit to your sources, you can decide whether to use foot-notes (at the foot of each page), endnotes (immediately after the text), or use the numbered bibliography or author's last name and publication year attribution method (omitting footnotes and using only a bibliography). The endnote page(s) is titled Endnotes and endnotes appear in the numerical order they are cited in the report.

Appendixes

An appendix contains material that is useful to the report but that might slow the reader if it appears in the text material. Items that would be part of an appendix are questionnaires, copies of interview questions, letters, memos, and other related (but not appropriate to the text) materials.

In a formal report, each appendix is preceded by a title page containing the label and the title of the appendix. Appendixes are lettered starting with *A* and placed in the order of their discussion in the text. They are identified in the table of contents.

Bibliography

The bibliography is a list of the sources you consult in preparing your report whether you actually cite the sources in your report or not. The bibliography assists your reader if additional information is needed; therefore, going beyond those sources cited can be valuable. If you cite all the sources you wish to list, the bibliography becomes a list of references.

Whether you use a bibliography or list of references, you can list your sources alphabetically either under one heading or under several subheadings. Subheadings classify your types of sources, such as books, periodicals, and government publications. The main title may be Bibliography, References, or List of References.

Index

Used only in lengthy reports, the index is an alphabetical list of key topics. This list includes the page number(s) for each topic. The index to this book is an example of the format you'll follow. Ask yourself whether the reader would benefit from an index as you decide whether to include it in your report.

The Preliminary Parts

A variety of items can be presented in the preliminary parts; generally speaking, the more items that are included, the more formal the report is. Other items are dependent on the situation and content of the report—obviously a list of tables is used only when there are tables, for example. The following, although not an exhaustive list, includes most of the formal preliminary parts: title fly, title page, authorization document, transmittal document, table of contents, list of tables, list of figures (or a combined list of illustrations), and the abstract.

The preliminary parts are the title page, authorization and transmittal documents, table of contents, and list of illustrations.

Title Fly

An optional part used in especially formal reports, the title fly contains only the report title. The title should be brief yet descriptive and should indicate either the report's depth or objective.

Title Page

Most business reports contain a title page. This page contains at least the following information: the report title, the name (and perhaps the title) of the person the report was prepared for, the author of the report (perhaps with title), and the date.

Authorization Document

If your report was authorized in writing, a copy of the letter or memo authorizing you to undertake the report should accompany the report. Showing authorizaton will add credibility to your work. This document is likely to be found in the more formal reports.

Transmittal Document

This is also likely to be seen in the more formal reports. This document—a letter or memo—transfers the report to the reader. The report recipient is likely to be the author of the authorization document; the author of the transmittal document (and the report) is probably the person authorized to do the report. These two items are closely related.

Your transmittal document should include:

a. The transmittal itself (first paragraph)
b. An overview of the report (second paragraph)
c. Optional acknowledgements to people who assisted you in preparing the report (third paragraph)
d. A courteous closing, in which you might discuss the next steps, express your pleasure at providing the report, or indicate your willingness to discuss the report in more detail (fourth paragraph)

Table of Contents

A required part of your formal business report, the table of contents lists the divisions of the report, such as the list of tables, bibliography, and the first- and second-level headings in the text.

The table of contents page(s) is titled Contents and usually uses dots to lead across the page to the page number of each item or heading. All items, except for the title fly, the title page, and the table of contents itself, are listed in the table of contents. The table of contents identifies the name and location of appendixes but not tables or figures which are identified on separate pages.

List of Tables

If tables are part of your report, then a list of tables is a separate page which follows the table of contents, even if you have only one table. The list of tables includes the table number, the table title, and the page where it is located.

List of Figures

The list of figures is also required if figures appear in your report. You don't have to separate your figures according to type such as, listing graphs first, then charts. Arrange the list of figures in order of their appearance in the report. The format of your list of figures is identical to the list of tables. Remember, however, that each list appears on a separate page. The list of figures may also be titled List of Illustrations.

Abstract.

The abstract, which may also be called Synopsis or Epitome, provides your reader with a summary of the entire text. The abstract may be considered the report in miniature; it is not just the conclusions of a report. An abstract (on a separate page) is included to help your receiver understand the text material before he or she reads it. Or it may be used as a time-saving summary after the entire report has been read. The single-spaced abstract has about a one to ten relationship to the text of the report, but it should seldom exceed one page.

Putting Your Report Together

So far we have discussed the writing of the text and preparation of the preliminary and supplementary parts. Now we are ready to put the report together. If your report is formal, it will have the following items, in this order:

    Preliminary parts
        Title fly*
        Title page
        Authorization document*
        Transmittal document*
        Table of contents
        List of tables
        List of figures
        Abstract
    Text (also sometimes referred to as the body)
        Introduction
        Body
        Conclusion
    Supplementary parts
        Endnotes
        Appendixes
        Bibliography
        Index*
    *Especially found in formal reports.

Before we conclude this chapter by showing you an entire report, there are some additional instructions that may affect your writing and typing of the report.

Pagination. Knowing when, where, and which type of number to place on a page is often a problem. Here are some guidelines:

□ The preliminary parts are treated differently than the balance of the report. Count every page but start your numbering with the table of contents. Thus, if the table of contents is the fifth page (after the title fly, the title page, the authorization document, and the transmittal document, each of which was counted but not numbered), it would be given the number *v*. This small Roman numeral is centered at the bottom of the page. The rest of the preliminary pages are numbered.

□ The first page of the body is numbered with an Arabic number centered at the bottom.

□ All pages after page 1 are numbered at the top of the page, probably in either the right corner or, less likely, centered. Be consistent in placing these numbers; if you center one page number, for example, center all page numbers.

□ In reports, paragraphs are usually indented with typically five or eight spaces of indention.

□ Do not use any punctuation or words with the page number. Use just the number 2, for example, and not Page 2, -2-, 2., two, or "2".

Spacing. Business reports are a combination of single and double spacing, as you will see in the complete report at the end of this chapter. Footnotes, for example, are single spaced with a space between citations. The text of the report may be either single or double spaced if you are consistent.

A double-spaced text promotes readability and leaves space for comments between lines. It also uses more paper, which may be important if many copies of your report will be duplicated. A single-spaced text adds an air of formality and precision while being more efficient.

Many organizations have standard formats for their reports (and letters and memoranda as well). You may be directed on which spacing is desired.

Cover. You may want to package your completed report inside a binder or prepare it with a special cover. Your organization may have printed covers for all reports. Covers can add uniformity, protection, and attractiveness.

Correct Procedures. We've stated frequently that two or more approaches might be acceptable or correct because authorities do not always agree and because organizations may have different goals for their reports. Different techniques have been presented when we thought they were important, such as the three attribution styles. There are, however, some other areas where experts differ. Knowledge of these views may be of value to you (see page 289).

Guidelines to pagination

□ The bibliography is sometimes the first item in the supplementary parts.

□ The abstract is sometimes placed before the table of contents in the preliminary parts.

□ Some reports use numbers before headings, such as 1, 1.1, or 3.12. Other reports use a combination of numbers and letters before headings, such as I, C, 2, a. Still other reports do not use these systems, but rely on the levels of the headings to help the reader.

□ The abstract is sometimes double spaced.

□ The table of contents does not always have leader lines and occasionally shows third- or even fourth-level headings. The page numbers for the additional levels may be presented.

□ There are other approaches to pagination, less often used, than the one we described.

Summary: A Sample Business Report

A complete business report in Figure 9.10 illustrates the writing principles discussed in Chapter 9 and the parts of a formal report. The sample report does not present every item since some of them are incongruous with others and some duplicate others. Of the preliminary and supplementary parts, only the index—which is exemplified at the end of this book—is omitted.

Careful examination of the writing tone of the report, as well as the appearance of the items, will guide you in preparing your business report.

This problem-solving report examines employee relations at Atlantic Electronics. Some of the items we have discussed, such as outlines and tables, are used again in the report.

Figure 9.10   An Example of a Long Report

EMPLOYEE RELATIONS PROBLEMS AT ATLANTIC ELECTRONICS:

NATURE, CAUSES, AND SOLUTIONS

EMPLOYEE RELATIONS PROBLEMS AT ATLANTIC ELECTRONICS:

NATURE, CAUSES, AND SOLUTIONS

Prepared for
Scott Millan, Personnel Director
Atlantic Electronics

by

Stephanie McQuiston, Personnel Assistant

January 30, 1985

ii

Atlantic Electronics
P.O. Box 138
Dover, Delaware 18717

November 10, 1984

Ms. Stephanie McQuiston
Personnel Assistant
Atlantic Electronics
P. O. Box 138
Dover, Delaware 18717

Dear Ms. McQuiston:

As explained in our conversation this morning, I am directing you to
research, analyze, and report on the current level of employee relations
at Atlantic Electronics. As members of the personnel office, we know there
have been an increasing number of grievances reported to us and the
company grapevine is carrying more negative information than usual.

You are to conduct research, both formal and informal, to adequately
appraise the employee relations situation. If the situation warrants it,
analyze solutions to our problem and propose them to me.

This matter is of major and immediate concern. Therefore, I need
your report by the end of January 1985. You have a budget of $10,000 for
supplies and can use the steno pool for duplication needs. Bill Parsons,
the new management trainee, is also assigned to you for this project.

Do let me know if you encounter problems or have questions.

Sincerely,

Scott Millan
Personnel Director

iv

Atlantic Electronics
P.O. Box 138
Dover, Delaware 18717

January 30, 1985

Mr. Scott Millan
Personnel Director
Atlantic Electronics
P. O. Box 138
Dover, Delaware 18717

Dear Mr. Millan:

Here is the report you directed me to prepare by letter on November
10, 1984. The report researches employee relations problems at Atlantic
Electronics, examines those problems, looks at solutions, and proposes
specific actions.

You will find that our employee relations problem is more serious
than you apparently thought when we discussed this project last November.
You'll want to pay particular attention to the implementation sections of
the report for ways to overcome these problems.

This has been a most interesting project. I'll be pleased to discuss
it with you, at your request.

Sincerely,

Stephanie McQuiston
Personnel Assistant

Contents

v

vi

List of Tables

List of Figures   vii

viii

Abstract

In the past five years, Atlantic Electronics has lost its position of employee relations leadership in the electronics industry. This report contains an analysis of the most important employee relations problems Atlantic currently faces. The analysis includes a careful definition of each problem, an assessment of causes, and recommendations for implementation of solutions. The solutions include hiring a consulting firm to develop job enrichment, starting a job rotation system, initiating supervisor training, and maintaining a follow-up plan.

EMPLOYEE RELATIONS PROBLEMS AT ATLANTIC ELECTRONICS:
NATURE, CAUSES, AND SOLUTIONS

<u>Background</u>

Atlantic Electronics is a young company yet a successful one. In 44 years, it has grown from 17 employees who produced vacuum tubes for radios to more than 2,000 employees who design and make 107 different electronic parts for home stereophonic applications and commercial computer uses. Gross income has increased as dramatically as the number of employees and the variety of products: 1940 produced a gross income of only $140,000 compared to 1983's $17 million.

These increases have not been without inherent costs. President and founder Claude William Rasnor has reminisced about the good old days when the first employees were close socially as well as vocationally. In 1941 Atlantic fielded an employee baseball team that won the city championship. Spouses of soldiers who died in World War II were voluntarily given pensions and other benefits.[1] Indeed, Atlantic Electronics was cited as a leader in the industry in low turnover rates only a few years ago.[2]

As this report will show, however, employee relations are no longer at this high level.

<u>Employee Relations in the Industry</u>

Almost since its inception, the electronics industry has been characterized by positive employee relations. One authority has gone so far as to say that the electronics industry has led the country in positive employee relations for the last 50 years.[3] An examination of employee relations in the industry will reveal the effects of good employee relations and the consequences of poor employee relations.

Effects of good relations. A company that has good relationships with its employees benefits both directly and indirectly. Direct results include higher quality products,[4] harder work by employees,[5] fewer injuries and days lost,[6] and less absenteeism and tardiness.[7] There are also a variety of indirect benefits from positive employee relationships: cleaner work areas,[8] happier, friendlier, and more energetic employees,[9] and lower turnover rates.[10]

Although there is a gray area between direct and indirect rewards and although there are other unmentioned benefits, the point is clear: the company benefits when relations with its employees are good.

1

2

Consequences of poor relations. When a company does not have good relations, not only does it lose the positive benefits, but it also acquires negative consequences. Included among these negative consequences are employee-family problems,[11] poor public image,[12] sabotage of facilities,[13] leaks of corporate secrets,[14] and the likelihood of labor/management distrust and alienation.[15] Distrust and alienation break down the existing channels of communication and, if none exists, a union is likely to seek admittance.[16]

Employee Relations at Atlantic Electronics

President Rasnor always has been concerned with good employee relations. Since he started the company in 1940, he has maintained turn-over rate records. In reviewing these company records, three major clusters of turnover rates emerged. For the 1940-1960 period, turnover was a mere 2 percent. For the 1961-1980 period, turnover rose to 6 percent, but this level was not considered especially serious.

Since 1981 our rate has been in the 20 percent and higher range. Because the rate had been creeping upward slowly since about 1970, the high level was not accurately recognized until recently. Particularly heavy demands on the company and the rapid changes in technology may have clouded the seriousness of the rate as well.

For the last six years, under the direction of Louise Alexander, personnel manager, these rates have been compared against our three major competitors, Burns, Dominion, and Southern. The precise results of Alexander's record-keeping are found in Table 1.

Table 1
1978–1983 Turnover Rates for
Atlantic Electronics and Selected Competitors

Company	Turnover Rate*					
	1978	1979	1980	1981	1982	1983
General	13%	17%	18%	21%	21%	23%
Burns	18%	21%	16%	12%	11%	7%
Dominion	15%	14%	17%	13%	12%	15%
Southern	17%	24%	18%	16%	15%	16%

*These percentages are the percentage per 1,000 employees for each company.

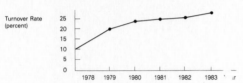

Figure 1
Percentage of Turnover Rates at
Atlantic Electronics from 1978–1983

Probably our fiercest competitor, the competitor closest to us in size, and the company which is often compared to us is Burns. For these reasons, we should examine our turnover rate to that of Burns; this information is presented in Figure 2.

Figure 2
Percentage of Turnover Rates at Atlantic Electronics
and at Burns from 1978-1983

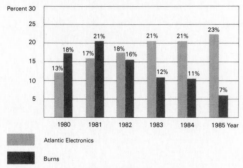

These percentages are the percentage per 1,000 employees for each company.

One can conclude from the information presented so far that good employee relations are to be sought, that there has been a major increase in turnover rates at Atlantic Electronics in the last ten years, and that our turnover rates are rising while our major competitor's rates are constant or slightly improving.

The balance of this report discusses the nature of the employee relations problem, examines its causes, presents solutions to the problem, and recommends implementation of specific solutions.

4

<u>Nature of Atlantic Electronics' Employee Relations Problem</u>

Our immediate problem has five major components: The number of grievances is high, turnover rates are excessive, absenteeism is unacceptable, morale is low, and unionization appears imminent.

<u>Grievances</u>

The personnel office is the destination for formal employee grievances. In addition to either acting on the grievance itself or directing it to the appropriate person, the personnel office codes the severity of the grievance. For example, 1 is for a valuable and legitimate grievance, a zero denotes a neutral grievance, or a -1 is given if the grievance has no apparent value, logic or point. The office admits this system is extremely subjective, and the office has kept the tally for only three years. However, in that three-year period, the ratio of 1-rated grievances per 100 employees per year has increased from 27 in 1981 to 41 in 1982 to 57 last year.

<u>Turnover</u>

Just knowing the rates of turnover is not enough. We also need to know the reasons for the turnover. Since the termination procedure for employees who choose to leave the company requires completion of separation forms, we know the stated reasons for turnover. The results of these inquiries are found in Figure 3. Almost three-quarters (72 percent) of the stated reasons for leaving were for one of three reasons: no job challenge, low pay, or no chance for promotion.

Figure 3
Reasons for Employee Separation at Atlantic Electronics

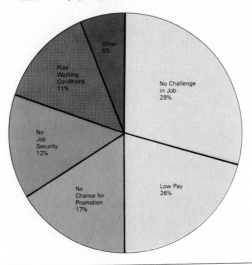

5

<u>Absenteeism</u>

We define absenteeism as missing a day or more of work without
authorization by a superior on a TP-8 form or without the knowledge or
consent of the company. An employee may receive permission to miss work,
for example, in the occurrence of an emergency, by phoning a superior. If
an employee misses work, even for an emergency, but does not notify a
company representative, absenteeism is reported to the personnel office.

This definition allows us to examine recent absenteeism levels.
Absenteeism levels from 1960 to 1977 did not vary from the average for
that period by more than five percent. In other words, in that 18-year
period, there was almost no variance in absenteeism. Table 2 compares that
rate to the last six years.

Table 2
Absenteeism Rates at Atlantic Electronics for
1978-1983 Compared to the Preceding 18 Years

Days Lost per Employee by Year						
Mean Absenteeism Rate	Annual Rate					
1960-1977	1978	1979	1980	1981	1982	1983
4.4	4.6	5.1	5.4	6.0	6.8	7.2

<u>Morale</u>

In order to determine the current level of employee morale as well as
causes for employee unrest, an employee survey was distributed to a random
sample of 500 employees. (See Appendix A.)

Methodology. To select the 500 employees, the card index of all
part- and full-time employees, found in the personnel office, was used.
From a random number table, the number 004 was drawn. Every fourth
name was selected from the file.

Return rate. Surveys were mailed to employees' homes. Of the 500
surveys distributed, 407 were returned completed, 9 were returned by the
post office, and 3 were returned uncompleted. The ratio of completed
surveys to delivered surveys (407/491) is 83 percent. This high rate is
attributed to the stamped, addressed return envelope, the survey
anonymity, and reader interest in the topic.

When respondents were asked to rate their current morale level on a
scale of 1 to 5 with 1 being the lowest possible score, the mean for all
respondents was 1.8. One interpretation is that any score less than 3.5,
the mid-point on the scale, is low morale. Clearly the 1.8 figure is low.

6

Unionization

  The electronics industry has relatively little unionization. Since there have been no overt efforts to keep unions out of the industry and since unions are most likely to emerge when conditions are poor, one can surmise that circumstances have not been ripe for unionization. At Atlantic, there has never been a proposal for unionization. However, in response to an open-ended survey question, 13 respondents mentioned unionization as the best way to improve working conditions and morale. Two comments stated that conversations have taken place with representatives of the Electronics Workers of America (EWA).

  A review of the current situation leads to the conclusion that the present situation is critical but not bleak. Grievances, turnover, and absenteeism are high, morale is low, and for the first time in Atlantic's history, unionization appears a possibility.

  Studying the nature of the employee relations problem is not enough. Statistics about turnover and absenteeism are symptoms of more deeply rooted problems.

    Causes of Atlantic Electronics' Employee Relations Problem

  The employee survey focuses on the causes of employee relations problems. Two major categories of problems emerge from the survey results: inadequate employee rewards and poor supervisory methods.

Inadequate Employee Rewards

  Within the survey, Question 2 asked respondents to check any item in a ten-item list that they believed was evident and important at Atlantic Electronics. Of the ten items, three were checked by over 50 percent of the respondents. Those three are (1) pay and benefits unsatisfactory, 71 percent; (2) work unfulfilling, 57 percent; and (3) feedback about performance nonexistent, 51 percent.

Poor Supervisory Methods

  The survey also uncovered two items of major concern about supervisory methods: inconsistent application of company rules and regulations, and lack of communication between supervisors and employees received a 50 percent notation level.

  Evaluation of these survey results leads us to conclude that although pay and benefits are seen as low, other nonmonetary concerns are also important. Money alone is not the prime motivator; meaningful work, communication, and praise are also important. Knowing the nature of the employee relations problem and its causes brings us to solutions to the problem.

7

<u>Solutions to Atlantic Electronics' Employee Relations Problem</u>

Employee concerns of unsatisfactory pay and benefits, unfulfilling work, lack of performance feedback, and inconsistent application of company rules and poor superior/subordinate communication are the causes of Atlantic Electronics' employee relations problems. These problems have surfaced in increased numbers of grievances, high turnover, high absenteeism, low morale, and discussion of unionization.

The solution to these employee concerns, and therefore to the symptoms of discontent, has two parts. First, we must offer more intangible rewards to the employees; secondly, we must provide more tangible rewards.

<u>More Intangible Rewards</u>

Intangible rewards are the most important aspect of the solution package. Most of the employee complaints and concerns, as uncovered by the employee survey, focused on the intangible aspects of their work. This finding is expected since extensive research has shown that once a worker's basic needs are met, the worker quickly turns to other forms of compensation, such as friendly working conditions, praise from supervisors, respect from peers, and so on.[17]

In improving the employees' intangible rewards, we need to improve the jobs and provide more feedback about employee performance.

Improving jobs. There are two aspects to improving the employee's jobs: job enrichment and job rotation.

Improving feedback. The feedback improvement solutions have three elements: formal quarterly performance reviews, informal monthly group feedback sessions, and informal day-to-day feedback.

<u>More Tangible Rewards</u>

In addition to the important improvements in the intangible rewards, Atlantic Electronics must also provide additional tangible rewards. These rewards are increased pay and improved benefits.

Increased pay. The employee survey found that respondents checked low pay and poor benefits as being of major concern to them; this heading was checked by 71 percent of the respondents. Although the survey presents clear-cut conclusions about the concern, it does not indicate the amount of improvement needed to reach acceptable levels.

We know that the average pay at Atlantic Electronics is somewhat lower than the industry average. For hourly employees, the industry average is $11.05 versus our average of $10.45. For salaried employees, we compare well with the industry: the industry average is $33,035 and our average is $31,985.[18]

8

The electronics industry is a highly competitive one and is somewhat unusual in that there are many professional associations which employees join, meet with peers in other companies, and compare their career situations. There is also substantial pride associated with pay in the industry. We might conclude that the high level of concern over a relatively small difference between Atlantic and the industry is the result of frequent cross-industry communication and personal pride. Therefore, although we need to improve the pay scale, the increases need not be exorbitant.

Fringe benefits. The situation with fringe benefits is closely aligned with that of employee pay: frequent comparisons with the industry and personal pride account for much of the employee concern. Less than one year ago the Atlantic benefits package was compared to that of the industry in an internal report prepared by our personnel office.[19] This report concluded that Atlantic is competitive with the industry in all areas except dental care, which is not included in our health insurance. About half of the companies in the industry provide dental care.

<u>Implementation of the Solutions</u>

Although Atlantic has a history of more than 40 years, which is relatively long in the electronics industry, it is still a newcomer to the diverse problems of rapid growth in employees, expanded product line, and technology. The interests of our employees, once exemplified as closeness and team spirit, have been lost recently. To regain this position we must implement improvements in both intangible and tangible rewards. However, we need expertise from outside our company to guide us in this implementation.

<u>Hire Consulting Firm</u>

A first step in improving the employees' jobs is to seek counsel on job-enrichment strategies. Although most employees in our personnel office are competent in most areas, no one professes experience in job enrichment or formal performance review systems. This void may well explain part of the reason the employees feel the need for such applications.

Initial contact has been made with Felix Graham and Associates, the consulting firm Atlantic has retained for four years. A copy of their response to our inquiry is in Appendix B.

<u>Begin Job Rotation System</u>

For some time we have been contemplating a job rotation system. For the past 18 months the supervisors have met to propose how such a system would work. Their conclusion is the system would be applied to all employees who are not classified E-3 (engineering specialist) or higher, or to employees who do not wish to be rotated. All employees would spend at least one week a year in a new job to be determined jointly with their supervisor and at least one week a year in seminars, short courses, and instruction for jobs other than the ones they currently hold. Members of management are encouraged to spend their week in college recruiting since this is an excellent opportunity to break the office routine, become knowledgeable of the company's goals, and still provide a valuable corporate service.

9

Initiate Supervisor Training

It is critical that we immediately initiate training sessions for our supervisors to learn how to give effective formal feedback and techniques of informal feedback. Amanda Lewis, a recent Ph.D. in psychology and counseling whom we hired one month ago as an industrial psychologist, has expertise and interest in developing these sessions. Permission would be required from her supervisor.

Implement Follow Up

We must not allow Atlantic to come this close to disaster again. Hopefully the implementation of the solutions outlined will overcome the current crisis. But we must launch a three-part follow-up system so we will not be caught off guard again. We must (1) survey employees regularly, both through attitude surveys and informally through discussions and interviews, (2) pay attention to what is happening in our industry in terms of pay and benefits as well as other unexpected developments that might affect the dedication of our employees to Atlantic Electronics, and (3) we must not fall behind again in maintaining--or even moving ahead of --industry averages for pay and benefits.

                                Conclusions

Atlantic Electronics has a proud history of employee relations. Recently, however, those relations have disintegrated as evidenced by problems with grievances, absenteeism, morale, and discussion of unionization. These symptoms, our employee survey determined, are related to major concerns about intangible and tangible rewards. To solve these problems we need to improve the employees' jobs, provide more feedback, and enhance their pay and benefits. Implementation of the solutions involves hiring a consulting firm, rotating jobs, training supervisors, and starting a follow-up system.

If these solutions are implemented as outlined, Atlantic should overcome its employee problems. The cost in achieving positive employee relations will be high in dollars, time, and effort. On the other hand, Atlantic cannot afford to allow the situation to continue.

10

Endnotes

[1]Claude William Rasnor, <u>The History of Atlantic Electronics, 1940-1983</u> (New York: Executive Press, 1984), p. 25.

[2]"A Review of the Industry," <u>Electronics Age</u>, December 1982, pp. 134-135.

[3]Mary Louise Harris, <u>Employee Relations in the Electronics Industry: A Review</u> (Chicago: A. J. Smith and Sons, Publishers, 1984), p. 421.

[4]Harris, p. 521.

[5]Henry Rosenblum, "Work and Working Relationships," <u>Labor Quarterly</u>, Spring 1983, p. 83.

[6]Sherry S. Quillan and Herman A. Quillan, "Injury in the Work Place," <u>Labor-Management Review</u>, 27 (1983), pp. 330-340.

[7]"Absenteeism and Tardiness: A New Perspective," <u>Labor Quarterly</u>, Fall 1981, pp. 35-60.

[8]Rosenblum, p. 85.

[9]Harrison Smith, "An Examination of Happiness on the Job" (PhD dissertation, University of Texas at Austin, 1979), pp. 221-254.

[10]Harris, p. 390.

[11]"The Effect of Poor Employee Relations on Job Performance," <u>Reflections on Employee Relations</u>, Carlos S. Gonzalez (ed.), (New York: Prestige Press, 1979), pp. 121-129.

[12]"The Effect of Poor Employee Relations on Job Performance," p. 135.

[13]Francis Lewis, et al., <u>The New Management</u> (San Francisco: Unicorn Publishers, 1983), p. 45.

[14]William R. Armstrong, Vice President for Production, Atlantic Electronics, personal interview, August 12, 1983.

[15]Rosenblum, p. 89.

[16]"When Unions Prefer to 'Make Their Move,'" <u>The Hickory Times-Dispatch</u>, April 18, 1982, p. 3.

[17]Smith, p. 207.

[18]These statistics are taken from company files and from statistics found in <u>U.S. Government Review of Employee Income</u>, No. 114, April 1982, pp. 1092-1107.

[19]Personnel Office, Atlantic Electronics, <u>Fringe Benefits Review</u> (Dover, Del., August 1983).

11

Appendix A

EMPLOYEE ATTITUDE SURVEY

EMPLOYEE ATTITUDE SURVEY

You are being asked to respond to a few questions about Atlantic Electronics. Only 500 of our employees are receiving this survey, so it is important that each is returned; your response reflects the opinions of many of your fellow employees.

Only about one minute of your time is required to complete the four questions. Your name is not needed; we are seeking only aggregate trends among our employees. You may use the stamped, addressed envelope that is enclosed to return your survey, or you may deposit it in any suggestion box.

The information we receive from this survey will be used to determine employee concerns. In turn, knowing these concerns will direct our attention to improving employee needs and benefits. Thank you for your help.

Stephanie McQuiston
Personnel Assistant

1. Please rate your current morale level on the following scale, which uses a 1 as the lowest possible level and a 5 as the highest possible level. Place a single check mark in one of the five locations.

My current morale level is:

```
___  ___  ___  ___  ___
 1    2    3    4    5
```

2. Listed below are ten items that relate to work conditions at Atlantic Electronics. Place a check mark beside any of the items that you feel represent your feelings about your job.

_____ Feedback about performance nonexistent
_____ Working conditions dirty
_____ Working conditions unsafe
_____ Not enough training sessions
_____ Pay and benefits unsatisfactory
_____ No choice in shift assignment
_____ Work unfulfilling
_____ Plant too far from home
_____ Poor parking situation
_____ Uniforms not supplied

3. Check any of the following items that you feel are current conditions at Atlantic Electronics.

_____ No time to talk to supervisors
_____ Lack of communication between supervisors and employees
_____ Not allowed to talk to peers

13

_____ Inconsistent application of company rules and regulations
_____ Employees don't seem to know their jobs

4.   In the space below, write any comments you wish to share with the
personnel office that you think might improve employee relations. (Use
additional paper if necessary.)

14

Appendix B

LETTER FROM FELIX GRAHAM AND ASSOCIATES

15

```
                    Felix Graham and Associates
                      Management Consultants
                          1414 Euclaire
                            Suite 100
                    Richardson, Delaware  18790
```

December 31, 1984

Ms. Stephanie McQuiston
Personnel Assistant
Atlantic Electronics
P. O. Box 138
Dover, Delaware 18717

Dear Ms. McQuiston:

As we discussed on the phone today, I am confirming our firm's interest in
working with Atlantic Electronics on review, analysis, and redesign of a
job enrichment program. I believe your president, Claude W. Rasnor, knows
of our expertise in this area.

Our financial arrangements would follow our usual approach. Your annual
retainer with us covers the first ten hours of consultation and after that,
each hour is billed at $75. The annual retainer of $1,000 for 1985 is
payable after December 31, 1984. We'll be billing you soon.

We'll be pleased to visit you at the Dover location, at no cost to you, to
discuss this project. Just let us know when you'd like to get together.

                         Cordially,

                         Felix Graham
                         President

cc: Claude W. Rasnor
```
```

16

Bibliography

"Absenteeism and Tardiness: A New Perspective." Labor Quarterly
     (Fall 1981).

Armstrong, William R. Vice President for Production, Atlantic
     Electronics, Dover, Delaware: August 12, 1983. Interview.

"The Effect of Poor Employee Relations on Job Performance." Reflections
     on Employee Relations. Carlos S. Gonzalez, ed. New York: Prestige
     Press, 1984.

Harris, Mary Louise. Employee Relations in the Electronics Industry: A
     Review. Chicago: A. J. Smith and Sons, Publishers, 1984.

Lewis, Francis, et al.. The New Management. San Francisco: Unicorn
     Publishers, 1983.

Personnel Office, Atlantic Electronics. Fringe Benefits Review. Dover,
     Delaware, August 1983.

Quillan, Sherry S., and Herman A. Quillan. "Injury in the Work Place."
     Labor-Management Review 27 (1983): 330-340.

Rasnor, Claude William. The History of Atlantic Electronics, 1940-1983.
     New York: Executive Press, 1984.

"A Review of the Industry." Electronics Age. (December 1982): 134-135.

Rosenblum, Henry. "Work and Working Relationships." Labor Quarterly.
     (Spring 1983): 35-60.

Smith, Harrison. "An Examination of Happiness on the Job. PhD
     dissertation. University of Texas at Austin, 1979.

U.S. Government Review of Employee Income. No. 114, April 1982.

"When Unions Prefer to 'Make Their Move.'" The Hickory Times-Dispatch.
     (April 18, 1982).

Review Questions

1. Identify the treatments of the first four levels of headings.
2. Differentiate between the three frequently used attribution styles. What are their strengths and weaknesses?
3. What are the differences between a footnote, an endnote, and a reference?
4. What is pagination? How is it applied to a business report?
5. What are the differences between illustrations and appendixes?
6. Describe the preparation of an abstract.
7. What are some techniques for increasing or decreasing the formality of a business report?
8. What are the differences between a business report and a term paper?

Case

The Long Report: Sunny Orange Juice
Robert J. Olney
Southwest Texas State University

As you arrive at Bennett Food Products Monday morning, you cannot resist stopping to admire the sign on the door of your new office. Below your name the sign reads assistant advertising manager. While you are admiring your new success, Mary Poplin, advertising manager, calls you into her office to confirm a rumor you have heard: the company wants to test the effectiveness of television advertising for Sunny Orange Juice. Sunny Orange Juice is a frozen concentrate of 100 percent natural juice and has had excellent acceptance in a limited test market. You are to recommend an advertising time period, and it is the first opportunity to prove yourself in your new position.

From your educational and work experience, you realize such decisions normally require extensive study, but you also know that the relatively young Bennett Food Products cannot afford such a study at this time. After a few minutes of thought you outline a plan of attack for this project:

1. Contact three area television stations which represent the three national networks to determine what advertising time is available.
2. Determine the viewer popularity of the shows around the available time periods.
3. Determine characteristics of the audience you want to appeal to in your television campaign.
4. Informally analyze characteristics of the audience viewing programs during each of the available times. Include age, sex, and marital status in your analysis.

5. Analyze the products currently advertised on these shows to determine the buying motives that current product advertising appeals to.
6. Produce a report that analyzes secondary and primary data which will help top management make its decision.

You call the area television stations to determine the commercial time periods that are available and discover that each station has a one-minute time period (listed as Eastern Standard Time) available in the prime viewing time: ABC, 8:15 Monday; CBS, 9:45 Friday; and NBC, 8:15 Wednesday.

■ ■ ■

Case Questions

1. Using your preliminary outline, begin your investigation.
2. Add to your preliminary outline any other factors you believe should be considered in the analysis of a time period.
3. In determining viewer popularity for the shows in the available time slots, you may want to trust the Nielsen ratings of the shows (published weekly in Wednesday's edition of *USA Today*), or you may want to conduct your own telephone survey of households in your area. If you elect the second alternative, carefully plan your telephone interview. Be prepared for a variety of responses.
4. Determine the cost per advertising minute for each of the available time periods. This information is published in *Standard Rate and Data Service.*
5. Use as many sources as possible to get other information to support your recommendations.
6. Present your problem data, analysis, conclusions, and recommendations in a report format specified by your instructor.

Case

Breaking the Lockstep
James M. Lahiff
University of Georgia

Curriculum development is a controversial topic in many schools. Administrators and faculty members devote much time and energy to developing the curriculum, but the results rarely satisfy everyone.

You attend Midwest State, where students must take many required courses. The program, known as the lockstep sequence, has been the subject of many student complaints. Most students believe that the program should be more flexible and that students should be allowed to select more of their courses.

Midwest State has decided to seek ideas from the students regarding possible changes in the program. The idea of allowing students to structure more of their program is under consideration. You have been appointed to the program evaluation committee, a group assembled to provide student input on this matter.

As a member of the program evaluation committee, you must select eight courses you believe would make up a good program for you. Prepare a report to be sent to the chairperson of the program evaluation committee. In this report describe eight specific courses and your rationale for including each one. Indicate what you consider to be the goal of your program and how each course contributes to that goal.

Use as many sources as possible to get the information necessary for this report. Interview professors, administrators, and other students. Perhaps someone in a field in which you hope to work would have some insights on the subject. Also, review the catalogs of other colleges which may be available in your college library. Use your imagination in developing your program. The courses that you suggest need not be presently available at your school.

■ ■ ■

Case Questions

1. Why did you organize your report the way that you did?
2. Describe one other way in which you might have organized it.

Memoranda and Short Reports

Learning Objectives

1. To recognize the important role played by short reports in facilitating organizational operations.
2. To identify the unique function of the memorandum and its advantages and disadvantages to the organization.
3. To recognize the underlying purpose of informational memorandum reports.
4. To develop effective progress reports and periodic reports.
5. To recognize the underlying purpose of analytical memorandum reports.
6. To develop effective justification reports and routine memorandum reports.
7. To identify situations for which a letter report would be appropriate.

As Joe Harrison neared retirement he became increasingly nostalgic. Thinking back over his 30 years with the company he often pondered how a person's perspective changed as one progressed along his or her career path.

The day after he graduated from college he had begun working as a sales representative. At that time he was usually traveling four days per week, and he devoted most of the fifth day to paperwork. His paperwork consisted mainly of a variety of short reports pertaining to customer orders, complaints, or future prospects. Throughout his years as a sales representative he always suspected that most of his reports were never read and that they were a waste of time.

After 12 years with the company he was promoted to assistant regional sales manager and his perspective began to change. He was surprised to discover that it was information from the sales representatives' reports that he relied on most when making decisions. Thinking back to the many small reports he wrote as a sales representative, he realized how wrong he had been in believing the reports went unread. A major part of his job consisted of abstracting reports from the ten sales representatives and reporting the completed results to the regional sales manager.

During his last eight years with the company, Joe Harrison was the regional sales manager. Any misgivings he had had about the importance of reports disappeared during this period. He recognized that through a variety of reports upper management was able to get the big picture and thereby make intelligent decisions.

Those short reports which individually may seem wastes of time and effort, collectively provide information without which organizations cannot function effectively. Because reports are so important there is no question that careers have been made and destroyed on the basis of one's ability (or inability) to write reports. ■

The Memorandum

Some people call it "memoitis," and others talk about "memomania." Many refer to it in terms that would never appear in textbooks. What they are all talking about is the excessive use of memoranda. In many organizations employees complain that they are swamped with memos. "If I read every memorandum that I received, I wouldn't have time for anything else," is a frequent complaint. While such statements may be exaggerations, it is true that memoranda are widely used but mostly for good reason.

A memorandum is a message written for use within the organization. Traditionally letters are used for external communication; ordinarily the memorandum is intended solely for communicating with others within the organization.

The memorandum is used primarily for internal communication.

The main explanation for the popularity of memoranda is that within large organizations there is a great need for communication. As organizations grow, problems of coordination become more severe; memoranda can help to keep the various parts of the organization in touch with each other. Memoranda have many different uses: to convey information from one department to another, to communicate between branches, or to file as records and reference. In fact, the memorandum is the most widely used form of written communication within the organization.

The Advantages of the Memorandum

Since memoranda are intended for internal communication, it might appear easier just to talk to the other person rather than to write a memorandum. While this is sometimes true, distinct advantages to using a memorandum are that it:

1. Provides a written record
2. Is suitable for transmitting complex information
3. Can reach many persons simultaneously.

Unlike a conversation, a memorandum can be filed for future reference. It serves as a written record for the writer or for the reader or for both. The more important the subject of the memorandum, the more likely that copies will be filed. By referring to the memorandum at a later date, one is reminded of specifics, such as date, individual responsibilities, and deadlines.

When a message contains a lot of very specific detail or is in some other way complex, the listener has difficulty remembering it. Complicated instructions are easily misunderstood under the best of circumstances, but when they are spoken, the chances for error are manifold. Consequently, a memorandum becomes an accurate memory-jogger.

If you must transmit some information to a number of coworkers, contacting each one individually is time consuming. Schedule conflicts may make it difficult to assemble the group for a meeting. A memorandum, however, can reach a large number of individuals easily.

At one time memoranda were considered to be economical. Then they were routinely handwritten and usually designated for individuals who were difficult to contact by telephone or face to face. Since many memoranda are now dictated and typed, the expense is almost as great as for actual letters. There is a savings in postage and envelopes, perhaps, but little more than that.

Memoranda have several advantages over oral communication.

Memoranda were once mainly handwritten and therefore economical. Now many memoranda are dictated and typed, thereby much less economical.

The Significance of the Memorandum to You

In larger organizatons the impression you make on your coworkers is determined partially by the memoranda you write. Your manner of communicating influences what others think of you. The further removed

In business organizations people are judged in part by the memos they write.

the other person is from you, the stronger the effect of the memoranda you write. For example, when Brenda Thornton sent a memorandum suggesting a change in pricing procedures, her superior Bill Hawley, did not have the authority to act on it. For that reason she provided more detailed information than Bill, who was familiar with the topic, would have required. Hawley forwarded the memorandum to his superior, Max Whitcomb, who had never met Brenda Thornton and knew little about her. In fact, his perception of her was created largely by her thorough memorandum.

When you are working in a large organization, the impression you make upon others goes beyond those with whom you personally interact. It extends to all who read your memoranda. For some, their sole link with you may be through your memoranda. In the example, Brenda Thornton's managerial potential was recognized in part through her effective use of memoranda.

Preparation of Memoranda

Chapters 8 and 9 detail the preparation of long reports, which consist of more parts and are written more formally than are short reports. The planning and the writing phases presented in Chapters 8 and 9, however, serve as a good guide in the preparation of short reports.

The memorandum has evolved to simplify communication within the organization. Some of the niceties of letter writing are sacrificed for the sake of conciseness. The format of the memorandum is also intended to simplify and speed up internal communication by ensuring consistency.

The memorandum is intended to ensure consistency in internal communication.

In order to guarantee consistency some organizations provide employees with preprinted forms that have the basic elements of any memorandum printed at the top of the page:

To:
From:
Date:
Subject:

By providing this format, a company can ensure that certain types of information always appear in the same place in memoranda. Finding a particular memorandum in a file is easier if all the memoranda are uniform in the placement of this information. You will know precisely where to look to find the subject of each memorandum.

Uniformity in the arrangement of memoranda makes them easier to comprehend.

Some organizations provide more structured forms which further simplify the memorandum-preparation process. Some structured forms consist of an original and two color-coded carbon copies and include space for the recipient to reply. This is the usual sequence of steps in using such a form:

1. The initiator writes the message, addresses the form, and removes one of the copies to keep as a reminder.
2. The recipient replies in the space provided, removes the second copy, and returns the original to the initiator.
3. The initiator now has the message and its reply on a form and can take whatever action is necessary.

Although such forms are intended primarily for internal communication, in exceptional instances they are sometimes used more broadly. Some organizations also use such forms for routine correspondence with people outside the organization. For example, suppose that you order a lightweight tent from a sporting goods company. Although the company does not have the model you ordered in stock, a comparable model is available. The company might use such a form to notify you and await your response.

> **Although memoranda are intended mainly for internal communication, they are sometimes used for external communication.**

Memoranda vary considerably in length. Some are brief, perhaps no more than a few sentences, while others may be three or four pages long. Some companies provide half-sheet memorandum forms for short messages, thus reducing the expense of paper. (Others feel that the savings from smaller forms are offset by the problems in filing and finding these smaller forms.) When a memorandum is more than one page long, each subsequent page should have a heading showing the addressee's name, the page number, and the date in a manner similar to the continuing page of a letter. In some organizations the subject of the memorandum is also included, as is done in the memorandum on the Delphi technique in Figure 10.1

> **Memoranda vary greatly in length.**

Despite the fact that memoranda may vary in appearance, they are alike in helping to facilitate internal communication. In order to ensure understanding the memorandum writer must conform to the principles of effective writing that were applied to letters. Because the memorandum is less formal than the letter and is designated for internal use mainly, some writers do not apply themselves properly in preparing memoranda. If a situation is important enough that a memorandum should be written, the memorandum merits care in both preparation and writing.

> **Since memoranda are less formal than letters, some writers mistakenly attach less importance to them.**

Memoranda are prepared for many different purposes. Among these purposes of routine memorandum reports are: (1) requesting information, (2) giving instructions, (3) serving as covers for all other messages, and (4) making announcements.

Requests for Information

Memoranda reports requesting information are a part of organization life. Sometimes the request will necessitate hours of research by the reader. At other times the reader may be able to write a paragraph in reply on

Figure 10.1 Example of a Memorandum

TO: All Exempt Employees

FROM: Bill Wendall, Chairperson, Evaluation Committee

DATE: September 30, 1985

SUBJECT: Explanation of Delphi Technique to Measure Clarity and
          Equity of Personnel Procedures

On October 1, 1985 20 percent of the exempt employees will be
invited to participate in an evaluation of personnel procedures within the
company. This memo is an explanation of the Delphi Panel procedure, which
will be used in investigating the subject.

Purpose of Delphi Technique

The Delphi technique is a method of combining the knowledge and
abilities of a diverse group to the task of reaching conclusions when
true values are not known. Exempt personnel from all departments will be
involved in presenting their thoughts on all aspects of personnel
procedures. It is expected that such company practices as recruitment,
selection, performance evaluation, and promotion will be among the topics
considered.

This study is intended to result in some modifications in current
personnel practices within the company. It is expected that subsequent
personnel operations will better meet the needs of exempt employees once
the personnel practices needing improvement are identified.

Advantages of Delphi Technique

During the past five years the company has conducted three company-
wide surveys. Although each survey had a unique purpose, the general
purpose of all was to improve upward communication within the company.

The Delphi technique is an upward communication format that has
several advantages over the questionnaires used in previous surveys. The
Delphi technique is less structured than the questionnaire and thus allows
for greater input from employees. Feedback is more immediate than it is
from questionnaires and, unlike questionnaires, the Delphi technique
allows respondents to refine their thinking.

In earlier studies within the company, interviews and group meetings
have been used to elicit employee attitudes and opinions. The Delphi
technique is not only less expensive but it provides an anonymity that is
lacking in interviews and group meetings.

Figure 10.1 (continued)

```
Memo To All Exempt Employees
(Explanation of Delphi Technique)
September 30, 1985
Page 2


    The feedback present in the Delphi technique exposes all of the
members to other points of view and stimulates everyone's thinking.  The
participants' anonymity means that the respondents need not take conventional
viewpoints nor follow a policy dictated by their superiors.  The Delphi
technique allows a participant to safely abandon long defended stands, and
the participant cannot be pressured into following the opinion of a well
known expert in the field.

    The Delphi technique is most effective for eliciting information from a
diverse collection of knowledgable respondents.

Procedures

1.   On October 1, 1985 20 percent of the exempt employees will
     receive several open-ended questions concerning personnel
     practices.  Participants will be asked to comment on those
     practices and to list the strengths and weaknesses of the
     practices.  Participants may suggest possible changes.
     Responses to these questions should be sent to me no later
     than October 8.

2.   On approximately October 22, the participants will receive
     returns from the first round of questions.  Responses will be
     arranged according to the frequency in which they were given.
     Participants are urged to reconsider and possibly modify
     their previous statements.  Suggestions previously given will
     be voted upon according to desirability and feasibility.
     Remember that a particular option could be desirable and
     unfeasible at the same time, or vice versa.  Participants
     should return their responses to Bill Wendall's office no
     later than November 1.

3.   On approximately November 15 the participants will receive
     returns from the second round of questions.  Responses will
     again be arranged in order of frequency.  Participants may
     modify their previous responses if they wish and return
     their responses to Bill Wendall's office by November 22.

4.   On approximately December 1 participants will receive
     results of the third round in summary form.  Appropriate
     action will be taken shortly thereafter.

    If you are selected to participate, you will be able to do so at your
convenience.  Each round will require only 30 to 90 minutes of your time.
Through the cooperation of those selected to participate, company
personnel practices will become more attuned to the needs of the employees.
```

the original memorandum and return it to the sender. This method of organization was followed in Figure 10.2

1. State the key idea, the request.
2. Present the details.
3. Remind the reader of the request and provide additional specific information.

Figure 10.2   A Memorandum Requesting Information

TO: Faculty, Business Education Department

FROM: Y. A. Young, Chairman, Business Education Department

DATE: January 8, 19__

SUBJECT: Film Catalog for Faculty Use

In order to reduce the time it takes to screen and select appropriate films, we are putting together a catalog of those films which have been used effectively in Business Education classes.

Please submit to this office the following information, using a separate sheet of paper for each film:

1. Film title and approximate length
2. One-paragraph description of the main points made in the film
3. One-paragraph description of how the film relates to the course in which it was used

Please provide this information by January 31. Shortly thereafter you will receive your copy of the completed catalog. Through the cooperation of all faculty members in this project, all of us will benefit.

The effectiveness of such a memorandum is determined largely by the clarity and reasonableness of its message as well as by the writer's explanation of purpose. After reading the message in Figure 10.2, the readers knew what they were to do and why they were to do it. They also should have recognized that their task would be accomplished easily and would result in benefits for them.

Giving Instructions

In giving instructions through a memorandum you must try to cover the subject so that the reader will not have any unanswered questions. At the same time you should avoid overwriting or belaboring the obvious. Figure 10.3 shows a sample memo of this type.

Transmittals

A transmittal memorandum is used to introduce the reader to a longer, accompanying message. At times you may go beyond a mere introduction and interpret the message for the reader or at least describe the main points of the message. Regardless of its length or brevity, however, the transmittal memorandum report introduces something.

When her boss asked her to learn the reasons for the high turnover among the custodial workers, Sharon Wilcox did extensive research and prepared a memorandum on the subject. The transmittal memorandum she wrote to accompany the report appears in Figure 10.4.
Had she felt that Bellamy might not even remember the problem, much less her assignment to do the research, Sharon would probably have written the body of the memorandum like this:

I have done some research on the high rate of turnover among custodial workers.

My report is divided into four parts, and each part is preceded by a brief abstract of its contents.

Part I clarifies the problem and its effects on operations; Part II presents a complication of the custodial supervisor's preceptions of the problem; Part III presents a compilation of the custodial workers' perceptions of the problem; Part IV presents conclusions based on the findings of the survey.

A memorandum of transmittal serves the purpose of covering another message.

Announcements

Memoranda may be used to announce such matters as personnel transfers, meetings, or policy changes. Such memoranda are sometimes

Memoranda may be used to announce a great variety of matters of interest to one or to many.

Figure 10.3   A Memorandum Giving Instructions

TO: Faculty, Sinclair College

FROM: J. R. Easton, Assistant Circulation Manager, College Library

DATE: March 15, 19__

SUBJECT: New Procedure for Reserving Books for Class Use

A new procedure for putting books on reserve will begin at the start of
the summer quarter. Remember to follow these guidelines:

   1.   Submit a list of books on the attached form(s) to the
      Reserve Department at least four weeks before the
      start of the quarter in which the books will be
      assigned.

   2.   Do not include more than ten books on a form.

   3.   Include the following in each entry on a list:

        a.   Call number
        b.   Book title
        c.   Author's name
        d.   Course number and name
        e.   Type of reserve desired--two-hour
           or overnight
        f.   Anticipated class size
        g.   Instructor's name, campus address,
           and office telephone number

By following these procedures you will be contributing to library
efficiency.

Figure 10.4   A Transmittal Memorandum

TO: James Bellamy, Personnel Director

FROM: Sharon Wilcox, Logistical Support Coordinator

DATE: August 1, 19___

SUBJECT: Research Report on Turnover Among Custodial Workers

Here are the results of the research I conducted pertaining to turnover among custodial workers.

(Had she felt that Bellamy might not even remember the problem, much less her assignment to do the research, Sharon would probably have written the body of the memorandum like this:)

I have done some research on the high rate of turnover among custodial workers.

My report is divided into four parts, and each part is preceded by a brief abstract of its contents.

Part I clarifies the problem and its effects on operations; Part II presents a compilation of the custodial supervisor's perceptions of the problem; Part III presents a compilation of the custodial workers' perceptions of the problem; Part IV presents conclusions based on the findings of the survey.

disseminated widely within the organization; in other instances they are sent only to a select few. Memoranda that make announcements are often posted prominently on company bulletin boards. The memorandum in Figure 10.5 would probably receive much exposure because it would interest all of the employees in the company.

The Memorandum Report Format

When discussing a memorandum, we usually think in terms of a brief message. You may also write reports, however, using the memorandum format. There are several differences between a memorandum and a memorandum report. A memorandum report is usually more structured; it will have a recognizable introduction, body, and conclusion; which a memorandum does not necessarily have. Like a memorandum, a memorandum report is used mainly for communication within the organization.

The memorandum report has the same advantages as the memorandum. We will consider a variety of reports that are often presented in the memorandum format. The broad purpose of all types of memorandum reports is to supply the information needed to keep the organization operating smoothly. The specific purposes of the reports will become obvious in the following sections.

Progress Reports

Progress reports are informational and are widely used throughout business, industry, and government. Depending upon the nature of the organization and the project being reported, a progress report may be made only one time or as one of a series. If there is to be a series of progress reports, the same format should be followed throughout the series for the reader's convenience.

Progress reports are ordinarily sent upward in the organization to inform management of: (1) rate of progress as compared to the schedule, and (2) goals for subsequent time periods and forecast for completion of the project. The more specifically this information is presented, the more helpful a progress report will be. In Figure 10.6 a banker described the progress being made in a campaign through a memorandum report to upper management.

The same format should be used for progress reports comprising a series.

Progress reports are intended to tell upper management the progress of a project compared to its schedule and to forecast future progress.

Figure 10.5   An Announcement Memorandum

```
TO:       All Management and Supervisory Personnel

FROM:     A. B. Kaster, Manager of Industrial Relations

DATE:     June 10, 19__

SUBJECT:  Paid Holidays for Full-Time Employees



Sizemore Industries will observe the dates listed below as official
holidays during the fiscal year beginning July 1, 19__.  These holidays
will apply to all regular employees, both exempt and nonexempt.  Part-
time employees and probationary workers are not considered regular and,
therefore, are not entitled to receive holiday pay.

     Independence Day, July 4, 19__
     Labor Day, Monday, September 3, 19__
     Thanksgiving, Thursday & Friday, November 22, 23, 19__
     Christmas, Monday & Tuesday, December 24, 25, 19__
     New Year's, Monday & Tuesday, December 31, 19__ and
        January 1, 19__

Please see that all personnel under your jurisdiction are made aware of
this official holiday schedule.
```

Figure 10.6   A Progress Report Memorandum

TO: Roger Davis, Director of Marketing

FROM: John Dartley

DATE: November 19, 19___

SUBJECT: Monthly Progress Report on Card-Bank Usage--Oakdale Branch

Summary

In this reporting period the percentage of customers using Card-Bank
has risen from 7.1 percent to 7.9 percent. Seventy percent of the
customers with new accounts (less than six months) have used Card-Bank
at least once.

Present Usage

There has been a 6.8 percent increase in the number of customers using
Card-Bank. Our goal for this date had been set at 8.0 percent. Among
those new customers with accounts for less than six months, 70 percent
have used Card-Bank at least once. The goal for new customer usage for
this date is 50 percent. The increased usage might be a result of our
policy of personal instruction of new customers.

Usage Forecast

Customer usage goal for the next period is 10 percent. A local media
blitz is scheduled for early December. Advertisements will emphasize
the 24-hour availability of Card-Bank. Our surveys have shown that
total availability is the least-known feature of Card-Bank.

Periodic Reports

In any organization there are reports that must be prepared on a regular basis. Whether daily, weekly, or monthly, the purpose of such reports is to keep others informed of some aspect of operations. Because a periodic report is ordinarily directed regularly to the same reader, the writer may assume the reader is generally knowledgeable about the subject. For that reason the writer need not provide much introductory information.

Periodic informational reports are prepared on a regular basis.

Figure 10.7 is an example of a periodic report on absenteeism in a manufacturing plant.

Justification Reports

Sometime you may have to write a memorandum report in order to justify something—a change in procedure, an increase in budget, or perhaps reasons for resisting any new policy. For whatever reason—and there are many—it is written, the justification report is a common type of memorandum report.

When Bob Rollins sought to justify a change in operating procedures, he took the direct approach. He organized his memorandum report in this way:

1. Proposal
2. Description of present system
3. Advantages of the change versus its costs to the organization.

Memorandum Guide

State your purpose early if the memorandum is informational.

State your purpose clearly. A memorandum should not leave the reader wondering why it was written. Readers should know what you want them to do.

Present only relevant information. Unless information is related to the purpose of the memorandum, it should not be included.

Organize your thoughts. Present points so that readers can easily follow the message.

If the memorandum is longer than a page, divide it into sections to aid the reader in retaining the main points.

Figure 10.7   A Periodic Report Memorandum

TO: R. T. Bowen, Plant Manager

FROM: Bill Hughes, Assistant Personnel Director

DATE: February 4, 19___

SUBJECT: Monthly Plant Absenteeism Record

During January the average rate of absenteeism was 6 percent. The average
rate of absenteeism last January was 7.5 percent. The average rate of
absenteeism during the past twelve months was 6.8 percent.

Here is a breakdown of absences according to shift and department. An
asterisk indicates those absences for which the absentee submitted a
written excuse from a doctor.

Shift	Production	Shipping	Yard Crew
1st	8 of 202	1 of 28	1 of 20
2nd	10 of 202	2 of 28	2 of 80
3rd	19 of 200	N/A	1 of 10
	*8	*3	*1

Supervisors are being urged to persuade workers to call in when they are
unable to come to work and to persuade workers to bring an excuse from a
doctor. Here is a breakdown of the absentees who did phone in advance.

Shift	Production	Shipping	Yard Crew
1st	6 of 8	0 of 1	0 of 1
2nd	10 of 10	0 of 2	2 of 2
3rd	12 of 19		1 of 1

If you have any questions about the records, please give me a call.

Since the memorandum report in Figure 10.8 is being directed upward
in the organization, Bob must remind the reader of the actual problem.
Rather than assume the reader is familiar with the existing system, Bob
wisely reminded him of it. The remainder of the memorandum was devoted to suggesting a change and to indicating the advantages to be
derived from it.

Figure 10.8 A Justification Report Memorandum

TO: John T. Bowers, Director of Personnel Research

FROM: Bob Rollins, Manager of Production

DATE: June 18, 19__

SUBJECT: Communication Problems at Shift Changes

Proposal

My proposal for improving the transmittal of instructions during shift
changes is for the company to require a five-minute overlap of all
production employees at shift changes.

Present System

At present the supervisors are responsible for communicating job related
information. Much of it is done through work logs which each supervisor
maintains. They make entries each day regarding orders and equipment
functioning. At the time of the shift change, the incoming supervisor
first reads the log and seeks any necessary clarification before the
outgoing supervisor departs.

There are several problems with this system. A supervisor will often
forget to record vital information, and the incoming supervisor will not
be aware of it. Supervisors are not always told by their people of
equipment problems, so such problems cannot be recorded. Some supervisors
are in such a rush to leave work that they are of little assistance to
the incoming supervisor.

Advantages of the Change

A five minute overlap would make the exchange of information at shift
changes easier and more thorough. Not only would the supervisors exchange
work related information, but individual production workers also would.
Being made aware of a machine's minor malfunctions upon coming to work
would enable a machine operator, for example, to adapt to the situation.
Machine operators would tell their replacements the important details of
their current efforts, and supervisors would no longer have to depend on
the work log for information from those on the previous shift.

The change would increase payroll costs by approximately 3 percent, since
each production employee would be paid for eight hours and ten minutes per
day rather than for eight hours. The benefits to the company would be
worth it. While it is difficult to determine how much the present policy
has cost the company, the expense has been considerable. Unclear
instructions in the work log plus order changes which were not conveyed to
the succeeding shift have cost the company much in terms of both dollars
and frustrated workers.

If Bob had anticipated strong opposition to his plan, he might have taken an indirect approach. If John had a reputation for resisting change, Bob might have been less direct. There is no rigid formula that the writer must follow. As the writer, you must look closely at the situation and adapt your approach to fit it.

Letter Reports

Many short reports are presented in the format of a letter report, which is intended for external communication. As is generally true of short reports, the letter report is usually less formal than longer reports.

Just as in any letter, the nature of the message and the response expected from the reader will determine the plan to be followed in writing a letter report. If the reader is likely to approve of the message, take the direct approach described in Chapter 8. Begin the letter with the main point, since the reader agrees with it, then construct the message as a good-news or neutral letter.

If the reader is likely to disapprove of the message, you should follow the letter of refusal sequence described in Chapter 6. Rather than stating your main point at the start of the letter, you should build up to it. In this type of letter a buffer and one or more reasons usually precede the main point.

A letter report is similar to a letter in appearance and includes many of the same features.

A letter report is similar to a letter in appearance. Since letter reports usually are sent outside of the organization, they are prepared on stationery with the company letterhead. Letter reports usually include many of the features of a letter, including sender's address, date, inside address, salutation, body, and signature. Some writers insert a subject line between the greeting and the body of the letter report.

The body of a letter report, like the body of the business letter, has three basic parts:

Most letter reports are comprised of introduction, body, and close.

1. *Introduction.* In this part the purpose of the report is described. If the report is based on a problem, the problem might be presented at this point. For longer reports a description of the way the report is organized is included in the introduction; however, a description is not necessary for most letter reports.
2. *Body.* This is the meat of any report. Here the reader's attention is directed at the findings or conclusions. If the report is somewhat involved, you may divide the report into sections and provide headings to aid the reader in following the flow of information.
3. *Close.* In most reports this is simply an offer of additional assistance if the reader desires it. The closing paragraph may deal with the relationship between the writer and the reader rather than with the contents of the report. If the letter report is for internal communication purposes, no such closing comments are necessary.

Elbert Cunningham hired National Insurance Analysts to appraise the health insurance plan provided by Falwick Industries for its employees. After investigating the plan, National responded with the letter report in Figure 10.9.

Preprinted Form Reports

Short reports perform many different functions in the business organization. Listing all of the different types of short reports would be a monumental task because of the great diversity.

The most common type of short report in most organizations is that which is required on a regular basis and which is informational. At the end of each week, for example, each sales representative for Falcon Products must send a customer contact report to the sales manager. Such information as number of customers visited, sales made, and service problems identified is included in the report. Since this report is submitted so frequently and by such a large number of representatives, Falcon Products provides a preprinted form for this purpose (see Figure 10.10). The form specifies the information needed and clearly indicates where the completed form should be sent.

From the company's perspective, the form ensures that the information provided will be uniform and hence easy to compile. From the individual respondent's perspective, it simplifies the process by indicating clearly what is to be provided on the form. Although the number of forms that must be completed is a source of complaint from many workers, preprinted forms save a great deal of time. If the workers had to develop and prepare individual reports instead of using preprinted forms, there would be much more complaining.

Preprinted forms constitute the greatest volume of short reports, and they play an important role in the smooth operation of any business. Without them the routine transmitting of information would be greatly complicated. Since this kind of report requires no particular expertise to complete, it has not been emphasized in this chapter.

> **The most common type of short report utilizes preprinted forms for the transmittal of routine information on a regular basis.**

Miscellaneous Short Reports

There is no shortage of short reports in most organizations. Because they are very functional, they are heavily used. Examples of easily recognized short reports include credit reports, reports of meetings, end-of-month production reports, and some reports to stockholders. As is generally true of short reports, each one has a distinct purpose and should contribute significantly to organizational operations.

Figure 10.9   A Letter Report

National Insurance Analysts
P. O. Box 940
Red Bank, New Jersey 07701

May 1, 19___

Mr. Elbert Cunningham
Director of Employee Benefits
Falwick Industries
Camden, New Jersey 08101

Dear Mr. Cunningham:

Having analyzed the health insurance plan provided by Falwick Industries
as you requested, I'm now reporting my findings, which you may find helpful.

Forecast of the cost of employee benefits

Your concern over the spiraling cost of employee benefits is justified.
During the last decade the cost of providing employee benefits has
increased at an average rate of 14 percent a year. Your employee benefit
plan is intended to cover growing medical costs and to replace lost job
income. As long as inflation continues to reduce the real income of
employees, benefit payments will rise proportionately. In other words,
this rate of increase is expected to continue for the foreseeable future.

One option: Pay-as-go insurance

In this direct self-funding approach the company pays claims directly from
the company's cash flow. The firm actually becomes its own insurer and
does not set aside any reserves for future claims. Most companies using
this plan purchase stop-loss insurance to protect against unexpectedly
severe claims. Since your company does not require employee contributions
to its plan, Falwick Industries is eligible, under ERISA restrictions, to
initiate such a plan.

Another option: Tax-exempt trust

In this self-funding approach a plan must be drawn to meet the unique needs
of the individual company. A tax-exempt trust is then set up and employer
and employee contributions are deposited into it. Claims and expenses are
paid from the trust and excess funds are invested in order to build up
reserves. There are several tax advantages of this trust. It may be
administered so as to qualify for exemption from federal income tax. The
contributions of the employer may be deductible as a business expense.
Usually the benefit payments are not taxable to the employees who receive
them.

Administration of self-funding benefit plan

Figure 10.9 (continued)

Falwick Industries
May 1, 19__
Page 2

Either of these self-funded plans can be administered within the
organization. Some companies prefer to have a professional outside
company handle the administration. Those companies which hire outside
administrators often feel that employees more readily accept the claims
decisions made by outside professionals. Whether the benefit plan is
administered by an employee or by an outsider, a company such as Falwick
Industries will enjoy considerable savings.

I hope that this report gives you a satisfactory picture of two options
open to your company. I shall be pleased to answer any questions that
you may have.

                    Sincerely,

                    Robert Simmons
                    Employee Benefit Analyst

Figure 10.10   A Sample Form Report

Customer Contact Report

Enter all visits with customers and potential customers each week. Indicate your time of arrival and departure as well as product(s) discussed. Describe any sale you made or service problem of which you learned. Describe any follow-up which you intend to perform.

Date	Time	Name of contact and company	Product discussed	Sales made	Service problems	Follow-up
Mon.	Arr. Dpt.					
	Arr. Dpt.					
	Arr. Dpt.					
Tues.	Arr. Dpt.					
	Arr. Dpt.					
	Arr. Dpt.					
Wed.	Arr. Dpt.					
	Arr. Dpt.					
	Arr. Dpt.					
Thurs.	Arr. Dpt.					
	Arr. Dpt.					
	Arr. Dpt.					
Fri.	Arr. Dpt.					
	Arr. Dpt.					
	Arr. Dpt.					

_____
Signature of Sales Representative

NOTE: Complete this form at the end of each work week and mail it immediately to the Sales Manager.

Summary

Much of the communication within any organization is in the form of memoranda. A memorandum is a message written for use within the organization. Some distinct advantages of the memorandum are that it: (1) provides a written record; (2) is suitable for transmitting complex information, and (3) can reach many persons simultaneously. The format of the memorandum is intended to simplify and speed up internal communication by ensuring consistency.

An organization requires a great deal of information in order to function smoothly. Much of this information is transmitted in the form of various types of short reports. In some organizations preprinted forms are provided to simplify reports that must be submitted frequently.

Short reports used for internal communication are often prepared as memorandum reports, which are more structured than memoranda. A memorandum report has a recognizable introduction, body, and conclusion; a memorandum is usually less structured. Short reports intended for external communication are often prepared in the format of a letter.

Review Questions

1. What is a memorandum?
2. What are the advantages of the memorandum?
3. In what ways does a memorandum differ from a memorandum report? How are they alike?
4. How do memorandum reports differ from letter reports?
5. What kinds of information might be included in a progress report?
6. What is a periodic report?
7. What are some possible purposes of justification reports?
8. Give two examples of routine memorandum reports.
9. What are the purposes of letter reports?
10. What are the advantages to an organization of providing preprinted forms for short reports? What are the disadvantages?

Exercises

1. As administrative assistant to the president of National Industries you have the job of getting contributions from the workers for the president's favorite charity, the Humane Society. It is the midpoint of the month-long campaign, and you must prepare a progress report for your boss. Thus far, 41 percent of the employees have contributed for an interim total of $1,180. Out of the total work force of 325 employees, 60 percent (195) have now been contacted, and 62 have indicated that they do not plan to contribute.

In planning this in-plant campaign your boss forecast a 100 percent rate of contributions totaling $3,250. Write a progress report to your boss, Richard Carlson, in the format of a memorandum report.

2. Prepare a progress report in letter form detailing your progress in this business communication course. In this report you are to indicate the goals you hope to attain in this course and the rate at which you are approaching these goals. Discuss your development in such areas as written communication, oral communication, and interpersonal relations. If you can cite grades as indicators of development, do so. Address this report to your instructor.

3. Prepare a preprinted form which would be appropriate to use in responding to Exercise 2. Assume that all of the students in your business communication class would complete this form several times during the course.

4. Prepare a periodic informational report at the end of each of the next three weeks. In these reports indicate the time that you spent on schoolwork during the week. These reports should be in letter form and will be sent to your business communication instructor. The reports should detail all your schoolwork, not simply the business communication course. Indicate the number of classroom hours for each course and the time you spent outside of class studying or doing assignments for each course. Also indicate any special circumstances, such as an examination, that may have led you to devote a disproportionate amount of time to a particular course. Include weekends as well as weekdays in these reports.

5. Assume that the school you attend, Boatwright University, is considering upgrading its football program. You have been asked to prepare a report on the annual expense of retaining a football coach. You have surveyed 20 schools of similar size and have learned that each school spends an average of $117,250 per year maintaining a football coach. The average salary is $46,000; $12,000 is contributed toward housing; $12,500 worth of club memberships are provided by the school; life insurance premiums of $2,000 are paid by the school as is a $1,250 auto insurance premium; the average school also pays for an administrative assistant ($21,000) and for a secretary ($14,000). In addition to those things, the average school guarantees $36,500 income from a television show and $6,000 from a radio show, as well as $7,500 from an annual football camp. Most schools also pay $5,400 for the lease of a new luxury auto.

Prepare a report in letter form for the 12 members of the Athletic Association, all of whom are alumni. Convey your findings as well as your belief that, if Boatwright is to succeed in its quest for football prominence, it must be more generous than are the average schools.

6. Various employees in the home office of Bastion Insurance Com-

pany have complained about the smoking habits of other employees in the building. The president has asked the department heads to poll their workers on their smoking habits and what the workers view as a solution to the problem. As manager of the accounting department you polled your 70 workers and learned the following: 37 do not smoke at all; 18 smoke between one and two packs of cigarettes at work each day; 7 smoke an average of ten cigarettes each work day; 3 smoke an average of five cigarettes a day; 5 smoke pipes only and they estimate that their pipes are lit for approximately three working hours per day.

Of the nonsmokers 19 suggested that smoking be allowed only in the restrooms; 8 said pipes should be banned and cigarette smokers should be allowed to smoke no more than six cigarettes a day; 5 said smoking should be limited to the two coffee breaks only; 5 said they didn't care because smoking didn't bother them. All of the smokers believed that it should be their right to smoke when and where they want; 12 of the cigarette smokers said the pipe smokers caused the problem and that pipes should be banned; 2 of the pipe smokers believed that most of the offensive smoke actually drifted over from the premium department, which is immediately adjacent to accounting.

Write a memorandum report to Charles Benson (the president) in which you present your findings, and attempt to justify whatever solution you suggest. After that, write a memo to the employees announcing the solution.

7. As personnel research director of Metro Bank, a large urban bank with many branches, you were assigned six months ago to investigate why there is such high turnover among the tellers and the clerks. You implemented an exit interview program and learned that of the 60 tellers and clerks who quit during that period 32 gave the heavy rush-hour traffic as the main reason; 20 said they wanted to get part-time jobs instead; 8 others gave personal reasons.

It seems to you that a good solution would be to introduce a more flexible schedule. By altering work schedules you believe that some workers could avoid rush-hour driving. Another possibility might be to hire more part-time employees and to allow full-time employees to become part-time if they wish.

The cost of training new employees is very high. Anything that can be done to reduce turnover, and thereby training costs, would be worthwhile, you believe. Prepare for Willard Petrol, vice president of personnel, a report in which you present your findings and make recommendations. Willard Petrol has a reputation for being against change. He believes that most modern personnel practices are actually harmful to the organization.

8. As head of the student activities committee you are in the process of developing a booklet for new students. You hope to include a

section on things students can do that are free. To compile this information you plan to contact the presidents of the social, civic, and all other clubs on the campus. You hope to come up with a long list of free things to do on campus and in town. Prepare a memorandum report to be sent to the club presidents. In it you will seek as much information about free activities as possible.

9. Students and faculty alike usually believe that registration procedures could be improved at their schools. List whatever changes you consider to be desirable, then prepare a memorandum report in which you detail the steps a student must follow in registering for classes under your improved system. This memorandum report will be sent to all students who are accepted by your school. If you are pleased with present registration procedures, your memorandum report should describe them.

10. Write a memorandum to the office personnel of Global Travel where you are employed as assistant manager. You believe that there is too much waste of office supplies. Several times you have found employees using the copy machine for personal use. You also believe that some employees make personal long-distance telephone calls. Lights are left on unnecessarily, and the office thermostat is often as high as 72 to 74 degrees. Write a memorandum to the employees and ask their cooperation in reducing waste.

11. As director of the college library you have received a growing number of complaints about the way the periodical room is managed. Twelve patrons have complained that magazines are allowed to pile up on tables before being shelved; eight complained that magazines are often put back on the wrong shelves. Also, many magazines are reported to be torn and no apparent attempt is made to repair them. Some students have been observed cutting articles out of magazines in violation of library policy. Write a memo to Curtis Farnsworth, periodical room manager, in which you describe the complaints and make recommendations.

12. You are a management trainee in a large (4,000 employees) manufacturing plant. The plant manager, Tom Collins, has asked you to write a report on the use of quality circles in business and industry. He wants to learn such things as what quality circles are, their uses, how widespread their usage is, and their benefits. Use the *Business Periodical Index* to locate several articles on quality circles in order to gain the knowledge necessary to write the report. Collins has little patience with long reports and will not read a report longer than three pages.

13. Prepare an informational report on the man of the year as selected by *Time* magazine in the past 20 years. In this report indicate the past 20 recipients, the year each was selected, the main reason each person won the award, and any trend which appears to be developing in bestowing the award. Lastly, predict the next recipient of the award and briefly defend your prediction.

14. Prepare a progress report describing the progress you are making in your education. Describe your goals and detail your plan for accomplishing these goals. Also, describe the major obstacles to accomplishing your goals and what you are doing to overcome the obstacles. Address this report to your adviser.

15. You are a member of a professional association (in your area of interest). You have been asked to suggest an appropriate topic for a 90-minute session at the national convention. You will not be responsible for giving any presentation but merely for suggesting an appropriate topic. Prepare a justification report in which you suggest a topic and present a rationale for it being a part of the convention. Indicate clearly why you believe this topic would appeal to the members of the professional association.

16. In order to actively include as many association members in the convention as possible (see Exercise 15) it is decided that each 90-minute session will feature four presentations. Prepare a justification report in which you suggest a topic for a session. Also, explain how the topic could be divided into four parts and what each speaker would cover. Explain in what ways the topic would interest the membership and defend your suggested division of the topic.

17. You have been an instructor of business communication for several years, and you have grown increasingly disturbed with the attire of your students in class. You believe that dress is much too informal and this casualness has a negative effect on classes. You believe that classroom atmosphere should be more businesslike and more suitable clothing is the first step to a more businesslike atmosphere. Prepare a memo for all of the business communication instructors in which you urge that they set and enforce certain standards of attire. Also, describe what you consider to be appropriate attire.

18. Keep a time log for one week. At 30-minute intervals throughout each day stop and write down what you did during the prior 30-minute period. At the end of the week prepare a letter report in which you describe your time usage. Divide your report into sections on the basis of your major uses of time. Conclude with a list of recommendations of how you could improve your use of time. Address the letter report to yourself.

19. Prepare a preprinted form which could be used for keeping a time log as described in Exercise 18. Prepare this form for college students to use.

20. You are to write a short report comparing the salaries paid to professional athletes in the NFL, NBA, and major league baseball. You researched the salaries paid by the three Atlanta professional athletic teams. You learned that in 1983 the Atlanta Falcons paid the following individual salaries: $400,000; $239,286; $165,000; $157,500; $148,000; $145,000; $135,000; $130,000; $128,725; $127,500; $127,000; $110,000; $105,000; $92,000; $86,833;

$76,500; $70,000; $62,000; $46,000; $41,167; $40,000; two players were paid $125,000; two were paid $120,000; two were paid $95,000; three were paid $85,000; three were paid $65,000; two were paid $50,000; two were paid $45,000; two were paid $44,000; three were paid $35,000 and four received $25,000.

In 1983 the Atlanta Braves paid the following individual salaries: $1,082,500; $600,000; $500,000; $400,000; $395,000; $383,333; $300,000; $280,000; $187,500; $185,000; $160,000; $150,000; $76,500; $60,000; $52,500; $37,000; two were paid $250,000; two were paid $75,000; two were paid $35,000 and five were paid $33,500.

In 1983 the Atlanta Hawks paid the following individual salaries: $625,000; $433,000; $421,000; $400,000; $351,666; $290,000; $225,000; $200,000; $120,000; $115,000; $55,000; $50,000 and $37,500.

In your report comment on such things as salary range, average salary, and speculate as to possible reasons for the differences.

Case

Why Students Choose a University
Anthony S. Lis
Professor of Business Administration
The University of Oklahoma
Norman, OK

The Division of Student Affairs at Urban University (enrollment 15,000) conducted a survey of incoming freshmen during the fall semesters of 1983, 1984, and 1985 to ascertain their reasons for having chosen Urban University.

The questionnaire contained 41 items for ranking by the freshmen.

Here is the list of the top 11 factors—ranked from highest to lowest—that were rated by the incoming students as either "Somewhat important" or "Very important":

Item	Percentage (1985)	Rank 1985	Rank 1984	Rank 1983
1. Curriculum in my major	94	1	1	1
2. Academic reputation of UU	92	2	2	2
3. Friendliness on campus	83	3	4	4
4. General character/image of Urban University	83	4	3	3
5. Reputation of department of my major	81	5	5	5
6. Social atmosphere/extra curricular activities	81	6	6	6
7. Prestige of UU degree	78	7	7	6
8. Reputation of faculty	77	8	8	8
9. Contacts with UU students and friends at UU	71	9	11	11

Item	Percentage (1985)	1985	Rank 1984	1983
10. Reputation of UU administration	71	10	10	10
11. Physical facilities	72	10	9	15

Incidentally, during the 1983–84 academic year, the new UU Physical Fitness and Recreation Center was put into service for students, faculty, and staff.

The above rankings are based on the means of the responses.

■ ■ ■

Case Questions:

1. Prepare an appropriate graph that you feel would present the above data even more effectively and vividly.

2. Prepare a memorandum report from the Director of the Student Affairs Division to the Vice President for Academic Affairs, Urban University. Include some conclusions and at least two recommendations for action that, in your opinion, should be taken by the university administration.

3. On the basis of your experiences at your own institution, what other use could and should be made of the above data?

Case

Clear and Concise Communication
Jeremiah J. Sullivan
University of Washington

August 3, 1985

Mr. John Smith
Vice President-Finance
Gotham Hospital
201 - 15th Avenue East
New York, N. Y. 10012

Dear Mr. Smith:

In line with our conversation earlier this week, we have set forth below
a framework for our proposed revolving credit facility for Mount Sinai:

Amount: $25,000,000.

Availability: $5 million available from January 1, 1986; increasing
                     to $10 million on July 1, 1986; increasing to $18
                     million on January 1, 1987; increasing to $25 million
                     on July 1, 1987; $25 million available through
                     December 31, 1988. Commencing January 1, 1989,
                     availability will decline in 14 equal semi-annual
                     amounts.

Revolving Nature
of Commitment: Until 12/31/88, Gotham Hospital may borrow, repay, and
                     reborrow under the line of credit so long as amounts
                     outstanding do not exceed in the aggregate the amount
                     of the bank's line of credit in effect at the time.

Purpose: Loan proceeds to be utilized for the acquisition and
                     improvement of land, the construction of new facilities,
                     and the purchase of equipment.

Final Maturity: 12/31/95

Loan Charges: 1. Interest Rate
                        Closing through 12/31/86:   Prime Rate
                        1/1/87 - 12/31/88:   Prime Rate +
                                                         1/4 percent
                        1/1/89 - 12/31/90:   Prime Rate +
                                                         3/4 percent

                     2. Availability Fee
                        3/8 of 1 percent per annum of $25 million payable
                        quarterly from date of closing to date of initial
                        drawdown; thereafter, 1/4 of 1 percent per annum
                        of the following amounts, fee payable quarterly in
                        arrears:

```
Gotham Hospital
August 3, 1985
Page 2



                   From 1/1/86 -  6/30/86:          $20 million
                   From 7/1/86 - 12/31/86:          $15 million
                   From 1/1/87 -  6/30/87:          $ 7 million

                3. Commitment Fee
                   ½ of 1 percent per annum payable quarterly in
                   arrears on the unused portion of the available
                   commitment commencing on the date of the committed
                   amounts become available; fee expires on the final
                   maturity date.

     Balances:      Average balances in an amount equivalent to 5 percent
                    of the available commitment plus 5 percent of average
                    borrowings are to be maintained in the form of a
                    noninterest-bearing time certificate of deposit.



                         Sincerely,


                         John Smith
                         City Bank of New York
```

■ ■ ■

Case Questions

1. Explain why the format of this memo is effective.
2. Does the writer use appropriate vocabulary for this short report? If so, give several examples.
3. How does the format lend itself to a clear presentation of a complex business problem?

Writing Policies and Procedures

Learning Objectives
1. To understand the nature of objectives, policies, and procedures.
2. To learn the five questions that a policy/procedure statement should answer.
3. To learn the correct format for writing policies and procedures.
4. To understand the application of characteristics of effective written communication to writing policies and procedures.

"*R*alph, it's company policy," said Paul, leaning back in his chair. "I can't help what they do in other departments."

"But, Paul, I've got a lot of unhappy people down there," Ralph responded. "When they called in, I told them we'd pay them only for the hours they put in. And Jean is paying all of her people for a whole day. Some of her folks didn't get here till three o'clock."

"I know," Paul replied. "Look, Ralph, this happened once before—long before you got here. Must have been 15, maybe 16 years ago. We had a terrible storm. Ice on the roads . . . hanging from the trees. Believe me. The whole town was just dead. But you know, we had 10 or 15 faithful employees show up, some of them after lunch. And that's when the man upstairs decided to give a full day's pay in circumstances like this. Jean knew about it because she was one of those people that got paid."

"Is that written down somewhere?" Ralph asked.

"The policy?"

"Yeah."

Paul shook his head. "I doubt it. We've got enough company policy, rules of conduct, standard operating procedures, and the like in writing as it is. Look, Ralph, I'm sorry you didn't get the word. But it's simple. Your people stayed home. They get paid nothing. If they'd shown up at even four o'clock, we'd have paid them for the whole day. But they didn't. Now you're going to have to work this out with them as best you can." ∎

It will probably happen to you some day—a policy that almost everyone in the business except you knows about. In Ralph's case he didn't know because the policy was unwritten. You may find yourself in Ralph's shoes even though the policy is written. In this chapter we'll introduce you to writing policies and procedures. At the same time, however, we'll try to give you some guidance about when those policies and procedures should be written and when they shouldn't be.

The Nature of Policies and Procedures

Every business is obviously concerned about its own success. In establishing and maintaining a successful operation, the owners or managers of the business set objectives for themselves. Examples of general objectives include:

□ Maximizing net profits
□ Keeping employees satisfied
□ Keeping customers satisfied
□ Maximizing market share
□ Being of service to the community

Although they change from time to time, these objectives are intended to channel the efforts of all employees toward similar ends. Yet, because they are so generally worded, objectives don't provide much guidance to employees in terms of exactly how they should behave. There are many different means to one end. Thus, policies and procedures enter the picture.

Policy Defined

A policy is a general guide to decision making. It is a framework consistent with organizational objectives which helps managers make decisions. Yet a policy is only a guideline as it usually gives the manager some degree of discretion in making decisions. To help you understand policies, here are some examples of them:

Objective	Policy	
Keeping customers satisfied	If any customer is dissatisfied with a purchase, then his or her money will be refunded.	**Policies help put objectives into operation.**
Being of service to the community	Managers will use every opportunity to become involved in community services such as the United Way, the Heart Fund, and the American Cancer Society.	
Keeping employees satisfied	All promotions to managerial positions will be from within the company.	

As you examine these policy statements, notice that they provide for discretion or flexibility in decision making. For example, the community service policy does not tell the manager which or how many community organizations to join, nor does it specify how extensively the manager should be involved in any one organization.

You'll find that the higher you move in a business, the more discretion you'll probably have. Policy statements for the top-level management are usually worded more generally than those for use at lower levels. Figure 11.1 shows the amount of discretion given managment levels in a small manufacturing plant.

Policies help to implement objectives. However, there are other advantages of policies as well, especially when they are written. First, policies enhance consistency in decision making. Had Ralph (in our story at the beginning of this chapter) been aware of the snow-day policy, then he and Jean would have made the same decision. Second, conflict

Advantages of policies

Figure 11.1 Policies Allow Different Amounts of Discretion

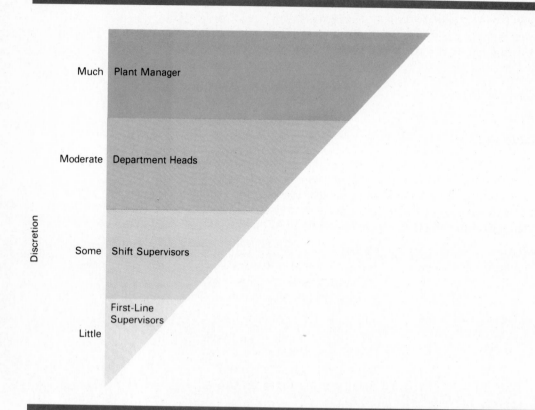

Discretion

Much — Plant Manager

Moderate — Department Heads

Some — Shift Supervisors

First-Line
Supervisors

Little

among employees may be prevented. Ralph already has conflict with his own employees because they found out that what he told them when they called in wasn't true. He probably feels conflict with Paul, who dumped the problem back in Ralph's lap. Finally, policies can save time. Without a formal snow-day policy, Ralph would need to make a new decision each time a heavy snowstorm occurred. Policies simply keep managers from having to make the same decision over and over again. Thus, they save time.

Despite the advantages of policies, they are not usually created for every decision. First, it is almost impossible to write a policy for every set of circumstances. To do so would require amazing foresight and would probably result in a policy manual hundreds of pages long (which many managers would not read). Second, although policies promote consistency in decision making, at the same time they reduce the amount of flexibility decision makers have. Exceptions to nearly every policy exist, and their existence often creates frustrated reactions like Paul's in our story: "I know there's no good reason. It's just company policy."

Disadvantages of policies

Policies, then, are general guides to decision making. They are created to help a business accomplish its objectives. If more specific decision-making guides are wanted, then procedures are written.

Procedure Defined

A procedure is a specific guide to decision making, a tool for implementing a policy. While the general wording of a policy allows discretion in making decisions, procedures provide little or no discretion. When procedures give discretion, they are called *guides.* If no discretion is allowed, then the procedure is a rule. The example below should help clarify this distinction.

Objective	Policy	Procedure (Guide)	Procedure (Rule)
Keeping customers satisfied	If any customer is dissatisfied with a purchase, then his or her money will be refunded.	Check the returned merchandise carefully to see if it has been misused.	The customer must sign the refund slip.

Guides and rules

For the policy statement we could develop a long list of both guides and rules. However, notice first that the guide we've listed gives the employee discretion, while the rule does not. Second, notice how we've worked from the general (the objective) to the specific (the rule). The farther we go toward the right side of the chart, the more control we exert over the behavior of our employees.

You may already have worked for a company that had no written policies or procedures. Many businesses don't. Generally, you'll find that the larger a firm is, the more written policies and procedures (sometimes called *standard operating procedures* or *SOPs*) the firm will have. You will also find that if the business has unionized employees, then no matter how large or small it is, most policies and procedures will be contained in what is called the *labor agreement* or *contract.*

Not all businesses have written policies and procedures.

Writing Policies and Procedures

As you pursue your career in business, you will most likely be involved in writing policies and procedures in one of three instances: (1) when a new business is formed, and you are part of it; (2) when a new policy or procedure is needed; or (3) when old policies or procedures are being rewritten. You'll probably have a chance to write policies and procedures on a variety of topics, including promotion and pay policies, actual work procedures for performing a task, and policies and procedures concerning employee grievances and discipline.

Occasions for writing policies and procedures

Here is a list of topics about which many organizations have policies and procedures:

1. Hiring new employees
2. Training new employees
3. Ensuring employee safety
4. Disciplining employees
5. Promoting employees
6. Hearing employee grievances
7. Handling customers
8. Dealing with employee absences
9. Terminating employees
10. Handling employee suggestions
11. Administering employee benefits
12. Evaluating employees

Policy and procedure topics

You can see from this list that most policies and procedures affect the internal operation of a company.

No matter for which topic you write a policy or procedure, there are several general guidelines that will help you.

Guideline 1: Answer All Possible Questions.

The next time you read a newspaper, notice that most stories begin by answering at least four basic questions: Who? What? When? Where? Here's an example:

WASHINGTON (UPI)—President Reagan is flying to Tokyo Saturday for a summit meeting with other Western leaders who also face angry, fuel-hungry citizens and a powerful oil cartel that is getting ready to raise prices again.

In the first sentence of the article the writer has told us who (President Reagan and other Western leaders), what (a summit meeting), when (Saturday), and where (Tokyo).

Your job as a writer of policy/procedure statements will be to answer five questions: Who? What? When? How? Why?

Who identifies all the people who are to act

What identifies exactly the action that should take place

When tells at what point in time actions are to occur

How tells in what way those actions will come about

Why justifies the action

Usually, you'll find the *why* answered in the policy statement. The following example of a sick leave policy/procedure answers our five questions.

Sick Leave Policy **As an employee of Burns Chemical Company you are allowed time off with pay when you are unable to work because of illness. Pay for sick leave is for the sole purpose of protecting you against loss of income when you are ill.**

Procedure   **1.** **If you are sick and unable to work, you should call your supervisor at least one hour before your shift begins.**
   2. **If you are unable to work for three or more days in a row, then you must bring a note from your doctor on the day you return to work. This note should be given to your supervisor.**

Although this example is only part of a sick leave policy/procedure, it clearly tells the employee who is involved (the employee, the supervisor, and possibly a doctor). *What* is a telephone call and bringing a physician's note. Two *whens* are in the procedure—one hour before the shift begins and the day the employee returns to work. The *how* is implicit in this procedure since it links the answers to the first three questions. *Why* is answered in the policy statement.

   As you write policies and procedures, remember to answer these five questions, and your communications will have a better chance of being understood by your receivers.

An effective policy/ procedure answers five basic questions.

Guideline 2: Follow a Specific Format.

One of the characteristics of effective written communication we identified in Chapter 3 was that writing should be mechanically sound. Your writing should be free of both errors in grammar and format problems. There are two format characteristics of a policy/procedure statement:

1.   Policies first, then procedures
2.   Procedures step by step.

As you write policy/procedure statements, you'll find that often more than one policy applies to a given procedure. If this is the case, you'll want to list all those policies first then follow them with the procedures. Here's an example that expands the sick leave policy we used earlier.

Sick Leave Policies **As an employee of Burns Chemical Company, you are allowed time off with pay when, because of illness, you are unable to work. Pay for sick leave is for the sole purpose of protecting you against loss of income when you are ill.**

A. You are allowed 18 paid sick days per calendar year.

B. If you do not need all of your sick leave days during a year, then you may add the days you don't use to your next year's total. A maximum of 90 paid sick leave days can be saved.

Procedures **1. If you are sick and unable to work, you should call your supervisor at least one hour before your shift begins.**

2. If you are unable to work for three or more days in a row, then you must bring a note from your doctor on the day you return to work. This note should be given to your supervisor.

In this example Policy A may seem to you to be a procedure because it appears to be a rule. However, don't forget that procedures are specific guides to decision making. They tell us how to take action to implement a policy.

When writing procedures, you should organize them step by step. Often, following procedures results in an end product of some kind. Therefore, to be sure that the product is correct, you should organize and label the steps clearly:

Customer Refunds

Policy **If any customer is dissatisfied with a purchase, then his or her money will be refunded.**

Procedures

1. **Check the customer's sales slip. Only the store manager may authorize returns on merchandise the customer has had for more than 30 days.**

2. **Check the returned merchandise carefully to see if it has been misused.**

3. **Fill out the customer refund slip, making sure that you enter:**
   a. **Customer's name and address**
   b. **Date of purchase**
   c. **Stock number and description of merchandise**
   d. **Sales number of salesperson who sold the merchandise**
   e. **Your sales number**
   f. **Reason for return**

4. **Take the customer refund slip to your immediate supervisor, who will approve the refund.**

5. **Have the customer sign the customer refund slip.**

6. **Refund the customer's money:**
   a. **If the purchase was by credit card, then tell the customer his or her account will be credited with the amount of purchase. Do not make cash refunds on credit card purchases.**
   b. **If the purchase was by cash, then refund the customer's money from your cash-register drawer. Place the audit copy of the credit refund slip in the drawer.**
7. **Take the remaining copies of the credit refund slip and the returned merchandise to the customer service department.**

Each step in the procedure requires a different action. Ideally, no two acts (unless they are closely connected, as in 6b) should be described in one step.

Typically, policies and procedures should follow this format:

Topic (if Policy/Procedure Statement)

General Policy
Specific Policies (A, B, C, etc.)
Procedures (1, 2, 3, etc.)

Guideline 3: Orient the Message to the Receivers.

Think back to the other characteristics of written communication which we discussed in Chapter 3: readable, tactful, personal, positive, active, unified, coherent, clear, and concise. Each of these characteristics applies in different ways to writing policies and procedures. Your analysis of the person(s) who will implement the policy/procedure statement will help you decide how they apply. Here are some examples:

Readability. Readibility is a serious problem in many existing policy/procedure statements. The example was taken from a labor agreement. It is a policy dealing with vending machines.

Food Services
Quality and quantity of automatically vended food items in the plant will be the subject of efforts for improvement and placed under strict surveillance by a Management representative who will confer periodically with the Union Committee. Such vending items will be available in the plant at convenient locations, as mutually agreed.

Many policies and procedures have readability problems.

Using Gunning's Fog Index, we can compute the readability of this policy:

1. 50 words
2. 2 sentences
3. Average sentence length = 25 words

4. 10 hard words; percentage of hard words is 20
5. 25 + 20 = 45
6. 45 × .4 = 18

The readability index for the policy is 18, far above the comprehension levels of the persons for whom the policy was written. If people can't understand policy/procedure statements, then how can they use the statements in their decision making?

Many businesses are aware of such readability problems and have tried, often successfully, to overcome them.

The U. S. Air Force recently completed an 18-year study undertaken to improve the readability of work procedures for its maintenance workers. Before the study began, these workers had to try to interpret lengthy, complicated repair procedures written by the product manufacturers. Air Force personnel rewrote these procedures, following several rules. Each step in a procedure had to be described in no more than three sentences. Each sentence could be no more than 25 words. By combining these simple rules with a picture of the step on a facing page of the repair manual, the Air Force found that even a new maintenance worker who used the manual could repair items as effectively as a worker who had years of experience.

You'll be writing policies and procedures for all levels of receivers. You should therefore control readability so that the least educated of your intended receivers can understand them.

Tact. Readable policy/procedure statements must be tactful as well. One other tact issue that deserves your special attention is imperial words.[1]

Imperial words are not tactful because they emphasize the superiority of the company over the employee. Two common imperial words in policy/procedure statements are *will* and *shall*. Unless you are describing some future action, these words are mere decoration on your statements. Consider the following:

Poor	**Better**
You will get a doctor's excuse for every illness.	Get a doctor's excuse for every illness.
All supervisors shall be responsible for safety in their work areas.	All supervisors are responsible for safety in their work areas.
Employees shall submit their suggestions in writing.	Submit your suggestions in writing.

Imperial words emphasize writer-reader differences unnecessarily.

Personal Approach. We emphasized using the "you" attitude in Chapter 3 because it is more personal. When writing policies and procedures, however, you'll sometimes want to avoid the personal approach, particularly when writing about unpleasant topics such as discipline, discharge, and layoffs. Compare the two discharge procedures below.

Personal   **A suspension form terminating you without pay will be completed by your department head when discharge is the only appropriate action.**

Impersonal   **A suspension form terminating the employee without pay will be completed by the department head when discharging is the only appropriate action.**

Active Voice.   Both policies and procedures demand use of the active voice since they are guides to an activity. If you want to de-emphasize an idea, then the passive voice is acceptable. However, you'll find the passive voice to be widely used for no apparent reason, as in this general grievance procedure:

General Grievances
In cases of general grievances by groups of employees in a department, those general grievances may be reduced to writing and filed with the department head. If the department head believes that the grievances justify a meeting, then a meeting will be arranged by the department head at a mutually agreeable time.

Conciseness.   In Chapter 3 we identified wordy expressions as one barrier to concise writing. Listed on the left are 14 verb phrases that procedure writers most often use.[2] All of them are wordy. When you write policies and procedures here are examples to avoid using:

Don't Say	Say
should be decided	decide
must be sent	send
may be requested	request
can be used	use
will be checked	check
shall be forwarded	forward
may be issued	issue
should be obtained	obtain
shall be placed	place
may be prepared	prepare
will be recorded	record

Sometimes the impersonal approach is better.

The unjustified passive voice.

Don't Say	Say
can be received	receive
must be shown	show
should be provided	provide

Summary

Policies and procedures are guides to decision making. They are intended to help a business meet its objectives by providing guidelines for more consistent decision making. Few people want to consult a policy or procedure manual, but they'll be more inclined to do so if, when you write your policy/procedure statements, you apply three specific guidelines:

1. Answer every possible question about the behavior wanted.
2. Follow an appropriate and consistent format.
3. Give careful attention to your receiver as you apply the qualities of effective written communication.

Footnotes

[1]Leslie H. Matthies, *The New Playscript Procedure* (Stamford, Conn.: Office Publications, 1977), pp. 29–30.
[2]Ibid., p. 76.

Review Questions

1. Explain the differences among an objective, a policy, and a procedure.
2. What is the role of discretion in writing policies and procedures?
3. Describe two basic kinds of procedures.
4. What questions does an effective policy/procedure statement answer?
5. What is the proper format for a policy/procedure statement? Describe it in detail.
6. Discuss the use of imperial words in writing policies and procedures.
7. How should the "you" attitude be applied when writing policies and procedures?

Exercises

1. Find a policy/procedure statement in the student handbook for your college or university.
   a. Evaluate the statement using the guidelines in this chapter.
   b. If the statement does not meet all the guidelines, rewrite it so that it does.
2. You work for a company that has decided to begin an employee suggestion system. Employees who submit useful suggestions will receive cash awards. Write a policy/procedure statement for all the hourly employees to follow in participating in the new system.
3. Write a set of procedures about one of the following:
   a. How to change an automobile tire.
   b. How to change a typewriter ribbon.
   c. How to fold and place a letter in an envelope.
   d. How to talk to customers on the telephone.
4. Write a policy statement for each topic:
   a. Employee vacations
   b. Employee coffee breaks
   c. Employee safety.
5. Choose one of those policy statements you wrote in Exercise 4 and write a set of procedures for it.
6. Write a set of procedures for some simple task one of your classmates might perform in class (for example, folding papers, working with columns of numbers). Give the procedures to a classmate and see how well that person can follow your instructions.

Case

Enthusiast or Maverick?
Basil Livingston Cleare, Ph.d.
Borough of Manhattan Community College,
City University of New York

Bailey was a new instructor in a technical college which provided training in air conditioning, carpentry, cosmetology, electrical installation, hotel services, industrial sewing, masonry, and welding. The institution was two years old and had a student enrollment of 250 and a full-time and part-time faculty of 17. The college staff included two clerk-typists, two secretaries, an aide, and the college director. Bailey impressed the director as being someone with drive, initiative, and innovative abilities, qualities the budding institution could use to accomplish its objectives.

When Bailey accepted his current post, administrators at the college where he had worked were pleased since they classified Bailey as someone who did not fit in. These innuendoes did not prejudice the director against Bailey, because people who were previously defined as misfits were now some of the director's most reliable and professional staff members.

The institution did some training for the armed forces. Thus close relationships developed between the director and training officers of the armed forces. On one visit to the college, the training officer for one of the naval bases produced a letter signed by Bailey and addressed to the commander of the base. The letter proposed structuring and offering courses in marine carpentry for personnel at the base. The courses were to be offered at the college where Bailey worked. The training officer asked if the letter was prepared and mailed with the director's knowledge and consent. The director knew nothing about the letter. However, the letter was typed by one of the school's staff members, and it was on the college letterhead.

■ ■ ■

Case Questions

1. How should the director handle the query about the letter?
2. How should the director handle the matter with Bailey?
3. How could similar situations be prevented in future? Give examples of specific policies and procedures.

Case

Policies in a Crisis
Smiley W. Weatherford, Jr.
President,
The Valmont Group, Inc.
Athens, GA

Mary Smith is employed by Mercy Hospital as a cashier in the emergency department. Her primary job is to register patients who report to the emergency room for treatment and to collect the emergency room fees for services provided by the hospital.

It is obvious to everyone working there that many of the people who come to the emergency room aren't really emergency cases. In fact more than a few seem to need no treatment at all.

Allan Swartz, the hospital business manager, has continuously voiced his opinion that the majority of emergency room patients are simply freeloaders who are trying to avoid paying doctor bills.

It appears that there might be something to Swartz's argument, since less than 20 percent of the patients seen in the emergency room pay for the services they receive.

Mercy Hospital has been in financial trouble for over a year. The problems have been so bad that the hospital's board of trustees recently fired the administrator who had held the position for the past nine years and replaced him with a much younger and aggressive man, David Hill. Hill was generally credited with saving a large city hospital from financial collapse prior to his arrival at Mercy Hospital.

At one of his first meetings with department heads, Hill announced, among other things, that it was essential for the hospital to reduce the amount of bad debts if it was going to survive financially. It has already been rumored throughout the hospital that a statement was made by Hill to the effect of "if the people we have doing this job can't do any better, then we'll get somebody else who can."

Swartz was obviously concerned after the meeting. In discussing it with the emergency room cashiers, he said it was up to them to see to it that people asking for emergency room treatment who were not emergency cases paid the emergency room fees before they were treated.

That night Louise Jones, a frequent visitor to the emergency room who had a large number of past-due accounts, showed up with a very general complaint of "just not feeling well." Mary Smith, recognizing the responsibility she had been entrusted with by Swartz, refused to admit Jones into the emergency room for treatment since she said she had no money.

Forty-five minutes later Louise Jones collapsed and died on a bus. She was reportedly en route to another hospital for treatment.

When questioned by reporters the next day, the hospital administrator, Hill, stated that it was definitely not the policy of Mercy Hospital to turn anyone away in need of medical care. In a similar statement Swartz said that he obviously never intended for Smith to turn away anyone seriously in need of care.

■ ■ ■

Case Questions

1. What was the policy of Mercy Hospital on treatment of patients who did not have the ability to pay?
2. Did Hill, Swartz, and Smith have the same understanding of this policy? If not, why not?
3. What procedures could have been established to prevent this unfortunate incident?

³ *Oral Strategies*

Listening as a Communication Tool

Learning Objectives
1. To understand the amount of time we spend listening.
2. To examine the potential relationships between effective listening and various individual characteristics.
3. To become aware of major perceptual barriers to effective listening.
4. To understand the valuable concept of active listening.
5. To learn how concentration, objectivity, questioning, and feedback can improve listening behavior.
6. To understand the difference between good listening behavior and poor listening behavior.

An irritating habit of mine, I've often been told by my closest friends or relatives, is to underline a passionate statement on whatever subject is under discussion with the question, "Do you HEAR me?" What I'm subconsciously asking the person, of course, is not just to listen but to "hear" my undertones, the implications.

On my desk now is a pioneering study which confirms that my question has not been as odd as it has appeared to be. For tests made as part of the study disclose that immediately after listening to a 10-minute oral presentation the average consumer or employee has heard, understood, properly evaluated and retained only half of what was said. Within 48 hours, that sinks by another 50 percent.

The final level of effectiveness—comprehension and retention—is only 25 percent! Even worse, as ideas are communicated from one person to the next, they can become distorted by 80 percent.

With 100 million workers in our nation, a simple $10 listening mistake by each would cost business $1 billion!

The financial toll of poor listening is enormous. Thus, more and more corporations are actively looking for solutions. Chairman and Chief Executive Officer J. Paul Lyet of Sperry Corp. (producer of Sperry Univac computers and other capital equipment products) is a leader in expanding the corporation's commitment to improve the quality of listening among its 87,000 employees.

"Poor listening is one of the most significant problems facing business today," says Lyet. "Business relies on its communication system, and when it breaks down, mistakes can be very costly. Corporations pay for their mistakes in lower profits, while consumers pay in higher prices."

If you're a poor listener, you're much more apt to make mistakes on important business matters. Letters must be retyped, appointments rescheduled and shipments reshipped—all because the proper information wasn't heard, or understood, when first given.

If you're among the majority, though, you don't overrate your own listening abilities. For instance, 85 percent of those asked rate themselves as "average" listeners or less, while fewer than 5 percent rate themselves as "superior" or "excellent."

But your listening ability can be improved. In the few schools which have adopted listening programs, listening comprehension among students has as much as doubled in a few months.[1] ∎

Surveys indicate that managerial people in organizations spend up to 80 percent of their work day in face to face conversations, in meetings, on the phone, or writing.[2] Others have suggested that approximately 60 percent of the work day is spent listening.[3] Estimates also indicate that less than 50 percent of the oral messages used in a day are fully understood.[4]

The purpose of this chapter is to become aware of how much of our day is spent listening, to identify some of the major barriers to effective listening, and finally to learn how concentration, objectivity, questioning, and feedback can improve listening behavior.

Many people spend 80 percent of the work day in some kind of communication.

Not only do we spend a large part of each day listening, we really do not do a very good job of listening to each other. As noted earlier, the average listener who hears a ten-minute presentation will hear, understand, and retain only half of what was said. Forty-eight hours later that portion drops another 50 percent. Or to put it another way we retain about 25 percent of what we hear.

Part of the reason for our poor listening ability is a result of our educational system. Our formal education system emphasizes the speaker at the expense of the listener. The system focuses major attention on reading, writing, and speaking skills—not listening skills. This emphasis may be misplaced when you realize that of our total working hours we spend 45 percent listening, 30 percent speaking, 16 percent reading, and 9 percent writing.

All of us have found ourselves in the situation of talking to another person and suddenly becoming aware that the other person is not listening. Not a very good feeling, is it? The fact is that most of us have no fundamental hearing deficiency, but we still do not listen very well. Why?

How can we become better listeners? Several researchers have examined the potential relationships between effective listening and other individual characteristics. The following conclusions can be drawn from research about listening:

1.   **Sex.** Although some research has shown that females comprehend slightly less from lectures than do males, the discrepancy is probably caused by the manner of testing, not inherent sex differences.

2.   **Personality.** Generally speaking, researchers have discovered no marked relationship between listening comprehension and personality characteristics; that is, a good listener does not possess a certain type of personality.

3.   **Intelligence.** Obviously, intelligence can be a determining factor in listening (aural) comprehension, but it is not the only element that affects aural proficiency. Intelligence alone does not produce listening skills.

4.   **Scholastic achievement.** Moderately positive correlations exist between listening ability and cumulative grade average. Such findings indicate that those who listen well get higher grades. Furthermore, since listening and reading have similar correlations with grade point average, it is reasonable to conclude that scholastic excellence depends equally upon aural and reading skills.

5.   **Verbal ability and vocabulary.** Verbal competence is an important part of listening comprehension. An adequate vocabulary facilitates listening and increases word retention. In fact, the effective use of words, through both listening and speaking, is a definite business and social asset.

6.   **Note taking.** Since most listeners take poor notes, note taking does not have a noticeable effect on listening comprehension and retention. However, if you listen carefully and synthesize as your write, you will probably perform better on examinations.

We retain 50 percent of what we hear and 48 hours later that drops another 50 percent.

7. **Motivation.** Motivation is one of the most significant elements of listening proficiency. Specifically, motivation, in terms of interest, emotional appeals and attitudes, and mind set, determines one's level of aural competence. A listener's comprehension improves if there is interest in the topic before the speech, if interest is created during the speech, or if the listener is to be tested after the speech. Comprehension is also determined by the intensity of the listener's emotional reaction to what is being said. Finally, a listener's level of understanding is influenced by various methods of producing an anticipatory mind set. For example, if you introduce your point by stating that it is going to be critical of, say, tax increases, your listeners are more apt to remember your criticisms. You have created, in the minds of your audience, a mind set to anticipate criticisms.

8. **Organizational ability.** Listening comprehension is directly related to the ability to organize and structure a message. The better organized the message, the higher the comprehension. This applies to speakers as well as listeners.

9. **Environment.** Research findings show that environmental factors influence comprehension. Good listeners will learn to allow for or adjust to distracting elements, such as poor lighting or extraneous noises, distance from the speaker, or other environmental shortcomings which the listener cannot control.

10. **Hearing ability.** Many think that those who suffer some hearing loss therefore are not good listeners; actually just the opposite is true. Those with moderate hearing loss usually are better listeners that those of us who have normal hearing.

11. **Usage.** While writing skills and, to a lesser extent, speaking skills, improve with usage, this is not necessarily the case with listening. Just because we have been hearing the spoken word all our lives does not mean we are good listeners. Instruction and practice in effective listening are needed for listening improvement.

We would like to provide more definite conclusions about listening from research studies, but listening ability is a complex combination of factors. The important point to remember is that, given stable personality and average IQ, there is no particular personality trait or intelligence level that excludes us from being good listeners. Listening is a skill that can be learned; we can become better listeners and better teachers of listening skills.[5]

Perceptual Barriers to Effective Listening

Before we consider suggestions for improving listening skills, let us examine some major barriers to effective listening.[6] The first barriers to listening are perceptual in nature, while the additional barriers are more general.

Major barriers to effective listening are perceptual in nature.

1.　People perceive stimuli according to their individual frames of reference. Have you ever heard the old cliche, "meanings are in people?" This saying means a message is composed solely of aural (hearing) and visual (seeing) stimuli. Although the speaker (message sender) may want to convey a particular meaning, it is the listener's individual frame of reference—that is, total life experience up to that point—that determines the actual meaning assigned to the message. The result is that the speaker and listener may share similar but never identical meanings through a given message.

We come from different cultures, and that fact can dramatically affect our frame of reference. For example, the belch after a meal that is considered a compliment in Arabia is socially unacceptable in the United States. Many other aspects of culture determine our frame of reference and how we apply it to our listening behaviors. These cultural differences increase in importance as we expand into international markets and employ global trade.

2.　People perceive stimuli according to their own expectations. Expectations are based upon experiences in similar situations. For example, picture two American businessmen in a waiting room of the headquarters building of a large business in a middle eastern country. This being their first visit to the region, they felt it appropriate to arrive 15 minutes early for their appointment with an executive. They have been waiting for an additional hour beyond their scheduled appointment. They are frustrated and upset by this apparent lack of punctuality. Finally, the executive appears and says, "Oh, there you are. Won't you please come in?"

The Americans think how rude of this person to not even apologize for the delay.

The executive thinks to himself, "Perhaps I should have kept them waiting a bit longer to emphasize my position above them even more."

What actually occurred in this example is a mix of cultural differences and forceful experiences that probably had overridden much of what took place in the meeting. In this case, the listeners' past climate of communication determined their perceptions of the immediate listening situation, the speakers, and the messages being sent.

Particularly in organizations, where position in a formal hierarchy may be highly defined, your vantage point may define your expectations. That is, you may approach a situation where you communicate with a superior differently than with a subordinate or a peer. If you are a line person, you may communicate in a different tone with staff personnel.

3.　People perceive stimuli according to individual attitudes and beliefs. Most of us have an almost innate ability to distort information so that it fits into our model of the world. This process is called *selective perception* and is very relevant to listening activity. For example, some employees may conveniently filter out criticisms from a supervisor to support the belief that their work is quite acceptable. They refuse to hear negative comments about their work, thus avoiding an unpleasant confrontation with reality. Selective perception serves as a protective device against unwelcome aural stimuli.

We selectively remember certain experiences (selective retention); we selectively pay attention to those things we find of value (selective attention); and we have comprehension skills in some areas and weaknesses in others (selective comprehension). Awareness of these attitudes is important if you are to overcome them.

4. The continuing relationship between speaker and listener plays an important role in perception. The relationship between superior and subordinate is the most relevant case in point. Subordinates will pay close attention to a respected, credible supervisor's comments and will be more conscious of how they perceive communication from that supervisor. However, subordinates are likely to attach minor importance to the comments of a supervisor with low credibility or little power.

5. Ineffective listeners are unaware of nonverbal cues. Nonverbal cues dramatically affect how we listen. As Chapter 13 shows, as much as 93 percent of our attitudes is formed by nonverbal cues. Knowing this should help you avoid undue influence from nonverbal communication.

6. "Signal" words can cause anxiety or raise your emotions. We all have certain words that get to us in either a positive or negative way. Check yourself and create an inventory of these influential words. Don't let specific words get in the way of effective listening.

In addition to these perceptual barriers, there are other barriers of a more general nature.

1. Faking attention. All too many of us have learned and apply our knowledge of how to appear as though we're listening. Outward appearance and actual listening may be quite different.

2. Listening only for facts. Watch out for hearing only "the trees and not the forest." That is, although individual facts may be important, check yourself to ensure that you are clear on the overall goal of the message as well.

3. Avoiding difficult listening. It's all too easy to turn off our listening when we encounter a topic we find difficult. The topics vary with individuals and depend on other circumstances such as our physical alertness and the context.

4. Dismissing the topic as uninteresting. "I've heard it all before," is an attitude certain to affect our listening detrimentally—so is the assumption that a topic is beneath us or beyond our sphere of interest.

5. Criticizing physical appearance or delivery. If you have ever not listened to an individual because the speaker's looks, dress, age, mannerisms of speech, or slight speech defects bothered you, you will realize that this is a common barrier to effective listening.

6. Yielding easily to distractions. We listen for many reasons. We listen for information, to evaluate the speaker, for esthetic appreciation of the voice, and to empathize with the sender. Research indicates that when we are not listening, we are likely to be daydreaming (about something totally unrelated to what is being said), detouring (from what was said to our own thoughts), debating (against what was said), or doing some private planning (on what to say when it's our turn). As we will see shortly, to overcome distractions we need to concentrate.

Now that we have examined some of the major barriers to effective listening, we are ready to suggest means for improving our ability to listen.

Hints for Active Listening

What do you visualize when you think of a person listening? Listening is frequently pictured as a passive activity. To improve our listening behavior, we must modify this view; the preferred approach pictures a good listener as actively involved in the listening process.

Listening is not a passive activity.

Several years ago Rogers and Farson introduced a concept of active listening. Basically, it requires that we grasp, from the speaker's point of view, just what is being communicated to us. More than that, we must convey to the speakers that we are seeing things from their viewpoint. To listen actively means there are several things we must do.

Active listening entails grasping the speaker's point of view.

Listen for Total Meaning

Any message a person attempts to convey usually contains two important and meaningful elements: content, and the attitude or feeling underlying this content. These two components make up the total meaning of the message, which is what we listeners try to understand. To illustrate, a machine operator tells a foreman, "I have finished the production run." This message has definite content and may be interpreted as a request for another work assignment. Suppose, instead, that the machine operator says to the foreman, "Well, I've finally finished that damned production run." The basic content is the same, but the total meaning of the message is quite different.

The difference in the meanings of the two statements has important implications for both the foreman and the machine operator. Listening sensitivity on the part of the foreman will determine whether this conversation is a successful exchange between the two parties. Suppose the foreman's reaction is simply to assign another production run. Would the employee believe that he had successfully communicated his total message? Would he feel free to talk to his foreman? Would he have a positive feeling about his work and be anxious to perform even better on the next job assignment?

On the other hand, the foreman could respond to the machine operator with such statements as "Worked under a lot of pressure, right?" or "Glad to have it over with, huh?" or "Guess I couldn't get you to do that again!" In this instance the foreman's listening sensitivity reacts in line with the employee's attitude or feeling about the completed task. In other words, the foreman responds from the employee's point of view. Such supportive replies don't mean that the next work assignment need be changed or that the way is open for the employee to complain about the pressure of the job. Listening sensitivity is simply a way to transform an average working climate into a more positive one.

Respond to Feelings

In some situations the message content is far less important than the feeling that underlies it. To interpret the full meaning of the message accurately, one must respond to the feelings or attitude component. For example, if our machine operator said, "I'd like to disassemble the production machine and sell its parts to our competitor," responding to content would obviously be absurd. The meaning of any message contains various degrees of feeling; each time the listener must be sensitive to possible variations. What is this person trying to tell me? What does this mean to him or her? What is this person's view of the problem?

Note All Clues

Communication is made up of verbal and nonverbal cues. Words alone do not reveal everything that the speaker is communicating. Sensitive listening requires an awareness of several levels of communication besides verbal. Voice inflection is one factor: a speaker may stress certain points loudly and clearly and only mumble others. The way a speaker hesitates reveals a great deal. The speaker's facial expressions, posture, hand gestures, eye movements, and breathing also help convey the total message.[7]

The concept of active listening has to do with the mental attitude that we should bring to the listening situation. In addition, several other basic concepts relate directly to our listening ability.

People are motivated to listen in varying degrees to a variety of messages. Simultaneously, they are demotivated from listening for many of the same kinds of reasons. Effective listeners are continually and consciously motivated to listen. From the effective listener's viewpoint, whatever other individuals wish to communicate is important. Though it

Motivation and demotivation affect the listening experience.

sometimes appears that nothing of great value may be gained through listening, effective listeners consciously strive to disprove this expectation. They become selfish listeners who look for potential economic benefits, personal satisfaction, or new interests and insights. In brief, each listener needs to say, "What is that speaker saying that I can use?"

There is a significant differential between average speaking rate (100 to 200 words per minute) and an average listener's ability to process messages (400 words per minute). Such a differential provides opportunities for mental tangents. The average listeners tend to tune in and out of conversations. As a consequence, they often fail to grasp what the speaker deems the important contents of a message.

Concentration is an important determinant of listening ability.

Concentration is the key to avoiding such counterproductive tangents. The listener should be aware of the difference between the rate of speech and the rate of thought and should use the time lag effectively rather than letting it destroy the listening process. Several tactics a listener can use to facilitate concentration are shown in the checklist for listening concentration.

Concentration consists of successfully managing the time lag between speech and thought. Certain tactics can be employed both to maintain attention to the speaker's message and to facilitate retention of that message.

In dyadic or paired communication, such as between a superior and subordinate, asking questions may often be an effective listening tactic. Such activity serves two purposes: it encourages the speaker by demonstrating that one is, indeed, actively listening, and it can clarify and develop points, thereby enhancing the listener's chances of clearly understanding the speaker's message.

The use of questions is an effective listening strategy.

Probing questions are highly useful types of questions to pose in improving one's listening capabilities. Here the listener simply asks ques-

Checklist for Listening Concentration

1. **Anticipate what the speaker will say next.** Whether or not one's anticipations are confirmed, such activity serves to focus the listener's attention upon the subject at hand.

2. **Focus on the message.** Weigh the speaker's evidence and search for the speaker's deeper meanings, especially connotative ones. Such a tactic will help bridge the time gap created by the speech-thought differential.

3. **Review previous points.** This activity involves recapitulating in one's mind the major points already covered by the speaker. Reviewing points can help to reinforce the ideas the speaker is explaining.

tions that build upon a speaker's words. Probing and other types of questions are discussed in Chapter 17.

Objectivity is a critical element in effective listening. Lack of objectivity can not only result in assigning distorted meanings to messages, but it may also jeopardize the relationship between speaker and listener. In terms of objectivity an effective listener should try to follow the principles in the checklist for objective listening.

Effective listeners follow the timeworn advice, "wait your turn." They allow others sufficient opportunity to satisfactorily communicate their position or ideas. By adhering carefully to the rule of taking turns, the listener becomes a more effective communicator.

Objectivity is crucial to effective listening.

Checklist for Objective Listening

1. Minimize the impact of emotion-laden words. Quite often a listener's perceptual process goes awry simply because the speaker utters a word or phrase that arouses an automatic emotional response. Words and phrases such as *sexism, reduction in force, strike,* and *grievance* can sometimes engender feelings of hostility or anxiety in a listener. When such feelings arise, the ability to think clearly and logically may be severely hampered.

2. Judge content, not delivery. Listeners often discount messages largely because of some distracting characteristic in the speaker's tone of voice, delivery, or pronunciation. Subjective impressions of the value of messages seriously endanger one's listening efficiency. An effective listener, therefore, focuses upon what is said, not upon how it is communicated.

3. React fairly and sensibly. One of the most difficult listening functions is to avoid reacting too soon to what one hears. For example, a department head was informed by the plant manager that his staff must be reduced by two people. Rather than wait for an explanation or justification from his superior, he immediately responded defensively. He plunged right in, offering every reason imaginable for not cutting back the number of people in his department. His defensiveness resulted only in the plant manager's defensive behavior and hostile feelings between them.

4. Overcome distractions. Don't let environmental factors affect your listening. For example, turn down a stereo or television that keeps you from hearing.

5. Detect the central message. Don't allow isolated facts to get in the way of the total meaning. Ask for clarification or rewording if you are unsure what is being said.

Take Notes

Note taking may be useful in some situations; it may be unnecessary in others; in some cases it may even be distracting. Your purpose in listening should determine whether or not you need to take notes. If you think you will need to refer to the information in the future, notes are probably necessary. If the information is for immediate use, you are probably better off to listen carefully and omit notes.

The usefulness of note taking depends on the situation.

Appropriate note taking may nonverbally convey to the speaker that you are paying close attention to what he or she is saying. Such note taking shows respect for the speaker and earnestness on the part of the listener.

Let us consider the major differences between good listeners and bad listeners. Lyman Steil, a well-known authority who serves as a listening consultant to major corporations throughout the country, summarizes the differences between good and bad listeners in Figure 12.1.

Figure 12.1   Ten Keys to Effective Listening

10 Keys to Effective Listening	The Bad Listener	The Good Listener
1. Find areas of interest	Tunes out dry subjects	Opportunizes; asks "what's in it for me?"
2. Judge content, not delivery	Tunes out if delivery is poor	Judges content, skips over delivery errors
3. Hold your fire	Tends to enter into argument	Doesn't judge until comprehension complete
4. Listen for ideas	Listens for facts	Listens for central themes
5. Be flexible	Takes intensive notes using only one system	Takes fewer notes. Uses 4–5 different systems, depending on speaker
6. Work at listening	Shows no energy output; Attention is faked	Works hard, exhibits active body state
7. Resist distractions	Distracted easily	Fights or avoids distractions, tolerates bad habits, knows how to concentrate
8. Exercise your mind	Resists difficult expository material; seeks light, recreational material	Uses heavier material as exercise for the mind
9. Keep your mind open	Reacts to emotional words	Interprets color words; does not get hung up on them
10. Capitalize on fact *thought* is *faster* than speech	Tends to daydream with slow speakers	Challenges, anticipates, mentally summarizes, weighs the evidence, listens between the lines to tone of voice

Source: Okum, Sherman K., "How to be a Better Listener," *Nation's Business,* p. 62. Reprinted with permission.

Provide Feedback

Although feedback is important to listening, it is frequently overlooked. Listeners should provide feedback at appropriate points to a speaker, who is sometimes unsure what is actually getting through to the listener. The speaker may start repeating the same ideas if the listener does not appear receptive. At this point the listener shows even less interest and comprehension, the speaker repeats even more, and the entire communication process quickly deteriorates. This problem can be alleviated when the listener provides appropriate and timely feedback to let the speaker know that an idea has been understood.

Feedback is important in the listening process.

Summary

This chapter provides an overview of the qualities that result in effective listening. One major concern was to highlight the importance of listening. While we spend most of our communication time listening, it is nevertheless the communication skill in which most of us are deficient and the skill we need to sharpen and develop. We suggested ways to overcome major perceptual barriers to effective listening. Various personality traits are associated with effective listening. Although personality factors are related to one's ability to communicate, effective listening is a skill that one can learn with practice.

Footnotes

[1]Sylvia Porter, "Now Hear This: Americans are Poor Listeners," *Tampa Tribune* (November 15, 1979), p. 15-A.

[2]Ibid.

[3]"The Act of Listening," *Royal Bank of Canada Monthly Letters* 60, no. I (January 1979).

[4]Eric H. Nelson and Jan Gypen, "The Subordinate's Predicament," *Harvard Business Review* (September–October 1979): 133.

[5]"The Act of Listening," *Royal Bank of Canada Monthly Letter* 60, no. I (January 1979).

[6]The review of listening research is based upon the following work: Charles R. Petrie, Jr., "Informative Speaking: A Summary and Bibliography of Related Research," *Speech Monographs,* 30 (1963): 79–91. See also Sam Duker, *Listening Bibliography,* 2d ed. (Metuchen, N.J.: Scarecrow Press, 1968); Sam Duker, *Listening Readings,* vols. 1 and 2 (Metuchen, N.J.: Scarecrow Press, 1966, 1971); Larry Barker, *Listening Behavior* (Englewood Cliffs, N.J.: Prentice-Hall, 1971); Carl Weaver, *Human Listening* (Indianapolis: Bobbs-Merrill, 1972); C. William Colburn and Sanford B. Weinberg, "An Orientation to Listening and Audience Analysis," *Modcom* (Chicago: Science Research Associates, 1976); Malra Treece, *Communication for Business and the Professions* (Boston: Allyn and Bacon, 1978); Rose V. McCullough, "Fight the Spread of Pessimism," *Rough Notes* 125, no. I (January 1982): 48–50; and Lyman K. Steil, Larry L. Barker, and Kittie W. Watson, *Effective Listening: Key to Your Success* (Reading, Mass.: Addison-Wesley, 1983).

[7]Carl Rogers and Richard Farson, "Active Listening," in *Readings in Interpersonal and Organizational Communication,* 3d ed. Richard Huseman, Cal Logue, and Dwight Freshley (Boston, Mass.: Holbrook Press, 1977), pp. 561–586.

Review Questions

1. On the average, how much of the work day do people spend in some type of communication? How much of that time is spent listening?
2. On the average, how much of what someone tells us do we remember immediately after we have heard it? Forty-eight hours after we have heard it? What do these facts tell you about the average person's level of listening retention?
3. Select what you believe are the six or seven more important individual characteristics that affect your ability to listen. Explain your decision.
4. Give an example in a business setting of each of the major perceptual barriers to listening.
5. What is active listening? Why is it so important?
6. What is a selfish listener?
7. What are the tactics a listener can use to facilitate concentration? In turn, how does concentration facilitate listening?
8. Is the use of questions an effective listening strategy? Explain.
9. Why is objectivity a critical element in effective listening? In terms of objectivity what should an effective listener do?
10. What are the major differences between good listeners and bad listeners?

Exercises

1. You and a classmate each choose a topic of considerable personal interest. Take turns discussing your topic for three minutes. After each discussion have the listener convey the content of the message and the attitude or feeling underlying that content.
2. If some memorable event is scheduled and if all class members have access, each member should attend or watch. Select an appropriate event, such as a presidential address on television, a presentation by a campus speaker, or an organization meeting. Students should listen but not take notes. The next day the instructor will quiz you on what you heard.
3. Present a five-minute speech on a business-related topic to a friend in the liberal arts. Ask your friend (the listener) to provide feedback at any point the speech is unclear. Reverse the roles so that you become the listener providing feedback to your friend's speech on some aspect of the liberal arts.

Case

The Drop

Smiley W. Weatherford, Jr.
President,
The Valmount Group, Inc.
Athens, GA

Pilot John Jones, copilot Sam White, and navigator Jack Smith are members of the United States Air Force and are assigned to a special operations wing in the Panama Canal Zone. All three are experienced aviation officers with excellent records that include combat tours in Southeast Asia. In fact, their achievement records are the reason they have been assigned to an organization with one of the most complicated missions in the Air Force (that is, counterinsurgency, training foreign air forces, public relations, and the protection of all official U.S. personnel in Central and South America).

They have been called in to fly a special mission on a beautiful Sunday afternoon. As they assemble to be briefed, they learn their weekend has been interrupted so that they can transport and drop an Army skydiving team at a community picnic.

Captain Jones is particularly irritated since the scheduling of this type of activity has been heatedly debated in recent weeks as an improper infringement on aircrew members' time. He believes that it is improper and that such a mission will only add to the controversy.

Captain Smith is equally irritated but for different reasons. His fiancee, an airline flight attendant, is visiting on a short, 24-hour layover in Panama. He had planned to spend the entire afternoon on the sunny beach near his apartment. He is afraid that there will not be enough time to enjoy the sand and surf.

While the three are briefed by a young Army officer, Captain White can't help but notice that the briefer is using incorrect English in his comments. He has always been somewhat egotistical about the fact that he had to satisfy higher educational requirements than his brother-in-law who is an Army officer. He notes that the Army briefer made at least seven grammatical mistakes in his presentation.

Later, the mission was fairly uneventful. The take-off was made on time, the aircraft performed well, the weather was clear enough to negotiate two mountain ranges without difficulty, and they made the drop within five minutes of the scheduled time. When they returned to the air base, however, they learned that they had dropped the skydivers on the wrong side of the town, at an outdoor religious ceremony instead of the community picnic.

■ ■ ■

Case Questions

1. Why did these competent aircrew members not remember the instructions they were given in their briefing?
2. What could the Army briefer have done to insure that a mistake didn't happen?

Case

Communication Mismatch

Martha Shoemaker
Coca-Cola Company U. S. A.

Andy Townsend, supervisor of the claims department of U.S.A. Insurance Company, believed his department was underproducing due to outmoded office equipment. He had thoroughly investigated sophisticated systems being used by competing insurance companies. Andy concluded that U.S.A.'s efficiency could be significantly improved if the company purchased three visual display terminals (VDTs).

Andy calculated that with the VDTs three operators could do the same amount of work presently being done manually by 12 employees. U.S.A. was growing dramatically, and Andy knew, thanks to his business education, that automation was the key to success in the long run.

Since Andy was aware that his boss, Cecil Vann, was concerned about costs, he thought there would be no problem getting his request approved. He believed the advantages were obvious. When he approached Vann for a go-ahead on the purchase, the following conversation took place:

Vann Andy, I've had a chance to look at your memo requesting three VDTs. Unfortunately, I need more information.

Andy The advantages are clear-cut. What more information could you possibly need?

Van Well, some cost figures are necessary to justify this expense to my superiors.

Andy Mr. Vann, my department is overworked—we never get the attention we deserve. Besides, why should you doubt my credibility? It's just not fair.

Vann   Andy, please calm down. All I'm asking for are some cost figures. If you're so certain of the benefits of these VDTs, those figures should be easy to produce. I'd really appreciate it.

Andy   I'm not an accountant. I work hard around here, you know. Why can't you take my word for it?

Two days later Andy received a letter from Vann. The request had been turned down.

■ ■ ■

Case Questions

1.   What went wrong in the exchange between Andy and Vann?
2.   Was Andy really listening to what Vann said? Substantiate your opinion.
3.   Could Andy have responded more appropriately to Vann's request? How?

Nonverbal Communication: Messages Beyond Words

Learning Objectives
1. To understand the importance of nonverbal behavior in the communication process.
2. To learn how paralanguage can affect the message you communicate.
3. To improve your perception of body movement in nonverbal communication.
4. To learn how space is used to communicate.
5. To recognize the impact of dress and appearance, color, and time on those around you.

Here are some examples of how nonverbal communication can influence our behavior.

Item: **You are strolling past the bakery in your local shopping mall. Isn't that the irresistible odor of fresh-baked chocolate-chip cookies wafting from the oven? Maybe not! International Flavors and Fragrances, Inc. has succeeded in synthesizing the mouth-watering aroma of not only chocolate-chip cookies but also hot apple pie, fresh pizza, baking ham, and even nongreasy french fries. IF & F packages the artificial odors in aerosol cans and markets them along with $25 to $30 timed-release devices that periodically fire a burst of scent out into the shopping mall to tempt potential customers.**

Item: **Claims are made about music's effect on us. Peppy music in the grocery store may encourage impulse buying or, in the fast-food restaurant, may speed us away after we quickly finish our sandwich. On the other hand, at the fancy French restaurant, the right musical mood may entice you to stay for dessert and another glass of wine. There are even claims that under certain conditions, music can affect production, job satisfaction, and extent of weariness.**

Item: **You arrive at your management class to find another student in the seat you usually occupy. Even though seats aren't assigned, you give the invader a stern look to let him know your displeasure. As you pass behind another student to get to a vacant seat, you need to touch her shoulder to get by. She jumps, startled, then turns, sees you, and smiles. You sit in a chair that obviously has been recently occupied; to your discomfort, you note that the seat is still warm. Not a word has been said.**

Item: **Don Watt and Associates Ltd., a consulting firm in Toronto, says it has found a powerful marketing tool in the use of the color yellow. Watt says that the philosophy of "big yellow" was conceived a few years ago for Loblaws, a Canadian supermarket chain, to strengthen the company's image as a bargain hunter's paradise. He advised Loblaws to put all feature price items under big yellow signs that said *Save*. Next, the company put all advertised items in a single aisle and hung yellow *Save* signs overhead. In 1977 the store began putting its generic foods in yellow packages. In 1975 they had introduced generics in black and white packages, and they were a failure, but the yellow containers were a success! Now, Loblaws has opened no-frills supermarkets in**

Canada and has painted these new stores yellow. Again, success. Watt says the yellow philosophy campaign draws on two psychological facts. First, yellow is striking and highly visible to the eye. Second, and most important, psychologists say that yellow has negative associations, meaning it connotes an image of cheapness—precisely the image that Loblaws wanted to communicate.[1]

We simultaneously use both verbal and nonverbal means to convey our messages. And all of the above items provide examples of the many ways that nonverbal communication influences us every day. More and more people who write about business communication stress the importance of nonverbal communication. For example, in your resume you communicate not only with words that describe your education and experience, but also with the quality and color of paper your resume is typed on, the neatness of the typing, and similar nonverbal qualities. Although we separately analyze several aspects of nonverbal communication, we should remember that in practice the verbal and nonverbal aspects of the message together comprise the total message that is communicated.

Nonverbal communication can be defined as all those messages that are not encoded with words. We will discuss the pervasive nature of nonverbal communication and examine its major categories, which include: paralanguage, how we say something; kinesics, how we communicate through body movement; proxemics, how we communicate with space; and communication through dress and appearance, color, and time.

In Chapter 2, where we discussed in some detail the nature of communication, our major concern was verbal communication—the use of language. In this chapter we give prime consideration to the nonverbal aspects of communication, which many authorities maintain is the key to most ordinary communication. Keep in mind, however, that usually verbal and nonverbal communication occur together instead of in a vacuum.

One authority, Mehrabian, states that our words convey a very small part of the message. He argues that 93 percent of the total impact of any given message consists of nonverbal factors. (See Table 13.1). If

Nonverbal communication is a message that is not encoded with words.

More than 90 percent of the message may be communicated nonverbally.

Table 13.1   Comparison of Verbal and Nonverbal Communication

Message Impact	Type of Communication
7 percent	Words
38 percent	Tone of voice and inflection
55 percent	Facial expression, body position, gestures

Adapted from Albert Mehrabian, "Communication Without Words," *Psychology Today* (September 1968), 2:53–55.

you carefully analyze the messages that others communicate, it may surprise you how much emphasis is placed on the nonverbal aspects of communication.

Paralanguage—How You Say It

Of the various components of nonverbal communication, paralanguage is most akin to verbal communication. While language deals with what is said, paralanguage deals with how it is said. To realize the importance of paralanguage you can perform a simple test. The next time a friend asks you to do something—go to a movie or to a particular restaurant for dinner—respond, "Sure, I would love to go," but let your tone of voice betray your words and convey that you have little or no interest in going. Watch the reaction of your friend to how you communicated your response.

> **Paralanguage can reinforce or undermine the verbal message.**

At times we mean to communicate a particular message through the use of paralanguage. For example, the phrase "I would like to help you" can convey several meanings, depending upon the paralanguage employed. Note the following types of emphasis.

1. *I* would like to help you.
2. I would *like* to help you.
3. I would like to *help* you.
4. I would like to help *you*.

In each case the emphasized word changes the meaning of the message.

To better understand paralanguage we can look at voice qualities, including volume, rate, rhythm, pitch, and resonance. All of us at one time or another have been made aware of the quality known as *rate*— how fast or slow someone is speaking. Depending on what other messages are being communicated, an increase in rate could indicate anger, impatience, or anxiety from the person sending the message. A decrease in rate can indicate thoughtfulness, a reflective attitude, or on the other hand, boredom or lack of interest.

> **Paralanguage voice qualities include rate, volume, rhythm, pitch, and resonance.**

Volume is another voice quality that frequently conveys meaning, especially in conjunction with rate. If a supervisor said softly, "I would like to talk with you in my office," you might feel somewhat at ease. But if your supervisor said loudly, "I would like to talke with you in my office," you would feel disturbed and ill at ease.

The qualities of rhythm, pitch, and resonance are more difficult to understand than rate and volume. When you consider voice qualities, the major point to note is a change or deviation from the speaker's normal voice quality. Noting differences in the sender's rhythm, pitch, and resonance can often increase your understanding of the message.

The voice qualities of rate, volume, pitch, and resonance in combination with vocal qualifiers cause paralanguage to become most apparent. Earlier we demonstrated the significance of accent as a vocal qualifier by changing the emphasis placed on words. Another example of that same kind of word emphasis is evident in the phrase "I am going to the boss's house for dinner tonight." Placing emphasis on different key words can greatly vary the meaning of the sentence.

The major function of paralanguage is to express emotions. Several researchers have demonstrated that it is possible to communicate various emotions solely with paralanguage. Actors who read the following ambiguous text made sure that the meanings communicated were solely the result of vocal cues rather than vocabulary:

You've got to believe it in time to keep them from hanging me. Every night you ask me how it happened. But I don't know! I don't know! I can't remember. There is no other answer. You've asked me that question a thousand times, and my reply has always been the same. It always will be the same. You can't figure out things like that. They just happen, and afterwards you're sorry. Oh, God, stop them . . . quick . . . before it is too late![2]

The actors repeated the statement to 64 student judges and attempted to convey contempt, anger, fear, grief, and indifference. The study concluded that all those emotions could be communicated. Average accuracy of identification for the five emotions was 88 percent for indifference, 84 percent for contempt, 78 percent for anger and grief, and 66 percent for fear.

Several more recent studies have demonstrated that paralanguage—*how* we say something—does convey emotions. These studies indicate that some emotions are more accurately transmitted than others. Frequently, it is easier to convey impatience, fear, and anger than satisfaction and admiration.

Paralanguage conveys emotion.

Kinesics—How We Communicate through Body Movement

Kinesics means communicating through body movement. The face and eyes are the most expressive means of body communication. Leathers, for example, states that ten basic classes of meaning can be communicated by facial expression.[3]

The face and eyes convey ten different types of meaning.

Class 1 Happiness
    2 Surprise
    3 Fear
    4 Anger
    5 Sadness

6 Disgust
7 Contempt
8 Interest
9 Bewilderment
10 Determination

The ability to interpret facial meaning is an important part of communication, since facial expressions can facilitate or hamper feedback. Leathers developed the Facial Meaning Sensitivity Test (FMST). Part I of the FMST contains photographs representing the ten basic classes of facial meaning. To test your ability to perceive facial expression, study the ten photos in Figure 13.1 and then place the numbers in the appropriate blanks of the accompanying chart.

Eye Contact

The eyes play an especially important role in facial communication. Eye contact is one of the most powerful forms of nonverbal communication. Authority relationships as well as intimate relationships are frequently initiated and maintained with eye contact. Looking directly at your listener is usually thought to convey openness and honesty. We usually believe it is easier to trust someone who looks right at us. On the other hand, we tend to distrust those who don't look directly at us. Less confidence is attributed to those who avoid eye contact. In addition, prolonged eye contact can signal admiration, while brief eye contact usually means anxiety. While more eye contact is usually better than

Eye contact is one of the strongest forms of nonverbal communication.

Figure 13.1   Facial Meaning Sensitivity Test, Part 1

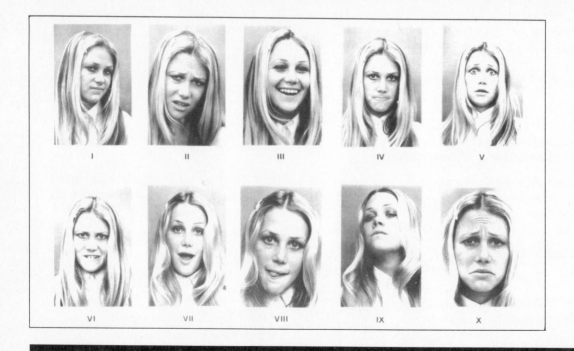

less eye contact, direct eye contact of more than ten seconds can create some discomfort and anxiety.

Gesture

Another important element of kinesic communication is the use of gestures. The language of gesture is usually thought of as hand and arm movements, but the entire body is capable of gesture.

Ekman and Friesen identify five types of body gesture: (1) emblems, (2) illustrators, (3) regulators, (4) affect displays, and (5) adaptors.[4] *Emblems* are thought of as sign language and are the equivalent of words or phrases. For example, the thumb and forefinger held in a circle say OK. The index and middle fingers held up in the form of a *V* indicate victory. *Illustrators* are directly tied to verbal language and illustrate the words a speaker is saying. When a speaker says, "My third and final point is . . ." and holds up three fingers, this gesture is an illustrator. When a baseball umpire calls someone out at home plate, he uses an illustrator as he points his thumb up and quickly jerks his hand upward. *Regulators* control oral communication by alerting the sender of the need to hurry up, slow down, or repeat something. Examples of regulators are frequently looking at your watch or drumming your fingers on the table when someone is talking with you.

Affect displays indicate emotional states, such as anger or embarrassment, and usually occur in facial expressions. Affect displays differ from the three previous categories in that people have far less control over them. Many of us, for example, have felt our face turning red because we were angry or embarrassed, but there is little we can do to control this affect display. *Adaptors* are another type of gesture that people have little control over. Frequently we are not conscious of performing such gestures. Stifling a yawn or clasping hands to face in fear illustrate adaptor gestures.

Posture

A person's general posture, even without specific gestures, communicates meaning. Posture frequently gives us clues to the self-confidence or status of a person. For example, superiors usually take a more relaxed posture than their subordinates.[5] Posture is also a way we demonstrate our interest in another person. Several writers have concluded that when you lean forward to the person you are speaking with, you demonstrate interest in that person. Sitting back, on the other hand, may communicate a lack of interest.

It is difficult to assess exactly how important gesture and posture are as modes of communication. Apparently, however, gesture and pos-

Posture of superiors and subordinates conveys meaning.

Some firms make selection decisions primarily on the basis of posture and gesture.

ture are assuming more importance in organizational life. A London-based management consultant, Warren Lamb, has developed his business based on the idea that a person's posture and gesture can tell much about how effectively a person will perform in an organization. Lamb claims that his program, called *movement analysis,* represents a new branch of applied behavioral science.[6] Corporations hire Lamb to help in the selection and promotion of managers. He conducts his work by holding an interview session and watching for the following body movements and their meanings.

Side-to-side movements are most evident when a person shakes hands. This person would normally move the arm in a sideways, circular motion and occupy a lot of space when talking. Such an individual is an effective informer and listener—in short, an effective communicator. According to Lamb this individual is best suited for companies seeking a sense of direction in their business ventures.

Forward and backward movements occur when an individual extends the hand straight forward when shaking hands and leans forward during an interview. The person using these forward and backward movements is described as an operator. Lamb would assign this type of person to an organization that needs a dramatic change or an infusion of energy.

Vertical movements take place during the handshake, when the person using vertical movements draws himself or herself up to the tallest posture possible. According to Lamb, this individual is the master salesman or presenter, an expert at selling himself or the company.

Again, no single gesture can always be accurately interpreted. However, Lamb asserts that the three categories of gesture—side-to-side, forward and backward, and vertical—enable him to identify and place executives where they will function most effectively.

While most of us will not make our living the way Lamb does, on a daily basis we will need to understand what people are communicating with their posture and gestures. Knapp has provided a useful scheme for classifying major types of body movements.[7] The following classifications are based primarily upon Knapp's work and are briefly presented to aid your understanding of how we communicate with our bodies.

Leathers has developed a method to measure the quality of nonverbal communication across many dimensions. This system—the Leathers Nonverbal Feedback Rating Instrument (LNFRI)—is presented in Figure 13.2 to show the diversity of meaning in gestural and postural communication.

We all have *attitudes,* since we all like or dislike particular elements in our environment. Many times these attitudes are reflected in body movement. The degree of like or dislike can be seen in terms of general body orientation by noting if the communicator's legs and shoulders are turned toward or away from the other person. When the body is turned fully toward the other person, it may indicate a liking, while the body turned away may indicate a degree of dislike.

Individuals in superior roles or positions have *status.* They frequently keep their heads raised when communicating with others. Those in lower or subordinate roles often lower their heads and shoulders when speaking.

Affective states of moods, which occur in various degrees of emotional conditions, are associated with body movements. The head and face are thought to convey information about anger, joy, and happiness; other body movements are thought to convey the intensity of the particular emotional state.

Approval seeking is evidenced by people who nod their heads and smile to secure approval from another person. In general, their bodies are more active than when they are not seeking approval. Frequently, one can observe this type of bodily activity by watching a subordinate present an idea to a superior.

Inclusiveness involves cues as to whose side you are on. The positioning of the body, especially the way the legs are pointed, will communicate, "I am on your side and not on their side." It can also indicate whether someone is open-minded or closed-minded to the other person's ideas.

Interaction markers are certain body movements that naturally accompany particular oral language. Frequently, at the end of a statement a person will move the head, eyelids, or hands downward. At the end of questioning statements, these movements will tend to be upward. Other types of interaction markers include leaning back when one is listening and leaning forward when one is speaking.

Although it is easy to oversimplify the classifications, it is important to realize that kinesic behavior affects the communication process. Having some basic understanding of how we communicate with our bodies will make us more effective communicators.

Proxemics—Communicating with Space

The third major type of nonverbal communication is proxemics or how we communicate with space. How close or far we stand in relation to the other person, where we sit in a room, or how we arrange the office furniture has a real impact upon communication. One of the major writers on this type of communication is an anthropologist, Edward T. Hall. He identifies three major types of space: feature-fixed space, semi-fixed feature space, and personal space.[8]

All of us communicate by the use of space around us.

Feature-Fixed Space

This type of space refers to buildings and other fairly permanent structures, such as walls. The manner in which buildings are laid out and the sequence of rooms and offices have a considerable influence on com-

Figure 13.2 Leathers Nonverbal Feedback Rating Instrument

Displeased 7 : 6 : 5 : 4 : 3 : 2 : 1

Spontaneous 7 : 6 : 5 : 4 : 3 : 2 : 1

Pleased 7 : 6 : 5 : 4 : 3 : 2 : 1

Deliberative 7 : 6 : 5 : 4 : 3 : 2 : 1

Uncertain 7 : 6 : 5 : 4 : 3 : 2 : 1

Withdrawn 7 : 6 : 5 : 4 : 3 : 2 : 1

Confident 7 : 6 : 5 : 4 : 3 : 2 : 1

Involved 7 : 6 : 5 : 4 : 3 : 2 : 1

Attentive 7 : 6 : 5 : 4 : 3 : 2 : 1 Unattentive

Responsive 7 : 6 : 5 : 4 : 3 : 2 : 1 Unresponsive

Clear 7 : 6 : 5 : 4 : 3 : 2 : 1 Confused

Analytical 7 : 6 : 5 : 4 : 3 : 2 : 1 Impulsive

Friendly 7 : 6 : 5 : 4 : 3 : 2 : 1 Hostile

Interested 7 : 6 : 5 : 4 : 3 : 2 : 1 Disinterested

Photographed by John Penrose

munication. You will probably communicate more with those individuals whose offices are closer rather than farther from yours.

Semifixed Feature Space

The placement and arrangement of movable objects, such as desks and chairs, is referred to as semifixed feature space. There is currently a great deal of emphasis on how business offices are arranged. Frequently, the superior person will come from behind the desk and sit face to face with the subordinate to make it easier to communicate. Several studies in hospital settings demonstrate that the arrangement of beds in a room will have a significant effect upon communication among the patients.

Personal Space

The physical distance we maintain in our encounters with others is known as personal space. Hall suggests four different zones or distances for different types of social interaction. These zones are intimate distance, personal distance, social distance, and public distance.

Figure 13.3 Nonverbal Communication of Interest Level

Intimate Distance. This distance ranges from actual physical contact to about 18 inches from another person. Communication and interaction within this distance are intimate activities. In organizations confidential information is often communicated within the intimate distance. The major form of intimate contact in business organizations is, of course, the handshake. Most people respond positively to men who give a firm handshake and negatively to men who give a limp handshake. Men respond positively to women who have either a firm or limp handshake. Many women, however, do not respond positively to a firm handshake from another woman.

Communication zones determine social interaction.

Personal Distance. Personal distance ranges from 18 inches to four feet. Interaction in this zone includes casual and friendly conversation.

Social Distance. A distance of from four feet to about eight feet is called social distance. Communication in this zone often occurs in the business setting. Much of the communication in organizations is done at social distance.

Figure 13.4 What Do These Photographs Suggest about the Status of These Persons in Their Organizations?

Photographed by Dan McClure

Public Distance.   This kind of distance ranges from 12 feet to the limits of visibility and hearing. Communication at public distance is considered public speaking. A good deal of communication within and outside an organization takes place at this range.

All of us are aware of some of the ways space is used to communicate in business organizations. Goldhaber, for example, has identified three basic principles about the use of space as it relates to status within the organization.[9]

1.   **The higher people are in the organization, the more and better space they are allotted.** In many organizations the president has the most attractive office, while the vice president, the department heads, and lesser officers have succeedingly smaller offices. The number of windows in the office and the way the office is furnished are also commensurate with rank or position.

2.   **The higher people are in the organization, the better protected their territory is.** Many times the more status a person has in the organization, the more difficult it is to see that person. Outer offices and secretaries often are used to protect the high-status person.

3.   **The higher people are within the organization, the easier it is for them to invade the territory of lower-status personnel.** The supervisor usually can enter the subordinate's office at will. The supervisor also has the ability to phone the subordinate at almost any time. However, the subordinate usually does not have this same access to the supervisor.

Now that we have discussed the three major categories of nonverbal communication, we can briefly examine some other areas that receive less attention, but nevertheless play an important role in communication.

The space we occupy in the organization communicates much about our status in the organization.

Dress and Appearance

All of us have heard the cliche, "clothes make the person." However, most of us are not aware of the impact that our clothing has on those around us. John Molloy, a consultant on executive dress with major corporations, has conducted several experiments to see what various types of clothing communicate.[10] In one of his studies Molloy compared the impact of black and beige raincoats. He took a set of twin pictures with only one variable: the pictures showed the same man in the same pose dressed in the same suit, the same shirt, the same shoes, the same tie. The only difference was the raincoat—one black, the other beige. Participants were told the pictures were of twin brothers and were asked to identify the more prestigious of the two brothers. Over 87 percent of the 1,362 people in the study chose the man wearing the beige raincoat as the more prestigious.

In another set of experiments Molloy found a group of 27 restaurants

Clothing communicates much about us to others.

in New York where ties are not required. In each restaurant he asked the head waiter to divide the dining room into two sample sections of most perferred seating areas and least preferred areas. Those areas near the street door and near the kitchen door were considered to be the least preferable. Invariably there was a disproportionate number of men who were not wearing ties in the less preferable areas; in fact, almost no men without ties were seated in the more preferable areas.

While the above experiments are interesting, the basic question remains: does the way a person dresses communicate something to others in the organization? The impact of dress is placed in perspective by Molloy early in his book, *Dress for Success:*

*O*ver the years I have conducted literally thousands of studies, experiments and tests to aid my corporate and individual clients in using clothing better and as an indispensable tool of business life. Immediately prior to beginning this book, and specifically for this book, I asked several series of questions of 100 top executives in either the medium-sized or major American Corporations. The first series was to establish the most up-to-date attitudes on corporate dress.

I showed the executives five pictures of men, each of them wearing expensive, well-tailored, but high-fashion clothing. I asked if this was a proper look for the junior business executive. Ninety-two of the men said no, eight said yes.

I showed them five pictures of men neatly dressed in obvious lower-middle-class attire and asked if these men were dressed in proper attire for a young executive. Forty-six said yes, fifty-four said no.

I next showed them five pictures of men dressed in conservative upper-middle-class clothing and asked if they were dressed in proper attire for the young executive. All one hundred said yes.

I asked them whether they thought the men in the upper-middle-class garb would succeed better in corporate life than the men in the lower-middle-class uniform. Eighty-eight said yes, twelve said no.

I asked if they would choose one of the men in the lower-middle-class dress as their assistant. Ninety-two said no, eight said yes.[11] ∎

Top executives have an unwritten code for corporate dress.

Molloy clearly finds that dress and appearance can communicate various messages in the business setting. Outside the business world, clothing communicates as well. For example, T-shirts, which have been called the "graffiti of the 1980s," often are used to show allegiance to our favorite rock group, to identify where we spent our last vacation, to publicize our college, club, or fraternity affiliation, or just to say something to the world.

Clothing styles and appearance change with time and depend on context. We might guess a man's military vocation, even out of uniform, by his short haircut. The jeans worn by working people for years took on a new and almost universal appeal with the advent of designer jeans in the early 1980s. Not too long ago businesswomen, particularly in executive roles, were encouraged by both fashion and some experts to wear the corporate uniform of the three-piece suit. Shortly afterward, the three-piece suit was no longer recommended, because the appearance was perceived as an invasion of the man's world, rather than an effort by women to be accepted in the corporate world. Furthermore, the look was unnecessarily and inappropriately unfeminine.

Whether or not we are correct in our evaluation of the wearer, certainly most of us are aware of others' clothing. Most of our own clothing decisions are not made on exclusively functional grounds.

Color

The communication involved in the choice of color can be related to dress because color in clothing affects communication. There is some evidence that there is a relationship between specific moods and color. This relationship, in terms of color, mood, and frequency of times chosen, is illustrated in Table 13.2.

Color is related to particular moods.

Colors that surround us affect us. In rooms with warm or hot colors, such as reds or oranges for example, we are likely to be more creative,

Table 13.2 Matching Colors with Moods

Mood Tone	Color	Frequency of Times Chosen
Exciting, stimulating	Red	61
Secure, comfortable	Blue	41
Distressed, disturbed, upset	Orange	34
Tender, soothing	Blue	41
Protective, defending	Red	21
	Brown	17
	Blue	15
	Black	15
	Purple	14
Despondent, dejected, unhappy, melancholy	Black	25
	Brown	25
Calm, peaceful, serene	Blue	38
	Green	31
Dignified, stately	Purple	45
Cheerful, jovial, joyful	Yellow	40
Defiant, contrary, hostile	Red	23
	Orange	21
	Black	18
Powerful, strong, masterful	Black	48

L.B. Wexner, "The Degree to which Colors (Hues) Are Associated with Mood-Tones," *Journal of Applied Psychology*, 38 (1954): 432–435. Table from *Nonverbal Communication in Human Interaction* 2 ed. by Mark L. Knapp. Copyright 1978 by Holt, Rinehart and Winston. Reprinted by permission of Holt, Rinehart and Winston.

stimulated, and prone to quick decisions. Rooms with cooler colors, such as blues, will likely engender solitude, slow, deep and methodical thinking, and detachment.

Men and women often describe colors with different language. Men may likely describe objects as being purple, blue, and yellow, while women might describe the same objects as, "fuchsia, robin's egg blue, and canary yellow.

Check the colors of a fast-food establishment, a church, and a classroom. There's a good chance that the colors enhance the desired image or mind set. If your classroom is devoid of color, that absence is probably not an accident but a carefully planned effort.

Time

Being early, on time, or late communicates much in our society. Setting and meeting deadlines is also important. The employee who is habitually late for work and misses deadlines communicates very little interest in the job. Another observation about time is that individuals with high status are usually able to get appointments sooner and their meetings with superiors usually last longer. They wait less in the waiting room. High-status people usually have more flexible work hours. We even hear about banker's hours as the working day for higher-status individuals.

Another way in which time communicates is the amount of time it takes to provide or receive feedback. For example, if we make a written request of someone and they respond too quickly, we may believe they have not carefully considered our request. On the other hand, if a long period of time lapses and we still have not had a response, we will believe it is because of a lack of interest even though formal communication has not taken place.

Among the major aspects of nonverbal communication that are influential in the business setting, there are some other items which can be given less attention. These include:

▫ Uniforms—such as bankers' clothes, nurses outfits, or your interviewing outfit, transmit special messages.

▫ Women's make-up, perfume, and jewelry and men's aftershave, beards, and even tattoos can be powerful communicators.

▫ The attention a teacher gives primarily to the front and middle section of the classroom is a unique form of interaction.

▫ The owner of the charcoal-cooked hamburger establishment knows quite well what effect the grill exhaust has on passersby when exhaust is blown into the street.

▫ The especially unusual behavior most of us exhibit on elevators—being quiet, avoiding physical and eye contact, and concentrating on the floor indicator numbers—can be fascinating to study.

▫ The high-status individual who doesn't have to face us but whose eyes we will try to contact, even if we must back out of their presence, is establishing or exercising authority.

It's important to be aware of how deception can be apparent in our communication. We are taught, over many years, how to manipulate our verbal communication. Some people become quite adept at lying with words. However, few can manipulate their nonverbal behavior much beyond such obvious changes as clothing or the surrounding environment. If we're experiencing stage fright, for example, it's hard for us to turn off our nonverbal messages of perspiration, white knuckles, or a cracking voice.

We receive little practice or instruction in how to modify our nonverbal communication, which makes the application of nonverbal communication to public presentations and speech making very important. Even though we know we have little effect over our emotions, and these emotions present themselves in recognizable nonverbal patterns, we can modify our behavior somewhat.

What are some nonverbal behaviors associated with effective oral presentations? Here are some, with some suggestions on overcoming nonverbal problems:

▫ A relaxed speaker tends to gesture, but not too much. A nervous speaker either avoids gestures and movement, or tends to overdo it.

▫ The confident speaker doesn't show perspiration; the nervous speaker is not so controlled. Dress lightly so you don't start out too warm.

▫ Visual contact with your audience enhances a presentation. This visual contact also scares many speakers. One well-known approach is to avoid direct eye contact by looking just above the eyes of your audience. Then, as you become more confident, you can work your way up to effective direct eye contact. A similar technique for using eye contact is to try to talk to and look at your audience one by one. Try not to think of the large group, but rather engage a person on one side of the room for a few seconds, then look at a person in the middle, and then one on the other side of the room. Most effective speakers use this technique not so much to overcome nervousness, but more for a personal touch.

▫ Effective voice control affects the impact of a speech greatly. An overrehearsed speech often comes out in a monotone no matter how enthusiastic the speaker. On the other hand, an ill-prepared speaker is likely to exhibit the cracking voice, gasping, or swallowing that we associate with nervousness. Try to pace yourself in terms of speed. A speaker who is unconfident is likely to change delivery speed in one of two directions: by either speeding up or slowing down. Aim for a normal delivery rate.

▫ Hands and fingers are not obtrusive for the confident speaker; they tend to shake for the nervous speaker. This shaking is amplified many times over if you point with a pencil at a transparency during overhead projector use. If you plant your pencil solidly on the film, you won't shake.

▫   Some effective speakers move around behind the podium somewhat but usually not too much. Beware of the speaker's shuffle. This side-to-side balancing often can be overcome if you remember to put one foot forward and one backward diagonally.

There are many other ways that nonverbal behavior affects the reception of an oral message. Our goal here is to view a few dimensions of the interplay between effective verbal and nonverbal communication.

Summary

After this discussion of paralanguage (how we say something), kinesics (how we communicate with our bodies), proxemics (how we communicate with space), and communication with dress and appearance, color, and time, we should be more aware of the impact of nonverbal communication. The importance of nonverbal communication is clear when you realize that about 90 percent of the total impact of a message can come from the nonverbal elements.

As we sharpen our skills at decoding nonverbal communication, we must avoid putting too much emphasis on any single cue. Just as one word out of context can be misleading, one nonverbal cue out of context can lead us astray. The more thoroughly one analyzes the entire context of the communication interaction, the less likely one is to decode the message inaccurately.

Finally, we should note that whenever there is a discrepancy between verbal and nonverbal messages, we favor the nonverbal cues because they are more spontaneous and free of deception. For example, when you tell a young man that you are interested in what he is saying but your tone of voice conveys a lack of interest, that lack of interest is what is received. This observation simply underscores the need for placing additional emphasis on nonverbal communication. We need to make sure that our nonverbal communication is consistent with our verbal message.

Footnotes

[1] *The Wall Street Journal,* Tuesday, April 17, 1979, p. 1.

[2] G. Fairbanks and W. Pronovost, "An Experimental Study of the Durational Characteristics of the Voice During the Expression of Emotion," *Speech Monographs,* 6 (1939): 88.

[3] Dale Leathers, *Nonverbal Communication Systems* (Boston: Allyn and Bacon, 1976), p. 24.

[4]P. Ekman and W. Friesen, "The Repertoire of Nonverbal Behavior: Categories, Origins, Usage, and Coding," *Semiotics* 1 (1969): 63–92.

[5]R. Harrison, *Beyond Words: An Introduction to Nonverbal Communication* (Englewood Cliffs, N.J.: Prentice-Hall, 1974), pp. 132–133.

[6]Jean Ross-Skinner, "Those Telltale Executive Gestures," *Dun's Review* (March 1970): 66–67.

[7]M. Knapp, *Nonverbal Communication in Human Interaction,* 2d ed. (New York: Holt, Rinehart and Winston, 1978), pp. 220–232.

[8]E. T. Hall, *The Hidden Dimension* (New York: Doubleday, 1966).

[9]G. Goldhaber, *Organizational Communication,* 3d ed. (Dubuque, Ia.: William C. Brown, 1983), pp. 192–194.

[10]John T. Molloy, *Dress for Success* (New York: Peter Wyden, 1975).

[11]Ibid., pp. 27–28.

Review Questions

1. Why do nonverbal messages play such a critical role in communication?
2. How can paralanguage reinforce or undermine the verbal message?
3. Cite examples of how facial expressions attach emotional meaning to our messages.
4. In what ways is gesture an important means of kinesic communication?
5. How can posture provide clues to the self-confidence or status of a person in a business organization?
6. How is space used as a communication device?
7. In what ways might your dress and appearance and the way you handle time impress your business colleagues?

Exercises

1. Identify some nonverbal rules such as books and coat in a library chair marking a person's territory. Then break the rule, in this case by moving the books and coat and sitting in the chair.
2. Observe and record people's behavior in elevators. List as many nonverbal behavior patterns as you can. Compare these patterns to those of people using escalators. What are the differences? Why do you think these differences exist?
3. Most of us feel comfortable in a classroom and think little about its nonverbal aspects. Identify the nonverbal patterns of students and instructors in typical classrooms.
4. What is the appropriate dress and appearance in a typical business setting? How much can you vary from this standard without being penalized?
5. What are the nonverbal aspects of music? Does music create different moods in different people at different times? How? Give examples. How is music used in business?

Case

The Disappointing Interview
Mary Jane Nelson Riley
Central State University

Dick Evans was out when Paula Winfield arrived early for her job interview. In two weeks Paula would complete her MBA. She had already interviewed with two of CMG's competitors. Although these other jobs were promising, a job with CMG had been her primary motivation for finishing an MBA.

Paula had an excellent academic record and experience which was more than adequate for the CMG position. Dick Evans's secretary ushered her into his office and said, "Dick had to go check on something in the shop. He's been having some difficulty out there for two weeks. I'm not sure how long he will be, so make yourself at home." It was an unusually large office with a desk and chairs on one side and a more comfortable area with a couch, table and magazines on the other side.

At first Paula took a chair near the desk, but as time passed the magazines on the table across the office looked inviting, so she moved to the couch. When Dick arrived 45 minutes later, she was so engrossed that he had to call her name before she realized he was in the room. Dick seemed a bit irritated and distracted throughout the interview. Although Paula responded well to his questions, Dick was not very receptive and at times was abrupt. She left 20 minutes later thinking she had blown the interview. On the way home, she went over the day's events in her mind, concluding that she wouldn't want to work for such a grouch and that one of the other jobs would have to do.

When the phone rang the next morning and Dick invited her back for a second interview, Paula was surprised. The man on the telephone seemed like a different person. Dick apologized for his bad mood and asked her to give him and CMG another chance. Paula agreed to the interview, but she continued to wonder how her first impression of Dick could have been so wrong.

■ ■ ■

Case Questions

1. What might have helped Paula form a more accurate perception of Dick and the interview?
2. Why was it difficult for Paula to be other than self-centered in this situation?
3. How might Dick have helped Paula?
4. What nonverbal miscues did Paula receive?

Case

Body Language
Mildred W. Landrum
Kennesaw College

Mike Thornton was seething. Everytime it looked as if he had finally straightened out his production supervisor, Steve Perkins, Steve managed to blow another situation with one of the workers. This time the worker had walked out, and the line had to be slowed down while a replacement was found.

This was a critical time for Mike. The vice president in charge of production was coming from New York for an inspection tour of the southeastern plant, and Mike wanted everything to go right. His future with the corporation depended on it.

For the third time he called in Steve to talk with him. Steve had better understand this time that he was really in trouble. Twelve years with the corporation gave him seniority, and the union would be difficult to handle if he fired Steve. Mike had to be sure Steve was impressed with the seriousness of the situation.

When the secretary buzzed Mike that Steve was in the waiting room, Mike said, "Let him cool his heels." Fifteen minutes later he asked Steve to come into the office. Mike did not raise his head and greet Steve, nor did he rise to shake hands as he would normally have done. Steve stood at his desk several moments before Mike looked up and said, "Sit down." The telephone rang, and Mike talked five minutes before putting down the receiver. He then turned to Steve, folded his arms, leaned back, and said, "Well, tell me about this one."

Steve was upset by the extremely negative attitude he felt from Mike. He dropped his eyes, lifted his hands in a hopeless gesture, and said, "Well, what can you do with some of these guys who think they know everything?"

■ ■ ■

Case Questions

1. Describe the negative nonverbal messages Mike sent to indicate his displeasure with Steve.
2. Describe the submissive nonverbal messages Steve sent to Mike.
3. Give a positive movement for each negative movement named in this interaction.

Public Presentations

Learning Objectives
1. To recognize the importance of public speaking to the individual, to the organization, and to society.
2. To identify audience characteristics that should influence your approach in speaking.
3. To learn several methods of organizing a speech and the benefits of each method.
4. To recognize stage fright as a normal phenomenon and to learn methods for controlling it.
5. To understand the different modes for delivering a speech and to identify settings in which each would be appropriate.
6. To integrate and practice the principles presented, thus learning how to give a superior public presentation.

Bill Jones had just finished his first six months as a supervisor. Today his six-month appraisal was scheduled with his boss, Hank Sims. Although Bill believed he had done a good job during his first six months, he was still a little nervous as he entered Hank's office for the appraisal session.

The appraisal session lasted 30 minutes. Hank was very positive about Bill's first six months as a supervisor. The session went even better than Bill had expected. At the end of the session Hank shook Bill's hand and as Bill started for the door, Hank said, "Oh, I almost forgot, we got a request from one of the local civic clubs to provide a speaker for their next meeting in two weeks—Bill, I want you to handle the speech." Bill had such a sinking feeling in his stomach he did not even hear the topic that Hank told him the group wanted to hear about.

Bill had never given a public speech, nor did he have any great desire to do so. Just the idea of standing in front of a group and talking was enough to make Bill break into a cold sweat. At first he looked for excuses to get out of the obligation, but the fact that his boss expected him to speak for him made it impossible to avoid.

After worrying about the speech for five days, Bill finally started working on it. He found the research fairly easy to do, but he had a difficult time trying to organize it in some logical way. How to make this dry subject interesting to the audience also presented problems.

The nearer the day of the speech came, the more apprehensive Bill was about it. He would lie awake nights thinking about it. When he was able to sleep, he would dream about the speech. One night he dreamed that he completely forgot what he wanted to say; another time he saw himself fainting at the speaker's stand. His most frequent dream was one in which he gave his speech and everyone in the audience fell asleep.

"If I can get through this speech," Bill thought, "I'm never going to give another one." To his own surprise Bill not only got through it, but several members of the audience were interested enough to ask him questions. He actually enjoyed handling the questions, but he vowed that there would be no more speeches for him.

Three days later, Bill received a letter from the company president praising his speech. In the letter the president said he hoped that Bill would "continue to serve as an effective representative of the company," and advised him, "Strive to become more visible in the local community." Bill started thinking that perhaps his speechmaking days were not over after all. ∎

The purpose of this chapter is to introduce you to a systematic approach to public speaking. Selecting and researching a topic will be discussed along with the way to analyze an audience. You will learn how to organize and outline a speech and how to deliver it effectively. This chapter will help you to develop your public speaking ability in any situation, whether you are the main speaker at a public event or one of several speakers in a symposium.

Public Speaking: The Individual, the Organization, and Society

A survey of 2,500 Americans indicated that speaking before a group was feared by over 40 percent of those surveyed.[1] Those surveyed were asked to pick the items from a list of many situations. The first ten items chosen were:

Speaking before a group	40.6%
Height	30.0
Insects	22.1
Financial problems	22.0
Deep water	21.5
Sickness	18.8
Death	18.7
Flying	18.3
Loneliness	13.6
Dogs	11.2

There is a widesprea
fear of public speakir
but it can be overcon
through a systematic
approach to the
problem.

Even though it may come as no surprise to learn that many people fear giving public speeches, the fact that the fear is so widespread is certainly impressive. Such a fear can be overcome, however, by learning to apply a systematic approach to the entire process of public speaking. By approaching the problem systematically you may remove much of the uncertainty and apprehension that routinely surrounds public speaking and replace it with the stability of following a planned approach. Until the uncertainties surrounding public speaking are resolved, you and a large portion of the population may continue to fear giving a speech.

A systematic approac
may reduce some of
the uncertainties
associated with publi
speaking.

Public speaking is important in many different ways. Becauses it encompasses so many aspects of our lives, we will consider public speaking from the standpoint of the individual, the organization, and the society.

The Individual

When you apply for a job, the employment interviewer evaluates you on the basis of certain characteristics. Your ability to communicate is one such characteristic, and it comes across clearly in an interview. Your ability to communicate not only influences whether you are hired, but it in part determines your progress on the job. Employers realize that

Guidelines for Establishing Credibility

Be knowledgeable about your subject and well-prepared to speak. (Expertise)

Develop and maintain a reputation for telling the truth. (Trust)

Display an urge to communicate through your genuine involvement with both subject and audience. (Dynamism)

Be open-minded to the views of others. (Objective)

Be considerate of the feelings of others. (Goodwill)

A message from a credible source is more likely to be accepted.

the ability to communicate often separates an exceptional employee from the average ones.

Being able to organize your thoughts and give a public speech is another significant determinant of your personal and professional success. When you speak and others listen and respond to your comments, it affects the way you see yourself and how others see you. Being able to give an effective public speech enhances your self-esteem; you feel good about yourself.

Your message is more likely to be accepted if you have credibility with your audience. Source credibility, discussed in Chapter 7, pertains to both oral and written communication.

Your credibility as a speaker and as a person will be recognized to the extent that you are perceived as expert, trustworthy, dynamic, objective, and being of goodwill.

Public speaking ability has a major influence on one's personal and professional success.

The Organization

It has been said that an organization is only as good as the individuals who comprise it. It could also be said that an organization communicates only as effectively as its individual members do.

When Robert Drake entered the management training program, there was very little that set him apart from the other trainees. In terms of educational background and technical ability the trainees were very similar. Robert soon displayed an ability to organize his thoughts and to express himself in a manner that was distinctly superior to that of the other trainees. By the end of the training program no one was surprised when he was awarded the choicest job assignment ever given to a trainee. That was 24 years ago, and today Robert is the president of the company. He is the first one to recognize the importance of technical ability, but as he sees it, "Unless a person is able to transmit

*information to others in a well-organized and convincing way, that per-
son is likely to remain a technician—and a mediocre one at that."* ■

There is a need in business for people who can effectively present the
organizational viewpoint to the public. The average business organization
does a poor job of acquainting the public with its contributions to
society.

From a communication standpoint it does not matter how pure the
motives of the organization are. What does matter is what the public
knows about such things and how the public responds to this knowledge. Unless the public is made aware of what business is doing and
why, the best intentions of business will be to no avail.

Only through effective external communication can business present
the information that is most likely to result in a desirable image. One of
the most important and effective formats used to present that information is the public speech.

**Unless business makes
the public aware of its
many contributions to
society, the public will
continue to see
business in a negative
light.**

**Business presents its
message to the public
through external
communication.**

The Society

We live in a society in which free expression of ideas is not merely
tolerated, but encouraged. Issues are analyzed and points of view are
presented in many different formats. Newspaper editorials, listener call-
in shows on radio, town hall meetings, and barroom discussions (or
arguments) are a few settings in which opinions are aired on subjects.

Our society thrives on this free expression of ideas, for it is through
such interchange that a balanced perspective is maintained. When a certain point of view ceases to be expressed, perhaps for the lack of
someone willing and able to speak out, that viewpoint no longer influences society.

Through public speaking ideas are presented for public evaluation.
This was as true in the preliminaries to the Declaration of Independence
as it is today in election campaigns. It is as evident at an annual meeting
of stockholders as at a monthly union local meeting.

For lack of an effective speaker a good idea may fail to be considered.
A lack of articulate opponents may result in the passage of legislation of
little merit. Our free society requires willing and articulate people of
every viewpoint.

**A well-balanced
society depends upon
the articulation of
varying viewpoints.
Effective public
speaking contributes
to this balance.**

The General Purpose

*A*s the crowd filed out of the lecture hall, Ted and Sue began to compare the notes each had taken on the speech they had just heard. They
had just listened to a candidate for the U.S. Senate give a speech entitled "The USA: Leader or Follower?" Ted and Sue were frustrated to
learn that they disagreed as to what the speaker had actually said.

Since their class had been assigned to hear the speech, it was the subject of the following day's class discussion. There was considerable disagreement within the class as to what the speaker had said. Approximately one third of the students believed that the need for a stronger national defense was his main point. Another third of the class maintained that a need for more social action programs was his main point. There was even greater disagreement among the remaining third of the class, in which two persons said that they had no idea what the speaker's main point had been. ■

These are some common responses to public speeches:

- "I'm not sure exactly what he meant."
- "I couldn't find any point to the speech."
- "I don't know what she was getting at."
- "What was the purpose of that speech anyway?"

The person who made the last comment got to the heart of a significant problem. Many speakers seem unable or unwilling to determine in advance the purpose of their speech. This is a great mistake. In planning a speech you should first decide what its purposes will be. This is a two-step process: determine the general purpose, then determine the specific purpose.

Most authorities recognize three possible general purposes: (1) to inform, (2) to persuade, and (3) to entertain. There are many possible specific purposes, since specific purposes are determined on the basis of a wide variety of factors.

> **The three general purposes are to inform, to persuade, and to entertain.**

To Inform

When you try to teach the listeners or to explain something to them, your general purpose is to inform. The classroom lecture is an example of an informative speech. Some informative speeches are intended to acquaint the listeners with something completely new to them. When Brenda White, a personnel director, explains to a group of new employees the company's benefits program, she is doing just that. Some informative speakers try to update listeners who are already somewhat knowledgeable about the subject. For example, when officers of credit unions attend the regional meeting of their trade association, they hear many informative speeches.

To Persuade

The second general purpose is to persuade the listener. Persuasive speeches range from those that seek to change the listeners' beliefs or attitudes to those that attempt to get the listeners to act in a certain way. Your purposes for giving a persuasive speech can be put into two very general but distinct categories: (1) to elicit a covert response, and (2) to elicit an overt response.

A covert response is, as the word implies, not readily apparent to the speaker nor to an observer. When a union leader seeks to convince the members that the union has their interests at heart, the speaker is seeking a covert response, acceptance of an idea. It is usually difficult to evaluate a speaker's effectiveness when the response being sought is covert.

Evaluating a speaker's effectiveness is easier when the speaker is seeking an overt response, one that is observable and measurable. The manager who tries to get the billing clerks to reduce their errors can check future error counts for evidence of effectiveness. The production manager who urges increased output from production workers can also measure results easily. In each of these examples the speaker is seeking an overt response.

> **It is easier for a speaker to measure effectiveness in seeking an overt response than in seeking a covert response.**

To Entertain

The third general purpose is to entertain—the response sought from the listeners is enjoyment. Many persons consider entertainment and humor to be synonymous, but that is not the case. Humor is certainly a common ingredient of entertainment, but it is not the only one. Perhaps you have had a teacher who thoroughly entertained and captivated the class with little or no humor. Some speakers who are enthusiastic about their subjects entertain their listeners. Others are able to entertain through their flair for drama or through their picturesque language.

The Specific Purpose

While there are only three general purposes for making a presentation, the number of specific purposes is virtually infinite. The specific purpose of a speech is constructed with both the subject and the audience in mind.

The following examples suggest the relationship among subject, audience, general purpose, and specific purpose.

Subject	**The collection of delinquent accounts**
Audience	**A class of undergraduate students of business administration**
General purpose	**To inform**
Specific purpose	**To explain techniques commonly used by business organizations to collect past-due bills from customers**

Subject	**The collection of delinquent accounts**
Audience	**Professional association of collection officers**
General purpose	**To inform**
Specific purpose	**To explain the latest approaches for collection of delinquent accounts**
Subject	**Use of nuclear energy for generating electrical power**
Audience	**Approximately 100 members of a neighborhood homeowners association**
General purpose	**To persuade**
Specific purpose	**To persuade listeners to write their senators and representatives to express their opposition to increased reliance on nuclear energy**

These examples indicate that while the general purpose may remain the same, the specific purpose will vary according to the audience. Although the three general purposes are usually considered separate and distinct, that is not actually true. Very few speeches are entirely informative, persuasive, or entertaining. Most speeches are in fact a combination of two or more of these general purposes.

Advance Audience Analysis

The more you can learn about your audience before your speech, the more appropriate your speech should be.

When Congressman Lilburn was invited to address the Wilbanks Employees Association at their monthly meeting, he immediately accepted. Since he would be seeking reelection soon, he was trying to get as much visibility as possible. His campaign theme was the need for more economical government, so he planned to speak on that issue.

He arrived at the auditorium barely on time, and he was introduced immediately. He spoke with vigor and emotion as he lashed out at excessive government spending. His special target was the social security system and the absurdity of it. To say that he got a cool response would be an understatement. Although the audience numbered nearly 200, only two persons asked questions, and both questions were hostile.

Had the congressman bothered to do research on the Wilbanks Employees Association in advance, he would have learned that most of the active members are retired employees. After the meeting he often wondered how many votes he lost because of that particular speech.

■

When you are asked to give a speech, there are some basic questions that you should ask immediately. The answers to these questions will facilitate the preparation of the speech:

- □ How large will the audience be?
- □ How educated are the listeners?
- □ What occupations will be represented?
- □ What is the age range represented?
- □ To which social, political, or religious groups do the listeners belong?

The answers to such questions will reduce some of the uncertainty surrounding the public-speaking situation.

Many speakers miss their target because they made no attempt to analyze the audience. A common shortcoming among speakers is a tendency to assume that what they find interesting will also interest the listeners.

In order to be a good speaker you must adopt a listener orientation. When preparing a speech, ask yourself how you would feel if you were in the listener's place. Before being able to answer that, you must learn as much about the listeners as possible, and this necessitates analyzing the audience.

The best way to analyze an audience is to talk personally with prospective audience members. Ideally you would accomplish this far enough in advance to give you ample time to tailor the material to the listeners. Unfortunately, this is an unrealistic approach to audience analysis—in most cases it would be difficult, time consuming, and impractical.

A satisfactory alternative is to talk to several persons who are likely to be in the audience. Assuming that these persons are similar to the rest of the audience members, you will get accurate insights into the nature of your listeners.

When it is not possible to talk with a likely member of the audience or even to talk with anyone familiar with the audience, you face a challenge. You will have to make some inferences about the audience from the information that is available.

The more similar your listeners are in terms of such factors as educational level, occupation, age, and group memberships, the easier it is to predict their attitudes toward you and your message. The more heterogeneous or diversified the audience is, the fewer inferences you can make about your listeners. The more you know in advance about an audience, the more effective a speaker you should be. Time spent in analyzing the audience is time well spent.

The audience for a business presentation is usually somewhat different than the audience for a public presentation. While the principles for making a public presentation also pertain to business presentations, certain differences in the two situations should be examined.

The audience for a business presentation is usually smaller. For that reason a speaker is able to take a more personal approach. It is easier to maintain eye contact with the smaller group and an informal climate is more likely.

The audience in a business presentation is generally more knowledgeable about the speaker's topic. Because the audience members are similar in interests, knowledge, and background, a speaker can make certain assumptions about the audience. As in any speaking situation, advance audience analysis is also important in making a business presentation.

Researching the Topic

Just as an athlete spends much more time practicing than actually competing, you will devote more time to preparation than to speaking. After determining the general purpose and the specific purpose, and after analyzing the audience, you should then take inventory of the sources of information available on the topic.

Much more time should be devoted to preparing a speech than to giving it.

In recent years many business organizations have developed speakers bureaus comprised of employees who volunteer to speak before local community organizations. In most cases these employees speak on subjects related to their areas of specialization. For speeches of this nature the speaker is probably the best source of information.

When Randall Best, assistant purchasing manager, was asked to speak to a civic club on purchasing and its effects on the local community, he spent hours in the library. He used many different sources including textbooks, trade journals, and government documents in preparing his speech.

He was disappointed with the audience's response to his speech—in fact, lack of response would be more accurate. At the end of his speech he offered to answer questions, but no one asked any. There was courteous applause, but the listeners seemed mainly interested in getting out of the room.

The next day he described the situation to Tom Long, his boss, who was sympathetic but who bluntly pointed out Randall's mistake. "Know thyself is the best advice I can give," Tom said. "As a purchasing agent you are recognized by these local groups as an expert. They want to learn about you and what you think on the subject. They don't want to be subjected to some list of figures that sounds like it's coming out of a computer. They want you." ∎

Many speeches given by representatives of business organizations are based almost entirely on the observations and knowledge of the speaker. This is not to discount the value of other types of research; however, many speakers need not go beyond themselves. The insights acquired over years in a given field will usually equip a person to speak knowledgeably about it. When a speech is about a subject the speaker is recognized as an authority on, the speaker is usually his or her own prime source of material.

Businesspeople who need more specific information for a speech can usually call on someone else in the organization for help. Either through personal observations and knowledge or with the assistance of colleagues, most business speakers can prepare an appropriate speech.

When speaking about one's own area of specialization, one seldom needs to rely on other sources of information.

Printed Sources of Information

Most students do not have the appropriate personal experiences for source material so the research process is complicated by the need to go beyond one's self for suitable ideas. This approach is not limited to students, naturally, since business speakers often look to outside sources for support of their ideas or to clarify knowledge of the subject. Students particularly, however, need to be aware of the printed sources of information available.

When you begin researching a topic, your first step should be the library's card catalog. The cards are arranged alphabetically according to the author's last name, book title, and general subject. In addition to the obvious title and author information, a catalog card also includes the book's date of publication, number of pages, and call number. By reading the card carefully you can save time and legwork.

By learning to use the card catalog, a person can greatly simplify the research process.

If you are looking for recent information, periodicals or newspapers will be more suitable. *The Reader's Guide to Periodical Literature* is a good starting point. This is an index of the articles published in more than 100 magazines and journals of general interest. The guide is published monthly and is arranged according to subject. The *Business Periodical Index* is another valuable source. Its format is similar to *The Reader's Guide* except it emphasizes publications of interest to the business community. Besides these two indexes there are indexes of articles published in specialized areas such as education, humanities, science, and others. The wide variety of indexes available can best be appreciated by visiting a college or university library.

When seeking information about specific companies, many sources are available. *Standard and Poor's Register of Corporations, Directors, and Executives* provides information about approximately 40,000 U.S. and Canadian firms, their directors, and executives. The *Million Dollar Directory* features hard-to-find information such as number of employees and sales figures for many public and private firms. *One Hundred*

Many library sources provide information about specific companies.

Thousand Leading U.S. Corporations provides rankings of corporations on the basis of many different factors. Detailed information on manufacturers is available in *The Thomas Register of Manufacturers.*

Many pamphlets and brochures on a wide variety of subjects are published by the government. *The Monthly Catalog of U.S. Government Publications,* an index of such sources, provides valuable information for researchers.

Newspapers are another helpful source of information on topics of general interest. *The New York Times* and *The Wall Street Journal* are indexed and are available on microfilm as are local newspapers at many libraries.

Vital Speeches is a magazine devoted to significant recent public speeches. By reading *Vital Speeches* you can identify possible speech topics and gain insights into the positions being taken by prominent speakers.

A knowledge of such information sources will facilitate smooth and systematic progress from preparation to presentation. Chapter 8 provides additional, helpful information on the research process. Throughout the preparation process keep in mind these questions which listeners will be seeking answers to:

1. How do you know?
2. Is this an accurate statement?
3. Does it agree with other sources?
4. What does it have to do with the subject?
5. What does it have to do with me?[2]

Organizing the Speech

Speakers often make the mistake of believing that they are ready to speak once they have completed their research. What usually results is a speech that is unclear in purpose and inconsistent in direction. Such speakers have overlooked the necessity of organizing their material.

When trying to organize the results of your research, you should have an overabundance of materials. While working on the organization you must select materials that are most appropriate. Inexperienced speakers often question the value of doing more research than is absolutely necessary; however, after preparing several speeches, they will find the reasons obvious. It is uncomfortable to a speaker and obvious to the listeners when a speech is short on ideas, for a speaker is then likely to include digressions, redundancies, and irrelevant statements.

The Body

A speech is made up of three main parts: introduction, body, and conclusion. Although the body follows the introduction, most speakers develop the body first. The body of a speech presents its actual message.

The body of a speech has three main components: central idea, main ideas, and supporting materials.

The *central idea* is the major theme of a speech: the speaker wants the listeners to remember it even if they forget all else. A campaigning politician may present many ideas in a campaign speech. The central idea, however, is usually "vote for me." Although central ideas are generally longer, they should be limited to one sentence. A training director recently gave an informative speech in which the central idea was this: a person should not be made a supervisor until having satisfactorily completed a course in interpersonal communication. A good central idea is, like the example, brief and clear. The central idea represents the minimum that you want the listeners to remember.

After determining the central idea, you seek ideas to support it; these are the *main ideas*. Since the main ideas are secondary in importance only to the central idea, speakers hope that the listeners will retain the main ideas, too. For that reason there should not be many main ideas; four or five are sufficient for most speeches.

Once the main ideas have been selected, look for ways to support them. Since an argument that convinces some listeners will not necessarily convince others, you should seek enough supporting materials to reach all of the listeners.

Among the methods of support most frequently used are quotations, examples, analogies, and statistics. In deciding the appropriateness of a given form of support, the speaker should consider these questions:

The body of a speech is comprised of the central idea, main ideas, and supports.

Several main ideas support the central idea, and there should be multiple supports for each main idea.

Quotations (or Testimony)

1. Will the person being quoted be recognized by the listeners?
2. Will the listeners regard the quoted person as an authority?
3. Does the person being quoted have credibility with the listeners?

Examples

1. Can the example be understood by the listeners?
2. Is the example clearly related to the main point?

Analogies

An analogy draws parallels between two different things. For example, when we use gasoline unnecessarily, we are reducing the number of future trips we will be able to take.

1. Is the analogy appropriate for the subject being considered?
2. Will the listeners be able to grasp the relevance of the analogy?

Statistics

1. Will the statistics be understandable to the listeners?
2. Will the listeners recognize the relationship between the statistics and the main point the statistics are intended to support?
3. Are the statistics recent and reliable enough to be acceptable to the listeners?

Sequence of Main Points

Once the central idea, the main points, and the supports have been selected, the speaker must decide the sequence in which the main points will be presented. Some of the most common organizational patterns are the chronological, topical, spatial, and logical sequences. The sequence that will be most appropriate depends on the topic, the purpose, and the listeners' interests. Effective speakers are equally adept in using any one of these sequential arrangements.

Chronological Sequence.   In this sequence the speech progresses from one given point in time to another. This sequence is regularly used when explaining a process.

When the plant manager explained papermaking to a class of undergraduates, he started by explaining how the lumber is purchased and what is done to it in the wood room. He described the entire process for the listeners up until the time when the paper is packaged and shipped out of the mill. ■

The chronological sequence might be used to describe the evolution of an idea or to explain how to do something.

Topical Sequence.   When a topic is divided into several different parts, it is arranged according to the topical sequence. The more natural the divisions, the easier it is for the listeners to understand and retain what the speaker is presenting.

At the annual meeting of stockholders of Tendril, Inc., the president spoke on the declining productivity of the Tendril employees. He first spoke about the causes of this problem as perceived by management, then he presented the causes as perceived by labor. He concluded by discussing those causes perceived differently by the two sides. ■

The topical sequence seems to be the one used more frequently. Some speakers tend to use it even though another sequence would be more effective.

Spatial Sequence.   As the name implies, the use of space determines the arrangement of ideas that the speaker presents. In the spatial sequence the speaker arranges the material according to physical location. Some approaches to the spatial sequence might involve describing something directionally, from east to west; another might be to describe a building from its first floor to the top floor.

When the city planner presented the board's first recommendations for a mass transit system, she talked about the unique ways each suburb would be affected by the system. She described the location of the main stations in the inner city and the system's accessibility to downtown

In selecting an appropriate sequence, the speaker must consider the topic, the purpose, and the interests of the listeners.

The spatial sequence involves presenting material according to physical location.

office workers and shoppers. She also described the major northern, southern, eastern, and western routes and the terminus of each route. ■

Speakers who use the spatial sequence describe the physical location of certain points and the relationship between them. The spatial sequence should enable the listeners to visualize what the speaker is telling them.

Logical Sequence. There are several different arrangement patterns included within the logical sequence. Among the most common patterns of the logical sequence are the causal and the problem and solution.

In using the causal approach, speakers have two options: one is to point out certain forces and the results that follow from them; the other is to describe events then explain the forces that caused them.

When a state chamber of commerce official spoke, he described the organized efforts made to attract new business to the state. He listed organizations that have moved to the state as a result of the efforts. In the presentation the efforts of the chamber were the forces and new business organizations the results.

When a representative of the Sierra Club discussed water pollution, she pointed out the growing health problems associated with it. She listed discharges from manufacturing plants and lax sewage control as the causes. In her argument she presented the results first then the causes.

The problem-solution approach is quite similar to the cause-effect approach because the speaker presents two main points. For example, in discussing an increase in customer complaints about sales personnel (the problem), the personnel director urged that greater emphasis be placed on employee training (the solution).

> **The causal and the problem and solution patterns are examples of the logical sequence.**

Introduction and Conclusion

Until you have decided what you will present in your speech, it is difficult to know how to get the listeners involved in it. For that reason the body of the speech should be developed before the introduction and the conclusion.

There are some speakers, however, who develop their ideas in the order they will present them. These speakers believe that by developing the introduction, body, and conclusion in that order, they will achieve better continuity between ideas.

The manner in which you introduce your speech will greatly influence the listeners' initial impressions. There are two purposes of the introduction: to establish rapport with the listeners, and to gain the listeners' attention.

> **An introduction should establish rapport with the listeners while gaining their attention.**

There are many different ways of introducing one's topic. These are among the approaches commonly used:

1. Make a startling statement
2. Refer to the audience
3. Refer to the occasion
4. Quote a recognized authority
5. Ask a rhetorical question
6. Use humor that is relevant

Regardless of the approach you use, you should remember the purposes of the introduction and of the speech: to indicate your subject and to gain the acceptance of the listeners.

In concluding a speech you should, at a minimum, restate the central idea of the speech. A good conclusion indicates to the listeners that the topic has been thoroughly covered. These are some of the most common ways a speaker may conclude a speech:

1. Summarize the main points
2. Propose a solution
3. Quote a recognized authority
4. Challenge the listeners to accomplish some specific goal
5. Visualize the future if your proposal is or is not accepted

Outlining the Informative Speech

In outlining an informative speech, arrange its different parts into a sequence that allows an orderly presentation of ideas. Through the use of an outline you can determine if the relationship between ideas is clear. An outline also helps the listener follow your train of thought. This is the outline of an informative speech given by a training director to an undergraduate professional management society:

By outlining a speech, the speaker is able to clarify the relationship between ideas.

I. Introduction
   A. Brief history of the training function within the business organization
   B. Increased specialization and automation changes as stimulants for training
II. Central idea: The job of the training director is varied enough to be challenging and very important to the organization
III. Body (main ideas)
   A. The training director must learn the training needs of the organization
      1. Through observation of operations
      2. Through interviewing upper management
      3. Through interviewing line workers
   B. The training director must develop training programs to meet organizational needs

    1.   Determine the target audience for the program

    2.   Locate and schedule competent instructors for the program

  C.   The training director must evaluate the effectiveness of the training programs

    1.   Test participants on the subject matter

    2.   Interview superiors of the participants and use other criteria to measure improvement

IV. Conclusion

  A.   Summary of speech body

    1.   Training director must learn training needs

    2.   Training director must develop appropriate training programs

    3.   Training director must evaluate the effectiveness of the programs

  B.   The job of the training director is important to the organization and challenging to the individual

Outlining the Persuasive Speech

Although the outline of the persuasive speech is similar to that of the informative speech, the two types are not developed in the same way. Since the informative speech is usually factual and not controversial, gaining the listeners' acceptance is usually not difficult.

Gaining the listeners' acceptance, however, is a challenge to the persuasive speaker. The more a persuader's ideas conform to the way people think, the more likely successful persuasion will occur.

The motivated sequence is a method of speech organization based on analysis of the thought process.[3] If you follow this sequence, you will present your ideas in the natural order that people follow when thinking through to a problem solution. Listeners who are led along these steps will be motivated to accept your proposition. The motivated sequence consists of five steps:

In the motivated sequence ideas are presented in a natural order.

1.   Getting attention

2.   Showing the need

3.   Satisfying the need

4.   Visualizing the results

5.   Requesting approval or action.

Just as readers become oblivious to magazine and newspaper advertisements, listeners also become oblivious when speakers try to persuade them. This is certainly not surprising; during an average day most of us are bombarded by numerous attempts to persuade. For these reasons a persuader must first get the attention of the listeners. There are a number of options available. The most appropriate approach depends on many factors, including the occasion and the nature of the audience.

The opening least likely to get the attention of the listeners is, "My topic today is . . . ."

In showing the need to the listeners, you describe a problem. Besides a mere description you may clarify the problem by using examples. The examples will be effective if they illustrate the seriousness of the problem. Listeners are more likely to recognize the need if you point out how the problem affects them.

In satisfying the need you present a solution to the problem raised in the previous step. You show how the solution will satisfy the need of which the listeners are now aware. At this point you clearly state the attitude or action the listeners are being asked to adopt. By using examples or other supporting materials, show that your proposal will work. As you explain how the solution will meet the need, you should anticipate likely objections and address them during this step.

By describing future conditions you help the listeners to visualize the results of the proposed solution. Some speakers describe the results likely if the solution is accepted. Others approach it negatively and describe future conditions if the solution is not accepted. The intended result of the visualization step is to intensify the desire of the listeners.

In requesting approval or action you focus the thoughts of the listeners on the theme developed in the speech. The speaker's request should be brief, to the point, and unmistakably clear.

This is the outline of a persuasive speech given by a production manager to a group of supervisors. In addition to the ideas presented, the steps of the motivated sequence are also indicated:

I. Introduction   **Attention**
    A. You have within you the power to grant yourself a pay increase
    B. You are in a position to generate more business for the company
II. Body (main ideas)
    A. Industry-wide research shows that we trail competitors in two significant factors
        1. We have the highest rate of lost-time accidents in the industry
        2. We have a worse than average rate of consumer complaints about product defects
    B. There are some actions you can take that will increase your earnings and improve the company's position within the industry
        1. Always enforce all safety regulations   **Satisfaction**
        2. Stress constant quality control and make more spot checks yourself
    C. If you follow our supervisory manual to the letter, lost-time accidents will be reduced by 50 percent and consumer complaints will be reduced by at least 30 percent. You will benefit directly by

    1. Increased earnings

    2. Less unproductive paperwork to complete concerning accidents   **Visualization**

III. Conclusion   **Action**

    A. Report all violations of safety regulations

Delivering the Speech

Many speakers believe if they have attended to all of the preliminaries leading up to a speech, the delivery will take care of itself. The advice they most likely give beginning speakers is, "Be natural." They tell speakers, "Imagine that you are carrying on a conversation with the audience and act accordingly."

Such advice, although well-intended, is not helpful, as it is difficult for you to be natural in what is an unnatural situation.

Bodily changes usually occur when you are about to give a public speech. Blood pressure and pulse rate increase, digestive processes slow down, perspiration increases, and breathing becomes irregular. These are some of the many different signs of anxiety that speakers may experience when facing an audience. Other signs may include trembling hands, dryness in the mouth, and butterflies in the stomach.

Feeling nervous in a public-speaking situation is to be expected—it is completely normal. As you become more experienced, such signs may become less apparent, but they never completely disappear. Even extreme nervousness—which you may be so aware of—is not nearly as noticeable to the listeners as you may think.

There is a positive aspect of nervousness: it gives you a slight edge, which is evident in greater alertness and sensitivity to the listeners. In fact, speakers who are more anxious very often give better speeches than do speakers who are less anxious. All in all, delivering a speech is a challenge that can provide satisfaction.

> **A certain amount of nervousness is to be expected in giving a public speech, but much of it can be overcome.**

Vocal Factors

While your primary message as a public speaker is verbal, there are many secondary channels through which you communicate. Volume, rate, and pitch of speech contribute to the impression you make.

Since noise pollution has become an issue in society, we have grown increasingly aware of the volume, or loudness, of those around us. When you speak to a group, adjust your volume according to such factors as room size and background noises.

*F*red Rosen was a well-organized and an articulate speaker. He had one overriding fault, however, which greatly reduced his effectiveness

Guide for Reducing Stage Fright

Select a topic in which you are genuinely interested.

Learn as much as possible in advance about your audience and about the setting in which you will speak. The more advance knowledge you have, the less uncertainty you will feel.

Prepare your speech thoroughly. Lack of preparation is a major cause of stage fright.

Write your main points on a notecard so you won't forget.

Practice, practice, practice—but do not memorize.

Space your practice sessions out. Rather than practicing for two hours the day before your speech, practice for shorter periods for six or seven consecutive days.

Each time you practice go through the entire speech. In this way you will get a feel for the whole mesage.

Throughout your preparation, always keep your main purpose in mind.

While awaiting your turn to speak, sit in a relaxed, even limp, position.

While waiting your turn, breath deeply.

Know your introduction especially well—this will ease you into your speech.

Refer to your notecard when necessary, but do not read to your listeners.

Focus your thoughts throughout your speech on your message and the response you seek rather than on yourself.

Use gestures and movement to emphasize important points and your tension will be reduced.

---

as a public speaker. He would begin each sentence with enough volume to be easily heard, then reduce his volume until many of the listeners were unable to hear the end of each sentence. It was this practice that led his subordinates to call him "Half-a-Sentence" Rosen. ■

A public speaker who regularly speaks more softly toward the end of each sentence is probably practicing improper breath control. If you have this problem, use shorter sentences or else consciously pause at natural breaks in the expression of your ideas to take a breath.

The speed, or rate, at which you speak will influence the way others respond to you and your message. Inexperienced speakers sometimes speak too quickly due to nervousness, and this causes other problems. Speaking too rapidly results in breath-control difficulties and a tendency to give all ideas equal emphasis. Your main ideas should leap out at the listener, but this will not happen unless you slow down . . . but not to extremes. By speaking much too slowly some people err in the opposite direction.

The high or low sound level of your voice is referred to as pitch. Although there is no one correct pitch, we each have a certain pitch level at which our voice is most effective.

Variety is the key to the successful use of these vocal factors. By varying your volume, rate, and pitch you will become more interesting to hear, and your message will be more memorable.

Rate of speech and pitch contribute to the impression made by a speaker.

Modes of Delivery

There are four main modes of delivery used in public speaking. They are:

1. Impromptu
2. Extemporaneous
3. Memorized
4. Manuscript

Delivery Guide

Record your speech at least once while practicing and carefully evaluate it.

Vary your rate, pitch, and volume so that you emphasize your main points.

Avoid vocalized pauses. Unnecessary *uhs* cause listeners to lose interest in the message. Silence is preferable to vocalized pauses.

Maintain eye contact with your listeners. Watch them to see how they are responding.

Develop an urge to communicate by selecting a topic in which you are interested. Unless you are obviously interested in your topic, your listeners will not be interested.

Lessen the distance between yourself and your listeners. Distance constitutes a barrier that must be overcome.

The impromptu speech is delivered with little opportunity to prepare. Its main virtue is that it is spontaneous; its main shortcoming is that it is usually not well-planned. When you are urged to say a few words without any advance warning, what results is an impromptu speech.

Extemporaneous speaking is somewhat more formal than impromptu speaking. You have an opportunity to plan, and the resulting speech is better organized than an impromptu speech. You will usually rely somewhat on notes, but you will not read to the listeners. Most public speeches are delivered extemporaneously.

A memorized speech allows for a well-planned expression of ideas. When presenting a speech from memory, however, speakers tend to lose a certain amount of naturalness and sometimes sound and look quite wooden. The possibility of forgetting the speech is another negative aspect of the memorized speech.

> **Each of the main modes of delivery has some advantages and some disadvantages.**

Manuscript speaking is relied on for more formal occasions. Speaking from a manuscript, you are able to be very precise, and you can carefully control the exact message the listeners receive. Of course, it takes longer to develop a manuscript speech, and frequently the manuscript becomes a barrier between you and the audience.

Visual Aids

Visual aids can help the communicator in at least four ways: by crystalizing vague ideas, by helping listeners remember information, by overcoming boredom and daydreaming, and by serving as signposts to keep the listener and speaker on track.[4]

> **Visual aids help keep the speaker and listeners on track.**

Photographs, charts, graphs, handouts, chalkboards, bulletin boards, and overhead projectors are frequently used by the speaker as visual aids. However they are also frequently misused. In addition to the suggestions presented in Chapter 9 on how to prepare charts, graphs and tables, we add these guidelines:

> **By following certain suggestions you can use visual aids effectively.**

1. Keep visual aids simple.
2. Make sure the visual presents the point clearly. Consider the use of color to assist in clarity.
3. Make sure everyone can see the visual.
4. Don't talk to the visual; look at your audience.
5. Display the visual, or refer to it, only when it is in use. For example, turn off an overhead projector when you have made your point.[5]
6. Learn in advance the most appropriate time to use a visual.
7. Be familiar with your equipment. Practice beforehand if you need to. Be sure the equipment is operable. Have a back-up machine if the aid is integral to your presentation.

Remember, the visual aid is just that: an aid. It is not a substitute for the speech itself. The burden is still on you to convey the message.

> **A very good visual aid will not compensate for a mediocre speech.**

Team Presentations

Although individual presentations are much more frequent, presentations by teams of individuals are not unusual. Continuity is especially important in a team presentation. The presentation should appear as a unified whole rather than as a series of individual presentations. Through careful planning the team members should avoid repetition and should structure the presentations so that each speaker paves the way for the succeeding speaker.

When the chamber of commerce sought to attract a major league baseball team, it assembled a group to present the city's case to the owners of the ball clubs.

The first speaker described the area from which the team would draw spectators. Through the use of flip charts the makeup of the population according to educational level was described.

The second speaker presented the findings of a wage survey done in the community. The various income levels were described, and the amount of discretionary income at each level was estimated. ■

Transportation facilities were described by the third speaker. Information about the airport and flight schedules was presented, as was a description of the city bus system. The urban freeway system was also shown with graphics.

The fourth speaker described the sports complex where the team would play and listed the specific financial incentives and tax benefits the city would provide the team that accepted its offer.

After agreeing to move to the city, the team officials cited the attractive package and persuasive presentations as major reasons. ■

The team presentation not only contains all the burdens of an individual presentation, but includes the need for coordination with your colleagues. Planning, therefore, is especially important with team presentations. Besides planning be sure to practice with visual aids, and time each speaker's presentation because a limited amount of time often is scheduled for team presentations.

Since people react differently to the stress of public speaking, it is sometimes hard to know exactly how much time each speaker may take. In their anxiety, some speakers speed up their delivery rate by as much as one third or more. Others do just the opposite; they slow down and therefore put pressure on other members to cut their presentations so that the team ends on schedule. Some system, such as placing a watch on the lectern or signaling the time remaining can help keep the presentation from continuing too long.

Team presentations can be effective if they are well-planned and if the individual presentations are mutually exclusive.

Planning and coordination are especially important in team presentations.

Team Presentation Guide

Plan the team presentation as a group, and divide the topics into logical and well-balanced divisions.

Anticipate questions and be prepared to respond to them.

Unless you are the first speaker, begin your speech by referring to the previous speaker to enhance the continuity of the team presentation.

Direct your speech primarily to the larger audience rather than to the other speakers.

Stay within your time limit. Do not infringe on the time of the other speakers or on the patience of the listeners.

While giving your speech, do not lose sight of the goal of the team.

Listen to the speeches of the other participants and refer to them where appropriate in your speech.

All of the principles of effective communication that we have discussed pertain to the team presentation also. Since the team format is somewhat different, however, the principles presented in the Team Presentation Guide are especially relevant.

Summary

The fear that many people express at the prospect of giving a speech can be overcome through careful preparation. Public speaking is not only important to an individual's professional growth, but it is also important to the organization the individual represents. In our free society the public speech is important for the expression of viewpoints.

These are the three main general purposes for public speeches: (1) to inform, (2) to persuade, and (3) to entertain. There are numerous specific purposes, of course, depending on what the individual speaker wants to accomplish.

After determining the general and specific purposes, the speaker should learn as much about the audience as possible. The more that is known in advance about the listeners, the more likely the speaker will be able to appeal to their interests.

In order to research a topic fully, a speaker should learn to use a library. By becoming familiar with *The Reader's Guide to Periodical Lit-*

erature, *The Business Periodical Index,* and other basic reference guides, a person can do research on most topics of current interest.

A speech is made up of three main parts: introduction, body, and conclusion. Since the body is the most important part, it should be prepared first. The body includes a central idea, several main ideas, and supporting materials. Quotations, examples, analogies, and statistics are among the most common methods of support. A speaker can choose from several different sequences of ideas. The topical sequence is used more than any of the others. Some of the other common sequences are chronological, spatial, and logical.

After the body of the speech has been prepared, the speaker is ready to develop an introduction and a conclusion. By outlining a speech a speaker can examine the relationships between the ideas to be presented and can provide for continuity.

The motivated sequence is a series of steps that a persuasive speaker can use to carry listeners along to the desired solution.

The primary message of a speech is the verbal one, but the speaker provides much additional information through other channels. The four modes of delivery are impromptu, extemporaneous, memorized, and manuscript. Through the use of visual aids or team presentations a speaker may attract greater interest in a subject.

Footnotes

[1]David Wallechinsky and Irving Wallace, *The Book of Lists* (New York: William Morrow, 1977).

[2]Robert T. Oliver, Harold P. Zelko, and Paul D. Holtzman, *Communicative Speaking and Listening,* 4th ed. (New York: Holt, Rinehart and Winston, 1968), p. 104.

[3]Alan H. Monroe and Douglas Ehninger, *Principles of Speech Communications,* 8th ed. (Glenview, Ill.: Scott Foresman, 1978), p. 252.

[4]Paul R. Timm, *Functional Business Presentations* (Englewood Cliffs, N.J.: Prentice-Hall, 1981), p. 131.

[5]Ibid., p. 136.

Review Questions

1. Why is public speaking so important to the individual, the organization, and to society?
2. Describe the two-step process used to arrive at the purpose of a speech.
3. What are the differences between a covert response and an overt response? Give three examples of each.
4. What is audience analysis?
5. What are the five basic questions you should seek answers to when analyzing an audience?
6. What types of information are available on a single catalog card?

7. How does *The Reader's Guide to Periodical Literature* differ from *The Business Periodical Index?*

8. Explain the relationship between central idea, main idea, and supporting materials in a speech.

9. What are four commonly used forms of support?

10. What are four commonly used sequences of main points?

Exercises

1. Select a speech from *Vital Speeches* magazine and analyze it to determine its general purpose, main points, and supporting materials.

2. Develop a five-minute informative speech to present to your class. Encourage comments and questions from the class members. Write a one- or two-page paper in which you describe the changes you would make in the speech if you gave it again.

3. Do a written audience analysis of your communication class. Detail the ways the class members are similar and ways they are different.

4. Develop a five-minute persuasive speech on a subject about which you feel strongly. Describe those factors from your audience analysis (as in Exercise 3) that most influenced your approach.

5. Give a one-minute impromptu speech on a topic selected by someone else in your class. Try to present one main idea and support it as well as you can.

6. Tape-record one of your speeches and write a two-page evaluation of it.

7. In groups of four or five prepare a team presentation to be given before the class. Select a subject, and divide it among the team members. Each team member should have a specific role, and the other class members should be told the kind of group they are to represent. Following each team presentation ask the class to do an evaluation.

8. Name two public figures who you have seen give a speech (either in person or on television). Describe what you think each should do to become a better public speaker.

Case

The Campus Planning Meeting
Julie C. Burkhard
Charlottesville, Virginia

Brian Wilson is President of the Student Government Association at Georgetown State College. Georgetown State has a student population of approximately 12,000 day students and 4,000 night students. The campus is spread over a two-mile stretch of land, and is located in the city of Georgetown which has a population of 40,000. Although there are residence halls on campus, most of the students live off campus and commute in by car. There is a city bus system that comes on campus, but most of the students prefer to drive.

For three years the Student Government Association has worked with the idea that more student parking is needed on campus. There are parking lots designated for faculty, staff, and handicapped, but very few for student parking. At present, if students drive, they must come to campus very early to get a parking place or park illegally during the day. Because the majority of students live off campus, the students feel the time has come for Georgetown State to provide more parking for students.

The Administration and Campus Planning Department of Georgetown State meet every week to discuss future plans for the development of the Georgetown campus. Their priorities for the campus range from a new Science complex to the construction of a new Performing Arts Center. For the past three years, the committee has not entertained the idea of additional parking for students. They feel that buildings and facilities must take presidence over parking lots. This year, Brian as President of SGA has been granted a place on the agenda to speak and present the students' views.

Brian has made many speeches and presentations before. With his facts and figures in mind, he must both educate the committee to the problem and persuade them to make one of their priorities campus parking for students. He must be the students' voice.

■ ■ ■

Case Questions

1. When analyzing his audience, what characteristics of the committee should Brian Wilson keep in mind?
2. Because Brian has to both educate and persuade the committee, how should he organize his presentation?
3. What modes of proof could Brian use to overcome the objections of the committee?
4. What visual aids could Brian use to add to his presentation?

Case

The City Council Meeting
Julie C. Burkhard
Charlottesville, Virginia

Jeffrey Faught is the director of the chamber of commerce in Eastman, a small town with a population of approximately 3,000. Although the town is relatively small, it is growing every year.

Faught has been working to bring industry to Eastman for about two years. Presently the town has no industries at all. Most of the people in Eastman are local businessmen or farmers. Faught believes the town needs some industry, because it would not only strengthen the economy, it would also create more jobs. With jobs come people, and people need homes to live in; therefore, real estate would gain from the industry as well.

Faught's problem is with the city council and the townspeople. The townspeople want a park and recreational area built where the plant would be built. The city council must decide whether to grant a zoning change for the new industry or the new park.

The second Tuesday night of every month, the city council meets. The public is invited, so anyone may attend. This particular Tuesday, both Faught from the chamber of commerce and the townspeople for the park plan to attend.

Faught decides he must make his stand known to both the council and the people. He has not given many speeches, but he knows this presentation must be very persuasive.

The townspeople have wanted a park for their children for years. They believe their town is doing just fine without industry. In the past, the city council has shared this same belief.

Fraught is faced with the job of convincing both the council and the people to change their views.

■ ■ ■

Case Questions

1. What should Jeffrey Faught take into consideration when analyzing his audience?
2. How might he organize his presentation to accomplish his persuasive purpose?
3. Knowing that Faught has to overcome the objections of the council and the people, what modes of proof should he attempt to employ?

Communication and Decision Making in Small Groups

Learning Objectives

1. To gain the skill necessary to participate more effectively in small-group communication situations.
2. To understand the purposes of small-group communication in organizations.
3. To become aware of the advantages and disadvantages of reaching decisions in small groups.
4. To learn about a problem-solving agenda to guide small groups toward effective decision making.
5. To understand the concept of brainstorming.
6. To understand the developmental phases of small groups.
7. To become aware of how individuals can distort group decision and how to overcome this problem.
8. To comprehend the critical concept of cohesion as it affects the successful functioning of small groups.
9. To examine the various styles of group leadership.
10. To increase awareness of how specific behaviors of group members can help move the group toward its goal.

"I've got a million things to do today," Tim was thinking as he entered the conference room; "The last thing I need is another meeting." The purpose of this meeting was to explain to the supervisors the new worker involvement program the company was about to implement.

Ron Ryan, the plant manager, conducted the meeting with the assistance of an outside consultant. In the first part of the meeting the consultant described the benefits other companies experienced through worker involvement programs. After that the consultant explained the process and the critical role the supervisor played. Tim found the concept of worker involvement interesting. He was skeptical, however, about it working in his company.

In accordance with what he had been taught, but with considerble apprehension, he called a meeting of his people. He explained the worker involvement program and described how everyone stood to benefit from the program's success.

"Concentrate on quality control," he told his workers. "What are some things you think should be done to improve quality control?" After an awkward silence a few members made halfhearted suggestions. Fortunately, the time had come to end the meeting. "Same time next week," Tim reminded his people, all the while dreading the prospect of another such meeting. "Between now and then, keep thinking of ways to improve quality control," he said.

At the next meeting, Tim realized that his fears had been unfounded. The group members required no prodding to participate. The members obviously had given some thought to quality control, and they were no longer hesitant about expressing their thoughts.

Tim was pleasantly surprised by the transformation of a collection of individuals into a group. As a result of his experience with the worker involvement program, Tim began to recognize the many values to be derived from working with groups. ∎

Small groups are an integral part of your business and social life. Your family is the first group to which you belonged. As you grew so also did the number and range of your groups. Neighborhood, school and church affiliations are all groups in which to interact.

The organizations within which you work, or will work, will be the source of additional groups. Most business organizations make extensive use of groups. In fact, many managers spend as much as half of each work day working in small groups. A large percentage of the decisions made in business organizations are made by groups.

The ability to lead and to participate in groups is an important skill in any business organization. It is also a skill that can be learned. The purpose of this chapter is to make you a more effective participant in small groups by making you more aware of factors that significantly influence group communication.

The Role of Groups in Today's Business Organization

Groups have played a major role in U.S. society since the nation's inception. The Declaration of Independence was forged through discussion and debate, and the same is true of virtually all pieces of legislation.

Business management also has traditionally made extensive use of groups. Until the last several decades, however, the makeup of such groups was exclusively managerial. Managers and staff participated in meetings and conferences for fact finding and for decision making. Plans were developed and policies made by groups which rarely included anyone else because the activities were considered the province of management alone.

Today the use of groups pervades all levels of the organization. In the quest for greater productivity and employee satisfaction, many companies have moved toward participative management. Through participative management, employees at every level become involved in job-related decision making. Worker involvement groups, described at the beginning of this chapter, are a technique of participative management.

The growth of the quality circle movement mirrors the growing emphasis on participative management. Quality circles are small groups of workers that meet regularly with management to discuss problems of productivity and of the work place in general. The impact of quality circles appears to be significant in terms of employee commitment to the organization as well as in organizational productivity and development.

Whatever job you eventually assume in a business organization, you will become a part of various work groups. Your ability to work and to interact effectively in groups will significantly determine your occupational success. While a knowledge of the contents of this chapter will not in itself turn you into a polished team player, it will help you move in that direction.

Until recently most decision-making groups were managerial in nature.

The emphasis on participative management has been accompanied by a greater emphasis on groups.

Characteristics of a Small Group

Imagine that you participated in two groups today. Your first group gathered in the plant cafeteria 30 minutes before starting work. The group consisted of you and five friends. This group met most mornings before work and usually discussed such topics as sports, politics, and the opposite sex, not necessarily in that order.

Your second group was the plant grievance committee, a group of seven members that meets weekly to consider employee grievances. You were selected to represent the shipping department.

Literally, each group is a small group; only one group, however, meets all of the criteria necessary to be designated a small group for our purposes. The characteristics of a small group are:

1. A common purpose
2. A small number of participants
3. Roles
4. Interdependency among members
5. Face to face interaction
6. A collective process.

Small groups have certain characteristics.

Common Purpose.   The members of the plant grievance committee gather with a common purpose to consider the grievances of employees. The individuals who met in the cafeteria did not share a common purpose. A few people were there because they especially enjoyed talking about sports; some like to talk about current events; you have your own interests also. The six individuals enjoy each other's company so they continue to meet most mornings although they do not share a common purpose.

Members must share a common purpose.

Small Number of Participants.   The size of a group has a significant impact on productivity as well as on the satisfaction of group members. A group that is too small will be limited in the quantity of information it can generate. Individual members may, however, have greater opportunities to participate because of the small size of a group. The increased opportunities will often result in more satisfied members.

Group size influences productivity and satisfaction of members.

   With greater size a group can generate more ideas. There will be fewer opportunities for individual participation, however, and members may be less satisfied with their groups. Although there is no magic number at which groups automatically achieve greatest effectiveness, groups of five members are often regarded as the ideal.

Interdependency among Members.   Groups are assembled with the intent of capitalizing on the combined efforts of the members. Members not only influence one another, but they also rely on one another for information and support. A bond develops between the members which leads to an interdependence which facilitates communication within the group. Members remain aware of the collective nature of the group.

There is an interdependency among group members.

Face to Face Interaction.   Another characteristic of a small group is that the members interact face to face. The members meet and exchange information verbally and nonverbally.

   The grievance committee possesses all of the characteristics of a small group. The cafeteria group does not since it lacks both a common purpose and interdependence among its members. A small group may be defined as a collection of a few individuals who interact face to face, verbally and nonverbally, for a common purpose and with interdependency among the members.

Interaction between members is face to face.

   Small groups are used in a wide variety of situations. However, there are really two basic purposes of the small group: (1) information sharing and (2) problem solving. Frequently, these two basic purposes are combined within the same group. For example, a group usually exchanges information before it reaches a decision about a certain problem.

Advantages and Disadvantages of Small Groups

When faced with a decision you should consider the advantages of using small groups. For many, participation in small-group communication is motivational. Most of us prefer to participate in a group and be a part of the decision-making process rather than have someone simply hand down a decision to us. The advantages of using small groups are:

1. **Quality of decisions.** As long as the group members have appropriate knowledge and expertise, a group decision is usually superior to the decision of an individual. A plant manager who expects first-line production supervisors to select the plant's new air-filtration system, however, is probably assuming too much about the supervisors' expertise.

2. **Acceptance.** Subordinates who are included in the decision-making process will usually accept the decision more readily. For example, suppose that the clothing manager in a retail store is faced with requests from three full-time salespeople for the same week of vacation. One of the three must be asked to reschedule so that the business can function normally. This is not a decision about quality—any one of the three salespeople could perform adequately alone. If the department manager makes the decision, the unlucky salesperson will be upset and may become hostile. However, by asking the three salespeople to work out a decision among themselves, each has the opportunity to discuss his or her own viewpoint. A group decision in this instance improves the chances that all the salespeople will accept the final agreement.

3. **Commitment.** The elements of acceptance and commitment are closely related. Commitment, however, goes beyond acceptance. When individuals are directly involved in analyzing a problem and formulating its solution, they become more committed to the effective implementation of the decision. Thus, a company considering such motivational tools as job enrichment, wage incentives, or profit sharing might benefit from involving employees in selecting the appropriate program.

4. **Status.** Participants gain a sense of heightened status and recognition from the responsibility and interaction in group decision making.

While the above advantages support the use of small groups, one must also be aware of the potential disadvantages of small-group decision making:

1. **Time.** It takes time to prepare for a meeting or conference, especially if you are responsible for leading the session: If you want to be an effective participant, you must devote some time to preparing. The

There are certain advantages in using small groups for making decisions.

actual meetings are time consuming. Many managers spend more than one third of their working hours in meetings.

2.   Cost. Expense is another disadvantage since group meetings take employees away from regularly assigned duties. When individuals make decisions, less time is lost from the job and, consequently, it is less expensive.

But using small groups also entails definite disadvantages.

3.   Unclear individual accountability. When an individual is assigned a task that person is accountable for its satisfactory completion. When a group is assigned a task, accountability is less clear. *Accountability* means the expectation that someone will do some specific things to accomplish a specific goal. When a group pursues a task, accountability is blurred.

Someone once said, "Success has a thousand fathers; failure has none." Although the person wasn't specifically referring to groups, the quotation suggests a disadvantage of groups. When a group effort is successful, individual members will often try to take credit for the success. When a group effort is unsuccessful, individual members will often seek to disassociate themselves from the results. From the standpoint of individual members, unclear accountability may be viewed as an advantage of small groups. From the standpoint of group productivity, however, unclear accountability is a definite disadvantage.

4.   Undue conformity. Sometimes a group is dominated by one individual with whom the other members acquiesce in order to avoid conflict and speed decisions. At other times a group may perceive a member as more knowledgeable than is the case and, therefore, go along with that person's opinions. The more a group interacts the greater the pressures on members to conform. Peer pressure, the influence of the other members, is likely to insure conformity. The greater the conformity, the less likely a group will benefit from all members' expertise. At the extreme, such conformity is called *groupthink*. This is discussed later in the chapter.

Solving Problems in Small Groups

Nearly every small group brought together to solve a problem follows a format or agenda. The most widely used format is based on John Dewey's Reflective Thinking Process.[1] These six steps are based on Dewey's work.

Step 1: Defining and Analyzing the Problem

During the initial meeting the precise nature of the problem should be specified and its underlying causes investigated. Consider, for example, a small retail firm that has low employee morale, a considerable decline

The most widely used format for group problem solving is based on Dewey's Steps of Reflective Thinking.

in sales, and an unusually high rate of employee turnover. The conference leader might begin by describing these problems and delineating them with available facts. By concisely depicting the present state of affairs, the leader is defining the problem.

Once each conference participant understands the nature and scope of the problem, the group can investigate potential causes. This is the crux of the first step in problem solving. In our example, group members would offer their perceptions of what might be causing the morale, sales, and turnover problems. These perceptions are discussed, modified (if necessary), and recorded by a leader or appointed group member. Suppose our group perceives the following four possible causes: (1) lack of communication between superiors and subordinates; (2) poor motivational programs; (3) conflict between the sales and delivery departments; and (4) insufficient advertising. After analyzing information from attitude surveys or grievance and exit interviews, the group might decide that inadequate motivation is the major cause of the problem. When the problem is defined and the suspected cause is identified, the group can move to Step 2.

1. Defining the problem

Step 2: Establishing Criteria for a Solution

The criteria step in the problem solving sequence is optional and may be safely postponed until solutions are actually evaluated. Suppose, however, that this group determines the criteria that any potential solution must meet. The criteria might be that the solution: (1) must include all nonmanagement employees; (2) must become effective within two months; and (3) must cost no more than two percent of the company's gross profits.

These criteria are derived, of course, from discussion among the conference members. Some proposed criteria were altered slightly, while some were rejected. In any event, the group has arrived at three criteria and is ready to begin Step 3 of the problem solving process.

2. Establishing criteria

Step 3: Proposing Possible Solutions

In this step participants suggest as many potential solutions as possible. Each participant attempts to propose solutions that meet the specified criteria. Although members may amend the solutions offered by others, no solutions are evaluated at this time. The third step is essentially brainstorming, and it is important to keep the basic rules of brainstorming in mind. These rules are:

3. Proposing solutions

1. Ideas are expressed freely without regard to quality. The emphasis is on quantity. Generate as many ideas as possible.

2. Criticism of ideas is not allowed until the brainstorming session is over.

3. Elaboration and combinations of previously expressed ideas are encouraged. The theory is that creativity will build as one idea triggers another. A record of the possible solutions generated is kept by the leader or appointee.

Suppose that the group suggests the following five potential solutions: (1) better fringe benefits; (2) increased commissions; (3) profit sharing; (4) a sales contest; (5) wage incentives. The group can now move to Step 4.

Step 4: Evaluating Possible Solutions

In Step 4 the conference members evaluate each of the proposed solutions. Each solution is weighed against the criteria outlined in Step 2 as well as against other proposed criteria. The group's aim is to identify the advantages and disadvantages of each solution. For example, the wage incentives might be pertinent to all nonmanagement employees and easily set up within two months but, nevertheless, too costly and irrelevant to the needs of the commission salespeople.

    Once the advantages and disadvantages have been assigned to each solution, the group can proceed to Step 5.

4. Evaluating solutions

Step 5: Selecting a Solution

A critical point to keep in mind is the group is not obligated to select only one of the proposed solutions. The most effective decision might combine two or three proposed solutions or an altered version of only one solution. Whatever the outcome, during Step 5 a final decision must be made concerning the best possible solution. The precise details of the solution should also be decided. Suppose, in this example, that the group chooses to increase commissions by one percent across the board. In addition, the group decides on a three-month sales contest between hard- and soft-line division, and the winners are to receive cash bonuses and gift certificates. The participants are now ready for the final step in the problem solving sequence.

5. Selecting a solution

Step 6: Plotting a Course of Action

This final step concentrates on how best to execute the solution. Before the conference can end, the participants must agree upon a specific, detailed method for enacting the solution. Conference members may

6. Action planning

volunteer to assume responsibility for certain aspects of the program, or the leader may assign specific tasks to group participants. Whatever approach is chosen, agreement must be reached before the problem solving process can terminate.

For the sake of illustration, suppose that two department heads have volunteered to direct the sales contest. Together they will work out the details and report to the store manager within one week. Finally, the store manager announces that the one percent commission increase will become effective at the beginning of the next month.

In summary, problem solving is a systematic approach that a group employs to solve a problem. The six distinct steps in the reflective thinking process are:

Checklist for Dewey Reflective Thinking Format

1. Defining and analyzing the problem

2. Establishing criteria for a solution

3. Proposing possible solutions

4. Evaluating possible solutions

5. Selecting a solution

6. Plotting a course of action

Although Dewey's six-step format is the best-known and most widely used approach to problem solving, there are other formats in use. One such format is the ideal solution form which was developed from observing the problem solving process followed by many business groups. In the ideal solution form group discussion follows this sequence of questions:

1. Are we all agreed on the nature of the problem?
2. What would be the ideal solution from the point of view of all parties involved in the problem?
3. What conditions within the problem could be changed so that the ideal solution might be achieved?
4. Of the solutions available to us, which one best approximates the ideal solution?[2]

The ideal solution form is another approach to problem solving.

The single question form is another approach to group problem solving. Groups which follow the single question form focus on a single objective and thereby are less likely to pursue digressions. In the single question form this sequence of questions is followed:

The single question form is sometimes used in problem solving.

1. What single question will yield the answer which is all the group needs to know to accomplish its purpose?
2. What subquestions must be answered before we can answer the single question we have formulated?
3. Do we have sufficient information to confidently answer the subquestions? (If yes, answer them. If not, continue.)
4. What are the most reasonable answers to the subquestions?
5. Assuming that our answers to the subquestions are correct, what is the best solution to the problem?[3]

The ideal solution form and the single question form appear to be more direct and to the point than the Dewey approach. The Dewey approach, however, is more thorough and is more likely to develop the group members' analytical skills. As a group matures and remains intact over long periods of time, the group adopts a more abbreviated approach to problem solving. The approach may be the ideal solution form or the single question form or it may be another approach specifically tailored to the environment and needs of that group.

Avoiding Defective Decision Making

Sometimes defective decisions are reached in small groups because of certain characteristics of individuals. For example, powerful individuals sometimes dominate groups and keep others from actively participating in the group process; poor decisions often result. You may encounter a group member who digresses and consumes valuable group time talking about unrelated topics. On other occasions individuals in the group may press for a quick decision before all the important aspects of the problem have been carefully considered. In numerous other ways also, individuals can dilute the decision making potential of groups.

There are several ways that individuals can distort group decisions.

One way to overcome some of these problems is to employ the nominal group procedure. The nominal group procedure is briefly outlined in three stages, which are discussed in terms of analyzing possible problem causes.[4]

The nominal group procedure is useful in problem solving.

Stage 1

The members who are going to participate in the small-group session are brought together and are asked not to speak to each other; thus, the term *nominal group* is used as the members are in a group setting, but no verbal interaction is permitted. After the individuals are seated, they are asked to write on a piece of paper what they believe are the

Nominal group members do not talk during the first stage of the nominal group process.

major causes of the problem under consideration. This task should take approximately 10 to 15 minutes. For example, if the problem-solving group has been brought together to discuss a high rate of absenteeism, each group member would be asked to list as many causes for the absenteeism as possible.

Throughout this first stage it is important that individuals in the nominal group not talk to each other.

Stage 2

After the members of the nominal group have had enough time to list the causes of the problem, the group leader asks someone to read one of the items he or she listed. As the person reads the cause aloud to the group, the leader writes the cause on a large pad of paper or blackboard placed in front of the group. The statement is written so that all group members can read it. The group leader proceeds to the next person and asks for another cause, continuing clockwise around the group until everyone's list has been read. When a cause is put on the master sheet that other members have also included on their lists, they should simply cross that item off their lists. In this way each cause is listed only once on the master list. If there is a question whether an item overlaps with an item already on the list, that item should be placed on the master list.

During the second stage a master list is developed.

Stage 3

At this point all individuals are asked to examine the master list carefully and to rank order the causes of the problem. If the list is long, the group members are asked to select the top five by secret ballot. After all individuals have completed their rankings, the information is collected and tabulated.

All three stages of this process can be completed in about one hour. When employed this way, the nominal group process can identify the major causes of the problem. The procedure also allows for the establishment of the most important causes. Since individuals rank the advantages by secret ballot, it is highly probable that the priority causes of the problem will be accurately established.

Some authorities think that the nominal group process is more effective than the interacting group process for identifying the major causes of a problem. There are several major factors that support the nominal group approach.

In newly-formed interacting groups, the members often do not know each other well and one strong member dominates; such domination

During the third stage the members rank order items in the master list.

A rationale exists for the nominal group approach.

sometimes persists within established groups. The nominal group approach, however, is more democratic, and tends to equalize the influence of the members. The equal opportunity to participate leads to greater acceptance by members of the group decision.

Interacting groups sometimes start evaluating and elaborating the problem dimensions too early. This may take so much time that other important dimensions are never brought to the group's attention. Again, the prohibition on verbal interaction is an advantage; it avoids evaluating and elaborating comments while the problem dimensions are being identified.

Third, interacting groups may tend to focus on one particular train of thought and not attempt to identify all of the problem dimensions. Many individuals find it easier to react to someone else's ideas rather than articulate their own. This problem becomes more severe when you realize that the early dimensions identified by the interacting group usually contain the obvious rather than the more subtle aspects of the problem. The nominal group method forces each individual to identify as many of the dimensions of the problem as possible; no one is permitted the luxury of simply reacting to dimensions generated by others in the group.

Time effectiveness is another advantage of the nominal group approach. There is a high degree of participation with a minimum investment of time. Nominal grouping elicits the active involvement of many more individuals, within a given period of time, than is possible through interacting groups.

When used the way we described, the nominal group enhances the advantages and minimizes the disadvantages of the interacting group. The following are among its major advantages:

- influence is more equal among members
- ideas are accepted more readily by group members
- members need not be acquainted for group to be productive
- premature evaluation of ideas is avoided
- more problem dimensions are identified
- time is spent more effectively
- can be used to involve very large groups.

The interacting group may keep all aspects of the problem from being identified, while the nominal group helps identify all problem areas. Furthermore, the interacting group may not allow enough creativity in suggesting solutions, while the nominal group contributes to the number and quality of proposed solutions.

In brief, the nominal group procedure is most useful for analyzing problem causes and proposing solutions. The interacting group procedure is best for information synthesis, evaluation, group consensus, and discussion of implementation of the final decision.

The nominal group method offers some distinct advantages.

Cohesion

In her five years as assistant planning director for the Metro-Quad Chamber of Commerce, Rita Branigan has attended hundreds of meetings. She has served on numerous task forces and committees in roles ranging from chairperson to recording secretary. She believes that some of the best and worst experiences of her life have occurred in groups. Rita believes that no two groups have exactly the same personality and that a group's personality determines its effectiveness. Rita claims she can accurately predict the effectiveness of a group after observing it for the first 30 minutes of its first meeting. "If the members introduce themselves, if they warm up to each other, and seem interested in one another, the group is off to a good start and is likely to be effective. When there is no warmth generated within a new group, no introductions, and little eye contact between members, that group doesn't have much of a future." That briefly describes Rita's theory about groups. ∎

Since people in business spend so much time working in groups, many of them have their own personal theories on how groups work (or don't work). While there may be little agreement between the various theories, most people believe if members feel loyal toward their group, it is destined to be more successful than groups which have no such loyalty. When members view a group as attractive, those members will be more loyal to the group. Such factors as loyalty, unity, and attractiveness as pertaining to groups are encompassed in the term *cohesion*. Specifically, group cohesion is the product of the mutual attractiveness of the members and the commitment of the members to the group.

> **Group cohesion is the result of the mutual attractivenss of the members and the commitment of the members to the group.**

Three factors which lead to greater cohesion are:

1. Agreement on goals
2. Frequency of interaction
3. Intergroup competition.

Agreement on Goals. Kim Murray quit her sorority after one year out of a sense of frustration. She, along with some other members, believed the sorority should pursue a small number of campus-improvement projects each year. Other members believed the group's main purpose should be to plan and hold as many parties as possible. Because this disagreement on goals was not resolved, group morale declined and several members left the sorority.

When a group agrees on goals, the members are more attracted to it. Just because there is agreement on goals, however, does not mean there will be no conflicts or disagreements among group members.

> **Cohesion is more likely to develop when there is agreement on goals.**

Deciding on the means of accomplishing a goal is the cause of many problems in groups. When there is agreement on goals, however, cohesion is likely to develop.

Frequency of Interaction.   The more frequently a group meets, the more likely that group is to become cohesive. As members get acquainted they become more interested in their colleagues and in their common tie, the group. Cohesion comes from familiarity, and familiarity from frequency of interaction.

Intergroup Competition.   Few situations bind a group as does a perceived threat to the group. In many business organizations, managers intentionally create a threat by developing competition between groups and increased cohesion results. When one group is pitted against another, both groups will usually benefit. In some plants, for example, competition is developed between shifts with the most productive shift receiving an award.

Frequent meetings and intergroup competition are also conducive to cohesion.

Just as there are factors which lead to greater cohesiveness, there are also factors which detract from cohesiveness. Among these negative factors are the following:

1.   Disagreement on goals
2.   Large number of participants
3.   Intragroup competition.

Certain factors detract from group cohesion.

Disagreement on Goals.   As long as group members cannot agree on what a group's goals should be, the group's effectiveness will be neutralized by a basic underlying conflict. Cohesion is virtually unattainable as long as such basic differences exist.

Large Number of Participants.   As discussed earlier, one characteristic of small groups is a small number of participants. As the size increases so do the pressures against cohesion. There is an inverse relationship between the size of a group and the probability of cohesion; that is, as a group grows, cohesion becomes less easily attained.

Intragroup Competition.   In the absence of a competitor, managers will sometimes divide one existing group into several subgroups. The purpose for the subdivision is usually to create competition for a certain project. Rather than developing cohesion, however, the opposite usually occurs: the members become polarized, one side against the other and interpersonal frictions develop. While competition between groups heightens cohesion, competition within groups results in division and discord.

Cohesion is a significant ingredient in effective groups. Some of the byproducts of cohesion are higher morale, better communication, and members' willingness to work hard. As is so often true, it is possible to have too much of a good thing, and cohesiveness is no exception.

Some of the byproducts of cohesion are higher morale and better commmunication.

Groupthink

Groups which are overly cohesive suffer from groupthink.[5] Groupthink occurs when agreement, rather than critical thinking, becomes most important. Under conditions of groupthink, a group may make decisions that the individual group members, acting alone, would probably not have made. The cliche, "Don't make waves," expresses a sentiment that often prevails in groups beset by groupthink.

Here are the symptoms of groupthink:

1.   An illusion of invulnerability, shared by most or all the members, which creates excessive optimism and encourages taking extreme risks;

2.   Collective efforts to rationalize in order to discount warnings which might lead members to reconsider their assumptions before they recommit themselves to their past policy decisions;

3.   An unquestioned belief in the group's inherent morality, inclining the members to ignore the ethical or moral consequences of their decisions;

4.   Stereotyped views of opposition leaders as too evil to warrant genuine negotiation or as too weak and stupid to counter whatever risky attempts are made to defeat their purposes;

5.   Direct pressure on any member who expresses strong arguments against any of the group's stereotypes, illusions, or commitments, making clear that dissent is contrary to what is expected of all loyal members;

6.   Self-censorship of deviations from the apparent group consensus, reflecting each member's inclination to minimize the importance of any doubts and counterarguments;

7.   A shared illusion of unanimity concerning judgments conforming to the majority view (partly resulting from self-censorship of deviations and augmented by the false assumption that silence means consent);

8.   The emergence of self-appointed mindguards—members who protect the group from adverse information that might shatter their shared complacency about the effectiveness and morality of decisions.[6]

Groupthink is both prevalent and destructive to genuine group efforts and its presence defeats the main reason for assembling groups—critical thinking. By adhering to these suggestions, however, it is possible to prevent groupthink:

1.   The leader of a decision-making group should assign the role of critic to each member. Doubts and objections are thus more likely to be exposed and discussed rather than suppressed. Group leaders must set the example by accepting criticism of their ideas and

Groupthink hampers decision making.

The symptoms of groupthink can be identified.

Suggestions exist for overcoming groupthink.

thoughts on the matter at hand. Acceptance of criticism does not often come naturally so it may have to be learned by group members.

2. When assigning a decision-making mission to a group, the leader should be impartial instead of stating preferences. When executives in an organization give guidance to decision-making groups, many times they introduce bias unwittingly by being too specific in outlining what they want accomplished. If the time is short, more guidance will hasten the decision. However, the less guidance there is, the less chance there is that the executive's preconceived notions will unduly influence the group's decision. Certainly the leader should not be so specific as to indicate which of several alternatives is personally preferable. Admittedly there is a delicate balance between just enough guidance to get the job done and too much guidance so that group members believe they have been manipulated. That balance is what a good group leader should strive for.

3. Members of the decision-making group should frequently seek advice and counsel from trusted associates in their own departments within the organization. Fresh perspectives on the problem can be gained by introducing thoughts from those outside the decision-making group. The reactions of these associates should then be taken back and introduced to the group. Discretion must be used in implementing this suggestion when the decision involves highly confidential planning of goals or policies which need to be kept from public dissemination.

4. The tendency to seek a consensus could be thwarted effectively by using a devil's advocate at each group meeting. The role of devil's advocate, to be most effective, should be rotated among the group members, and, in some cases, more than one may be desirable. Criticisms by the devil's advocate(s) should be taken seriously and discussed to the satisfaction of all present.[7]

Cohesion is desirable for the effective functioning of the group; too much cohesion, however, can result in groupthink and, in turn, to poor decisions.

Group Leadership

An important role in every group is that of the group leader. Because of the importance of leadership, there has been a great deal of research done on it. Researchers have identified the following styles of group leadership:

There are various styles of group leadership.

1. Authoritarian leadership
2. Supervisory leadership
3. Democratic or participative leadership
4. Laissez-faire or group-centered leadership.

Authoritarian Leadership. Authoritarian leaders usually determine the specific task for each participant because they often believe that group participants are limited in ability and need strict guidance and control. This style of leadership, therefore, is rigid and inflexible. Authoritarian leaders often dominate discussion and are usually reluctant to acknowledge those who disagree with them. Such leaders discourage member participation, causing members to resign themselves to the fact that the leader will make all the decisions no matter what anyone else might have to contribute. Leaders who employ the authoritarian style may very quickly reach the solution they want, but in terms of group morale, the costs are very high.

Authoritarian leaders exercise strong control.

The emotional consequences of authoritarian leadership are serious. One might wonder why any group leader would use this style of leadership. The simple fact is, in many situations, leaders want the group to know beyond any doubt that they are in control. Because such leaders so completely dominate their groups they remain unaware or unconcerned about the members' perception of them as leaders.

There are some situations for which authoritarian leadership would be appropriate. When there is an immediate crisis, or when time is extremely limited or the matter under discussion trivial, authoritarian leadership might be the most appropriate style of leadership. Authoritarian leadership, however, is overused and counterproductive.

Supervisory Leadership. This style of leadership, which stops short of autocratic control, is useful when efficiency is critical. Supervisory leaders almost always introduce the problem for discussion with a lengthy description. They usually decide what problem will be discussed in the meeting and frequently summarize what has taken place in the group. Such leaders are not as formal or as rigid as the authoritarians, but they give little attention to the needs of the group.

Supervisory leaders are slightly more flexible than authoritarian leaders.

Democratic or Participative Leadership. Both authoritarian and supervisory leaders depend upon methods that limit the participation and freedom of other group members. These two styles restrict the participation of group members. Democratic or participative leaders, on the other hand, encourage group members to participate actively in discussion. Rather than restricting group members, this style of leadership has a positive effect. A leader who employs the participative style seeks to accomplish the following:

Democratic leaders relinquish some control and encourage group participation.

1. All group members should participate freely.
2. Communication should be directed to all members, not just the leader.
3. Group decisions should be perceived as group achievements.
4. Group members should be able to satisfy some personal needs in the group environment.
5. Group members should be able to identify with the group.

Employing the participative style of leadership is a difficult assignment. The leader must be able to coordinate both the task and the group maintenance functions (discussed later in this chapter). This type of leadership is most frequently used because it promotes a high degree of group cohesion and at the same time spurs the group toward accomplishing the task.

Laissez-Faire or Group-Centered Leadership. Laissez-Faire leaders expect group members to be self-directed. Leaders in this group must refrain from structuring the group in any way. They listen but do not show approval or disapproval, and although they may clarify on occasion, they must be careful not to inject their own thoughts. The group atmosphere is extremely permissive. The leader of a group-centered group always tries to view the discussion from the frame of reference of the member who is speaking.

> **Laissez-faire leadership is permissive.**

The relationship between the styles of leadership can be seen on the continuum in Figure 15.1.

As we suggested, participative leadership is usually desirable. Although the group usually takes longer to reach a consensus, member satisfaction is highest. Each group has its own needs, however, and each leader will want to select a style that is in keeping with these needs and with his or her personality.[8]

Functions of a Leader

After considering which style of leadership fits your personality, you must give some attention to the two major functions of the leader of the small group: the task function and the maintenance function. These two functions are broken down as follows:

> **A leader of a small group has a task function and a maintenance function.**

Group Task Function

1. Defining the problem to be discussed
2. Ordering the sequence of topics
3. Asking for information about the problem
4. Clarifying the contributions of group members
5. Asking for evaluation of information

> **The task function pertains to completing the group task.**

Figure 15.1 Styles of Leadership

Minimum Control	Leaderless Group	Group-Centered Leadership	Participative Leadership	Supervisory Leadership	Authoritarian Leadership	Maximum Control

6. Asking for solutions
7. Asking for evaluation of solutions.

Group Maintenance Function

1. Encouraging participation by all members
2. Developing a permissive and informal group atmosphere
3. Seeking to make group members feel secure
4. Ensuring that contrasting views are presented
5. Providing for release of tension
6. Resolving differences among group members

The behaviors included under the task function have to do with completing the group task. The behaviors included under the maintenance function keep the group working together.

The presence or absence of effective leadership is especially obvious in the way meetings are conducted. The group leadership guide lists behaviors which are characteristic of effective leaders.

The maintenance function pertains to keeping the group working together.

Functions of Group Members

The success of small-group decision making also depends upon the group participants. They can make the leader's job easier by trying to follow the agenda and by being aware of the flow of the discussion. Group members can help move the group toward its goal.

Contributing Information. The problem-solving group needs information to reach decisions. Effective group members bring information they have gathered about the topic. Some participants have a tendency to

Contributing information is an important function of a group member.

Group Leadership Guide

In conducting a meeting you should:

Start the meeting on time.

Keep the group aware of the goal(s) of the meeting.

Control the discussion by discouraging digressions.

Encourage quiet group members to participate.

Provide frequent internal summaries as a means of clarifying what has transpired thus far.

End the meeting by summarizing what has been accomplished.

divulge all their information the first time they have the opportunity to speak; this leads to disorganization. People need to develop the ability to see where their information on the topic applies. Timing is a critical element in presenting information.

Evaluating Information.   Group participants need to bring several critical skills to the problem-solving situation. One of the most important is the ability to carefully examine all information presented to the group. Participants should offer additional supporting evidence when they have it and contradictory evidence when it is available. Fallacious reasoning and unsupported assertions should be exposed. Good reasoning and accurate information are essential to the group problem-solving process. Participants should resist the tendency to accept everything that is said during the discussion.

Group members should be prepared to evaluate information.

Asking Questions.   Group participants perform an important function by asking pertinent questions at appropriate times. Such questions help to expose inaccurate information or to clarify a point that one of the other members is attempting to make. The use of questions encourages feedback, aids the understanding of all group members, and helps keep the participants on the main subject of the discussion. The attention of the entire group can be focused upon the central issue of the discussion by a well-phrased, pertinent question.

Asking pertinent questions is another function of group members.

Empathetic Listening.   Earlier we stressed the importance listening has in the total communication process. Effective group participants will listen to the content of what other members are saying and will also be

A good group participant listens between the lines.

Group Participation Guide

As a participant in a meeting you should:

Be on time.

Be alert in both attitude and physical bearing.

Participate early in the meeting and as often as you have something relevant to say.

Keep your comments brief. It is better to contribute several times making one point at a time than to make a series of points at one time.

Take notes to retain specific information.

alert to listen between the lines. The empathetic listener tries to see the topic from the other members' frames of reference as they speak. It's important to be sensitive to the attitudes and feelings of the other group members.

Group Thinking.　The group member needs to be aware that group thinking (not groupthink) is different from individual thinking. Participants need to relate their comments to the group's thinking. People should refer to what their fellow group members have said and what has already been agreed. Usually the longer people participate in a group, the more skilled they become in group thinking. It's not a good idea to try to move ahead too quickly. For the group to function effectively, the group must think together.

Participants should relate their comments to the group's thinking.

Certain behaviors at meetings distinguish superior participants from the others. The group participation guide lists behaviors which are characteristic of effective participants.

Summary

There can be little question small groups play an increasingly important role in organizations. There are significant advantages and disadvantages in making decisions through the small-group format. While small groups are not the answer to all problem solving, there are times when using small groups will result in a better decision, wider acceptance of the decision, or stronger commitment to the decision.

Small group decision making is more effective when a problem-solving agenda is followed. The most widely used format is the six-step sequence based on Dewey's Reflective Thinking Process. The ideal solution form and the single question form are other formats groups sometimes use.

The nominal group approach can overcome some of the potential problems of interacting groups. This approach is especially useful in identifying causes of a problem and in suggesting potential solutions.

While cohesion is important to effective group functioning, it can result in groupthink or in poor decisions when carried to an extreme. Finally, some specific behaviors for effective leadership and participation in small groups were suggested. The growing emphasis on the use of groups in business organizations is evident in a variety of worker involvement schemes such as quality circles.

Footnotes

[1]John Dewey, *How We Think* (Boston: D.C. Heath, 1933).

[2]Carl Larson, "Forms of Analysis and Small Group Problem Solving," *Speech Monographs*, 36 (1969):453.

[3]Ibid., p. 453.

[4]Richard C. Huseman, "The Role of the Nominal Group in Small Group Communication,"

Readings in Interpersonal and Organizational Communication, Richard C. Huseman, Cal M. Logue, and Dwight L. Freshley, eds. (Boston: Holbrook Press, 1977), pp. 493–502.

[5]Irving L. Janis, *Groupthink,* 2d ed., (Boston: Houghton Mifflin Company, 1982).

[6]Ibid., pp. 197–198.

[7]Ibid., pp. 198–199.

[8]This discussion of leadership styles is adapted from Charles R. Gruner, Cal M. Logue, Dwight L. Freshley, and Richard C. Huseman, *Speech Communication in Society,* 2d ed. (Boston: Allyn & Bacon, Inc., 1977), pp. 258–260.

Review Questions

1. What are the identifying characteristics of small group communication?
2. In what specific ways can the small group format be utilized in organizations?
3. There are major advantages and disadvantages of reaching decisions in small groups. Discuss them and give an example of each.
4. Briefly explain the six distinct steps in the problem-solving agenda.
5. What is brainstorming?
6. What are the developmental stages of most groups?
7. Discuss how the nominal group procedure can prove useful to group decision making.
8. In what three ways is the nominal group approach to problem solving superior to the interacting group approach?
9. Define the concept of cohesion as it relates to small-group decision making. Why is it such a critical factor in determining successful group problem solving?
10. What is groupthink? How does it contribute to irrational and poorly formulated decisions?
11. As the leader of a small decision-making group, you are anxious to achieve a consensus without ignoring alternative courses of action. How might you and your group members prevent groupthink from obstructing a successful outcome?
12. What are the major styles of group leadership? Which style best fits your personality? Why?
13. Most of the time participative leadership style is the most desirable. Why?
14. Group members play a vital role in successful group decision making. In what ways can the participants help move the group toward its goal?

Exercises

1. Divide the class into groups of five or six and use the brainstorming technique to generate solutions to a problem that confronts your school.

2. Attend a meeting of the local city council and observe the interaction of council members. Record your observations.

3. Critically evaluate a meeting connected with your interests at school—student government, fraternity or sorority, professional honor society, or the like. Include both pros and cons of the proceedings in your evaluation.

4. Select a problem that is common to yourself and a peer group. Reach a decision on your own, then discuss it with the group. Record any new viewpoints that the group brought up which you overlooked in your original decision.

5. Lead a group discussion about a pertinent issue such as job placement or course curriculum degree requirements. How did your role as a group leader differ from that of a participant? Rotate the leadership role among other group members and describe how individual styles produced various types of interaction.

6. Assemble two groups of four to six people. Discuss an issue. How did the conclusions and decision-making procedures differ between the two groups?

7. Gather together with 11 classmates. Split up into two groups of four and eight, then attempt to resolve the same problem. Did the size of the two groups affect the communication process and the eventual outcome? How?

8. Divide the class into three groups and select a single problem in which the participants are interested. Assign each group to take a different approach to solving the problem. One group uses the Steps of Reflective Thinking; another uses the single question form; the third uses the ideal solution form. Following the exercise, discuss the differences and similarities of the three approaches.

9. Have everyone in class make a list of the problems one experiences as a new member of an established group. Then divide into groups of five or six and, using the individual lists, construct a master list for each group. Each group should then identify ways in which group members can overcome these problems.

10. Using the problem lists generated in Exercise 9, groups should identify ways that group leaders can assist members in overcoming those problems.

Case

The Realty Tangle
Doris D. Phillips, Ph.D.
School of Business Administration
University of Mississippi

Kilgore and Mitchell, Realtors, is a Mississippi real-estate firm with two realtors, six full-time salespeople, two part-time salespeople, and two full-time secretaries. The firm has been in business for 15 years and has a strong local and regional reputation.

Recent problems have arisen that are having a detrimental effect on the usual harmonious atmosphere of the company office.

Virginia Bolt, 55, has been with the firm in part-time sales for less than five years, but she has built a reasonably large clientele. She has worked for 25 years in various clerical positions in banks and with governmental agencies. She successfully passed the state real-estate examination and received her license as salesperson at age 50.

Virginia has done a very good job in her previous positions because of her excellent clerical skills, but she has been unable to remain in any job for any great length of time due to an inability to get along with other people. She has a very aggressive personality and is a people manipulator—traits that would normally seem to be assets in the sales field.

Her recent actions in the real-estate firm indicate a renewal of the old people problem. In addition to antagonizing other salespeople in the firm by undercutting and backstabbing, she has allegedly violated an important point in realty ethics by advertising property in her own name with no reference to Kilgore and Mitchell as her employers.

Realtor Donald O. Mitchell, the junior partner in the firm, wants to release Virginia from her position with the firm. He indicates that her unethical actions could damage the firm's good name. He also believes that her personality is disrupting an otherwise smooth operation.

Senior partner James J. Kilgore disagrees with Donald and wishes to give Virginia another chance. His reasoning is that her successful record in sales outweighs her shortcomings in other areas.

Evidently, interpersonal human relations skills are needed in communication concerning this situation.

■ ■ ■

Case Questions

In a group of five persons, analyze the case study, keeping in mind the field of human relations and psychology in communication.

1. Considering the feelings of all the individuals involved, make the management decision as to what should be done about Virginia's tenure with the firm.
2. What method(s) should be used to communicate the decision reached in Question 1 to Virginia and to other personnel that will provide the greatest degree of acceptance and harmony?
3. Using the method(s) of communication decided upon in Question 2, draft messages to Virginia and to other employees of Kilgore and Mitchell, Realtors, informing them of the decision reached in Question 1.

Case

The Hemphill Company
Elizabeth Plunkett
West Georgia College

One of the nation's leading shirt manufacturers, the Hemphill Company, a moderate size, family-owned business, has recently acquired a highly sophisticated Japanese pressing system. As Hemphill's purchase of this state-of-the-art equipment represented the introduction of this technology into the United States, the Japanese electronics manufacturer will provide specialized training for Hemphill's mechanics. The Japanese firm will assume all costs—except for transportation to and from Japan—for an unlimited number of Hemphill's mechanics to participate in this three-week program.

The company president called a meeting to determine who should attend this training program. Present at the meeting are: Mr. Hemphill, the company president/general manager; Mr. Cates, the production manager, who assists the president with many management decisions (he is ambitious to become general manager and considered by Mr. Hemphill to be capable); Mr. Day, the personnel manager, whose responsibilities uniquely but appropriately include overseeing maintenance personnel, equipment needs, and small parts procurement; Mr. Miller, the research and development manager, who is responsible for managing training programs; and Mr. Lee, the chief engineer, who is responsible for setting rates and pay-back figures on new equipment.

The management group considers the following individuals as possible candidates: Candidate 1, the mechanics' foreman, respected by his subordinates, has refused previous training opportunities, believing that they required too much personal time. Candidate 2 was stationed in Japan in the military, and his familiarity with Japan is considered an asset. Even though Candidate 2 is highly skilled on manual equipment, electronic machines under his supervision have not performed well. Candidate 3 has consistently been Hemphill's top performer in training programs, and while extremely successful with electronic equipment, he appears to be negligent in routine maintenance of equipment. Candidate 4 has previously received additional training to become the company specialist on one piece of electronic equipment. Candidate 5 works exceptionally well with Candidate 4 and the electronic machinery under their joint supervision has attained optimal productivity. A dedicated employee, Candidate 5 has had personal problems with drug addiction and marital difficulties. Although he appears to have conquered his drug problem, his marital situation still conflicts with his job. Recently, his wife objected to his absence while he attended a two-day training session. Despite this conflict, he excelled in the course. All of the above candidates are from 28 to 34 years of age, except Candidates 1 and 5 who are 40 to 42 years old.

The managers agreed that Candidate 1 should be included in the program, in spite of his previous reluctance to accept training. They felt that he needed updating in this technology and that his leadership could influence the success of this program. Candidate 1 enthusiastically accepted the challenge of this important project. When asked for his suggestions regarding Candidates 2 through 5, he responded that he had no preference among them and that he had no additional names for consideration.

After much deliberation, the managers reached a standstill in the decision-making process. Since Mr. Hemphill was adamant that performance and teamwork were essential factors in candidate selection, Candidates 4 and 5 met these particular requirements. Faced with the issue of Candidate 5's marital conflict, Mr. Hemphill emphasized that management must be careful about making decisions for subordinates based on how they (managers) judge subordinates' non-work environment. He felt that Candidate 5 should have the opportunity to choose whether or not to accept the assignment.

Mr. Cates supported Candidates 2 and 3, believing that Candidate 2's knowledge of Japan was invaluable and that Candidate 3's proficiency and success with electronics equipment made him a natural choice. On the other hand, Mr. Day suggested that the foreman should make the final decision but that personally he would eliminate Candidates 3 and 4 from consideration. He objected to Candidate 3's maintenance record and stressed that Candidate 4, with his specialized training, could not be spared. Mr. Day also indicated that a company's extensive investment and dependence on any single individual could create unnecessary vulnerability.

Conversely, Mr. Miller proposed that Candidates 3 and 4 were the only logical selection based on their strong training performance records. Mr. Lee, however, firmly believed that all the candidates should attend the course. He felt this solution not only would assure the payback on this expensive system but also would resolve the deadlock in this discussion.

What course(s) of action would be best for the Hemphill Company?

■ ■ ■

Case Questions

1. What could be done to facilitate the decision-making process?
2. What interpersonal factors influence the decision makers in their selection?
3. Which candidate(s) would you select to attend the conference? Support your recommendations.

Communication and Conflict

Learning Objectives
1. To understand the nature and role of conflict in organizations.
2. To become aware of the characteristics of conflict behavior.
3. To examine the role of perception in conflict situations.
4. To understand when conflict is useful and when it should be reduced or eliminated.
5. To recognize the different styles of conflict management.
6. To learn guidelines for communicating in conflict situations.

DeWitt County, Texas, was the scene of an intense five-year conflict. From 1868 to 1873 this Texas county was the setting for a bitter struggle between the Taylor and Sutton families. Frequently during this five-year period there were bloody gun battles between members of the opposing families that would also include friends of the two families. General stores, taverns, and even the streets became the scenes of ambushes, knife fights, and shoot-outs. Late in 1873 there was a week-long battle between the Taylor and Sutton families. When the smoke had cleared, the heads of both families were dead. In addition, dozens of other family members and friends of the two families were also dead.

Interestingly enough, no one could really say what had caused this intense conflict. It was known, however, that tension had existed since before the Civil War, when the two families lived close to each other in South Carolina and Georgia.[1] ∎

It seems strange to us that the Suttons and Taylors could continue their deadly conflict for years without really knowing why. Most of us find it difficult to imagine ourselves participating in such bloody fighting. However, all of us experience some type of conflict each day of our lives.

Tensions, antagonisms, and frustrations always occur when people work together. Think about any part-time or summer jobs you have held. You will probably remember disagreements, perhaps even fights, between employees and supervisor or between coworkers. Aside from personality clashes, people simply have different viewpoints about the way things should be done. Conflict is thus an appropriate topic for a business communication text because conflict is directly related to communication. While we can have communication without conflict, we cannot have conflict without some form of communication. More important, through communication we can correct conflict when it occurs. Whether verbal or nonverbal, communication can soothe tempers, settle misunderstandings, and get the organization back to a normal work schedule.

We become aware of conflict through some form of communication.

In this chapter we examine communication and conflict, discuss the nature of conflict and the role of perception in conflict, and finally make some suggestions for managing communication in conflict situations.

The Nature of Conflict

Conflict can be either constructive or destructive. For example, constructive conflict occurs when the adrenal glands deliver extra energy. We are in a state of tensed readiness in which hearing and vision become more acute. On the job this type of constructive conflict, or stress—properly channeled—can stimulate a person to put forth superior effort. Many active people thrive on conflict. Conflict is an inevitable

Conflict can be constructive.

byproduct of having an interesting and challenging job. For some of us conflict is the spice of life, and it can have a beneficial effect on our physical and mental health. Competition between your organization and a competing company can be healthy for the members of both organizations and can be beneficial to your company.

On the other hand, conflict can be damaging. Too much conflict can be harmful when your overmobilized body refuses to relax and assume normal activity. Your blood pressure remains high, your back muscles develop spasms, and your judgment is impaired. Excessive conflict over time can make one unable to work. **Conflict can be destructive.**

Competition within an organization is potentially dangerous because it can divide loyalties and hamper cooperation. Even competition as apparently harmless as an interdepartmental bowling league should be examined carefully.

Conflict is like one of the modern miracle drugs: the correct dosage can be good for you, but too much can bring damage. We need to be able to distinguish between constructive and destructive conflict. One level of conflict may key you up for superior performance. Too much conflict may cause worry or fear, hamper your work performance, and in some cases lead to ulcers and other forms of physical and mental illnesses.

Realizing that moderate conflict can be constructive while more intense or prolonged conflict can be destructive, we are ready to look at the conditions that can lead to conflict situations. What causes conflict? Does conflict simply happen, or do certain conditions make conflict more likely to occur? In fact, there are certain social relationships that characterize various kinds of conflict behavior. Each one could occur in your work area. As future managers, the more aware you are of these conflict settings, the better your chances of correcting them and running a smooth operation: **Certain conditions may lead to conflict.**

1.   **Ambiguous jurisdictions.** Conflict will be greater when the lines separating each employee's jurisdiction (area of job responsibility) are unclear. When two people have related job tasks which have ambiguous boundaries, the potential for conflict between them increases. For example, consider the case of a department head to whom three first-line supervisors report. Each of these supervisors should have clearly defined job responsibilities so that the potential for overlap among the three is reduced. Otherwise, confusion and conflict result as the supervisors all try to do each other's job. In addition, the boundaries between the department head and the supervisors must also be clearly spelled out, otherwise the supervisors may resent the department head's interference in their work responsibilities. The result is a department full of discord and conflict over unclear limits of authority. Such an antagonistic situation can be avoided if job descriptions are clarified so that all employees know the extent of their work responsibilities.

2.   **Conflict of interest.** Conflict will be greater where people's interests diverge. Consider the following example of a conflict between

the marketing manager and the plant (production) manager of a leading producer of chocolate. Each manager would like to have more control over the factors that affect the company's profitability. In the face of fierce competition from other chocolate manufacturers, the marketing manager occasionally wants to run a sampling campaign to support a new candy bar. This manager needs to act fast before competitors match the new chocolate product. However, when the marketing manager asks for sharply increased production capacity during the sampling campaign, the plant manager refuses. The hiring and training of new workers would only be temporary. After the sampling campaign is completed, the company would lay off the new workers. The result is a conflict of interest between the marketing and plant managers and a competitive edge for rival chocolate manufacturers.

3.   Communication barriers. Conflict will be greater when barriers to communication exist. If parties are separated from each other physically or by time—for example, the day shift versus the night shift—the opportunity for conflict is increased. To illustrate, suppose a company employs only one plant supervisor, who works the day shift and leaves orders at the beginning of each week for the workers on the night shift. By the end of the week, however, these orders have been only partially carried out. The supervisor can't figure out why. Obviously, the supervisor's absence from the night shift has posed a communication barrier, which in turn causes decreased output. Thus, space or time separations can promote isolated group interests rather than advance a common effort toward joint goals.

4.   Dependence of one party. Conflict will be greater where one party is dependent upon another. Where parties are dependent, they must rely on each other for performance of tasks or for provision of resources. Thus, the opportunity for conflict to occur is increased. For example, a supervisor who depends upon the preparation of a cost-effectiveness report by a subordinate in order to make a marketing decision, may monitor the subordinate's progress. The subordinate resents this close supervision and in retaliation takes a long time to prepare the report. The supervisor, in turn, reminds the subordinate of a forthcoming performance evaluation. Thus, the interdependence of both supervisor and subordinate fuels the potential for serious conflict.

5.   Differentiation in organizations. Conflict will be greater as the degree of differentiation, or the division of labor, in an organization increases. When people work together in a complex organization, there is evidence that conflict is related to the number of organizational levels, the number of distinct job specialties represented, and the degree to which labor is divided in the organization. For example, consider the administrators in your college: most likely there is a dean, an associate dean, department heads, program advisors, and secretaries. All of these people administer some aspect of your curriculum and other educational needs. However, they are at different levels of the organizational hierarchy and handle specialized tasks. Although these university employees share a common focus, their different positions and job concentrations can lead to overlap and conflict.

6.   Association of the parties. Conflict will be greater as the degree of interaction of the parties increases. As used here, degree of association, or interaction, refers both to the parties' participation in decision making and to informal relations between them. When parties make decisions jointly, the opportunity for conflict is greater, which may explain why some managers are reluctant to involve others in decision making. These managers would prefer to make decisions on their own rather than risk a difference of opinion with a colleague. However, there is a trade-off between the possibility of gaining valuable suggestions and the possibility of an argument. Thus, the association of parties has constructive and destructive possibilities.

7.   Need for consensus. Conflict will be greater when consensus between the parties is necessary. When all parties must agree on a decision so that no individual believes the decision is unacceptable, it is possible to avoid conflict by having mechanisms such as voting to make decisions without the confrontation of consensus. However, such mechanisms themselves may have undesirable consequences. They may offer an easy way out of the immediate conflict but may not solve the problem. Settling the matter haphazardly may only postpone the hard decisions until a true crisis occurs. The point is that when consensus is difficult to achieve, the resultant conflict should not be avoided but used in a constructive manner.

8.   Behavior regulations. Conflicts will be greater when behavior regulations are imposed. Regulating mechanisms, which include standardized procedures, rules, and policies, seem to do two things at once. On the one hand, they reduce the likelihood of conflict because they make relationships predictable and reduce the need for arbitrary decisions. Some individuals need specific guidelines explaining how to perform their jobs. They are only comfortable making routine decisions about their work. Other individuals have a greater need for autonomy and self-control. Regulating mechanisms that increase the degree of control may be resisted by some workers and welcomed by others. For either type of individual, if the adherence to or the imposition of rules becomes discretionary, further sources of disagreement are created. If behavioral regulations fail to match individual needs of employees, conflict is bound to occur.

9.   Unresolved prior conflicts. Conflicts will be greater as the number of unresolved prior conflicts increases. That is, the longer problems are ignored or postponed, the worse new conflicts become. Suppression of conflict through the use of power or compromises to which the parties are uncommitted creates conditions and expectations that may lead to further conflict.[2]

Suppose the people in an office want to streamline operating procedures and rearrange desks and other office furniture to fit this new office reorganization. The workers are not content with the present office organiza-

tion and their lack of input into office policy. For some time their complaints have been ignored by the division manager, who hoped they would tire of asking for changes and drop the matter once and for all. Together with their supervisor, the employees seek permission from the division manager to draw up reorganization plans. In an effort to placate them, the manager approves their request. The office members and their supervisor earnestly devise new guidelines and office rearrangement. They submit the guidelines to the division manager, who rejects their proposals because he doesn't have sufficient time to review the plans properly and he fears unsatisfactory changes. The staff becomes very angry and seeks outside help in organizing a union. Thus, the manager's attempt to suppress conflict by the use of power has simply increased the original conflict to a crisis point. This example underscores the idea that unresolved prior conflicts are active breeding agents for future crises.

The conditions that can lead to conflict need not always do so. However, these conditions create the opportunity for conflict to occur. Being aware of the conditions for discord will help us to avoid some potential conflicts and to understand other conflicts once they become apparent.

Having determined the conditions that can lead to conflict, we can examine the nature of conflict in greater detail. When we experience a particular conflict, we may feel frustration or even anger. Sometimes it is difficult for us to know exactly why we experience this conflict. Furthermore, we are not sure exactly how to remedy the situation.

A convenient perspective for examining conflict is what Pondy has termed the *conflict episode,* which consists of five distinct stages:

> The conflict episode provides a perspective for viewing the conflict situation.

The Conflict Episode

□ 1. **Latent conflict** deals with underlying sources of organizational conflict. Among these sources are competition for scarce resources (e.g., materials, money, labor), drives for autonomy, and differing subunit goals within the organization.

□ 2. **Perceived conflict** can supposedly occur whether or not latent conflict is present. When no latent conflict exists but conflict is nevertheless perceived, it is said to be a result of the parties' misunderstandings of one another's true positions. When latent conflict exists but fails to

A Personal Conflict Episode

□ 1. **Latent conflict:** You attend a university that has a very limited number of tennis courts. During the last few years more and more students have started playing the game. You have become an avid tennis player and two or three nights a week you try to play.

□ 2. **Perceived conflict:** On Monday evening, you and a friend decide to play tennis. As the two of you take your rackets and get in the car, your friend remarks, "Boy, I sure hope we can get a court." You glance at your watch and notice that it is almost 6:30—a time when the

The Conflict Episode
(continued)

reach the level of awareness, it is not because such conflict is not actually perceived, but because certain individual defense mechanisms tend to suppress it.

□ 3. **Felt conflict** may also be termed *the personalization of conflict,* because at this stage the conflict actually affects the individual directly. Felt conflict is normally a function of either: (a) individual anxieties created by organizational demands that the individual perceives as limiting personal growth; or, (b) total involvement in a relationship, making an individual necessarily more aware of the occurrence of conflict.

□ 4. **Manifest conflict** is identified simply as the actual occurrence of conflicting behavior. It may range from aggression to apathy or even extremely rigid adherence to rules with the intention of frustrating another party to the relationship. So long as both parties perceive a specific behavior to be conflicting, and so long as the party indulging in the behavior persists, a clear case of manifest conflict has developed.

□ 5. **Conflict aftermath** is a function of how well the entire episode or sequence of episodes has been resolved. Perhaps this stage will reveal that bases for a more cooperative relationship have been established;

A Personal Conflict Episode (continued)

few tennis courts are likely to be in use. Suddenly, you perceive a potential conflict situation.

□ 3. **Felt conflict:** As you approach the tennis courts, you observe that all the courts are occupied. Then you notice that the group on the last court has apparently finished and the players are leaving the court. Just then another car speeds into the parking lot. Two players quickly jump out and rush toward the court. You and your partner make a dash for the court.

□ 4. **Manifest conflict:** Your partner wins the race and secures the court. As you and your partner begin play, the two players that lost the footrace come onto the court and sit down close to the playing area. During the match the two other players make comments when you or your partner miss a shot. Your match stands one set to one set. As you begin the third set, your two friends stand up and start bouncing tennis balls with their rackets. On your first serve you double fault. You eventually lose the set 6–4.

□ 5. **Conflict aftermath:** As you drive home, you and your friend discuss the possibility of trying to play tennis again on Thursday. Neither of you displays much interest as you both recall the conflict that frequently

The Conflict Episode
(continued)

or it may suggest how newly perceived problems might be handled; or, if the latent conditions were merely suppressed instead of resolved, they may emerge at this time to foster more serious difficulties. The aftermath stage suggests the dynamic nature of conflict; that is, a conflict between or among two or more individuals in an organization is not likely to consist of only one episode, but it is made up of a sequence of such episodes. Each one results from the resolution of conflict in the previous episode.

A Personal Conflict Episode (continued)

results from the limited number of courts available. Early the next morning your tennis friend calls you and excitedly tells you that his parents have just given him a birthday present—a membership in a new tennis club. The membership guarantees six hours of court time each week. Suddenly your interest in the game of tennis is renewed.

L.R. Pondy, "Organizational Conflict Concepts and Models," John M. Thomas and Warren Bennis, eds., *Management of Change and Conflict* (Middlesex, England: Penguin Books, 1972), pp. 360–366.

The conflict episode provided by Pondy and the personal conflict episode that paralleled it are useful in helping to view conflict situations. Since we have defined the conditions that can lead to conflict and the conflict episode, we are ready to discuss the role of perception as it relates to conflict.

Perception and Conflict

The adage, "beauty is in the eye of the beholder," makes the point that what one person perceives as beauty may not be thought beautiful by another. We have all observed situations where two people observe the same event yet later describe two different situations. People do not behave according to the facts as other people interpret them. Our behavior is based on our unique perceptions of ourselves and the world in which we live. Indeed, all behavior is completely determined by the way we perceive the events around us.

In conflict situations perception also plays a major role. In some cases perception may be the cause of conflict. Whatever the cause of a conflict situation, those involved must be aware of the conflict in order for it to exist. Perception as it relates to conflict can be illustrated by the following five conflict situations:

Conflict must be perceived for it to exist.

1.   **Intra-individual conflict** occurs when the designated perceiver experiences conflict within himself or herself. Such conflict may arise from personal or job responsibilities and may influence, either directly or indirectly, job performance.

2.   **Inter-individual conflict** exists between the designated perceiver and another individual within the organization. Although the other person need not be aware of the conflict, the perceiver of the conflict situation recognizes the present or future impact it can have on job performance.

3.   **Intra-group conflict** occurs between the ·designated perceiver and his or her immediate group within the organization. The immediate group can consist of one's work team, department, or union. Whether fully or only superficially aware of the conflict issue, the perceiver realizes that it can directly or indirectly affect job performance.

4.   **Inter-group conflict** arises between the designated perceiver's immediate group and another group within the organization. Again, the perceiver's involvement may not be critical, but he or she must be aware of the situation and the potential impact it can have on work performance.

5.   **Organization-environment conflict** arises between the perceiver's organization and the environment it is part of. Environment may refer to the city, country, or world in which the organization exists. For example, if the environment consists of a home office and a number of branches, each branch may be viewed as a single entity within its local environment or as part of the entire organization within a state, nation, or worldwide setting. Whatever the context, the environmental boundary should be defined so that the conflict situation is accurately understood. As with the other four conflict circumstances, the perceiver may be acutely or only casually aware of the conflict and its effect upon job performance.

To illustrate these five levels of perceiving conflict, take the case of a second-year business student at a leading two-year college.

Two conflict case studies

*T*his student has worked hard throughout her college career, maintained a high grade point average, and, as she nears graduation, is anxious about getting a good job. She has recently gotten a very low grade in one of her courses and is worried that the grade will lower her overall average. Furthermore, she believes that the grade is unfair since she always completed her homework on time and had worked hard to write an excellent term paper. She wants to discuss the matter with her professor in hopes of a grade change, but she wonders if she dare take the time away from job hunting (intra-individual conflict). Furthermore, her professor is known to be an insensitive person who reacts poorly to any student's request for a grade change (inter-individual conflict). If the student gets her grade changed, then her classmates might *start squabbling about who else deserves a raise in grade (intra-group conflict). If several grades are changed and word gets back to students from previous semesters, they might complain about unequal grading standards among the different classes (inter-group conflict). Finally, if word of the discrepancy gets to the board of examiners which accredits the college's business program, then the business department risks having its accreditation reviewed (organization-environment conflict).* ■

Then there's the example of Jeff, the assistant manager of production for a medium-size company that makes pleasure sailboats.

Although not a yacht designer, Jeff sees a modification to the keel of the top of the line boats as an idea with potential. He prepared a proposal and submitted it to his immediate supervisor.

Jeff received no response to his proposal for four months. Then he heard through the grapevine that some major modifications were to be made to the larger boats. The production line was halted for those models.

When Jeff asked his boss about what was going on, his supervisor was evasive. The following week, the company announced a breakthrough in keel design for their large offshore boats. This design would be incorporated immediately in selected models. At the same time the company announced Jeff's boss would be promoted to vice president.

Jeff was unsure whether to do or say anything about his report (intra-individual conflict). He was tempted to speak to his boss, who was the only person he had given his report. Jeff knew there was potential here for inter-individual conflict since he believed his idea had been stolen.

Jeff didn't want to let others in the department know of his anger for he knew it could create unrest (intra-group conflict). He also was wary of talking to acquaintances in the yacht design department which had been mentioned as deeply involved in the keel design project (inter-group conflict). Jeff considered going to the editor of the employee newspaper, the trade journal, or even the local daily newspaper, but reconsidered (organization-environmental conflict). ■

Table 16.1 summarizes the five levels of analyzing the various sources of conflict involved in the first case study—the student's deciding whether or not to ask the professor for a grade change. Although the example does not provide entries for each column of the table, it is easy to imagine other examples that would illustrate those areas.

Now that we have examined the role of perception in several types of conflict situations, we are ready to discuss specific suggestions for using communication to manage conflict situations.

Table 16.1   An Analysis of Conflict (Designated Perceiver: A College Student)

	Perceived Impact of Source of Conflict			
	Direct (Impact on Student)		**Indirect (Impact on Extra-Organizational Concerns)**	
Perceived Source of Conflict	**Current (Operating Now)**	**Potential (Likely to Operate)**	**Current**	**Potential**
1. Intra-individual	Student wonders whether to spend time getting grade changed.			Possible loss of time for job search.
2. Inter-individual		Conflict with student and professor over grade change.		Strained relationship with professor.
3. Intra-group	Concern over the furor in class over changing only one student's grade.	Students argue among themselves about who deserves a higher grade, and the conflict becomes worse.	Low ticket sales to end-of-school party because of tension caused by grade controversy.	
4. Inter-group	Class groups from previous semesters quarrel over why their grade changes weren't granted.	Class groups from different semesters may complain to dean about unfair grade distribution.		
5. Organization-environment	Board of examiners has the power to investigate irregular grading policies.	Angry students contact board of examiners.		Loss of accreditation by board of examiners.

Managing Conflict Situations

We established earlier that in some cases a certain level of conflict will produce better performance. The concept of conflict management is based on this premise. In other words, managers in organizations need to distinguish between conflict that is useful and conflict that should be reduced or eliminated. The objective of conflict management is to see that conflict remains creative and productive. Besides requiring manag-

Conflict management can improve performance.

ers to be able to distinguish between functional and dysfunctional conflict, conflict management also requires that managers develop individuals who can work under conflict and tension and still be productive members in the organization. Realizing that conflict management must allow some types of conflict and must reduce or eliminate other types, we can consider approaches to conflict reduction.

In deciding how to handle a particular conflict situation, we first need to understand it. The following suggestions are a method for analyzing conflict situations.

1.   Assess the importance and impact of the conflict. Is the conflict useful and motivational in nature and likely to improve the performance of one or several members of the organization? Or is the conflict damaging and in need of resolution? If the conflict is harmful, the remaining steps of analysis should be used.

Analyzing conflict situations can aid in conflict management.

2.   Identify the type of conflict. *Intra-individual conflict* is conflict individuals experience within themselves.   *Inter-individual conflict* is conflict the individual experiences with another.   *Intra-group conflict* is conflict between the individual and his or her immediate group within the organization.   *Inter-group conflict* is conflict between the individual's immediate group and another group within the organization. *Organization-environment conflict* is conflict between the individual's organization and the larger outside environment.

3.   Select an overall strategy for dealing with the conflict. *Controlling the conflict.* Perhaps at this time it is either impossible to resolve completely, or it would take too much time and energy to do so. *Resolving the conflict.* If the conflict is serious, you will want to resolve it.

4.   Identify methods for reducing the conflict. Decide on the basic approach to conflict resolution. Select particular communication strategies.

Now that we have briefly identified the major steps in analyzing a conflict situation, we are ready to discuss Step 4 in greater detail. At this point let us identify some basic styles of conflict management.

There are at least two major concerns in every conflict situation. The first is the extent to which an individual wants to meet personal goals. A second concern is the extent to which the individual wants to maintain a relationship with another individual or group or wants to be accepted by that individual or group.[3] The way these two concerns interact is demonstrated in Figure 16.1. Concern for personal goals is scaled from one to nine representing the increasing degree of importance in the mind of the individual (1 = low concern; and 9 = high concern). The concern for relationships is also scaled from one (low concern) to nine (high concern). Given this scale, Blake and Mouton identify the following styles: high concern for personal goals and low concern for relationships (9, 1); low concern for personal goals and high concern for relation-

Two major concerns exist in every conflict situation.

Figure 16.1 The Conflict Grid

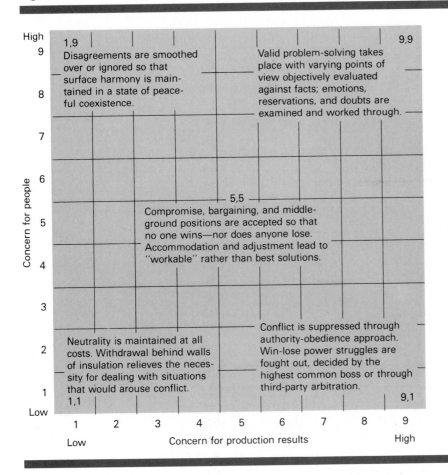

High
9 | **1,9**
Disagreements are smoothed over or ignored so that surface harmony is maintained in a state of peaceful coexistence.

Valid problem-solving takes place with varying points of view objectively evaluated against facts; emotions, reservations, and doubts are examined and worked through.
9,9

5,5
Compromise, bargaining, and middle-ground positions are accepted so that no one wins—nor does anyone lose. Accommodation and adjustment lead to "workable" rather than best solutions.

Neutrality is maintained at all costs. Withdrawal behind walls of insulation relieves the necessity for dealing with situations that would arouse conflict.

Conflict is suppressed through authority-obedience approach. Win-lose power struggles are fought out, decided by the highest common boss or through third-party arbitration.

1,1
Low

(Y-axis: Concern for people, 1–9)
(X-axis: Concern for production results, Low 1 ... 9 High)
9,1

ships (1, 9); low concern for personal goals and low concern for relationships (1, 1); moderate concern for personal goals and moderate concern for relationships (5, 5); and high concern for personal goals and high concern for relationships (9, 9). With this overview we are ready to examine each style in more detail.[4]

The Tough Battler Style. The win-lose style (9, 1) is the trademark of the tough battler who seeks to meet goals at all costs without concern for the needs of others. For this type of individual losing means the loss of self-image. This type of person is willing to sacrifice individuals or groups to be a winner.

The Friendly Helper Style. The yield-lose style (1, 9) involves the friendly helper who overvalues relationships with others and undervalues the achievement of personal goals. People of this type desire acceptance by others so much that they give in to the desires of others almost all the time. They always avoid conflict in favor of harmony.

The Loser Style.   The lose-leave style (1, 1) is used by the person who sees conflict as a hopeless and useless experience. Rather than be a part of any conflict, this type of person simply withdraws either physically or mentally from the conflict.

The Compromise Style.   The compromise style (5, 5) is exemplified by the middle-of-the-roader who takes the position that half a loaf is better than none. The person using this style looks for a position that allows each side to gain something. This individual always looks for the middle ground when confronted with a conflict situation.

The Problem-Solver Style.   The integrative (9, 9) style is the approach of the problem solver, who seeks to satisfy his or her own goals as well as the goals of others. The individual who takes the problem-solving approach has the following views:

1.   Conflict is natural and helpful and can even lead to a more creative solution if handled properly.
2.   The attitudes and positions of everyone need to be aired when attempting to resolve conflicts.
3.   No one is ever sacrificed simply for the goal of the group.

Filley reports on research that shows the relative effectiveness of three different conflict styles. He cites the work of Cummins, who identified three types of bargainers: the tough bargainer, the soft bargainer, and the equalizer. Filley points out that the tough bargainer is equivalent to the tough battler (9, 1); the soft bargainer equates to the friendly helper (1, 9); and the equalizer is like the problem solver (9, 9).

Filley also describes the consequences when the tough battler, the friendly helper, and the problem solver interact with each other. This is his summary of the interaction of these conflict styles:

Interaction of conflict styles results in various consequences.

▫ When one tough battler meets another tough battler, a stalemate results 80 percent of the time.
▫ When the tough battler meets the friendly helper, the battler wins 90 percent of the time.
▫ When the tough battler meets the problem solver, the battler wins over 50 percent of the time.
▫ Strangely enough, when two friendly helpers meet, a stalemate results 80 percent of the time.
▫ When a friendly helper meets a problem solver, the problem solver usually wins.
▫ When two problem solvers interact, they frequently arrive at an agreeable solution.[5]

Filley concludes that the problem-solving style of conflict resolution is the preferred style in that it provides advantages relative to possible agreements reached through the use of other styles.[6]

Given that the problem-solving approach has the greatest potential for resolving conflict, we can now offer some specific suggestions for communicating in conflict situations. The suggested pattern for communication in conflict is based on Rapoport's Region of Validity Technique.[7] It is illustrated by a common scenario that you may have experienced as a college student. Whether you communicate orally or in writing, the following is useful as an overall approach to communicating with someone in a conflict situation.

1. Communicate to the other people that they have been carefully heard and that understanding exists. If misunderstanding still exists, ask the other party to express their position again. Keep in mind that it is important that the other people are convinced that you understand their exact position.

Suppose you have spent hours writing a term paper for your favorite class. You are expecting a high grade for your extra effort, hence you are very upset when the paper is returned with a low mark. You decide to communicate to the professor that you would like him to reread your paper and raise the grade or at least provide a critique. The professor thinks you are criticizing his grading standards and reacts defensively. To clear up this misunderstanding, you reiterate that you are asking the professor simply to reread the paper and change the grade only if he feels it is justified. The professor relaxes and is more open to discussion about your paper.

2. At this point you enumerate the valid points in the other person's position. Concentrate on the valid points in the other person's position, not the inadequacies of the position.

In explaining your paper's content, you want to make sure the professor understands that you followed his instructions. You avoid criticizing the inadequacies of his assignment and concentrate instead on enumerating his instructions and the corresponding points in your paper.

3. At this stage in the process you invite the other party to participate in the process, as you did in Steps 1 and 2.

Hoping that you have convinced the teacher of your sincere scholarly interest, you ask if you correctly understood his instructions. After he answers this question, then ask your professor to discuss the valid points of your paper to make sure he understood your explanation. The conflict is resolved through open communication about both parties' perceptions of the term paper.

See if you can differentiate these same three stages in this example:

Problem-solving approach is the preferred style.

*Y*ou have been called to the director of personnel's office, and you know several others in your department have also been called in. They were reprimanded for making personal calls on the company's long-distance telephone line. They had to reimburse the company and a disciplinary letter was placed in their personnel files.

You have never used the telephone system for personal calls. Once you did find a colleague using your extension for a private call and although you made it clear not to use your extension again, you let the matter slide since other employees were taking advantage of the system.

The personnel director brings you into the office, points to a chair, and coldly states, "I'm sure you're aware of the policy statement of November 12 about inappropriate use of the company phone system. That policy is the subject of this conversation." You volunteer your position regarding personal use of the system and explain that you have never misused the system. Indeed, you believe in the policy and support it.

You mention that you know of the disciplinary actions on the others and that on one occasion you found someone misusing your extension. You don't volunteer the person's name.

You then say, "I suppose you want to discipline me, too, because an inappropriate call showed on my extension. Is that the purpose of this meeting?"

"Yes and no," is the response. "Alicia told me last week she misused your phone. To get to the bottom of this situation, I asked the others who were involved about your participation. I'm pleased to report they all verify your story. Congratulations—you're one of the few in the department to follow company policy. I just wanted you to know we appreciate your honesty and loyalty. I'm sorry I don't sound more enthusiastic with my praise. I've got a toothache that's killing me!" ■

These guidelines can be applied to a number of communication situations that you will face using both written and oral formats. It is essential to understand how the other party perceives the conflict situation. After this perception, our communication needs to be directed openly and honestly in a manner that promotes trust and confidence from the receiver.

Summary

In this chapter we examined the nature of communication and conflict by noting that conflict is present to some degree in all organizations. A certain amount of conflict can actually make us perform better, while too much conflict can hamper our work. While we cannot always prevent conflict, we can become aware of conditions that are likely to lead to conflict. We examined various interpersonal settings that characterize different kinds of conflict behavior. A convenient perspective from which to examine conflict, the conflict episode, will give you a more thorough understanding of the nature of conflict. The role of perception in conflict was emphasized, and five conflict situations were presented to illustrate this point.

Finally, we presented major steps to help you analyze a conflict situation when it occurs. Several basic styles of conflict management were identified and described. We gave particular emphasis to the friendly helper, the tough battler, and the problem solver styles. In most cases the problem solver style is most appropriate. This style promotes the climate that everybody wins, which is most helpful in airing differences that contribute to conflict situations. Regardless of the style you select to manage conflict, you can use Rapoport's Region of Validity Technique as a suggested pattern for communicating in conflict situations.

Footnotes

[1] Adapted from a condensation of *Bloodletters and Badmen* by Jay Nash (New York: Newsweek Books, 1975), pp. 253–254.

[2] These nine characteristics of conflict are adapted from Alan C. Filley, *Interpersonal Conflict Resolution* (Palo Alto, Calif.: Scott Foresman and Co., 1975), pp. 9–12. Reprinted by permission.

[3] The remainder of this section is based on Robert R. Blake and Jane Srygley Mouton, "The Fifth Achievement," *Journal of Applied Behavioral Science* 6, No. 4 (1970): 413–426 and Jay Hall, *Conflict Management Survey* (Houston: Teleometrics, 1968).

[4] Reproduced by special permission from Robert R. Blake and Jane Srygley Mouton, "The Fifth Achievement," *Journal of Applied Behavioral Science* 6, No. 4 (1970):418, NTL Institute for Applied Behavioral Science.

[5] Filley, Ibid., pp. 55–56.

[6] Ibid., p. 56.

[7] A. Rapoport, *Fights, Games, and Debates* (Ann Arbor: University of Michigan, 1960).

Review Questions

1. All conflict is harmful and should be reduced or eliminated whenever possible. Comment on this statement.

2. You manage a large department of employees with different backgrounds, skills, and job responsibilities. Within the context of Filley's nine characteristics of social relationships associated with conflict behavior, provide an example of each kind of conflict situation that could arise in your department.

3. Discuss the five distinct stages of a conflict episode.

4. How does perception play a major role in conflict situations? Provide original illustrations of the five possible conflict circumstances that could occur in a business organization.

5. What is conflict management? What steps might a manager take to analyze a particular conflict situation?

6. Describe the different styles of conflict management. Which style is the most preferable? Why?

References

Robert D. Nye, *Conflict Among Humans* (New York: Springer Publishing Company, 1973).

Klaus R. Scherer, Ronald P. Abeles, and Claude S. Fischer, *Human Aggression and Conflict* (Englewood Cliffs, N.J.: Prentice-Hall, 1975).

Conflict Resolutions: Contributions of the Behavioral Sciences, Clagett G. Smith, ed. (South Bend, Ind.: University of Notre Dame Press, 1971).

The Structure of Conflict, Paul Swingle, ed. (New York: Academic Press, 1970).

Exercises

1. The next time you have a disagreement with a friend, see if you can identify the various stages of the conflict. Does this identification process help you better understand how the conflict arose?

2. Conflict can occur in student work groups. The next time you observe group conflict, see if you can help resolve that conflict by following the guidelines presented in this chapter.

3. Identify as many situations from your experience as you can where conflict was beneficial. Are there similarities between these positive experiences? What are they?

4. Of the various styles of conflict management, which would be easiest for you to assume? The most difficult? Why do you lean in the direction you do? Will this leaning hinder your ability to be an effective conflict resolver?

Case

Communication and Conflict

Sherry Rhodes
Human Relations Consultant
Sherry Rhodes and Associates
Dallas, Texas

Bob Taylor has been the regional marketing manager for a national insurance company for 15 years. Bob is 50 years old, and he is having personal problems and has begun to drink quite heavily.

One year ago, Bob hired Barbara Johnson as executive secretary. Barbara is 28 years old and has an excellent work history. Having graduated from college with a degree in liberal arts, Barbara has brought to this position excellent secretarial skills as well as knowledge in human relations and communication interactions.

During her period of employment, Bob and Barbara have developed a close working relationship. Because of Bob's position, Barbara has often been asked to work late in the evenings and on weekends. Recently, Bob has treated Barbara in a manner which she believed was unprofessional.

During the last two months, Bob made numerous verbal suggestions which contained sexual innuendos. Barbara was uncomfortable with these statements but chose not to express her discomfort to Bob. On several occasions, Bob has touched Barbara in a manner which is both intimate and sexual. Barbara has resorted to making excuses to avoid staying late in the office or working alone with Bob.

When she was hired, Barbara was promised a salary review at the end of one year. This morning she made an appointment with Bob to discuss the salary review. Bob's reply to her request suggested that her compensation would not be based solely on her professional performance. This time, Barbara responded by laughing and treating the matter lightly.

However, Barbara was very upset with Bob's behavior. Upon returning to her desk, Barbara placed a call to a local recruiting firm to seek other employment.

■ ■ ■

Case Questions

1. Do you think that Barbara responded appropriately to Bob in the situations outlined?
2. What do you feel prompted the change in Bob's behavior?
3. How should Barbara have responded to Bob's verbal and nonverbal behavior?
4. Do you think Barbara should seek other employment? Why or why not?

Case

Boss Man
Karen L. Reiter
Walsh College

Your supervisor (Boss Man) is a technically capable employee who lacks effective managerial skills. He has a good five-year record with the company. He has the final word for hiring, firing, and raises, but for all practical purposes you have this power over your subordinates.

You were hired six months ago. Since that time you've become very capable in your job. You have good interpersonal skills, high visibility, and some ideas of your own about how the department should be run. You've tactfully presented your ideas to Boss Man, but nothing has been done about them. At a social gathering MGR (Boss Man's supervisor) asks you how things are going, and you mention that you have some good ideas that you'd like to see tried. Word of this communication gets back to Boss Man.

Since then (you think) Boss Man is acting a little paranoid about his job security. You notice some unusual happenings that could be interpreted as Boss Man trying to undermine your authority with your subordinates.

It all became unbearable when you learned the following: you've had a little trouble motivating one of your subordinates to pick up some technical skills you think he should have. You've told him that in six months you will give him a $250-per-month raise if by his next performance appraisal he has picked up these skills. A week later you hear through the grapevine that your supervisor gave this subordinate the raise without consulting or telling you. You believe that your authority and motivational techniques have been grossly undermined. What should you do?

■ ■ ■

Case Questions

1. What are the facts in this case?
2. Which of your superiors and subordinates must you consider in deciding what action to take or not to take?
3. What is the real conflict in this case?

Interviewing as a Management Tool

Learning Objectives

1. To recognize the prevalence of the interview as a business communication format.
2. To identify the different types of questions and the advantages and disadvantages of each.
3. To understand the basic structure of all interviews.
4. To learn how to conduct effective employment interviews.
5. To learn how to conduct effective performance appraisal interviews.
6. To understand the purposes of those types of interviews regularly conducted in business organizations.
7. To recognize the obstacles to effective interviews and the ways to overcome those obstacles.

*A*s manager of a medium-size manufacturing plant, Bill Thatcher had many demands placed upon his time. As far as he was concerned, there were not enough hours in the day. When asked where his time went, he would place most of the blame on meetings. "Most every workday," Bill would say, "is nothing but a succession of meetings." He continued to feel that way until he was introduced to the time log.

In an attempt to become more productive Bill had his secretary keep notes on everything he did during the course of a week. He reasoned that the time log might suggest some ways in which he could make better use of his time. Some of the things she reported back to him at the end of the week truly astonished him.

One of the big surprises was that he actually spent much less time in meetings than he had thought. Another surprise was the large blocks of time in which he dealt with a single person. Here are a few of the more significant entries.

Monday, 11:00–12:00, talked with the person production wants to hire as assistant production manager. Tried to learn if he was likely to stay for a while or if he was only looking for a training program.

Tuesday, 8:30–10:00, talked with night shift supervisor about severe absenteeism problem. Discussed the eight most flagrant violators and counseled her on possible approaches to take with each. Told her that her career with company depends on solving this problem.

Thursday, 3:00–4:00, conducted semiannual performance appraisal with production manager. Discussed extent to which goals we had set had been met. Agreed upon goals for next time period.

Friday, 3:30–4:30, talked with shipping manager about his plans to leave company. Discussed opportunities for advancement here but made little progress. Only reason he gives for leaving is "personal reasons."

These entries were similar to many others included in the time log. Many of the entries described brief conversations with individual employees, only some of which had been scheduled in advance. Also included were references to three meetings which totaled seven hours.

In inspecting his secretary's notes, Bill was surprised to learn how much more time he spent talking to individuals than he did in meetings. "All the authorities say that a manager has to be able to plan, organize, direct, and control," Bill now says, "but something else they should say is that a manager must be able to interview also." ■

In this chapter we will investigate all aspects of the interview. Since the question is the interviewer's main tool, different types of questions with their advantages and disadvantages will be presented. You will learn the steps to follow in conducting many different types of interviews. This chapter emphasizes the role of the interviewer. In Part 4, we will discuss how to be an effective job applicant and how to be interviewed successfully.

Interviewing as a Managerial Activity

The interview is a most useful tool in communicating with others. As used by management it has a wide variety of purposes. Job applicants are hired on the basis of interviews. Employees who experience personal problems may be counseled in an interview. In many organizations managers evaluate the performance of their workers in regularly scheduled appraisal interviews. Disciplinary interviews are conducted with workers who are involved in job-related problems. Through an exit-interview program a company will seek to learn the reasons why employees leave the company. New employees are often oriented to their duties through an interview. The interview is an important managerial tool, for through it management acquires and transmits much of the information necessary for efficient operations.

The interview has several purposes.

An interview was once considered no different from a conversation, and it was thought that anyone who could carry on a conversation could conduct an interview. Today it is recognized that this is not true. To understand the need for trained interviewers one need only look within any organization to see that a large number of employment interviews have resulted in the selection of unsuitable individuals. Counseling interviews that do not resolve problems and disciplinary interviews that do not result in changed behaviors are additional evidence that trained interviewers are necessary.

There is a need for trained interviewers.

The Interview Defined

There are some characteristics of an interview that clearly differentiate it from a conversation. An interview is purposeful, while a conversation may not be. The intent of a conversation is frequently satisfaction with the conversation and nothing more. Not only does the interview have a definite purpose, but that purpose is determined in advance of the interview. Because the interview has a predetermined purpose, it is more formal than a conversation.

An interview has a predetermined purpose and a structure. It is held for the exchange of information.

Another characteristic of an interview is that it is clearly structured. Unlike many conversations which appear formless, an interview has definite parts. Regardless of the interview's purpose, it is comprised of an opening, body, and closing. Adding to the structure is the fact that the participants have specific roles.

While interviews may have a variety of specific purposes, the general purpose is usually the exchange of information. This does not make interviews unique since it is true of many conversations also. However, the exchange is a universal characteristic of the interview.

To summarize, an interview is a purposeful exchange of information for a predetermined purpose in a structured situation.

Types of Questions

Generations of schoolchildren have been taught that the verb is the motor of the sentence. Without a good verb, a sentence will wander rather than move purposefully. An interview also has a motor—the question. Without appropriate questions an interviewer accomplishes little. Unless you are able to recognize and use the variety of questions available, you will not utilize the full potential of the interview.

An interviewer must be aware of the variety of questions available.

Open and Closed Questions

Questions fall into one of two general categories—open or closed. Open questions allow the interviewee much freedom to respond. An open question is broad in scope and usually requires more than a few words in response. When you ask an open question, you are often merely specifying the topic to be covered. The interviewee may decide on the quantity and the type of information to provide.

Open questions allow the interviewee more freedom to respond; closed questions are more restrictive.

Open questions are not all alike. They may differ in their degree of openness. The following questions are very open:

- Tell me about yourself.
- What are you seeking in a career?
- How do you feel about the present candidates?

Other questions are less broad. Although still open, they restrict the interviewee's response somewhat:

- What do you like about your present job?
- Tell me how you feel the problem developed.
- Why did you apply for this job?

Advantages of Open Questions

1. Interviewer has greater opportunity to observe.
2. They are considered non-threatening because they are usually easy to answer.
3. They suggest interest by the interviewer.

Disadvantages of Open Questions

1. They take more time.
2. It is often difficult to record or to quantify the information.
3. Controlling the interview is more difficult.

Closed questions are somewhat restrictive in nature and generally call for a brief and limited response. By using closed questions you limit the answer options available to the interviewee. The following questions are moderately closed as they call for only a brief bit of information:

Closed questions are more restrictive than open questions.

▫ Who is Peter Drucker?
▫ What is your main duty on your present job?
▫ For what reason do you wish to leave?

Very closed questions are even more restrictive in that the interviewer has few answer options. These are some more very closed questions:

▫ Rank the following courses in terms of their value to you: business mathematics, English composition, American history.
▫ How would you rate the present governor in terms of his concern for the unemployed: very concerned, neutral, or unconcerned.
▫ Do you drink alcoholic beverages?

<table>
<tr><td colspan="2">**Advantages of Closed Questions**</td><td colspan="2">**Disadvantages of Closed Questions**</td></tr>
<tr><td>**1.**</td><td>Less training is required of interviewers.</td><td>**1.**</td><td>They provide too little information.</td></tr>
<tr><td>**2.**</td><td>They take less time.</td><td>**2.**</td><td>They sometimes inhibit communication.</td></tr>
<tr><td>**3.**</td><td>They make it easier for the interviewer to exert control.</td><td>**3.**</td><td>They provide little opportunity for the interviewee to offer additional information.</td></tr>
<tr><td>**4.**</td><td>It is easier to tabulate the answers.</td><td></td><td></td></tr>
</table>

Neutral and Leading Questions

When you ask a neutral question, you make no attempt to direct the interviewee's response. Since such questions do not exert any pressure, they may elicit more accurate responses. Neutral questions are phrased so that possible responses are not indicated and alternatives are presented in a balanced fashion. These are some typical neutral questions:

Neutral questions are completely unbiased.

▫ How would you feel about work that requires a considerable amount of traveling?
▫ Why are you leaving the company?
▫ Who do you think is responsible for the problem?
▫ Which one of the following sports do you enjoy participating in most—baseball, football, basketball, tennis or soccer?

Leading questions enable you to guide the interviewee in a certain direction. There are many appropriate uses for leading questions. They are especially useful when you are trying to verify factual information. When used carelessly, leading questions may result in biased responses. With care, however, you may secure accurate information quickly.

Through leading questions an interviewer can guide the interviewee in a certain direction.

Leading questions are sometimes regarded negatively because they are often misused. But they are useful tools and should not be neglected. These are some leading questions:

- You have a driver's license, don't you?
- You are at least 16 years of age?
- You have a telephone, don't you ?
- Do you believe, as most students do, that you are overworked?

Loaded Questions

A loaded question is even stronger in direction than a leading question. While a leading question may be somewhat subtle, a loaded question tends to be hard-hitting. Some interviewers use loaded questions to create stress by using language likely to draw an emotional response or by inquiring into topics about which the interviewee feels strongly. In most interviews there is no need for loaded questions; they should be left to skilled interviewers for the exploration of emotional issues. Some examples of loaded questons are:

Loaded questions are strongly directional.

- What do you think of the government's foolish waste of the tax dollar?
- Do you mean to tell me that you have no work experience? (to a new college graduate who has been rejected by other interviewers for lacking experience)
- How do you like the company's ridiculous policy about vacations?

Mirror Questions

A mirror question reflects an interviewee's previous answer with the intent of drawing out additional information. Through the use of mirror questions more information can be obtained without biasing the interviewee's responses. When you believe a response is incomplete, you may draw the interviewee out more by simply restating that response. This is called *mirroring* a response. When you do it, you are trying to get the interviewee to elaborate on a particular topic. Mirror questions are employed in these examples:

With a mirror question an interviewer can get an interviewee to elaborate on a topic without introducing any structure.

Interviewee **I liked my last job a lot. It was interesting and the pay was good. I'd still be there if it weren't for my problems with my supervisor.**

Interviewer **Problems with your supervisor?**

Interviewee **You'll see that I do good work so long as people don't hassle me.**

Interviewer **Hassle you?**

Probing Questions

A probing question is stimulated by the interviewee's previous response. Some interviewers prepare a schedule, or list of questions, in advance. No probing questions would be included in such a list for probing questions are unplanned. An interviewee's response or responses may lead you to use probing questions. For example, in an employment interview the applicant says, "In my present job I had to learn how to assume responsibility." The interviewer might then use probing questions such as these:

□ Exactly how did you assume responsibility?
□ How much responsibility did you assume?
□ Why did you have to learn that?

A probing question is unplanned and asked in order to follow up on a response. Through probing questions you may elicit important information that had not been anticipated.

Probing questions are unplanned questions stimulated by the interviewee's previous response.

Pauses

Although it is not exactly a question, the pause may serve the same purpose. When you want the interviewee to elaborate, instead of following a response with another question you may simply remain silent. The pause is the most neutral approach of all, since it neither structures the answer nor even suggests a topic for discussion. There is a point at which your pause may turn into an embarrassing silence which the interviewee will find threatening. With experience you will become comfortable and proficient in the use of pauses to stimulate the interviewee.

The types of questions discussed are commonly used by interviewers. Regardless of the types of questions asked, interviewers must draw out the desired information while motivating the interviewee to cooperate. In order to develop as an interviewer you should learn the different types of questions and the purposes of each. The questions comprise the most crucial component of the interview structure.

By pausing, the interviewer can draw out the interviewee.

The Interview Structure

*S*oon after Bill Slayton was promoted to supervisor, he decided to take a management course. After he enrolled in night school, he was surprised to learn that the course textbook included only one chapter on communication.

"When you are a supervisor, communication is the name of the game," Bill said. *"Your success depends on your ability to deal with your workers. Instead of devoting so much attention to activities that upper management is mainly responsible for, more emphasis should be given to the basics.*

"Look at our textbook," he exclaimed. *"Four hundred pages and only 30 of them are on communication. Only 10 of the 30 are on interviewing. My most important contacts with my workers are one-on-one interviews. There are so many different possible purposes for interviews you can't possibly learn how to conduct them all in just a few pages."*

■

Bill makes some good points, although he is operating under one misconception. While there are many different possible purposes, interviews are very much alike in structure. Awareness of this structure will make interviewing of all types more productive and more pleasant for you.

Regardless of the purpose of interviews they are similarly structured.

There are five distinct phases of the interview. Your strategy differs in each one. Since the interview process is continuous, however, there is no apparent separation between phases. The phases follow in their usual sequence.

1. Planning

The planning phase is actually not a part of the interview itself. Planning is so vital to the success of an interview, however, that it must be included. Here's what you do in planning an interview:

1. Determine the purpose or purposes of the interview.
2. Identify the type of response(s) being sought from the interviewee.
3. Learn as much about the interviewee and about the subject in advance as possible.
4. Determine the amount of structure to employ and on that basis develop whatever questions are necessary.
5. Select an appropriate setting for the interview and communicate this information to the interviewee.

The extent of planning to be done for an interview depends on the reasons the interview is conducted. Before a performance-appraisal interview some managers spend several hours familiarizing themselves with the interviewee's work records. An employment interviewer should read the completed application form. The clerk in the clothing store, however, may have no advance information about a customer but will be prepared to discuss the merits of the clothing available.

Planning is vital to the success of most interviews.

2. Establishing Rapport

For many individuals an interview is a unique occurrence and as such is a cause of tension. In order to reduce the tension and make it easier to exchange information, you should first strive to establish rapport with the interviewee. Rapport means an agreeable relationship between you and the interviewee. Greeting the interviewee graciously and extending simple courtesies will help you to establish rapport. Many interviewers make small talk at the start in order to accomplish that. Some interviewers talk about topics of mutual interest.

Establishing rapports should result in a better climate.

You will devote more time to establishing rapport in some types of interviews than others. The success of a counseling interview, for example, depends upon the climate established. Since rapport is so important in a counseling interview it merits more time than it would in most other interview types. The relationship between you and the interviewee also influences the amount of time for establishing rapport. If you and the interviewee are friends or if you work together regularly, there is ordinarily little need to devote attention to establishing rapport.

Establish rapport early in the interview, and it will pave the way for what is to come. Even after the interview has started smoothly, however, you should remain aware of the importance of rapport. Differences of opinion may surface in an interview, or tension may increase for other reasons. In any case, through rapport, a climate conducive to open communication can be developed and maintained.

3. Stating the Purpose

Jan Rowan enjoys her job as a programmer. Even though she has held the same position for two years, she is continuing to learn in it. Practically the only thing that upsets her about the job is the fact that her boss is rather vague. Two weeks ago he asked her to reserve an hour at 3:30 so he could talk to her. They talked for over an hour, but Jan left without knowing what the purpose of the interview had been. She was asked questions about how she liked her job, problems in the organization, the condition of the lunchroom, and even her vacation plans. As Jan expressed it, "It's nice to have a boss who is interested in you, but it would also be nice to know what your boss is getting at."

■

Interviews such as the one described above are, unfortunately, common because interviewers assume their purposes are as clear to the interviewee as they are to themselves. At the risk of belaboring the obvious, you should prevent problems by simply stating the purpose of

Although it is often obvious, the interviewer should clearly state the purpose of the interview.

the interview. Employment interviewers who neglect this are the kind who will persist in describing the duties of a secretary level 1 to an applicant who is applying for the job of clerk level 2. It is so easy to clarify the purpose of an interview to the interviewee's satisfaction that there is no reason for any interviewer to ignore this duty.

4. Asking Questions

At this point the actual business of the interview commences. As described earlier, the question is the main tool of the interviewer; through appropriate questions you seek to accomplish some predetermined goal.

Through questions and answers the actual business of an interview is accomplished.

You come into this phase having determined in the planning phase the types of questions to ask and the sequence in which you will ask them. You would have developed the extent of the structure to be employed. Now it's time to implement the strategy.

This phase constitutes the largest part of the interview. It consumes the most time, appropriately, since it is here that the actual business of the interview is conducted.

5. Summarizing

In general, interviewer and interviewee exchange a considerable amount of information. Some of the information may be highly relevant, and some may be less so.

At the end of an interview the interviewer should summarize the conclusions that were reached.

Irrelevancies, redundancies, and unanticipated interruptions may blur some of the conclusions. To remedy this you should summarize what the interview accomplished. Since you and the interviewee may not perceive the conclusions identically, clarify what you consider these conclusions to be. Without such a summary the interview may end with the parties unaware that differences actually exist. Such differences may not be recognized until one of the parties does something that appears to be contrary to a conclusion reached in the interview. It is simple to avoid such occurrences by agreeing on the conclusions before the interview ends.

By consciously structuring interviews according to the five phases, you will become a more systematic and productive interviewer. The same five phases constitute the structure of the different types of interviews.

Types of Interviews

There are different ways of classifying the various types of interviews since there are numerous variations of interviews and their purposes. Interviews are often classified into three types: information getting, information giving, and problem solving. Since interviews are so diverse, however, they can be more clearly identified on the basis of specific purpose. In this section we will review types of interviews conducted most frequently in business organizations.

The Employment Interview

The employment interview is the most important tool in the selection process of most organizations. Most selection decisions are made on the basis of the selection interview. Because of the widespread use of the interview, you should know how to conduct an employment interview.

The interview is used more than any other method for selecting employees.

*B*y *the time Wanda Metcalf graduated from college, she had been interviewed by 20 different employment interviewers. Although most of the interviewers represented large national organizations, they were far from equally competent.*

Some of the interviewers were well-organized and businesslike: others were not. A recruiter for a paper company began the interview by saying to Wanda, "Tell me all about yourself," and said little else. A recruiter for a chemical company must have asked 100 questions, all of them of the yes or no variety. Several interviewers did not seem to know anything about the job they were trying to fill. Although none of the interviewers was actually unfriendly, two did not seem to be the least bit interested in Wanda.

Talking about her experiences as a job applicant, Wanda said, "Most companies don't realize the importance of the interviewer's job. The way applicants feel about a company is influenced by their impression of the company's representative. In fact, as far as most applicants are concerned, the interviewer is the company." ∎

Interview Goals. As an employment interviewer your main goal should be to determine an applicant's suitability for the job. That is not the only goal, however. You should also tell the interviewees enough about the job so that they will clearly understand the scope and duties of the job.

Usually, the applicant's knowledge of the job is slight. What the interviewee knows about the job is probably based on a newspaper ad or a brief job description posted on a bulletin board. Therefore you must

The employment interviewer's main goal is to select the applicant best suited for the job.
The interviewer must educate the applicants about what the job entails.

educate the applicant about what the job actually entails. The more thorough you are in performing this function, the less likely it is that new employees will quickly grow disillusioned with their jobs.

You should also be aware of the importance of good public relations. Seek to create and maintain goodwill for the company. Often numerous applicants are interviewed before there is a single hiring. One study showed a ratio of 37 interviews to a single hiring.[1] You have the opportunity to influence how the applicant, whether successful or not, will view the company and its products or services in the future.

As an employment interviewer you should have three goals:

1. Principally, to determine a person's suitability for employment.
2. To present an accurate description of the job to the applicant.
3. To create and maintain goodwill for the company.

Topics usually covered in an employment interview are:

1. Work experience emphasizing jobs recently held.
2. Educational background, including both formal and informal training.
3. Outside interests, especially those that might affect the individual's job performance.
4. Physical characteristics, if such factors are important for the job.

The interviewer should be aware of the importance of public relations.

Employment Interview Guide

Learn the applicant's background by reading the completed application form and the applicant's resume (if it's available).

Know enough about the job so that its most important requirements are clear to you.

Schedule the interview so that sufficient time is available and so that there will be no interruptions.

Scan the topics to be covered early in the interview, and proceed through each topic in an organized manner.

Determine that the interviewee is aware of the most important aspects of the job.

Relate your questions to the job the interviewee is applying for, and ask the same questions of each applicant.

Summarize what has been accomplished at the close of the interview and indicate specifically what the interviewee can expect next.

In order to comply with the guidelines of the Equal Employment Opportunity Commission you should: (1) ask questions that are directly related to the job being sought, and (2) ask the same main questions of all the applicants.

Throughout the interview you should encourage the applicant to ask questions, and you should respond to the questions with as much detail as necessary. In closing the interview you should briefly summarize the main points covered as well as clearly indicate to the applicant what will follow. At the end of the interview the applicant should know exactly what to expect. If the applicant will be expected to take further tests, you should explain that. If some organizational policy dictates the next step in the selection process, you should make the applicant aware of that. It is an interviewer's responsibility to remove as much of the applicant's uncertainty as possible.

In closing the employment interview the interviewer should tell the interviewee what to expect next.

After the Employment Interview. Since interviewers often meet many applicants in a single day, record the findings from each interview as soon as possible after the interview. Many companies provide forms on which interviewers rate applicants. If forms are not available, you should develop one of your own so that you are sure to note your reactions immediately following the interview.

The Performance-Appraisal Interview

In many organizations performance-appraisal interviews are conducted on a regular basis, often annually or semiannually. The interview is conducted by a worker's immediate superior. It is intended to provide the worker with feedback concerning how the company thinks the worker is performing.

Performance-appraisal interviews are usually conducted by a worker's immediate superior.

The performance-appraisal interview is strongly evaluative in nature and is sometimes difficult to conduct. Adding to the sensitivity of the situation is the effect that the appraisal could have on the subordinate's pay. The specific goal of each performance-appraisal interview depends on how the interviewee has been performing on the job.

*W*erner Nelson was relieved to have finally completed his tenth and final performance-appraisal interview for the year. Evaluating ten subordinates was a difficult and a time-consuming process. No two workers were exactly alike, and the goals of each interview differed according to the nature of the individual worker.

As Werner saw it, he had conducted three different types of appraisals. In interviewing five of the subordinates he believed his main task was to recognize their good work and to express the company's appreciation. At the same time he attempted to point out ways they could improve. He was trying to develop two other subordinates for higher-

level jobs, so he used the appraisal interviews with them mainly for that purpose.

Since the other three subordinates were still on probation and had been performing poorly, Werner warned each one of them that some improvement was necessary. The remaining time in these appraisals consisted of discussing specific ways each interviewee could improve.

In discussing the appraisal interviews Werner said, "My people seem to think that I like evaluating them, but they're dead wrong. I don't like it any better than they do. No one likes to play God, but it's a method of developing people, of helping them become better at their jobs." ■

Before the Performance-Appraisal Interview. You must decide what the specific purposes of a performance-appraisal will be on the basis of what the interviewee's performance has been.

After determining the purposes, you decide the extent the interviewee should participate in the preliminaries. In some organizations employees are given copies of the evaluation forms in advance and are requested to evaluate themselves. They bring their completed forms to the interview so there can be discussion of how the supervisor's rating differs from their own and the possible reasons for the differences. At the very least workers are told well in advance of the pending appraisals so they can organize their thoughts.

The main purpose of a performance-appraisal interview depends on how the interviewee has been performing.

During the Performance-Appraisal Interview. The evaluation form should certainly not be the sole focus of the performance-appraisal interview. Emphasis should be on involving the subordinate in two-way communication rather than telling the subordinate what is to be done. If the discussion of problems is to be meaningful, the subordinate must first acknowledge that problems exist. In setting goals for the future there must be agreement between the superior and the subordinate. The main strength of the performance-appraisal process lies in human interaction. Unless both parties work together, the strength of the performance-appraisal process is not being utilized.

Goal setting is an important aspect of the performance-appraisal interview. The goals should be agreed upon mutually.

In closing the performance-appraisal interview you should summarize the main points covered. By now there should be agreement on: (1) the areas in which the subordinate is performing well; (2) the areas in which the subordinate needs improvement; (3) what the subordinate must do to attain that improvement. If there is disagreement between the parties after the summary, the interview should not end until the points of disagreement are resolved.

After the Performance-Appraisal Interview. You must follow up the interview in whatever way has been agreed upon. In some organizations the subordinate is given a copy of the final evaluation form. If additional paperwork is to be completed, you should do that immediately. If the subordinate complained during the interview about the standards used for measurement, you should look into the matter immediately rather than wait for it to surface again in the next appraisal interviews.

The Correction Interview

Managers who dislike conducting performance-appraisal interviews react even more negatively to the correction interview. In this type of interview the superior seeks to get the subordinate to substitute some desirable behavior for behavior that is undesirable. Even though negative information might be presented to the interviewee in the performance-appraisal interview, at least it is a regularly scheduled event in which all employees routinely participate. The correction interview, however, is not a part of every employee's schedule. The irregular nature of the correction interview adds to the suspicion and hostility that usually accompany it.

Before the Correction Interview.   Correction interviews deal with sensitive matters. For that reason before the interview the supervisor should collect as much information as possible concerning the employee's alleged infraction. The supervisor should also be aware of what corrective measures might be appropriate and should then schedule the interview as soon as possible.

During the Correction Interview.   A correction interview is a serious matter, and both parties know it. Little time need be devoted to establishing rapport, since both parties, especially the subordinate, are anx-

Since the correction interview is of such a sensitive nature, preparation by the interviewer is important.

Openness and candor are vital for an effective correction interview.

Performance-Appraisal Interview Guide

Notify subordinates well enough in advance to allow them to prepare for the interview.

Encourage written or oral self-evaluation by the subordinates.

Involve the subordinates in every aspect of the discussion.

Separate salary matters and discussion of promotional possibilities from the appraisal itself.

Identify and solve, together with the subordinate, any performance problems.

Set specific, short-term objectives with the subordinate and discuss methods of attaining them.

ious to get on with it. As the interviewer you should state the interview's purpose and describe the violation in as much detail as necessary. The subordinate should be encouraged to describe his or her version of the problem, and both parties should work together to arrive at a solution. In closing the correction interview, you should summarize what has been accomplished and restate the corrective action to be taken.

*W*hen it became apparent to Ellen, a supervisor, that George's productivity was dropping, she began to observe George more closely. George did not manage time well. When he arrived at work at exactly 8:00 a.m., he would devote 15 or 20 minutes to straightening up his desk. Each afternoon he quit work 15 minutes early to prepare to leave. For several weeks Ellen kept records of all her subordinates' time usage habits. It became obvious that the misuse of time was causing George's decreased productivity.

Following her research Ellen conducted a correction interview in her office with George. At first George disputed Ellen's findings; however, her carefully kept records soon convinced him that a problem existed and that his misuse of time was the cause. Ellen and George agreed that George would become more aware of how he used time. Within three weeks George had regained his previous high level of productivity. ∎

After the Correction Interview. If it is decided that a description of the violation should go into the employee's file, this should be done

Correction Interview Guide

Obtain all of the relevant facts in advance and get verification where possible.

Conduct the interview out of earshot of others.

Concentrate on the subordinate's behavior in describing the problem, and avoid any discussion of personality traits.

Encourage the subordinate to describe the infraction as it occurred.

Discuss any discrepancies that occur between the superior's version and the subordinate's version.

Discuss possible corrective actions with the subordinate.

Summarize what has occurred and the corrective action that will be taken.

immediately. You should ascertain not only that corrective action is being taken, but also its apparent effect. This might be accomplished through any or all of the following: observation, judicious discussion with the associates of the subordinate, or discussion with the subordinate.

The Counseling Interview

Since counseling interviews are directed at personal problems, many believe that only social workers and psychologists conduct them. Although counseling is not always recognized as a manager's duty, most managers do counsel their subordinates. Even if a problem is personal or family related, it will have some effect on the employee's job performance; this is why most managers have counseling interviews with their subordinates.

At the age of 23 Bob Wiggins became a supervisor. After two years on the job Bob believes that he is finally getting a good grasp on it. When he first started he expected to encounter many on-the-job problems. He envisioned that the problems would mainly involve equipment, raw materials, and the manufacturing process. As Bob had expected, there were many such problems. What Bob had not expected was the high incidence of personal problems among workers. Bob found that personal problems make many workers less effective than they would otherwise be. Bob estimates that he devotes ten percent of his work week counseling employees with problems. "It's time well-spent," says Bob, "if it results in a more productive worker." ■

Because of the personal nature of the subject of the interview, the climate that is established is very important. You should try to create a situation which will allow a free exchange of information. Such a climate is more likely if you:

The effectiveness of a counseling interview depends largely on the climate established.

1. Secure the trust of the interviewee, possibly by assuring that what the interviewee says will remain confidential.
2. Create an atmosphere in which the interviewee will feel free to bring up any subject without fear of offending or alienating the interviewer.
3. Maintain a nondirective approach so that the interviewee, rather than the interviewer, determines the subjects to be considered.
4. Do not evaluate, either verbally or nonverbally, what the interviewee is saying.

The Orientation Interview

Among the dozen or more typist jobs that Bob Porter has held, the most memorable one was with Allied Industries. On his first day with Allied, Mae Rosen, his supervisor, introduced him to his duties. She told him that she hoped Bob would like his job. "The only really bad thing about this work," she said, "is that it is so repetitive. You do the same thing from nine until five. Until you learn how to think about other things while typing, you'll be pretty bored." Bob soon discovered what Mae had meant. He probably never gave the job a chance as he was led to expect to be bored and he immediately was bored. He quit that job after the longest two weeks he can remember. ■

Orientation interviews acquaint new employees with their jobs and with the range of duties involved. A good orientation interview will provide the new employee with a desire to learn and an interest in succeeding. This type of interview is unique because the interviewer's primary role is that of information giver. The interviewer tells the new employee about the job and the company. Organizational policies and procedures may be discussed, as will any other topic that is pertinent to orienting a new worker to the environment. Initial opinions, attitudes, and expectations are formed, at least partly, as a result of orientation interviews. As in Bob Porter's case, these initial expectations can significantly influence the behavior of the new employee.

The orientation interview can profoundly affect the way new employees view the job and the organization.

The Exit Interview

An exit interview is conducted in order to learn why employees who leave voluntarily are doing so. The interview is usually conducted by a personnel specialist, who also may use the opportunity to explain the organization policies on such matters as letters of recommendation and continuation of insurance.

The exit interviewer intends to discover if the employee's reasons for quitting indicate some organizational problem that merits investigation. For example, if several departing employees cite the supervision on the night shift as their reason for leaving, an actual problem exists.

This is a difficult interview to conduct because there are several obstacles to frank disclosure of the true reasons for leaving. Interviewees are often suspicious of the company's sudden show of interest. There is always the chance that the employee may want to return to the organization and therefore is unwilling to speak negatively of it.

The exit interviewer must overcome such obstacles by securing the interviewee's trust. The suggestions for creating an appropriate climate for the counseling interview are equally pertinent to the exit interview.

If conducted properly, the exit interview can yield information that is likely to improve the organization.

A good exit program can be the source of information that leads to significant organizational improvements.

Charlie Bennings considers exit interviews to be one of the most time-consuming activities. Rarely a week goes by that Charlie, as assistant personnel manager, does not conduct several exit interviews. Some of these interviews last for an hour or more. Charlie observed that he elicits more relevant information if he devotes some time to establishing rapport. "After doing several exit interviews, I have a tendency to stick to the company interview form and rush through it. If I take my time in establishing rapport and keep the interview conversational, I get more helpful information. ■

The Information-Getting interview

Jerry Sloan's job title is project coordinator; he is responsible for keeping three construction projects on schedule. "Bringing them in on time is what I'm paid to do," explains Jerry enthusiastically. Most of his time is spent talking to each of the three site managers to ensure that deadlines will be met. When bottlenecks seem likely, Jerry talks with the subcontractor responsible and tries to solve the problem. "I'm a coordinator," says Jerry, "and coordination is communication; I'm also an interviewer, since I get most of the information I need through interviews." ■

Many of the interviews conducted in organizations do not fall into any of our major categories. As in Jerry Sloane's case, they are conducted to elicit information for a specific purpose. An interviewer from the news media would conduct an information-getting interview with witnesses to an accident. An interviewer for a public opinion poll would conduct an information-getting interview, as would an automobile service manager when talking with the owner of a car that requires service.

Numerous such interviews are routinely conducted, many of them so unstructured that they resemble conversations rather than interviews. The information concerning questions and phases of the interview is applicable to all types of interviews.

Although many interviews do not fall into the major categories, they resemble others in structure.

Styles of Interviewing

Styles of interviewing can be thought of in terms of two concepts: freedom and control. The extent to which these two concepts are balanced determines interviewing style. There are three distinct styles of interviewing: (1) highly directive, (2) directive, and (3) nondirective.

Figure 17.1 Interview Styles as Related to Freedom and Control

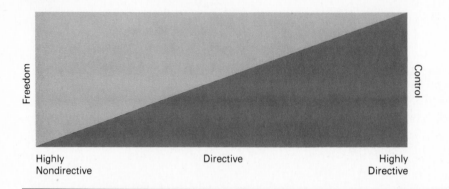

Freedom   Control

Highly Nondirective   Directive   Highly Directive

Rather than viewing each style as unique and separate from the others, they should be thought of as existing on a continuum. The differences among styles are matters of degree and are determined by the extent that the interviewer emphasizes freedom and control. This continuum is illustrated in Figure 17.1.

In the highly directive style of interviewing the interviewer exerts strong control. Typically little time is devoted to establishing rapport. Most of the questions are closed, and the responses elicited are often recorded. The highly directive style is frequently used for gathering factual information. Many, if not all, of the questions asked by the highly directive interviewer may be prepared in advance.

The directive style of interviewing is characterized by the interviewer's balance between freedom and control. A more flexible approach allows the interviewer more leeway in terms of approach. Directive interviewers usually prepare their main questions in advance and they rely on a balance of open and closed questions.

In the nondirective style, open questions are used almost exclusively. The nondirective interviewer may list in advance some topics for discussion, but the style is mainly an unstructured one. Considerable control of the interview is given to the interviewee, who does most of the talking. This style is appropriate only for skilled interviewers; otherwise it takes much time and the results are largely unclear.

The style of interviewing is determined by the emphasis placed on freedom and control by the interviewer.

Summary

There are many different ways that organizations use interviews, and there is a shortage of trained interviewers. Until recently, few people recognized any differences between interviews and conversations. Unlike conversations, however, interviews are characterized by a predetermined purpose and a clear structure; they are conducted to exchange information.

There are many different types of questions available to a skilled interviewer. Questions fall into one of two general categories, open and closed. Open questions allow the interviewee more freedom to respond; closed questions call for narrow, restrictive answers. Neutral questions, which are completely unbiased, are usually desirable. Leading questions allow an interviewer to guide the interviewee's response. Loaded questions are stronger in direction and draw an emotional response. A mirror question reflects a previous answer in order to draw additional information. Interviewers should also use probing questions and pauses to attain their goal.

The way an interviewer handles control and freedom in conducting an interview determines the interviewer's style. There are three distinct styles of interviewing: (1) highly directive, (2) directive, and (3) nondirective.

Although interviews may be used for many different purposes, they are alike in structure. An interview may be divided into five phases: (1) planning, (2) establishing rapport, (3) stating the purpose, (4) questions and answers, and (5) summarizing.

Interviews are used for many different purposes. The major uses of interviews are for employment, performance appraisal of subordinates, and correction of subordinates.

The main goal of the employment interviewer is to select the best applicant for the job. Secondary goals are to describe the job accurately to the applicants and to maintain goodwill for the company.

As interviewer you should prepare for an employment interview by learning as much about the interviewee as possible from the application form and the resume, if available. When conducting employment interviews, you should relate the questions to the job for which the person is applying. You should ask the same main questions of all applicants for a given job.

Performance-appraisal interviews are intended to let a worker know how the worker is performing on the job. A worker's immediate superior is usually the interviewer. Both participants should be involved in setting future goals. A key to successful performance appraisal is the involvement of superior and subordinate.

The purpose of a correction interview is to get the interviewee to substitute desirable behavior for undesirable behavior. This type of interview is usually conducted by an employee's immediate superior. Openness and candor are necessary if the problem is to be resolved.

There are many other purposes for interviews besides the ones presented in this chapter. Some of the more common purposes for interviews are for counseling, orientation, exit, and information gathering.

Footnotes

[1]Cal W. Down, "Perceptions of the Selection Interview," *Personnel Administration* (May–June 1969): 8–23.

Review Questions

1. What is an interview?
2. How does an interview differ from a conversation?
3. How do open questions differ from closed questions?
4. How do leading questions differ from loaded questions?
5. What are the five phases of the interview structure?
6. What must you do when planning an interview?
7. Why does the importance of rapport vary with the purpose of the interview?
8. What are the four main topics usually covered in an employment interview?
9. By the end of the performance-appraisal interview there should be agreement between interviewer and interviewee regarding three main points. What are these three points?
10. What are the three main styles of interviewing? Describe each style.

Exercises

1. Interview someone who has a job you are interested in. In the interview you should emphasize such aspects of the job as:
   a. Qualifications necessary to do the job
   b. Opportunity for growth and advancement
   c. Likely starting salary and future earning potential.
   Prepare a letter report in which you describe your findings. Prepare the report for the director of the placement office at your school.
2. Conduct two interviews, one with a person who works primarily with his or her hands and another with someone who mainly uses his or her mind. Determine what they like and dislike about their respective jobs. Prepare a report in which you compare and contrast your two interviewees.
3. Conduct an interview with a person in business concerning that person's letter-writing practices. Find out the kind of writing that your interviewee does most. What is the purpose of it? What are the most important principles in doing that kind of writing? Prepare

a brief informational report for your professor. Prepare an oral report to present before your business communication class.

4. Interview someone who graduated from your school within the past three years. Find out what your interviewee considered the strengths and shortcomings of his or her program. Find out any changes that your interviewee would suggest. Prepare a short informational report for your professor.

5. Your business communication professor has a policy of conducting performance-evaluation interviews with each student midway through the term. Prepare a form that would insure that the same topics are covered with every student.

6. Form a pair with another student. Participate in two interviews, once as interviewer and once as interviewee. Each interview should last five minutes. Each interviewer should try to learn as much as possible about the other person's background and interests. The first interviewer should ask only closed questions; the second interviewer should ask only open questions. Write a one-page report on the interview you conducted and the effect of asking only one type of question.

7. Interview someone who conducts employment interviews. Try to learn the interviewing techniques that your interviewee uses. Compare what your interviewee says to what is presented in this chapter. Write a one-page report on this subject.

8. Visit a factory or office in your community and learn the performance-appraisal techniques used. Interview someone who conducts performance-appraisal interviews and write a report on the approach used.

9. Keep a diary for one day of all your contacts with others. How many of these were interviews? How many were conversations? Write a report explaining what made you label some interviews and others conversations.

10. Select a national figure and make a list of 20 questions you would like to ask this person.

11. Have another student role play the part of the interviewee in Exercise 10. Ask that person your 20 questions. After each response, ask two probing follow-up questions.

12. Select a topic about which people are concerned. Write two lists of closed questions—one of ten neutral questions; the other, ten leading questions. Ask five persons your ten neutral questions and record their answers. Ask five other persons your ten leading questions and record their answers. Write a one-page report in which you compare the responses to the neutral questions with the responses to the leading questions.

13. Interview someone in a personnel office who conducts exit interviews. Find out the purpose of the exit interviews and the kinds of information obtained from them. Prepare a report on this topic.

Case

A Hair-Raising Situation

Amanda Copeland
Southwestern Oklahoma State University
Kathy B. White
University of North Carolina at Greensboro

Jean, a young woman of approximately 20 years of age, walked into a nationally franchised hair-care center in a town of approximately 30,000 and asked for the owner.

Marie, the woman at the desk, had noted her entrance and reflected upon her self-confident and poised manner. "I'm the owner; what can I do for you?"

Jean explained that she was new in town and was looking for a job in her trained profession—hairdressing and styling. She offered proof of her ability and previous employment by producing check stubs from a hair-care center of the same franchise in a large metropolitan center. Substantial earnings, as shown on the stubs, indicated that Jean was a good hairdresser. As the conversation continued, Marie became more and more favorably impressed with both Jean's personality and apparent skill.

Although impressed, Marie decided the better part of valor was to defer any positive commitment. She told Jean that she had no immediate opening, but that things looked promising and that she would let her know in a week's time whether business would let her afford another hairdresser.

The next morning Jean returned to the shop and asked for Marie. Sue, the shop manager, came forward and told Jean that Marie would not be in that day and asked if she might help.

Jean drew some papers out of her purse and asked Sue to complete them for her so she could return them immediately. The papers were from a local apartment complex, asking for confirmation on Jean's employment date and salary.

Sue told Jean that she could not complete the papers for she knew nothing of her hiring. Jean insisted that she had to have the papers, that she had talked with Marie the day before, and that she was going to work there. She was so insistent that Sue felt inept; she did not know what to do about the papers or how to handle the situation. Finally she told Jean that she really was sorry but she could do nothing except take the papers and ask Marie to take care of them when she returned to the shop the following day. Plainly perplexed and exasperated, Jean left and left the papers for Marie.

When Marie entered the shop the following day, Sue gave her the papers and told her about the incident. Marie was dumbfounded.

She could not imagine what had gone wrong or why Jean would actually think that a job offer had been made.

■ ■ ■

Case Questions

1. What do you think went wrong?
2. Who failed to communicate what properly and/or adequately and to whom?
3. What could be done to ensure that no similar incident happens again?

Case

The Interview Dilemma

Ann Maloy Kane
Rose State College
Midwest City, Oklahoma

Scott, a computer expert; his wife, Leann, an excellent secretary; and their friend, K. C., an investor, formed the Home Computer Corporation (HCC). Leann performs necessary office tasks. K. C. greets customers and maintains good public relations. Only Scott can answer computer-related questions and demonstrate capabilities of the systems and of the software.

Recently several prospective customers became impatient and left before Scott could talk to them. K. C. did his best to build goodwill, but potential customers were lost. To serve more customers, HCC must hire a person who has enough computer knowledge to assist Scott.

Neither Scott nor Leann have time during normal business hours to interview applicants. K. C. has delightfully accepted the task. He quickly researches methods of interviewing and prepares to use a patterned approach for each one of the 48 applicants.

Below are his prepared questions:
1. Do you have any experience with computers?
2. Can you work long, irregular hours?
3. Do you get along with others?
4. What is your long-term goal?

If the applicant is a woman, K. C. will ask two additional questions:
5. How many children do you have?
6. Do you have a babysitter?

By the end of the week K. C. had interviewed all of the 48 applicants and had eliminated 42 of them. Most of them had taken computer classes, but they did not have any practical experience with home computers. The remaining six candidates seemed to be equally qualified for the job.

K. C. thinks Scott should interview the six candidates and make the final decision. Scott thinks K. C. should complete the task because no one would be able to answer customers' questions if Scott were interviewing.

■ ■ ■

Case Questions

1. Who should interview the six candidates? Why?
2. Was it necessary to interview 48 applicants? How could HCC have handled the situation more effectively and efficiently?
3. How could the questions be improved? Should any questions be asked of women that are not asked of men? Explain.

Using the Electronic Office

Learning Objectives
1. To recognize the importance of the electronic office in today's business world.
2. To understand the components of the electronic office.
3. To identify the advantages and disadvantages of different methods of electronic communication.
4. To understand how the electronic office functions.
5. To become familiar with the terminology used in the electronic office.

This chapter was written by Professor Janette Reints, Grossmont College, El Cajon, California 92020.

*F*rom the day the rumor surfaced there was a feeling of deep concern in the office of Central Industries. The rumor was that the office was to be modernized and word processing equipment would be installed. As the rumor spread some of the employees became preoccupied with the effect that word processing equipment might have on their jobs and their lives.

After the rumor was confirmed by a formal announcement, employees expressed their fears more openly. There were two main concerns among the typists and the secretaries. Some felt that word processing equipment was so complicated that they would not be able to understand it. Having seen the sophisticated office equipment advertised on television, some employees felt that a higher intelligence than theirs was required to master it.

Another source of apprehension was due to misconceptions about the capabilities of modern electronic office equipment. Those who were newer on the job feared that their jobs would be eliminated. They assumed that one word processing unit was capable of doing the work of several people and that their services would no longer be necessary.

Once the equipment was installed it became obvious that some employees had failed to anticipate the actual effects of the processing equipment. While it did require effort to learn how to use the new equipment, those employees who were offered the opportunity learned quickly. Upon being introduced to it their initial apprehension soon disappeared and, to their surprise, they enjoyed the challenge. After a short time office productivity had exceeded all previous levels.

Those employees who had feared the loss of their jobs soon realized that their concerns were unfounded. As management became comfortable with the new equipment, its expectations rose and its greater demands upon the staff resulted in continued full employment.

As everyone had expected, there was a period of uncertainty following the installation of the new equipment. Before long, however, all agreed that the electronic office was a significant improvement over its predecessor. ■

The Need for the Electronic Office

The paperwork explosion, ever-increasing costs, and the declining availability of skilled office workers have combined to exert heavy pressure for higher productivity rates in the office. The office has been called the most labor intensive and least cost effective domain.[1] Fortunately, in the midst of the concern for increasing office productivity, technology has been applied to the problems.

In the 1950s approximately 1,000 computers were operating in the United States. These computers were large, costly, and had limited capabilities. Today more than 1 million computers are operating. A video display terminal or VDT (also called a cathode ray tube or CRT) is installed every 13 minutes. Now there is one VDT for every 20 desks. By 1990 there will be one VDT for every three desks.[2] Beyond 1990, a "tube in every cube" has been predicted.

Even though business must use electronic technology to remain competitive, the process is becoming easier and less expensive. New storage media can hold vast amounts of information cheaply. Best of all, the movement away from special computer languages means these new electronic tools are becoming easier to operate. In the electronic office, all employees will be responsible for improving office productivity.

New equipment is less expensive and easier to operate.

This chapter describes the four components of the electronic office—input, processing, storage, and output. Within the input stage the writer of business documents can be most effective; therefore, as we discuss this input component, we will show you how to input documents efficiently. The processing, storage, and output components are described so that you can recognize their functions and importance.

Components of the electronic office

The Traditional Office

The traditional office looks something like this: One boss employs one secretary who performs a variety of duties such as answering the phone, greeting visitors, taking dictation, typing, running errands, filing, arranging meetings, and keeping records. The office has the usual filing cabinets, electric typewriter, and office desks. The desks are stacked high with file folders, loose papers, calendars, and telephone message reminders. An electronic calculator is buried somewhere. The office supply cabinet holds a large quantity of typewriter erasers, correction paper, white correction fluid, carbon paper, file folders and labels, along with several different types of office paper.

Poor procedures and uneven workloads cause delays.

At times work piles up. The manager must get out an important report; the secretary is working at top speed—missing coffee breaks, lunches, and working overtime. Other secretaries in the company are not available to help. At last the secretary places the completed report on the boss's desk and heaves a sigh of relief. But while the secretary was busy typing the report, the boss found information to add to it. At this point the working relationships become strained as the secretary begins to retype the document completely.

At other times, the work in the office is slack. Down the hall another office may be extremely busy, but since there is no supervision of the secretarial staff, the uneven division of work continues. When the secretary is on vacation or ill, the work often piles up because no one else is trained to fill in.

A New Look for the Office

In the middle 1960s IBM developed an automatic typewriter called the MT/ST (magnetic tape selectric typewriter). By using the MT/ST, a typist could record keystrokes on magnetic tape as well as on paper. Once the keystrokes had been captured on tape, revising documents was easier because only the changes had to be rekeyed.

The production of form letters was made easier because the machine could type the same text repetitively at the rate of over 180 words a minute. Also, errors could be corrected by merely striking over the previously typed character(s). This revolutionary device launched the office into the electronic age, and the term *word processing* entered the language.

About the time the MT/ST was developed, studies were made of the use of the traditional secretary's time. Table 18.1 shows how the typical secretary's time is allocated.[3]

Table 18.1 shows the secretary's day to be filled with interruptions and task switching. One solution to increasing the productivity of the secretary is to divide the work in a different manner. Those tasks involving document preparation are given to one group of secretaries, and all other secretarial tasks are assigned to another group. Those secretaries who choose document preparation are designated as word processing specialists or correspondence specialists. These specialists are freed from the many daily interruptions and can concentrate on streamlining the flow of documents.

Those secretaries who choose the nontyping activities are designated as administrative specialists. The managers, too, are now sometimes referred to by new titles which vary from *word originator,* or *principal,* to *knowledge worker* (a term generally reserved for professionals).

New titles have emerged.

Table 18.1   Typical Secretary's Day

Activity	Time Spent (percent)
Typing	20
Clerical Duties	19
Communicating by phone or in person	11
Filing, taking shorthand, handling mail, composing documents, etc.	10
Away from desk[a]	31
Waiting for work[a]	9

[a]*Unproductive time*

Figure 18.1   Work Flow in the Traditional Office

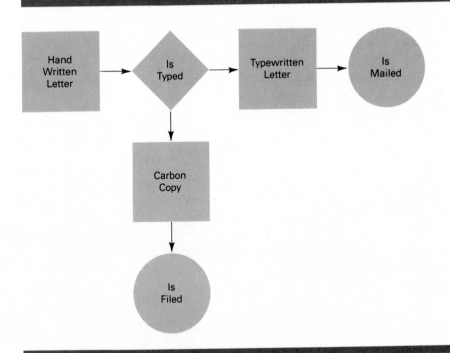

The administrative specialists are assigned such duties as helping management with reports, composing letters, answering phones, filing, and planning meetings and itineraries. An administrative specialist can provide assistance to more than one principal. The word processing specialists are gathered together into one work area equipped with automatic typewriters and designated as a word processing center. Most all document preparation for the company is taken care of in the center. This arrangement is called a *centralized system.*

As companies gained experience with word processing centers, they recognized that the centralized approach was not always the most satisfactory arrangement. The work group structure emerged. The work group is a small number of support personnel who function as a team. The group, composed of word processing specialists and administrative specialists, is assigned to a department or other entity.

Work group approach is an effective structure.

Both the word processing specialists and administrative specialists are managed by supervisors. These word processing supervisors and administrative support supervisors oversee the specialists, coordinate work flow, schedule working hours, and generally ensure a smoothly running system. These supervisors report to either a word processing manager or an administrative support manager, who both report to the information manager.

Supervised office staff operates more efficiently.

The advantages of this new office structure are many. Managers are not dependent upon just one person for support services. An entire team is trained to keep the work flowing. Documents can be prepared more quickly and professionally. The greatest advantage to management, however, is that many of the routine duties can be delegated to administrative specialists. Managers are given freedom to address pressing problems. The secretaries benefit because their careers are no longer tied to the success of their employers. A definite career ladder exists, and the specialist can be promoted on the basis of skills and abilities.

Input Alternatives

Input is the beginning step in the creation of a business communication. The most often used method of input is longhand. The writer drafts the communication in longhand, then gives it to a typist who prepares the final copy. Longhand input is the slowest, most ineffective input method. The average person writes at the rate of between 10 and 20 words a minute, sometimes in handwriting that is hard to decipher.

Longhand input is too slow.

If a handwritten or other draft is submitted to the word processing specialist, a request slip, such as shown in Figure 18.2, would be attached to the rough draft copy. Figure 18.3 is a sample page from a word processing center's user's guide. This guide describes the procedures used in operating the center.

Dictation to a shorthand writer is another method of input. With this method two people are involved in creating a document. This type of dictation is two to three times faster than longhand input, but the time of two people is used.

Dictation to a secretary is expensive.

A third, and most efficient, method of input is machine dictation. By using a machine to record dictation, the rate of input can be increased to over 100 words a minute. If a writer is going to function efficiently and contribute to the electronic office's overall effectiveness, it is imperative that he or she develop the skills of machine dictation. Dartnell Institute of Business Research found that the use of dictation equipment can cut the cost of the average business letter by 25 percent—a savings that cannot be overlooked.[4] The advantages of machine dictation far outweigh the advantages of other presently available means of input. These advantages include:

Dictation to a machine is simple and cost effective.

The skill is easily developed.

A secretary does not have to be available to take notes; thus, the dictator is free to dictate at any time.

Anyone in the office can transcribe the dictation.

Transcription from machine dictation is faster than from longhand notes.

Time is not wasted trying to decipher rough drafts.

Figure 18.2 Work Request Form

```
                        Word Processing
                         Request Slip


    Originator's Name:  _____

    Department:         _____

    Date In:  _____    Date Needed:  _____

    Draft:    _____    Final:        _____

    Check below:  (Paper to be used)

        □ Bond Paper
        □ Internal Communication
        □ Operations Bulletin
        □ Operations Manual
        □ OPC
        □ Employee Relations Manual
        □ Training Manual
        □ Directors Handbook
        □ Other
        □ Accounting Manual
        □ Legal
        □ Accounting Statements

    Special Instructions:  _____

    _____

    _____

    _____


    Operator's Initials:  _____

    No. of Pages:  _____

    Date Completed:  _____
```

Designed by Gayle Harper, Security Pacific Finance Corporation

Dictation Equipment. Reasonably priced dictation equipment is available in a variety of designs. Choose the type of equipment that will best meet your needs.

Portable dictation units are small and easily carried in a pocket or briefcase. These units are battery operated and are especially popular for use away from the office. Although these units are small, they have many features found on larger pieces of dictation equipment (see Figure 18.4).

There is a piece of dictation equipment for every need.

Figure 18.3 Sample Page from a Word Processing User's Guide

User's Guide

I. Word Processing Operations

A. Hours: Monday - Friday 8:00 a.m. to 4:45 p.m. The dial access dictation system is available 24 hours a day, 7 days a week.

B. Turnaround Time:

Routine work:

1-3 pages	24 hours (max)
4-9 pages	48 hours (max)
9+	Schedule with WP Supervisor
Special Projects	Schedule with WP Supervisor

Priority: Requests for priority status are evaluated by the Word Processing Supervisor on an individual basis. The highest priority will be assigned to documents that affect the Bank's liability (e.g. court filing deadlines, prime interest rate letters, etc.). Users will receive the best service when they plan ahead so that the Word Processing Center is not placed in the position of establishing priorities across departmental/ group lines which could result in less than satisfactory services for all concerned.

II. Documents

A. Input: The Word Processing Center will accept machine dictation; longhand copy; marked and edited copy including correspondence, interoffice memoranda, fill-in forms, statistical reports, form letters and standard paragraphs. For other services call the Center at x6283.

B. Output: The Center will always use standard block correspondence style unless specified otherwise. Drafts will always be double-spaced unless specified otherwise. For samples of expected copy see the Sample Manual.

C. Storage: All input will be stored for a minimum of one week. Periodically you will receive a list of documents being stored in your name. Please line through documents that can be deleted and return the list to Word Processing.

D. Proofreading: The word processing proofreader will proofread all final output for typographical errors, misspellings and grammatical errors in punctuation. The Center will do minor editing for inadvertant grammatical and rhetorical errors. The proofreader will not proofread drafts unless requested to do so. The reference source for grammar: Reference Manual for Stenographers and Typists, Fourth Edition, Gavin & Sabin.

E. Revisions: When a revision is needed, please follow these guide-lines:

Include original document name (found on the Work Request form - MIS-35). (Refer to the Sample Manual for examples.)

If you have any questions please call the Center at x6283.

Developed by Trudy Travis, San Diego Trust & Savings Bank

Desk-top units are used in the traditional dictator-secretary arrangement. These units are available in models for dictation only or in models that can be used for transcription as well as dictation (see Figure 18.5).

Central recording systems are designed to handle large volumes of dictation. The telephone or a permanently wired handset is used for input. The system can be accessed from virtually any telephone in the world.

The dictation is recorded in a central location. Transcription would normally be handled in a centralized word processing center (see Figure 18.6).

The standard recording media for dictation equipment are cassettes. Standard cassettes can hold from 30 to 180 minutes of recording time. Many systems require standard cassettes; but mini- or microcassettes, which hold 30 to 60 minutes of recording time, are becoming more popular. Some central recording systems use media called endless loop. The endless loop is recording tape that is housed in a tank. The tape continually circulates in the tank, and there is no need to change or handle the medium in any way. The dictator need not worry about how long the tape will last.

Cassettes are the recording media.

Dictation Procedures.   The business communicator can make his or her most important contribution to efficient document production in the office by following an effectual method of dictating. In fact, some companies set up their word processing procedures to give top priority to dictated documents. With training and planning, dictation will become automatic. Here are some hints to help make dictation comfortable:

- Become thoroughly familiar with your equipment. The vendor will provide help, but read the instruction manual carefully. Your company may also conduct dictation training sessions.
- Get rid of mike fright by simply reading a passage into the machine. Listen to your voice to evaluate the speed and clarity of your speech. Keep practicing until your voice can be easily understood.

Becoming at ease with the equipment and dictating are easy with practice.

Figure 18.4   Sony BM–550 Portable Dictation Unit

Source: Courtesy of Sony Corporation of America

Figure 18.5   Dictaphone Desk-top Dictation Unit Featuring Electronic Cuing

Source: Courtesy of Dictaphone Corporation, Rye, New York.

Planning to Dictate.   Set aside a certain time of the day to dictate. Mornings are recommended so that documents can be transcribed and mailed the same day.

Plan to dictate the rush items first. Gather information pertaining to the correspondence, and it is often helpful to jot down an outline for the message.

Many companies will have dictation procedures manuals that describe how documents should be dictated. Be sure to follow those procedures. Generally, these guidelines should be followed:

- Identify yourself, your title, your department, and your phone number.
- Indicate the type of document—letter, memo, report, and so on. Be sure to specify whether the document is to be a rough draft or in final form.
- Indicate when the document is required and how many copies are needed.
- Specify special stationery or paper if necessary.

Figure 18.6 Dictaphone's Nucleus Central Dictation System

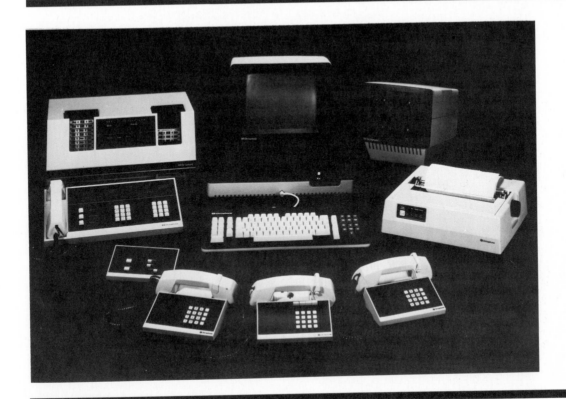

This system can dictate or transcribe remotely over ordinary telephone lines.
Source: Courtesy of Dictaphone Corporation, Rye, New York.

▫ Give an estimation of the length of the document, whether it is a short one-page letter or a four-page report.

Dictating the Document.   Speak distinctly at a natural speed. Hold the microphone two to three inches from your mouth, and emphasize past tenses and plurals.

Punctuation can be indicated by voice inflection, but it is a good idea to dictate commas, periods, question marks, and paragraphing. *Be sure* to dictate such unusual punctuation as quotes, underscoring, and dashes. Capital letters should be dictated, too.

Spell out difficult or confusing words or names. If necessary, tell the transcriber where to find reference material.

Indicate document end, errors, special instructions, or insertions in dictation by using the cuing devices on the equipment. The manual accompanying the machine will explain how to use the features of your particular model. Marking the corrections is a great help and time saver to the transcriber.

Using the cuing device is of importance.

When dictating charts or lists, always prepare the transcriber for them by indicating how many columns and column headings there will be. Dictate from left to right and from top to bottom. If possible, provide a written sample of the desired format.

The transcriber, or proofreader, will undoubtedly proofread your documents before returning them to you. However, the documents are sent out with your name on them, and it is *your* final responsibility to see that the document is acceptable.

Correction of the copy is the author's responsibility.

The more dictating you do, the easier it will become. Make the effort to become at ease with the microphone. If, in the beginning, you find it easier to write the letter in longhand and then dictate the letter to the machine, go ahead. You will soon be able to dictate with only a guide or outline of the message.

Other Input Alternatives

Optical Character Readers. Another type of input is the optical character reader, which is commonly referred to as OCR. Optical character readers, when used in combination with word processing equipment, can be a rapid means of input. The OCR reads pages of previously typed documents, converts what it reads to electronic information, and places that information on a magnetic medium, usually a disk. The disk can then be placed in a word processing machine; the document is called onto the screen and is edited.

For example, you receive a report from another branch of your company. You are asked to update the report. The needed changes are few; you write the changes directly on the report. The report is scanned by the OCR, and the information is transferred to a disk. The word processing specialist inserts the disk in the word processing machine, views the document on the screen, incorporates the changes you have indicated, and prints a revised copy of the report.

Use the OCR to reduce keyboarding time.

There are several advantages to OCR: (1) previously typed documents do not have to be rekeyed; (2) any typewriter could be used to keyboard information, the document is scanned by the OCR, and then word processing equipment is used for subsequent editing; (3) word processing equipment is better utilized because it is used solely for editing purposes; and (4) optical character readers can read 350,000 to 450,000 characters an hour while operators key 10,000 to 12,000 characters hourly.

These scanning devices are able to give input to small business computers, phototypesetters, computer mainframes, communication devices, as well as word processing machines. Future scanners will be small enough to fit into a briefcase.

Prewritten Messages. In Chapter 5 you studied the uses and advantages of prewritten messages such as form paragraphs, form letters, and form letters containing blanks for variable information. One of the optimum functions of the electronic office is the expediting of these types of documents. Figure 18.7 shows a work request for a letter containing form paragraphs. These form letters and paragraphs are stored electronically in the word processing system for use when needed. After the word processing specialist has keyed the receiver's name and address, the prewritten paragraphs can be recalled with just a few strokes, and a personalized document is ready to be sent. Total time necessary to produce the document is probably less than three minutes.

A form letter containing variable information can be requested by use of a form shown in Figure 18.8. The word processing specialist keys in the variable information, calls up the form letter, and the equipment automatically merges the document with the variable information. Once again, very little time is used to produce the document.

Form letters speed up the communication process.

Writer Keying.   As terminals become more widely available, another input alternative is for the writer to do the keying. You may have a word processing specialist do the final formatting, editing, and production, but composing at the terminal is an effective means of input. Composing at the keyboard is two to three times faster than composing in longhand. The writer can create the report on the computer terminal and save a great deal of time both for the writer and for the word processing specialist.

Processing Alternatives

The type of document processing equipment that is available in your company depends on many factors. Among the most important are the type of documents that are generated, the size of the company, the amount of money available for equipment, and the way the company is organized. You may find that your company uses more than one of the following alternatives. It is important that the users of the electronic office understand the capabilities of the equipment.

The electronic typewriter is rapidly taking the place of the more customary electric typewriters. The electronic typewriter, at first glance, looks similar to traditional typewriters, yet there are significant differences. For instance, the electronic typewriter has fewer moving parts and possesses at least a few automatic features, which may include a limited memory, automatic lift-off of errors, automatic centering, automatic carrier return, automatic decimal alignment, and a choice of printing in 10-, 12-, 15-pitch, or proportional spacing.

Many electronic typewriters are designed for easy upgrading to more powerful capabilities, such as a larger memory. Some electronic typewriters are designed to communicate with other pieces of equipment, such as computers, or to be used as a printer. Conversion to electronic

The standard office typewriter is now electronic.

Figure 18.7 Work Request for Letter Containing Form Paragraphs

Word Processing Products

Word Processing

Work Request

	Operator:	Received (date / time)
	Sales	

The attached material may be stored for:

☑ One week   ☐ Permanent file

   (correspondence)   (updated periodically)

☐ One month   ☐ Other _____

Deliver to:	
Author Name	*Toby*
Job Title	*letter*

Delivery Instructions:

☐ Call to pick up _____

☑ Deliver by in-house mail

Date Required (please specify *May 6, 198—* date in full)	Ext. *774*
Do you wish: ☐ Draft ☑ Final	Document no.

Instructions

Standard ¶'s 1, 2, 3, 7 to
Garman Freight Lines, Inc.
939 West 14 Street
San Deigo, CA 92101

Delivered: (date / time)

For Center Use Only (Round total time to nearest quarter)

Date & Time Started	Time		Keystrokes	Pages	Comments
	Hrs.	Mins.			
Totals					

Document ID	Diskette	Operator	☐ New Input ☐ Change	Turnaround	Delivered Pages

Figure 18.8   Work Request for Form Letter Containing Variable Information

Word Processing Products

Word Processing

Work Request

	Received (date / time)
Operator:	
Deliver to: Nels Toby	
Author Name Nels Toby	
Job Title First reminder collection letter –	

The attached material may be stored for:

☐ One week   ☒ Permanent file

  (correspondence)   (updated periodically)

☐ One month   ☐ Other _____

Date Required (please specify May 5, 198- date in full)	Ext. 774
Do you wish:	Document no.
☐ Draft ☒ Final	

Delivery Instructions:

☒ Call to pick up _____

☐ Deliver by in-house mail

Variables: A

1. Mr. Ted Sheldon _____

   5657 Vinton _____

   San Antonio, Texas 78207 _____

2. Mr. Sheldon _____

3. $1,225.75 _____

4. Sales Rep. Jose Chavez _____

5. _____

6. _____

7. _____

8. _____

9. _____

10. _____

Variables: B

1. Dr. Franklin Myers _____

   76 Country Club Drive _____

   Denver, Colorado 80201 _____

2. Dr. Myers _____

3. $225.00 _____

4. Sales Rep. Darrell Smith _____

5. _____

6. _____

7. _____

8. _____

9. _____

10. _____

typewriters is one of the first steps in automating the office. This equipment is designed for original letters, memos, and short documents that probably need no revision.

The stand-alone word processor is more sophisticated than the electronic typewriter. The stand-alone word processor, shown in Figure 18.9, consists of a central processing unit (commonly referred to as a CPU), a disk drive, a keyboard, a screen, and a printer. This equipment is capable of performing a large variety of text editing and repetitive processing tasks. A major advantage of such a system is that the operator can be keying a document while other documents are being printed. Productivity is greatly improved by this capability.

Stand-alone word processors are versatile and able to handle many tasks.

With a stand-alone system only one person can use the equipment at a time. Therefore, it is useful in small businesses or departments of larger businesses.

A shared or distributed logic system (also referred to as a cluster system) operates in much the same way as does a stand-alone system, except one CPU is connected to two or more keyboards and printers. Some large systems are capable of supporting up to 132 pieces of equipment on one central processing unit. Shared systems are appropriate for companies that employ more than one word processing operator. Because just one CPU controls the system, all work stations can share the same data base. When long documents must be processed in a

Shared systems save money when several stations are needed.

Figure 18.9   NBI OASys 4000S Stand-Alone Word Processing System

Source: Courtesy of NBI, Inc.

hurry, the work can be divided so that several operators are working on the one document. When all keying is completed, the document can be easily assembled and printed.

In a shared-logic system, all pieces of equipment are dependent on one CPU for computer logic and memory. If the CPU develops trouble, no part of the system can function until repairs have been made. Terminals in this system are called *dumb terminals.*

A distributed-logic system may look like a shared-logic system, but there is an important difference. In a distributed-logic system, the individual pieces of equipment have their own intelligence. If the central processing unit malfunctions, the other pieces of equipment may continue to operate. Both the stand-alone word processors and the cluster systems are capable of handling heavy text editing and repetitive typing tasks.

Some companies may find it advantageous to have the document processing done on the mainframe computer. The computer equipment that handles the firm's data processing applications would also be capable of word processing tasks. The word processing could be done on a remote terminal that is connected to the large computer. In this case, the document printing may be done on a remote printer or perhaps the document would be printed elsewhere and delivered.

Companies that would like the benefits of data and word processing, but do not feel like making the financial commitment needed to purchase the equipment, may choose a time-shared system. The firm can subscribe to a system and pay for only the time that is used. A terminal connected by a telephone connector (modem) would be installed in the subscribing firm's office. One advantage of this arrangement is that it gives access to sophisticated capabilities that a firm might not otherwise afford.

Functions

Some text editing functions are commonly available on word processing systems. It is essential for a writer to know what automatic functions he or she can use when revising documents. Many changes that used to call for retyping an entire document can now be made with just a few keystrokes. A writer need no longer feel terribly apologetic about asking an operator to make document changes.

Automatic functions make document revision easy.

The functions available on individual equipment vary according to the needs of the firm and the amount of money invested in the system. The following features are among the most commonly used:

Delete/Insert allows characters, words, sentences, paragraphs, etc., to be deleted or inserted anywhere in the text.

Copy/Move allows any amount of information to be copied or moved anywhere within the document or to any other document that is on the system. For instance, a paragraph(s) that appears in one document but needs to be repeated in another document can easily be moved or copied.

Pagination/Repagination allows the selection of the number of lines to appear on each page. The operator keys in the desired number, and the system counts the lines and indicates the page breaks. When a document has been edited and text has been added or deleted, new page breaks can be automatically inserted and the revised document printed rapidly.

Format change allows the line length and tabs to be reset at anytime. The system automatically adjusts all lines to the requested format. Vertical spacing can also be changed; single, double, triple, one and a half, and quarter spacing are among the options.

Justified right margin directs the system to produce a document with a straight right-hand margin. This feature is especially useful in newsletters and manuals.

Document assembly allows previously keyed paragraphs to be assembled in any order to create a new document. Form paragraphs would be used with this function.

Merge allows the combining of previously keyed text, such as form letters and lists of names, to create repetitive letters that appear to be originals. Form letters containing variables that change with each name are also produced by use of the merge function.

Columnar interchange allows columns to be switched around. For example, when a statistical report needs to be updated, one column could be deleted entirely, the other columns moved left, and new information added in a far right-hand column.

Global search and replace locates a specified character string wherever the string appears in the document. The characters can then be replaced with another set of characters. For example if a proposal has been composed for the ABC Company and later the same proposal is to be made to the XYZ Company, the global search and replace function will find each occurrence of *ABC Company* and replace it with *XYZ Company*. A new customized document is created, but the costly re-keyboarding and proofreading is held to a minimum.

Headers and footers allow, for instance, section titles to be placed automatically at the top of each page and consecutive page numbers to be placed at the bottom of each page.

Glossary/Phrase library storage allows the storing of frequently used words or phrases. These phrases are coded so that they appear fully spelled out in the document, but the input is accomplished with just two keystrokes. The date, company names, and frequently used words or phrases can be stored in the glossary and called on when needed.

Dictionary allows spelling to be checked automatically. When a page has been keyed, the dictionary function can be accessed. The keyed words are automatically checked. Incorrect words are highlighted, and the operator can correct errors. This function is not to be used as a replacement for proofreading the document. For example, the dictionary does not know that *their* was used when the correct word should have been *there*. Neither can it check for word omissions or transpositions. The dictionary function takes care of a great deal of the proofreading, but it does not check for errors in agreement of nouns and verbs, and other grammar or syntax errors.

Grammar/Syntax verification software is available to check for such errors as capitalization of the first word of a sentence, capitalization of the word *I,* balanced quotes and parentheses, and inconsistent capitals, such as SUsan. This software can check for words and phrases that are considered wordy, archaic, or trite and suggest alternatives.

The document is reviewed for the number of sentences and words. The average word and sentence length is computed. The number of sentences containing more than 30 words is counted as is the number of sentences containing fewer than 14 words. It counts how many times words are repeated and the number of questions and prepositions. With this information, a writer can revise the text to make it more readable. In the future, even more sophisticated grammar/syntax software will be developed.

Thesaurus software allows the writer to ask for alternative words. The writer identifies the word that he or she would like to change, and the computer supplies a number of choices. The writer makes a selection, and the new word automatically replaces the previous one.

Subscripts and superscripts allow numbers to be placed slightly above or below lines for use in footnoting or keyboarding formulas. For example, 2^4 CO_2.

Footnote tie-in automatically allows space at the bottom of the page for the footnotes indicated in the text. Some systems keep the footnote number and footnote together automatically. For instance, if the footnote number is transferred to another page, the footnote will be transferred automatically to the bottom of the same page.

Table of contents update automatically updates the table of contents of a document when new sections are added, deleted, or moved. Outline update and index update work in the same manner.

Forms allow a form, such as an invoice, to be created on the system. A *forms mask* is called up on the screen, and the operator fills in the blanks. The mask is used over and over as many times as needed and is stored for future use.

Advanced Features

Some optional sophisticated features available on a system include:

Files capabilities allow lists to be created and updated. The lists can be printed according to any category in the list. For example, a list containing names, addresses, birth dates, and social security numbers can be printed to list those people who were born in January.

Sort capability allows lists to be rearranged in any order. For example, the previously mentioned list could be used to sort out the people who live in a particular state and arrange their names according to zip code.

Mathematics support expands the system's capabilities into data processing. Math packs add, subtract, multiply, and divide columns of figures, as well as perform other functions. This option is used to verify previously computed figures.

Graphics capability is available as a software option on many systems. With this function such documents as graphs and charts can be completed quickly. An especially useful application of this feature is to produce organizational charts. When the organization changes, the charts can be updated easily.

Storage Alternatives

When documents have been processed using the functions just described, they must then be stored. Electronic technology has done wonders for data storage. Today more than a million bits (a bit is the smallest piece of electronic information) can be stored on a computer chip that is no larger than a fingertip. This chip is referred to as a *microcomputer*.

Internal Storage

The chip, which is located inside the equipment, constitutes internal storage. Another type of internal storage called *bubble memory* offers promise for future use. The bubble can hold the equivalent of 100 pages of the Manhattan telephone directory in just one square inch.[5]

Hard disks represent another type of internal storage medium that holds many millions of characters (megabytes). The disks are able to store information inexpensively. The advantage of the hard disk, as well as other types of internal media, is that the media are not touched by humans and damage is avoided. Hard disks are becoming more popular as prices decrease and storage capabilities increase.

The type of storage will depend on the firm's needs and kind of equipment used.

External Storage

Magnetic tapes and cards are early examples of external media. A magnetic tape cassette is able to hold 25 to 60 pages of information. The magnetic card is useful for storing one page of information per card. Magnetic tapes and cards, which are rather cumbersome to access and edit, have been replaced by floppy disks in more up-to-date systems.

Floppy disks are available in 8-, 5¼-, and 3½-inch sizes and hold from 70 to 130 or more pages of information, depending on size and density of the particular disk. Individual pieces of information stored on a floppy disk can be accessed instantaneously, making the editing process easy. The floppy disk is presently the most popular storage medium because it costs only a few cents a page to store information on it. The trend is to use smaller spaces of media to store more information.

The storage media discussed so far are used to store information while the documents are being processed. Long-term storage of documents will probably be by file cabinets, or in more sophisticated settings, by microforms.

Paper creates a major bottleneck in storage. What can we do with all the stacks and stacks of paper? Where can we put all the metal file cabinets that are required to house the stacks and stacks of required information? Microfilm has been used for many years; its main use was to store documents which were seldom referred to. Now, however, the technology called *micrographics* is expanding because large amounts of information can be packed into small amounts of space. The term *microforms* is used to cover any type of microdata such as microfilm, microfiche, and ultrafiche.

Costly storage of paper can be avoided by using microforms.

Microform storage takes up only five percent of the storage needed by paper. One filing cabinet of microforms can store the contents of 50 filing cabinets of paper. A 1,000-page report costs $1 to store on microforms and $29 to store on paper. In addition, the cost of paper is expected to rise at twice the inflation rate.[6]

Micrographics encompasses not only microfilm but also *microfiche,* which holds several hundred pages in an area 4 by 6 inches, and *ultrafiche,* which holds 10,000 pages in a strip 8 inches long. These microforms can be produced quickly and inexpensively. They are read by use of a microform reader or by hard copy produced by a microform printer.

Output Alternatives

Although electronic storage is available in many forms, the majority of documents are presently produced on paper. The type of output alternative that you choose for any particular document depends on how the document will be used. In many cases it will be up to you to specify the type of output.

Impact Printers

Impact printers are familiar to you because a typewriter is an impact printer. An image is produced when a device strikes the paper. For many years typewriters used typebars to print the letters. In the 1960s IBM

The kind of document and its use will determine the type of output.

developed the ball or Selectric element. This device is more properly called a *single-element font*. Other manufacturers now use these elements on their products. The single-element was a boon to printing on early word processing devices. The element printer could print at approximately 15 characters per second (cps) or 180 words a minute—far faster than most skilled typists.

In the early 1970s the daisy print wheel was developed. The daisy wheel resembles a multispoke wheel with characters on the ends of each spoke. The daisy wheel is capable of faster printing than the single-element font. The speed ranges between 30 to 55 cps or 350 to 650 words a minute. The daisy wheel is replacing the single-element font as the most popular impact printing device. Many electronic typewriters use a daisy wheel.

Another impact device is the Spinwriter or thimble printer. The device resembles a thimble with characters along the outside edge. The Spinwriter is durable and capable of printing at the rate of 55 cps.

All the impact devices—typebar, single-element, daisy wheel and thimble—produce what is called *letter-quality printing*. When you want a document to look originally and individually typed, you will probably specify the output to be printed from one of these types of impact printers.

There are other types of impact printers that do not produce letter-quality documents. These are called *line printers* or *chain printers*. These printers are high-speed devices that are commonly used for computer output. Quality is sacrificed for speed, and speeds range from 100 to 3,800 lines per minute (lpm).

The dot matrix printer produces characters by use of dots. Low-density dot matrix printing is considered sufficient for draft printing. Some companies may use lower cost matrix printers to produce draft copies; the letter-quality printer is then used for final copies. High-density dot matrix printers are available. Output from these printers can resemble letter-quality print. The advantage to a dot matrix printer is that, in addition to printing alpha-numeric characters, it can also produce symbols and graphic representations. These high-density printers are becoming popular as inexpensive, yet versatile, printers.

Nonimpact Printers

The electrostatic (xerographic) copier is a familiar piece of equipment. The photocopier has replaced carbon paper as the choice method of reproducing either one copy or many copies. Businesses with high document production requirements may find that an intelligent copier/printer will meet their high output demands.

An intelligent copier/printer (IC/P) can be activated by the word processing specialist. The operator keys the document, and when the copy is ready, it is transmitted electronically to the IC/P. The IC/P can store the document for printing later or produce the output immediately. The IC/P can produce the document in a wide variety of type styles, sizes,

Intelligent copiers may be the high-speed printers used by many firms.

and line spacing. The IC/P produces letter-quality documents at the rate of up to 120 pages per minute.

This printer could possibly replace more conventional forms of printing for many firms. In addition to printing words, the copier has a highly sophisticated graphics capability. Not only does the IC/P accept electronic information from the word processing machine, but input can also come from computers and other IC/Ps.

Typesetting once was the exclusive domain of professional printers. Documents, such as annual reports, that required a highly professional look were sent outside the firm to a printer. Today over 50 percent of large businesses find it cost effective to do their printing in-house. Savings can be realized through streamlined procedures that work like this:

Typesetting moves inside the office.

A rough draft copy is given to the word processing specialist who keys the document. The writer edits the document, and corrections are made by the word processing specialist. When the final copy is approved, the document is transmitted electronically to the phototypesetting machine. The special typesetting codes are entered on the document, and the phototypesetter produces a camera-ready copy. The copy is then run, often in multicolor, on a printing press.

Advantages to this system are that a professional-looking document is produced; the document is keyed only once; the document never has to leave the premises; confidentiality can be maintained; deadlines can be more easily met; and the material is stored in-house for future use and revision. In addition to the savings and more efficient procedures, there is another important advantage: a document that is phototypeset takes about half the space of a typed document. Paper costs are thereby cut in half.

Phototypesetting saves time and paper.

Computer output microfilm (COM) is a process that can be used to cut down the mountains of stored paper. Output from the computer can be put directly onto microfilm without first being printed on paper. Computer output systems can convert 200 to 400 pages of computer output a minute to microfilm. Figure 18.10 depicts computer output microfilm equipment.

The computer made it possible for you to have computer output microfilm, and a computer can also help you find your documents. The process is called *computer-assisted retrieval* (CAR). With the help of the computer, records can be retrieved in seconds. The days of tedious searching through file folders full of paper are rapidly drawing to a close for many businesses.

Distribution Alternatives

At the moment the U.S. Postal Service carries most of the mail generated in this country. However, hand-delivered mail may not always reach its destination in time. Also hand delivery of the mail is the most time-consuming link in the document cycle.

Figure 18.10 ARIS™ II, the Advanced Remote Imaging System from Datagraphix, Inc.

This system features dry-heat development processing and unique raster scan laser imaging. The system records COM output at speeds up to 12,000 lines per minute.

Source: Courtesy of Datagraphix, Inc.

For many years businesses have been communicating by way of telex/TWX machines. This system operated by Western Union has made it possible for a firm with a telex machine to communicate instantly with another firm that has a telex machine. To send a telex message, an operator must key the information into the machine.

Another device that has been used for many years is the facsimile (FAX) machine. The FAX is essentially a copier that takes an already prepared document, copies it, and sends it electronically to a receiving FAX machine. The FAX equipment transmits alpha-numeric data as well as handwritten information, pictures, and graphs. Portable facsimile equipment is available to be taken on field assignments or trips.

Electronic mail speeds document delivery and lowers costs.

Both telex/TWX and FAX are examples of electronic mail or tele-communications. Although these technologies have been used for a number of years, they weren't described using these terms until recently.

Other methods of electronic mail are also available. Word processing machines can be equipped to communicate with other word processing machines to achieve what is called *communicating word processors.* For example, a branch office in Atlanta, Georgia, develops a marketing plan that must be approved by the corporate office in Dallas, Texas. The plan is keyed on a word processing machine in the Atlanta office. The information is transmitted electronically to a compatible word processing machine in Dallas. No paper is used; no valuable time is lost waiting for the mail to be delivered. When the plan is received in Dallas, it can be printed, or it can be read from the screen. Suggestions can be made, approval given, and the plan transmitted back to Atlanta within a short time. Companies can save thousands of dollars a month through the use of electronic mail.

Word processing machines can deliver electronic mail.

Telephone cables are used as the workhorse of the electronic mail transmissions, but satellites are the transmission devices with the greatest potential. Private companies, such as Satellite Business Systems, provide services to allow firms to transmit voice, video, data, and graphic communications. It is expected that satellite transmission will be available at the cost of 1.5 cents a page. Therefore, it is reasonable to believe electronic mail will become the pipeline for business communications.

Satellites are the carriers of the future.

Computer-based message systems are a part of the electronic mail cycle. Messages that are transmitted electronically are stored in an electronic "mailbox" and can be read and responded to at the user's convenience. Not only written messages can be stored, but also voice messages. This feature is an extension of the familiar telephone-answering device. The advantage to the computer-based message system is that all messages are received unattended: secretaries need not take time to answer the phone or write down and transmit messages. Communications from anywhere in the world can be received anytime and held for the recipient's action.

Computers can deliver phone messages.

We have been discussing the rapid transmission of information to the outside world, but what can be done to speed up information transmission within the individual company? From 60 to 90 percent of communications are confined to a moderately sized geographical area, such as an office building or a campus.[7] Local area networks have been developed to link the company to an electronic network. Cables are strung to enable the different types of electronic devices—computers, word processors, facsimile machines, multifunction work stations, personal computers, intelligent copier/printers, phototypesetters—to communicate with one another. Examples of these local area networks are the Wangnet, developed by Wang Laboratories, and Ethernet, developed by Xerox.

Interoffice communications can be improved by local area networks.

Emerging Developments

Multifunction Work Stations

Estimates indicate that 15 to 40 percent of the executive's time is spent on less productive activities, such as clerical tasks, finding and screening information, and waiting while traveling. At least 15 percent of this time can be saved through automation.[8] The multifunction work station is an electronic device designed to improve the productivity of executives.

The work station is linked to the local area network. With a multifunction work station, the executive can view the day's appointment calendar electronically. Reminders that are in the tickler file will appear at the touch of a button. If a meeting with associates must be called, the associates' calendars will appear on the screen, a time for the meeting is set, and the notices for the meeting will be distributed electronically. Incoming messages and mail will appear on the screen—no paper to shuffle or message slips to lose. Electronic files, sometimes called *hot files* can be called to the screen at will; there is no need to rummage in the files or call the secretary to find a document.

Multifunction work stations help the executive to work productively.

If a report must be updated, these steps may be followed: the company's data base, or a subscription data base, such as Dun and Bradstreet or the New York Times Information Bank, is accessed for the needed information; the previous report is called to the screen and revised; charts and graphs are generated, and the document transmitted to the word processing center for new formatting or printing if necessary.

The multifunction work station should be considered a tool to enhance management's productivity. Office functions and data processing activities are integrated to enhance management control efficiently. With more than 75 percent of a manager's time devoted to communications and with management and professional labor accounting for more than half of the total office labor costs, the use of a multifunction work station to increase productivity is certainly worth investigating. Figure 18.11 depicts a multifunction work station in use.

The personal computer (PC) can also be considered a multifunction work station. The personal computer can perform the same functions as the multifunction work station; the main difference is a personal computer can operate as a stand-alone device as well as being linked into a network. Personal computers can be used by small businesses as the total electronic office. Such functions as word processing, accounts receivable and payable, payroll, financial statements, inventory control, and billing can be performed on a personal computer.

Figure 18.11   Wang Alliance 250

The Wang Alliance 250 provides data base power and information management techniques to the entire office team, without requiring a knowledge of computers. The first
human-engineered office system for information access and retrieval, the Alliance inte-
grates data processing, word processing, audio processing, image processing, human
factors, and networking.

Source: Courtesy of Wang Laboratories, Inc.

The executive who is used to having electronic technology as a tool
in the office will also want access to electronic technology outside the
office. The office in the briefcase fulfills this need. Computers, word
processors, dictating equipment, and printers are now miniaturized to
fit in a briefcase, as shown in Figure 18.12. The executive can transmit
orders, reports, letters, or memos from any telephone with this equipment.

**As technology
progresses, the tools
become more portable.**

Figure 18.12 Sony Typecorder

The Sony Typecorder takes transcription and dictation and communicates. The compact printer is available for on-the-spot printing.

Teleconferencing

Teleconferencing is an electronic tool designed to cut the need for business travel. Business travel is not only costly in terms of dollars spent, but also in terms of the time it requires. Teleconferencing can be accomplished by conventional closed-circuit television technology in which the participants are able to see each other on a screen.

When participants need not see each other, but there is a need to transmit and discuss sketches, maps, charts and the like, the *electronic blackboard* can be used. At other times a *computer conference* can be arranged. Computer conferencing uses terminals, printers, and telephone lines to access a computer for direct communication. Participants need not be at their communications instruments simultaneously, but they can read others' input and give their own at their convenience.

The advantages of teleconferencing are travel is reduced, there are fewer meetings, more can be accomplished in less time, issues can be dealt with immediately, the quality and quantity of feedback is im-

proved, and there is increased job satisfaction by allowing more participants in the decision-making process.

Advances in Computers

Breakthroughs in voice processing will enable us to speak to the computer for information rather than using a keyboard. The computer will
understand what we are saying and convert our speech into alpha-
numeric symbols on our screen. This dramatic advance will replace the
need to key information.

Artificial intelligence is another emerging electronic technology. Artificial intelligence will react to memo-like requests, sort through knowledge stored in a computer, and carry out a line of reasoning. It is predicted that a system will read our mail and tell us which messages are
important. The system will generate its own notices, monitor responses, and coordinate managers' schedules.[9] Optical videodisks will
store our data on light-sensitive materials, and laser beams will read and
write the data. Prototype optical disks can hold over 10 billion bits of
data on a single 30-centimeter disk. The disks will probably cost about
$10 each.[10]

Figure 18.13   Work Flow in the Electronic Office

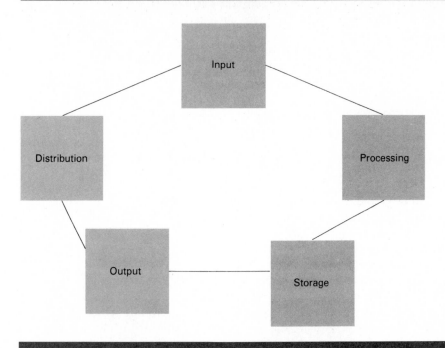

These technologies are available now and will make work in the electronic office very different from the traditional office. Compare the work cycle in Figure 18.1 with the cycle in Figure 18.13. Inevitably, the processes will be refined, equipment production costs will decrease, and these sophisticated devices will be feasible for many businesses.

Summary

The traditional boss-secretary, one-to-one relationship in the office is giving way to a new office structure. This new structure is designed to increase office productivity and provide more timely information to managers. To accomplish these goals, new job descriptions and titles have been developed. Word processing specialists have taken on the duties of document production, and administrative specialists act as assistants to the word originators or knowledge workers. New procedures have been designed to improve the work flow and streamline operations.

A profusion of electronic equipment is entering the office. Dictation equipment allows documents to be dictated from any place at any time. Word processing equipment records documents on magnetic media so that editing and repetitive production is made quick and easy.

The movement toward the "paperless office" is underway with the introduction of electronic files, electronic mail, local area networks, microfiche, ultrafiche, and computer output microfilm. Multifunction work stations enable an executive to do research, receive and answer mail and messages, keep track of calendars, search files, access data bases, and construct charts and graphs by simply touching a few buttons.

Teleconferencing makes it possible to communicate with colleagues in distant locations without travel. Decisions are more timely and relevant, and valuable time is saved.

In the future we look forward to speaking to the computer in our natural spoken language. The computer will recognize what we say and help us reason. We will be able to keep in contact with our office when we are at home or when we are away with our electronic "office in a briefcase." Instead of reporting to the office, you may instead work in a neighborhood satellite center. You will be linked electronically to headquarters. These electronic tools will enhance the quality of our work and shorten our working hours.

Footnotes

[1]"Stepping into Tomorrow's Office," *The Office* (November 1981): 119.

[2]Paul H. Witting, "For Better or Worse," *Words* (June-July 1982): 22.

[3]Based on information from Paul Truax and Jean Strong, "Think Before You Leap into

Word Processing," *The Office* (November 1976) 73–75, 123; Harold Tepper, "The Private Secretary: A Company Liability," *Management Review* (February 1973): 23–42; and Mona Casady, *Word Processing Concepts* (Cincinnati: South-Western Publishing, 1980).

[4]Bella G. Clinkscale and Kenneth R. Mayer, "The Art of Dictation: More than Just Lip Service," *Management World* (November 1981): 13.

[5]Marly Bergerud and Jean Gonzalez, *Word Information Processing Concepts, Careers, Technology and Applications* (New York: John Wiley and Sons, 1981), p. 68.

[6]"New Directions for COM," *Administrative Management* (September 1981): 45–46, 48–49.

[7]"LAN Provides Needed Link for Today's Office," *The Office* (February 1982): 113.

[8]"How to Boost Your Office Productivity," *Infosystems* (August 1980): 27.

[9]"Artificial Intelligence: The Second Computer Age," *BusinessWeek* (March 8, 1982): 66–69.

[10]"Optical Disk Study Planned by IGC," *Information Management* (May 1983): 12.

Review Questions

1. What are the four components of the electronic office?
2. Give an example of each of the four components of the electronic office.
3. Describe three advantages of "the new look of the office" recommended for the electronic office.
4. What is a work group? Discuss its advantages.
5. Which method of input would you choose for business documents? Why?
6. Who should assume ultimate responsibility for the correctness of a business document? Why?
7. Why should the business communicator understand the functions performed by word processing equipment?
8. To what extent do you believe electronic mail will be used in business in the future?
9. Is it reasonable to expect that executives will use multifunction work stations? Why or why not?
10. If office productivity is to be improved, who is responsible for improving productivity? Explain.

Exercises

1. You are employed by Datatech, Inc. Accounting Associates, 5326 Portland Avenue, Oklahoma City, Oklahoma 73112, has just placed a $7,500 order for an accounting software package. This is Accounting Associates' first order with Datatech. You are asked to write an acknowledgment letter.

   a.   Jot down a guide for the letter.

   b.   Dictate the letter into a dictating machine or tape recorder. Be sure to adhere to the procedures given in this chapter.

   c.   Ask someone to transcribe your letter.

   d.   Evaluate the transcribed letter to see if the transcriber could follow your directions.

   e.   Indicate how you can improve your next dictated letter.

2. Ask a dealer who sells dictation or word processing equipment for sales brochures on one piece of equipment. After studying the materials, either write a two-paragraph report on the equipment or give a brief oral report to the class.

3. You work for a small firm that employs two typists. Each month the company sends out hundreds of form letters which are pre-printed, and a typist types the date and cutomer's name and address on each letter as needed. One day your boss says it is time to buy a new typewriter for the office and asks you to make a suggestion.

   a.   What type of machine would you recommend?

   b.   Defend your choice.

4. In your position as technical writer for a large electronics manufacturer, you are writing a technical manual. As you complete sections, the word processing specialist keys the document. You have the following output equipment available: low-density dot matrix printer, letter-quality daisy wheel printer, and phototype-setting equipment.

   a.   Which output method would you choose if you wanted a rough draft of the manual? Why?

   b.   Which output method would you choose if you wanted 100 final copies of the manual? Why?

5. Universal Engineering is a company that has 10 branches in the United States and 8 branches in foreign countries. All branches are equipped with the same brand and model of word processing equipment. Corporate headquarters in Minneapolis is concerned about the high cost of postage spent communicating with the branches and the length of time necessary to receive the mail. The executive committee is looking for a solution.

   a.   What would you suggest?

   b.   What problems would there be in implementing your suggestion?

6. Universal Engineering believes it must meet with its branch managers four times a year. Each time they meet, approximately five days, including travel time, are used. These meetings cost about $225,000 each or $900,000 annually.

   a.   Does Universal have any alternative to bringing their managers together for meetings?

   b.   If so, what is the alternative and its advantages?

References

Bergerud, Marly and Jean Gonzalez. *Word Information Processing Concepts, Careers, Technology, and Applications.* New York: John Wiley and Sons, 1981.

Connell, John J. "Managing the Electronic Office." *Nation's Business* (February 1982): 59–60.

Datapro Reports on Word Processing. (looseleaf) Delran, NJ: Datapro Research Corporation.

Kleinschrod, Walter A., Leonard B. Kruk, and Hilda J. Turner. *Word Processing: Operations, Applications, and Administration.* Indianapolis: Bobbs-Merrill Educational Publishing, 1980.

Long, Jeffrey E., Joseph McKendrick, and Lou Pilla. "Strategies for Successful Office Systems." *Office Administration and Automation* (January 1983): 23–42.

Pomerantz, David, and Steve Saunders. "Tracking OA in 1983." *Today's Office* (December 1982): 21–30.

"The Office of 1990: Management, Human Resources, Automation." *Management World* (January 1982).

Case

The Expanding System
Mike Rausenberger
MBS Software
San Diego, California

A few years ago, a medium-size, rapidly growing company recognized the need to expand their customer service operations. Their growth was deemed by management to be largely the result of the company's concern for customer satisfaction.

Increased sales and projections indicated a significant rise in customer contacts could be expected. The national customer relations manager, who was responsible for the company's responsive image regarding customers' problems, was faced with a dilemma. His staff of six people handled 800 customer contacts a month.

One time honored approach was to add to existing staff, and add again tomorrow, and add again and again as sales continued to increase. The manager reasoned, however, that there would be a time when sales, in their historic cycles, would fall off. He knew that, regardless of work load, those slumps brought layoffs, and staffing for today's needs might well cause other problems later, such as the inability to maintain the effectiveness that was a cornerstone of the company's success.

After thoroughly reviewing the situation, the manager decided against temporarily increasing his staff, but something had to be done. Since answering letters and keeping records took most of the staff's time, automation seemed the answer.

The manager spent a great deal of time evaluating word processing equipment and chose a system that, while very powerful, could be learned quickly (operator friendly) and could be expanded as the need arose. The result was a word processing system that, in the early stages, included only one CRT and a letter-quality daisy wheel (40 cps) printer.

In a matter of weeks it became obvious that the system was "input clogged." Additional work stations were added to alleviate this condition. It then became apparent that the system could do much more than just speed responses to customers. Record keeping was added to the system, which allowed automation of the manual monthly reports required to monitor the department's activities (and requirements). Dictating equipment further increased efficiency.

Implementation was successful. In fact, the department's work load over a period of two years increased by 260 percent without adding one staff member.

■ ■ ■

Case Questions

1. Create a memorandum to management to request and justify the expense of purchasing an initial word processing system.
2. Show how expansion of such a system could benefit the company. (Consider initial investment, personnel efficiency, and corporate image.)
3. What additional equipment could further increase efficiency?
4. How would adding telecommunications to the company's mainframe computer affect reporting to management?

4 *Career Strategies*

Interviewing for a Job

Learning Objectives
1. To learn different techniques for getting job interviews.
2. To learn how to write job search letters.
3. To learn how to write interview follow-up letters.
4. To learn how to plan for the job interview.
5. To understand the kinds of questions job interviewers typically ask.
6. To learn how to improve performance during a job interview.

*I*t was the thirtieth day of May. Tom Solomon would graduate in ten days, but he didn't have a job yet. He'd been through three interviews at the campus placement center, each of which he thought had gone extremely well. Yet in the past week he'd received rejection letters from all three companies. The letters had said much the same thing: "You have fine qualifications, but at present you don't fit the position we are filling. Please keep us in mind in the future."

"So much for a college degree," Tom thought, as he packed his now huge collection of textbooks in boxes for shipment home. "Here I am, a 3.5 average, and I can't even get a job. Maybe I should go to graduate school." ∎

Each year thousands of junior college and senior college students have an experience like Tom's. Desperation sets in as graduation approaches and no job offers appear. Thousands of other students have found jobs, many of them because they majored in a field where jobs are abundant. Yet most students who have found attractive entry-level positions in business have done so because they carefully planned and carried out a strategy to find the best possible job. Our purpose in this chapter is to help you plan and implement your search.

Getting a Job Interview

At the beginning of Chapter 20 we list several techniques that students use in finding a job. Among them are personal contacts, employment agencies, mail campaigns, college placement centers, and responding to newspaper advertisements. No matter how many of these techniques you use, your primary goal should be to schedule as many job interviews as you possibly can. There are two reasons for this strategy:

1. **Experience.** Most students have little or no experience in interviewing for a career position. Such interviews can be ego-threatening and even traumatic, especially when an interviewer asks you a question you are not prepared to answer (for example, "What is your major weakness?"). As you progress through a number of interviews, however, you'll become more confident and be able to sell yourself because you have learned from practice and from your own mistakes.

2. **Probability.** The more interviews you have, the greater the likelihood that you'll be offered a job. Tom, in our story, had only three job interviews. His approach is tragically similar to that used by many students. You will be offered a job only when your qualifications match the position being filled and you are better qualified than all the other individuals who have applied for that position.

The more interviews you have, the greater your chances of finding an attractive position.

Strategies in Getting Interviews

There are many ways to get job interviews. Perhaps someone you know tells you about a job opening. Maybe you apply to a company that you have worked for before. Most job openings, however, are found through direct-mail approaches, newspaper advertisements, or your college placement office.

Direct-Mail Campaigns. In seeking interviews, you will either contact companies that have not announced an opening or respond to a known opening. The letter of application sent to the company with a known job opening is a solicited letter. The knowledge of the opening need not be formal; you may have learned of the job from family members or announcements on bulletin boards, as well as through newspaper advertisements or from company employees. The letter of application sent to companies without known openings is called an *unsolicited,* a *surveying,* or a *prospecting letter.* The direct-mail approach likely involves writing unsolicited letters.

The direct-mail approach is akin to a "shotgun" approach. Even though you may write to many companies, your chances of actually acquiring an interview are not particularly good. Nevertheless, if jobs are scarce in your major or if you wish to maximize your chances for acquiring interviews, the approach might be explored.

There are three steps in the direct-mail campaign:

1. Select the companies.
2. Prepare and mail cover letter and resume.
3. Follow up as necessary.

Obviously, you can't mail your resume to every existing company, so in Step 1 you should narrow your list of prospects down to companies that fit your job objective and, if important, your geographic preference. For example, if you want to work for an insurance company in Chicago, then you might search the Yellow Pages in the Chicago telephone directory for the names of prospective employers. Should you want a personnel position, then you might consult a journal called the *Personnel Administrator.* Published by the American Society of Personnel Administrators, this journal prints an annual directory of its membership. Other key sources for selecting companies are:

College Placement Annual. Published by the College Placement Council, it contains a list of companies in both the U.S. and Canada who are seeking college graduates.

Dun & Bradstreet Million Dollar Directory. Provides information about more than 30,000 companies whose net worth exceeds $1 million.

Sources of companies for a direct-mail campaign

Dun & Bradstreet Middle Market Directory. Similar to the *Million Dollar Directory,* but information is about more than 30,000 companies whose net worth is between $500,000 and $999,999.

Moody's Manual of Investment. Contains information about a variety of companies, including banks, public utilities, insurance firms, and industrial firms.

Standard & Poor's Register of Corporations, Directors, and Executives. Contains an alphabetical listing of more than 35,000 corporations in the U.S. and Canada. Provides listing of products and services, officers, and telephone numbers.

Thomas' Register of American Manufacturers. Contains a list of manufacturers under headings of 70,000 products. Information includes addresses and telephone numbers of manufacturers.

Some students select as many as 500 companies for their direct-mail campaign; more typically, 100 or fewer key prospects are chosen. If you send your application to 100 such firms, you can expect a rejection rate of approximately 85 percent. You won't hear at all from some of the other companies. However, should you get six or seven job interviews from such a campaign, then your strategy has been successful.

Much of the reason for the low number of positive responses in a direct-mail campaign lies in the breadth of the approach. The more you narrow the focus of your campaign, the greater your success. Here are some ways to narrow your list of prospects:

1. Pick companies that offer the type of job in which you're interested.
2. Select companies with jobs for which you're qualified.
3. Locate companies that are known to provide advancement in your field.
4. Find companies that are centered or have branches in geographical locations of interest to you.
5. Omit companies where you are sure you would not accept a job.

Once you have selected your prospects, then preparing and mailing your resume and cover letter are the next steps. We discuss resume preparation in Chapter 20. In the direct-mail campaign, your cover letter is just as important as the resume.

First, get the name and address of the person to whom you intend to mail your application letter. Never send campaign letters to *Dear Sir or Madam* or *To Whom It May Concern.* A personal touch is critical in your campaign. Usually, the person whose name you want is the personnel officer of the company. Often you can obtain this name by consulting the sources we listed above or by calling the firm and asking for the name and title of the personnel officer (for example, personnel manager, vice president for personnel, or recruiting officer).

Second, decide on a reason for applying with each specific company. You can include this reason in your cover letter as a way of showing interest in the firm. You can also get this type of information from the sources listed earlier.

Preparing the cover letter in a direct-mail campaign

Third, write the actual letter. Since it is a persuasive letter, you might use the AIDA format discussed in Chapter 7. As always, you should use the "you" attitude, as well as the other characteristics of effective communication.

One authority suggested that the cover letter should accomplish these things:

1. Ask for a job; be specific about what you want.
2. Explain how your experience, as outlined on your resume, relates to the desired job and to the company.
3. Tell how you were attracted to the company.
4. Ask for the interview. Tell the reader you'd like to arrange a meeting at a time and place convenient for the employer.[1]

An example of a cover letter is shown in Figure 19.1.

Usually responses from your prospects arrive about two weeks after you mail your letter and resume. If you don't hear from a company after about 14 days, you might consider following up by phone or letter. The phone call is quicker, but it may be perceived as too aggressive. If you decide to call, try to reach the person to whom you addressed the letter. Ask about the progress of your application. With the letter, you can organize your thoughts to achieve your goal.

A sample follow-up letter appears in Figure 19.2. Notice first that the writer uses tact by mentioning the earlier contact without placing blame for inaction. Second, another resume is enclosed in case the original is misplaced. Third, another summary of relevant qualifications is provided. New information can be added at this time as it is another opportunity to emphasize your qualifications. Finally, available times for receiving phone calls are repeated.

Responding to Newspaper Advertisements. When you respond to a help-wanted advertisement in a newspaper, be assured that literally scores of other applicants are responding to the same ad. Thus, you must prepare a most convincing cover letter and resume. The cover letter you send can be basically like the one you use in the direct-mail campaign. However, in the first paragraph you should refer to the ad, identifying where and when you read it and the position for which you are applying. Again, be sure to follow up if the firm doesn't respond to your letter within two weeks.

If a firm grants you an interview as a result of your direct-mail campaign or your response to a newspaper advertisement, then you might write a letter confirming the date, time, and place for the interview and expressing your appreciation for being given the interview. Here's an example of the body of such a letter:

Thank you for scheduling an interview with me about opportunities in Able Computers' manager trainee program. I am looking forward to our meeting.

Sample interview-confirmation letter

Figure 19.1   Example of a Cover Letter

March 12, 1984

Ms. Patricia Markham
Personnel Manager
Able Computers, Inc.
P. O. Box 1511
Columbus, Ohio 45453

Dear Ms. Markham:

The reputation and growth of Able Computers have led me to apply for a
position in your management trainee program. Information in the College
Placement Annual indicates you hire college graduates with business
degrees. The Annual states you prefer computer, management and sales or
marketing majors.

The fact that you were rated number one in a poll as the most promising
company of the 1980's by Electronic Industry Magazine is impressive. The
challenge of helping you maintain your position of leadership in the
volatile computer industry is especially exciting.

My BBA degree from the University of Arkansas incorporates a major in
management and a minor in marketing. Further, my two years of part-time
work for the Bank of New England in the data processing department utilized
capabilities acquired in my three college computer classes.

As you will note on my attached resume, I am willing to accept challenges
and carry them through to successful completion. Grover Jefferson, of the
Bank of New England, has offered to support this view. His address, and
the names and addresses of other references, are on the resume.

May I have an interview at your convenience? I am available at the phone
number on the resume between 2 and 6 p.m. weekdays.

Sincerely,

As you requested during our telephone conversation [or As you re-quested in your letter], I'll be in Room 117 of the Able Building at 10:00 a.m. on Thursday, August 9.

I appreciate your interest in my application.

The direct-mail campaign and responding to newspaper advertisements are only two approaches to getting job interviews. Other strategies you might consider, especially if the job market in your particular field is tight, include: (1) calling personnel officers directly and asking for an interview; (2) making unannounced visits to the firms where you seek

Figure 19.2   Example of a Follow-Up Letter

April 1, 1984

Ms. Patricia Markham
Personnel Manager
Able Computers, Inc.
P. O. Box 1511
Columbus, Ohio 45453

Dear Ms. Markham:

Several weeks ago I wrote you applying for a management traineeship with
Able. I do wish to ensure that you know of my enthusiasm for Able. As
my March 12 letter stated, I am impressed with your position of leadership
in your industry.

You are interested, I understand, in recruits with computer, management,
and marketing abilities. My management major, marketing minor, and data
processing job experience meet those qualifications. Last week I was
honored as the most promising senior in the University of Arkansas
Management Club, a group of over 120 students.

The enclosed resume presents more information about how my educational, job,
and extracurricular activities well prepare me for your traineeship.

An interview with you, at your convenience, is still my goal. My schedule
remains the same; I am available by phone weekdays from 2 p.m. until
6 p.m.

Sincerely,

employment; (3) placing your own ad in a newspaper; and (4) attending conventions or trade shows of industries you've selected as potential employers.

Using the College Placement Office.   Using the placement office in acquiring interviews is much different than direct mail or newspaper advertisement techniques. The direct mail and newspaper advertisement approaches are general in tone, frequently cannot be personalized, and are used on the assumption that if you apply to enough companies, you'll receive some interviews.

The placement office, on the other hand, is more individualized and, in some cases, leads directly to an interview. One valuable way to use the placement office is as a library. Often the latest publications on how to interview or write resumes are available. Many companies send placement offices their annual reports and other recruiting literature. In addition to the library function, the personnel often can help you with career decisions or know the most recent trends in industries. They may also know of the latest job openings. Some placement offices maintain your records, including letters of reference and resume. The personnel can even review your resume or application letter.

A second major activity of the placement office is scheduling on-campus job interviews. Companies frequently visit the campus to interview 13 to 15 students a day in a series of 30-minute interviews. The placement office coordinates room scheduling and time-period assignments, makes company literature available, and gathers interviewees' resumes.

Signing up for an interview through the placement office is far easier than having to use the letter of application to schedule an interview. For this reason, as well as the other benefits mentioned, regular communication with your placement office is usually wise.

Job Interview Performance

Your actual, face-to-face interaction with a representative of the company is the most critical step in your job search process. For many years companies used two basic approaches to selecting new employees: the job interview and psychological testing. Now, however, many companies no longer use these tests because of new federal laws; a company must be able to provide evidence that a psychological test can differentiate between good and poor performers on the job. Because gathering such evidence is extremely difficult, especially for smaller companies, the job interview is now the major selection tool for most organizations.

A successful job interview involves three steps:

1. Planning
2. Performing
3. Following up.

Interview Planning

Throughout this text we have emphasized planning in every business-communication situation. Such planning is of paramount importance to the job interview. Here are some suggestions to help you better prepare for your interview:

1. **Review Your Qualifications.** Your job search will be successful when the employer's representative realizes that there is a match between your qualifications and the requirements of the position being filled. The question, "Is this person qualified?" will remain uppermost in every interviewer's mind. Your goal is to show this match during the interview, to demonstrate that the pieces of this job-selection puzzle do fit together.

Your qualifications for a job include not only your previous applicable work experience, education, and extracurricular activities, but also any salable personal characteristics you have. Here is a list of qualities that employers consider to be important. As you place a checkmark in the appropriate blank next to each quality, don't forget to consider all your work- and school-related experiences.

You should be able to justify *clearly* any high rating you have given yourself. Trained interviewers are not interested in statements, such as "I'm a self-starter," unless you can give evidence of your initiative. Be prepared to *show* that you are dependable, adaptable, mature, and so on.

Be able to document your best qualities.

Any activity in which you have been involved can provide the necessary evidence. For example, playing basketball or any other team sport requires the ability to work with others. Earning part or all of your college expenses shows initiative. A clear and logical explanation of why you changed majors or transferred from one school to another can indicate decision-making ability and, perhaps, adaptability. Leadership skills can be shown through various activities, including offices in organizations, working as a counselor in a summer camp, or training your replacement for a job you left.

In short, pick your major qualifications, document them, review them, and be prepared to talk about them during the interview.

2. **Research the Company.** One of the most important preparation steps for an interview is to research the company. You need to know the size of the company, its products or services, position in the

Figure 19.3 Match Your Qualifications with the Job Requirements

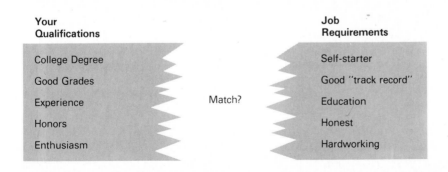

Your Qualifications		Job Requirements
College Degree		Self-starter
Good Grades		Good "track record"
Experience	Match?	Education
Honors		Honest
Enthusiasm		Hardworking

Am I Qualified?	Superior	Above Average	Average	Below Average	Poor
Leadership skills	_____	_____	_____	_____	_____
Initiative (self-starter)	_____	_____	_____	_____	_____
Decision-making abilities	_____	_____	_____	_____	_____
Written communication skills	_____	_____	_____	_____	_____
Oral communication skills	_____	_____	_____	_____	_____
Adaptability	_____	_____	_____	_____	_____
Professional appearance	_____	_____	_____	_____	_____
Working with others	_____	_____	_____	_____	_____
Enthusiasm	_____	_____	_____	_____	_____
Dependability	_____	_____	_____	_____	_____
Self-confidence	_____	_____	_____	_____	_____
Maturity	_____	_____	_____	_____	_____

industry, some historical perspectives, locations from which it operates, financial considerations, employment situation, types of jobs being filled, the subsidiary situation, and its plans for the future. Articles by or about recruiters that discuss major problems or errors in interviews inevitably point to the interviewee's lack of knowledge about the company as a serious shortcoming. One recruiter for a nonprofit institution received comments about his company's products. Another recruiter was startled that an $80,000-a-year executive did not bother to read a prospective employer's annual report.[2]

In addition to the sources mentioned earlier in the direct-mail campaign, look also to the *Wall Street Journal,* the company annual report, recruiting literature, and the *Business Periodicals Index.*

3. Anticipate What Will Happen in the Interview. Knowledge of interviews will help you prepare for the interview and reduce your anxiety as well. Background knowledge of interviews has four main components: (1) the types of interviews, (2) the types of interviewers, (3) the flow of the interview, and (4) the types of questions asked.

Most interviews or interview situations fit into one or more of the following six classifications: (a) screening interview, (b) open-ended interview, (c) panel interview, (d) group interview, (e) stress interview, and (f) office visit interview.

The *screening interview,* as its name implies, screens prospects into groups to interview further, groups to reject, or groups to hold for future decision. These interviews usually occur before other categories of interviews and typically last about 30 minutes.

An *open-ended interview* (or *unstructured* or *nondirective interview*) follows no discernible pattern. Your answer to an initial question may determine the next question. The interactions and responses form the direction of the interview.

A *panel interview* involves one interviewee and more than one interviewer. Occasionally you may feel outnumbered when there is only one interviewer; imagine the pressure you might feel with several people questioning and observing you. On the other hand, if the company believes an interview with you is important enough to justify the time of two or more recruiters, perhaps they are already impressed with you.

The *group interview* is the antithesis of the panel interview—several interviewees are present with one interviewer. You're likely to encounter a group interview in a social setting, such as a party to which many job prospects are invited, or a mass screening when there is a large number of applicants for few positions. Since these interviews may not last long, each interviewee seeks to make a quick and positive impression—often at the expense of other applicants. Do try to impress your interviewer, but avoid direct comparison to others in the room if possible.

The *stress interview,* probably the most unpleasant of the six categories, places the interviewee in a stressful situation which the interviewer then carefully observes. Inviting you to smoke but not supplying an ashtray or putting you in a lengthy business simulation full of tricks and pitfalls are examples of stress activities. Questions the interviewer knows to cause stress may also be used. At one time stress questions and stress interviews were fairly common. Today they are less frequent. For high level, high stress executive jobs and positions (high pressure sales, for example) you are more likely to encounter stress interviews.

The *office* (or plant or headquarters) *visit* is not a single interview but a series of interviews that may incorporate many of the other categories discussed. Some interviews may be stressful, others may be conducted by a panel, and still others may be open ended. A six- or seven-hour day, including lunch and coffee breaks with company officials, is not unusual. Although the day will range from formal interviews to casual, informal discussions, you are constantly being evaluated; never let down your guard. Other activities you may encounter include psychological or ability testing, building tours, discussions with potential peers or subordinates, and completion of application or travel reimbursement forms.

Just as there are many types of interviews, there are also different types of interviewers; the major categories are the practitioner and the personnel office representative. These categories may be encountered in either a screening interview, which is usually the first interview, or the office visit, which is usually the culmination interview.

The *practitioner* is a person who is currently doing the type of job for which you would be hired. The term, *field interviewer,* is also used. For example, an accountant interviews prospective accountants, and so on. The practitioner may be the person who would be the immediate superior of the new hire. The practitioner is not likely to have formal training in interview procedures; therefore, it is difficult to predict the course of the interview. The area of expertise and background about the job are likely to be discussion topics. Because of their naivete, practitioners are more likely to ask stress questions at inappropriate times or ask questions deemed illegal by Equal Employment Opportunity Act guidelines.

The *representative of the personnel office* or *personnel recruiter* probably has, as part of their job description, the role of recruiter. Training in selection methods, appraisals, and interviewing prepare them for this role. Because of their training, representatives of personnel offices are difficult to read. They will be pleasant and courteous, but seldom will you be certain that you have blown the interview or that you have aced it.

A description of a typical screening interview will help you prepare for it. The interview may last from 15 to 45 minutes, but 30 minutes is traditional. A typical 30-minute period might be broken down as follows:

First 5 minutes	Introductions, small talk, questions of low priority.
Next 10 minutes	Focus on interviewee's abilities and responses to interviewer's questions.
Next 10 minutes	Responses by interviewer to interviewee's questions and description of company and job.
Last 5 minutes	Closing comments, explanation of next steps.

A full day office visit depends on the organization and type of job. However, a visit to an office for a management job might proceed through these steps:

9–10 a.m.	Breakfast with the interviewer who conducted the screening interview.
10:15–11 a.m.	Introductions to other personnel office employees.
11 a.m.–12 p.m.	Meeting with vice president of related area.
12–1:30 p.m.	Lunch with two members of personnel office and prospective immediate superior.
1:30–2:30 p.m.	Meeting with prospective immediate superior.
2:30–4 p.m.	Half-hour meetings with three potential peers.
4–5 p.m.	Completion of company forms and tour of facilities with personnel office representative.
5 p.m.	Depart with screening interviewer for the airport for flight home.

As you can see, by the time you get home, you will have had a long, tiring, and eventful day.

The fourth way you can help yourself through anticipating what will occur in an interview is by knowing the types of questions you may be asked and when they usually occur in an interview. Of five major categories of questions, four will be asked of the interviewee.

Most interviews start off with questions to which the answers—that is, the content per se—are really inconsequential. Their purpose is to break the ice and get the interview moving. Trained interviewers know that you'll be anxious about the interview. After all, much rides on how you perform in a short period of time; you'll be in a strange and perhaps bleakly appointed interview room; you're meeting a total stranger and talking, in some cases, about personal thoughts and feelings.

For these reasons questions about the weather or last Sunday's football game occur first. The recruiter doesn't care too much about what you say but rather about how you say it. Your enthusiasm for a certain football team is more impressive than which team you prefer.

Shortly after you start to relax, the questions will focus on your interests, knowledge of the company or the job, and why you think you can do the job. The recruiter will listen carefully to your responses to these *important answer* questions and is likely to build on your answers with related follow-up questions. You are evaluated on the speed, depth, and quality of your answers, as well as other ingredients.

The third type is the *stress* question which is designed to pressure you. These questions may occur at any time in an interview, but they are most likely to appear after some important answer questions. By definition, it is hard to plan on how to respond to a stress question; their intent is to catch you off guard. Still, just knowing they may occur should help you.

The fourth category of question is the *inappropriate* question, one that is either illegal or unrelated to the job. Rules keep interviewers from asking questions that might discriminate against you. For example, questions about your age, marital status, or religion are seldom allowed. Exceptions occur when this or other information is directly related to the job, such as hiring a parent instead of a childless person for a child-care center. Other questionable topics include race, political affiliation, club memberships, handicapped status, national origin, and veteran status.

What should you do when you are asked one of these questions? You have several options. If you do not find the question offensive or the answer potentially damaging, you can answer it. If the answer to the question is personal or you think it is not related to the job, politely tell the recruiter so. Perhaps you will wish to ask the purpose of the question; there may be a good reason for it that you did not anticipate.

The final type of question encompasses those you ask of the recruiter. Most interviewers allow time for you to learn more about the job and the organization. Two reasons exist for asking truly valuable questions: the better the question, the better its reflection on you; and you should have some questions to which the answers are important. Prepare yourself before the interview with five or six questions. The interviewer may answer some of these in the company or job description segments of the interview. Then, when given the opportunity, you can raise several probing questions. Avoid trite or shallow questions. Aim for open-ended questions rather than those that yield only a yes or no answer. Consider questions about the extent of responsibility you would be given, the types of assignments encountered, and even queries about the negative aspects of the job.

Here are some example questions you might ask:

1. Where does your typical manager trainee wind up in five years' time?
2. How important are advanced degrees, such as an MBA or a law degree, to advancement?
3. Do you normally promote from within the company?
4. What kind of orientation program or training do you provide for new employees?

Be sure to avoid questions that might create ego-threat or other negative feelings in the interviewer. For example "Are you having much trouble with EEOC?" is inappropriate unless you are interviewing for a personnel job. "Will I have to work much overtime?" might characterize you as having little initiative. You should avoid questions about salary unless starting salaries are the same for all incoming employees (for example, some teaching positions, government jobs, and even management trainee programs).

Besides the five types of questions just discussed, you will also find it valuable to review three categories of interview questions. They are:

Open-ended questions. Open-ended questions allow the interviewee to talk freely on any topic.

Direct or closed questions. Direct or closed questions allow the interviewer to probe for information when the interviewee has not thoroughly answered a question. (If the interviewer asks many direct questions, this should suggest to the interviewee that his or her open-ended answers are not satisfying the interviewer).

Indirect questions. Indirect questions are disguised requests for information and may tell more about the interviewee than he or she wishes known. The unsuspecting interviewee should be warned that questions such as, "What does your best friend think of your boss?" are really asking, "What do you think of your boss?"

Listed below are 50 questions that are frequently asked by college recruiters. Examination of the questions will give you the flavor of an interview. Since some of these questions are likely to be asked of you, you may want to think of your answers to them. As you read the questions you will notice that many seek your opinions and others ask for facts. Most interviewees have much more difficulty with the opinion questions since a correct answer isn't clear.

Questions Most Frequently Asked by College Recruiters in Interviewing College Students

1. What are your future vocational plans?

2. In what school activities have you participated? Why? Which did you enjoy most?

3. How do you spend your spare time? What are your hobbies?

4. In what type of position are you most interested?

5. Why do you think you might like to work for our company?

6. What jobs have you held? How were they obtained? Why did you leave?

7. What percentage of your college expenses did you earn? How?

8. Why did you choose your particular field of work?

9. What courses did you like best? Least? Why?

10. How did you spend your vacations while in school?

11. What do you know about our company?

12. Do you feel that you have received a good general training?

13. What qualifications do you have that make you feel that you will be successful in your field?

14. What extracurricular offices have you held?

15. What are your ideas on salary?

16. How do you feel about your family?

17. How interested are you in sports?

18. If you were starting college all over again, what course would you take?

19. Can you forget your education and start from scratch?

20. Do you prefer any specific geographic location? Why?

21. Do you have a girlfriend? [boyfriend?] Is it serious?

22. How much money do you hope to earn at age 30? 35?

23. Why did you decide to go to this particular school?

24. How did you rank in your graduation class in high school? Where will you probably rank in college?

25. Do you think your extracurricular activities were worth the time you devoted to them?

26. What do you think determines a person's progress in a good company?

27. What personal characteristics are necessary for success in your chosen field?

28. Why do you think you would like this particular job?

29. What is your father's [mother's?] occupation?

30. Tell me about your home life during the time you were growing up.

31. Are you looking for a permanent or temporary job?

32. Do you prefer working with others or by yourself?

33. Who are your best friends?

(continued)

Questions Most Frequently Asked by College Recruiters in Interviewing College Students (continued)

34. What kind of boss do you prefer?

35. Are you primarily interested in making money or do you believe that service to your fellow human beings is a satisfactory accomplishment?

36. Can you take instructions without feeling upset?

37. Tell me a story.

38. Do you live with your parents? Which of your parents has had the most profound influence on you?

39. How did previous employers treat you?

40. What have you learned from some of the jobs you have held?

41. Do you have recommendations from previous employers?

42. What interests you about our product or service?

43. What was your record in military service?

44. Have you ever changed your major field of interest while in college? Why?

45. When did you choose your major in college?

46. How do your college grades after military service compare with those previously earned?

47. Do you believe you have done the best scholastic work of which you are capable?

48. How did you happen to go to college?

49. What do you know about opportunities in the field in which you are trained?

50. How long do you expect to work?

Source: Reprinted with permission of New York Life Insurance Company.

Although we can't tell you how to answer each of the 50 questions, here are some suggestions for dealing with several questions students have found difficult.

Question 7: What percentage of your college expenses did you earn? How? It is a paradox of our society that most of us envy the wealthy, such as a college student who doesn't need to work during the summer or after school hours. However, job experience and indications of industriousness are paramount in employee selection. All things being equal, the recruiter is more impressed with the student who worked to pay education expenses, even doing menial or activities that are not job related, than with the wealthy student who does not indicate a willingness to work. Therefore, the stronger a case you can build for yourself in percentage of expenses earned, the better your evaluation. If your parents give you all your expenses, you earned zero percent. If your spouse is paying the expenses, you can claim 100 percent. If you are using a loan that you will repay, claim that as a percentage from you.

Question 19: Can you forget your education and start from scratch? Your goal in answering this question is to underline the importance of your education but at the same time to show a willingness to learn new things. Thus an answer such as this might be appropriate: I can't really forget my education, because I think I've learned some things that will be helpful to me in my work. However, I know that my education isn't completed yet. I'm willing and eager to learn new things.''

Question 37: Tell me a story. Many of our students have heard this question in job interviews. One approach to answering this question is to tell a factual story containing a moral about yourself or someone you know. For example, you might describe a conflict situation with a roommate where you became so frustrated that you finally sat down and leveled with your roommate. Because your interaction had a healthy outcome, you realized the importance of simply communicating with someone with whom you're in conflict. Or you might tell a story about a relative you have who, although lacking formal education, started a business, worked long hours, and succeeded. You can draw morals from a story like this one about persistence, perseverance, initiative, energy, or optimism.

4. Know What the Recruiter Is Seeking. You can prepare for an interview better if you have some feeling about how and on what you will be evaluated. Many students are surprised to learn that often they are not evaluated for what they know. Instead, recruiters assume that your college degree has given you some basic information and shows you have the ability to learn. It also indicates an interest in specific areas. If the recruiter hires you, the company supervisor will teach you, in depth, the specifics that he or she wants you to know. Therefore, few questions are asked about your knowledge of subjects, such as, the difference between municipal bonds and corporate bonds or the application of Maslow's Theory to a management trainee job. Questions are asked to determine such characteristics as tact, enthusiasm, industriousness, maturity, human relations skills, leadership ability, motivation, congeniality, or communication ability. How directed you are, your initiative, competitiveness, and intelligence will be scrutinized as well.

Most companies use an interviewee evaluation form which the recruiter completes after the interview. Since attributes of importance differ by company, there is no standard form. To better understand the content of these forms, visit your college placement office. The sample form in Figure 19.4 is typical in the type of attributes evaluated, and the length and depth of response requested.

5. Consider Your Appearance. Don't let the simplicity of this suggestion mislead you. One survey of practicing interviewers found that in a 20-minute interview the average interviewer had made a selection decision within the first four minutes of the interview.[3] Some interviewers claim that they can decide whether an applicant is suitable for a job the very instant that applicant enters the room. Obviously, these early decisions are based in large part on physical appearance.

Generally, you should dress as you would in the job for which you are applying. This guideline means that, as graduates of a two- or four-

Appearance shouldn't cost you a job, but it might.

Figure 19.4 Interview Appraisal Form

Name _____ School _____

Campus Address _____ Phone Number _____

Post Graduation
Mailing Address _____ Phone Number _____

Geographical Career
Availability _____ Preference _____ Interests _____ G.P.A. _____

Date _____

Selection Standard	Observations	Exceeds	Meets	Does Not Meet
	Relates to selection standards and to information reported by applicant or			
Presentation	Forcefulness, Organization, Conciseness—ask related questions.			
Achievements	Academic, Technical, Professional Contributions to previous employers. Do they relate to our needs?			
Ambitions	Career Goals, Financial Goals—are they realistic?			
Contributions	Long- and short-term, what can the candidate add to the organization?			
Is Candidate Sold on Pizza Hut	Understands Career Opportunity.			
Overall Reaction				

_____ Highly Recommended _____
Recruiter's Signature Recommended _____
Reject _____

Source: Courtesy of Pizza Hut.

year college, males wear a coat and tie and females a dress or suit and heels. If you aren't sure how to dress, then it is probably better to dress simply in business attire, giving consideration to what is socially acceptable in the area.

6. **Prepare for the Unusual.** Stories abound about "tricks of the trade" that interviewers use to catch an applicant off guard. Although it is unlikely that you will be confronted with any of these tricks, you should nevertheless be aware of and be prepared for them. Examples are:

Silence	**The interviewer says absolutely nothing at the beginning of the interview. Instead, he or she simply looks at you. You, therefore, must begin the interaction.**
Sell Me	**If you are interviewing for any kind of sales or marketing position, the interviewer slides an ashtray or a pencil across the desk to you and says, "Here. Sell this to me."**
Turnabout	**The interviewer says, "I've been interviewing people all day. I'm tired. Why don't you interview me?"**
No Smoking	**You are a smoker. You're nervous. The interviewer asks, "Would you like to smoke?" You light a cigarette and discover that there is no ashtray in the room.**
Choose a Chair	**When you enter the interviewer's office, there are two chairs from which to choose. One is near the interviewer's desk, the other is several feet away from the desk. The interviewer says simply. "Have a seat," but doesn't tell you which chair.**

Tricks of the trade are not used by most interviewers.

If these examples seem frightening to you, remember that very few interviewers use such tricks. Most contemporary interviewers are highly trained, competent businesspeople who want to evaluate your qualifications in a straightforward manner.

In summary, our first step in successful job interviewing is to plan for the interview. The five suggestions we've offered should help build your confidence before an interview and improve your actual interview performance.

Interview Performance

The second step in your strategy for a successful job interview is your behavior during the interview. Here are several suggestions you might want to consider:

1. **Arrive Early or on Time.** Being late for a job interview shows lack of dependability (one of the qualities we discussed earlier). If you must be late, call the interviewer and explain why. Consider making a trial run prior to the interview to determine travel time, parking facilities, and exact location of the interview. Arriving late will put unneeded pressure on you.

2. **Have a Firm Handshake.** First, *do* shake hands with the interviewer. A handshake is a sign of acceptance and greeting in a business situation. Also, a weak fishlike handshake is perceived by some interviewers to be characteristic of a similarly weak personality.

   Don't be afraid to offer your hand first. The job interview is not a social situation steeped in rules of etiquette. Many interviewers have expressed the same uneasy feeling about the handshake as you might experience: do I shake hands first? You can relieve much interviewer uneasiness and show some assertiveness if you'll simply extend your hand as you approach the interviewer.

3. **Establish and Maintain Eye Contact with the Interviewer.** Like the weak handshake, an absence of eye contact connotes a weak personality to many interviewers. To a few of them it also indicates that the interviewee may be lying.

4. **Consider Your Posture.** Interviewers will sometimes unconsciously form negative perceptions of applicants who slouch in a chair, cross their arms and legs, and face away from them. Consider sitting erect, facing the interviewer. Don't cross your legs and arms at the same time. Some interviewers are victims of a stereotype that people who sit in such a closed position are trying to shut the other person out.

5. **Don't Fiddle with Objects.** Playing with objects (for example, a pen or pencil) during the interview communicates unusual nervousness to many interviewers. Often they will translate your nervousness during the interview to mean that you cannot perform well in stress situations on the job. Of paramount importance: do not fiddle with objects on the interviewer's desk.

6. **Don't Criticize Past Employers.** An interviewer can interpret your criticism of past employers as an indication that you are a complainer who criticizes all your employers. Also, such criticism can be interpreted as a rationalization for the real (and damaging) reasons you left your previous employers.

7. **Don't Evaluate Previous Jobs—Simply Describe Them.** Because many college students have work experience they consider to be simple or menial, they are often inclined to communicate that perception during the interview: "Well, really all I did was fry hamburgers," or "The job really wasn't much—I just waited on people." Yet, no matter how unimportant you think a job might have been, an interviewer will ask questions about it in order to assess a number of qualities, among them dependability, leadership skills, working with others, and initiative.

Successful interview performance involves a combination of verbal and nonverbal behaviors.

8. **Ask Questions about the Company.** During interview planning you prepared questions about the company. Remember to ask them before the interview ends.

9. **Be Honest.** Don't try to be someone or something you're not. Allow your true personality to emerge and try to make a good impression, but avoid developing an image that is inaccurate. Recruiters are making hiring decisions on what they see in the interview. Problems may occur if the real you who shows up for work is substantially different.

10. **Express Appreciation for the Interview.** As the interview closes and you are about to leave, remember to thank the interviewer for discussing employment opportunities with you. If possible, express appreciation for any constructive suggestions the interviewer has made, especially if you think you will not be considered for the job.

    In summary, this second step in successful interviewing involves polished, professional behavior during the actual interview. You can gain the needed skills by practicing the suggestions we've mentioned with anyone (classmates, friends, relatives) who will take the time with you.

Interview Follow Up

A job interview follow up consists of three steps: (1) immediate follow up, (2) delayed follow up, and (3) follow up to letters of acceptance or rejection.

1. **Immediate Follow Up.** As soon as possible after the interview, write the interviewer a follow-up letter. Basically, this letter consists of three paragraphs:

> *Immediate follow up should occur within one to two days after your interview.*

Paragraph A　**Express appreciation for the interview and your continued interest in the position.**

Paragraph B　**Add any important information about yourself that you failed to mention during the interview. Or emphasize one of your qualifications that the interviewer stressed as being important, especially if you feel personally confident about the qualification. Or emphasize some information you learned about the company during the interview which impressed you.**

Paragraph C　**Communicate your willingness to answer further questions about your qualifications. Assume a positive attitude toward hearing from the interviewer.**

Try to say something that will remind the reader of you and the interview; pick something that would not have been discussed with other interviewees. You may mention also, as appropriate, that you have completed and enclosed an application form. An example of such a follow-up letter appears in Figure 19.5

Most companies use their own standard application forms which ask for much of the same information supplied on your resume. Your resume is used to catch the recruiter's eye and to achieve an interview.

Figure 19.5   Sample Follow-Up Letter to an Interview

Dear Ms. Markham:

Thank you for the time you spent with me on Thursday discussing employment opportunities in Able Computers' manager trainee program. Your description of Able's program is impressive and reinforces my serious interest in the position.

You mentioned during the interview that Able is interested in individuals who can assume responsibility. Both my work experience (where I trained new employees and replaced the manager when she was out of town) and my extracurricular activities (where I assumed leadership positions in three different campus groups) show the kind of responsible experiences you might be seeking in an applicant.

If you wish to discuss any questions about my qualifications for the manager trainee position, please call. I look forward to hearing from you.

Sincerely,

You may be asked to complete the organization's form before a screening interview, immediately after the screening interview, or at the office visit. Frequently at the completion of a successful screening interview, you will be asked to take a form with you and return it by mail. This is an indication that you are proceeding through the job-getting process. As you complete the form, keep in mind that neatness, spelling, grammar, and punctuation are important. A sample application form appears in Figure 19.6.

2.   Delayed Follow Up: Most interviewers will close a job interview by telling you how soon a selection decision will be made: "We'll let you know something by the fifteenth of next month." If you don't hear from the company by the deadline they specify, then telephone the interviewer to check on the progress of your application. In situations where a decision has not yet been made, you will have simply gained the advantages of immediate follow up. If a decision has been made and you have not been chosen, then you will at least know where you stand.

If you are turned down, you have little to lose by remaining diligent. Perhaps you can revise your application to a different area of the company, ask for a re-evaluation, or seek to have your file remain active in case another position opens. Recruiters sometimes talk about the employee they hired who they couldn't shake—who wouldn't take no for an answer.

A final note on follow ups: you might have wondered why we have emphasized the follow up so extensively. Certainly, it will create much more work for you. However, the follow up (whether by letter or telephone) has two purposes. First, it is a public relations device designed to enhance your relationship with the interviewer. Second, it is a means of bringing your name back to the interviewer's attention. Many interviewers, especially those who visit your school's placement center, will interview as many as 15 applicants in one day. You'll want your name to stand out among the applicants as a qualified person who is genuinely interested in the position.

Advantages of the follow up

3.   Follow Up to Letters of Acceptance or Rejection. You'll probably get both of these kinds of letters—some offering you a position and others turning you down. You should respond to both types of letters. In your answer you'll either accept or refuse the position. Your letter of acceptance should:

    a.   Formally accept the position.
    b.   Express appreciation for the offer.
    c.   Confirm the details of the offer, including:
        1.   Salary
        2.   Starting time
        3.   Location of position
        4.   Name of person to whom you'll be reporting.
    d.   Show anticipation of doing good work.

Figure 19.6 Application Form for Sears, Roebuck and Co.

PLEASE PRINT

Personal Data

Print Name in full (Last) (First) (Middle) Social Security Number

Home address (Street) (City) (State) (Zip Code) Telephone

Temporary Address (Street) (City) (State) (Zip Code) Telephone

If hired, can you furnish proof of age? ☐ YES ☐ NO Licensed to drive car? ☐ Yes ☐ No Is license valid in this State? ☐ Yes ☐ No
(Answer only if position for which you are applying requires driving.)

Are you a U.S. Citizen ☐ YES ☐ NO or Resident Alien ☐ YES ☐ NO

Have you ever been employed by Sears? ☐ Yes ☐ No If so, when and where last employed? ______ Position ______

Former employes of Sears and certain subsidiaries may be entitled to service credit under the Pension Plan based on prior employment with Sears, Roebuck and Co., Homart Development Co., Sears Investment Management Co., Sears Roebuck Acceptance Corp., Sears, Roebuck de Puerto Rico, Inc., Sears Roebuck Overseas, Inc., Terminal Freight Handling Co., Allstate Insurance Company and their subsidiaries, Lifetime Foam Products, Pacific Installers, and Sears, S.A. (Central America).

Are any of your relatives employed by Sears in the unit(s) where you want to work? ______

Type of position desired? Date available for work State salary you will consider

Are you willing to relocate? What initial location would you prefer?

Have you been convicted during the past seven years of a serious crime involving a person's life or property? NO ☐ YES ☐

If yes, explain. ______

Physical Data

A PHYSICAL DISABILITY OR HANDICAP WILL NOT CAUSE REJECTION IF IN SEARS MEDICAL OPINION YOU ARE ABLE TO SATISFACTORILY PERFORM IN THE POSITION FOR WHICH YOU ARE BEING CONSIDERED.

Do you have any physical condition which may limit your ability to perform the job applied for? If so, please give details. ______

To protect the interests of all concerned, applicants for certain job assignments must pass a physical examination before they are hired. Alternative placement of an applicant who does not meet the physical standards of the job for which he/she was originally considered is permitted.

Education

	No. of Years	Name of School	City and State	Course or College Major	Average Grades	Did you Graduate?	Type of Degree
Senior High School							
College							
Graduate Studies							
Other—Give Type							

Military Service

Branch of Service	Date Entered Service	Date of Discharge	Service Related Disability	Highest Rank Held	Service-Related Skills and Experience Applicable to Civilian Employment
			YES ☐ NO ☐		

Activities

Professional Organizations ______

What are your hobbies or special interests? ______

Experience

Please give a detailed account of your previous experience and training. Specify the type of work done and the type of work you would prefer to do. If more space is needed, continue on a supplementary page.

RECORD OF EMPLOYMENT AND REFERENCES

LIST BELOW YOUR FOUR MOST RECENT EMPLOYERS, BEGINNING WITH THE CURRENT OR MOST RECENT ONE. IF YOU HAVE HAD LESS THAN FOUR EMPLOYERS, USE THE REMAINING SPACES FOR PERSONAL REFERENCES. IF YOU WERE EMPLOYED UNDER A MAIDEN OR OTHER NAME, PLEASE ENTER THAT NAME IN THE RIGHT HAND MARGIN. IF APPLICABLE, ENTER SERVICE IN THE ARMED FORCES ON THE REVERSE SIDE.

☐ It is not satisfactory to contact my present employer. ☐ It is satisfactory to contact my present employer.

1

NOTE: State reason for and length of inactivity between present application date and last employer.

Name

Address Tel. No.

City State Zip Code

Nature of Employer's Business | Name of your Supervisor

What kind of work did you do?	Starting Date	Starting Pay	Date of Leaving	Pay at Leaving	Why did you leave? Give details
	Month / Year	$ ☐ Mo. ☐ Wk. ☐ Hr.	Month / Year	$ ☐ Mo. ☐ Wk. ☐ Hr.	

2

NOTE: State reason for and length of inactivity between last employer and second last employer.

Name

Address Tel. No.

City State Zip Code

Nature of Employer's Business | Name of your Supervisor

What kind of work did you do?	Starting Date	Starting Pay	Date of Leaving	Pay at Leaving	Why did you leave? Give details
	Month / Year	$ ☐ Mo. ☐ Wk. ☐ Hr.	Month / Year	$ ☐ Mo. ☐ Wk. ☐ Hr.	

3

NOTE: State reason for and length of inactivity between second last employer and third last employer.

Name

Address Tel. No.

City State Zip Code

Nature of Employer's Business | Name of your Supervisor

What kind of work did you do?	Starting Date	Starting Pay	Date of Leaving	Pay at Leaving	Why did you leave? Give details
	Month / Year	$ ☐ Mo. ☐ Wk. ☐ Hr.	Month / Year	$ ☐ Mo. ☐ Wk. ☐ Hr.	

4

NOTE: State reason for and length of inactivity between third last employer and fourth last employer.

Name

Address Tel. No.

City State Zip Code

Nature of Employer's Business | Name of your Supervisor

What kind of work did you do?	Starting Date	Starting Pay	Date of Leaving	Pay at Leaving	Why did you leave? Give details
	Month / Year	$ ☐ Mo. ☐ Wk. ☐ Hr.	Month / Year	$ ☐ Mo. ☐ Wk. ☐ Hr.	

I certify that the information contained in this application is correct to the best of my knowledge and understand that any misstatement or omission of information is grounds for dismissal in accordance with Sears, Roebuck and Co. policy. I authorize the references listed above to give you any and all information concerning my previous employment and any pertinent information they may have, personal or otherwise, and release all parties from all liability for any damage that may result from furnishing same to you. In consideration of my employment, I agree to conform to the rules and regulations of Sears, Roebuck and Co. and my employment and compensation can be terminated with or without notice, at any time, at the option of either the Company or myself. I understand that no unit manager or representative of Sears, Roebuck and Co. other than the President or Vice-President of the Company, has any authority to enter into any agreement for employment for any specified period of time, or to make any agreement contrary to the foregoing. In some states, the law requires that Sears have my written permission before obtaining consumer reports on me, and I hereby authorize Sears to obtain such reports.

Applicant's Signature ______

Source: Reprinted with permission of Sears, Roebuck and Co.

Here is an example of such a letter:

Dear Ms. Markham:

Your offer of a position in Able Computers' manager trainee program is enthusiastically accepted. Thank you for your confidence in my potential to perform well in the program.

In confirming your letter offering the position, I understand that the starting salary is $16,150 per year to be paid monthly. I will report to Room 236 of the Able Building at 8 a.m. on Monday, January 4, and ask for Phillip Slone, who is to be my training coordinator.

As we discussed earlier, I am impressed with the opportunities Able Computers provides qualified applicants. I will do all I can to justify your trust in my potential.

Sincerely,

Sample letter accepting a job offer

If you refuse a position offered by a company, then your letter of refusal should:

- **a.** Express appreciation for the offer.
- **b.** Compliment the interviewer or the company offering the position.
- **c.** Clearly refuse the position *and* explain your refusal.
- **d.** Express appreciation for the offer again.

Here is an example of a letter refusing a job offer:

Dear Ms. Markham:

Thank you for your letter of September 23 offering a position in Able Computers' manager trainee program. I am sincerely impressed by both your confidence in my potential and the opportunities Able offers to qualified applicants.

Just this morning Stover Chemicals offered me a training position in their employee relations department. Because of Stover's closeness to my home and the immediate opportunity to work directly in the employee relations field, I have decided to accept their offer.

Your interest in me and your consideration of my application are appreciated.

Sincerely,

Sample letter refusing a job offer

If you receive a letter rejecting your application for a position, you should follow it up, especially if you might reapply with the company in the future. Such a letter should:

- **a.** Express appreciation for considering your application.
- **b.** Express appreciation for the learning experience the application process has provided you.
- **c.** Introduce future application possibilities.

Here is an example of a response to a letter of rejection:

Dear Ms. Markham:

Your letter of September 23 indicating that I will not be offered a position in Able Computers' manager trainee program arrived today.

Your time and effort in considering my application are appreciated. Interviewing with you has also been a learning experience that provided me with valuable insight into my qualifications and opportunities for improvement.

As we discussed earlier, I am genuinely impressed with the opportunities Able provides qualified applicants. Therefore, as my qualifications you mentioned in your letter become better, I intend to reapply for a position with Able. Please keep my application on file.

Sincerely,

Sample response to a letter of rejection

Comparing Companies and Delaying Decisions

Sometimes you may receive a job offer from one company but will want to wait to see if you receive other, better offers. When this is the case, you may wish to write a letter seeking a delay in your decision. Recruiters assume you are interviewing elsewhere and are not embarrassed nor disconcerted by a request for a delay. On the other hand, they often have deadlines to meet or other applicants to whom they would like to offer the job. Therefore, your request must be tactful. Your letter should:

a. Express appreciation for the offer.

b. Indicate that your goal is to select the company where you can be of the most benefit and where your career will be most enhanced.

c. Explain that your interviewing process is not quite complete and you wish an extension of the decision date (from __ to __).

d. Do not explain that if forced into an immediate decision you would turn them down; this is better left unsaid.

e. Reaffirm your interest in the job and the company.

Here is a sample delay request letter:

Dear Ms. Markham:

Last week you offered me a position at Able Computers as a management trainee, starting June 1, at a salary of $16,500. I am very pleased to receive this offer and am giving it much thought. With your offer, you asked that I decide by February 1.

Sample letter requesting a delay in decision making

As discussed during my visit to Columbus, I am seeking a position where I can make a valuable contribution while moving toward my career goal of high-level management. To be fair to myself and the company I will work for, it is necessary to explore the job market fully. My exploration is about over but is not yet complete.

Would it be convenient, Ms. Markham, to delay my decision about your offer from February 1 until February 20?

Your job offer impresses me and I am excited by it. This delay will enhance the quality of my decision—a decision that is important to both of us.

Sincerely,

Hopefully, you will have the opportunity to compare many job offers, although it is sometimes difficult to weigh the organizations evenly. One company, realizing this, supplies a form for comparison. Their form is shown in Figure 19.7.

Summary

Obviously, the job search calls for persuasion—you are trying to shape the decision-making behavior of a company representative. In this chapter, we've suggested several strategies in getting a job interview, among them the direct-mail campaign and responding to newspaper advertisements.

Your actual job interview performance involves three steps: planning, performing, and following up the interview. When planning for the interview, you should review your qualifications, prepare questions about the company, think through all possible questions, and prepare for the unusual.

We gave you ten suggestions for performing during the interview. Practicing these suggestions in mock interviews with classmates, relatives, or friends should help you prepare for actual interviews and help you feel more relaxed when those interviews take place.

The interview follow up has three steps: immediate follow up, delayed follow up, and follow-up letters of acceptance or rejection. As a public relations device, the follow up should help improve your relationship with the interviewer and keep your name in the interviewer's active files.

The strategies we discussed in this chapter should not be taken as a prescription that, if not followed, will cost you a job. However, the strategies are based upon our own experience consulting with and training personnel managers and college recruiters. Our perception is that your qualifications should get you the job. The strategies described here will help you communicate your qualifications more compellingly.

Figure 19.7 The Main Hurdman Career Guide

The Main Hurdman
Career Guide

Despite the fact that accounting opportunities are expanding rapidly, there are many accounting graduates who never fully examine the range of options which are open to them.

From a student's viewpoint, the major accounting firms bear a striking resemblance to each other. Most of the well-known firms were founded within a decade of each other. All have a number of appealing but similar qualities—a record of growth, expanding opportunities, and attractive clientele.

Sorting it out.
A key to effectively planning your career lies in developing a systematic approach to assessing a variety of firm attributes. Certainly, this is no easy task. The Main Hurdman career guide on the next two pages should help you place into perspective various firms and to compare career options.

Before you begin.
The Main Hurdman career guide suggests several important variables, and provides space for applying these variables to different accounting firms. One column, which contains facts about Main Hurdman, has been completed.

Answers in many of the categories will require subjective judgments based upon your own experiences. When you are finished, you will have a set of organization profiles for comparison, analysis and further consideration.

It's Your Decision
If you have made an effort to use this guide, you will have organized some of your thoughts about the firms which you are considering. But there are many variables which cannot be compared objectively. Such qualities as reputation and leadership in the profession are difficult to assess on your own. Speak with your professors, your career counselors, or friends in the profession. They may be able to provide you with specific insights into the firms you are considering.

There is not a great deal of advice we can give you about analyzing the profiles you have developed. You must compare your own goals, values, and abilities with what a firm has to offer,

and then make your own decision. This is an intensely personal process and one that can never be accurately structured, except on an individual basis.

Each firm has a distinctive personality which will become evident to you during the recruitment process as you talk with various firm representatives. If you feel comfortable and interface well with these representatives you will probably be able to achieve maximum self-development in that firm's environment. In the final analysis a firm is nothing more or less than its people.

KMG Klynveld Main Goerdeler–International firm

Source: Courtesy of Main Hurdman

Figure 19.7 (continued)

	Main Hurdman	Firm A	Firm B	Firm C	Firm D	Firm E
Firm image	Recognized for its high quality work and leadership in the profession.					
Professional environment	Staff accountants are highly visible members of their local offices. They work directly with partners and managers. Firm stresses individual development and judgment.					
Firm growth	Dramatic growth over the last decade. Outstanding opportunities available as firm attains its growth goals.					
International scope	Services are provided throughout the world. Opportunities are available for international assignments at advanced levels.					
Firm size	An international accounting firm, but not so large as to lose sight of the individual.					
Client orientation	Main Hurdman provides professional services to a wide range of organizations, from "Fortune 500" multinational firms to small businesses, unions, governmental bodies and other entities.					
Career development	Staff members at all levels participate in an active career counseling and development program. Specialization is available.					
Evaluation and advancement	Promotion solely on merit. Comprehensive written evaluations after assignments.					
Professional education	Formal national professional education programs, regional and local office seminars and intensive on-the-job training.					

Footnotes

[1]"Goof-Proof Your Resume," *Changing Times* (September 1983): 43–46.

[2]Ibid.

[3]Robert L. Dipboye, Richard D. Arvey, and David E. Terpotra, "Equal Employment and The Interview," *Personnel Journal* 55 (October 1976): 521.

References

Bolles, Richard Nelson. *What Color Is Your Parachute? A Practice Manual for Job-Hunters and Career Changers.* Berkeley, Calif.: Ten Speed Press, 1975.

Boros, James M., and Parkinson, J. Robert. *How to Get A Fast Start in Today's Job Market.* Englewood Cliffs, N.J.: Prentice-Hall, 1980.

Bostwick, Burdette E. *Finding the Job You've Always Wanted.* New York: John Wiley and Sons, 1977.

Djeddah, Eli. *Moving Up: How to Get High-Salaried Jobs.* Berkeley, Calif.: Ten Speed Press, 1978.

Donaho, Melvin W., and Meyer John L. *How to Get the Job You Want.* Englewood Cliffs, N.J.: Prentice-Hall, 1976.

Einhorn, Lois J., Bradley, Patricia Hayes, and Baird, John E., Jr. *Effective Employment Interviewing.* Glenview, Ill.: Scott, Foresman and Co., 1982.

Erdlen, John D., and Sweet, Donald H. *Job Hunting for the College Graduate.* Lexington, Mass.: DC Heath & Co., 1979.

Figgins, Ross. *Techniques of Job Search.* San Francisco: Canfield Press, 1976.

Gootnick, David. *Getting a Better Job.* New York: McGraw-Hill, 1978.

Lederer, Muriel. *Guide to Career Education.* New York: New York Times Book Co., 1974.

Lindquist, Victor R., and Endicott, Frank S. *Northwestern Endicott Report, 1983.* Evanston, Ill.: Northwestern University, 1983.

Medley, H. Anthony. *Sweaty Palms: The Neglected Art of Being Interviewed.* Belmont, Calif.: Lifetime Learning Publications, 1978.

Robertson, Jason. *How to Win in an Interview.* Englewood Cliffs, N.J.: Prentice-Hall, 1978.

Rogers, Edward J. *Getting Hired.* Englewood Cliffs, N.J.: Prentice-Hall, 1982.

Straub, Joseph T. *The Job Hunt.* Englewood Cliffs, N.J.: Prentice-Hall, 1981.

U.S. Civil Service Commission. *Career Planning Handbook; A Guide to Career Fields and Opportunities.* Washington, D.C.: Government Printing Office, n.d.

Review Questions

1. What steps are involved in the direct-mail campaign? Describe them.
2. What are the steps in planning for a job interview?
3. Describe five nonverbal behaviors you should be conscious of during the job interview.

4. Discuss the importance of follow up as it applies to job interviews.

5. What are three situations where you would be likely to use a follow up?

Exercises

1. You are a campus recruiter for Goldwin's, a chain of department stores with locations in Dallas, Atlanta, Chicago, and New York. You are looking for an applicant who shows three major qualities: dependability, initiative, and willingness to assume responsibility. The chosen applicant will become a manager trainee at Goldwin's in Atlanta.

    a. Interview one of your classmates for this position.

    b. Write a brief (no more than two pages) report that summarizes the following:

        1. How you assessed your classmate against the three qualities.

        2. What your classmate said that made you believe that he or she possessed each of the qualities.

        3. How your classmate's nonverbal communication affected your perception of him or her.

2. Form a trio with two of your classmates. Person A is the interviewer, Person B is the interviewee, and Person C is the observer. A should interview B for approximately ten minutes, asking any of the 50 interview questions listed in this chapter. A and C should give feedback to B about both his or her answers and nonverbal communication. Allow B to practice answering difficult questions. Then switch roles for the next 20 minutes, making sure that each member of your trio plays each person in the exercise.

3. Fill out the qualifications checklist presented in Figure 19.3. Then write a brief report justifying your rating on each qualification. Use your work experience, activities, honors, and interests as evidence.

4. Make an appointment to interview the personnel officer of a local company. Your purpose in this interview is to find out:

    a. What kinds of questions the person likes to ask in job interviews.

    b. The role this person thinks nonverbal communication plays in the job interview.

    c. The most difficult problem this person has in selecting among applicants.

    d. What qualities this person looks for in people with your level of education. Write a brief report or make a short oral presentation to the class summarizing your findings.

Case

Who's Interviewing Whom?

Jim Stull
San Jose State University

Carla Chavez has landed an interview with Tom Coates, regional sales manager for Nirvana Computers. During the interview, Tom asks Carla, "Why do you want to work for Nirvana?" Carla replies:

"Well, Mr. Coates, that's why I asked for the opportunity to meet with you today. I want to be sure that Nirvana *is* the right company for me.

"I've read a great deal of literature about Nirvana. I've met a few of your employees. I listened to a presentation by one of your campus recruiters. Everything that I've heard and read has been extremely positive. I'm especially impressed by your concern for employees and service to customers.

"But I need to see some of this for myself. I'm not sure that I can get a true feeling for the Nirvana culture without visiting and finding out how I would fit the profile of a Nirvana sales representative. I have a few questions that I need answered before I can be sure."

Tom says, "Sure, go ahead and ask and I'll answer them as best as I can."

Carla asks a few specific questions about various Nirvana policies, and she probes until she is satisfied that she has gotten the information she needs.

Tom leans back in his chair, puts his feet up on the coffee table, clasps his hands behind his head and says, "I like your style, Carla, and I think you've got the makings of a top-notch Nirvana sales representative."

■ ■ ■

Case Questions

1. What do you think it is in Carla's verbal behavior that Tom likes? Be specific and identify some of Carla's words that you believe were particularly effective in winning Tom over.

2. Some interviewers might perceive Carla's statement, "I want to be sure that Nirvana *is* the right company for me," as threatening. Why do you think that they might?

3. Carla used an information-getting technique called *probing*. Explain why this is effective when used by the interviewee. Why is this technique especially effective for Carla, in view of her objective to be a sales representative? Write a brief dialogue between Carla and Tom showing how Carla would use the probing technique.

Case

Lost Opportunity
Michael T. O'Neill
Personnel Finders of Arlington, Inc.

On the advice of his college placement center, Sid Flaccus called Data Preparation Associates to set up an interview for the entry-level technical writing position DPA advertised in the placement center's *Job Hot Line.*

Flaccus is 22 years old and has a BA in English. He works part-time for Personnel Service of Arlington, Texas, where he writes manuals, letters, memos, and reports.

Sid arrived 15 minutes early for his interview with Betty Boman, the chief editor at DPA. He had dressed in a suit and tie and had even shined his shoes. Two days earlier he had had his hair styled and cut short.

Betty was dressed casually and appeared relaxed. Sid could see that she was an experienced interviewer. She let Sid do most of the talking, but interrupted his digressions about his writing experiences to ask pointed questions about Sid's knowledge of computers and computer software.

Sid knew a little about computers from his required course in computer science, and he added that he "didn't see much difference between journalism and tech writing." He even recommended a recent article to Betty that took computer software writers to task for their jargon. Sid quoted several humorous examples from it.

When the conversation turned to Sid's writing, he quickly pointed out that he had published a short story in the campus magazine and was writing a scholarly paper on poetry. He also mentioned that his English professors had praised his writing and encouraged a writing career.

The interview lasted nearly an hour; for the last half hour Betty asked no questions. She and Sid discussed the novels of William Faulkner, in whose work they shared an interest. The interview ended cordially, and Betty told Sid to call in about a week.

When Sid called a week later, he was surprised to find that another applicant got the job.

■ ■ ■

Case Questions

1. What do you suspect caused Betty to turn Sid down?
2. What would you have done differently at the interview that might have changed its outcome?
3. Would you tell Sid to do anything differently at his next interview? What?

Writing a Resume

Learning Objectives
1. To understand the components of an effective resume.
2. To learn several ways to compile a resume.
3. To learn how to package the resume.

*B*ob Pfeiffer, personnel manager for Barrington Industries, pulled open his file drawer and quickly flipped through it. Pulling out a file marked Applications—Manager Trainees, he returned to his desk and emptied onto it 250 resumes, which he'd received in the past two months.

He began sorting the resumes into piles. During his 15 years in personnel work, he had developed a system for choosing potential employees by looking at their resumes. In just 45 minutes he had selected 25 resumes from the stack. He placed the remaining 225 resumes into the file, slid it to one side of his desk, and began calling 25 fortunate applicants to schedule job interviews with them. ∎

Whether you're a student about to finish school, a person reentering the job market after a period of time, or someone simply wanting to find a more attractive position than the one you have now, you'll find that people use a variety of techniques to find a job:

- Personal contacts through family
- Personal contacts through close friends and acquaintances
- Employment agencies
- College placement centers
- Mass mailings
- Responding to newspaper advertisements
- Unannounced visits to businesses
- Community surveys of existing employers.

People use many techniques in their job searches.

No matter which technique you use, your success in convincing a company to hire you instead of someone else depends on three factors: your background, your effectiveness in presenting that background, and your performance in the job interview.

The resume and cover or application letter which accompanies the resume are usually the first contact between you and the organization; therefore, you will be evaluated through these documents. In reading a resume and the letter of application, the recruiter seeks three types of information: (1) do you have the basic credentials for the job, such as a business degree for a business job? (2) do you have background information that elevates you beyond the basic qualifications, such as related job experience? and (3) are you good at what you do?

This third background qualification is the most important to most recruiters. Many recruiters prefer an applicant who is good at ditch digging, for example, to one who is only mediocre in a job. The enthusiasm, leadership, or responsibility that emerges when you hold a job indicates your effectiveness. This effectiveness is sometimes referred to as your track record. If you can show your winning background, recruiters will anticipate your continued success. Most resumes transmit the first information type; many transmit the second type. Few, however, take full advantage of the third type, even though the background information warrants its inclusion.

Resumes are defined by three characteristics: they are factual, categorized, and tabulated. The information in resumes can be substantiated and is not opinion. The date and location of your high school graduation, for example, can be verified. Your belief that you're enthusiastic cannot be verified. The information is categorized or grouped under headings, such as education or job experience. The headings tend to be mutually exclusive. Information in a resume is not presented in sentence form; it is *tabulated* much like a balance sheet with headings and subheadings and responses to queries, such as *Health: excellent.*

Chapter 19 provides a list of detailed suggestions for succeeding in the job interview. In this chapter you learn how to write an effective resume that will not only help you obtain an interview, but will be of value in the interview. We will discuss the components of a resume and show you how to fit these components into a format suited to your specific needs.

The resume is a required part of your job search.

Components of an Effective Resume

Just as resume formats vary widely, so do resume components. Further, the order of the components may determine the image or tone of the message. Just as we organize persuasive letters differently than positive letters, we need to plan the organization of the resume. Even though you probably won't use all the components in your resume, we'll discuss each one, so that you can choose the components you think best represent your accomplishments. These components are not necessarily presented in the order that is always most efficient for all job applications.

Component 1: Resume Heading

A required part of every resume, the heading should contain the word *Resume,* your name, address, and telephone number. *Resume* is an optional part of the heading, but since your resume is likely to be copied and passed among members of the organization where you apply, the word in the title will help them quickly identify your resume. If you have two addresses, one at school and one at home, put both in the heading. Listing your home address will help an employer contact you when you are no longer in school.

Here is an example of a resume heading:

RESUME

Robert J. Anderson

Address (until June 1, 1985)

134 Ansley Street
Atlanta, Georgia 30324
(404) 863-2717

Address (after June 1, 1985)

1897 Clearwater Road
Duran, Iowa 52242
(319) 422-5799

If you have only one address, place it either where you see the Ansley Street address or directly beneath your name.

You may wonder why there is no picture called for at the top of your resume. Approximately ten years ago pictures were standard items on resumes. However, federal laws now prohibit employers from discriminating on the basis of several factors, including race, sex, and age. If you put your picture on your resume, someone at the company that receives it will likely obscure it. In short, don't put your potential employer in an embarrassing position; omit the picture.

Leave the picture off your resume.

Component 2: *Availability Date*

Companies budget many of their position openings to coincide with graduation dates. For example, Bob Pfeiffer's organization might have five openings beginning July 1 (for May and June graduates), two September 1 openings (for August graduates), and two January 1 openings (for December graduates).

Availability dates help employers find you an opening.

Openings may occur in every month of the year, of course, but as a convenience for your potential employer, place your date of availability on the resume. If you do so, the employer can more easily fit you into a budgeted position.

Give both the month and year and, if possible, specific day for your availability.

AVAILABLE: June 1, 1985

If you are available for a position at the time you complete your resume, you might write the availability component like this:

AVAILABLE: Immediately

If you know that the availability date is not important to the company, place this information lower in the resume, perhaps with personal data.

Component 3: *Objective*

The impression you make upon your potential employer is due in large part to how clearly defined your goals are. As Chapter 19 explained, interviewers will normally ask about both your short-term and long-term

The objective shows your potential employer that you have planned for the future.

goals. To many interviewers applicants with clear-cut goals show more maturity and readiness to pursue a profession than applicants who have no clear goals in mind.

Here's an example of a goal statement:

<u>OBJECTIVE</u>: **Responsible career position in accounting or finance**

Choose your words carefully. The word *responsible* says that you want and are willing to assume responsibility. Don't let a potential employer wonder whether you are responsible.

The word *career* says that you want to stay with the company that hires you. Employees are expensive to replace. In some organizations the cost of replacing you if you quit could be as high as $2000 or $3000 for such things as severance pay and hiring and training your replacement. Therefore, in the front of every interviewer's mind will be the question: how long will this applicant stay with my company?

Be sure that the position you list in the goal statement is as specific as you can make it. Accounting and finance are fairly closely related. Try to avoid general statements (for example, general business) or statements that represent you as the proverbial jack-of-all trades (for example, accounting or real estate).

Are you willing to relocate or to travel? If so, then state your willingness after your objective:

<u>OBJECTIVE</u>: **Responsible entry-level position in personnel management with ample opportunity for advancement. Willing to relocate and travel.**

Although not actually part of your career or job objective, this information may be placed in this part of your resume so that every reader will notice it.

Relocation and travel information is tremendously important to some businesses. In recent years many managers in large companies have turned down promotions and salary increases simply because relocation was involved. If you are willing to relocate, let the reader know as soon as possible. Such willingness is simply a part of many sales positions. However, no matter what position you seek, there may be some traveling involved, especially during the training and orientation period.

A willingness to relocate and travel will help you make a better impression.

Component 4: Education

The education section of your resume contains five important items:

a. When you received your degree(s) or diploma(s)
b. Where you earned your degree(s) or diploma(s)
c. Your major or field of concentration
d. Relevant course work
e. Your grade point average, if appropriate.

Where you place this component in your resume will depend upon which format you decide to use. However, most students just finishing school place their education directly beneath their objective.

If you have or are expecting to receive a four-year degree, you might write your education component like this:

EDUCATION:

June 1984	Bachelor of Business Administration, Southern University, Atlanta, Georgia. Major in Personnel Management. Minor in Marketing. Course work included wage and salary administration, personnel selection, personnel administration, EEO, and ERISA. GPA of 3.8 on a 4-point scale. Graduated summa cum laude.
June 1980	Graduated with honors from Southwestern High School, Roanoke, Virginia.

If the location of your college or university is well known, then omit the city and state, but always include the city and state for your high school entry.

Place of education

The course work you list should be related to the objective in the previous section of your resume. Be careful about listing courses by name as often the name of a course is misleading or ambiguous. For example, if a course called *Human Resource Management* focused primarily upon such topics as Equal Employment Opportunity (EEO) and the Occupational Safety and Health Act (OSHA), then your course work statement should read *EEO and OSHA*.

Listing course work

Finally, list your grade point average (GPA) only if you want to call attention to it. Many employers are more interested in your major, work experience, and activities than in your GPA. Be sure to show the scale on which your GPA is computed (for example, 3-point scale, 6-point scale). Also, if your overall GPA is not high but the GPA in your major is, then state, "GPA in major of 3.6 on a 4-point scale."

Listing the GPA

If you are a graduate of a two-year college, then you might use this format for your education component:

EDUCATION:

June 1985	Associate of Arts in Business Administration, Atlanta Junior College, Atlanta, Georgia. Concentration in General Business. Forty hours of business course work, including Administrative Practices, Business Communication, Marketing Principles, and Accounting Theory. GPA of 3.4 on a 4-point scale.
June 1983	Graduated with honors from Central High School, Atlanta, Georgia.

Finally, if you have a four-year degree but also attended a two-year school during your college career, you can work both colleges into your resume like this:

EDUCATION:

June 1985 (Expected)	Bachelor of Business Administration, Southern University, Atlanta, Georgia. Major in personnel management. Minor in marketing. Course work included wage and salary administration, personnel selection, personnel administration, EEO, and ERISA. GPA of 3.8 on a 4-point scale. Graduated summa cum laude.
September 1981 to June 1983	Attended Wolfson Junior College, Roanoke, Virginia. Concentration in general business. GPA of 3.9 on a 4.0 scale.
June 1981	Graduated with honors from Southwestern High School, Roanoke, Virginia.

If you write your resume before you receive your final degree, you can place the word *expected* beneath the date when you expect to receive the degree. If that date is only two or three months away, however, you might omit *expected*. Most potential employers reading your resume before the date will understand that the date listed is the expected date.

Component 5: Work Experience

For any full-time or part-time job that you have had, include the following information:

- **a.** When you held the job
- **b.** Your job title
- **c.** Who your employer was
- **d.** Your responsibilities
- **e.** Your accomplishments.

Here is an example:

WORK EXPERIENCE:

Example of a work experience section

September 1983 to present	Part-time Registration Clerk, Holiday Hotel, Atlanta, Georgia. Responsibilities include registering hotel guests, making reservations, processing check-outs, and handling guest problems. Earned approximately 30 percent of college expenses.
Summer 1983	Sales Representative, Eastern Book Company, Baltimore, Maryland. Responsibilities included calling on potential customers, processing orders, and delivering merchandise. Was top salesperson in 12-person territory. Earned 70 percent of college expenses for 1983–1984 year.

First, notice that the jobs are listed in reverse chronological order—most recent job first. Second, if you held a number of jobs during college and high school, you may not want to list them all. Choose those most related to your objective. Remember that no matter how menial the job seemed to you, to a potential employer your having worked says two things: (1) this applicant has been out in the real world and therefore has actual business experience, and (2) this applicant shows initiative and responsibility.

Dates of Employment. Notice that the dates in the example are not exact—you don't need to list the actual days you began and ended your employment. If you held the same job at different times, you can state "Summers 1982, 1983," or "Summers 1982, 1983, and Christmas 1983."

Job Title. Some jobs don't have specific titles. If you had such a job, simply make up a descriptive title for it. For example, if your job was serving customers at the counter of a fast-food restaurant, then you can call your position "counter clerk." Notice each job title is underlined so that it stands out.

Name of Employer. When you list employers, show both their names and locations. If your potential employer wants to call for a reference or verify your employment, this will make that job easier.

Responsibilities. Notice that we called them *responsibilities,* not *duties.* Again, your purpose is to show that you are capable of assuming responsibility. You need not list all of your responsibilities, just those you think are the most important.

Accomplishments. Any accomplishment that your potential employer can verify belongs in your list of accomplishments. In the example we illustrated two kinds of accomplishments: earning money to attend school and succeeding as a salesperson. Other types of accomplishments you can list include supervising other people or training your replacement, both of which show leadership skills to many potential employers. If you assumed your supervisor's duties while he or she was absent, include that information. Perhaps you made some suggestion that was adopted by your employer. If so, then list it. Even seemingly minor accomplishments, such as an employee-of-the-month award, being placed in charge of other student summer help, or being assigned security or cash-handling duties, can impress the person who reads your resume.

Accomplishments will help set you apart from other applicants.

It is the accomplishments section—also called *results*—that spotlights your track record, the third and most important type of information found in a resume.

Component 6: Honors

Any school-related honor you received belongs in the honors section of your resume. If you have no honors, simply omit this section. If you have only one honor, then you should consider including it in the activities section and renaming that section *honors and activities*. You can look outside school activities for honors as well. Here's a sample honors section:

HONORS: <u>College</u>
Sigma Iota Epsilon (National Management Honorary), 1984
Phi Kappa Phi (Scholastic Honorary), 1984
Cardinal Club (Freshman Honorary), 1983
<u>High School</u>
Beta Club (Scholastic Honorary), 1982
National Honor Society (Languages), 1982

<u>Others</u>
Selected social director of neighborhood bicycling group.
Chosen to represent senior high-school-aged students from area at national church convention.

Notice that a brief explanation of each honor is provided as well as the year the honor was received. Never list your honors in paragraph form. An interviewer is likely to forget what honors you have received. If you list them as in the example, the interviewer might at least remember how many honors you have.

Component 7: Activities

After your major and work experience, the activities in which you have been involved constitute an important part of your resume. Honors differ from activities in that honors are bestowed upon you by others; activities are things you decide to do. To most potential employers, activities you list show interest in other people, practice in developing interpersonal relationships, and social skills. If you have served as an officer in some organization, you may also have leadership skills. Include organizations at school as well as church, volunteer, and other outside activities.

ACTIVITIES: <u>College</u>
Society for the Advancement of Management (vice president, 1982–1984).
Member, Democrats in Action, 1982–present.
Chairperson, campus Red Cross Blood Drive, 1983.

Your activities show many skills that interest your potential employer.

High School
Spanish Club, 1981–1982 (president, 1982).
Tennis team (lettered three years).

Component 8: Interests

You may have wondered, when filling out an application for a job, why you were required to list your hobbies or interests. To many potential employers your interests are as important as your activities. Many employers seek a person who has a balance of individual and group interests. Consider the following:

INTERESTS: Reading, jogging, skiing, photography

Show a mix of group and individual interests.

Some interviewers will perceive a person with interests like these to be an isolate. There are no real group activities listed.

Other interviewers will have an equally negative perception of:

INTERESTS: Tennis, basketball, chess, backgammon

Interests such as these might depict a total group orientation. The interviewer may perceive you as too dependent upon others.

In short, your interests should include a mix of group and individual activities. However, do not list interests that you don't actually have. An interviewer will ask you to discuss the most recent book you've read or how often you jog. If you don't actually read or jog, you've placed yourself in an embarrassing predicament.

You may use hobbies instead of or with interests, if you wish. A slight distinction exists between the two: interests are those things that interest you, even though you may not do them often. Hobbies are usually done with some regularity or frequency.

In presenting your hobbies or interests, keep these points in mind:

Seek a balance between individual and group activities. For example, include *read science fiction* with *play intramural football.*

Seek a balance between athletic and more cerebral activities. Contrast *avid jogger* with *enjoy classical piano concertos.*

Avoid items that appear average, or make you appear average, such as *watch TV* or *go to football games.*

Try to find job-related items, such as writing programs for home computer, or charting marketing trends in some industry.

Be specific in your description if possible. *Sorority tennis team co-captain* is better than just *tennis.*

Job-oriented organizations, such as a business fraternity or a real-estate club, are valuable assets. Volunteer work, such as blood drive worker, or hospital candy striper, also carries a positive message.

Don't overdo it. A list of too many items suggests you may not have enough time or interest for the job. A total of about six hobbies, interests, or activities is probably the maximum.

Component 9: Achievements

If you have at least three major achievements, consider illuminating them. These achievements might be found in more depth elsewhere on your resume but are highlighted here.

Make sure your items are true achievements. It's quite negative to emphasize achievements and then present weak items. For that same reason, having only one or two items under the heading shows a weakness in achievements, not a strength; that's why we suggest at least three items. Don't overdo your list, either. Five or six items should be the most you present; more tend to diminish your entries.

Here are some sample achievements entries.

Earned 90 percent of college expenses.

Achieved 3.8 GPA (on 4.0 system) for four-year period.

Elected president of Finance Club.

Dean's list (three semesters).

Re-employed each of four summers by same company.

Selected by (college/dean/fraternity/sorority/business organization/ church group, etc.) to represent them at (convention, meeting, seminar, etc.)

Component 10: Personal Data or Background Information

Businesses are prohibited from making selection decisions based upon your age, race, sex, marital status, and other personal data unless the data are bona fide occupational qualifications. Thus, this section of your resume is optional. You should include personal data only if you think it will help you get the position. For example, if you are an unmarried female who is also willing to relocate, then your marital status might help you although legally it should not.

Don't include personal data unless you think it will help you.

Personal data on a resume usually includes the following:

PERSONAL: Age: 22   Birth Date: August 15, 1962
                    Health: Excellent

If you have only one address at the top of your resume, then you might place your personal data in the top right corner to create balance and to save space:

Age:	22
Birth Date:	August 15, 1962
Health:	Excellent
Marital Status:	Single

By giving both age and birth date, the reader doesn't have to calculate your age from your birth date and overcomes the problem of updating your age if a birthday occurs during the job-seeking process.

Other items sometimes found with background information, are:

Geographic preference

Date of availability

Percentage of college expenses earned

Hometown

Social security number

Physical characteristics (height, weight)

Religious preference

Family background (number of children, information about spouse or parents, etc.).

Many of these items are inconsequential to the job, thus you would only include those items you believe might reflect favorably upon you. You should also be aware that you are volunteering this information. Current laws are clear that you are not required to give information about such items as religion or family background.

Component 11: Military Service

An entry pertaining to your military service is appropriate only if you received an honorable discharge. Also, persons with military service receive bonus points on aptitude tests when applying for many civil service positions.

If your military service is extensive (more than two years) and relates closely to your objective, then you might enter it as part of your work experience components. Otherwise, the entry should be brief:

MILITARY SERVICE   U.S. Navy, 1978–1980. Served as supply officer on a destroyer. Discharged as lieutenant (junior grade).

Component 12: Licenses and Other Accreditations

Possessing a license or some professional certificate may be important to your getting a position. For example, if you are applying for a real-estate salesperson's position, then having your real-estate license should help. Other examples of licenses or accreditations that might be entered on your resume are: licensed practical nurse, registered nurse, certified public accountant, certified nuclear safety engineer, certified life underwriter, and any teaching certificate relevant to your objective. An entry for this component can appear like this:

<u>PROFESSIONAL</u>   Licensed Practical Nurse, State of Illinois.
<u>LICENSES</u>:   Certified Nurse-Midwife, State of Illinois.

Component 13: Special Skills

Some jobs you may apply for require special skills. For example, many computer programmers are expected to know several computer languages as well as different types of computer systems. If you are one of these persons, then your special skills component can appear like this:

<u>COMPUTER</u>   <u>Languages</u>: COBOL, FORTRAN, SYSTEX
<u>SKILLS</u>:   <u>Systems</u>:   IBM 360, 720, and 1030; CYBER 370
                and 380

Many applicants for positions in international business must know one or more foreign language. These special skills can appear on the resume in the same format as the computer skills:

<u>FOREIGN</u>   Can speak and read German and Spanish fluently.
<u>LANGUAGES</u>:   Can read and write Italian.

Any special skill you possess should be entered on your resume provided that the skill is relevant to your objective.

Component 14: Professional Memberships

Many college students are members of campus chapters of professional organizations. Your membership in such organizations can be listed under the activities component, unless you'd like to draw special attention to it. Here's an example:

<u>PROFESSIONAL</u>   American Marketing Association, 1983–present
<u>MEMBERSHIPS</u>:   American Society for Personnel
                Administration, 1982–present

Component 15: References

Unless you are changing jobs and want to keep your decision private as long as possible, consider listing your references on your resume. Phrases such as *References available upon request* are inconvenient to the personnel specialist, who must either call or write you, ask for your references, then contact them. You'll save the specialist time if references are on the resume. He or she may be more inclined to consider you if your references are easy to check.

List the names of your references on the resume.

References are supplied for possible verification of the facts you have presented on the resume or for additional information. References fall into three main categories: (1) professional references, who can speak about your professional ability for this job, such as your knowledge of accounting or computer science; (2) character references, who know your personality, such as your industriousness or ambition; and (3) educational references, who can respond to questions about your scholarly achievements and background, such as your performance in a management class.

Use professional, character, and educational references.

Former employers are frequently used as professional references; friends, neighbors, or colleagues are used as character references; and teachers are used as educational references. Keep in mind, though, it's how they know you that determines the category of reference. A boss may be a friend (character reference), for example. Of course, one reference may be found in several categories.

There are some types of people generally to avoid as references. Family members, clergy, or students are assumed to be biased in your favor. Their opinions, therefore, are discounted.

You may wish to categorize your references under subheadings in the references component. Since educational references are close to professional references in the type of information they supply, the two can be combined under the professional references subheading.

When you use references subheadings, supply an equal number of references under each subheading to show you're balanced. That is, supply two professional references to equalize two character references.

Never list a person as a reference until you have obtained permission to do so.

Here is an example of a reference section from a resume:

REFERENCES (with permission)

Professional	Character
Dr. Lillian Patterson	Ms. Betty Weatherford
Department of Business	Department of English
Southern University	Southern University
P. O. Box 3561	P. O. Box 3561
Atlanta, Georgia 30723	Atlanta, Georgia 30723
(404) 731-8265	(404) 731-8143

Mr. William Lucey   Dr. John L. Harper, DDS
Distribution Manager   Harper Dental Center
Eastern Book Company   Maguire, Georgia 30703
4324 Brownsboro Road   (404) 737-2245
Baltimore, Maryland 13426
(713) 926-5333

Be sure each of your references has a title (for example, Dr., Mr., Mrs., or Ms.) so that the personnel specialist who telephones them will know how they are to be addressed. Give the complete business address and telephone number. Never list the reference's home address unless the reference prefers it.

What your references say about you will not—unless it is negative—have a great impact on your evaluation. Some potential employers will not even contact your references, although others will. Employers expect that anyone you list as a reference will support your application. Nevertheless, you will be required normally to submit at least three names of people who are willing to recommend you.

Should you decide not to list your references on the resume, you might use one of the following statements:

REFERENCES: Excellent references available upon request.

REFERENCES: Excellent references available at:
                Career Planning and Placement Center,
                Southern University, Atlanta, Georgia 30723.

In summary, you can choose from among 15 components those that you think will best show your accomplishments. In the rest of this chapter we'll show you how to package these components into a compelling resume format.

Resume Formats

You can select from a variety of formats for the one you think presents your resume components in the best way. We'll introduce you to three such formats: basic, chronological, and functional.

Basic Resume Format

The basic resume format is especially useful if you are graduating from school and entering the job market with little work experience. The basic resume format incorporating most of the 15 components described appears in Figure 20.1.

Notice first that most section headings are capitalized, underlined, and set apart in the left-hand margin. A reader can quickly find the infor-

Figure 20.1   **Example of a Basic Resume**

```
                              RESUME

                          Robert J. Anderson


Address (Until June 1, 1985)              Address (After June 1, 1985)
134 Ansley Street, Apartment 4-B          1897 Clearwater Road
Atlanta, Georgia  30723                   Duran, Iowa  63217
(404) 863-2717                            (612) 422-5799

AVAILABLE:      June 1, 1985

OBJECTIVE:      Responsible career position in accounting or finance.

EDUCATION:      Bachelor of Business Administration, Southern University,
                Atlanta, Georgia.  Major in Accounting.  Minor in Finance.
                Course work included Accounting Principles, Tax Accounting,
                Accounting Law, Financial Analysis, and Financial
                Planning.  GPA of 3.7 on a 4-point scale (4.0 in major).
                Graduated summa cum laude, June 1985.  Graduated with
                honors from Southwestern High School, Roanoke, Virginia,
                June 1981.

WORK
EXPERIENCE:     Part-time Registration Clerk, Holiday Hotel, Atlanta,
                Georgia.  Responsibilities include registering hotel
                guests, making reservations, processing check-outs, and
                handling guest problems.  Have earned approximately 30
                percent of college expenses.  September 1984-present.
                Sales Representative, Eastern Book Company, Baltimore,
                Maryland.  Responsibilities included calling on potential
                customers, processing orders, and delivering merchandise.
                Was top salesperson in twelve-person territory.  Earned 70
                percent of college expenses for 1984-1985 year.  Summer
                1984.

HONORS:         College
                - Beta Alpha Psi (National Accounting Honorary), 1985
                - Phi Kappa Phi (National Scholastic Honorary), 1985
                - Cardinal Club (Freshman Honorary), 1982
                High School
                - Beta Club (Scholastic Honorary), 1981
                - National Honor Society (Languages), 1981

ACTIVITIES:     College
                - Alpha Kappa Psi Business Fraternity (Vice President,
                   1984-1985, 1983-1984)
                - Member, Democrats in Action, 1983-present
                - Chairperson, campus Red Cross Blood Drive 1984.
                High School
                - Spanish Club, 1980-1981 (President, 1981)
                - Tennis team (lettered three years)

INTERESTS:      Reading, tennis, basketball, photography
```

mation that is most important. For example, some will want to read about your work experience first; others, your education.

Second, the actual information you present about yourself is blocked attractively, several spaces in from the section headings. The appearance of your resume is almost as important as its contents.

Finally, the references are listed across, not down, the bottom of the page to save typing space and to make your references easier to identify.

Another example of the basic resume format, written for a different person, is shown in Figure 20.2.

Figure 20.1 (continued)

```
PERSONAL:       Age 22; married, no children; excellent health

REFERENCES:     Professional
                Dr. Lillian Patterson        Ms. Betty Weatherford
                Department of Business       Department of English
                Southern University          Southern University
                P. O. Box 3561               P. O. Box 3561
                Atlanta, Georgia 30723       Atlanta, Georgia 30723
                (404) 731-8265               (404) 731-8143

                Character
                Mr. William Lucey            Dr. John L. Harper, D.D.S.
                Distribution Manager         Harper Dental Center
                Eastern Book Company         Maguire, Georgia 30703
                4324 Brownsboro Road         (404) 737-2245
                Baltimore, Maryland 21426
                (713) 926-5333
```

Chronological Resume Format

Both the chronological and functional resume formats are typically used by persons with extensive work experience. In the chronological resume the work experience component appears early and describes each position in detail. An example appears in Figure 20.3.

With this resume format the individual's work experience consumes the most space. Work experience also precedes education, since it is more important.

Figure 20.2 Basic Resume Format

```
                          RESUME

                       Holly M. Clark


       1554 Westside Drive
       Atlanta, Georgia  30110
       (404) 638-2176

       AVAILABLE:     July 1, 1985

       OBJECTIVE:     Responsible entry-level position in computer programming.
                      Willing to relocate.


       EDUCATION:
       June 1985      Associate of Arts in Computer Sciences, Northrup Junior
       (Expected)     College, East Point, Georgia.  Concentration in Computer
                      Analysis and Design.  Course work included Computer Design,
                      Computer Programming, COBOL, and FORTRAN.  GPA in
                      concentration of 5.4 on a 6-point scale.

       June 1981      Graduated from Southwest High School, East Point, Georgia.

       WORK
       EXPERIENCE:
       September 1983 Part-time Computer Programmer, Northrup Junior College
       to present     Computer Center.  Responsibilities include programming,
                      checking system malfunctions, assisting students with
                      computer jobs, keeping time-sharing records on all users.

       Summers and    Salesperson, Annette's Dress Shop, East Point, Georgia.
       Christmases    Responsibilities included assisting customers, stocking
       1982 to 1983   merchandise, creating displays, and inventory.  Trained
                      replacement at the end of Summer 1983.

       ACTIVITIES:    - Baptist Student Union, 1984 to present
                      - Staff Writer, The Blue and Gold (Northrup Junior College
                        Newspaper)

       COMPUTER
       SKILLS:        - Languages:  COBOL, FORTRAN
                      - Systems:  IBM 360, CYBER 370

       PROFESSIONAL
       MEMBERSHIPS:   - National Computer Science Association, 1983 to present
                      - Computer Users of America, 1984 to present

       INTERESTS:     - Writing computer programs for home computer
                      - Singing in church choir
                      - Playing intramural tennis (doubles)

       PERSONAL:      - Age:  22   Birthdate:  August 15, 1963
                      - Marital Status:  Single
                      - Health:  Excellent

       REFERENCES:    - Available upon request
```

Functional Resume Format

The functional resume is quite different from the basic and chronological formats; its purpose is to summarize a diversity of work experience that, when combined, give the person more general qualifications. As you read Figure 20.4, notice that work experience is broken down by functional areas, and the actual positions are listed.

Using the functional format, you can chose the qualifications you

Figure 20.3 Chronological Format

```
                              RESUME

                        Wilma G. Peterson


    4255 Tufts Road                  Age:  27
    Troy, Illinois  62234            Marital Status:  Married, 2 children
    (316) 614-8432                   Health:  Excellent

    AVAILABLE:     Immediately

    OBJECTIVE:     Responsible and challenging management position in
                   health-care administration.

    EXPERIENCE:
    May 1984       Assistant Administrator, Cowans County Medical Center,
    to present     Troy, Illinois
                   Responsibilities
                   - Directly responsible for hiring all hourly employees to
                     staff 100-bed hospital.
                   - Administer wage and salary program for all staff members.
                   - Write policies and procedures for employee handbook.
                   - Supervise four department heads, two clerical workers.
                   Accomplishments
                   - Implemented technical training program for all
                     health-care employees.  Received highest possible
                     rating from Hospital Accreditation Board.
                   - Implemented employee suggestion system which has
                     resulted in net savings to hospital of $75,327.00

    September      Nursing Supervisor, Cowans County Medical Center, Troy,
    1983 - April   Illinois
    1984           Responsibilities
                   - Scheduled working hours for all nursing staff
                   - Supervised three shift supervisors
                   Accomplishments
                   - Promoted use of paraprofessionals to assist nursing staff
                   - Awarded the Illinois Nurses's Association "Supervisor of
                     the Year Award," 1983

    June 1980 -    Nurse, Groveland Hospital, Chicago, Illinois
    August 1983    Responsibilities
                   - Patient care and medication, Intensive Care
                   - In charge of 12 other nurses on night shift (June-
                     August 1983)
                   Accomplishments
                   - Promoted to nurse-in-charge after three years
                   - Recommended changes in patient care were implemented
                   - Salary increased 110 percent in 39-month period

    EDUCATION:
    1984 to        Working toward a Master's Degree in Hospital Administration,
    present        Acton College, St. Louis, Missouri.  Have completed 35 hours
                   of course work.
```

think are important for the position you want, list them separately, and show how you possess each of the qualifications. In Figure 20.4 an individual with little formal education and work experience was able to show himself to be highly competent.

In summary, the three resume formats are the basic (widely used for entry-level positions), the chronological (used to provide extensive details about work experience related to the objective), and the functional (used to emphasize expertise in separate functional areas).

Figure 20.3   (continued)

```
June 1980      Bachelor of Science Degree in Nursing, St. Mary's School
               of Nursing, Chicago, Illinois.  Graduated with high honors.

PROFESSIONAL
MEMBERSHIPS:   - National Association of Hospital Administrators
               - Illinois Association of Health Care Administrators
               - National Association of Nursing Administrators

COMMUNITY
ACTIVITIES:    - American Cancer Society
               - American Red Cross
               - United Way (Campaign Chairperson, 1983)

INTERESTS:     - Collecting antiques
               - Playing golf
               - Listening to light opera

REFERENCES:    - Available upon request
```

There are five dimensions in effectively preparing your resume that set you apart from—and above—the crowd.

1.   Present positive information with positive phrasing.
2.   Order your components and the items under the components with most important (to the reader) information first.
3.   Show your track record. Indicate that you're good at what you do, whatever it may be.
4.   Avoid being average or saying average things. Look for information that sets you apart from the crowd.

Figure 20.4   Functional Format

```
                           RESUME

                      Harold D. Williams

   25 Clarkston Place              Age:  25
   Salem, Oregon  80135            Marital Status:  Married, no children
   (817) 236-5926                  Health:  Excellent

   AVAILABLE:      Immediately

   OBJECTIVE:      Responsible general management position in textile or
                   related field.  Willing to travel or relocate.

   EXPERIENCE:
   General         Have supervised more than 100 hourly workers in two textile
   Management      plants.  Responsible for scheduling and employee-relations
                   problems.

   Quality         Met or exceeded quality standards 95 percent of the time.
   Assurance       Helped establish quality standards for new product.

   Production      Assisted in introduction, set-up, and operation of new
                   machines.  Am familiar with Crossland and Weaveright
                   equipment.

   Motivation      Have used MBO, goal-setting, and piece-rate systems.

   WORK HISTORY:  - 1984 to present:  Production Manager, Bostick Mills,
                     Salem, Oregon
                  - 1981 to 1984:  Production Supervisor, Quality Fabrics,
                     Inc., Salem, Oregon

   EDUCATION:
   June 1983       Graduated from Owens Technical School, Salem, Oregon (one-
                   year program).  Concentration in Textile Management.
                   Course work included Production Planning, Quality Control,
                   Supervisory Methods, Machine Design, and Human Factors
                   Engineering.

   June 1981       Graduated from Northside High School, Salem, Oregon.

   COMMUNITY
   ACTIVITIES:    - Lion's Club, 1983 to present (Sergeant-at-Arms, 1983)
                  - Toastmaster's International, 1980-1983

   SPECIAL
   QUALIFICATIONS:- Four years related job experience
                  - Supporting technical education
                  - Record of achievement

   INTERESTS:     - Fish hunting with bow and arrow, playing Pente, and old
                    movies

   REFERENCES:    - Available upon request
```

---

5.   Aim for consistency and balance. Try to present equal numbers of items or to handle items similarly.

As you have seen in the sample resumes, margins are about one and one-half inches at the top and bottom, and at least one inch on each side. Typing includes a combination of single and double spacing. There are not standardized rules on how to indent, underline, or space the content of the resumes. Remember, keep your resume balanced, clean, and esthetically pleasing.

Preparing Copies of Your Resume

You can use one of two approaches to getting your final resume prepared. First, you can take your final draft to a printing shop and have the resume set in type. A less expensive alternative is the second—to hire a professional typist to type your final resume.

Try to keep your resume to one page in length unless you have extensive work experience or other information that creates a need for more than one page. Many interviewers are not offended by two-page or longer resumes as long as all the information is important and relevant.

One way to help get a lot of material on one page is to use reduction. If your resume takes more than one page and you are using a professional typist, have your final draft typed on 8½ by 14-inch paper with no margins at the top or sides. Many print shops can reduce this long copy to standard-size paper when the resume is copied. If your long copy requires no more than a 20 percent reduction, the final resume should have an attractive appearance.

Reduce the resume to one page.

The final copies of your resume should be printed on quality white or off-white bond paper. Many print shops have a variety of bright colors from which to choose; however, colors are not as important as they once were. Your potential employer must be able to demonstrate that you were selected (or rejected) upon some other criteria than the color of your resume. Your goal is to present a document that is esthetically pleasing.

Color of the resume

Summary

In this chapter we've introduced you to 15 components of a resume. As you write your resume, you might go back and choose the components you think will best represent your accomplishments. Although many of the components are a necessary part of any resume, some will require your judgment concerning their appropriateness.

We also introduced three resume formats—basic, chronological, and functional. The basic format is most useful if you have little work experience. Should you have extensive work experience related to your objective, you might choose between the chronological and functional formats.

Finally, we suggested how to package your resume. Clearly, the components and format are important, yet the resume's appearance will make an important first impression. Your goal is to have a professionally packaged product that will not only help you get interviews, but will also have a lasting, favorable impact on your potential employer.

Review Questions

1. What does the education component of a resume contain? The work experience component?
2. What is meant by a balance of interests on your resume? Why is this balance important?
3. Describe and differentiate among three different resume formats.
4. What are special skills on a resume?
5. Briefly discuss the final printing and copying of a resume.

Exercises

1. Write a draft of your own resume using the basic format. Exchange your resume for a classmate's. Evaluate one another's drafts, suggesting changes you think will help.
2. Rewrite your resume using either the chronological or functional format. Do you see any advantages in this format for your resume?
3. Make an appointment to interview a personnel officer in a company in your community. Your purpose in this interview is to find out:
   a. What he or she considers most important in a resume.
   b. How he or she uses the resume in making selection decisions.
   c. What he or she does not like in a resume.
   Write a brief report summarizing your interview findings.

Case

Accomplishments Lead to Interviews

Ann Perry
Assistant Director for Placement Services
University of Louisville, Belknap Campus

A good resume is a sales tool which clearly demonstrates your abilities and skills. It should show the prospective employer that you can produce the results the organization is seeking.

Proof that you can produce those results will come primarily from your record of past accomplishments. Focus on how you performed in your previous jobs and activities by starting phrases with action verbs like *coordinated, implemented, increased,* and *supervised.* Whenever possible point to some tangible results of your work; for example, *exceeded sales quota 13 of 14 weeks of summer job* or *assisted in redesign of office information system resulting in 20 percent reduction in costs.*

Emphasize the most relevant work experience. Consider summarizing those jobs that are not as significant.

Figure 20A.1

```
                            JIM SMITH
                          1302 Oak Street
                     Louisville, Kentucky  40233
                          (502) 588-6708


        OBJECTIVE

        Staff Accountant

        EDUCATION

        Bachelor of Science in Business Administration, University of Louisville,
        May 1984.  Major:  Accounting

        EXPERIENCE

        Karpster and Halbrand, CPAs, Louisville, Kentucky.  As intern, gathered
        and analyzed vast amounts of data on clients for Senior Auditor.  Had
        responsibility for auditing three small businesses.  Wrote yearly and
        monthly financial statements.  Trained several clerical workers.
        Responsible for developing new business.  (Spring 1983, 1984)

        Louisville Gas and Electric Company, Louisville, Kentucky.  Accounting
        Clerk II.  Duties included processing accounts payable for data entry.
        (June - September 1983)

        Young Men's Christian Association, Shelbyville, Kentucky.  Life Guard.
        Duties included teaching swimming and diving lessons.  Responsible for
        safety.  (Part-Time 1977 - 1980)

        Harold's Restaurant, Shelbyville, Kentucky.  Bus Boy.  Cleared tables and
        shelved equipment.  (Summer 1980)

        Camp Cheerio, Blowing Rock, North Carolina.  Unit Counselor.  Responsible
        for supervising and coordinating activities for 14 campers.  (Summer 1976)

        ADDITIONAL INFORMATION

        Membership Chairman, University of Louisville Accounting Club
        Chairman, Fraternity Fundraising Drive
        Selection Committee for new Dean of School of Business
        U. L. Elite Club (Campus honor society)
        Interested in water sports, certified diver


                       REFERENCES FURNISHED UPON REQUEST
```

Review the two resumes in Figures 20A.1 and 20A.2. Imagine you are the accounting manager for a medium-size industrial firm which is projected for a great deal of growth in the next three to five years. You have an opening for an entry-level accountant. The person you select must have the potential for moving on to greater responsibility very quickly if the anticipated growth materializes. Your recruiting budget is limited, and because of the distance, you can bring only one of the following two candidates in for an interview.

■ ■ ■

Figure 20A.2

JOAN A. CLARK

1704 Mills Lane   (502) 425-1212 (Home)
Louisville, Kentucky 40223   (502) 636-3232 (Message)

OBJECTIVE

Entry level position in Accounting with industrial firm. Long-range goal
Financial Management. Willing to travel and relocate.

EDUCATION

Bachelor of Science in Business Administration, University of Louisville,
May 1984. Major: Accounting

3.8/4.0 Grade Point Average in Major Field. Earned 75 percent of college
expenses.

EXPERIENCE

Karpster and Halbrand, CPA's, Louisville, Kentucky. As intern, analyzed
vast amounts of data into relevant financial statistics for 25 business
and individual clients. Performed detailed customer audits for three
small businesses, and produced clear monthly and yearly financial
statements. Trained several clerical workers on firm's newest computerized
system. Developed two new business clients for firm. (Spring 1983, 1984)

Louisville Gas and Electric Company, Louisville, Kentucky. Accounting
Clerk II. Processed accounts payables for data entry. Designed new form
subsequently adopted by management. (June – September 1983)

Other work experience includes: Lifeguard, Bus Boy, and Summer Camp
Counselor.

ADDITIONAL INFORMATION

Membership Chairman, University of Louisville Accounting Club. Increased
   membership by 20 percent.
Chaired sorority fund raising drive which raised $5,000 for American
   Cancer Society.
Served on Selection Committee for new Dean of Business School.
Selected to membership in Mortar Board (scholastic and leadership).
Interested in water sports, certified diver

REFERENCES FURNISHED UPON REQUEST

Case Questions

1. If you were the accounting manager, which student would you choose to interview? State reasons the resume you selected aroused your interest.
2. Develop at least three descriptive phrases which demonstrate your own achievements in work, school or college, and community activities.

Case

The Resume: Path to an Interview—and a Job
Richard J. Barnhart
San Francisco State University

Now that you are familiar with the theory of resume writing, you should be able to pinpoint the devices that distinguish an acceptable resume from a truly effective one.

Figures 20B.1 and 20B.2 show two resumes prepared by a young marketing graduate who set for himself the goal of landing a job in sales with IBM.

He updated the resume he had used in his senior year in college and mailed it directly to IBM's San Francisco area marketing manager. When he received no reply after two weeks, he phoned and learned from the secretary that the company had no sales openings.

Using his marketing experience—he was, after all, selling himself—he revised his résumé and resubmitted it. This time he received a phone call from the marketing manager asking him to come in for an interview. And he did get the job he wanted.

■ ■ ■

Case Questions

1. Place yourself in the marketing manager's position. You don't have any current openings, but you can make room for an exceptional applicant. Which version would arouse your interest enough to call the applicant for an interview?
2. Why? Defend your selection with specific examples.

Figure 20B.1   Resume A

NAME

Street Address
City, State Zip Code

Phone Number

EXPERIENCE:

1981 to
present
American Greetings Corporation
Hayward, California
Accounts Manager: Promoted from sales representative in
supermarket division to accounts manager of a top national
drug chain. Maintained customer satisfaction with
successful sales through the development of innovative
merchandising techniques and analysis of market trends.
Supervised six employees.
Accomplishments
Over forecast in 1983 by 32 percent and 1984 by 71 percent
with eleven new accounts opened. Percentage of new stores
successfully prospected is up 40 percent in 1984 over
previous two years.

1973 to 1981
Magic Chef Delicatessen
Daly City, California
Night Manager: Worked up from apprentice clerk to night
manager with responsibilities for preparing and closing
the store. Paid for all school and traveling expenses
with job.

EDUCATION:
Bachelor of Arts in International Business from
San Francisco State University, June 1981. Member of the
Student World Trade Association

AWARDS:
Earned Business Achievement Award from the Bank of
America in 1979 on the basis of scholastic accomplishments
and debating skills.

INTERESTS:
Building fine furniture, playing golf and racquetball

REFERENCES:
References available upon request

Figure 20B.2   Resume B

```
Resume of                                            Telephone
                                                      (415)


Occupational
Objective:     To be an active participant in sales with a progressive
               company

Experience
Highlights:
1981 to        American Greetings Corporation
present        Cleveland, Ohio
               Accounts Manager:  Initially employed as a sales
               representative in the supermarket division.  Promoted to
               accounts manager, requiring supervision of merchandisers,
               sales analysis, development of innovative merchandising
               techniques and customer relations.

1975 to 1981   Magic Chef Delicatessen
               Daly City, California
               Sales Clerk:  Worked up from apprentice clerk to night
               manager with the responsibilities of preparing for the
               next day and closing the store.  Paid for all school and
               traveling expenses with job.

Education:     B.A. in International Business from San Francisco State
               University, June 1981.
               Played on college golf team.  Member of the Student World
               Trade Association.  Earned Business Achievement Award from
               the Bank of America in 1979.

Military
Service:       Completed six years of service in the California National
               Guard

Personal
Interests:     Building fine furniture, playing golf and handball

Personal Data: Age 26; married, no children; height 6'0"; weight 170 lbs.;
               excellent health

References:     Personal and business references available upon request.
```

Recognizable Patterns
of Language

Learning Objectives
After reading and understanding this section, you will be able to write a correct sentence. More specifically, you will be able to:
1. **Identify grammatical patterns.**
2. **Follow the formal guidelines for usage.**
3. **Punctuate in accordance with established guidelines.**
4. **Spell correctly.**

Richard David Ramsey, of Southeastern Louisiana University, Hammond, Louisiana, prepared Appendix A.

To some folks the word *grammar* conjures up images of frowning schoolmarms who rap children over the knuckles for every conceivable infraction of the rules. The fact is, nonetheless, that grammar, rather than being a laborious, frustrating maze of useless rules, is actually a necessity if we are to communicate efficiently with one another. Grammar provides the logical, mutually recognizable patterns in which our language operates.

Recognizable Patterns

Consider the following two sequences of numbers:

a. 5 3 9 1 4 0 8 2 7 6.
b. 9 8 7 6 5 4 3 2 1 0.

Which sequence puts less of a burden on the reader? Which sequence is easier to remember? Why? Sequence b is the answer, of course, because it follows a recognizable pattern. We look for such patterns in every aspect of life—in our daily schedule, in the professor's lectures, in the music we listen to, in the way we drive our cars, in certain matters of social protocol, and in the grammar of our language.

Take a look at the following two sentences:

c. audited accountant ledger The the.
d. The accountant audited the ledger.

Which of these sentences communicates more efficiently? Which is easier to remember? Why? The answer is d, because it follows the grammar (recognizable patterns) of the English language, whereas c is nonsense.

As you might guess, the student who is likely to have the most problems with grammar is the one who lacks recognizable patterns in the other areas of life. Take, for example, the case of Joe Kool. Joe boozes until the wee hours almost every night, occasionally smokes pot, eats anywhere from zero to six meals a day (and never on schedule), attends class sporadically, changes majors at least three times per year, simultaneously dates two different women, and constantly changes lanes when he drives his green-and-pink convertible on the highway. Joe Kool is not very likely to be a whiz in writing recognizable patterns of grammar.

Of course, not all the problems we discuss in this chapter are as flagrant as those in sentence c above or those of Joe Kool, but the fact still remains that we look for recognizable patterns in grammar as in everything else. Further, the burden is on the writer (or speaker), in adopting the you viewpoint, to identify with the reader's (or listener's) interests and concerns and therefore to make the grammar everything that it should be for the reader's (or listener's) ease. This point is especially critical in business, where there is money to be made. The better one communicates, the more likely one is to make that money.

As we proceed, we will follow a basic assumption that our audience in business is usually literate; that is, the audience will be most favorably disposed toward us, our message, and our product, if we use the guidelines (recognizable patterns) of formal English. There are times when we might break some of these guidelines; when that need arises, we want to do so deliberately, not in ignorance. The writers of a widely circulated advertising campaign were well aware that *we,* not *us,* is the proper pronoun to serve as a subject of verb, but still they used, "Us Tareyton smokers would rather fight than switch." Perhaps the writers reasoned that an audience of fighters wouldn't really care about grammatical formalities.

Units in Grammar

"Give me a place to stand," said Archimedes, "and I will move the world." By analogy, in grammar we could say, "If I can write a sentence, I can move the world." The chief objective of this chapter is to enable you to write a sentence. An English sentence has four elements:

1. Entire sentence
2. Clause(s)
3. Phrase(s)
4. Word(s).

Entire Sentence

The entire sentence may be of any length provided that it contains the following:

   a. A capital letter
   b. A clause that can stand alone without being subordinate to or dependent on another thought. (For example, the clause *The accountant audited the ledger* is a sentence, but a clause beginning with a subordinating word, as in *When the accountant audited the ledger,* is not, by itself, a complete sentence.)
   c. A period or other appropriate terminal punctuation mark.

Clause

A clause must contain two things:

a. A subject (which in commands is often understood, as in [*You*] "Type this letter.")

b. A verb (that is, a full verb such as *audit,* not an infinitive [*to audit*]).

Clauses may be of two kinds: (1) independent *(the accountant audited the ledger)* or (2) dependent *(when the accountant audited the ledger).* A dependent clause may function as an adverb (*When the accountant audited the ledger,* the judge dismissed the lawsuit); as an adjective (The accountant *who audited the ledger* is Laurie Sosebee); or as a noun (The judge could see *that the accountant had audited the ledger*).

Phrase(s)

A phrase is a cluster of words that works together grammatically and that functions as a single word might serve, if available. Some of the more common types of phrases are:

a. Noun (nominal), as in *the accountant*
b. Verb, as in *is auditing*
c. Infinitive, as in *to audit*
d. Participial: *Auditing the ledger,* the accountant had difficulty with some entries; *Audited in accordance with the specifications,* the ledger was returned to the file.
e. Gerundive: *Working late* is something that accountants often do during the first two weeks of April.
f. Prepositional, as in *from the ledger.*

Noun phrases always function as nouns, verb phrases always function as verbs, and participial phrases always function as adjectives (modifiers of the meaning of nouns). The present participle always ends in *-ing,* and the past participle of most verbs ends in *-ed.* An infinitive phrase may function as a noun (Laurie decided *to audit the ledger*), as an adjective (the accountant *to audit the ledger* is Laurie), or as an adverb (*to audit the ledger,* you will need to see the bursar). A gerundive phrase always contains an *-ing* word formed from a verb and used as a noun (unlike the present participle, which is used as an adjective). A prepositional phrase may function as either an adverb (the accountant testified *on the witness stand*) or an adjective (the accountant *on the witness stand* is Laurie Sosebee).

Word(s)

Words serve various functions. Some of the most common of these functions are the following:

a. Substantives

(1) *Nouns* serve as subjects and complements of verbs and as objects of prepositions. Nouns generally form the plural by adding an *-s* to the singular *(girl→girls)*, but a few are irregular *(woman→women, datum→data, series→series)*.

(2) *Pronouns* are stand-ins for nouns. There are at least four common pronoun types:

(a) *Personal pronouns* are summarized in Table 1.

(b) *Relative pronouns* appear in clauses used as adjectives, to relate the clause to the noun antecedent. There are five relative pronouns: *that,*[1] *which,* and *who,* which has a possessive form, *whose,* and an objective form, *whom.* (Can you find the relative clause you are now reading?)

(c) *Interrogative pronouns* ask questions: *who, whose, whom,* and *which* appear here as well; *what* is another interrogative pronoun.

(d) *Indefinite pronouns (one, anybody, anyone, everybody, everyone, somebody, someone)* are the only pronouns that use the apostrophe to form the possessive *(one's, anybody's,* etc.).

b. Verbs

Verbs express action or states of being. Each verb has three

Table 1 Personal Pronouns

	Nominative	Singular Objective	Possessive	Nominative	Plural Objective	Possessive
First person	I	me	my/mine	we	us	our/ours
Second person	you(thou)	you (thee)	your/yours (thy/thine)	you* (ye)	you*	your/yours
Third person						
Neuter	it	it	its	they	them	their/theirs
Feminine	she	her	her/hers	same as neuter		
Masculine	he	him	his	same as neuter		

*Common regional variants in speech are *y'all* (a contraction of *you all*), *yous*, and *you guys*, all of which have possessive forms as well. In speech these forms compensate for the distinction lost several centuries ago when *you*, historically a plural, replaced *thou* and *thee*, which have always been singular.

parts: (1) the stem *(audit/write)*, the past *(audited/wrote)*, and the past participle *(audited/written)*. Verbs have two basic tenses—present *(audit)* and past *(audited)*. With the use of auxiliaries, verbs can express future time *(is going to audit, will audit)* as well as shades of present time *(is auditing)* and past time *(has audited, had audited)*. Most verbs have a passive form *(is audited)*, which differs from the active in that the passive contains (1) some form of *be (be/am/is/are/was/were/being/been)* plus a past participle and (2) directs its action toward the grammatical subject *(the ledger was audited)*.

c. Modifiers

(1) *Adjectives* modify or clarify nouns: I audited *the* red ledger, and *the* ledger *that* I audited was red. Two classes of adjectives—the demonstratives *(this/that/these/those)* and the articles *(a/an/the)*—must always precede the noun. They also differ from other adjectives in having to agree with the noun in number. *(These book* is not grammatical English, and neither is *a books)*.

(2) *Adverbs* modify verbs. Most end in *-ly (I wrote quickly)*, but some don't *(I wrote fast)*. Occasionally adverbs team up so that one modifies the other (I wrote *unusually fast*).

(3) *Intensifiers* generally emphasize the meaning of adjectives, participles, or adverbs (the case history was *very interesting*). *Very,* incidentally, is not an adverb, because *very* cannot modify a verb: For example, we can say *the bookkeeper was very deceitful,* but not *the bookkeeper deceived very.*

d. Prepositions

Prepositions are the headwords in prepositional phrases. There are many prepositions, and they always connect a substantive to the rest of the sentence. The combination of preposition with substantive is a prepositional phrase (I went *into my office* to audit the ledger).

e. Conjunctions

The most important class of conjunctions is the coordinating conjunctions, so named because they conjoin two or more units that are *grammatically equivalent* (two prepositional phrases, two verbs, two nouns, etc.). The coordinating conjunctions are *and, or, nor,* and *but.* When used to combine two independent clauses, the coordinating conjunction should be preceded by a comma (the ledger contained mistakes, *and* the accountant had to work overtime to find them.).

f. Expletives

The two common grammatical expletives are *it* and *there.* Both serve merely to get a clause moving *(it is raining)*, but *there* can never be the subject. (Say *there* **are** *two ledgers on the desk* and *there* **is** *one ledger on the table*).

g. Other words

In the other category our language has one perhaps significant group—the interjections. These include *oh* and *well* used at the beginning of a clause.

Quiz

The following quiz may assist you in ascertaining the strength or weakness of your knowledge in applying specific guidelines of English grammar. Please use the following list to designate the problem in each sentence:

A. Error in grammar or usage
B. Error in punctuation
C. Correct, no error
D. Error in spelling or capitalizing
E. Erroneous statement about grammar or punctuation.

1. _____ The chapter discussing the principal of a loan was entitled "Principals and Interests."

2. _____ The ledger was kind of illegible.

3. _____ A comma should appear before the coordinating conjunction joining two independent clauses.

4. _____ According to Mark Lester, "Grammar is a way of talking about how words are used to make units that communicate a meaning." (*Introductory Transformational Grammar of English,* 2d ed. [New York: Holt, Rinehart, and Winston, 1976], p. 13.)

5. _____ The city's four industries, Burroughs, Data General, Datapoint, and Halliburton, were expanding rapidly.

6. _____ The financial planner applied the new formula and the long-term forecast became much more optimistic.

7. _____ John's writing 32 instead of 23 in the last column caused the total to be $9 too high, however, he found the error quickly.

8. _____ B. F. Skinner was born in Susquehanna, Pennsylvania in 1904.

9. _____ Susan B. Anthony and Carrie Nation both supported womens' suffrage.

10. _____ Rensselaer Polytechnic Institute is a technological university. The oldest one in the United States.

11. _____ Metathesis is when someone transposes or reverses the letters in a word.

12. _____ The speaker's habit of inserting *you know* into virtually every sentence sort of weakened the impact of the presentation.

13. _____ I would urge you to sell that stock now and you should reinvest the money in a computer company.

14. _____ A worker must pay their union dues by payroll deduction.

15. _____ The accomodations were inadequate.

16. _____ On 16 December 1979 the "Lubbock Avalanche-Journal" had a Sunday circulation of 79,354.

17. _____ Attending the class, a cadaver was used for experiments.

18. _____ Gillian claimed, in her resume, that she had taught at the University of Leeds, England, from 1979–1980.

19. _____ The passive voice in grammar is a combination of some form of *be* plus a past participle.

20. _____ After receiving fair warning from the instructor, George finally learned to separate *a lot* into two words.

21. _____ The contract is to expire at noon on July 1, 1987 when the new contract takes effect.

22. _____ You should remember to add in the deposits that have arrived by mail, you should never send out notices of bad checks until you have considered all deposits for the day.

23. _____ Attending the meeting were Joseph Biggs, Laramie, Wyoming, president, David L. Carson, Troy, New York, secretary, and Allen White, Duncan, Oklahoma, treasurer.

24. _____ Laurie felt badly about the erroneous entries in the ledger.

25. _____ Now that we have finished the quiz, is there any questions?

The answers and corrections for the quiz are as follows:

1. **B** → The chapter discussing the principal of a loan was entitled "Principals and Interests."

2. **A** → The ledger was rather illegible.

3. **C**

4. **B** → According to Mark Lester, "Grammar is a way of talking about how words are used to make units that communicate a meaning" (*Introductory Transformational Grammar of English,* 2d. ed. [New York: Holt, Rinehart and Winston, 1976], p. 13).

5. **B** → The city's four industries—Burroughs, Data General, Datapoint, and Halliburton—were expanding rapidly.

6. **B** → The financial planner applied the new formula, and the long-term forecast became much more optimistic.

7. **B** → John's writing 32 instead of 23 in the last column caused the total to be $9 too high; however, he found the error quickly.

8. **D** → B. F. Skinner was born in Susquehanna, Pennsylvania, in 1904.

9. **D** → Susan B. Anthony and Carrie Nation both supported women's suffrage.

10. **B** → Rensselaer Polytechnic Institute is a technological university—the oldest one in the United States.

11. **A** → Metathesis is the transposing or reversing of the letters in a word. OR Metathesis occurs when someone transposes or reverses the letters in a word.

12. **A** → The speaker's habit of inserting *you know* into virtually every sentence somewhat weakened the impact of the presentation.

13. **A** → I would urge you to sell that stock now and to reinvest the money in a computer company.

14. **A** → Workers must pay their union dues by payroll deduction. OR A worker must pay his or her union dues by payroll deduction.

15. **D** → The accommodations were inadequate.

16. **B** → On 16 December 1979 the *Lubbock Avalanche-Journal* had a Sunday circulation of 79,354.

17. **A** → Attending the class, I used a cadaver for experiments. OR When I attended the class, a cadaver was used for experiments.

18. **A** → Gillian claimed, in her resume, that she had taught at the University of Leeds, England, during 1979–1980. OR . . . from 1979 to 1980.

19. **C**

20. **D** → The correct spelling is *receiving;* the other frequently misspelled expressions—*separate* and *a lot*—are correct as given.

21. **B** → The contract is to expire at noon on July 1, 1987, when the new contract takes effect.

22. **B** → You should remember to add in the deposits that have arrived by mail; you should never send out notices of bad checks until you have considered all deposits for the day.

23. **B** → Attending the meeting were Joseph Biggs, Laramie, Wyoming, president; David L. Carson, Troy, New York, secretary; and Allen White, Duncan, Oklahoma, treasurer.

24. **A** → Laurie felt bad about the erroneous entries in the ledger.

25. **A** → Now that we have finished the quiz, are there any questions?

Guidelines

Having now laid out some framework to analyze the recognizable patterns of English, we are ready to proceed toward a more detailed discussion of guidelines to reinforce these recognizable grammatical patterns. The guidelines, if followed, will enhance your ability to communicate, especially in writing, so that the reader can understand you more easily. Remember: we follow the you viewpoint in language to minimize the burden on the reader (or listener).

In addition to the notations used in the guidelines, the following symbols are often used in proofreading to correct various errors:

◯	Close up, as in *partner⁀ship*
⌀	Delete material slashed and close up, as in *judgₑ̃ment*.
ℯ	Delete the material circled, as in *July⌀1974 was President Nixon's last full month in office.*
¶	Make a new paragraph.
No¶	Do not begin a new paragraph.
∨ ∧	Insert missing material, as in *The TVA began during the* *Franklin* *Presidency of ∧ Roosevelt.*
⊢	Move the item to the left.
⊣	Move the item to the right.
⦵	Spell out the abbreviation in the text. (This notation usually appears in the margin.)

Guidelines for Usage

A/An Confusion. Use *a* before consonants, *an* before vowels.   **A/An**

Colloquial	**The company requested a audit.**
Standard	**The company requested an audit.**

Adjective/Adverb Confusion. Do not misuse an adjective for an adverb or an adverb for an adjective.   **Adj/Adv**

Misleading	**Laurie felt badly about the erroneous entries in the ledger.**
True	**Laurie felt bad about the erroneous entries in the ledger.**
Colloquial	**You done real good.**
Standard	**You did really well.**
Nonstandard	**I could sure use a new calculator.**
Standard	**I could surely use a new calculator.**

Some of the oppositions cited later, in guidelines WW–3f and Sp–2, are adjective/adverb confusions (for example, *because of/due to* and *all together/altogether*).

Adverbial Noun

Do not use an adverb clause where a noun clause is needed. The words *if* and *because* are adverbs and in standard English should not be used to introduce noun clauses. *When* and *where* are also subject to this error when they are used in definitions.

Instead of	**I'll see if she is here.**
Use	**I'll see whether she is here.**
Instead of	**The reason is because I'm penniless.**
Use	**The reason is that I'm penniless.**
Instead of	**Metathesis is when two letters are transposed.**
Use	**Metathesis is the transposition of two letters.**
or	**Metathesis occurs when two letters are transposed.**

Dangling Expressions *(see also guideline MM).*

Make sure that a participle has a substantive logically to modify. Participles are verbal forms ending in *-ing* (present) and *-ed* (past) and used as adjectives. If the substantive that the participle is to modify is not actually named, the participle is said to dangle.

DglP

Dangling participle	**Rejected by the management, a strike began at midnight.**
Correct	**Rejected by the management, the union went on strike at midnight.**

The most vexing problem is with a present participle at the beginning of a sentence (often passive). Here is how such a dangling participle develops:

Thought 1	**I attended the class.**
Thought 2	**I used a cadaver for experiments.**
Thought 1a	**Attending the class** *(present participle)*
Thought 2a	**A cadaver was used for experiments. (Note that the passive sentence, in eliminating the need to mention the doer of the action, simultaneously eliminates the word which** *attending* **needs to modify.)**
Dangling participle	**Attending the class, a cadaver was used for experiments.**
Correct	**Attending the class, I used a cadaver for experiments.**
Correct	**When I attended the class, a cadaver was used for experiments.**
Correct	**In one of my classes, a cadaver was used for experiments.**

Name the doer of the action of a gerund.   DglG

Dangling gerund	**By standing on the riverbank, a steamboat could be seen.**
Correct	**By standing on a riverbank, I could see a steamboat.**

Incomplete Constructions

Do not leave out any word that is necessary to make a statement or   IC
a comparison logical and complete.

Incomplete   **Richard wanted to pass not only the CPA examination but the bar examination.**

Complete   **Richard wanted to pass not only the CPA examination but also the bar examination.**

Incomplete   **Be specific as possible.**

Complete   **Be as specific as possible.**

*Misplaced Modifiers (*see also *guideline DgIP.)*

Position a modifier and the word modified as close together as possible.   MM

Misplaced   **It is unwise to carry an electromagnet into a computer center that is activated.**

Better   **It is unwise to carry an electromagnet that is activated into a computer center.**

Better still   **It is unwise to carry an activated electromagnet into a computer center.**

A particular problem arises with use of certain words such as *almost, just, nearly,* and *only.* Observe how *only* effects a different meaning in each of the following positions noted by the caret (ˇ):

1   2   3   4   5
ˇThe ˇhouse ˇcosts ˇ$90,000 ˇ.

1. You'll pay an additional fortune for the garage!
2. There's no other house on the block.
3. The house really isn't worth that much.
4. The house doesn't cost any more than that.
5. There's no additional charge in pesos or yen.

Parallelism, Faulty

Make concepts that are parallel in thought parallel in grammatical form. In particular, since a coordinating conjunction must coordinate, be careful to keep coordinate elements on either side of it.   //

Faulty	**Keypunching the cards and to write the program might take all week.**
Parallel	**To keypunch the cards and to write the program might take all week.**
Parallel	**Keypunching the cards and writing the program might take all week.**

Also, be sure to follow each member of correlative pairs *(both . . . and, either . . . or, neither . . . nor, not only . . . but also)* with the same grammatical structure as the other member of the pair.

Faulty	**Both in cost and space, this computer is best.**
Parallel	**In both cost and space, this computer is best.**
Parallel	**Both in cost and in space, this computer is best.**

Passives, Needless *(see also guideline DglP.)*

Avoid needless passives when actives will do the job.   PX

Passive (and stilted)	**The audit was conducted.**
Active (and dynamic, specific)	**Arthur Young conducted the audit.**

Preposition at End of Sentence

Since prepositions at the end of a sentence are native to the English   PrepX
language, avoid them only if by doing so you gain some rhetorical
advantage.

Flat	**This is the desk our best accountant worked herself to death at.**
Periodic	**This is the desk at which our best accountant worked herself to death.**

For most intents, however, this is a rule that you can just forget
about.

Pronoun Problems

Give each pronoun a specific noun to refer to. This problem occurs most often with *it, that, this, they,* and *which.*

PRef

Vague | The accounts had not been audited. This brought about many problems with the Internal Revenue Service.

Proper | The accounts had not been audited. This failure brought about many difficulties with the Internal Revenue Service.

Proper | Failure to audit the accounts brought about many difficulties with the Internal Revenue Service.

Make each pronoun agree with its antecedent in number and gender.

PAgr

1. Use a plural pronoun to refer to a plural noun and a singular pronoun to refer to a singular noun (*see also* guideline SVAgr).
2. If the antecedent is two substantives joined by *and* (as in *X and Y*), make the pronoun plural (such as *they*), unless X and Y form a single unit, as in *bacon and eggs (it).*
3. If the antecedent is two substantives joined by *or* or *nor,* make the pronoun agree with the nearer antecedent.
4. In American usage[2] use a singular pronoun (e.g., *it*) if a collective-noun antecedent is unitary, but if the use of a plural pronoun with a collective-noun antecedent is awkward, then you may wish to recast the sentence.

Unitary | The management agrees with the union about the need for a stock-option plan.

Individual | The management are going to the meeting in separate cars and airplanes.

5. Avoid sex bias in use of pronouns. Commentators sometimes have strong feelings on this matter, but probably you are best advised to avoid the controversy by being sensitive to it.

Don't say | A student should pay his fees.
But say | Students should pay their fees.

Don't say | Call the operator and ask her.
But say | Call the operator and ask.

Don't say	**The employee gradually becomes more concerned about his retirement benefits.**
But say	**The employee gradually becomes more concerned about the retirement benefits.**

6. Treat words following *every (everybody, everyone)* as singular *(every man, woman, and child has his or her problems)*.

7. Understand foreign plurals *(data, memoranda)* as plural in English, too.

Use the proper case of pronoun.   **PCase**

1. Remember that a pronoun takes the case it has in its own clause.

Instead of	**Give the file to whomever asks for it.**
Use	**Give the file to whoever asks for it** *(Whoever* **is the subject of** *asks;* **the object of the preposition** *to* **is the entire clause** *whoever asks for it.)*
Instead of	**This is her you're speaking with.**
Use	**This is she you're speaking with. (The object of** *with* **is an understood** *whom* **or** *that.*)

2. In the formal context use nominative pronouns for all nominative uses.

Say	**Susan and I wrote the program.**
Say	**This is he, speaking.**

3. Use objective pronouns for all objective uses.

Say	**The secretaries gave a party for John and me.**
Say	**Between you and me there is an understanding.**

4. Use the possessive case before a gerund.

Don't say	**I was displeased with him resigning so abruptly.**
But say	**I was displeased with his resigning so abruptly.**

5. Be conscious of courtesy in sequence of pronouns; if you can put yourself last, do so.

Say	**Janice and I are the top salespersons.**

Sentence Fragment

Give each sentence a subject and a verb that do not have any initial subordinating word to prevent them from forming a complete sentence.

FRAG

Fragment	**Because the bookkeeper was drunk**
Sentence	**The bookkeeper was drunk.**

Many times a fragment is actually a clause or phrase that belongs with the preceding sentence but has (erroneously) been punctuated as a sentence by itself. Note the utility of the dash in correcting the problem.

Not this	**Rensselaer Polytechnic Institute is a technological university. The oldest one in the United States.**
But this	**Rensselaer Polytechnic Institute is a technological university—the oldest one in the United States.**

Split Infinitive

A split infinitive is often awkward; if it is, try to avoid it.

Sinf

Awkward	**Virginia decided to, at the last minute, take the CPA review course.**
Better	**At the last minute, Virginia decided to take the CPA review course.**

Subject-Verb Disagreement (see also *guideline PAgr.*)

Make each subject and verb agree in number.

SVAgr

1. Use a singular verb with a singular subject, a plural verb with a plural subject.
2. If the subject is two substantives joined by *and,* as in *X and Y,* make the verb plural, unless *X and Y* forms a single unit (as in *Ham and eggs is a common breakfast*).

Don't say	**Dallas and Houston is the largest cities in Texas.**
But say	**Dallas and Houston are the largest cities in Texas.**

3. If the subject is two substantives joined by *or* or *nor,* make the verb agree with the nearer substantive. (For verbs, this rule applies to agreement in person as well as to agreement in number.)

   Don't say   **Either the accountants or the manager have objected to the new policy.**

   But say   **Either the manager or the accountants have objected to the new policy.**

4. In American English use a singular verb (e.g., *is*) if a collective-noun subject is unitary. If a collective-noun subject is acting as individuals, and a plural is awkward, you should recast the sentence. Instead of *The committee have,* say *The committee members have.*

   Unitary   **The committee has remained firm in its resolve.**

5. In sentences beginning with *there* or *here,* be careful to make the verb agree with the logical subject.

   Colloquial   **There is too few accounting professors.**
   Formal   **There are too few accounting professors.**

6. Treat words after *every (everybody, everyone)* as singular *(every man, woman, and child was present).*

7. Understand foreign plurals *(data, memoranda)* as plural in English, too.

   Don't say   **This data is . . . .**
   But say   **These data are . . . .**

8. Make the verb agree with the real subject, not with the object of an intervening prepositional phrase.

   Not this   **Yesterday's balance of the accounts were correct.**

   But this   **Yesterday's balance of the accounts was correct.**

Tense Problems

1. Use English tenses properly with regard to time.   **TNS**
   a. The present tense describes current happenings *(I am studying accounting),* facts that are always true *(Only women can give birth),* or historical events discussed in

present time *(Hildebrand goes to Canossa and begs for mercy)*.

b.   The past tense describes events in past time.

c.   English expresses future time by using the present tense
   (1) With an adverb of time *(I study accounting tomorrow)*.
   (2) With modal *will* or *shall (I will study accounting)*.
   (3) Through other means, usually the present participle of *go (I am going to study accounting)*.

2.   Use tense consistently.

Don't say	**Geraldine adds up the columns and advised her supervisor about the overrings.**
But say	**Geraldine added [or adds] up the columns and advised [or advises] her supervisor about the overrings.**

3.   If events happen at different times, use auxiliary verbs logically.

Not this	**Peri has been a good skier before she has broken her leg.**
But this	**Peri had been a good skier before she broke her leg.**

Word Misuse

1.   Use logical comparisons. Some adjectives and adverbs are absolute in meaning and do not logically submit to comparison. Examples are *complete, full, perfect,* and *unique.* Instead of saying *fuller/fullest* or *more/most unique,* use *more/most nearly full* or *unique.*   **WL**

2.   Avoid needless use of ink (verbiage).   **WORDY**

Don't write	**Due to the fact that . . . .**
But write	**Because . . . .**
Don't write	**Fill the tank up.**
But write	**Fill the tank.**
Don't write	**Utilize**
But write	**Use**
Don't write	**The ledger which was returned to me was Tom's.**
But write	**The ledger returned to me was Tom's.**

Don't write	**Consensus of opinion**
But write	**Consensus**
Don't write	**And etc.**
But write	**Etc.**

3. Use standard expressions.   **ww**
   a. There is no -*s* on *anywhere, nowhere,* or *a long way.*
   b. The adverbial *kind of* and *sort of* (or *kinda, sorta*) should be omitted or changed to a standard expression such as *rather, somewhat,* or *a little.*
   c. The infinitive sign *to* is preferable to *and* after *try* (i.e., *try to come,* not *try and come*).
   d. Some words in colloquial speech are out of place in formal usage.

Colloquial	**Correct**
Complected	Complexioned
Enthused	Enthusiastic
Irregardless	Regardless or irrespective
Yourn, Yous	Yours
Illiterate past tenses and past participles, such as brung, clumb, knowed, have went, and have wrote	*Correct past tenses and past participles, such as* brought, climbed, knew, have gone, and have written

   e. Some words are more specific than others.

Inexact	**Exact**
Contact	Communicate with, telephone, visit
Great	Famous, large, wonderful
Nice	Attractive, congenial, easygoing, thoughtful

   f. Some expressions that seem alike in some way are actually different. Learn to discriminate between the following words:

Almost	Most
Among	Between
Amount	Number
An	And
As . . . as *(with positive comparison)*	So . . . as *(with negative comparison)*
Because of	Due to
Can	May
Continual	Continuous
Each other	One another
Fewer	Less
Farther	Further
Imply	Infer
In	Into
Lay *(transitive verb)*	Lie *(intransitive verb)*
Oral	Verbal
Raise	Rear *(verb)*
Set *(transitive verb)*	Sit *(intransitive verb)*
Whereas	While

Guidelines for Punctuation

Apostrophe

1. Use the apostrophe to indicate the possessive (genitive) case of all nouns. If the noun ends in *-s,* add only the apostrophe. If the noun does not end in *-s,* add *-'s* for the singular possessive, or end the word with *-s'* in the case of the plural possessive.   **Apos**

Singular Nominative	Singular Possessive	Plural Nominative	Plural Possessive
Thomas	Thomas'	Thomases	Thomases'
Jane	Jane's	Janes	Janes'
company	company's	companies	companies'
woman	woman's	women	women's

2. Use the apostrophe only with the last noun in a series citing joint ownership.

    Individual ownership   **John's and Mary's clothes**

    Joint ownership   **Derrill and Suzanne's advertising agency**

3. Use the apostrophe to indicate the possessive case of *indefinite* pronouns *(everybody's, one's).*
4. Use the apostrophe to stand for the missing elements in contractions *(doesn't, don't, y'all).*
5. Do not use needless apostrophes. The most flagrant violation of this rule is the confusion of the contraction *it's* (for *it is*) with the possessive pronoun *its.* Although some educated people use apostrophes in simple plurals of letters or numbers, there seems to be little justification for the practice. The following procedure is acceptable for indicating simple plurals: *1920s* or *CPAs.*

Brackets

1. Use brackets to insert material into a quotation, as in the following example (*see also* guideline EI):   **Brack**

    Senator Fogbound claimed that "unemployment is no longer an anecdote [sic, *antidote*] *to inflation."*

2. Except in mathematics and in computer languages, use brackets for parentheses inside of parentheses: for example,

   According to Mark Lester, "Grammar is a way of talking about how words are used to make units that communicate a meaning" (Introductory Transformational Grammar of English, *2d ed.* [New York: Holt, Rinehart and Winston, 1976], *p. 13).*

Colon

1. Use a colon to introduce an enumeration, explanation, list, or long quotation (particularly one that contains commas). Guideline Col–2, below, is an example. **Col**

2. Use a colon in the following particular places:
   a. Between title and subtitle, as in Grinder and Elgin's *Guide to Transformational Grammar: History, Theory, Practice.*
   b. Between place of publication and publisher in a citation, as in *New York: Holt, Rinehart, and Winston, 1973.*
   c. Between hours and minutes, as in *11:05 a.m.*
   d. Between sentences, if there is a cause-effect relationship. (This guideline is similar to guideline Semi-1, and should be used sparingly.)
   e. After the salutation (greeting) in a business letter.

3. Do not use a colon that interrupts the syntax.

Unnecessary colon	**We sent technicians to: Birmingham, Leeds, and Manchester.**
Correct	**We sent technicians to Birmingham, Leeds, and Manchester.**
Correct	**We sent technicians to the following: Birmingham, Leeds, and Manchester.**

Comma

1. Do not use a comma to join two independent clauses unless the comma is followed by a coordinating conjunction. This error, called a *comma splice* or *comma fault,* is one of the most serious in punctuation. **Com**

Wrong	**John did not study, therefore he did not pass.**
Right	**John did not study, and therefore he did not pass.**

2. Do not use a comma merely because it "feels good." There are rules that govern the use of commas. In particular, do not use a comma needlessly between subject and verb or between verb and complement:

Not this	**Anne and Tyrone, studied together.**
But this	**Anne and Tyrone studied together.**

3. Do not use a comma before an indirect quotation or before a quotation that runs on with the sentence:

Indirect quotation	**Eleanor said that she would not go.**
Running text	**Paul urged the Romans to be "Not slothful in business" (Romans 12:11 KJV).**

4. Use a comma before a coordinating conjunction *(and, or, nor, but)* joining two independent clauses. For example:

The financial planner applied the new formula, and the long-term forecast became much more optimistic.

5. Use the comma after any verbal material that precedes the independent clause.

Correct	**When Bonnie finished the examination, she forgot to hand in the answer sheet.**
Correct	**In preparing this form, you should write everything in ink.**

6. Use the comma to set off an appositive (*see also* guideline DASH–1).

Correct	**Kimberly Shipman, our last supervisor, transferred to Alaska.**

7. Use the comma to set off a nonessential relative clause.

Correct	**Thomas Darden Willis, who sits in the back row, gave an excellent presentation.**

8. Use the comma to separate words in a series.

Correct	**Mark wrote the COBOL program quickly, neatly, and accurately.**

9. Use the comma to separate adjectives that independently modify a noun.

   Correct   **Gretchen became involved in a long, expensive lawsuit.**

10. Use the comma to set off a noun of address.

    Correct   **What do you think, Trevor, about this solution?**

11. Use the comma before a short direct quotation.

    Correct   **John Paul Jones said, "I have not yet begun to fight."**

12. Use the comma to separate contrasted elements.

    Correct   **Take the blue form, not the red one, to the bursar.**

13. Use the comma for the following purposes:
    a. To set off *yes* or *no* from the rest of a sentence.
    b. To set off conjunctive adverbs—particularly *however.*
    c. To set off tag questions:

       Correct   **Thaddeus is stupid, isn't he?**

    d. To separate certain items in dates.

       Correct   **July 1987 is the termination date.**
       Correct   **July 1, 1987, is the termination date.**
       Correct   **The termination date is 1 July 1987.**

    e. To separate items in addresses (except state and zip code).
    f. To stand for nonrepeated elements.

       Correct   **The red form goes to the registrar; the blue one, to the bursar.**

    g. To aid clarity as needed.
14. Remember that a comma on one side of an item to set it off generally requires a complementary comma on the other side of the item.

    Correct   **The contract is to expire at noon on July 1, 1987, when the new contract takes effect.**

Dash

1. Use the dash to set off an appositive that   DASH
   a. Has commas inside of it.
   b. Is separated from the substantive to which it refers.

   John's book was widely read—a bestseller for months.

2. Use dashes, instead of parentheses, if the material set off is to be emphasized.
3. Remember that a dash on one side of an item to set if off generally requires a complementary dash on the other side of the item.

Ellipsis Marks

1. Use ellipsis marks (spaced periods) to show an omission within   EI
   a quotation (*see also* guideline Brack–1).
2. Type ellipsis marks to conform to the following:
   a. Three spaced periods show an omission within a sentence.
   b. Four periods show an omission that crosses over a sentence boundary; one period marks the end of the sentence, and it is followed by three spaced periods.
   c. An entire line of spaced periods indicates the omission of at least a paragraph.

Exclamation Point

Use the exclamation mark only occasionally to show strong emotion.   Excl

Hyphen

1. Use the hyphen to separate the whole number from the fraction   Hyph
   in a mixed number, as in *3-5/16.*
2. Use the hyphen in compound words, such as *self-actualization.*
3. Use the hyphen between compound (unit) modifiers, as in a *36-inch pointer* or a *computer-scored answer sheet.*

4. Do not use the hyphen
    a. Between words that merely follow each other.

    - Compound modifier   - 20-dollar bills (= $20 × ?quantity)

    - Separate modifiers   - 20 dollar bills (= 20 × $1)

    - Compound modifier   - A deep-dredged canal

    - Adverb and adjective   - A deeply dredged canal

    b. In hyphenation at the end of a line if
        (1) The entire word is less than seven letters.
        (2) The division does not occur between syllables.
        (3) The word is part of a proper name.
        (4) The line is at the end of a page.
        (5) The hyphenated word comes immediately after or before another hyphen or dash.
        (6) There are several other hyphenated words on the page. (Hyphenation is at best a privilege to be used sparingly.)
        (7) The manuscript is to be submitted to a publisher.

Parentheses (Round Brackets)

1. Use parentheses for supplementary remarks or for references in the text (Joseph N. Ulman Jr. and Jay R. Gould, *Technical Reporting,* 3d ed. [New York: Holt, Rinehart and Winston, 1972], pp. 197–198).   **Paren**
2. If the sentence element before the parentheses requires a mark of punctuation, place the mark of punctuation after the closing parenthesis. Ulman and Gould (page 197), while discussing parentheses, also cite this rule.
3. Use parentheses to enclose the area code for a telephone number: (504) 345–2063.
4. Use parentheses in pairs.

    Not this   1)
    But this   (1)

Period (Full Stop)

1. Use the period at the end of a declarative or unemotional imperative sentence or after a polite *would-you-please* request.   **Pd**
2. Use the period with certain abbreviations (U.S., f.o.b., I.O.O.F.,

P.D.Q.), but not with others (CIA, CYA, NCR, TVA). If use of the period is optional, then be consistent (if am, then pm; if a.m., then p.m.).

3. Use the period for a decimal point.

Question Mark

1. Use the question mark for a direct question, but not for an indirect question.   QM

> Correct   **Judy asked, "Did I hurt someone's feelings yesterday?"**
>
> Correct   **Judy asked whether she hurt someone's feelings yesterday.**

2. Use the question mark in parentheses to express doubt about the material preceding the parentheses.

    John's new (?) car was a Model T.

3. Do not follow the question mark immediately with a comma, a period, or a semicolon.

Quotation Marks

1. Use quotation marks to enclose a speaker's or writer's exact   Quo
    words.
2. If a quotation extends over more than one paragraph, use opening quotation marks before each quoted paragraph, closing quotation marks only at the end of the quotation.
3. Use quotation marks to enclose the title of a work that is published as part of a book—for example, the titles of short stories, chapters, poems (*see also* guideline Und–1).
4. Position the closing quotation marks as follows if there is an immediately adjacent mark of punctuation:
    a. The comma or the period *always* goes inside (to the left of) the closing "quotation marks."
    b. The colon or the semicolon *always* goes outside (to the right of) the closing "quotation marks":
    c. The exclamation point or the question mark goes inside if part of the quotation, outside if part of the sentence surrounding the quotation.

Correct	**Mary said, "When will I see you again?"**
Correct	**Did Mary say, "I will see you again tomorrow"?**
Correct	**Did Mary say, "When will I see you again?"?**

5. Use single quotation marks for quotes within quotes; inside the single quotes revert to double quotation marks.

Correct	**John said, "Bill claimed, 'I have read the section entitled "Recognizable Patterns of Language." ' "**

6. Use quotation marks only sparingly to indicate words used in a special (sometimes satiric) sense; do not use quotation marks as decorations.

7. Although quotation marks may be used in tabular columns to indicate repetition, do not use quotation marks for other abbreviations. (For *inches* and *feet,* spell the words out or use the standard abbreviations *in.* and *ft.*)

8. Do not use quotation marks to surround material that is separated from the text, indented and single spaced, unless these quotation marks are in the original quote. (The layout by itself indicates that the material is being quoted; quotation marks are therefore redundant.)

Semicolon

1. Use the semicolon to separate independent clauses that are intimately joined in logic.   Semi

Correct	**Semicolons are one thing; commas are another.**

2. Use the semicolon to join clauses or items that have internal commas.

Confusing	**Attending the meeting were Joseph Biggs, Laramie, Wyoming, president, David L. Carson, Troy, New York, secretary, and Allen White, Duncan, Oklahoma, treasurer.**
Clear	**Attending the meeting were Joseph Biggs, Laramie, Wyoming, president; David L. Carson, Troy, New York, secretary; and Allen White, Duncan, Oklahoma, treasurer.**

Guideline Semi–2 sometimes works together with guideline Com–4, as in

> *Suzanne, afraid of the final examination, studied frantically while drinking tea, coffee, and Royal Crown Cola; and, in the end, she fell asleep during the test.*

3. Use the semicolon only between grammatically equal units. Do not use it, for example, between a dependent clause and an independent clause:

Wrong	**While Sara studied to be a CPA; her boyfriend found a new lady.**
Right	**While Sara studied to be a CPA, her boyfriend found a new lady.**

Sentence Punctuation Error

Use only a period, a semicolon, a colon, a dash, or a comma plus coordinating conjunction to join two independent clauses.   **SPE**

See also guideline Com–1.

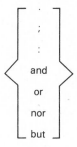

S_1
This is the first
independent clause.

and

or

nor

but

S_2
This (or this) is the
second independent
clause.

Spacing

In typewritten work be careful to use spaces as follows: **#**

1. Space twice after the period that ends a sentence.
2. Insert spaces between the dots in ellipses.
3. Space at least twice between the state and the zip code (or postal zone).

Correct	The vendor is The Bible Shop, Post Office Box 2491, Hammond, Louisiana 70404-2491.
Correct	Mr. W. R. O'Donnell lectures in the Department of Linguistics and Phonetics, The University of Leeds, Leeds, West Yorkshire LS2 9JT, England.

4. Do not space before or after either the hyphen or the dash.

Underline (Underscore) Errors

Use underlining (underscoring) for the same functions as italicizing in print.   **Und**

1. Underline the titles of separately published works such as books and periodicals (*See also* guideline Quo–3).
2. Underline expressions used as themselves.

Correct	The word <u>word</u> should be underlined when used as a word.
Correct	John's writing <u>32</u> instead of <u>23</u> in the last column caused the total to be $9 too high.

3. Underline foreign words and expressions that have not become fully anglicized.

Correct	The evaluator claimed that Ian's argument was <u>post hoc ergo propter hoc</u>.

4. Underline the names of vehicles, particularly ships.

Correct	David received valuable business experience while serving as disbursing officer aboard USS <u>Berkeley</u> (DDG 15).
Correct	Charles Lindbergh's <u>Spirit of St. Louis</u> is now in the Smithsonian Institution.

Virgule (Slash)

Use the slash to indicate alternative possibilities.   **Slash**

- Alternative telephone numbers
- One may telephone the message to Richard at (504) 345-3682/2063.

Guidelines for Spelling and Capitalization

Spelling

1. Spell words in accordance with the dictionary. English spelling　Sp
   is more or less regular, but rules to describe it usually become
   submerged in exceptions. It is a fact that people who read a lot
   tend to spell well; it's partly a matter of pattern recognition.
   Some of the most troublesome words are listed below (Table
   2). Thirty of the most troublesome words are underlined.

2. Differentiate between expressions that are alike in pronunciation but different in meaning or syntactical function. The following similar sounding expressions are sometimes confused:

Accept / except	**Led / lead**
Affect / effect	**May be / maybe**
All ready / already	**Passed / past**
All together / altogether	**Principal / principle**
Any one / anyone	**Right / write**
Capital / capitol	**Some time / sometime**
Cede / seed	**Stationary / Stationery**
Cite / sight / site	**Their / there / they're**
Faze / phase	**To / too / two**
Its (*possessive pronoun*) /	**Who's / whose**
**　it's (contraction for *it is*)**	**your / you're**

3. Spell out the words for symbols unless you really need to save
   space.

Not this	@	But this	at
	¢		cent *or* cents
	#		number (*or* tons)
	%		percent

   The # symbol has different meanings and in any case is often
   redundant before a number. Why should one write *Apartment
   #B727* when *Apartment B727* will suffice?

4. Leave the name of an organization exactly as it is officially—for
   example, *Texas Tech University,* not Texas Tech. University
   and not *Texas Technological University.* (This guideline also
   applies to punctuation—for example, *Holt, Rinehart & Winston,*
   not *Holt, Rinehart, and Winston.*)

Table 2 Potential Spelling Difficulties

a lot	convenience	interest	performance	repetition
absence	coolly	interface	permissible	rhythm
accessible	cylinder	interpret	persistent	ridiculous
accidentally	decision	irresistible	personal	schedule
accommodate	definitely	irritable	personnel	seize
accommodation	definition	laboratory	picnic	sense
accurate	define	ledger	picnicking	separate
achievement	describe	leisure	possession	separation
acquaintance	description	license	possible	sergeant
acquire	desirable	lose	practical	sheriff
among	despair	loose	precede	shining
analogous	development	losing	predictable	similar
analyze	disappear	maintenance	preference	studying
apparent	disappoint	maneuver	preferred	succeed
appropriate	disastrous	marriage	prejudiced	succession
arguing	discriminate	mere	prepare	suddenness
argument	drunkenness	misspelling	prevalent	superintendent
assistant	efficiency	moral	privilege	supersede
attorneys	embarrassment	morale	probably	supposed
balloon	environment	mortgage	procedure	surprise
beginning	equipped	necessary	proceed	technique
belief	exaggerate	newsstand	profession	than
believe	exceed	ninety	professor	then
beneficent	excellence	noticeable	prominent	thorough
beneficial	existence	occasionally	pronunciation	through
benefited	existent	occurred	propeller	tragedy
carburetor	experience	occurrence	psychology	transferred
category	explanation	occurring	ptomaine	tries
changeable	fascinate	offered	pursue	truly
choose	forty	offering	quantity	undoubtedly
chose	government	omitted	questionnaire	unnecessary
coming	grammar	opinion	quiet	until
committee	grievous	opportunity	realize	using
comparative	guarantee	original	receipt	vacuum
conscience	height	paid	receive	varies
conscientious	holiday	pamphlet	receiving	vicious
conscious	imagine	panicky	recommended	villain
consensus	immediately	parallel	referred	weird
consistent	incidentally	paralyze	referring	woman
controversial	indispensable	part-time	relevant	writing
controversy	insistent	pastime	renowned	written

Numbers and Numerals

Use numbers and numerals according to the business writing con-   **Num**
ventions. (The following numbered guidelines are arranged in increasing power or importance.)

1.   Write as numerals all numbers above ten (*11* and up) whether
     positive or negative.
2.   Express all numbers containing decimals as numerals.

3.   Use a cipher (even if *0*) to fill decimal notation (i.e., write 1.0, not 1., and 0.1, not .1).

4.   As a general rule use numerals with any unit of measure, even if below 11. Units of measure include money, time, dates, addresses, age, volume numbers, and arithmetic calculations, in addition to bushels, inches, meters, etc.

5.   Differentiate series running together:

George had five 12-column ledgers and twelve 9-column ledgers.

6.   Spell out any number coming immediately at the beginning of a sentence. (There are no capital numerals.)

7.   Be consistent. (For example, if you type a paper that has the fractions 1/2 and 3/16, you must type the ½ as 1/2, and not by using the ½ key on the typewriter, since there is no *3/16* key.)

See also guideline Hyph–1.

Capitalizing

1.   In material to be capitalized, except in headings and other situations in which you use all capitalization (ALL CAPS), capitalize the first letter of nouns, verbs, adjectives, and adverbs.

   a.   Capitalize the first letter of the first word in such material even if the word is not a noun, verb, adjective, or adverb.

   b.   You may capitalize prepositions longer than four letters, if you wish, but be consistent.

Inconsistent	***Communicating through Letters and Reports** was written after the War Between the States.*
Consistent	***Communicating through Letters and Reports** was written after the War between the States.*
Consistent	***Communicating Through Letters and Reports** was written after the War Between the States.*

2.   Capitalize the following:

   a.   Names of deities and of titles of scripture books.

   b.   Works such as books, articles, poems, stories.

   c.   Important documents (the *Magna Carta,* the *Declaration of Independence.*)

   d.   Days, holidays, months, and historical periods (*the Enlightenment).*

   e.   First word in a sentence.

f.   Languages (*see also* guideline 1c–4b).

g.   Organizations *(IBM, Ku Klux Klan, Roman Catholic Church),* but preserve the capitalization that the organization uses officially (for example, *E. I. du Pont de Nemours & Company,* not *E. I. DuPont De Nemours and Company*).

h.   Places and regions *(the Sahara, the South)* (*see also* guideline 1c–4c).

i.   Names of streets and other thoroughfares.

j.   Title when followed by a name *(Miss Alice Young, Professor Yaney).*

k.   *Father, Mother, Brother, Sister,* etc., when used like a given name, as in the salutation or greeting of a friendly letter *(Dear Mom).*

l.   *President* whenever used with reference to the chief executive of the United States of America.

m.   Certain nouns if followed by numbers, as in *Apartment B727.*

n.   Nouns intended to stand for an entity that would be capitalized. *(College,* for example, would be capitalized if intended to stand for the College of Business Administration in a particular university, but not if used in the sense of *Joe went to college.)*

3.   Be consistent in capitalization of comparable words.

Wrong	**The class contained both blacks and Whites.**
Wrong	**The class contained both Blacks and whites.**
Acceptable	**The class contained both blacks and whites.**
Acceptable	**The class contained both Blacks and Whites.**
Correct	**The officers present were Bonnie Campbell (President) and Pat Underwood (Treasurer).**
Also correct (consistent)	**The officers present were Bonnie Campbell (president) and Pat Underwood (treasurer).**

4.   Use lower-case (small) letters for   lc

a.   Seasons of the year *(winter).*

b.   Academic subjects not otherwise capitalized.

Correct	**Brenda, Dee, and Terry respectively studied management, Roman history, and English.**

c.   Simple directions, as on a compass (*see also* guideline Cap–2h).

Correct	**When he worked in the North, John's office was on the south side of a busy street.**

Footnotes

[1]Additionally, *that* may function to introduce a clause used as a noun, or function as a demonstrative adjective: The ledger *that I audited* is on the desk (relative clause); I saw *that the ledger was audited* (noun clause); *That ledger* is the one I audited (demonstrative adjective).

[2]Note that British standards differ from American standards in some pronunciations, and in several other ways. A few examples:

a.   British collective nouns (e.g., *committee, company*) are always plural.

b.   British occasionally exercises different syntactical choices *(Have you got the time?* and *Is our policy different to yours?* as opposed to American *Do you have the time?* and *Is our policy different from yours?).*

c.   British has certain vocabulary items which are unknown in American, and *vice-versa.* Examples are *bloke* and *zebra crossing* (crosswalk) in British and *sidewalk* and *automobile* in American.

d.   Words have different meaning in the two dialects. *e.g.,* in American *to table a motion* usually means, in effect, to kill it; but in British *to table a motion* means to schedule it for a vote.

e.   British punctuation uses single quotation marks where American uses double quotation marks.

f.   Spelling is often different *(civilization/civilisation, color/colour, connection/connexion, maneuver/manoeuvre).*

We should be aware of these and other differences, and exercise special care in international business communications.

The Legal Environment of Business and Business Communications

Wesley C. King, Jr., J.D., University of Georgia;
Member Georgia Bar prepared Appendix B.

In this appendix we will clear up some misconceptions about the law and alert you to particular areas within the law which have a direct bearing on business communication, both written and oral, and on business. To accomplish these objectives, however, you must first understand both the role of the courts in our government and the process of making law.

The Judicial System

The judicial system in our government consists of two independent court systems: federal and state. On the federal level, the judicial hierarchy ranges from district court to circuit court to the supreme court. In addition, the U.S. court of claims and federal tax court handle specialized questions dealing with claims against the federal government and federal tax disputes with the Internal Revenue Service. By constitutional authorization, the supreme court has the ultimate authority to decide any question of federal law which reaches the supreme court through the appeals process.

On the state level, the hierarchy is more varied but generally ranges from superior court to court of appeals to state supreme court. The state supreme court generally has state constitutional authority to decide any questions dealing with state law. Interaction between state and federal courts occurs only when a conflict arises between state law and federal law; otherwise, each court system acts autonomously.

Law comes in two forms: statutory law and common law. Statutory law comes into being through passage of a statute by the state legislature on the state level or by Congress on the federal level. Common law is judicial, judge-made law which comes into being either by judicial interpretation of a statute or by judicial decision of a case when no applicable statute exists. Whereas statutory law has the express approval of the legislature, the common law is simply those principles, usages, and rules of action which do have authority upon any express and positive declaration of the legislature's will.

To compare and contrast statutory law with common law, consider the following hypothetical statute: A debtor shall be considered in default of any bill which is legally due if the creditor has not received payment by the due date. This statute would seem to establish a rather hard and fast rule easily applied to all situations. Imagine, however, the insurance premium for your business is due December 31, and on December 27, you mail a check for the full amount due. Because of the holiday mail lag, the insurance company does not receive your check in its accounting office until January 4. Are you in default of your payment? Can the insurance company, relying on the statute, cancel your policy because of the delay in receiving your payment?

A strict interpretation of the statute would favor the insurance company's cancellation. However, if you have acted in good faith in complying with the statute, the court will probably invoke the common law Mail Box Acceptance Rule which says that the law deems the payment to be received by the insurance company once the payment is in the mail and thus is beyond your control.

Business and the Law

Now that you have a general understanding of the two court systems and the two types of law, you are ready to consider the particular areas of law which have a direct bearing on the business world and on business communications. These areas include:

1. Defamation
2. Right of privacy
3. Fraud (misrepresentation)
4. Interference with advantageous relations
5. Warranties and other consumer protections
6. Products liability
7. Employment.

Defamation

The question is not can you speak your mind, but rather to whom and to what extent can you do so. Composed of the twin wrongs of libel (written or printed defamation) and slander (spoken and heard defamation), defamation is the offense which tends to injure a person's reputation or character by false statements. To prove defamation, you must show four elements:

1.   The language must be *defamatory;* that is, the language must adversely affect one's reputation or good standing within the community. Generally, words which tend to impeach one's honesty, integrity, virtue, sanity, or financial soundness are defamatory. Some words are defamatory per se, such as *criminal, liar, cheat,* or *bastard.*

Other words are defamatory only when judged by the tenor of the times. For example, a 1917 Texas case declared the words *having brainstorms* to be defamatory; today, these same words would be complimentary. Other examples which today might not prove to be defamatory include *rascal* (1843—Tennessee), *skunk* (1887—Wisconsin), and *hypocrite* (1889—Florida). Still others which today we find more humorous than defamatory include: "My opinion of you is that you are the sort of man that would steal his mother's bones from the grave and sell them to buy flowers for a harlot" (1910—

New York) and "Leave the old skunk to himself to stink himself to death" (1887—Georgia).

2. The words must be communicated to a third person—that is, to a person other than the person defamed. Thus, you may tell Employee X to his face with no witnesses that he is a thief and a crook, but you would not be able to tell anyone else that Employee X is a crook without being liable for defamation. To be slanderous, the words need only be spoken to a third person in a language understood by that person. To be libelous, the communication need only be embodied in some permanent form which a third person can see; thus, a motion picture or a statue can be libelous.

3. The defamatory language must be of or concerning the person defamed; the language must identify the person defamed to a reasonable reader, listener, or viewer. Thus, to say "All people are crooks" is not defamatory, since the reasonable person will not impute dishonesty to the reputation of all people. On the other hand, to say "All clerks at XYZ Department Store are crooks" is defamatory, since the reasonable person will impute dishonesty to this identifiable group of people.

4. Actual damage to the reputation of the person defamed must occur among a substantial segment of the community, although most courts allow damage among a small group to suffice.

Four categories of words that the courts have generally declared defamatory per se are:

1. Words affecting a person in his trade, business, or profession. The words must directly relate to the person's trade, business, or profession to be defamatory per se. Examples include calling a doctor a quack, a lawyer a shyster, a surgeon a butcher, a merchant a cheat, or an office holder an accepter of bribes.

2. Words attributing a loathsome and communicable disease to the plaintiff. The courts have historically limited this category to venereal disease or leprosy.

3. Words imputing a crime to the plaintiff. To be defamatory, the crime must involve moral turpitude (adultery, sodomy, murder, etc.) and not simply be a violation of the law (for example, a parking ticket).

4. Words imputing unchaste behavior to a woman. This category is operative only in some jurisdictions.

Assume, then, that you have spoken words which are defamatory. There are defenses available to you. Truth, consent, and privilege (absolute and qualified) provide a defense against charges of defamation.

1. **Truth** is an absolute defense to defamation. Defamation involves injury to reputation through false statements. Thus, a statement cannot be both true and defamatory. You should be aware, however, that even though a true statement cannot give rise to defamation liability, it can give rise to liability for an invasion of privacy or for intentional infliction of emotional distress.

2. **Consent** from the defamed person to publish or speak the defamatory words is an absolute defense.

3. **Privilege** denotes a legal right to do something, in this case to communicate defamatory information. A privilege can be either absolute or qualified.

 a. **Absolute privilege.** In judicial, legislative, and executive proceedings, an absolute privilege generally applies. Thus, in a trial, all statements made in relation to that trial are deemed not to be defamatory, as are all remarks by legislators made during hearings or floor debates. Similarly, a government executive official is privileged while performing part of the duties of the office. The officials, however, have no privilege when they willingly speak defamatory words which do not pertain to the performance of official duties.

 An absolute privilege likewise applies to communication between spouses and to broadcasters of compelled broadcasts, such as equal time political broadcasts compelled by federal regulation.

 b. **Qualified privilege.** Under the Supreme Court's 1964 *New York Times* rule, you have a qualified privilege to defame either a public official or a public figure so long as the defaming is without actual malice (an intent to injure or an actual knowledge of injury). A public official is one holding public office or one who is voluntarily in the public eye. A public figure is one who has involuntarily achieved fame or notoriety; for example, a sports figure, a university athletic director, or a retired general voluntarily involved in school integration.

 Other situations in which a qualified privilege against defamation will apply are reports of public meetings or hearings, fair comment and criticism of general public interest, and comments made between two parties concerning a third party in which both have an interest in the information and neither is acting as a busybody (for example, a reference letter from a former employer to a prospective employer about a job applicant).

Realizing how the law of defamation operates, you can see how it affects communication in a commercial setting. Obviously, business communication should be devoid of malice, not only because malice is inappropriate, but also because it generally is evidence of defamation. Instead of violent or abusive language, you should remain objective and rational. Furthermore, you should stick to the subject at hand; if a prospective employer requests information concerning a former employee who has applied for a custodial job, do not exceed the scope of the inquiry by relaying the rumor that the former employee is an alleged spouse beater. This information has no bearing on custodial abilities. On the other hand, if the position is for a counselor in a marriage crisis unit, rumors of spouse abuse, if substantiated, are germane to the inquiry; you should not be reluctant to relay this information.

If you are aware of some damaging, although pertinent, information about a job applicant, you have both a duty to communicate this information as well as a duty to protect yourself from a defamation suit. Since truth is a defense to defamation, you should have sufficient documentation to substantiate any specific claim. Do not simply level a charge ("Former employee X is a thief.") without being able to go to some official records for verification. Also, when giving information about a job applicant, look for an open-ended question which will allow you to state your opinion concerning the former employee. Such questions are often phrased: Are you aware of any other information which will assist us in evaluating the applicant? Likewise, when requesting information, ask an open-ended question so the respondent will feel free to divulge all relevant information— both positive and negative—about the applicant.

You should also make the receiver of your communication aware that you prefer that your communication remain confidential. Marking the envelope *personal* or *confidential* is a good idea; also be sure that the envelope is not transparent enough to reveal the contents of the letter when held up to a light.

Probably the best safeguard against defamation is to have the person who is the subject of the communication sign a waiver (consent form) releasing all parties from liability for all information provided. If the applicant does not sign such a waiver, then the federal Freedom of Information Act may allow access to the file, which makes a lawsuit possible.

Above all, let good faith and fair dealing dictate the content and motivation of your communication. Provide accurate information, do not be negligent, act without malice, and employ integrity and circumspection in all your communication, and the law will protect you.

Right of Privacy

A former U.S. supreme court justice declared the right of privacy to be based on the right of every American "to be let alone." An invasion of privacy is a violation of this right to be let alone and to remain unnoticed if so chosen. The right of privacy encompasses four distinct wrongs:

1. Intrusion into a person's physical solitude is an invasion of the right of privacy. Examples include wiretapping a telephone or bugging a bedroom.

2.   Disclosure of private facts about a person is a violation of the right of privacy even though the facts are true. Unlike the truthfulness defense to defamation, the truth of the statement is immaterial in violation of the right of privacy because the right to be protected here is simply the right to be let alone.

3.   Appropriation of a person's name or likeness for another's commercial advantage is an invasion of the right of privacy. Generally, the courts limit recovery to the use of a person's name or picture in connection with promotion or advertisement of a product.

4.   Any publication which places a person in a false light in the public eye is a violation of the right to privacy. To place a person in a false light, you need only attribute views that the person does not hold or actions that he or she did not take.

For example, two professional models pose for a shoe ad and sign releases (consent forms) consenting to unrestricted use of their photographs. When the ad appears the legend reads: "Walk the streets at night in Streetwalker Shoes. We do." Has the advertising company invaded the privacy of the two models? Probably so. Even though the models consented to unrestricted use of their photographs, they never contemplated that the ad would attribute the world's oldest profession to them personally. They consented to their photograph in a shoe ad, not to a promotion of prostitution.

In a commercial setting, the two most common defenses to a violation of the right of privacy are either that the person consented to the alleged violation of the right of privacy or that the person is a newsworthy public figure by virtue of public notoriety. If the models in the shoe ad had signed a waiver which included the copy of the ad as it appeared, they would have consented to what would otherwise be a violation of their right of privacy. Likewise, public figures like Ronald Reagan, the Rolling Stones, Bette Midler, and to an extent, very visible corporate executives like Ted Turner do not enjoy the same immunity from public scrutiny that the ordinary citizen enjoys simply because they have voluntarily placed themselves in the public eye.

Note that the four distinct wrongs which make up the right of privacy deal with rights of the individual. Therefore, you should not find it surprising that the right of privacy is not available to either a partnership or to a corporation. In recent years, industrial espionage has used technological wonders, such as telephoto lenses, infrared cameras, and sonic wave measuring devices, to spy on everything from the competition's models of new products and designs left on a desk beside a window to the computer activity inside a windowless building. These wrongs are not violations of privacy. Other remedies (larceny, constructive conversion, etc.) are available to the wronged corporation; however, a claim of a violation of the right of privacy is not, since it is strictly a right of an individual.

Fraud

Fraud is a false representation of a matter of fact which deceives and is intended to deceive. The fraud can be by words or conduct, by false or misleading allegations, or by concealing some fact that should have been disclosed. To prove fraud, you must prove these elements:

1. The defendant made a misrepresentation of a past or present material fact.
2. The defendant made the misrepresentation knowing it was false or made it with a reckless disregard for its truth or falsity.
3. The defendant intended to induce the deceived person to rely on the false statement.
4. The deceived person must have actually relied on the false statement and must have been justified in so doing.
5. The deceived person must have suffered some actual monetary damage as a result of relying on the false statement.

Generally, statements of opinion are not fraudulent because such statements are not fact and because you cannot justifiably rely on them.

Take, for example, a used car salesperson's pitch: "This is a clean car; it will get the job done for you. Yes sir, this is a fine automobile. The best thing on the road." Such statements are simply puffing (seller's talk to bolster a product) and are not meant to misrepresent a material fact. However, if the same salesperson said, "Yes sir, 15,000 miles is the total actual mileage of this car," and knew that the actual mileage was 115,000, then this statement would be grounds for fraud if you reasonably relied on the statement and suffered damages because of it. (The monetary damages here would be the loss of the bargain from buying a car with 100,000 more miles on it than you were lead to believe.)

On the other hand, if you were familiar with the actual mileage yet bought the car anyway, you could not successfully claim fraud. The wrong the law seeks to remedy here is being induced to be an unwilling victim of fraud. If you have superior knowledge but nonetheless choose to become a willing victim, the law will allow you to suffer the consequences.

Some cases of fraud are not so clear cut as the used car example. Suppose you have built a house with a septic tank system installed by competent workers. You sell the house and tell the buyer that the septic system is adequate. To your surprise and the buyer's dismay, the workers had failed to seal an outlet pipe and the resulting leak contaminated the well water used in the house. The buyer sues you for fraud.

Obviously, you have made a misrepresentation of a material fact, but you neither knew that your statement was false nor intended to deceive. In cases like this where the law of fraud would provide an inadequate remedy, the courts look to the equities involved and attempt to balance the scales. The question the court will ask is: Who should bear the loss, the builder/seller or the completely innocent purchaser? In this case, as you might expect, the court ruled for the purchaser.

Interference with Advantageous Relations

Just as individuals have a right to be let alone, they also have a right to run a business and to make and to perform contracts without wrongful interference by another. If you intentionally interfere with the performance of a contract or if you engage in unfair competition, you are guilty of interference with advantageous relations. Unfair competition applies to all dishonest or fraudulent rivalry in business but particularly to the substitution of your goods for those of another by unethically imitating or counterfeiting the distinctive characteristics of the dominant goods—for example imitating the color, shape, wrapping, name, logo, or any other distinctive characteristic.

For the businessperson, interference with advantageous relations is more a protective shield from the unscrupulous than a sword of attack to be used against competitors. The courts try to protect the legitimate interests of time and expenditure that a business invests in engineering, testing, and marketing a product. The courts do not attempt to squelch either legitimate competition or a valid competitive edge in bargaining for the best contract terms available. Just as in defamation and the right of privacy, the courts simply police the interference and intermeddling of one person (or business) into the affairs of another.

Warranties and Other Consumer Protections

Caveat emptor (let the buyer beware) has historically been the rule not the exception. However, as commerce became more global and more complex, Congress and various state legislatures realized that the average consumer needed uniform protection and that businesspersons needed consistency within the law to be able to carry on commerce more effectively. The Magnuson-Moss Warranty Act of 1975 epitomized congressional concern, and the Uniform Commercial Code (passed in all states except Louisiana) reflects this concern on the state level. Both acts are attempts to standardize what was otherwise a fragmented, piecemeal approach to consumer protection.

The Magnuson-Moss Warranty Act attempts to sort out the various types of consumer products warranties, to specify warranty provisions and minimum standards, and to spell out the legal remedies available to consumers. Specifically, the Act provides that:

in order to improve the adequacy of information available to consumers, prevent deception, and improve competition in the marketing of consumer products, any warrantor warranting a product to a consumer by means of a written warranty shall . . . fully and conspicuously disclose in simple and readily understood language the terms and condition of such warranty.

The Act specifies that a warranty for any consumer product costing $5 or more shall comply with the Act's provisions. Furthermore, if the product costs more than $10 and has a warranty, the warranty must be labeled either a *full warranty* or a *limited warranty*. A full warranty guarantees repair or replacement without charge of a defective product within a reasonable time. A limited warranty guarantees repair or replacement without charge of a defective product within a time specified by the warranty. To avoid the requirements of the Act, some manufacturers, however, prefer limited warranties because they can spell out the particulars of the warranty including any exclusions.

The Uniform Commercial Code (UCC) is state law passed: to simplify, clarify, and modernize the law governing commercial transactions; to permit continued expansion of commercial practices through custom, usage and agreement of the parties; and to make uniform the laws among the various jurisdictions.

The UCC deals with two types of warranties: express and implied. Both the full and the limited warranties under the federal Magnuson-Moss Act are express warranties in that they express the terms of each. An implied warranty is a warranty imposed by law and is either a warranty of merchantability (that is, the goods are fit for the ordinary purpose for which such goods are normally used) or a warranty of fitness for a particular purpose (that is, the goods are fit for the particular purpose at the time of the sale, and the buyer relies on the seller's skill or judgment to select suitable goods). Under either of the UCC's implied warranties, a consumer as well as a businessperson purchasing inventory has a remedy for defective or unsuitable goods even if the product itself has no warranty under the Magnuson-Moss Act.

Products Liability

Products liability refers to the legal liability of manufacturers and sellers to compensate buyers, users, and even bystanders for damages or injuries suffered because of defects in a product. Products liability makes a manufacturer and oftentimes a seller liable if a product has a defective condition that makes the product unreasonably dangerous to the consumer. There is a distinction between the interests that the warranty law protects and the interests products liability law protects. The warranty law safeguards the monetary interest in the consumer good itself. The products liability law looks to the physical interest of a consumer in not being injured by an unreasonably dangerous product.

Some manufacturers attempt to avoid liability for their products by including in the sales contract *sold as is, sold with no warranty as to safety of the product,* or *sold with all faults.* Courts most often treat such disclaimers of the implied warranty as void because the disclaimer runs against public policy which requires manufacturers to take all reasonable precautions to make products safe for normal use.

Recognizing that some federal mechanism was necessary to police safety standards for consumer products, Congress established the Consumer Products Safety Commission in 1972. The commission has authority over all consumer products except tobacco products, poisons, foods, drugs, cosmetics, aircraft, boats, motor vehicles and equipment, and firearms and ammunition; other regulatory agencies oversee the safety standards of these products. The commission's five commissioners are appointed by the President to set safety standards for consumer products, to research and investigate product safety, and to take action against products deemed hazardous. The commission has the authority to ban a product it deems unsafe, to compel a recall for repair of a product, to order a replacement, or to require a pro rata refund of the purchase price. Penalties for violation of the safety standard imposed by the commission are stiff: $2,000 for each individual product violating the standard, and the total is not to exceed $500,000. Any consumer may petition the commission to review a safety rule for any product.

As a consumer, you should realize that the law has taken steps to protect both your monetary interest and your safety with regards to consumer products. As a manufacturer, distributor, or retailer of consumer products, you should realize that the law simply requires you to do that which you should already be doing, i.e., making and selling products that are reasonably safe for their intended uses so that unsuspecting consumers will not lose the benefit of the bargain or be injured.

Employment

Congress passed the Civil Rights Act of 1964 in part to eliminate employment discrimination. Title VII of the Act covers the entire gamut of employment: hiring, firing, compensation, conditions of employment, and privileges. The law's aim is not to inhibit businesses from employing the most qualified people but rather to prohibit unjustified employment discrimination based on race, color, religion, sex, or national origin. The law seeks to have employers treat people as individuals, not as members of a group which have a certain set of physical characteristics or which adhere to a particular religious belief.

Keep in mind that what you say is evidence of what you think and of your intent. Thus in an employment interview, if you ask questions that have a discriminatory angle, your intent would also seem to be discriminatory. Examples include:

Race, color, or national origin

Avoid pre-employment inquiries about citizenship, national origin, or ancestry if these characteristics are not directly related to job performance. Likewise, avoid requesting a photograph of the applicant, and avoid questions of skin, eye, or hair color. Any questions which gives the applicant cause to believe that a particular race or national origin is a prerequisite to employment will be grounds for an employment discrimination suit.

Religion and group affiliation

Unless the job is religiously oriented (a church pastor, for example) or unless the applicant must be a member of an organization to hold the position (international president of the Lion's Club, for example), you should not inquire about religious affiliation or association with any group. Positions which are religiously oriented or which require membership in a group are exempt from the Civil Rights Act as long as these requirements are reasonably related to the job.

Questioning an applicant about religious conviction or affiliation with organizations is grounds for an employment discrimination suit, as is asking if the applicant attends church or observes any religious holidays.

Sex

A particular sex will seldom be a valid prerequisite to employment. Exceptions might include a modeling agency that employs only male models or an entertainment producer who has only female roles to fill. However, if physical characteristics are not reasonably related to the job, avoid questions that elicit such information. Inquiries about height, weight, sex, age, pregnancy, or handicaps fall within this prohibited range if these characteristics are not reasonably related to job performance.

Other areas

Questions about the applicant's family or family life, spouse's employment and salary, marital status, number of children, criminal convictions, or residence may likewise be grounds for an employment discrimination suit unless these questions are reasonably related to job performance. However, inquiries about the applicant's ability to meet the demands of the job are legitimate, job-related questions. The nature of the job determines whether you may ask some questions. Thus, while you may not ask, "Are you married?" and consider marital status as a condition of employment, you may ask, "This position is for a task force which will work as a team for at least 12 months. Our company needs a cohesive group whose members are willing to commit themselves to the position for at least this long. Do you have any obligations, including family responsibilities, that will prohibit you from committing yourself fully to this group for a minimum of 12 months?"

Summary

In summary, to preserve your rights and the rights of others, be honest and fair in all your dealings, bridle your tongue when tempted to speak ill of another, and respect the privacy of others. Additionally, keep abreast of current legal developments which affect you and your business, and consult an attorney when necessary. Follow the spirit of the law in all you do, and the letter of the law will give you protection.

Index